AUSTRALIA
Law Book Co.
Sydney

CANADA and USA
Carswell
Toronto

HONG KONG
Sweet & Maxwell Asia

NEW ZEALAND
Brookers
Auckland

SINGAPORE and MALAYSIA
Sweet & Maxwell Asia
Singapore and Kuala Lumpar

CONFIDENTIALITY

CONFIDENTIALITY

SECOND EDITION

by

R. G. TOULSON, M.A., LL.B.
A Justice of the High Court and Master of the Bench of the Inner Temple

and

C. M. PHIPPS, M.A.
A Barrister of the Middle Temple

LONDON
SWEET & MAXWELL
2006

First edition published in 1996 by
Sweet & Maxwell Limited of
100 Avenue Road
London NW3 3PF
http//www.sweetandmaxwell.co.uk

This edition published in 2006.
Typeset by Interactive Sciences Ltd, Gloucester
Printed in England by MPG Books Ltd, Bodmin

No natural forests were destroyed to make this product:
only farmed timber was used and re-planted

ISBN 10 0 421 87630 1
ISBN 13 978 0 421 87630 9

A CIP catalogue record for this book is available
from the British library

ACKNOWLEDGEMENTS

We might be tempted to dedicate this edition to Sisyphus, who was punished in the underworld (as it happens, for an indiscretion over the relationship between Zeus and Aegina that might now be termed a breach of confidence) by having to roll a huge stone up a hill, only for it to roll down again as he was reaching the top. The plan was to complete the book in stages during the legal vacations, but each time we returned to it we would find that fresh legal developments meant that there was more climbing and rolling to do. As a result it has taken us far longer to complete the book than we had intended and, worse, our families have suffered the prolonged antisocial consequences. Respect for private and family life may have become a prominent feature of the law of confidentiality through Article 8 of the European Convention, but for our long-suffering wives, Elizabeth and Polly, "confidentiality" has become a byword for unwarranted interference with family life. It is to them that dedication of this edition is due. We are hugely grateful to them for their patience and support.

R.G.T.
C.M.P.

PREFACE TO THE FIRST EDITION

Nearly a hundred and fifty years ago, on October 20, 1848, the Prince Consort applied, *ex parte,* for an injunction against Mr William Strange, a printer and publisher carrying on business at 21 Paternoster Row, to restrain him from exhibiting or reproducing a collection of etchings made by Queen Victoria and the Prince for private use. The matter eventually came before the Lord Chqancellor, Lord Cottenham, who began his judgment[1] with the statement that the importance which had been attached to the case arose entirely from the exalted station of the plaintiff and not from the facts, which fell so clearly within the established principles as to present no difficulty. He went on to declare that "a breach of trust, confidence or contract would of itself entitle the plaintiff to an injunction", and with those words he ushered in a jurisdiction broader than had ever previously been recognised.

Development of the jurisdiction was slow over the next hundred years. In 1948 *Saltman's* case[2] gave it a new injection of life. In the last half century it has grown much faster. It is no accident that this period of growth has coincided with a time of unprecedented change in methods of information storage and copying, communication and surveillance, which have brought with them the computer hacker, the electronic eavesdropper and the peeping Tom with a telephoto lens.

Unlike patent and copyright law, which are governed by statute (and are outside the scope of this book), the law of confidentiality is almost entirely judge made. In 1981 the Law Commission proposed the abolition of the action for breach of confidence and its replacement by a new statutory tort, but the proposal was not adopted.

Much water has flowed under the bridge since the Law Commission's recommendations. The absence of a statutory framework has allowed flexibility in the development of the law. But it has to be recognized that such development has not always been coherent or consistent, and that it has left fundamental issues unresolved. The jurisprudential foundation and essential ingredients of the law of confidentiality still involve matters of debate. On them depend questions who may sue whom and what remedies are availabe. There are also major uncertainties regarding defences, including bona fide purchase, change of position and "public interest".

Roscoe Pound,[3] writing more than half a century ago, distinguished between text books containing doctrinal writing and those which were a

---

[1] (1849) 1 Mac. & G. 25 at 40.
[2] (1948) 65 R.P.C. 203.
[3] Dean of Harvard Law school, 1916 to 1936.

mere key to the cases, he observed that there was a great need for doctrinal writing in modern times as in the formative period of the law, because whereas in its formative period the courts had little to go on and much to bring about, in modern times judges have too much to go on to permit working over the vast mass of available material:

> "The labours of counsel, with the aid of the modern apparatus of digests and cyclopaedias, put before them an enormous mass of authoritative matter in which they must find starting points for reasoning or analogies or rules."[4]

The law of confidentiality is in many ways still in its formative period, despite a large mass of material.

The objects of this book are to examine the historical origins of the action for breach of confidence and its development through the more important cases; to attempt an analysis of the present state of the law, its foundations and principles (although to try to rationalize all the authorities would be an impossible task); and to discuss particular areas of difficulty and possible answers. We also consider certain relationships involving duties of confidence and confidentiality in the legal process.

Confidentiality is a fascinating and absorbing, as well as an important, branch of the law. The cases are varied and full of interest, and it would be an ideal subject for law students. Unfortunately it is not widely taught at universities. Perhaps if it were taught more, some of the present doctrinal confusion would have been dispelled.

April 1, 1996   R.G.T.
                                                                     C.M.P.

---

[4] Roscoe Pound, *The Formative Era of American Law* (1938, p.165).

PREFACE TO THE SECOND EDITION

The changes which have occurred during the 10 years since the publication of the first edition of this book have required a substantial re-writing of the first part of the book (dealing largely with origins, foundations, key elements and remedies). The changes to the second part (dealing with particular relationships) and third part (dealing with confidentiality in the legal process) include some significant new material but are more in the nature of updating.

The most radical development has been in the area of personal information. Significant protections were introduced by the Data Protection Act 1998, but its provisions are cumbersome. That Act has been overshadowed by the broader jurisprudence of the Human Rights Act 1998 and the European Convention on Human Rights (notably the provisions of Article 8 regarding the right to respect for private and family life and the provisions of Article 10 regarding freedom of expression).

The introduction of the Human Rights Act caused debate whether the courts should give "horizontal" as well as "vertical" effect to Article 8.

At the European level that issue has been determined in principle by the European Court of Human Rights in a number of cases which have held that Article 8 involves a positive obligation on the part of states to provide legal protection of a person's rights under that article from unjustifiable interference by others, although the extent of that obligation remains to be mapped.

Domestically the response of the courts so far to the challenge of Article 8 has been the hatching of a fledgling law of privacy in the nest of confidentiality. It is not a perfect nesting place (for confidentiality and privacy are not identical), and sooner or later the fledgling is likely to find the nest too small (for breaches of Article 8 may occur which do not involve use of personal information, and these will not necessarily be limited to cases where the violation was at the hands of public officials, as in *Wainwright v UK*).

For all that the issues about privacy and its relationship with confidentiality are important, and for all the publicity which has attached to recent high profile cases about the lives of celebrities, there is much more to the law of confidentiality, and its key principles need to be clear and coherent.

The objects of this book remain as stated in the preface to the first edition: to examine the historical origins of the action for breach of confidence and its development through the more important cases; to attempt an analysis of

the present state of the law, its foundations and principles (although to try
to rationalise all the authorities would be an impossible task); and to discuss
particular areas of difficulty and possible answers.

The law is stated at October 1, 2006.   R.G.T.
                                                                         C.M.P.

CONTENTS

Chapter 4—DURATION OF CONFIDENTIALITY

Chapter 5—PUBLIC SECTOR CONFIDENTIALITY

Chapter 6—PUBLIC INTEREST

CHAPTER 7—CONFIDENTIALITY AND PRIVACY

CHAPTER 8—DATA PROTECTION AND FREEDOM OF INFORMATION

CHAPTER 9—REMEDIES

CHAPTER 10—CONFIDENTIALITY AND FOREIGN LAW

CHAPTER 20—METHODS OF PARTIAL PROTECTION

CHAPTER 21—CHILDREN

CHAPTER 22—ARBITRATIONS

TABLE OF CASES

TABLE OF STATUTES

TABLE OF STATUTORY INSTRUMENTS

TABLE OF CIVIL PROCEDURE RULES

PART I

Origin and Principles of Confidentiality

CHAPTER 1

Historical Introduction

Early Origins

In *Coco v A.N. Clark (Engineers) Ltd* Megarry J. said[1]:   **1–001**

> "The equitable jurisdiction in cases of breach of confidence is ancient; confidence is the cousin of trust. The Statute of Uses, 1535, is framed in terms of 'use, confidence or trust'; and a couplet, attributable to Sir Thomas More, Lord Chancellor avers that
>
>> 'Three things are to be ... in Conscience: Fraud, Accident and things of Confidence.'
>
> (See 1 Rolle's Abridgement 374). In the middle of the last century, the great case of *Prince Albert v Strange* (1849) 1 Mac. & G. 25 reasserted the doctrine."

It is doubtful, however, whether "confidence" in the time of Sir Thomas More bore any resemblance to its present day meaning. Bacon in his "Essay on the Statute of Uses" explained the meaning of confidence as follows:

> "The special trust lawful is, as when I infeoff some of my friends, because I am to go beyond the seas, or because I would free the land from some statute, or bond, which I am to enter into, or upon intent to be reinfeoffed, or intent to be vouched, and so to suffer a common recovery, or upon intent that the feoffees shall infeoff over a stranger,

---

[1] [1969] R.P.C. 41 at 46.

and infinite the like intents and purposes, which fall out in men's dealings and occasions; and this we call confidence, ... "

Moreover, for more than a century before *Prince Albert v Strange* courts of equity were decidedly cautious in their approach to cases which would now be regarded as involving confidence and did not proceed on any broad or general jurisdiction.

1–002   The early reported cases concerned letters, literary works and recipes for medicines. In *Pope v Curl*[2] Alexander Pope obtained an injunction against the bookseller Curl restraining him from selling a book entitled "Letters from Swift, Pope and others". The Lord Chancellor, Lord Hardwicke, continued the injunction in relation to the letters from Pope to Swift but not vice versa. The basis of the distinction was that property in such letters belonged to the author; that the sending of a letter did not constitute a gift to the receiver; that the receiver had only a "special property", possibly property in the paper and at most joint property with the writer; and that such limited property did not give to the receiver licence to publish to the world.

1–003   In *Duke of Queensberry v Shebbeare*[3] the personal representatives of Lord Clarendon obtained an injunction restraining the defendant from publishing a previously unpublished history by Lord Clarendon. Dr Shebbeare's case was that he had acquired the manuscript from his co-defendant Mr Gwynne, whose father had been given it by Lord Clarendon. The injunction was continued on the ground that it was not to be presumed that Lord Clarendon had thereby intended Mr Gwynne to "have the profit of multiplying it in print".

1–004   These and other cases of unauthorised publication of writings were analysed in *Millar v Taylor*.[4] The importance of this copyright case lies in its discussion of common law rights of property and in the reliance placed on it in *Prince Albert v Strange*.[5] The facts were simple. Millar claimed ownership of a book of poems by James Thompson, entitled "The Seasons", copies of which he printed and sold. Taylor also printed and sold copies of the work, acting without Millar's permission. Millar sued for damages for trespass on the case. He brought the action in the Court of King's Bench, presided over by Lord Mansfield.

1–005   The case was argued first in June 1767, but the judges were unable to agree and it was ordered to be re-argued. It was argued for the second time in 1768. Judgment was finally delivered in April 1769, the plaintiff having, in the meantime, died. Lord Mansfield recorded that it was the first occasion since his appointment on which the court had been unable to reach unanimity despite repeated attempts to do so. Lords Mansfield, Willes and Aston JJ. found for the plaintiff. Yates J. dissented.

---

[2] (1741) 2 Atk. 342.
[3] (1758) 2 Eden 329.
[4] (1769) 4 Bur. 2303.
[5] (1849) 1 De G. & Sm. 652, (1849) 1 Mac. & G. 25.

There were three issues:

(1) whether copyright existed at common law;
(2) if it did, whether it was lost on first publication;
(3) whether any such common law right was removed by the Statute of Anne 1709, under which authors of unpublished works could obtain a copyright for a term of 14 years, renewable for a further 14 years.

On the common law questions, the defendant's argument was that there was no common law right of property detached from a physical object, and therefore no right of literary property. The owner of a document had the right to its use, but once he transferred to another the ownership of the physical document, or a copy of it, that person acquired at common law an equal right to make such use of it as he pleased.

This argument was rejected by the majority. Lord Mansfield who had **1–006** great experience of the subject, having (as he said) appeared as counsel in most of the cases cited in Chancery, said[6]:

"I use the word 'copy' in the technical sense in which that name or term has been used for ages, to signify an incorporeal right to the sole printing and publishing of somewhat intellectual, communicated by letters. It has all along been expressly admitted 'that, by the common law, an author is intitled to the copy of his own work until it has been once printed and published by his authority;' and 'that the four cases in Chancery,[7] cited for that purpose, are agreeable to the common law; and the relief was properly given, in consequence of the legal right.'

The property in the copy, thus abridged, is equally an incorporeal right to print a set of intellectual ideas or modes of thinking, communicated in a set of words and sentences and modes of expression. It is equally detached from the manuscript, or any other physical existence whatsoever. . . .

From what source, then, is the common law drawn, which is admitted to be so clear, in respect of the copy before publication? From this argument—because it is just, that an author should reap the pecuniary profits of his own ingenuity and labour. It is just, that another should not use his name, without his consent. It is fit that he should judge when to publish, or whether he ever will publish. It is fit he should not only choose the time, but the manner of publication; how many; what volume; what print. It is fit, he should choose to whose care he will trust the accuracy and correctness of the impression; in whose honesty he will confide, not to foist in additions: with other reasonings of the same effect. . . ."

[6] *Millar v Taylor* (1769) 4 Bur. 2303 at 2396.
[7] *Webb v Rose* May 24, 1732, cited 4 Bur. 2330; *Pope v Curl* (1741) 2 Atk. 342; *Forrester v Waller* June 13, 1741, cited 4 Burr. 2331 and *Duke of Queensberry v Shebbeare* (1758) 2 Eden 329.

> But the same reasons hold, after the author has published. He can reap no pecuniary profit, if, the next moment after his work comes out, it may be pirated upon worse paper and in worse print, and in a cheaper volume."

Yates J., dissenting, observed that no logical distinction could be drawn between literary compositions and any other production of the brain, such as mechanical inventions.

1–007   The matter was considered by the House of Lords in *Donaldson v Beckett*,[8] on appeal from a decree of the Court of Chancery founded on the decision in *Millar v Taylor*.[9] The opinions of the judges were taken. A majority agreed with *Millar v Taylor* on the common law questions, but not on the effect of the Statute of Anne 1709. The House of Lords voted to reverse the decree. On the common law questions, the views of the majority of the judges in *Millar v Taylor* were ultimately to be reversed by the House of Lords, but not until 80 years later in *Jefferys v Boosey*.[10]

1–008   In *Thompson v Stanhope*[11] Lord Apsley L.C. granted an injunction to restrain the publication of letters, following the precedents of *Forrester v Waller*, *Webb v Rose*, *Pope v Curl* and *Duke of Queensberry v Shebbeare*. No reference is made in the report to *Donaldson v Beckett*, decided by the House of Lords four weeks earlier, nor to *Millar v Taylor*.

1–009   Those cases and the principles on which they rested were considered in a trio of cases in equity between 1813 and 1818 — *Percival v Phipps*, *Southey v Sherwood* and *Gee v Pritchard*.

1–010   In *Percival v Phipps*[12] the defendant Phipps had published in a newspaper a letter purportedly written by the plaintiff to the defendant Mitford. The plaintiff had subsequently stated publicly that it was a forgery. Mitford asserted that it was genuine and that he had passed it to Phipps with the plaintiff's consent. To corroborate his version Mitford passed to Phipps a number of other letters from the plaintiff, which Phipps wished to publish in order to rebut the allegation that he had published false information on spurious authority. The plaintiff sought an injunction to restrain him from doing so. The application was based on grounds both of literary property and that the publication would amount to a breach of confidence. The application failed.

1–011   The Vice-Chancellor expressed doubt whether a court of equity could restrain publication of private correspondence on grounds of breach of confidence, independent of contract or a right of property in the correspondence. He also took a restricted view of the class of correspondence in which there could be a right of property based on the concept of a literary work, and he held that the defendants' reasons for publication were sufficient for a court of equity not to intervene.

---

[8] (1774) 4 Bur. 2408.
[9] (1769) 4 Bur. 2303.
[10] (1854) 4 H.L.C. 815.
[11] (1774) Amb. 737.
[12] (1813) 35 E.R. 225.

In *Southey v Sherwood*[13] Lord Eldon L.C. refused the poet Southey an **1–012** injunction to restrain the publication of a poem which he had placed with a publisher 23 years earlier, holding that such injunctions were only granted to prevent the use of that which was the exclusive property of another.

Gee v Pritchard[14] was another case of an injunction to restrain the **1–013** publication of letters. The plaintiff claimed both that the letters were her property and that their proposed publication would be a breach of private confidence. Lord Eldon granted the injunction, following the precedents of his predecessors Lord Hardwicke and Lord Apsley, but he did so expressly and only on the ground of the plaintiffs' right of property.

Lord Eldon also took a cautious approach to claims for injunctions to **1–014** restrain misuse of secret medical recipes for which either there was no patent or the patent had expired. He refused injunctions in *Newbery v James*[15] and *Williams v Williams*,[16] observing in the latter that he did not think that on general principles the court ought to struggle to protect such secrets. In *Yovatt v Winyard*[17] Lord Eldon granted an injunction restraining the defendant from using or communicating certain recipes for veterinary medicines, but on the ground (according to the headnote) that he had obtained knowledge of them by a breach of trust. The defendant had been employed by the plaintiff and during his employment surreptitiously obtained access to the plaintiffs' books of recipes, which he copied. The report does not give Lord Eldon's reasons beyond stating that he granted the injunction upon the ground of there having been a breach of trust and confidence.

Green v Folgham[18] also involved a breach of trust in relation to a medical **1–015** recipe, but in that case the recipe was the subject of an express trust.

In *Abernethy v Hutchinson*[19] the plaintiff was a distinguished surgeon **1–016** and lecturer at St Bartholomew's Hospital. The defendants were publishers and sellers of *The Lancet*. The action was brought for an injunction to restrain them from reproducing the plaintiff's lectures, the text of which must have been taken down in shorthand by a student and supplied to the defendants for publication contrary to the plaintiff's express wishes.

After days of argument, during which various possible grounds of relief **1–017** were canvassed, Lord Eldon finally granted an injunction on the ground that there was an implied contract between the plaintiff and his students that they would not publish his lectures for profit; and that, although there was no implied contract between the plaintiff and the defendants, they must have procured the text of the lectures in an undue manner from those who were under a contract not to publish, and that this was a form of fraud in

[13] (1817) 2 Mep. 435.
[14] (1818) 2 Swans. 402.
[15] (1817) 2 Mer. 446.
[16] (1817) 3 Mer. 157.
[17] (1820) 1 Jac. & W. 394.
[18] (1823) 1 Sim. & St. 398.
[19] (1824) 3 L.J.Ch. 209.

a third party sufficient to enable the court to grant an injunction against them.[20]

1–018   In summary, the cases before *Prince Albert v Strange*[21] did not establish any general right of relief in respect of misuse or threatened misuse of confidential information. The cases in which the courts intervened may be classified as cases of actual or threatened:

> (1) infringement by the defendant of a right of property recognised at common law;
> (2) breach of contract by the defendant;
> (3) breach of trust by the defendant; or
> (4) use by the defendant of information knowingly obtained from a party who was himself acting in breach of contract or trust in supplying it.

Prince Albert v Strange

1–019   In *Prince Albert v Strange*[22] the plaintiff obtained an injunction against the defendant restraining him from publishing a catalogue of private etchings made by Queen Victoria and Prince Albert. As well as describing the etchings, the catalogue announced a proposed exhibition of them and implied falsely that the publication had royal consent. The catalogue was compiled from copies surreptitiously made by an employee of a printer in Windsor, to whom plates of the etchings had been sent for the purpose of making copies for the Queen and Prince.

1–020   The plaintiff's principal argument was that publication of the catalogue infringed their right of property in the etchings on the basis of *Millar v Taylor*[23] and similar authorities. Secondly, it was argued that the information in the catalogue was derived from a breach of trust, and therefore the plaintiff was entitled to an injunction against a knowing recipient by analogy with *Abernethy v Hutchinson*.[24] The defendant's argument was that mere description of the etchings did not infringe any property right of the Queen and Prince at common law and that he was not party to any breach of trust.

1–021   The Vice-Chancellor, Sir Knight Bruce, held in favour of the plaintiff on both grounds and his judgment was upheld on appeal by Lord Cottenham L.C. On the issue of property, the Vice-Chancellor adopted Yates J.'s argument in *Millar v Taylor* that there was no difference between literary works and other products of the brain, such as mechanical or artistic creations. He held also that the owner's common law right of property was

[20] See also *Tipping v Clarke* (1843) 2 Hare 383. A person who surreptitiously obtained information which he could only have obtained from a person in breach of contract in communicating it could not be permitted to avail himself of that breach of contract.
[21] (1849) 1 De G. & Sm. 652, (1849) 1 Mac. & G. 25.
[22] (1849) 1 De G. & Sm. 652, (1849) 1 Mac. & G. 25.
[23] (1769) 4 Bur. 2303.
[24] (1824) 3 L.J.Ch. 209.

infringed as much by description without consent as by copying without consent. On the second issue the Vice-Chancellor regarded the circumstances as so obviously redolent of the etchings having been obtained by a breach of trust as to warrant an injunction on that ground.

Lord Cottenham L.C. said at the outset of his judgment that the **1–022** importance attached to the case arose entirely from the exalted station of the plaintiff, and not from the facts, which so clearly fell within established principles as not to cause any difficulty. After summarising the facts, he said[25]:

> "It was said by one of the learned counsel for the Defendant, that the injunction must rest upon the ground of property or breach of trust; both appear to me to exist. The property of an author or composer of any work, whether of literature, art or science, in such work unpublished and kept for his private use or pleasure, cannot be disputed, after the many decisions in which that proposition has been affirmed or assumed."

He continued[26]:

> "Upon the first question, therefore, that of property, I am clearly of opinion that the exclusive right and interest of the Plaintiff in the composition or work in question being established, and there being no right or interest whatever in the Defendant, the Plaintiff is entitled to the injunction of this Court to protect him against the invasion of such right and interest by the Defendant, which the publication of any catalogue would undoubtedly be; but this case by no means depends solely upon the question of property, for a breach of trust, confidence, or contract, would of itself entitle the Plaintiff to an injunction . . . .
>
> If, then, these compositions were kept private, except as to some given to private friends and some sent to Mr Brown for the purpose of having certain impressions taken, the possession of the Defendant, or of his intended partner Judge, must have originated in a breach of trust, confidence or contract, in Brown or some person in his employ taking more impressions than were ordered, and retaining the extra number, or in some person to whom copies were given, which is not to be supposed, but which, if the origin of the possession of the Defendant or Judge, would be equally a breach of trust, confidence or contract, *Duke of Queensberry v Shebbeare* (2 Eden 329); and upon the evidence on behalf of the Plaintiff, and in the absence of any explanation on the part of the Defendant, I am bound to assume that the possession of the etchings by the Defendant or Judge has its foundations in a breach of trust, confidence or contract, as Lord Eldon did in the case of Mr Abernethy's lectures (3 Law J. Chanc. 209); and upon this ground also

---

[25] *Prince Albert v Strange* (1848) 1 Mac. & G. 25 at 42.
[26] *ibid.* at 44.

I think the Plaintiff's title to the injunction sought to be discharged, fully established."

Lord Cottenham's observation that the case fell clearly within established principles did less than justice to the defendant's arguments. On the question of property, there was substantial force in the argument that the case went significantly beyond *Millar v Taylor*[27] or any other precedent and that mere description of the etchings did not involve any usurpation of the plaintiff's ownership. On the question of equity, the case fell within the principle of *Abernethy v Hutchinson*[28] if the circumstances were such that the defendant must have known of the unlawful conduct of the person showing him the etchings, for in that case (as in *Abernethy v Hutchinson*) his own conduct would be regarded in equity as a form of fraud by a third party. The circumstances were suspicious, but the defendant denied on affidavit any knowledge or suspicion of unlawfulness.

1–023   The decision has been treated as authority for the grant of an injunction against someone who has acquired information to which he was not entitled, without notice of any breach of duty on the part of the person who imparted it to him, but who cannot claim to be a purchaser for value.[29] In this respect also the case did not fall within any previously settled principles.

1–024   More generally it has been seen as a landmark case because of the broad statement that "a breach of trust, confidence or contract would of itself entitle the plaintiff to an injunction", although it is questionable whether Lord Cottenham was there intending to lay down three independent categories in which an injunction would be granted, or merely using a compendious phrase wide enough to cover the facts of the case without intending or attempting any precise definition of the legal requirements. The trust or confidence owed by Brown to the plaintiff arose from his contract, and Lord Cottenham's judgment does not suggest that he was intending to consider them in isolation.

The century after *Prince Albert v Strange*

1–025   During the 100 years between *Prince Albert v Strange* and *Saltman Engineering Co. Ltd v Campbell Engineering Co. Ltd*,[30] the main cases on confidentiality are significant for their lack of any uniform jurisprudential basis. The confidences were mostly commercial and arose generally in the context of contracts, such as contracts of partnership, employment, agency or sale.

---

[27] (1769) 4 Bur. 2303.
[28] (1824) 3 L.J.Ch. 209.
[29] *Printers & Finishers Ltd v Holloway* [1965] R.P.C. 239 at 253 and 257, *per* Cross J.
[30] (1948) 65 R.P.C. 203.

In *Morison v Moat*[31] the action arose from a partnership to manufacture **1–026** and sell "Morison's Universal Medicine". The medicine was not the subject of any patent. The original partners were the plaintiffs' father, who was the inventor of the medicine, and the defendant's father. The plaintiffs' father disclosed the secret of the recipe to the defendant's father on terms that he was not to tell anyone else. Shortly before his death, the defendant's father gave the recipe to the defendant. After the expiry of the partnership the defendant manufactured and sold the medicine for his own account. The plaintiffs, to whom the recipe had been bequeathed under their father's will, obtained an injunction to restrain the defendant. Turner V.C. said[32]:

> "That the Court has exercised jurisdiction in cases of this nature does not, I think, admit of any question. Different grounds have indeed been assigned for the exercise of that jurisdiction. In some cases it has been referred to property, in others to contract, and in others, again, it has been treated as founded upon trust or confidence, meaning, as I conceive, that the Court fastens the obligation on the conscience of the party, and enforces it against him in the same manner as it enforces against a party to whom a benefit is given the obligation of performing a promise on the faith of which the benefit has been conferred; but, upon whatever grounds the jurisdiction is founded, the authorities leave no doubt as to the exercise of it."

The approach of taking the jurisdiction as established, without further **1–027** inquiry into its jurisprudential basis, has been followed in many subsequent cases with the consequence that the uncertainty to which the Vice-Chancellor referred has continued. The Vice-Chancellor did, however, provide the earliest judicial definition of what was meant by "trust or confidence" for the purposes of this jurisdiction.

The Vice-Chancellor dealt with the defendant's argument that the effect **1–028** of an injunction would be to give the plaintiffs a better right than that of a patentee by saying that[33]:

> " . . . what we have to deal with here is, not the right of the Plaintiffs against the world, but their right against the Defendant. It may well be that the Plaintiffs have no title against the world in general, and may yet have a good title against this Defendant . . . ."

Despite the language of title, it would seem that the injunction must have been based on a personal obligation of the defendant towards the plaintiffs, rather than a property right in the plaintiffs; for if they had a right of property, it is difficult to see why it would not be good against the world.

The Vice-Chancellor also commented, without having to decide the point, **1–029** that it might have been different if the defendant were a purchaser for value

---

[31] (1851) 9 Hare 241, affirmed (1852) 21 L.J.Ch. (N.S.) 248.
[32] (1851) 9 Hare 241 at 255.
[33] *Prince Albert v Strange* (1851) 9 Hare 241 at 258.

of the secret without notice of any obligation affecting it. This too remains an unsettled question.

1–030   *Gartside v Outram*[34] is best known as the origin of the "defence of iniquity", but it also involved consideration of the basis of the jurisdiction. The plaintiff brokers filed a bill for an injunction to restrain a former clerk from disclosing any of their dealings. The defendant in his answer stated that the plaintiffs were in the habit of defrauding their principals, and in support of his answer he filed interrogatories, to which the plaintiffs objected. It was held that there was no privilege to prevent them from answering, the discovery being relevant to the defendant's answer which, if proved, would be a defence to the bill.

Wood V.C. said[35]:

> "The equity upon which the bill is founded is a perfectly plain and simple one, recognized by a number of authorities and most salutary to be enforced, by which any person standing in the confidential relation of a clerk or servant is prohibited, subject to certain exceptions, from disclosing any part of the transactions of which he thus acquires knowledge. But there are exceptions to this confidence, or perhaps, rather only nominally, and not really exceptions. The true doctrine is, that there is no confidence as to the disclosure of iniquity. You cannot make me the confidant of a crime or a fraud, and be entitled to close up my lips upon any secret which you have the audacity to disclose to me relating to any fraudulent intention on your part: such a confidence cannot exist."

This places the jurisdiction on the relationship between the parties, although at the end of his judgment Wood V.C. said[36]:

> "The real ground of the jurisdiction, as it is properly put, is founded first upon property, because the Court attempts not to interfere with morals, except in administering civil rights connected with rights of property. There is the property of the employer in those secrets of his business which he is obliged to communicate to others, and which are not to be trifled with. It is a sacred and solemn deposit, but there is no property in these transactions with this gentlemen which were of the character I have been describing, and in his answer he has made no disclosures except as to these fraudulent transactions."

Although Wood V.C. said that the court was concerned with the administration of civil rights connected with rights of property and not morals, he was clearly influenced by considerations of public interest in holding that there could be no property in secrets of an iniquitous character.

---

[34] (1857) 26 L.J.Ch. (N.S.) 113.
[35] *ibid.* at 114.
[36] *Gartside v Outran* (1857) 26 L.J.Ch. (N.S.) 113.

In *Pollard v Photographic Company*[37] North J. took a different **1–031**
approach. The plaintiff had photographs of herself taken by the defendant.
Without her consent, the defendant used one of the negatives to make a
form of Christmas card and displayed a copy of it in his shop window for
sale. The plaintiff obtained an injunction to restrain the defendant from
selling copies of the photograph. North J. dismissed as irrelevant the
defendant's argument that his conduct did not injure any property right of
the plaintiff. He said[38]:

> "The right to grant an injunction does not depend in any way on the
> existence of property as alleged; nor is it worth while to consider
> carefully the grounds upon which the old Court of Chancery used to
> interfere by injunction. But it is quite clear that, independently of any
> question as to the right at law, the Court of Chancery always had an
> original and independent jurisdiction to prevent what that Court
> considered and treated as a wrong, whether arising from a violation of
> an unquestionable right or from breach of contract or confidence, as
> was pointed out by Lord *Cottenham* in *Prince Albert v Strange*."

North J. compared the photographer to a person who obtained confidential
information in the course of his employment and who would not be
permitted to make improper use of it; and he held that it was an implied
term of the defendant's contract that prints from the negative would be
appropriated only to the plaintiff's use.

In *Merryweather v Moore*[39] Kekewich J. cited part of the passage from **1–032**
North J.'s judgment in *Pollard v Photographic Company* set out above and
went on to say[40]:

> " . . . it is sometimes difficult to say whether the Court has proceeded
> on the implied contract or the confidence, for I will put aside once for
> all any cases arising on express contract. Perhaps the real solution is
> that the confidence postulates an implied contract: that, where the
> Court is satisfied of the existence of the confidential relation, then it at
> once infers or implies the contract arising from that confidential
> relation—a contract which thus calls into exercise the jurisdiction to
> which I have referred."

Implied contract can be a useful device, as in *Abernethy v Hutchinson*,[41] but
it is not apparent why a relationship intended to be confidential need
involve the postulation of a fictitious contract in order for equity to
intervene. On the other hand the terms (whether express or, more usually,
implied) on which any confidential relationship came into existence should
rightly be regarded as fundamental whether in contract or in equity.

[37] (1888) 40 Ch.D. 345.
[38] *ibid.* at 354.
[39] [1892] 2 Ch. 518.
[40] *ibid.* at 522.
[41] (1824) 3 L.J.Ch. 209.

1–033   This approach was taken by the Court of Appeal in *Lamb v Evans*.[42] The plaintiff engaged the defendants on a commission basis to obtain advertisements for publication in a trade directory. The advertisers provided the defendants with blocks for printing their advertisements. The defendants subsequently went to work for a rival publication and used the same blocks for identical advertisements. The plaintiff obtained an injunction to prevent them from doing so.

1–034   The Court of Appeal decided the case on the basis of principles of agency. Lindley L.J. said[43]:

> "What right has any agent to use materials obtained by him in the course of his employment and for his employer against the interest of that employer? I am not aware that he has any such right. Such a use is contrary to the relation which exists between principal and agent. It is contrary to the good faith of the employment, and good faith underlies the whole of an agent's obligations to his principal."

Bowen L.J. went back to the source of the relationship. He said that the plaintiff's entitlement to an injunction[44]:

> " . . . depends entirely, I think, upon the terms upon which the employment was constituted through which the fiduciary relation of principal and agent came into existence. I think my Brothers have already during the course of the argument expressed what I fully believe, that there is no distinction between law and equity as regards the law of principal and agent. The common law, it is true, treats the matter from the point of view of an implied contract, and assumes that there is a promise to do that which is part of the bargain, or which can be fairly implied as part of the good faith which is necessary to make the bargain effectual. What is an implied contract or an implied promise in law? It is that promise which the law implies and authorises us to infer in order to give the transaction that effect which the parties must have intended it to have and without which it would be futile . . . It seems to me that in this case the proper inference to be drawn would be that it was part of the understanding that these materials were not to be used otherwise than for the purposes of the employment in the course of which they were obtained."

Lindley and Bowen L.JJ. both referred to the misuse of "materials", a point further emphasised by Kay L.J. After considering *Morison v Moat*,[45] *Abernethy v Hutchinson*[46] and *Prince Albert v Strange*,[47] he said[48]:

[42] [1893] 1 Ch. 218.
[43] *ibid.* at 226.
[44] *ibid.* at 229.
[45] (1851) 9 Hare 241.
[46] (1824) 3 L.J.Ch. 209.
[47] (1849) 1 De G. & Sm. 652, (1849) 1 Mac. & G. 25.
[48] [1893] 1 Ch. 218 at 236.

"So that I think the doctrine . . . does extend to every case in which a man has obtained materials (I use the word advisedly, because it would be very difficult indeed to grant an injunction to prevent a man using his knowledge)—where a man has obtained materials while he was in the position of agent for another—materials which were obtained by him in the course of that agency and were to be used for the purposes for which his principal had employed him."

Subsequent development of the law has not been so confined. In *Reid and Sigrist Ltd v Moss and Mechanism Ltd*,[49] for example, Luxmoore J. said: **1–035**

"Undoubtedly there is a well recognised rule in the law relating to Master and Servant that a servant cannot use to the detriment of his master information of a confidential or secret nature entrusted to the servant or learnt by him in the course of his employment. There are many cases in the books on the subject. In some of them it has been debated what is the precise ground to be assigned for the exercise of the jurisdiction of the Court. Is it to be referred to property or contract, or is it to be founded upon trust or confidence? But whatever may be the true ground on which the jurisdiction is founded there is no doubt as to its existence."

"Information of a confidential or secret nature" is potentially much wider than "materials". In *Printers & Finishers Ltd v Holloway*,[50] Cross J. said: **1–036**

"The mere fact that the confidential information is not embodied in a document but is carried away by the employee in his head is not, of course, of itself a reason against the granting of an injunction to prevent its use or disclosure by him."

Nevertheless, Kay L.J. touched on a major problem when he referred in *Lamb v Evans* to the difficulty of extending the doctrine to the use of knowledge. There is not only the difficulty of enforcement, but also a potential clash between legitimate competing interests: on the one hand that secrets should be respected, and on the other hand that a skilled person should not be restricted from making use of his skills. The boundary between knowledge of particular secrets derived from confidential sources and more general knowledge may be elusive, particularly since the latter may be derived to a greater or lesser extent from the former. This topic has been considered in many subsequent cases, including notably *Herbert Morris Ltd v Saxelby*,[51] *Printers & Finishers Ltd v Holloway*[52] and *Faccenda Chicken Ltd v Fowler*.[53]

[49] (1932) 49 R.P.C. 461 at 480.
[50] [1965] R.P.C. 239 at 255.
[51] [1916] A.C. 688.
[52] [1965] R.P.C. 239.
[53] [1987] 1 Ch. 117.

1–037　　No such problem arose in *Robb v Green*,[54] in which Kay L.J. was again a member of the Court of Appeal. An employee surreptitiously copied his employer's customer list for the purpose of soliciting orders from them after setting up in business on his own account. The claim was for damages, delivery up of the list and an injunction to restrain him from making use of the information so obtained.

1–038　　The court followed the analysis of Bowen L.J. in *Lamb v Evans*, but, whilst he had said in that case that there was no distinction between the law and equity as regards the law of principal and agent, the court in *Robb v Green* did distinguish between the remedies available. Kay L.J. said that an injunction ought to be granted "either on the ground of breach of trust or breach of contract", and that "a document surreptitiously made in breach of the trust imposed in the servant clearly ought to be given up to be destroyed." He continued[55]:

> "As to the damages, I think there is more difficulty. The right to them depends on whether the conduct of the defendant can be regarded as a breach of an implied contract. According to the view taken by Bowen L.J. in *Lamb v Evans*, it can; and in the result I come to the conclusion that the judgment in that respect must be upheld."

This is in accordance with classical doctrine that damages cannot be awarded for breach of an equitable obligation except under the jurisdiction derived from Lord Cairns's Act.[56]

1–039　　The crucial fact in *Robb v Green* was that the defendant copied the customer list while still in the plaintiff's employment. This point was emphasised in *Wessex Dairies Ltd v Smith*[57] by Maugham L.J. who noted that in *Robb v Green* the defendant was not restrained from sending out circulars to customers whose names he could remember.

1–040　　The availability of equitable relief to restrain misuse of confidential information, not only by the confidant but also by a third party recipient, was reaffirmed by the Court of Appeal in *Ashburton v Pape*.[58] Copies of privileged letters written by Lord Ashburton to his solicitor had been obtained by the defendant from a clerk employed by the solicitor. Swinfen Eady L.J. said[59]:

> "The principle upon which the Court of Chancery has acted for many years has been to restrain the publication of confidential information improperly or surreptitiously obtained or of information imparted in confidence which ought not to be divulged. Injunctions have been granted to give effectual relief, that is not only to restrain the disclosure

---

[54] [1895] 2 Q.B. 315.
[55] *ibid.* at 320.
[56] Chancery Amendment Act 1858 (now s.50 of the Supreme Court Act 1981).
[57] [1935] 2 K.B. 80 at 89.
[58] [1913] 2 Ch. 469.
[59] *ibid.* at 475.

of confidential information, but to prevent copies being made of any record of that information, and, if copies have already been made, to restrain them from being further copied, and to restrain persons into whose possession that confidential information has come from themselves in turn divulging or propagating it."

In *Herbert Morris Ltd v Saxelby*[60] there was no misconduct by the **1-041** defendant during his employment, but the plaintiffs, who were manufacturers of lifting machinery, sought to enforce against him a covenant against being involved as principal, agent or employee, in the sale or manufacture of lifting machinery of various types within the United Kingdom for a term of seven years after the end of his employment. The plaintiffs had a leading position in the market. The defendant was an engineer. The covenant was held to be unenforceable.

The employers' argument was that the covenant was a reasonable **1-042** provision for the protection of their property, namely trade secrets and customer connection. The argument of counsel for the employee conceded that it was permissible for a clause to protect "the filching of the employer's property such as trade secrets or customers' connection" but objected to the covenant on the ground that its real object was to protect against mere competition. This argument was essentially adopted by the various members of the Judicial Committee.

Lord Atkinson contrasted, on the one hand, "trade secrets . . . , such as **1-043** secret processes of manufacture, which may be of great value" and documents containing commercially sensitive information, such as lists of customers and their requirements, all of which were to be regarded as "private and confidential documents, the property of the [plaintiffs]" from, on the other hand, more general employee know-how, saying[61]:

> "The respondent cannot, however, get rid of the impressions left upon his mind by his experience of the appellants' works; they are part of himself; and in my view he violates no obligation express or implied arising from the relation in which he stood to the appellants by using in the service of some persons other than them the general knowledge he has acquired of their scheme of organisation and methods of business."

Lord Parker said that[62]:

> " . . . the reason, and the only reason, for upholding such a restraint on the part of an employee is that the employer has some proprietary right, whether in the nature of trade connection or in the nature of trade secrets, for the protection of which such a restraint is—having regard to the duties of the employee—reasonably necessary. Such a restraint has,

[60] [1916] A.C. 688.
[61] *ibid.* at 703.
[62] *ibid.* at 710.

so far as I know, never been upheld if directed only to the prevention of competition or against the use of personal skill and knowledge acquired by the employee in his employer's business."

Lord Shaw also used the language of property[63]:

"Trade secrets, the names of customers, all such things which in sound philosophical language are denominated objective knowledge—these may not be given away by a servant; they are his master's property, and there is no rule of public interest which prevents a transfer of them against the master's will being restrained. On the other hand, a man's aptitudes, his skill, his dexterity, his manual or mental ability—all those things which in sound philosophical language are not objective, but subjective—they may and they ought not to be relinquished by a servant; they are not his master's property; they are his own property; they are himself."

1–044   In *Mechancial and General Inventions Co. v Austin*[64] the plaintiffs were patentees of a system for installing sun roofs in cars. They provided details to the defendants with a view to entering into a licence agreement, which did not materialise. The House of Lords upheld a finding by the jury that there was a contract whereby the information disclosed to the defendants was to be used only under a licence agreement and also its award of £35,000 damages.

1–045   From the note of the defendants' argument,[65] it appears that the contract alleged was an implied contract. It was argued on their behalf that no such contract should be inferred and that,

"The appellants are really complaining of something in the nature of a breach of trust or confidence, for which relief, if there be any, must be sought in a Court of equity, and not by way of damages at common law."

Lord Atkin said[66]:

"It is quite sufficient to support the contract averred that the terms upon which the information was disclosed were that it was to be used for a particular purpose only. The giving of the information is ample consideration, and use for any other purpose would be a breach. The analogy of a contract of bailment I think supports this view."

---

[63] *Herbert Morris Ltd v Saxelby* [1916] A.C. 688 at 714.
[64] [1935] A.C. 346.
[65] *ibid.* at 350–351.
[66] *ibid.* at 370.

Saltman

Saltman Engineering Co. Ltd v Campbell Engineering Co. Ltd[67] is a **1–046**
landmark case, both because of its re-affirmation of the equitable doctrine
of confidence independent of contract, and because of its attempt to define
the quality of confidence necessary for the doctrine to apply. The plaintiffs
supplied the defendants with drawings of tools for the manufacture of
leather punches. After supplying punches to the plaintiffs, the defendants
retained the drawings, which they used for manufacturing and selling other
punches to other purchasers. The plaintiffs alleged breach of contract and
breach of confidence, and claimed relief including an order for delivery up
of the drawings and all tools made from them, an injunction and an inquiry
as to damages.

The Court of Appeal held that it was unnecessary to decide the question **1–047**
of breach of contract, because there was a plain breach of confidence in that
the drawings had been supplied for the limited purpose of manufacturing
punches for the plaintiffs, and (*per* Somervell L.J.[68]) that the plaintiffs' relief
under that head was as great as it could be under any other.

Lord Greene M.R. said[69]: **1–048**

> "The information, to be confidential, must, I apprehend, apart from
> contract, have the necessary quality of confidence about it, namely it
> must not be something which is public property and public knowledge.
> On the other hand, it is perfectly possible to have a confidential
> document, be it a formula, a plan, a sketch, or something of that kind,
> which is the result of work done by the maker upon materials which
> may be available for the use of anybody; but what makes it confidential
> is the fact that the maker of the document has used his brain and thus
> produced a result which can only be produced by somebody who goes
> through the same process."

The court declined to order the destruction of the tools made by the
defendants but ordered an inquiry as to damages, to cover both past and
future acts, under Lord Cairns Act.

The decision in *Saltman* provided a great impetus for the use of the action **1–049**
to prevent industrial piracy,[70] from which its use spread to the protection of
personal confidences (*Argyll*[71]) and government secrets (*Attorney-General v
Jonathan Cape Ltd*[72]).

In 1981 the Law Commission produced a report on Breach of Con- **1–050**
fidence[73] in which it commented on the many uncertainties concerning the

---

[67] (1948) 65 R.P.C. 203.
[68] *Saltman* (1948) 65 R.P.C. 203 at 217.
[69] *ibid.* at 215.
[70] See Lord Oliver's summary of the history of the breach of confidence action in "Spycatcher:
Confidence, Copyright and Contempt", *Israel Law Review* (1989) 23(4) 407.
[71] [1967] Ch. 302.
[72] [1976] 1 Q.B. 752.
[73] Law Com No.110, Cmnd. 8388 (1981).

ultimate legal foundation of the jurisdiction, its ambit and the remedies available, and recommended that the law be placed on a statutory basis. It drafted a Breach of Confidence Bill, which would have created a statutory tort of breach of confidence and abrogated all principles of equity and common law relating to breach of confidence, except in cases of proceedings for breach of contract or contempt of court. The recommendations were not accepted and the law has continued to develop on a case by case basis.

Developments since *Saltman*

1–051 Since *Saltman* there has been considerable development of the action for breach of confidence, induced by changes in the political and social landscape. Three factors have been particularly significant—the writing of memoirs by ex-spies, spymasters or politicians containing information regarded as secret by the Government; the use of increasingly sophisticated means of obtaining information covertly; and increased media appetite for publishing details of the private lives of well known figures, often obtained by intrusive methods.

Public sector confidentiality

1–052 A number of cases have resulted from Government attempts to use the law of confidentiality to prevent, or provide a remedy against, publication by former public office holders or employees of material which the Government considered should be kept secret in the public interest.[74] It is now established that the law of confidentiality is not confined to the private sector, but in the case of public sector confidentiality the Government has to show that the public interest requires the relief claimed to be granted. The *Spycatcher* case is of particular importance for its analysis of the cause of action.[75]

Covert and intrusive ways of obtaining information

1–053 In Britain and elsewhere the use of invasive methods of obtaining information has become common. Kirby J. and Callinan J. referred to it in *Australian Broadcasting Corporation v Lenah Game Meats Pty Ltd.*[76]

1–054 Kirby J. said:

> "The phenomena of 'cheque-book journalism', intrusive telephoto lenses, surreptitious surveillance, gross invasions of personal privacy, deliberately deceptive 'stings' and trespass to land 'with cameras rolling' are mainly phenomena of recent times."

[74] *Att-Gen v Jonathan Cape Ltd* [1976] 1 Q.B. 752; *Commonwealth of Australia v John Fairfax & Sons Ltd* [1969] R.P.C. 41; *Att-Gen v Guardian Newspapers Ltd (No. 2) ("Spycatcher")* [1990] 1 A.C. 109; *Att-Gen v Blake* [2001] 1 A.C. 268.
[75] See especially [1990] 1 A.C. 280–289 (Lord Goff).
[76] (2001) 208 C.L.R. 199, paras 172 and 255.

Callinan J. said:

> "The means and sources of information (both legitimate and unlawful) available to the media are more numerous and diverse today than ever before; spy cameras, telephone interception devices, access to satellites, night vision equipment, thermal imaging, parabolic listening devices, telephoto lenses, and concealable video cameras to name some only."

The courts have recognised that a person who uses underhand methods to obtain information which he knows that the target intends not to allow to become publicly available (or not until it chooses to do so) may be held to be under a duty of confidentiality. The courts have also recognised that a design may be regarded as a form of information which may be protected from underhand reproduction.[77]

Personal privacy

The most radical development of the law has been in relation to personal privacy. Article 8 of the European Convention on Human Rights provides that everyone has the right to respect for his private and family life, his home and his correspondence. **1–055**

In *Von Hannover v Germany*[78] the European Court of Human Rights held that Art.8 imposes on a state both negative and positive obligations. A state must not only abstain from unwarranted interference with the private lives of individuals but must also take appropriate measures to secure respect for private life in the sphere of the relations of individuals between themselves. **1–056**

The court held that Germany was in breach of Art.8 in that its laws failed to give adequate protection to the applicant from the actions of paparazzi photographers, and that her rights had been breached by the publication of photos showing her in scenes from her daily life, engaged in activities of a purely private nature such as practising sport, walking, leaving a restaurant or enjoying a holiday. **1–057**

The Human Rights Act 1998, s.6 provides that it is unlawful for a public authority (which includes a court) to act in a way which is incompatible with a Convention right. **1–058**

In a series of important cases[79] the courts have enlarged the action for breach of confidence to include infringement of a person's right to privacy under Art.8 by unwarranted publication of material of a personal nature. The full extent and implications of this development have yet to be worked out. **1–059**

---

[77] *Shelley Films Ltd v Rex Features Ltd* [1994] E.M.L.R. 134; *Creation Records Ltd v News Group Newspapers Ltd* [1997] E.M.L.R. 444.
[78] (2005) 40 E.H.H.R. 1, para.57.
[79] *A v B Plc* [2002] EWCA Civ 337; [2003] Q.B. 195; *Campbell v MGN Ltd* [2004] UKHL 22; [2004] 2 A.C. 457; *Douglas v Hello! Ltd (No. 3)* [2005] EWCA Civ 595; [2006] Q.B. 125.

CHAPTER 2

Foundations

Different species of action

2–001   No single concept satisfactorily explains or encompasses all species of the action for what has traditionally been called breach of confidence.

2–002   The Law Commission in its 1981 Report[1] observed that there was uncertainty as to the nature and scope of the action for breach of confidence owing to its somewhat obscure legal basis, and quoted the words of Professor Gareth Jones[2]:

> "A cursory study of the cases, where the plaintiff's confidence has been breached, reveals great conceptual confusion. Property, contract, bailment, trust, fiduciary relationship, good faith, unjust enrichment, have all been claimed, at one time or another, as the basis of judicial intervention. Indeed some judges have indiscriminately intermingled all these concepts. The result is that the answer to many fundamental questions remains speculative."

Since then the field has been enlarged. A claimant's action may, but need not necessarily, be based on a breach of confidence in the ordinary sense. Aside from cases where there is an underlying relationship giving rise to a duty of

---

[1] Law Com No.110, Cmnd. 8388 (1981), para.3.1.
[2] Jones, "Restitution of benefits obtained in breach of another's confidence" (1970) 86 L.Q.R. 463.

confidentiality, the law may recognise an obligation to treat information with confidentiality if it is obviously of a confidential nature and was obtained by the recipient by dishonest or discreditable means or, possibly, by an obvious accident. Since the Human Rights Act 1998 the action has also become available to protect, within limits, a person's rights under Art.8 of the European Convention to respect for his private and family life, his home and his correspondence.

The action can therefore cover very different types of case giving rise to different considerations.   2–003

In the Art.8 type of case, English law now provides what is in substance (but not yet in name) an action for breach of rights of privacy, the limits of which are at present uncertain.   2–004

In *Campbell v MGN Ltd*[3] it was said that the cause of action for breach of confidence has now shaken off the limiting constraint of the need for an initial confidential relationship; in so doing it has changed its nature; it is now a tort; and it is now better described as misuse of private information.   2–005

The view advanced in this book is that under the label of breach of confidence (or misuse of private information) there are now significantly different types of cause of action.   2–006

Where there is an underlying relationship of confidentiality, the law has not changed as a result of the Human Rights Act (subject to possible arguments by a defendant under Art.10 of the European Convention, which protects freedom of expression). The basic value which underlies the law in such circumstances is that a person ought to be able to entrust information to another without having that trust abused. This vital concept affects both the range of information which may be protected and the scope of potential defences.   2–007

The jurisprudential basis of a duty of confidence arising from a confidential relationship may be contractual or equitable.[4]   2–008

The range of information which may be protected by reason of such a relationship is potentially wide and certainly far wider than information which would be protected under Art.8. It may include trade secrets or Government secrets, and the claimant may be a business organisation or public authority.   2–009

In cases where there is an underlying relationship of confidentiality, the focus of the court's inquiry is on the requirements properly arising from it. These may vary according to the nature of the relationship but the general principle in such cases, and the value underlying it, were stated by Lord Goff in the *Spycatcher* case[5]:   2–010

> "I start with the broad principle (which I do not intend in any way to be definitive) that a duty of confidence arises when confidential

[3] [2004] UKHL 22; [2004] 2 A.C. 457, paras 13–14 (Lord Nicholls).
[4] *Saltman* (1948) 65 R.P.C. 203; *Att-Gen v Guardian Newspapers Ltd (No. 2)* [1990] 1 A.C. 109; *Kitchenology BV v Unicor Gmbh Plastmaschinen* [1995] R.P.C. 765 at 778.
[5] [1990] 1 A.C. 109 at 281.

information comes to the knowledge of a person (the confidant) in circumstances where he has notice, or is held to have agreed, that the information is confidential, with the effect that it would be just in all the circumstances that he should be precluded from disclosing the information to others. I have used the word 'notice' advisedly, in order to avoid the (here unnecessary) question of the extent to which actual knowledge is necessary; though I of course understand knowledge to include circumstances where the confidant has deliberately closed his eyes to the obvious. The existence of this broad general principle reflects the fact that there is such a public interest in the maintenance of confidences that the law will provide remedies for their protection."

2–011   The same public interest and the same general principle apply to an original confidant and to a subsequent recipient who knows that the information has been passed to him in breach of confidence. As Dillon L.J. said in the *Spycatcher* case[6]:

" . . . anyone who receives information from a person bound by an obligation of secrecy or confidence, and who knows that the information has been passed to him by his informant in breach of that obligation, becomes automatically prima facie himself bound by a like obligation of secrecy or confidence which will prevent his disseminating the information any further, or making any use of it without the consent of the person to whom the obligation of secrecy or confidence was owed by the informant."

It is not difficult to apply by analogy the same principle to a person who obtains what he knows to be confidential information by dishonest or discreditable means or, possibly, by accident. In the *Spycatcher* case Lord Goff deliberately stated the broad principle underlying breach of confidence in terms wide enough to cover such situations, although he observed that in the vast majority of cases a duty of confidence would arise from a transaction or relationship between the parties.[7]

2–012   In cases where there is no such transaction or relationship, but the recipient is alleged to have obtained the information by dishonest or discreditable means, or possibly by accident, the focus of the inquiry will be on the nature of the information and whether the recipient obtained it in such circumstances that he should in conscience be required to treat it as confidential.

2–013   Where Art.8 is engaged the focus is different. The European Court of Human Rights has stated that the primary purpose of Art.8 is to enable the development, without outside interference, of the personality of each individual in his relations with other human beings.[8] This extends beyond

---

[6] [1990] 1 A.C. 109 at 201.
[7] [1990] 1 A.C. 109 at 281.
[8] *Botta v Italy* (1998) 26 E.H.R.R. 241, para.32; *Von Hannover v Germany* (2005) 40 E.H.R.R. 1, paras 50, 69.

the family circle and includes a social dimension. The court has recognised that there is a "zone of interaction with others, even in a public context, which may fall within the scope of 'private life'".[9] An aspect of a person's right to enjoyment of that zone of privacy is the right to control personal information about himself, including information about his personal relationships with others.

The difference between confidentiality and privacy as concepts was **2–014** discussed by Lord Mustill in *R. v Broadcasting Standards Commission, Ex p. BBC*.[10] It was held that under the Broadcasting Act 1996 a company could make a complaint of unwarranted infringement of its privacy in the obtaining of material included in a broadcast programme. But the court emphasised that this conclusion was based on the particular language of the statute and its underlying purpose, which was concerned with establishing broadcasting standards rather than legal rights. Lord Mustill said:

"I do . . . wish to emphasise the degree to which this conclusion is dependent on the language and purpose of this particular statute, for in general I find the concept of a company's privacy hard to grasp. To my mind the privacy of a human being denotes at the same time the personal 'space' in which the individual is free to be itself, and also the carapace, or shell, or umbrella, or whatever other metaphor is preferred, which protects that space from intrusion. An infringement of privacy is an affront to the personality, which is damaged both by the violation and by the demonstration that the personal space is not inviolate. The concept is hard indeed to define, but if this gives something of its flavour I do not see how it can apply to an impersonal corporate body, which has no sensitivities to wound, and no selfhood to protect.

There will, it is true, be many occasions where grounds for complaint maintainable by a company will be of the same kind as those which could be presented by an individual as a breach of privacy. For example the clandestine copying of business documents would be actionable by a company and an individual alike as civil wrongs, amounting to a breach of confidentiality, copyright and the like. But privacy and confidentiality are not the same. For example, the reading and copying of personal diaries, letters to relatives or lovers, poems and so on could ground not only an allegation of tortious conduct but also an additional complaint that the privacy of the writer and perhaps also of the recipient have been intruded upon. Such conduct is specially objectionable, not because legal rights have been infringed but because of the insult done to the person as a person. No such complaint would, I believe, be feasible when made by a company, not for the obvious reason that a corporation does not create documents of this kind, but because an intrusion into such matters has an extra dimension, in the

---

[9] *Von Hannover v Germany*, para.50.
[10] [2001] Q.B. 885, paras 48–49.

shape of the damage done to the sensibilities of a human being by exposing to strangers the workings of his or her inward feelings, emotions, fears and beliefs—a damage which an artificial 'person', having no sensibilities, cannot be made to suffer. A company can have secrets, can have things which should be kept confidential, but I see this as different from the essentially human and personal concept of privacy."

In Art.8 cases concerning disclosure of personal information, the focus of the court's inquiry will be on the extent to which the disclosure interferes, or would interfere, with the objective of Art.8 (when balanced against Art.10).

2–015   As Lord Hoffmann put it in *Campbell v MGN Ltd*,[11]

"The result . . . has been a shift in the centre of gravity of the action for breach of confidence when it is used as a remedy for the unjustified publication of personal information . . . Instead of the cause of action being based upon the duty of good faith applicable to confidential personal information and trade secrets alike, it focuses upon the protection of human autonomy and dignity—the right to control dissemination of information about one's private life and the right to the esteem and respect of other people."

Given the differences in concepts and objectives between breach of confidence and breach of privacy, to attempt to meld the different types of case into a uniform cause of action risks doctrinal and practical confusion.

2–016   It is understandable that courts are more willing to make new law when it can be viewed as adapting and extending existing doctrine rather than creating a new branch of law. It has been easier for the courts to develop the law incrementally by expanding the action for breach of confidence than by declaring a new cause of action for breach of privacy, especially in view of a strong line of authority denying a cause of action for breach of privacy, of which the high watermark was *Wainwright v Home Office*.[12]

2–017   A mother and son were strip searched for drugs on a prison visit. The search was conducted in a manner which contravened prison rules and was gratuitously humiliating. It included indecent touching of the son. They sued the Home Office. The events pre-dated the Human Rights Act but the Act was in force by the time that the case reached the House of Lords. The son recovered damages for battery in respect of the indecent touching, but otherwise their claim in respect of their degrading treatment failed. It was argued that there was a common law tort of invasion of privacy, and that recognition of its existence was necessary for the United Kingdom to conform with its international obligations in respect of Art.8. The House of Lords rejected both parts of this argument.

---

[11] [2004] UKHL 22; [2004] 2 A.C. 457, para.51.
[12] *Kaye v Robertson* [1991] F.S.R. 62; *Wainwright v Home Office* [2003] UKHL 53; [2004] 2 A.C. 406.

The Wainwrights took their case to the European Court, which held that **2–018** there had been a violation of Art.8.[13] Strip searching involved an interference with the applicants' right to personal privacy which required to be justified in terms of the second paragraph of Art.8 by showing that it had a legitimate objective and was proportionate to that objective. The court accepted that the prevention of smuggling drugs into prison was a legitimate objective, but held that the searches were not proportionate to the legitimate objective in the way that they were carried out. Because English law (as held by the House of Lords) did not did not provide the applicants with a remedy, except in respect of the indecent touching of the son, the United Kingdom was held also to be in breach of Art.13.

If the same facts were to occur today, the Wainwrights would be entitled **2–019** to damages by virtue of ss.7 and 8 of the Human Rights Act for the violation of their Art.8 rights by the prison officers, since their mistreatment was at the hands of public officials. In those circumstances there would therefore no longer be a breach of Art.13. But Art.8 may also impose on the state an obligation to safeguard a person's rights of privacy from interference by companies or private individuals,[14] and ss.7 and 8 of the Act would not provide a remedy in that situation.

In relation to the publication of information about a person's private life, **2–020** the Court of Appeal took a bold approach by declaring in *A v B plc*[15]:

"[Articles 8 and 10] have provided new parameters within which the court will decide, in an action for breach of confidence, whether a person is entitled to have his privacy protected by the court or whether the restriction of freedom of expression which such protection involves cannot be justified. The court's approach ... has been modified because, under section 6 of the 1998 Act, the court, as a public authority, is required not to act 'in a way which is incompatible with a Convention right'. The court is able to achieve this by absorbing the rights which articles 8 and 10 protect into the long-established action for breach of confidence."

This approach was approved by the House of Lords in *Campbell v MGN Ltd*,[16] but there are limitations and difficulties in trying to absorb breach of rights of privacy within breach of confidence, as has been noted by commentators[17] and courts.[18]

---

[13] *Wainwright v UK* [2006] ECHR 807.
[14] *Von Hannover v Germany* (2005) 40 E.H.R.R. 1 at para.57.
[15] Para.4 (Lord Woolf, C.J. giving the judgment of the court); [2002] EWCA Civ 337; [2003] Q.B. 195.
[16] [2004] UKHL 22; [2004] 2 A.C. 457.
[17] See, in particular, Phillipson, *Transforming Breach of Confidence? Towards a Common Law Right of Privacy under the Human Rights Act* (2003) 66 M.L.R. 726.
[18] See, in particular, the judgments of the New Zealand Court of Appeal in *Hosking v Runting* [2004] NZCA 34 and *Douglas v Hello! Ltd (No. 3)* [2005] EWCA Civ 595, [2006] Q.B. 125, para.53, "We cannot pretend that we find it satisfactory to be required to shoe-horn within the cause of action for breach of confidence claims for publication of unauthorised photographs of a private occasion" (Lord Phillips M.R. giving the judgment of the court).

2-021   First, for Art.8 rights to be brought under the umbrella of confidentiality, the case must involve use of information of a private character, but there may be invasions of privacy which do not involve publication of information.[19] Secondly, although there is obvious potential overlap in cases concerning personal information between rights of confidentiality founded on pre-Human Rights Act law and rights under Art.8, the concepts of privacy and confidentiality are neither identical nor mutually exclusive. There are thus differences of foundation of the different species of action presently grouped under the heading of breach of confidentiality (or misuse of private information).

Relationships giving rise to a duty of confidentiality

2-022   A duty of confidentiality may arise from express or implied terms of a contract. Aside from contract, the courts have also long recognised that an equitable duty of confidentiality may arise out of a relationship under which information is imparted. The basis on which breach may give rise to a claim for compensation is discussed below.

Information obtained by dishonest or discreditable means

2-023   A person who obtains confidential information by dishonest or discreditable means (such as electronic eavesdropping) should be, and is, in no better legal position than if the information had been imparted to him voluntarily in confidence. Equity acts on the conscience, and the conduct of a person who obtains confidential information improperly is as reprehensible to the conscience as that of a person who violates the confidence in which he received it.

Information obtained by accident

2-024   The law in this area is less developed. The cases considered have been ones where a person has received a document of a confidential nature which was plainly not intended for him. A person has no right to retain or make use of a document which does not belong to him and to read what he knows is not intended for him may well be regarded as unconscionable.

Article 8 cases

2-025   Cases under Art.8 need not be founded on a relationship of confidentiality, nor need they involve any conduct by a defendant of a discreditable kind

---

[19] As Lord Nicholls noted in *Campbell v MGN Ltd* [2004] 2 A.C. 457 at para.15, referring to the example of *Wainwright*; [2004] UKHL 22.

(although they sometimes do). It would be artificial to try to base such cases on the concept of unconscionability.

In *Campbell v MGN Ltd*[20] the claim for damages for publication of photographs of the claimant leaving premises of Narcotics Anonymous was regarded by Lord Nicholls as an action in tort. **2–026**

A contrary view was taken by the Court of Appeal in *Douglas v Hello! Ltd*.[21] The court considered the nature of the Douglasses' claim for the purpose of determining the appropriate choice of law. It observed that their claim in relation to the invasion of their privacy might seem most appropriately to fall within the law of delict. But it concluded, with hesitation, that the effect of shoe-horning this type of claim into the cause of action for breach of confidence meant that it did not fall to be treated as a tort under English law. It regarded as persuasive the suggestion of *Dicey & Morris on the Conflict of Laws*[22] that a claim for breach of confidence fell to be categorised as a restitutionary claim for unjust enrichment. **2–027**

There may well be cases in which an infringement of a person's rights may cause damage, physical or psychological, unrelated to any enrichment of the wrongdoer. Instances might include cases where the publication of the identity and address of a person could place them in physical danger, but there could be less dramatic examples. Indeed, the damages awarded to the Douglasses were based on personal distress, cost and inconvenience, rather than any estimation of enrichment of the defendants. Far from making a profit, the court noted that the defendants made a loss on the whole exercise, and this was one ground on which the court rejected the suggestion of a notional royalty as basis for assessing damages.[23] **2–028**

It is suggested that the court's natural inclination towards tort as the basis of the claim was sound, and that the problem which troubled the court about the "shoe-horning" of breach of privacy within breach of confidence is best addressed by recognising the differences between them. **2–029**

Conflicting views on information as property

There has been a long standing debate whether confidential information is or should be regarded by the law as property. If so, it would give rise to proprietorial remedies which could be exercised against a third party, regardless of whether he was or ought to have been aware that the information was confidential. **2–030**

In the *Spycatcher* case Lord Goff said[24]: **2–031**

"I have ... deliberately avoided the fundamental question whether, contract apart, the duty lies simply 'in the notion of an obligation of

---

[20] The action was so described in *Campbell* [2004] 2 A.C. 457, para.15 by Lord Nicholls; [2004] UKHL 22.
[21] [2005] EWCA Civ 595, [2006] Q.B. 125, at paras 96–97.
[22] 13th edn, 2000, para.34–029. See now Dicey, Morris and Collins (14th edn, 2006), para.34–040.
[23] Paras 243–245.
[24] [1990] 1 A.C. 109 at 281.

conscience arising from the circumstances in or through which the information was communicated or obtained' (see *Moorgate Tobacco Co. Ltd v Philip Morris Ltd (No. 2)* (1984) 156 C.L.R. 414, 438, *per* Deane J., and see also *Seager v Copydex Ltd* [1967] 1 W.L.R. 923, 931, *per* Lord Denning M.R.), or whether confidential information may also be regarded as property (as to which see Dr Francis Gurry's valuable monograph on *Breach of Confidence* (1984), pp.46–56 and Professor Birks' *An Introduction to the Law of Restitution* (1985), pp.343–344)."

2–032   The question whether (statute apart) there can be property in ideas or information goes back to the issues debated in *Millar v Taylor*[25] (in which the judgments repay reading). Now, as then, opinions are divided.

2–033   The question depends on what is meant by property, a matter of complexity upon which much has been written. As Professor Cornish has commented:

"The root difficulty of such a question is the flexibility of the property notion in English law and the many ends to which it is applied."[26]

It is therefore not surprising that different views have been expressed. However, there are formidable difficulties in the way of any treatment of the action for breach of confidence as an action in tort based on infringement of a proprietary interest. The objections may be grouped under the headings of precedent, conceptual analysis and logical consequence.

2–034   As a matter of precedent, the latest decision of the Court of Appeal (in *Douglas v Hello! Ltd (No. 3)*[27]) and the weight of previous authority are against the proposition that confidential information is to be regarded as property.

2–035   The view held by Lord Mansfield and the majority of the judges in *Miller v Taylor*[28] that the common law recognised an incorporeal right to a set of ideas was ultimately rejected by the House of Lords in *Jefferys v Boosey*.[29] Lord Brougham said[30]:

"Whatever can be urged for property in a composition, must be applicable to property in an invention or discovery. It is the subject matter of the composition, not the mere writing, the mere collection of words, that constitutes the work. It may describe an invention, as well as contain a narrative or poem, and the right to the exclusive property in the invention, the title to prevent anyone from describing it to others,

---

[25] (1769) 4 Bur. 2303. See para.1.
[26] Cornish & Llewellyn, *Intellectual Property: Patents, Copyright, Trade Marks and Allied Rights* (5th edn, 2003, Sweet & Maxwell) para.8–50.
[27] [2005] EWCA Civ 595, [2006] Q.B. 125.
[28] (1769) 4 Bur. 2303.
[29] (1854) 4 H.L.C. 814. For a valuable description of Lord Mansfield's contribution to the development of the law of intellectual property, see Professor James Oldham, *The Mansfield Manuscripts* (1992, University of North Carolina Press) Vol.1, Chap.12.
[30] (1854) 4 H.L.C. 814 at 966.

or using it himself (before it is reduced to writing) without the inventor's leave, is precisely the same with the right of the author to exclude all men from the multiplication of his work. But in what manner has this ever been done or attempted to be done by inventors? Never by asserting a property at common law in the inventor, but by obtaining a grant from the Crown."

Lord Brougham recognised that the author of an unpublished manuscript **2–036** had a right to the manuscript, and was entitled to publish the composition, or not, as he saw fit.[31] In later authorities it was held that the "so-called copyright that remains in an author in respect of an unpublished work" at common law could be passed to another independently of the manuscript.[32] But the right so recognised was in the *form* of the composition, not the ideas or information which it contained, as was explained by Lord Oliver in a lecture given to the Hebrew University of Jerusalem in 1989[33]:

"Now the action of confidence is entirely an equitable invention . . . . The common law recognised the right of property of an author in his unpublished work, but what it protected was the mode of expression not the information expressed. The idea that information imparted or acquired in confidence or as a result of a confidential relationship, such as a doctor and a patient, could be legally protected by the courts seems to have arisen only in the early nineteenth century."

He also referred to the basis of the action being[34]:

" . . . that equity intervenes to preserve the confidentiality of information not because information is susceptible of a *proprietary* claim but because its use in the hands of the defendant is unconscionable."

In *Nichrotherm Electrical Co. Ltd v Percy*[35] Lord Evershed M.R. also **2–037** rejected the suggestion of property in ideas, saying:

" . . . a man who thinks of a mechanical conception and then communicates it to others for the purpose of their working out means of carrying it into effect does not, because the idea was his (assuming that it was), get proprietary rights equivalent to those of a patentee. Apart from such rights as may flow from the fact, for example, of the idea being of a secret process communicated in confidence or from some contract of partnership or agency or the like which he may enter into

---

[31] (1854) 4 H.L.C. 814 at 962.
[32] *Re Dickens* [1935] 1 Ch. 267 at 286.
[33] "Spycatcher: Confidence, Copyright and Contempt", *Israel Law Review* (1989) 23(4) 407 at 413.
[34] *ibid.* at 421.
[35] [1957] R.P.C. 207 at 209.

with his collaborator, the originator of the idea gets no proprietary rights out of the mere circumstance that he first thought of it."[36]

2–038   It may be argued that this is hard to reconcile with the concept of a secret recipe as capable of being the subject of a trust (see *Green v Folgham*[37]). But it is perfectly possible to recognise a fiduciary relationship (e.g. between trustee and beneficiary or between partners) involving obligations in relation to confidential information, without regarding such information as property in the strict sense of the word.[38]

2–039   In *Phipps v Boardman*[39] a solicitor to the trustees of a will and a beneficiary under the will trust bought shares in a company in which the trust had a substantial holding. At the time of the negotiations the purchasers were in the position of agents of the trustees and, as such, learned information relevant to the company, which they did not fully report to the trustees. From their special position they gained the opportunity to make a profit from the purchase of the shares and the knowledge that it was there to be made. The House of Lords held by a majority that the purchasers were liable to account for their profits from the purchase as constructive trustees, having used their position to make a personal profit without the full knowledge and consent of their principals.

2–040   The judges were divided on the question whether the information obtained by the purchasers was to be regarded as trust property in the strict sense. Lords Dilhorne,[40] Cohen[41] and Upjohn[42] considered that it was not; Lords Hodson[43] and Guest[44] that it was. Lord Upjohn said[45]:

> "In general, information is not property at all. It is normally open to all who have eyes to read and ears to hear. The true test is to determine in what circumstances the information has been acquired. If it has been acquired in such circumstances that it would be a breach of confidence to disclose it to another then courts of equity will restrain the recipient from communicating it to another. In such cases such confidential information is often and for many years has been described as the property of the donor, the books of authority are full of such references; knowledge of secret processes, 'know-how', confidential information as to the prospects of a company or of someone's intention or the

---

[36] See also *Federal Commissioner of Taxation v United Aircraft Corporation* (1943–1944) 68 C.L.R. 525 at 534 (High Court of Australia), *per* Latham C.J.: "I am unable to regard the communication of information as constituting a transfer of property . . . It is only in a loose metaphorical sense that any knowledge as such can be said to be property."
[37] (1823) 1 Sim. & Stu. 398.
[38] *Phipps v Boardman* [1967] 2 A.C. 46 at 102, *per* Lord Cohen, and at 127–128, *per* Lord Upjohn.
[39] [1967] 2 A.C. 46.
[40] *ibid.* at 89–90.
[41] *ibid.* at 102.
[42] *ibid.* at 127–128.
[43] *ibid.* at 107 and 110.
[44] *ibid.* at 115.
[45] *ibid.* at 127.

expected results of some horse race based on stable or other confidential information. But in the end the real truth is that it is not property in any normal sense but equity will restrain its transmission to another if in breach of some confidential relationship."

Lord Hodson disagreed. He said[46]:

" . . . I dissent from the view that information is of its nature something which is not properly to be described as property. We are aware that what is called 'know-how' in the commercial sense is property which may be very valuable as an asset."

Lord Hodson also cited[47] a passage from the judgment of Bowen L.J. in *Aas v Benham*,[48] in which he commented on an observation of Cotton L.J. in *Dean v MacDowell*[49] that:

"Again if he" (that is, a partner) "makes any profit by the use of any property of the partnership, including, I may say, information which the partnership is entitled to, there the profit is made out of the partnership property."

Bowen L.J. commented:

2–041

"He is speaking of information which a partnership is entitled to in such a sense that it is information which is the property, or is to be included in the property of the partnership—that it to say, information the use of which is valuable to them as a partnership, and to the use of which they have a vested interest."

It is suggested that Lord Upjohn's analysis is to be preferred and it was cited as an accurate summary by the Court of Appeal in *Douglas v Hello! Ltd.*[50] The passages cited by Lord Hodson from *Dean v MacDowell* state the sense in which information has sometimes been referred to as "belonging to" a partnership (i.e. information valuable to the partnership and which the partnership has a right to use), but the basis of such right lies in the relationship between the partners.

The information in *Phipps v Boardman* was of the same character in that **2–042** its use was of potential value to the trustees and it was obtained by the purchasers in the capacity of agents for the trustees.

Similarly in *Bell v Lever Bros*[51] Lord Blanesbury said, in relation to **2–043** private cocoa speculations by directors of a company engaged in the cocoa market, that:

---

[46] *Phipps v Boardman* [1967] 2 A.C. 46 at 107.
[47] *ibid.* at 109–110.
[48] [1891] 2 Ch. 244 at 258.
[49] (1878) 8 Ch.D. 345 at 354.
[50] [2005] EWCA Civ 595; [2006] Q.B. 125, at para.127.
[51] [1932] A.C. 161 at 194.

" . . . the company has no concern in his profit and cannot make him accountable for it unless it appears—this is the essential qualification—that in earning that profit he has made use *either* of the property of the company *or* of some confidential information which has come to him as a director of the company." (Emphasis added.)

2–044 The director's liability in the latter case would arise not from the confidential information constituting property, but from use of his fiduciary position to make a personal profit without his principal's knowledge.

2–045 In *Seager v Copydex Ltd*[52] the plaintiff entered into negotiations with the defendants with a view to their marketing a carpet grip invented by him and for which he had a patent. During the negotiations the plaintiff suggested to the defendants an alternative form of grip. After the negotiations fell through, the defendants marketed a grip closely similar to the plaintiff's suggested alternative. The plaintiff claimed an injunction and damages. The defendants were found to have made use unconsciously of information supplied to them in confidence. The Court of Appeal declined to grant an injunction or an account of profits but ordered an inquiry as to damages.

2–046 Following the precedent of *Mechanical and General Inventions Co. v Austin*[53] the plaintiff would appear to have had a good case for relying on breach of an implied contract, but there is no reference to that authority being cited; and the decision of the Court of Appeal was expressly based not on any theory of implied contract, but on the principle of equity that a person who receives information in confidence shall not take unfair advantage of it.

2–047 In *Seager v Copydex Ltd (No. 2)*[54] the Court of Appeal directed that the damages be assessed, by analogy with damages for conversion, on the basis of the market value of the information misused by the defendants. Lord Denning M.R. said that just as a satisfied judgment in trover transferred the property in the goods, so the confidential information would belong to the defendants once the damages were paid.

2–048 This has prompted the comment:

"The Court of Appeal had already held . . . that the confidence was purely equitable. What it was now doing was to hold that equity would condone, nay facilitate, the compulsory acquisition by the defendant of the plaintiff's property; a state of affairs that would have exceeded the comprehension of the masters of equity who spoke in England before darkness enveloped all."[55]

---

[52] [1967] 1 W.L.R. 923.
[53] [1935] A.C. 346.
[54] [1969] 1 W.L.R. 809.
[55] *Meagher, Gummow and Lehane on Equity: Doctrines and Remedies* (4th edn, 2002 Butterworths LexisNexis), para.41–090. Contrast also *Franklin v Giddins* [1978] Qd.R. 72 (see para.3–034, below).

The analogy of conversion has also been criticised by others including **2–049** Professor Cornish[56]:

> "Altogether, the analogy to damages for misappropriation of a single tangible article is inept, given in particular the more obvious comparison to patents and copyright and the more flexible approach to damages which applies to their infringement."

While it seems entirely just that the plaintiff should have been compensated for the fact that information supplied by him to the defendants in confidence was used by them without his permission to their commercial advantage, the *Seager v Copydex* decisions present difficulties of analysis. **2–050**

A possible interpretation of *Seager v Copydex* is that it established a new **2–051** head of tortious liability for breach of confidence, analogous to conversion and based on the plaintiff's proprietary right in the information.[57] However, that is difficult to reconcile with the fact that the judgment of the Court of Appeal on liability was expressly founded on "the broad principle of equity that he who has received information in confidence shall not take unfair advantage of it".[58] That principle does not require any underlying proprietary right.

Lord Denning M.R. expressed the same view in *Fraser v Evans*[59]: **2–052**

> "The jurisdiction is based not so much on property or on contract as on the duty to be of good faith. No person is permitted to divulge to the world information which he has received in confidence, unless he has just cause or excuse for doing so."

A similar view was expressed in the High Court of Australia in *Moorgate* **2–053** *Tobacco Co. Ltd v Philip Morris Ltd (No. 2)*[60] by Deane J. (with the concurrence of Gibbs C.J. and Mason, Wilson and Dawson JJ.):

> "It is unnecessary, for the purposes of the present appeal, to attempt to define the precise scope of the equitable jurisdiction to grant relief against an actual or threatened abuse of confidential information not involving any tort or any breach of some express or implied contractual provision, some wider fiduciary duty or some copyright or trade mark right. A general equitable jurisdiction to grant such relief has long been

---

[56] Cornish & Llewelyn, *Intellectual Property: Patents, Copyright, Trade Marks and Allied Rights* (5th edn, 2003, Sweet & Maxwell) para.8–48.
[57] For a critique of this interpretation and its problems see Prof. P. M. North, "Breach of Confidence: Is there a New Tort?" 12 J.S.P.T.L. 149.
[58] [1967] 1 W.L.R. 923 at 931, *per* Lord Denning M.R. Lord Goff in the *Spycatcher* case treated *Seager v Copydex Ltd* as founded on obligation of conscience rather than proprietary rights. See [1990] 1 A.C. 109 at 281.
[59] [1969] 1 Q.B. 349 at 361.
[60] (1984) 156 C.L.R. 414 at 437–438.

asserted and should, in my view, now be accepted: see *The Commonwealth v John Fairfax & Sons Ltd*.[61] Like most heads of exclusive equitable jurisdiction its rational basis does not lie in proprietary right. It lies in the notion of an obligation of conscience arising from the circumstances in or through which the information was communicated or obtained."

2–054 It has also been held that the information in an examination paper does not constitute "intangible property" capable of falling within s.4 of the Theft Act 1968.[62]

2–055 In *Douglas v Hello! Ltd (No. 3)* the question arose directly whether confidential or private information, capable of commercial exploitation, constituted as such a form of property. Lindsay J. found that the claimants had a right to control pictorial information about their wedding because it was a private event; and that because it was commercially exploitable, their right to exclusivity of photographic coverage of the event was a form of property right which could be shared with another and enforced by the other, at any rate where the defendant knew or could be taken to know of the co-ownership before acting in breach and where all entitled to the confidence asserted it. The Court of Appeal agreed with the first but disagreed with the second part of the judge's ruling. It held that the claimants had a right of protection of information about their wedding because it was private but rejected the argument that their right was based on some form of proprietary interest.[63]

2–056 Although some forms of confidential information bear some similarity to some forms of intellectual property, any broad concept of confidential information as property would be hard to encapsulate. Confidential information involves information about some fact or idea, but a mere fact or private idea is not susceptible of ownership.[64] It would be a strange form of property which would come into existence on the confidential acquisition of information about a fact or idea and cease to exist on its wider publication.

2–057 As Professor Gareth Jones has commented[65]:

"Confidential information is conceptually very much *sui generis*. It is an intangible; and, consequently, it would be 'wrong to confuse the physical records with [the information] itself . . . ; for if you put them on a duplicator and produce one hundred copies you have certainly not

---

[61] (1980) 147 C.L.R. 39 at 50–52.
[62] *Oxford v Moss* (1979) 68 Cr.App.R. 183.
[63] [2005] EWCA Civ 595; [2006] Q.B. 125, at paras 119, 126–127.
[64] *Jefferys v Boosey* (1854) 4 H.L.C. 814; *Nichrotherm Electrical Co. Ltd v Percy* [1957] R.P.C. 207; *Federal Commissioner of Taxation v United Aircraft Corporation* (1943) 68 C.L.R. 525 at 534.
[65] "Restitution of benefits obtained in breach of another's confidence" (1970) 86 L.Q.R. 463 at 464.

multiplied your asset in proportion'.[66] It has, too, the quality that it may be transmitted to a limited class without destroying its value; so, know-how 'can be communicated to or shared with others outside the manufacturer's own business,' for example, under licence.[67] Conversely the nature of confidential information is such that no one, save the person who imparted it, may realise for some time that it has been communicated in breach of confidence. For similar reasons it is not always easy to protect a purchaser of confidential information from his seller who subsequently sells the same information to another innocent third party.

Information is not like other choses in action, such as debt or copyright, which lend themselves more easily to a classical analysis in terms of property."

There is a danger of circularity of reasoning in concluding, because equity intervenes by injunction or other remedy, that the reason for the intervention lies in the protection of a proprietary interest. This point was recognised by Gummow J. in *Smith Kline & French Laboratories (Australia) Ltd v Department of Community Services*,[68] citing *Colbeam Palmer Ltd v Stock Affiliates Pty Ltd*[69] and *E.I. Du Pont de Nemours Powder Company v Masland*,[70] where Holmes J. said: **2–058**

"The word property as applied to trade-marks and trade secrets is an unanalysed expression of certain secondary consequences of the primary fact that the law makes some rudimentary requirements of good faith."

These objections, powerful though they are, would be no compelling reason for the courts not to recognise confidential information as a form of property, if to do so would resolve problems and assist the development of the law on a principled and rational basis. But, if anything, the opposite would be the case.   **2–059**

Professor Finn has observed[71]:   **2–060**

"Certain types of information and particularly trade secrets doubtless can have certain of the attributes of property. Information can for example be intrinsically valuable; it can be the subject matter of a trust; it can be communicated for a consideration; it can be included in the 'property' which passes to a trustee in bankruptcy.

[66] *Rolls-Royce Ltd v Jeffrey (Inspector of Taxes)* [1962] 1 All E.R. 801 at 805, *per* Lord Radcliffe.
[67] *ibid.*
[68] [1990] F.S.R. 617 at 673–674; (affirmed (1991) 28 F.C.R. 291).
[69] (1968) 122 C.L.R. 25 at 34, *per* Windeyer J.
[70] (1917) 244 U.S. 100 at 102.
[71] Finn, *Fiduciary Obligations* (1977) paras 295–296. Note also his comment at para.293, "Perhaps the most sterile of debates which have arisen around the subject of information received in confidence is whether or not such information should be classified as property".

But even if from such similarities one wishes to create a form of abstract property, difficulties immediately arise. If all information is described as property, it is nonetheless meaningless to give a property basis to the jurisdiction relieving against misuse of information. All such 'property' is not protected by the courts. The information, and the circumstances of its communication must, as will be seen, possess certain characteristics before protection will be given. If only some information is described as property, i.e. information protected by the courts, to call that information property is merely to add yet another consequence to a decision taken for reasons quite unrelated to property considerations."

2–061   Nowhere are the difficulties of adopting property as a basis of the jurisdiction more acute than in relation to the "innocent" third party. The concept of an action for breach of confidence based on a broad principle that one should not break, or co-operate with another in breaking, a personal duty of confidence is fundamentally different from the concept of an action based on tortious infringement of a property right analogous to trespass to goods.

2–062   If the concept is based on equitable principles, no liability would be expected to attach to a third party recipient of confidential information for acts done by him in ignorance that there had been any breach of confidence. So, it has been held that, in order to be fixed with an obligation of confidence, a third party must know that the information was confidential.[72] On discovering that there had been such breach the third party would ordinarily then come under a duty of confidence, at least if he were a volunteer.[73] On the other hand, it might be unfair to impose such a duty on him if he had paid in good faith for the information, or had subsequently incurred effort or expense in putting it to use, or had otherwise undergone a change of circumstances, except possibly on terms compensating him for the loss or prejudice which he would otherwise suffer.[74]

2–063   However, if the concept is based on a tort of infringement of property analogous to conversion, the mental innocence of the third party would be no defence and he would be liable in damages for his past innocent misuse of the plaintiff's confidential information,[75] a liability analogous to the statutory liability to damages of an infringer of copyright.[76]

2–064   The only way of avoiding strict liability for innocent misuse of confidential information would be for the courts to create a special defence not ordinarily available in cases of tortious infringement of property rights.

[72] *Fraser v Thames Television* [1984] 1 Q.B. 44 at 65. *Valeo Vision S.A. v Flexible Lamps Ltd* [1995] R.P.C. 205 at 226–228. *Thomas v Pearce* [2000] F.S.R. 718. See also the Report of the Law Commission, Law Com No.110, Cmnd. 8388 (1981), para.4.12.
[73] *Printers & Finishers Ltd v Holloway* [1965] R.P.C. 239 at 253 and 257, *per* Cross J. and *Fraser v Thames Television* [1984] 1 Q.B. 44.
[74] See paras 3–054–3–062, below.
[75] Compare *Marfani & Co. Ltd v Midland Bank Ltd* [1968] 1 W.L.R. 956.
[76] *Paterson Zochonis & Co. Ltd v Merfarken Packaging Ltd* [1986] 3 All E.R. 522.

In *Douglas v Hello! Ltd (No. 3)* Lindsay J. tentatively followed this path **2–065** when he held that the benefit of a confidence could be shared between and be enforceable by co-owners or by a successor in title, but added "at any rate where the defendant knew or could be taken to have known of the co-ownership or sharing before acting in breach".[77] But, as the Court of Appeal held, if the claimants had a proprietary right in information about the events at their wedding, it would be a right which could be exercised against a third party regardless of whether he ought to have been aware that the information was private or confidential.[78]

As Professor Gareth Jones has said[79]:   **2–066**

> "No property theory can satisfactorily determine, even with the aid of equity, the question of the liability of the person who innocently exploits a secret. For example, there may be circumstances where it is just that a volunteer should be free of any liability to account for profits made through the use of confidential information. Conversely, it may not be difficult to imagine a case where even a bona fide purchaser ought to be enjoined, albeit on terms, from using information which he later learns was given him in breach of another's confidence."

Conflicting views on damages

For a long time there was uncertainty about the foundation on which **2–067** damages could be awarded for breach of confidence.

If a duty of confidentiality arises simply from an equitable obligation of **2–068** conscience, according to traditional authority the remedies would not include damages (except under the jurisdiction derived from Lord Cairns' Act and now contained in s.50 of the Supreme Court Act 1981). So, for example, in *Robb v Green*[80] the Court of Appeal held that the plaintiff's entitlement to damages depended on whether he could establish a breach of an implied contract or only a breach of an equitable duty of confidence.

In *Nichrotherm Electrical Ltd v Percy,*[81] Harman J. ordered an inquiry as **2–069** to damages for breach of confidence and breach of copyright. In the Court of Appeal the matter proceeded, by agreement, on the basis that the breach of confidence relied upon by the plaintiff involved breach of an implied contract, and on that ground the court did not have to consider further the basis of the enquiry as to damages. But the court was clearly troubled by the form of order at first instance, and Lord Evershed M.R. observed[82]:

---

[77] [2005] EWCA Civ 595; [2006] Q.B. 125 at para.123.
[78] *ibid* at para.126.
[79] "Restitution of benefits obtained in breach of another's confidence" (1970) 86 L.Q.R. 463 at 465.
[80] [1895] 2 Q.B. 315.
[81] [1956] R.P.C. 272.
[82] [1957] R.P.C. 207 at 213.

"If the confidence, breach of which is alleged or proved, is imposed by or arises out of contract, express or implied, then the remedy would, I assume, be by way of damages at law as upon a breach of contract. If, on the other hand, the confidence infringed is one imposed by the rules of equity, then the remedy would be, prima facie, by way of injunction or damages in lieu of an injunction under Lord Cairns' Act."

2–070   In *Seager v Copydex Ltd*[83] the Court of Appeal held that the defendant was in breach of an equitable duty for which it declined to order an injunction or account of profits but ordered an inquiry as to damages, which it later directed should be assessed on the basis of the market value of the information misused.[84] The two decisions caused much academic debate but their historical significance was in setting a precedent for an award of damages for breach of an equitable obligation.

2–071   In the telephone tapping case of *Malone v Metropolitan Police Commissioner*[85] one of the grounds on which the plaintiff sought, unsuccessfully, a declaration that it was unlawful for the defendant to tap his telephone line was based on a claimed right of confidentiality. Sir Robert Megarry V.C. said[86]:

"This is an equitable right which is still in the course of development, and is usually protected by the grant of an injunction to prevent disclosure of the confidence. Under Lord Cairns' Act 1858 damages may be granted in substitution for an injunction; yet if there is no case for the grant of an injunction, as when the disclosure has already been made, the unsatisfactory result seems to be that no damages can be awarded under this head: see *Proctor v Bayley* (1889) 42 Ch.D. 390. In such a case, where there is no breach of contract or other orthodox foundation for damages at common law, it seems doubtful whether there is any right to damages, as distinct from an account of profits. It may be, however, that a new tort is emerging (see *Goff and Jones, The Law of Restitution* (6th edn 2002), pp.518, 519 and Gareth Jones (1970) 86 L.Q.R. 463, 491), though this has been doubted: see *Street, The Law of Torts* 6th edn (1976), p.377. Certainly the subject raises many questions that are so far unresolved . . . "

2–072   In its Report on Breach of Confidence in 1981[87] the Law Commission expressed the different view, in para.4.76, that:

"It is a reasonable inference from the decision in *Seager v Copydex Ltd* that damages are awardable for a past breach of confidence."

---

[83] [1967] 1 W.L.R. 923.
[84] [1969] 1 W.L.R. 809.
[85] [1979] 1 Ch. 344.
[86] *ibid.* at 360.
[87] Law Com No.110, Cmnd. 8388 (1981).

But it qualified that view by adding:

> "On the other hand it can be argued that it is not clear from that case whether the damages which were ordered to be assessed were intended to include loss suffered in respect of the past breach of confidence or only to provide compensation in lieu of an injunction. The subsequent decision in *Seager v Copydex Ltd (No. 2)*, in which the Court of Appeal had to determine the basis of assessment for the damages ordered in the earlier case, has not clarified the position in this respect."

In *English v Dedham Vale Properties*[88] Slade J. said that he read *Seager v Copydex Ltd* as a case in which the court granted damages in lieu of an injunction.

In *Dowson & Mason Ltd v Potter*[89] an employee of the plaintiffs in   **2–073** breach of duty divulged confidential information to another company, who used it to compete with his employers. The plaintiffs sued the employee and the company. Both submitted to an order for an inquiry as to damages. Subsequently an issue arose as to the basis on which damages were to be assessed. The company contended that damages should be assessed by reference to the value of the information, following *Seager v Copydex Ltd*. The plaintiffs contended successfully for assessment by reference to their loss of profits. The Court of Appeal held that *Seager v Copydex Ltd* laid down no general rule as to the appropriate basis of assessment in such a case, and applied the principle stated by Lord Wilberforce in *General Tire and Rubber Co. v Firestone Tyre & Rubber Co. Ltd*[90]:

> "As in the case of any other tort (leaving aside cases where exemplary damages can be given) the object of damages is to compensate for loss or injury. The general rule at any rate in relation to 'economic' torts is that the measure of damages is to be, so far as possible, that sum of money which will put the injured party in the same position as he would have been in if he had not sustained the wrong."

However, there was no analysis of the underlying basis of the order for damages, which had not been articulated in any judgment, since the order was made by consent.

In the *Spycatcher* case Lord Goff said[91]:   **2–074**

> "An important section of the law of restitution is concerned with cases in which a defendant is required to make restitution in respect of benefits acquired through his own wrongful act—notably cases of waiver of tort; of benefits acquired by certain criminal acts; of benefits acquired in breach of a fiduciary relationship; and, of course, of

[88] [1978] 1 W.L.R. 93 at 111.
[89] [1986] 1 W.L.R. 1419.
[90] [1975] 1 W.L.R. 819 at 824.
[91] [1990] 1 A.C. 109 at 286.

benefits acquired in breach of confidence. The plaintiff's claim to restitution is usually enforced by an account of profits made by the defendant through his wrong at the plaintiff's expense. This remedy of an account is alternative to the remedy of damages, which in cases of breach of confidence is now available, despite the equitable nature of the wrong, through a beneficent interpretation of the Chancery Amendment Act 1858 (Lord Cairns' Act) . . . "

2–075   In *Universal Thermosensors Ltd v Hibben*[92] Sir Donald Nicholls V.C. referred to *Seager v Copydex Ltd* and, in particular, the passage in Lord Denning's judgment to the effect that a recipient of confidential information should not get a start over others by using it, at any rate without paying for it, even if the case was not one for an injunction. The Vice-Chancellor added:

> "An award of damages in such circumstances would not be a novelty. There are several fields where the courts have awarded damages to a plaintiff whose property is wrongfully used by another even though the plaintiff has not suffered pecuniary loss by such user. The cases concerning this principle, sometimes called 'the "user" principle', can be found gathered together in *Stoke-on-Trent City Council v W & J Wass Ltd* [1988] 1 W.L.R. 1406, 1416–1418."

2–076   *Stoke-on-Trent City Council v W. & J. Wass Ltd* is authority for the proposition that as a general rule damages in tort are to be assessed by reference to the loss sustained by the plaintiff; but that exceptionally in certain cases (such as trespass to land, patent infringement and certain cases of nuisance or detinue) the user principle may apply to enable the plaintiff to recover a reasonable sum for the use made of his property.

2–077   The principle was approved in *Inverugie Investments Ltd v Hackett*,[93] where Lord Lloyd said:

> "The principle need not be characterised as exclusively compensatory, or exclusively restitutionary; it combines elements of both."

2–078   It would be deeply unsatisfactory that monetary compensation should be capable of being awarded for past misuse of confidential information only where there was a case for the grant of an injunction (as Sir Robert Megarry V.C. observed in *Malone v Metropolitan Police Commissioner*[94]) and, probably because that is so obvious, it has become accepted in practice that compensation can be awarded generally for breach of confidence. The surprise is that the courts should still be grappling for a satisfactory explanation on what basis (other than breach of contract) this may be done.

[92] [1992] 1 W.L.R. 840 at 856.
[93] [1995] 1 W.L.R. 713 at 718, PC.
[94] [1979] 1 Ch. 344 at 360.

Lord Goff's suggestion in the *Spycatcher* case[95] that damages are now **2–079** available for breach of confidence, despite the equitable nature of the wrong, through a "beneficent interpretation" of Lord Cairns' Act, is not entirely satisfactory.

In neither *Seager v Copydex Ltd* nor *Seager v Copydex Ltd (No. 2)*[96] did **2–080** the Court of Appeal make any reference to Lord Cairns's Act providing the basis for damages. Further, it is not difficult to imagine cases in which there could be no grounds for the grant of an injunction, for example, because there was no threat to repeat a past breach, or because the information had ceased to be confidential for reasons which might be quite independent of the defendant's breach (as in *Mustad & Son v Dosen*[97]). In such a case, to describe an award of damages for a past breach as being in lieu of an injunction would involve more than a beneficent interpretation of Lord Cairns's Act. It would be a fiction.

An alternative partial solution might be advanced under the rubric of **2–081** restitution, under which a wrongdoer may be required to restore benefits obtained through his own wrongful act. In *Spycatcher*[98] Lord Goff recognised this principle as applying to benefits obtained in breach of confidence. This would justify the wrongdoer being ordered to pay over the value of the benefit received, regardless of the availability of an injunction; and so, on the facts of *Seager v Copydex Ltd*, would afford a legitimate basis for the defendants being required to pay the "market value" of the information misused.

That would have the same effect as a *quantum meruit* award, which Goff **2–082** and Jones[99] suggest would have been a happier basis of the award in *Seager v Copydex Ltd*. However, the authors recognise that it is difficult to square that approach with an award of damages. It would be still more difficult to justify expectation damages (i.e. damages for loss of anticipated profits), as in *Dowson & Mason Ltd v Potter*,[1] on a restitutionary basis.

Equitable compensation

A more satisfactory solution (not dependent on Lord Cairns's Act or on the **2–083** developing principles of restitution) is to recognise that equitable compensation may be awarded for breach of an equitable duty of confidence, just as it may be awarded for breach of duty by a fiduciary (*Nocton v Ashburton*[2]).

---

[95] [1990] 1 A.C. 109 at 286.
[96] [1967] 1 W.L.R. 923; [1969] 1 W.L.R. 809.
[97] [1964] 1 W.L.R. 109.
[98] [1990] 1 A.C. 109 at 286.
[99] Goff and Jones, *The Law of Restitution* (6th edn, 2002), para.34–013.
[1] [1986] 1 W.L.R. 1419.
[2] [1914] A.C. 932.

2–084   This approach accords with the view expressed by Professor Finn that[3]:

> " . . . no great violence to principle is wrought if they [i.e. awards of damages for breach of an equitable obligation of confidence] are regarded as modern developments in the compensatory jurisdiction of Equity which was so forcefully reaffirmed by Viscount Haldane L.C. in *Nocton v Ashburton.*"

It is also consistent with the decision of the Court of Appeal in *Kitchenology BV v Unicor Gmbh Plastmaschinen.*[4] The court held that claims for breach of confidence do not arise in tort and that it was clear beyond doubt that the jurisdiction to "restrain and, if necessary, award damages for breach of confidence" was an equitable jurisdiction.

2–085   The law relating to fiduciary relationships is one of the least clearly defined areas of the law,[5] but there is a close parallel between a person owing an equitable obligation of confidence and a person owing a fiduciary obligation, and there seems no good reason in principle why a person should not be required to provide compensation in equity (sometimes called equitable damages) for breach of an equitable obligation of confidence as in a case of breach of a fiduciary obligation.

2–086   *Seager v Copydex Ltd* was explained in this way in *U.S. Surgical Corporation v Hospital Products International Pty Ltd* by McLelland J., who said[6]:

> "Apart from the limited power to award damages in addition to or in substitution for equitable relief, conferred by the Supreme Court Act, 1970, S.68 (following Lord Cairns' Act), which is of no present relevance, the court has an inherent power to grant relief by way of monetary compensation for breach of a fiduciary or other equitable obligation: see *Nocton v Lord Ashburton* [1914] A.C. 932 at pp.946, 956, 957; *McKenzie v McDonald* [1927] V.L.R. 134 at p.146; *Holmes v Walton* [1961] W.A.R. 96; *cf. Seager v Copydex Ltd* [1967] 1 W.L.R. 923; [1967] 2 All E.R. 415; [1969] 1 W.L.R. 809; [1969] 2 All E.R. 718."

2–087   Just as the doctrine of fiduciary duty is not limited to direct relationships[7] but extends to a person who dishonestly assists in a breach of trust by

---

[3] Finn, *Fiduciary Obligations* (1977), para.388.

[4] [1995] F.S.R. 765 at 777–778.

[5] See *Henderson v Merrett Syndicates Ltd* [1995] 2 A.C. 145 at 206, *per* Lord Browne-Wilkinson.

[6] [1982] 2 N.S.W.L.R. 766 at 816. (Reversed on other grounds (1984) 156 C.L.R. 41.) See also Davidson, "The Equitable Remedy of Compensation", 13 *Melbourne University Law Review* 349.

[7] *White v Jones* [1995] 2 A.C. 207 at 271, *per* Lord Browne-Wilkinson: " . . . the special relationship (i.e. a fiduciary relationship) giving rise to the assumption of responsibility held to exist in Nocton's case does not depend on any mutual dealing between A and B, let alone on any relationship akin to contract. Although such factors may be present, equity imposes the obligation because A has assumed to act in B's affairs".

another (*Royal Brunei Airlines v Tan*[8]), or who receives (by accident or misconduct) assets emanating from another in the knowledge that he was not intended to do so (*Chase Manhattan Bank N.A. v Israel-British Bank (London) Ltd*[9]), there seems no reason in principle why equitable compensation for breach of a duty of confidence should not equally be awarded against a person who knowingly assists in a breach of confidence by another,[10] or who knowingly receives confidential information by mistake or misconduct and misuses it.[11]

Although there is considerable historical authority on the difference between compensation in equity and damages at common law,[12] the House of Lords held in *Target Holdings Ltd v Redferns*[13] that the principles underlying both are the same, the fundamental object being to compensate the innocent party for the loss caused by the wrong. **2–088**

In Art.8 cases, it is established that damages may be awarded, including damages for distress (as in *Campbell v MGN Ltd*[14] and *Douglas v Hello! Ltd*[15]). But it is suggested that, depending on the relationship between the parties, it may be more realistic to regard such damages as based in tort than on a strained concept of an equitable obligation. **2–089**

New Zealand, Canada and Australia

It is instructive to compare the development of the law in New Zealand, Canada and Australia. In *Aquaculture Corporation v New Zealand Green Mussel Co. Ltd*[16] the defendants misused confidential information, supplied by the plaintiff, in manufacturing and marketing a product. The plaintiff claimed that its own business prospects had been injured by the defendants' irresponsible marketing campaign. Damages for the plaintiff's loss were assessed at $1.5 million, but the trial judge held that he had no power to award compensatory damages. This ruling was reversed on appeal. Delivering the judgment of the Court of Appeal of New Zealand, Cooke P. said[17]: **2–090**

> "There is now a line of judgments in this Court accepting that monetary compensation (which can be labelled damages) may be awarded for breach of a duty of confidence or other duty deriving historically from equity . . . In some of these cases the relevant observations were arguably obiter, but we think that the point should

---

[8] [1995] 2 A.C. 378.
[9] [1981] Ch. 105.
[10] See paras 3–066 — 3–074, below.
[11] See paras 3–030 and 3–043 — 3–047, below.
[12] See Meagher, Gummow and Lehane, *Equity: Doctrines and Remedies* (4th edn, 2002), Ch.23.
[13] [1995] 3 W.L.R. 352.
[14] [2004] 2 A.C. 457; [2004] UKHL 22.
[15] [2005] EWCA Civ 595; [2006] Q.B. 125.
[16] [1990] 3 N.Z.L.R. 299.
[17] *ibid.* at 301.

now be taken as settled in New Zealand. Whether the obligation of confidence in a case of the present kind should be classified as purely an equitable one is debatable, but we do not think that the question matters for any purpose material to this appeal. For all purposes now material, equity and common law are mingled or merged. The practicality of the matter is that in the circumstances of the dealings between the parties the law imposes a duty of confidence. For its breach a full range of remedies should be available as appropriate, no matter whether they originated in common law, equity or statute."

Cooke P. drew support from this approach not only from New Zealand authorities but also from the decisions of the Supreme Court of Canada in *LAC Minerals Ltd v International Corona Resources Ltd*[18] and of Rogers J. in the Supreme Court of New South Wales in *Catt v Marac Australia Ltd.*[19]

2–091   In *Lac Minerals* the plaintiff owned mining rights on land on which it was drilling exploratory holes. In the course of negotiations with a view to a possible partnership or joint venture (which never materialised), the plaintiff revealed to the defendant information about the drilling results, from which it was clear that an adjacent property was likely to have valuable deposits. The plaintiff attempted to acquire the mining rights in the adjacent property but was out bid by the defendant, which developed the mine on its own account. The plaintiff sought a declaration that the defendant held the mining rights on constructive trust for the plaintiff on the grounds either of breach of fiduciary duty or of breach of confidence. It was found that, but for the defendant's use of the relevant information, the plaintiff would have obtained the mining rights and developed the mine for itself.

2–092   Three issues therefore arose: first, whether the defendant acquired the mining rights in breach of fiduciary duty (in which case there could be no dispute about the defendant holding the rights on trust for the plaintiff); secondly, whether the defendant acted in breach of confidence; and thirdly, if so, what remedy was available.

2–093   The Supreme Court held (by a majority) that the parties were not in a fiduciary relationship, but (unanimously) that the defendant acted in breach of confidence. On the question of remedy, the majority (La Forest, Lamer and Wilson JJ.) upheld the plaintiff's argument in favour of the imposition of a constructive trust. The minority (Sopinka and McIntyre JJ.) considered damages a more appropriate remedy. There was, however, no difference between the judges as to the range of remedies which it lay within the court's power to award. On this the most detailed analysis was that of Sopinka J. He said[20]:

---

[18] [1990] F.S.R. 441.
[19] (1986) 9 N.S.W.L.R. 639.
[20] [1990] F.S.R. 441 at 495–497.

"The foundation of action for breach of confidence does not rest solely on one of the traditional jurisdictional bases for action of contract, equity or property. The action is *sui generis* relying on all three to enforce the policy of the law that confidences be respected: see Gurry, *Breach of Confidence* (Clarendon Press, Oxford, 1984) at pp.25–26, and Goff & Jones, *The Law of Restitution*, (3rd edn, Sweet & Maxwell, 1986) at pp.664–667.

This multi-faceted jurisdictional basis for the action provides the court with considerable flexibility in fashioning a remedy. The jurisdictional basis supporting the particular claim is relevant in determining the appropriate remedy . . . . A constructive trust is ordinarily reserved for those situations where a right of property is recognised . . .

Although confidential information has some of the characteristics of property, its foothold as such is tenuous . . .

As a result, there is virtually no support in the cases for the imposition of a constructive trust over property acquired as a result of the use of confidential information . . .

Although unjust enrichment has been recognised as having an existence apart from contract or tort under a heading referred to as the law of restitution, a constructive trust is not the appropriate remedy in most cases . . .

While the remedy of the constructive trust may continue to be employed in situations where other remedies would be inappropriate or injustice would result, there is no reason to extend it to this case.

The conventional remedies for breach of confidence are an accounting of profits or damages. An injunction may be coupled with either of these remedies in appropriate circumstances. A restitutionary remedy is appropriate in cases involving fiduciaries because they are required to disgorge any benefits derived from the breach of trust. In a breach of confidence case, the focus is on the loss to the plaintiff and, as in tort actions, the particular position of the plaintiff must be examined. The object is to restore the plaintiff monetarily to the position he would have been in if no wrong had been committed: see *Dowson & Mason Ltd v Potter* [1986] 2 All E.R. 418 (CA) and *Talbot v General Television Corp. Pty Ltd* [1980] V.R. 224. Accordingly, this object is generally achieved by an award of damages, and a restitutionary remedy is inappropriate."

The majority considered that the imposition of a constructive trust was **2–094** the appropriate remedy as the surest way of putting the plaintiff in the position that it would have been in but for the defendant's breach of confidence; and that the restitutionary principle, which enables a court to give to a plaintiff something which has been wrongly taken from him (a restitutionary proprietary award), or its monetary value (a personal restitutionary award), should by analogy apply equally in the situation in which the wrongdoer has acquired a benefit which would otherwise have accrued for the benefit of the plaintiff.

2–095   In *Cadbury Schweppes Inc v FBI Foods Ltd*[21] Binnie J., delivering the judgment of the Supreme Court, rejected criticisms of Sopinka J.'s *sui generis* characterisation of the action for breach of confidence. He observed that the concept had been adopted to recognise the flexibility that had been shown by the courts to uphold confidentiality and in crafting remedies for its protection. On the jurisdiction of the court to award damages he said[22]:

> "Equity, like the common law, is capable of ongoing growth and development . . . In my view, therefore, having regard to the evolution of the equitable principles apparent in the case law, we should clearly affirm that, in this country, the authority to award financial compensation for breach of confidence is inherent in the exercise of general equitable jurisdiction and does not depend on the niceties of Lord Cairns' Act or its statutory successors. This conclusion is fed, as well, by the sui generic nature of the action. The objective in a breach of confidence case is to put the confider in as good a position as it would have been in but for the breach. To that end, the Court has ample jurisdiction to fashion appropriate relief out of the full gamut of available remedies, including appropriate financial compensation."

2–096   In Australia there has been searching analysis, particularly by Meagher, Gummow and Lehane[23] and (in his judicial capacity) by Gummow J. in *Corrs Pavey v Collector of Customs*[24] and *Smith, Kline & French Laboratories (Australia) Ltd v Secretary to the Department of Community Services and Health*.[25] Meagher, Gummow and Lehane have observed that[26]:

> " . . . the equitable duty of confidence has now sufficiently developed (as has the law of trusts to a much greater degree) to be regarded as occupying a specific field of its own, but subject always to the caveat that where there are questions as to the direction of further development (for example, in dealing with third parties who receive information) these can best be answered by looking to the source whence the stream has sprung. Thus, it will be contended that the third party who participates in breach of a duty of confidence is accountable under the second limb of *Barnes v Addy* (1874) 9 Ch.App. 244 at 251, no less than is a participant in a breach by a delinquent fiduciary within the strict modern acceptance of that term."

---

[21] (1999) 167 D.L.R. (4th) 577 at 591.
[22] *ibid.* at 604.
[23] Meagher, Gummow and Lehane, *Equity: Doctrines and Remedies* (4th edn, 2002), Ch.41.
[24] (1987) 74 A.L.R. 428.
[25] [1990] F.S.R. 617, affirmed [1991] 28 F.C.R. 291.
[26] Meagher, Gummow and Lehane, *op. cit.*, para.41–035.

In *Smith, Kline & French* Gummow J. said[27]: **2–097**

> "It seems clear enough that knowledge *per se* is not proprietary in
> character; see *Moorgate Tobacco Co. Ltd v Philip Morris Ltd* (1982)
> 64 F.L.R. 387 at 404–405, affirmed (1984) 156 C.L.R. 414; *Boardman
> v Phipps* [1967] 2 A.C. 46 at 89–92, 102–103, 127–129, but compare
> 106–107, 115. Further, it is clear in Australia that the equitable
> jurisdiction to grant relief against an actual or threatened abuse of
> confidential information, not involving any tort or breach of contract,
> fiduciary duty, copyright or trade mark, is based not in pre-existing
> proprietary right, but in an obligation of conscience arising in the
> circumstances of the case: *Moorgate Tobacco Co. Ltd v Philip Morris
> Ltd (No.2)*."[28]

Gummow J. also held it to be established law in Australia that the court **2–098**
had an inherent jurisdiction to award monetary compensation, independent
of its statutory powers under any derivative of Lord Cairns's Act, for breach
of an equitable duty of confidence, as appears from the following part of his
judgment[29]:

> "I should have hoped that any controversy as to the applicability of
> Lord Cairns's Act and its derivatives to claims in respect of purely
> equitable rights (rather than tortious or contractual rights) had been
> quelled by the recent analysis by Mr Dean in his work, *The Law of
> Trade Secrets* (1990), pp.317–320, 329. I have indicated my views in
> *Concept Television Productions Pty Ltd v Australian Broadcasting
> Corporation* (1988) 12 I.P.R. 129 at 136. This Court is, by statute, a
> court of equity as regards matters otherwise within its jurisdiction . . .
> This brings with it, in a case such as the present, the inherent
> jurisdiction to grant relief by way of monetary compensation for
> breach of an equitable obligation, whether of trust or confidence. After
> all, long before the birth of Lord Cairns, delinquent trustees were
> brought to book in Chancery and, independently of any tracing remedy
> *in rem*, were obliged to make up from their own pockets the value of
> trust funds which had been lost: *Re Dawson dec'd* [1966] 2 N.S.W.R.
> 211. And as to the personal liability of fiduciaries other than trustees,
> see *Catt v Marac Australia Ltd* (1986) 9 N.S.W.L.R. 639. If it
> transpires that the applicants are entitled to an inquiry [as to pecuniary
> loss], it would, in my view, be on this basis in the inherent equitable
> jurisdiction . . . "

The High Court of Australia and the Court of Appeal of New Zealand have
also both considered the relationship between confidentiality and privacy.

[27] [1990] F.S.R. 617 at 673.
[28] (1984) 156 C.L.R. 414.
[29] [1990] F.S.R. 617 at 634.

2–099   In *Australian Broadcasting Corporation v Lenah Game Meats Pty Ltd*[30] trespassers made a secret video recording of the killing of possums at the respondent's abattoir. The film was passed to the appellants, who proposed to broadcast it. The respondent applied for an injunction to prevent the broadcast. The High Court held by a majority of five to one that no injunction should be granted. The respondent conceded that it had no claim under the law of confidentiality because the nature of the process filmed was not secret. But it argued among other grounds that the court should recognise a tort of breach of privacy, to which an earlier decision of the High Court in *Victoria Park Racing and Recreation Grounds Co. Ltd v Taylor*[31] was generally considered to be an obstacle. The court left the question open.

2–100   Gleeson C.J. accepted that the law should be more astute than it had been in the past to identify and protect interests of a kind which fell within the concept of privacy, but expressed caution about declaring a new tort of breach of privacy, partly because of the lack of precision of the concept of privacy and partly because of the availability of breach of confidentiality as a way of protecting images and sounds of private activities. Gummow, Hayne and Gaudron JJ. did not consider that the *Victoria Park* case should stand in the way of the possible development of a tort of breach of privacy, but suggested that any such development should be by adapting recognised forms of action to meet new situations rather than searching to identify ingredients of a generally expressed wrong. Kirby J. described it as a difficult question whether, so many years after *Victoria Park*, the court should declare the existence of an actionable wrong of invasion of privacy. Callinan J. (who would have granted an injunction) was strongly critical of the *Victoria Park* case and considered that the time was ripe for consideration whether a tort of privacy should be recognised.

2–101   In *Hosking v Runting*[32] parents brought an action to prevent publication of pictures of the mother pushing their 18-month old twins in the street. The couple were celebrities who had recently separated. The pictures were taken without the mother's knowledge by a photographer commissioned by a magazine. The claim was brought on the ground that publication of the photographs would amount to a breach of the twins' right of privacy. The Court of Appeal of New Zealand was unanimous in rejecting the claim but divided on the issue of the existence of a cause of action for breach of privacy. The majority (Gault P. and Blanchard and Tipping JJ.) held that there was. Keith and Anderson JJ. disagreed.

2–102   Gault P. (giving the judgment of himself and Blanchard J.) analysed the English authorities and summarised the position as follows:

> "It seems then that there are now in English law two quite distinct versions of the tort of breach of confidence. One is the long-standing cause of action applicable alike to companies and private individuals

[30] [2001] HCA 63; (2001) 208 C.L.R. 199.
[31] (1937) 58 C.L.R. 479.
[32] [2004] NZCA 34.

under which remedies are available in respect of use or disclosure where the information has been communicated in confidence ... The second gives a right of action in respect of the publication of personal information of which the subject has a reasonable expectation of privacy irrespective of any burden of confidence, but only where that publication is likely to be highly offensive to a reasonable person."[33]

He continued:

" ... we consider that it will be conducive of clearer analysis to recognise breaches of confidence and privacy as separate causes of action ... Privacy and confidence are different concepts. To press every case calling for a remedy for unwarranted exposure of information about the private lives of individuals into a cause of action having as its foundation trust and confidence will be to confuse those concepts."[34]

Tipping J. said:

2–103

"In the United Kingdom the Courts have chosen incrementally to develop the equitable remedy of breach of confidence. But, in so doing, it has been necessary for the Courts to strain the boundaries of that remedy to the point where the concept of confidence has become somewhat artificial. The underpinning element of the breach of confidence cause of action has conventionally been that either by dint of a general or a transactional relationship between the parties, one party can reasonably expect that the other will treat the relevant information or material as confidential and will not publicly disclose it.

 ... It ... seems to me ... that it is more jurisprudentially straightforward and easier of logical analysis to recognise that confidence and privacy, while capable of overlapping, are essentially different concepts. Breach of confidence, being an equitable concept, is conscience based. Invasion of privacy is a common law wrong which is founded on the harm done to the plaintiff by conduct which can reasonably be regarded as offensive to human values. While it may be possible to achieve the same substantive result by developing the equitable cause of action, I consider it legally preferable and better for society's understanding of what the Courts are doing to achieve the appropriate substantive outcome under a self contained and stand-alone common law cause of action to be known as invasion of privacy...

The result in substantive terms of recognising a separate tort is not significantly different from the extended form of the breach of confidence cause of action as it is being developed in the United Kingdom. What is at stake is really a matter of legal method rather than substantive outcome."

[33] Para.42.
[34] Paras 45, 48.

Conclusion

2–104   Common to the approach adopted in New Zealand, Canada and Australia is the recognition that the essential foundation of the law of confidentiality lies in an obligation arising from the circumstances under which the information was obtained. This is consistent with the historical development of the action for breach of confidence in England.

2–105   In cases of contract, such obligation may arise from an express or implied term of the contract. Such obligation may also arise by imposition of law. Just as a duty of care or a fiduciary duty may arise both under the terms of a contract and by imposition of law,[35] similarly a duty of confidence may arise both under a contract and by imposition of law.[36]

2–106   It may not appear to make a practical difference whether, contract apart, the action for breach of confidence:

  (1) is founded on an equitable obligation, for breach of which the court may now award monetary compensation in addition to or instead of other equitable remedies, or
  (2) is founded on a multi-faceted jurisdiction under which the court may award a full range of equitable and common law remedies.

It is suggested that the first is the preferable analysis, both historically and conceptually. The action for breach of confidence has come to occupy its own area within the law, and it may in that sense be described as *sui generis*, but it is desirable for its coherent development that its underlying foundation should be clear.

The circumstances in which a person may obtain confidential information vary widely. Broadly they may be divided into the following classes:

  (1) *Direct receipt.* A discloses confidential information to X. This is the simplest case.
  (2) *Indirect receipt.* A discloses confidential information to B, who passes it to X. X may know that it is confidential at the time or he may not discover that until later, by which time he may have incurred expense or otherwise altered his position in the belief that he was entitled to use the information or he may himself have passed on the information.
  (3) *Accidental receipt.* X obtains information regarded by A as confidential as a result, directly or indirectly, of accident, carelessness or mistake on the part of A or some person to whom A has passed the information.

---

[35] *Henderson v Merrett Syndicates Ltd* [1995] 2 A.C. 145 at 206, *per* Lord Browne-Wilkinson:
   "The existence of a contract does not exclude the co-existence of concurrent fiduciary duties (indeed, the contract may well be their source); but the contract can and does modify the extent and nature of the general duty that would otherwise arise".
[36] e.g. *Lamb v Evans* [1893] 1 Ch. 218; *Robb v Green* [1895] 2 Q.B. 315.

(4) *Surreptitious receipt.* X obtains information regarded by A as confidential as a result, directly or indirectly, of reprehensible conduct, to which X may or may not be a party.

It can be seen that in some instances there will be an obvious, direct **2–107** relationship of confidentiality between A and X; in some instances, there may be said to be an indirect relationship of confidentiality between A and X; in some instances the information has not reached X under or by reason of any relationship of confidentiality.

Insofar as all these types of case may involve breach of what has been **2–108** recognised as an equitable obligation, it is established that monetary compensation is now in principle available for all of them.

There is also now developing in English law a different species of action **2–109** under the same name for the protection of information about a person's private life within the meaning of Art.8. There are conflicting views how this is best classified. It is suggested that it is best seen as an action based in tort, but the content is more important than the classification.

CHAPTER 3

Essential Features of Confidentiality

GENERAL PRINCIPLES

3–001 Aside from cases founded on a person's right to privacy under Art.8, the core principles of the law of confidentiality may be stated in broad terms as follows:

(1) A duty to treat information as confidential may arise by the express or implied terms of a contract or as an equitable obligation.

(2) Key factors in establishing an equitable obligation are the nature of the information, the circumstances in which it was obtained and notice of its confidentiality.

(3) The circumstances must have been such as to import an obligation of confidentiality.[1] Such circumstances include cases where information

---

[1] *Coco v A N Clark (Engineers) Ltd* [1969] R.P.C. 41 at 47; *Att-Gen v Guardian Newspapers Ltd (No. 2)* [1990] 1 A.C. 109 at 281.

    (a) is received in the course of a relationship or venture which a reasonable person would regard as involving a duty of confidentiality[2];

    (b) is received for a limited purpose in the exercise of a legal power or furtherance of a legal duty[3];

    (c) is obtained by improper or surreptitious means[4] or, possibly, by accident or mistake[5];

    (d) is received directly or indirectly from another person under a duty of confidentiality.[6]

(4) The recipient must have notice that the information is confidential.[7] The degree of notice or knowledge required may vary according to the circumstances. Where information is imparted in the course of a relationship or venture which a reasonable person would regard as involving a duty of confidentiality, it is enough that a reasonable person in the recipient's position would regard the information as confidential.[8] But a third party recipient of confidential information will not be under a duty of confidentiality unless he knows of (or is deliberately blind to) its confidentiality.[9]

(5) The nature of the information must be such as to warrant the recipient being under an obligation to treat it as confidential.

(6) It is an essential ingredient of the action for breach of confidence that confidential information has been, or is threatened to be, misused.[10] What constitutes misuse will depend on the circumstances of the case and the scope of the duty owed.

(7) A duty of confidentiality may be negated or qualified by public interest.[11]

---

[2] *Coco v A. N. Clark (Engineers) Ltd* [1969] R.P.C. 41 at 48.

[3] *Marcel v Commissioner of Police* [1992] Ch. 225 at 262; *Hellewell v Chief Constable of Derbyshire* [1995] 1 W.L.R. 804 at 807; *R. v Licensing Authority Established under Medicines Act 1968 Ex p. Smith Kline & French Laboratories Ltd* [1968] A.C. 910 at 946; *Woolgar v Chief Constable of Sussex Police* [2000] 1 W.L.R. 25 at para.6.

[4] *Lord Ashburton v Pape* [1913] 2 Ch. 469 at 475; *Franklin v Giddins* [1978] Qd. R. 72 at 79–80; *The Commonwealth v John Fairfax* (1980) 147 C.L.R. 39 at 50; *Shelley Films Ltd* [1994] E.M.L.R. 134; *Creation Records Ltd v News Group Newspapers Ltd* [1997] E.M.L.R. 444.

[5] *English & American Insurance Ltd v Herbert Smith* [1988] F.S.R. 232 at 237–238; *Att-Gen v Guardian Newspapers Ltd (No. 2)* [1990] 1 A.C. 109 at 281.

[6] *Abernathy v Hutchinson* (1824) 3 L.J.Ch. 209; *Prince Albert v Strange* (1848) 1 Mac. & G. 25; *Printers & Finishers Ltd v Holloway* [1965] R.P.C. 239 at 253; *Att-Gen v Guardian Newspapers Ltd (No. 2)* [1990] 1 A.C. 109 at 201; *Lancashire Fires Ltd v S.A. Lyons & Co. Ltd* [1996] F.S.R. 629 at 676.

[7] *Att-Gen v Guardian Newspapers Ltd (No. 2)* [1990] 1 A.C. 109 at 281.

[8] *Printers & Finishers Ltd v Holloway* [1965] R.P.C. 239 at 256; *Coco v A. N. Clark (Engineers) Ltd* [1969] R.P.C. 41 at 48.

[9] *Valeo Vision S.A. v Flexible Lamps Ltd* [1995] R.P.C. 205; *Thomas v Pearce* [2000] F.S.R. 718.

[10] *Coco v A. N. Clark (Engineers) Ltd* [1969] R.P.C. 41 at 47.

[11] *Att-Gen v Guardian Newspapers Ltd (No. 2)* [1990] 1 A.C. 109; *W v Egdell* [1990] 1 Ch. 359 at 419–420; *Imutran Ltd v Uncaged Campaigns Ltd* [2002] 2 All E.R. 385 at para.20.

(8) A duty of confidentiality may be subject to other qualifications either by agreement or by operation of law.[12]

(9) Where an action is based on the court's equitable jurisdiction, the court may decline to grant relief (or limit the terms of any relief) on equitable grounds. These may include:

(a) that the claim is stale;

(b) that the claimant's own conduct is not such as to merit relief[13]; or

(c) that the relief claimed would cause injustice to a defendant who has acted in good faith.[14]

(10) As a general rule an action for breach of confidentiality may be brought only by a person to whom the duty in question is owed, but exceptionally an action for protective relief may be brought by someone having responsibility to protect the welfare of that person.[15]

CONTRACT

3–002   A contract may contain express terms restricting a person's use of information. This may include information about matters which are common knowledge or easily ascertainable.[16]

3–003   In *Saltman*[17] Lord Greene M.R. emphasised that:

"The information, to be confidential, must, I apprehend, apart from contract, have the necessary quality of confidence about it, namely, it must not be something which is public property and public knowledge."

In *Attorney-General v Barker*[18] Lord Donaldson M.R. observed that a contractual promise not to publish information, even if not inherently confidential, is a form of negative covenant for consideration which the court will enforce "provided only that the covenant itself cannot be attacked for obscurity, illegality or on public policy grounds such as that it is in restraint of trade".

---

[12] *Tournier v National Provincial and Union Bank* [1924] 1 K.B. 461.

[13] *McNicol v Sportsman's Stores* (1930) McG.C.C. 116, at 125; *Hubbard v Vosper* [1972] 84 at 99–101; *Church of Scientology v Kaufman* [1973] R.P.C. 627 at 654–656.

[14] Compare *Lipkin Gorman v Karpnale Ltd* [1991] 2 A.C. 548 at 577–580.

[15] *Fraser v Evans* [1969] 1 Q.B. 344; *Broadmoor Special Hospital Authority v Robinson* [2000] Q.B. 775; *Green Corns Ltd v Claverley Group Ltd* [2005] EWHC 958, QB; *A Local Authority v W* [2005] EWHC 1564, Fam.

[16] As the Law Commission noted in its Report on Breach of Confidence, Law Com. No.110 (Cmnd 8388), 1981, at para.4.15 and fn.140.

[17] (1948) R.P.C. 203 at 215.

[18] [1990] 3 All E.R. 257 at 259.

In *Attorney-General v Blake*[19] the House of Lords declared that the **3–004** Attorney-General was entitled to an account of profits made by the spy, George Blake, by breach of his contractual undertaking not to divulge any official information gained by him as a result of his employment in the Secret Intelligence Service either in the press or in book form. Blake broke the undertaking by writing his autobiography. At the time of its publication none of the information relating to his activities as a secret service officer was secret, nor was it alleged that the publication would damage the public interest. The contractual undertaking was nevertheless still binding.

A contract will be unenforceable if and to the extent that: **3–005**

(1) It would prevent an ex-employee from making proper use of his skills[20] or otherwise amounts to an unreasonable restraint on trade[21];
(2) It conflicts with English or European competition law;
(3) It would prevent publication justified in the public interest, including the right to freedom of expression protected by Art.10 of the European Convention[22];
(4) It would be otherwise unlawful.

Where a relationship of a confidential nature arises from a contract which does not contain an express confidentiality term, the courts will imply a contractual duty of confidentiality,[23] but it is suggested that the scope of the duty will be the same whether viewed as an implied term or an equitable obligation.[24] The duty of confidentiality between a doctor and patient, for example, will be the same whether the patient is treated privately or under the National Health Service. The extent of an equitable obligation of confidentiality arising from a relationship governed by contract will fall to be determined by reference to the underlying contractual relationship.[25]

It has been suggested[26] that an obligation of confidence expressly **3–006** assumed under a contract might carry more weight than an obligation that is merely implied or equitable in origin. As stated above, express contractual terms may impose a duty of confidentiality where none would otherwise exist. They may also assist a claimant in identifying and defining information that can properly be characterised as confidential. Otherwise, it is

---

[19] [2001] 1 A.C. 268.
[20] *Herbert Morris Ltd v Saxelby* [1916] A.C. 688; *Faccenda Chicken Ltd v Fowler* [1987] 1 Ch. 117.
[21] *Maggbury Pty Ltd v Hafele Australia Pty Ltd* (2001) 210 C.L.R. 181.
[22] *London Regional Transport v Mayor of London* [2001] EWCA Civ 1429; [2003] E.M.L.R. 4.
[23] *Faccenda Chicken Ltd v Fowler* [1987] 1 Ch. 117 at 135.
[24] This is expressed as a suggestion rather than a dogmatic statement because of dicta in *Hilton v Barker* [2005] UKHL 8 and *Booth & Eastwood* [2005] 1 W.L.R. 567, discussed below at para.3–132.
[25] As in the case of a fiduciary duty: see *Henderson v Merrett Syndicates Ltd* [1995] 2 A.C. 145 at 206 *per* Lord Browne-Wilkinson.
[26] *Campbell v Frisbee* [2002] EWCA Civ 1374; [2003] E.M.L.R. 76, at para.22; *HM Att-Gen v MGN Ltd* [2002] EWHC 3201, Ch, at para.14 *per* Lewison J.

difficult to see on what basis and how a court could attach greater legal force to an express contractual term than to an implied one or an equitable obligation.

CIRCUMSTANCES IMPORTING AN OBLIGATION OF CONFIDENTIALITY

Information imparted in the course of a relationship or venture which a reasonable person would regard as involving a duty of confidentiality

3–007   It would be impossible to compile a list of all relationships likely to give rise to duties of confidentiality. They include agents, trustees, partners, directors and employees; professional people; holders of public and private offices; people in close personal relationships; and many others. The common thread is that a reasonable person would understand them as involving an obligation of confidentiality.

3–008   In *Printers & Finishers Ltd v Holloway*[27] Cross J. said that the law would defeat its own object if it sought to enforce standards which would be rejected by the ordinary man. Conversely, it would be defective if it failed to protect information imparted in trust in the course of a relationship which a reasonable person would regard as involving an obligation of confidentiality. Such a relationship may be enduring, or may be limited to a single transaction or may arise where parties are in pre-contractual negotiations.[28]

3–009   In *Mars UK Ltd v Teknowledge Ltd*[29] the claimant company had developed a "Cashflow" machine for testing the validity and denomination of coins. Despite the claimant's use of an encryption system, the defendant had succeeded in reverse engineering the claimant's machine and had used the information thereby gained to compete with the claimant. Jacob J. held that the defendant had infringed the claimant's copyrights and database rights but had not acted in breach of confidence.

3–010   Turning to the requirement of communication in circumstances importing a duty of confidence, Jacob J. said:

> "Mars say that such circumstances are to be inferred from the fact that the student of the Cashflow finds encryption. They say the fact of encryption is equivalent to a notice saying 'confidential—you may not de-encrypt'. And they go on to say that if such an express notice were given, the examiner of the machine would come under a duty of confidence. I think they are wrong on both counts. As pure matter of common sense I cannot see why the mere fact of encryption makes that

---

[27] [1965] R.P.C. 239 at 256.
[28] *Seager v Copydex Ltd* [1967] 1 W.L.R. 923.
[29] [2000] F.S.R. 138.

which is encrypted confidential or why anyone who de-encrypts something in code, should necessarily be taken to be receiving information in confidence. He will appreciate that the source of the information did not want him to have access, but that is all. He has no other relationship with that source. Nor do the circumstances have an analogy with eavesdropping or secret long-lens photography . . . or telephone tapping . . . There is nothing surreptitious in taking a thing apart to find out how it is made. In so holding I am applying the 'reasonable man' test suggested by Megarry J. in *Coco* . . . "[30]

Information received for a limited purpose in the exercise of a legal power or furtherance of a legal duty

Where information of a personal or confidential nature is obtained or received in the exercise of a legal power or in furtherance of a legal duty, the recipient will in general owe a duty to the person from whom it was obtained or to whom it relates not to use it for unrelated purposes. Tax payers, for example, are required to disclose details of their income to the revenue. The revenue owes a duty of confidence to every tax payer in respect of such information.[31] There need not therefore be a voluntary imparting of information in order for the recipient to be under an equitable obligation of confidence arising from the nature of the information and the circumstances of its receipt.   **3–011**

Just as a photographer employed to take a person's photograph owes a duty of confidence to the customer in respect of the material obtained,[32] so a police authority empowered to take a "mug shot" of an arrested person owes an equitable obligation to that person under the law of confidence not to make improper use of the material obtained.[33]   **3–012**

The scope of the duty may vary from one case to another according to the circumstances in which, and purpose for which, the material was obtained. In *Hellewell v Chief Constable of Derbyshire*[34] Laws J. held that the police might make reasonable use of the photograph for the purpose of the prevention and detection of crime, the investigation of alleged offences and the apprehension of suspects or persons unlawfully at large. Limited circulation of the mug shot of the plaintiff (who had 32 convictions   **3–013**

---

[30] The use of reverse engineering to analyse products supplied confidentially was considered by Peter Smith J. in *EPI Environmental Technologies Inc v Symphony Plastic Technologies plc* [2004] EWHC 2945, Ch. See also the decision of the New South Wales Court of Appeal in *Industrial Rollformers Pty Ltd v Ingersoll-Rand (Australia) Ltd* [2001] N.S.W.C.A. 111, at paras 114–116.

[31] *R. v Inland Revenue Commissioners Ex p. National Federation of Self-Employed and Small Businesses Ltd* [1982] A.C. 617 at 654, *per* Lord Scarman; *R. v Inland Revenue Commissioners Ex p. Preston* [1985] A.C. 835 at 864, *per* Lord Templeman; *Lonrho plc v Fayed (No. 4)* [1994] Q.B. 775; *Mount Murray Country Club Ltd v Macleod and others* [2003] UKPC 53, (2003) S.T.C. 1525, at para.33.

[32] *Pollard v Photographic Company* (1888) 40 Ch.J. 345.

[33] *Hellewell v Chief Constable of Derbyshire* [1995] 1 W.L.R. 804.

[34] *ibid.*

including 19 for offences of dishonesty) to shopkeepers who were considered to have legitimate cause for apprehension if he were to visit their premises, was not improper use of it.

3–014   The general principle was stated in *Marcel v Commissioner of Police*[35] by Sir Christopher Slade:

> "In my judgment, documents seized by a public authority from a private citizen in exercise of a statutory power can properly be used only for those purposes for which the relevant legislation contemplated that they might be used. The user for any other purpose of documents seized in a draconian power of this nature, without the consent of the person from whom they were seized, would be an improper exercise of the power. Any such person would be entitled to expect that the authority would treat the documents and their contents as confidential, save to the extent that it might use them for the purposes contemplated by the relevant legislation."

The Court of Appeal recognised that the duty in that regard lay not only in public law but also in the private law of confidentiality. But just as the recipient of information voluntarily imparted to him in confidence may be compelled to disclose it by process of law, so may the recipient of information which was itself supplied to him under compulsion.

3–015   In *Marcel's* case a development company sued a purchaser for default in contracts for the purchase of some flats. The purchaser alleged that he was induced to enter the contracts by misrepresentations made by three agents of the company. The three were arrested by the police on suspicion of conspiracy to defraud the purchaser (with which they were later charged, but the charges were dropped) and documents were seized from them. The purchaser served a *subpoena duces tecum* on the police requiring them to produce the seized documents at the trial of the action brought by the company. The police allowed the purchaser's solicitor to inspect and copy some of the documents before the subpoena was formally served. The three agents issued proceedings against the police, the purchaser and his solicitor, to prevent use of the documents in the civil action.

3–016   The Court of Appeal held that voluntary disclosure of the seized documents by the police to the purchaser, without a *subpoena*, would have been a breach of duty of confidence; but that the police might be compelled to produce them on *subpoena*, just as the owners of the seized documents might themselves have been compelled to produce them on *subpoena*. The Court expressed differing views about the propriety of the disclosure of the documents after issue of the *subpoena* but prior to the requirement for their formal production in court. Dillon L.J. said that he could see the practical sense of producing them prior to the trial so that they could be sifted and administrative arrangements made to facilitate the conduct of the civil proceedings, provided that it was remembered that the documents were not

[35] [1992] Ch. 225 at 262.

the property of the police. Sir Christopher Slade, while having sympathy with the course taken by the police, said that they should not have disclosed the documents without the consent of the owners or the authority of the court.

The plethora of powers given to different bodies for obtaining informa-   **3–017** tion under the Police and Criminal Evidence Act 1984, the Companies Act 1985, the Insolvency Act 1986, the Criminal Justice Act 1987, the Financial Services and Markets Act 2000, the Serious Organised Crime and Police Act 2005 and other statutes, and the potential for the powers of compulsion under one statute to be used to obtain information supplied by compulsion under another, have combined to produce almost as many possible permutations as a football pools coupon. This has given rise to some complex questions of confidentiality, especially in cases where the facts are complicated, the documents are voluminous and various regulatory bodies are involved.[36] In the case of *BCCI*, for example, the group carried on business through 365 branches and agencies in about 70 countries. The group's records were scattered throughout the world. In the United Kingdom alone there were 100 million documents, of which by January 1992 some 40 million documents in 26,000 boxes had been logged on computer.[37]

The principles and potential complexities are illustrated by *Re Arrows*   **3–018** *Ltd (No. 4)*.[38] N was a director and principal shareholder of Arrows Ltd. When the company collapsed he was examined by the liquidators, under s.236 of the Insolvency Act 1986, and transcripts were made. A person examined under that section may not refuse to answer questions on the ground that his answers would be self-incriminating.[39] At the time of his examination N was also under investigation by the Serious Fraud Office (SFO). The SFO subsequently served a notice on the liquidators, under s.2(3) of the Criminal Justice Act 1987 requiring the liquidators to produce the transcripts to the SFO for use as evidence in criminal proceedings against him.

It was argued on behalf of N that the *Marcel* principle applied, and that   **3–019** the liquidators owed a private law duty to him not to produce the transcripts to the SFO. The House of Lords rejected that argument. They recognised the validity of the *Marcel* principle within its limits, i.e. to prevent voluntary disclosure otherwise than for the purposes for which the information or material was obtained. But, said Lord Browne-Wilkinson[40]:

> "In my view, where information has been obtained under statutory powers the duty of confidence owed on the *Marcel* principle cannot

---

[36] *Re Esal (Commodities) Ltd* [1989] B.C.L.C. 59; *Re Esal (Commodities) Ltd (No. 2)* [1990] B.C.C. 708; *Morris v Director of Serious Fraud Office* [1993] B.C.L.C. 580; *Re Maxwell Communications Corporation Plc (No. 3)* [1995] 1 B.C.L.C. 521; *Marlwood Commercial Inc v Kozeny* [2004] EWCA Civ 798; [2005] 1 W.L.R. 104.
[37] *Morris v Director of Serious Fraud Office* [1993] B.C.L.C. 580.
[38] [1995] 2 A.C. 75.
[39] *Bishopsgate Investment Management Ltd v Maxwell* [1993] Ch. 1.
[40] [1995] 2 A.C. 75 at 102.

operate so as to prevent the person obtaining the information from disclosing it to those persons to whom the statutory provisions either require or authorise him to make disclosure."[41]

3–020 Moreover, even though the statutory provisions under which the first body (i.e. the liquidators) obtained information by compulsion might not require or authorise that body to pass it on to a second body (i.e. the SFO), the second body might be empowered to require its disclosure under its own statutory powers. This was so in *Re Arrows Ltd*, where the SFO claimed production under the Criminal Justice Act 1987, under which its powers were wide. Lord Browne-Wilkinson said[42]:

> "Subject to limited exceptions the Act of 1987 expressly overrides any duty of confidence 'imposed by or under' any statute other than the Taxes Management Act 1970: section 3(3) of the Act of 1987. Similarly, the fact that section 2(9) and (10) of the Act of 1987 expressly preserves two specific duties of confidence (legal professional privilege and banking confidence) shows that all other common law duties of confidence are overridden."

3–021 N also relied on public interest immunity.[43] It was argued that although his own *private law* right in the confidentiality of information extracted from him under statutory powers was subject to the statutory powers of the SFO under the Act of 1987, there was a wider *public* interest in ensuring that information extracted was used only for the purpose for which the statutory power to obtain it was conferred (*Conway v Rimmer*[44]; *Alfred Crompton Amusement Machines Ltd v Customs & Excise Commissioners (No. 2)*).[45] So it was submitted that N's transcripts, having been obtained under s.236 of the Insolvency Act 1986, could be used only for the purposes of the liquidation.

3–022 This argument caused the House of Lords to examine the extent of the duty of confidentiality owed by liquidators to persons examined under s.236. They concluded that the Act of 1986 contemplated liquidators disclosing information and documents obtained by them to others, including disclosure for the purposes of criminal proceedings. Accordingly, liquidators could not give any assurance to a person examined under s.236 that his answers would not be disclosed to prosecuting authorities and the claim that the answers enjoyed public interest immunity also failed.[46]

---

[41] See also the analysis by the Court of Appeal in *Sutton v GE Capital Commercial Finance Ltd* [2004] EWCA Civ 315, at paras 39–43, of the purposes for which administrative receivers may use documents obtained pursuant to requests under ss.234–236 of the Insolvency Act 1986.
[42] *ibid.* at 99.
[43] For fuller discussion of public interest immunity see Ch.19, below.
[44] [1968] A.C. 910 at 946.
[45] [1974] A.C. 405.
[46] In relation to material obtained under s.235 of the Insolvency Act 1986, see *R. v Brady* [2004] EWCA Crim 1763; [2004] 1 W.L.R. 3240, at paras 23ff.

In *Woolgar v Chief Constable of Sussex Police*[47] the Court of Appeal **3–023** accepted that what a person says to the police during an interview under caution after arrest is confidential, subject to qualifications. It may obviously be used in the course of a trial if charges are brought, since that is a primary purpose of the interview. The court also held in that case that the police were entitled on grounds of public interest to disclose a transcript to a nursing regulatory body in connection with a wider investigation being carried out into the treatment of patients at a nursing home where the claimant was the matron.

A similar duty of confidentiality is owed to a witness who gives voluntary **3–024** information to the police. In *Taylor v Director of the Serious Fraud Office*[48] Millett L.J. said in the Court of Appeal:

"Members of the public who volunteer information to the police are entitled to expect that it will be used only for the purpose of the investigation and subsequent criminal proceedings. Their expectations should be respected."

Even if the information itself is not of a confidential nature, the fact that the witness has given it may well be so.

There are also cases in which disclosure of otherwise confidential **3–025** information is obligatory if a person wishes to pursue a particular activity (e.g. to carry on a business for which a licence is required). Many examples could be given. Such disclosure may be described as voluntary in one sense but obligatory in another. Whichever way it is classified, the recipient will owe to the confider a duty of confidentiality, the extent of which will depend on the purposes for which it is provided.

In *R. v Licensing Authority Established under Medicines Act 1968 Ex p.* **3–026** *Smith Kline & French Laboratories Ltd*[49] the applicants were manufacturers of a drug used in the treatment of gastric ulcers. The Medicines Act 1968 prohibits the manufacture or sale of any medicinal product except in accordance with a product licence granted by the appropriate licensing authority. By a combination of the provisions of the Act, regulations made under it and EC directives, an application for a licence had to be supported by a large amount of information of an obviously confidential nature. The applicants sought declarations to the effect that the licensing authority was not entitled to have regard to information supplied by the applicants, when considering applications by other companies for licences to market generic versions of the drug. The application failed. Lord Templeman said[50]:

"If the appellants choose to apply for a product licence under the Act, they choose to provide information to the licensing authority for the purposes of the Act. It is not unconscionable for the licensing authority

---

[47] [2000] 1 W.L.R. 25 at para.6.
[48] [1999] A.C. 177 at 198.
[49] [1990] 1 A.C. 64.
[50] *ibid.* at 104.

to make use of that information in the public interest for the purposes of the Act, although it would be unconscionable for the licensing authority to disclose that information to third parties for other purposes."

Looking at the purposes of the Act, Lord Templeman concluded that,

" . . . it is the right and duty of the licensing authority to make use of all the information supplied by any applicant for a product licence which assists the licensing authority in considering whether to grant or reject any other application, or which assists the licensing authority to perform any of its other functions under the Act of 1968."

A similar question arose under different statutory provisions in New Zealand[51] and in Australia[52] with a similar result in each case.

3–027   In Australia the court rejected "the test of confider's purpose" (argued for by the company) as governing the scope of the confidant's duty in such a case. The confider's purpose in disclosing the information was narrow (to obtain a licence). The authority's purpose was wider (to protect public health and safety). In considering whether the confidant's use of the information was unconscionable, it was necessary to consider the purpose of the regulations under which the information was provided, rather than merely the purpose of the provider.

3–028   In New Zealand, Jeffries J. approached the question whether there had been a breach of a duty of confidentiality by considering the nature of the relationship between the parties. He said[53]:

"It is not a bilateral commercial relationship. It has no contractual base whatsoever. . . . The parties are forced into the relationship by statute law. The Minister and his departmental officers are responsible for consenting to the use of new medicines which if faulty can have catastrophic effects of which thalidomide is an example. The Minister and Department are acting on issues in granting consent of the foremost public importance being the health of the nation . . .

In the circumstances, as disclosed by this case, I would think it wrong to impose such a strict and narrow duty of confidentiality on a Government Department so as to prevent access to its own records of prior applications, and its accumulated knowledge and experience when performing the task of approving another pharmaceutical product which is identical, or nearly so."

---

[51] *Smith Kline and French Laboratories Ltd v Att-Gen* [1989] 1 N.Z.L.R. 385.
[52] *Smith Kline and French Laboratories (Australia) Ltd v Department of Community Services* [1990] F.S.R. 617, *per* Gummow J.; affirmed (1991) 28 F.C.R. 291 (Full Court of the Federal Court).
[53] [1989] 1 N.Z.L.R. 385 at 396–397.

Information obtained by improper or surreptitious means

In *Prince Albert v Strange* the Solicitor-General argued that: **3–029**

> "The information, which has been here made use of by the Defendant was improperly obtained; either there was a breach of contract or there was a crime committed. In neither case could the Defendant obtain a title to use the information so acquired."[54]

Lord Cottenham L.C. said[55] that on the affidavit evidence the collection of royal etchings described in the catalogue published by the defendant could only have been formed by "impressions surreptitiously and improperly obtained", and that since the defendant was unable to suggest any mode by which they could have been properly obtained, so as to entitle the possessor to use them for publication, it must be assumed that the defendant's possession had its foundation in a breach of trust, confidence or contract. The tenor of the judgment does not suggest that he would have taken a more favourable view if the etchings had been surreptitiously obtained in some other way.

The principle in *Ashburton v Pape*

In *Ashburton v Pape*[56] the defendant surreptitiously obtained copies of   **3–030**
letters between the plaintiff and his solicitor from a clerk employed by the solicitor, so there was both surreptitious behaviour and breach of a confidential relationship. Swinfen Eady L.J. expressed the principle as follows:

> "The principle upon which the Court of Chancery has acted for many years has been to restrain the publication of information improperly or surreptitiously obtained or of information imparted in confidence which ought not to be divulged."[57]

However, as the Law Commission noted in its Working Paper on Breach of Confidence in 1974,[58] in *Ashburton v Pape* there was a breach of duty by one of the parties to the confidence. In its Report in 1981[59] the Law Commission concluded that:

> " . . . under the present law it is very doubtful to what extent, if at all, information becomes impressed with an obligation of confidence by reason solely of the reprehensible means by which it has been acquired,

---

[54] (1848) 1 Mac. & G. 25 at 38.
[55] *ibid.* at 41–45.
[56] [1913] 2 Ch. 469 at 475.
[57] Cited by Mason J. (later Mason C.J.) in *Commonwealth of Australia v John Fairfax & Sons Ltd* (1980) 147 C.L.R. 39 at 50.
[58] Working Paper No.58 at para.21.
[59] Law Com. No.110: Breach of Confidence (Cmnd. 8388) at para.4.10.

and irrespective of some special relationship between the person alleged to owe the obligation and the person to whom it is alleged to be owed."

The Law Commission's doubts were based partly on the absence of precedent for the imposition of such a duty and partly on the judgment of Sir Robert Megarry V.C. in *Malone v Metropolitan Police Commissioner*.[60]

3–031   Malone had sought a declaration that the tapping of his telephone line by the police, on the authority of the Home Secretary, was unlawful on various grounds, including confidentiality. In dismissing the claim, Megarry V.C. said that one of the requirements of the action for breach of confidence was that information must have been "imparted in circumstances importing an obligation of confidence" and in this connection he contrasted the facts with those of *Coco v A. N. Clark (Engineers) Ltd*,[61] where his own decision had been based on the communication by an inventor to a manufacturer of information which the manufacturer misused. He continued[62]:

> "In the present case, the alleged misuse is not by the person to whom the information was intended to be communicated, but by someone to whom the plaintiff had no intention of communicating anything: and that, of course, introduces a somewhat different element, that of the unknown overhearer.
>
> It seems to me that a person who utters confidential information must accept the risk of any unknown overhearing that is inherent in the circumstances of communication. Those who exchange confidences on a bus or a train run the risk of a nearby passenger with acute hearing or a more distant passenger who is adept at lip-reading. Those who speak over garden walls run the risk of the unseen neighbour in a tool-shed nearby. Office cleaners who discuss secrets in the office when they think everyone else has gone run the risk of speaking within earshot of an unseen member of the staff who is working late. Those who give confidential information over an office intercommunication system run the risk of some third party being connected to the conversation. I do not see why someone who has overheard some secret in such a way should be exposed to legal proceedings if he uses or divulges what he has heard. No doubt an honourable man would give some warning when he realises that what he is hearing is not intended for his ears; but I have to concern myself with the law, and not with moral standards. There are, of course, many moral precepts which are not legally enforceable.
>
> When this is applied to telephone conversations, it appears to me that the speaker is taking such risks of being overheard as are inherent in the system. . . .

---

[60] [1979] 1 Ch. 344.
[61] *Coco v A. N. Clark (Engineers) Ltd* [1969] R.P.C. 41.
[62] *ibid.* at 376.

No doubt a person who uses a telephone to give confidential information to another may do so in such a way as to impose an obligation of confidence on that other: but I do not see how it could be said that any such obligation is imposed on those who overhear the conversation, whether by means of tapping or otherwise."

The contrast drawn in this passage between a person to whom con-   **3–032** fidential information is consciously confided and the unintended overhearer suggests that Megarry V.C. considered that a duty of confidentiality required some deliberate act of confiding. If so, subsequent authorities show that the duty is not so confined.

Malone was distinguished by the Court of Appeal in *Francome v Mirror Group Newspapers*.[63] The plaintiff, a well-known jockey, sought and obtained an interlocutory injunction to restrain the defendants from publishing information derived from unauthorised tapping of his telephone. The tapping was a criminal offence under the Wireless Telegraphy Act 1949.[64] The defendants contended that there could be no right of action against them, or against the eavesdroppers who recorded the plaintiff's conversations, and relied for that proposition on *Malone*. Sir John Donaldson M.R. described it as a "rather surprising proposition". The court rejected the argument that the decision in *Malone* negatived the right to confidentiality alleged by the plaintiff, and stressed that Megarry V.C. had been dealing only with a case of authorised tapping by the police; but because the matter was before the court on an interlocutory application, it was unnecessary for it to make a final decision whether there had been a breach of a duty of confidentiality.[65]

In Australia the courts have recognised the applicability of an equitable   **3–033** obligation of confidentiality to a person who obtained confidential information by improper or surreptitious means. In *Concrete Industries (Monier) Ltd v Gardner Bros & Perrott (WA) Pty Ltd*[66] Fullager J. said that it is not a defence that the plaintiff did not impart the information to the defendant and that he got it by his own hard work as an industrious eavesdropper.

Obtaining confidential information through trespass

In *Franklin v Giddins*[67] the defendant trespassed on the plaintiff's orchard   **3–034** and stole some budwood cuttings from a new and commercially valuable strain of nectarine (called "Franklin Early White"), which the plaintiff had developed by selective cross-breeding over a considerable number of years. The plaintiff could have sued in trover, but the consequence of judgment being satisfied would have been that property in the subject-matter would then have vested in the defendant (see the observations of Lord Denning

---

[63] [1984] 1 W.L.R. 892.
[64] See now the Regulation of Investigatory Powers Act 2000.
[65] See also *R. v Preston* [1994] 2 A.C. 130 at 150.
[66] Vic S.C., August 18, 1977, unreported. The citation is taken from Meagher, Gummow and Lehane, *Equity: Doctrines and Remedies* (4th edn, 2002) para.41–045.
[67] [1978] Qd.R. 72.

M.R. in *Seager v Copydex (No. 2)*[68]), and this would have given the defendant an unassailable right thereafter to propagate trees from the cuttings and sell them in competition with the plaintiff. The plaintiff sued for delivery up of all trees in the defendant's possession which had been propagated from the stolen cuttings and for injunctive relief, basing his claim on misuse of confidential material by the defendant.

3–035   If the defendant had been employed by the plaintiff to work in the orchard, there could be no doubt that the plaintiff would have been entitled to such relief. The case would have fallen squarely within such authorities as *Lamb v Evans*[69] (misuse of printers' blocks for use in compiling a trade directory) and *Robb v Green*[70] (surreptitious copying of the employer's customer list). The plaintiff's budwood was not for sale, precisely because he wished to preserve to himself the technique which he had developed for propagating Franklin Early White nectarines, as the defendant knew. By stealing the budwood the defendant acquired the ability to use that technique by dishonest means. The judge accepted that the parent tree could be likened to a safe in which were locked a number of copies of a formula for making a nectarine tree with special characteristics, and when budwood was stolen it was as if a copy of the formula was taken out of the safe. The formula was genetic, the result of cross-breeding, and was contained in (and inseparable from) the budwood.

3–036   The defendant relied on the absence of any consensual relationship between himself and the plaintiff, and he contended that an equitable obligation of confidence could only arise from the imparting of confidential matter by the plaintiff. It would be most unsatisfactory if that were so in relation to a formula of commercial value, which the plaintiff was not prepared to impart to the defendant, and which the defendant therefore resorted to dishonest means to obtain.

3–037   Dunn J. upheld the plaintiff's claim. After reference to *Prince Albert v Strange*,[71] *Saltman*[72] and *Argyll*,[73] he said[74]:

> "[Counsel for the defendants] argued that the budwood twigs were not 'information confidentially imparted' and that therefore no obligation of confidence deserving of protection had arisen, challenging the proposition that 'it would be extraordinary if a defendant, who acquired by eavesdropping or other improper covert means the secrets of the plaintiff because he would not have been able to get them by consensual arrangement, could defend proceedings by the plaintiff on the ground that no obligation of confidence could arise without communication of the information by the plaintiff.' (Meagher, Gummow and Lehane's book, at p.719.)

---

[68] [1969] 1 W.L.R. 809 at 813.
[69] [1893] 1 Ch. 218.
[70] [1895] 2 Q.B. 315.
[71] (1848) 1 Mac. & G. 25.
[72] (1948) 65 R.P.C. 203.
[73] [1967] Ch. 302.
[74] [1978] Qd.R. 72 at 79–80.

I find myself quite unable to accept that a thief who steals a trade secret, knowing it to be a trade secret, with the intention of using it in commercial competition with its owner, to the detriment of the latter, and so uses it, is less unconscionable than a traitorous servant. The thief is unconscionable because he plans to use and does use his own wrong conduct to better his position in competition with the owner, and also to place himself in a better position than that of a person who deals consensually with the owner.

I have already expressed the opinion that, when the male defendant stole budwood from the plaintiff's orchard, what he got was a trade secret. The secret was the technique of propagating Franklin Early White nectarines, using budwood from the plaintiff's orchard. The technique of budding was no secret, but the budwood existed only in the plaintiff's orchard, where the plaintiffs guarded it by exercising general surveillance over fruit-pickers and visitors, and by bruiting it abroad that it was theirs and theirs alone. The 'information' which the genetic structure of the wood represented was of substantial commercial value, much time and effort had been expended by the male plaintiff in evolving it and it could not be duplicated by anybody whatsoever."

More recent authorities in England have followed the same approach. In *Shelley Films Ltd v Rex Features Ltd*[75] an injunction was granted on the ground of breach of an equitable duty of confidence against use of photographs surreptitiously taken of a confidential costume design.

The plaintiffs were producers of a film, *Mary Shelley's Frankenstein*, starring the actor Robert De Niro as the Frankenstein "creature". He wore a highly distinctive costume made up of prostheses described as analogous to a rubber sculpture. The plaintiffs, who had invested over $40 million in the film, were anxious that the appearance of the creature should remain a secret until the film was released. Filming took place in a secure area, manned by security guards and with notices stating that the taking of photographs was not permitted. A freelance photographer managed to gain access to the set and took photographs depicting the "creature" on the scaffold, which he supplied to the defendant photographic agency. A picture of the scene was published in the *Sunday People*.   **3–038**

Two days later the plaintiffs obtained, ex parte, an order against the defendants requiring them to disclose the identity of the photographer, but Rattee J. set aside the order, on an inter partes hearing, on the ground that the information relating to the film which the plaintiffs sought to protect could not be said to have been communicated to the photographer in confidence, when it was the plaintiffs' case that he had obtained it clandestinely and without the plaintiffs' knowledge. The judge appears not to have been referred to any of the authorities showing that a duty of   **3–039**

[75] [1994] E.M.L.R. 134.

confidence may be owed by a person who obtains confidential information surreptitiously or by accident or mistake.

3–040   The plaintiffs continued with the action and applied for an interlocutory injunction restraining the defendants from publishing any photograph or reproduction depicting any costume design made for use in the film. The injunction was granted after fuller argument.

3–041   The judge, Martin Mann Q.C., cited *Franklin v Giddins* and added:

> "Although Dunn J. characterised the information involuntarily imparted to the defendant as a trade secret, there is in my judgment no relevant distinction for present purposes between such information and less secret information similarly or analogously obtained provided always that it is properly to be regarded as confidential."

He further held that the steps taken by the plaintiffs to maintain security and prevent photography, the circumstances in which the photographs were taken, and the plaintiffs' evidence about the value which they attached to keeping the film costumes secret for commercial reasons, established against the defendant agency a serious issue to be tried that it was under an equitable obligation not to publish the photographs, sufficient for the grant of an interlocutory injunction.

3–042   In *Creation Records Ltd v News Group Newspapers Ltd* [76] the plaintiffs had a recording contract with the pop group Oasis and planned to take photographs for an album sleeve featuring a white Rolls Royce in a swimming pool with members of the group around it. The filming was to be done at a hotel. Security staff were employed to see that members of the public who were at the hotel did not take photographs of the set, but a newspaper photographer managed to take photographs of it which were published. Lloyd J. granted an interlocutory injunction against further publication of the photographs, holding that it was arguable on the evidence that the photographer must have acted surreptitiously, knowing that there was no consent to the taking of photographs, and that the album design was a form of confidential information. It was not entirely secret since members of the public would be able to describe what they had seen, but still had significant confidentiality because they were not permitted to record it photographically.

3–043   *Douglas v Hello! Ltd* [77] was another case of surreptitious photography. After citing *Shelley Films Ltd v Rex Features Ltd* and *Creation Records Ltd v News Group Newspapers Ltd*, the Court of Appeal stated:

> "Where an individual ('the owner') has at his disposal information which he has created or which is private or personal and to which he can properly deny access to third parties, and he reasonably intends to profit commercially by using or publishing that information, then a

---

[76] [1997] E.M.L.R. 444.
[77] [2005] EWCA Civ 595; [2006] Q.B. 125, at para.118.

third party who is, or who ought to be, aware of these matters and who has knowingly obtained the information without authority, will be in breach of duty if he uses or publishes the information to the detriment of the owner. We have used the term 'the owner' loosely."

There is today no doubt that equitable principles of confidentiality apply where a person improperly or surreptitiously obtains confidential information. Moreover, if a duty of confidence can be owed by the recipient of obviously confidential information obtained by accident (discussed below), the same must apply with added force where it has been obtained improperly. It would be absurd if a duty were owed in equity by a finder of a private diary dropped in the street, but not by a pickpocket, whose conscience should be more greatly affected.

Extension of *Ashburton v Pape* to mistake

A series of cases have now confirmed the principle stated by Swinfen Eady   **3–044**
L.J. in *Ashburton v Pape*[78] and have extended it to information obtained by mistake known to the recipient.[79]

In *English & American Insurance Ltd v Herbert Smith*[80] papers which a   **3–045**
barrister intended to be sent to solicitors instructing him in litigation were by a clerical error sent instead to the defendants, who were the solicitors acting for the other side. The defendants read them and took copies before sending on the original documents to the intended recipients, acting upon guidance given by the Law Society and in the belief that their paramount duty was to their clients. Sir Nicolas Browne-Wilkinson V.C. held that their conduct was in breach of an equitable obligation of confidentiality. He rejected the argument that the jurisdiction did not apply where there was "an accidental escape of information to the third party" or that the recipient need be "improperly implicated in the leakage of the information".

He also drew a distinction between innocent receipt of a document and   **3–046**
innocent receipt of the information contained in it, saying:

> "If somebody is handed a letter addressed to another marked 'Private and Confidential', that letter having been handed to him in error, and he chooses to read it notwithstanding seeing that it is marked 'Private and Confidential', and as a result acquires the information contained in that letter, I find it difficult to say that he is not implicated in the leakage of the information contained in that letter."[81]

[78] [1913] 2 Ch. 469 at 475.
[79] *Goddard v Nationwide Building Society* [1987] 1 Q.B. 670; *Guiness Peat Ltd v Fitzroy Robinson* [1987] 1 W.L.R. 1027; *English & American Insurance Ltd v Herbert Smith* [1988] F.S.R. 232; *Webster v James Chapman & Co.* [1989] 3 All E.R. 939; *Derby & Co. Ltd v Weldon (No. 8)* [1991] 1 W.L.R. 73; *Fayed v Commissioner of Police of the Metropolis* [2002] EWCA Civ 780; *The Times*, June 17, 2002.
[80] [1988] F.S.R. 232.
[81] *ibid.* at 238.

3–047   In *Spycatcher* Lord Goff, after stating the general principle that a duty of confidence arises when confidential information comes to the knowledge of a person in circumstances where he has notice that the information is confidential, with the effect that it would be just in all the circumstances that he should be precluded from disclosing the information to others, added[82]:

> "I realise that, in the vast majority of cases, in particular those concerned with trade secrets, the duty of confidence will arise from a transaction or relationship between the parties—often a contract, in which event the duty may arise by reason of either an express or an implied term of that contract. It is in such cases as these that the expressions 'confider' and 'confidant' are perhaps most aptly employed. But it is well settled that a duty of confidence may arise in equity independently of such cases; and I have expressed the circumstances in which the duty arises in broad terms, not merely to embrace those cases where a third party receives information from a person who is under a duty of confidence in respect of it, knowing that it has been disclosed by that person to him in breach of his duty of confidence, but also to include certain situations, beloved of law teachers—where an obviously confidential document is wafted by an electric fan out of a window into a crowded street, or where an obviously confidential document, such as a private diary, is dropped in a public place, and is then picked up by a passer-by."

In *English & American Ltd v Herbert Smith* and the hypothetical cases instanced by Lord Goff there would be no room for doubt in the recipient's mind that the document was not meant to be read by him before he read its contents.

3–048   Other cases have occurred where there has been an intended delivery to the recipient, but there has been a mistake in the document enclosed. The mistake may not be apparent to the recipient until after he has read it or until some time later. In such situations an equitable obligation of confidentiality may still arise when the recipient realises that he has been sent a confidential document by mistake, but whether it does will depend on all the circumstances of the case. The yardstick is what standard of behaviour is reasonably and practicably to be expected of the recipient. There may be cases where it is reasonable and practicable to expect the recipient to return the document and make no use of it, but there may be other cases where this would be unrealistic or unjust.

3–049   There is now a complex body of case law on the relationship of confidentiality and legal professional privilege, particularly where one party in the course of litigation mistakenly discloses privileged documents to an opposing party. This subject is discussed in Chapter 18.

---

[82] [1990] 1 A.C. 109 at 281.

Information received directly or indirectly from another person under a duty of confidentiality

Information properly disclosed

A third party may receive confidential information or material for a proper **3–050** purpose. A general practitioner might, for example, provide medical information about a patient to a consultant for the purpose of obtaining the consultant's opinion or send a specimen of the patient's blood to a laboratory for the purpose of testing. The consultant or analyst receiving the information or specimen would as a general proposition be under a duty of confidentiality to the patient not to use the information or material otherwise than for the purpose for which it was provided.

Information improperly disclosed

A third party may also receive confidential information or material in **3–051** circumstances where the supplier is in breach of a duty of confidence to another (the confider). Where the third party receives information knowing that it has been disclosed by his informant in breach of confidence, he will himself owe a duty of confidence to the confider.[83] This principle is derived from the doctrine that it is equitable fraud in a third party knowingly to assist in a breach of trust, confidence or contract by another: *Abernethy v Hutchinson*[84] and *Prince Albert v Strange*.[85] In *Lancashire Fires Ltd v S. A. Lyons & Co. Ltd*[86] Sir Thomas Bingham M.R. said:

> "In *Seager v Copydex Ltd* [1967] 1 W.L.R. 923 Lord Denning M.R. at p.931 considered the nature of a claim for breach of confidence and stated 'The law on this subject does not depend on any implied contract. It depends on the broad principle of equity that he who has received information in confidence shall not take unfair advantage of it.'
>   That principle would be defeated if a third party to whom the secret information had wrongfully been disclosed could as a matter of course make use of it."

Innocent recipient with subsequent knowledge of improper disclosure

The position of a third party who receives confidential information inno- **3–052** cently and subsequently learns that it was supplied to him in breach of confidence is more difficult. In principle, lack of notice at the time of its receipt that the information was subject to a duty of confidence should not prevent the recipient from himself coming under such a duty as from the time of his discovering the true position, *provided* that he had not in good faith incurred detriment by paying for the information or perhaps by

[83] *Spycatcher* [1990] 1 A.C. 109 at 201, *per* Dillon L.J. at 261, *per* Lord Keith at 281, *per* Lord Goff.
[84] (1824) 3 L.J.Ch. 209.
[85] (1848) 1 Mac. & G. 25.
[86] [1996] F.S.R. 629 at 676.

incurring expense of money or effort in consequence of obtaining it (for example, in further research or development).

3–053   Leaving the proviso aside, the principle accords with authority. In *Printers & Finishers Ltd v Holloway*[87] Cross J. said:

> "If authority is needed for the grant of an injunction against someone who has acquired—or may have acquired—information to which he was not entitled without notice of any breach of duty on the part of the man who imparted it to him but who cannot claim to be a purchaser for value, I think that it can be found in the case of *Prince Albert v Strange* (1850) 1 MacN. and G. 25. There the court granted an injunction against a defendant who was not—or at all events was assumed by the court not to have been—implicated in the breach of confidence in question. There again, however, the precise wording of any injunction will require careful consideration."

Where the proviso applies, the position is unclear.

"Bona fide purchase" and change of position

3–054   In *Morison v Moat*[88] Turner V.C. in granting an injunction against the defendant, observed,

> "It might indeed be different if the Defendant was a purchaser for value of the secret without notice of any obligation affecting it; and the Defendant's case was attempted to be put upon this ground . . . but I do not think that this view of the case can avail him . . . So far as the secret is concerned he is a mere volunteer deriving under a breach of trust or of contract."

3–055   In *Stevenson Jordan & Harrison Ltd v MacDonald & Evans*[89] the defendant publishers resisted a claim for an injunction to prevent publication of a book allegedly containing material obtained in breach of confidence on the grounds that they were bona fide purchasers for value. At first instance Lloyd-Jacob J. ruled against the existence of such a defence and granted an injunction. His decision was reversed on other grounds and the Court of Appeal declined to express an opinion on the point, although Lord Evershed M.R. observed,[90] *obiter*, that it would be "somewhat shocking" if a third party purchaser persisted in plans to implement use of confidential material after becoming aware of the breach of duty by which it had been supplied to him.

---

[87] [1965] R.P.C. 239 at 253; see also *Fraser v Evans* [1969] 1 Q.B. 349 at 361 and *Surface Technology plc v Young* [2002] F.S.R. 387 at 399, *per* Pumfrey J.
[88] (1851) 9 Hare 241 at 263–264.
[89] (1951) 68 R.P.C. 190.
[90] (1952) 69 R.P.C. 10 at 16.

In *Wheatley v Bell*[91] Helsham C.J. in the Supreme Court of New South   **3–056**
Wales granted an injunction against a bona fide purchaser, holding that the
defence of bona fide purchase only applied to property rights and that there
were no property rights attached to equities involved in the protection of
confidence.

In *Spycatcher (No. 1)* Nourse L.J. said in interlocutory proceedings: **3–057**

> "As for the newspapers and any other third party into whose hands the
> confidential information comes, an injunction can be granted against
> them on the simple ground that equity gives relief against all the world,
> including the innocent, save only a bona fide purchaser for value
> without notice."[92]

This passage was cited at first instance by Sir Nicolas Browne-Wilkinson
V.C. in *Spycatcher (No. 1)*[93] and by Lord Donaldson M.R. in *Spycatcher
(No. 2)*, who said[94]:

> "Since the right to have confidentiality maintained is an equitable right,
> it will (in legal theory and practical effect if the aid of the court is
> invoked) 'bind the conscience' of third parties, unless they are bona fide
> purchasers for value without notice (*per* Nourse L.J. on 25 July, 1986
> in the interlocutory proceedings: *Attorney General v Observer Ltd*
> Court of Appeal (Civil Division) Transcript No.696 of 1986)."

Professor Gareth Jones, in an article entitled "Restitution of Benefits
Obtained in Breach of Another's Confidence", observed[95]

> "Judicial dicta, and the Reporters of the *Restatement of Torts*, accept
> that a good-faith purchaser who has no notice of any breach of
> confidence should be free to use and exploit confidential information
> even though he is subsequently told that it has been sold to him in
> breach of another's confidence.
>
> Superficially this is an attractive conclusion which marks off the
> position of the bona fide purchaser from that of the innocent volunteer,
> such as the donee. Moreover, it preserves the certainty of commercial
> transactions. Bona fide purchase would certainly be a good defence if
> the plaintiff's action was based on the defendant's infringement of the
> plaintiff's equitable property in the particular information. But it is
> questionable whether the mere payment of money should, in itself,
> defeat a restitutionary claim whose essence is a duty of good faith, a

---

[91] [1984] F.S.R. 16; [1982] 2 N.S.W.L.R. 544. See also *AG Australia Holdings Ltd v Burton*
[2002] N.S.W.S.C. 170 at paras 224–227 *per* Campbell J.
[92] Nourse L.J. used the same words in *Goddard v Nationwide Building Society* [1987] 1 Q.B.
671 at 685.
[93] [1987] 1 W.L.R. 1248 at 1265.
[94] [1990] 1 A.C. 109 at 177.
[95] (1970) 86 L.Q.R. 463 at 478–479.

duty not to take unfair advantage of the plaintiff's confidence. Contrast these two cases,

(a) D, a business man, pays R for some information which, unknown to D, R has imparted to D in breach of P's confidence. Two weeks later P discovers the true facts and tells D, at which time D has incurred no further expenditure.

(b) D, a business man, pays R for certain information which, unknown to D, R has imparted to D in breach of P's confidence. D begins to develop a grip, using this information. His expenditure on plant, machinery and leasehold premises has been very substantial. D is then told by P, who has just discovered R's duplicity, the true facts. Three years have elapsed since he paid R for the information.

If bona fide purchase is accepted as a defence, then P will fail in both these cases. In (b) it is right that he should do so. But is there not a great deal to be said for granting him relief in (a), on the terms that he reimburses D his expenditure? This expenditure apart, there has been no detrimental change of position. In such a case, certainty of transaction can be preserved by the recognition of a strong rebuttable presumption that a good-faith purchaser is deemed to have changed his position to his detriment; and the financial interests of the defendant can be safeguarded by the condition that the plaintiff reimburses him his expenditure, with interest, before he is granted relief. The application of a flexible notion of change of position may, it is suggested, balance more effectively than an absolute defence of bona fide purchase the competing equities of the honest purchaser and the deceived plaintiff."

Other writers have also argued for a flexible approach in cases where an innocent third party has suffered detriment by expending resources in obtaining or exploiting information supplied to him in breach of another's confidence.[96]

3–058   In *Lipkin Gorman v Karpnale Ltd*[97] the House of Lords held that in principle a defence of detrimental change of position is available in restitutionary claims to:

"a person whose position has so changed that it would be inequitable in all the circumstances to require him to make restitution, or alternatively to make restitution in full",[98]

the explanation being that:

---

[96] Cornish & Llewelyn, *Intellectual Property: Patents, Copyright, Trade Marks and Allied Rights* (2003, 5th edn), para.8–33; Meagher, Gummow and Lehane, *Equity: Doctrines and Remedies* (2002, 4th edn), para.41–110.
[97] [1991] 2 A.C. 548 at 577–580.
[98] *ibid.*

"where an innocent defendant's position is so changed that he will suffer an injustice if called upon to repay or repay in full, the injustice of requiring him so to repay outweighs the injustice of denying the plaintiff restitution."[99]

If that defence is available to one who has received money belonging to another, there is at least as strong an argument for saying that it should be available to one who has received information in breach of a duty of confidence owed to another. Indeed, the case for the latter may be stronger, because (as Lord Goff recognised in *Lipkin Gorman*) a claim to recover money at common law is made as a matter of right, whereas the obligation of the third party recipient of confidential information supplied in breach of confidence to another is founded on an obligation of conscience, which *ex hypothesi*, cannot bind him to do (or abstain from doing) that which it would in all the circumstances be inequitable to require him to do (or abstain from doing).

Although the expression "purchaser for value" of confidential informa-   **3–059** tion is of respectable antiquity, going back to *Morison v Moat*,[1] and has been used by distinguished judges, it is apt to mislead because of its implication of transfer of property.

If confidential information were a form of equitable property, there   **3–060** would be logic in affording to the bona fide purchaser of such property an absolute defence to any claim based on his use of the property, regardless of the adequacy of the consideration which he paid or any other circumstances.

Since confidential information is not a form of equitable property in   **3–061** English law,[2] "bona fide purchaser" is merely a loose description of a person who pays money for the supply of information in ignorance that it is being supplied to him in breach of another's confidence. In principle, his position on discovering the truth should be governed by considerations of conscience rather than misleading analogies with transfer of property rights.

The fact that he innocently acts to his detriment by paying for the supply   **3–062** of the information should not automatically afford him an absolute right in all circumstances to continue to use the information after discovering the truth, but is, and should be regarded as, a form of detrimental change of position. In any case where there has been a detrimental change of position in good faith by the recipient of information supplied in breach of another's confidence, it should be for the court to decide in all the circumstances whether, balancing the parties' respective interests and the justice or injustice which would result to each from the grant or refusal of the relief claimed, any such relief should be granted and, if so, on what terms.[3]

---

[99] *ibid.* at 580.

[1] (1851) 9 Hare 241.

[2] *Douglas v Hello! Ltd* [2005] EWCA Civ 595; [2006] Q.B. 125, at paras 119 and 126. See Chap.2 for a fuller discussion.

[3] This approach is consistent with the views of Goff and Jones, *The Law of Restitution* (2002, 6th edn), paras 34–016 – 34–018.

Notice of confidentiality

3–063 In *Spycatcher*[4] Lord Goff stated in his formulation of the general principle that a duty of confidence arises when confidential information comes to the knowledge of a person in circumstances where he "has notice or is held to have agreed" that the information is confidential. He added that he used the word "notice" advisedly in order to avoid the question of the extent to which actual knowledge is necessary, although he understood knowledge to include circumstances where the confidant has deliberately closed his eyes to the obvious.

Direct relationship between confider and confidant

3–064 Where information is imparted in the course of a relationship or venture which a reasonable person would regard as involving a duty of confidentiality, it is enough that a reasonable person in the recipient's position would regard the information as confidential.

3–065   Cross J. in *Printers & Finishers Ltd v Holloway*,[5] gave the following example in the case of an ex-employee:

> "Suppose such a man to be told by his new employers that at this or that stage in the process they encounter this or that difficulty. He may say to himself: 'Well, I remember that on the corresponding piece of machinery in the other factory such-and-such a part was set at a different angle or shaped in a different way': or again, 'When that happened we used to do this and it seemed to work,' 'this' being perhaps something which he had been taught when he first went to the other factory, or possibly an expedient which he had found out for himself by trial and error during his previous employment.
>
> Recalling matters of this sort is, to my mind, quite unlike memorising a formula or list of customers or what was said (obviously in confidence) at a particular meeting. The employee might well not realise that the feature or expedient in question was in fact peculiar to his late employer's process and factory; but even if he did, such knowledge is not readily separable from his general knowledge of the flock printing process and his acquired skill in manipulating a flock printing plant, and I do not think that any man of average intelligence and honesty would think that there was anything improper in his putting his memory of particular features of his late employer's plant at the disposal of his new employer. The law will defeat its own object if it seeks to enforce in this field standards which would be rejected by the ordinary man."

The same concept is echoed in the judgment of Megarry J. in *Coco v Clark*[6]:

---

[4] [1990] 1 A.C. 109 at 281.
[5] [1965] R.P.C. 239 at 256.
[6] [1969] R.P.C. 41 at 48.

"It seems to me that if the circumstances are such that any reasonable man standing in the shoes of the recipient of the information would have realised that upon reasonable grounds the information was being given to him in confidence, then this should suffice to impose upon him the equitable obligation of confidence. In particular, where information of commercial or industrial value is given on a business-like basis and with some avowed common object in mind, such as a joint venture or the manufacture of articles by one party for the other, I would regard the recipient as carrying a heavy burden if he seeks to repel a contention that he was bound by an obligation of confidence: see the *Saltman*[7] case at 216."

Third party recipient

In order to be fixed with an obligation of confidence, a third party must know that the information was confidential; knowledge of a mere assertion of confidentiality is not sufficient.[8]   **3–066**

There has been debate over what constitutes sufficient knowledge for the conscience of a third party to be bound. The relevant equitable principle is the same as applies to accessories to a breach of trust. In *Royal Brunei Airlines v Tan*[9] the Privy Council re-examined the principle in relation to that subject and reviewed the authorities, including the much cited judgment of Lord Selborne L.C. in *Barnes v Addy*.[10] Lord Nicholls, delivering the judgment of the Board, held that failure to exercise reasonable diligence was insufficient to establish liability against a third party who procured or assisted in a breach of trust, and that it was necessary to establish that he had failed "to observe the standard which would be observed by an honest person" placed in his circumstances. He preferred that formulation to posing the test in terms of whether the third party had "knowingly" assisted in a breach of trust, because a question posed in the latter form led too often into tortuous convolutions about the sort of knowledge required.   **3–067**

Dishonesty is a natural word to use in relation to misappropriation of trust assets. It is an equally natural word to use in relation to misuse of confidential information of a commercially valuable kind. In the case of confidential information of a non-commercial character other expressions might more naturally be used to convey the gravity of misconduct required, such as wilful or reckless disregard of its confidentiality.[11] Unconscionable is another word which reflects the root of the jurisdiction in an equitable duty of conscience, but suffers from the disadvantage referred to by Lord   **3–068**

---

[7] (1948) 65 R.P.C. 203.
[8] *Fraser v Thames Television* [1984] 1 Q.B. 44 at 65.
[9] [1995] 2 A.C. 378.
[10] (1874) L.R. 9 Ch.App. 244.
[11] In *Hivac Ltd v Park Royal Scientific Instruments Ltd* [1946] 1 Ch. 169 at 172 Lord Greene M.R. said, "The defendants and the employees on the evidence appear quite clearly to have known exactly what they were doing, and they knew that, at any rate, it was morally reprehensible, if not legally wrong".

Nicholls of not being in everyday use by non-lawyers and requiring its own definition.

3–069   The important thing is that for a third party to be held liable in equity for a breach of confidence, more is required than merely careless, naive or stupid behaviour; there must be awareness of the fact that the information was confidential or willingness to turn a proverbial blind eye. This test was applied by the Court of Appeal in *Thomas v Pearce*.[12]

3–070   Where the supply of confidential information to a third party involves the supplier in a breach of a contractual duty of confidence, the third party will be liable for the tort of inducement of breach of contract if he makes himself party to the receipt of the information with knowledge that the supplier is acting in breach of contract.[13] Conversely, the third party will not be liable if he lacks that knowledge, unless he deliberately shuts his eyes to suspicion.[14]

3–071   There is no comparable action in tort for inducement of a breach of trust or, by analogy, breach of an equitable duty of confidence, because the position of secondary parties to a breach of an equitable duty is adequately dealt with by the principles developed in *Barnes v Addy*[15] and *Royal Brunei Airlines v Tan*.[16] The Court of Appeal so held in relation to inducement of breach of trust in *Metall und Rohstoff A.G. v Donaldson Lufkin & Jenrette Inc.*[17]

3–072   In *Valeo Vision S.A. v Flexible Lamps Ltd*[18] the plaintiffs supplied confidential information to M, who wrongly disclosed it to the defendants. The defendants, unaware of M's breach of confidence, used the information in competition with the plaintiffs. The plaintiffs claimed damages from the defendants, not on the basis that the defendants were party to M's misconduct, but on the simple basis that it was inequitable that they should retain the benefit of their innocent misuse of confidential information. Aldous J. dismissed the claim, holding that the conscience of the defendants could not be bound, and therefore any claim against them in equity failed, in circumstances in which they had no knowledge of the breach of confidence.

3–073   In *Thomas v Pearce*[19] a letting agency sued a former employee and her new employer, another letting agency, for breach of confidence. On changing her employment the employee took with her a list of landlord clients of the first firm and showed it to P, another employee of the second firm. P arranged for letters to be written to some of those on the list to tell

---

[12] [2000] F.S.R. 718.

[13] *Hivac Ltd v Park Royal Scientific Instruments Ltd* [1946] 1 Ch. 169. *Ansell Rubber Co. Pty Ltd v Allied Rubber Industries Pty Ltd* [1972] R.P.C. 811.

[14] *British Industrial Plastics Ltd v Ferguson* [1940] 12 All E.R. 479, HL. *Printers & Finishers Ltd v Holloway* [1965] R.P.C. 239. Compare *Emerald Construction Co. Ltd v Lowthian* [1966] 1 W.L.R. 691 at 700.

[15] (1874) L.R. 9 Ch.App. 244.

[16] [1995] 2 A.C. 378.

[17] [1990] 1 Q.B. 391.

[18] [1995] R.P.C. 205; see too *B v H Bauer Publishing Ltd* June 14, 2001, QBD, *per* Eady J. at para.23.

[19] [2000] F.S.R. 718.

them that the employee had joined the second firm. The trial judge found that the employee had acted in breach of confidence but dismissed the claim against the second firm. His assessment of P's evidence was that she had not acted dishonestly, and, although a reasonable estate agent in her position would have made further inquiries, she had not deliberately refrained from asking questions in case she learned something which she would rather not know. On those findings of fact the Court of Appeal upheld his judgment.

In *Campbell v MGN Ltd* the defendants sought to take the mental **3–074** requirement further. They argued that a third party could not be liable for breach of confidence if it believed publication to be in the public interest. This "ambitious" submission was rejected by the Court of Appeal and not renewed in the House of Lords.[20]

Accidental recipient

Although there is no direct authority on the point, an accidental recipient of **3–075** confidential information should not be under an equitable obligation unless he knows that the information is confidential or is deliberately blind to the likelihood of it being confidential. It is difficult to see why there should be a more onerous obligation on a person who unwittingly receives confidential information by accident than on a person who unwittingly receives confidential information from someone who is under a duty of confidentiality.

Improper or surreptitious receipt

A person who obtains confidential information improperly or surrepti- **3–076** tiously behaves in a way which by its nature is contrary to "a properly formed and instructed conscience" (to use the expression of Gleeson C.J. in *Australian Broadcasting Corporation v Lenah Game Meats Pty Ltd*[21]). It is hard to imagine circumstances in which such a person could resist the application of the equitable jurisdiction on grounds of lack of notice of the confidentiality.

Confidential nature of the information

The requirements for a duty of confidentiality that the information must be **3–077** confidential, and that it must be obtained in circumstances giving rise to a duty of confidentiality, are closely linked. Both are determined from the viewpoint of a reasonable person; and the circumstances in which information is received may be relevant to whether a reasonable person would regard the subject matter as confidential. But it does not necessarily follow

---

[20] [2002] EWCA Civ 1373; [2003] Q.B. 633 at paras 66–70.
[21] (2001) 208 C.L.R. 199 at para.45.

that information will have the objective quality of confidentiality because it is imparted in the course of a confidential relationship.

3–078   Sir Robert Megarry V.C. referred to the difficulties of definition, in a commercial setting, in *Thomas Marshall Ltd v Guinle*[22]:

> "It is far from easy to state in general terms what is confidential information or a trade secret. Certain authorities were cited, but they did not carry matters very far. Plainly 'something which is public property and public knowledge' is not confidential: see *Saltman Engineering Co. Ltd v Campbell Engineering Co. Ltd* (1948) 65 R.P.C. 203, 215, *per* Lord Greene M.R. On the other hand, 'something that has been constructed solely from materials in the public domain may possess the necessary quality of confidentiality: for something new and confidential may have been brought into being by the application of the skill and ingenuity of the human brain. Novelty depends on the thing itself, and not upon the quality of its constitutent parts': *Coco v A. N. Clark (Engineers) Ltd* [1969] R.P.C. 41, 47, a case that was not cited, but in part draws on the *Saltman* case, which was. Costs and prices which are not generally known may well constitute trade secrets or confidential information: see *Herbert Morris Ltd v Saxelby* [1916] 1 A.C. 688, 705, referring to prices."

He went on to suggest, as a matter of principle, certain elements which might assist in identifying confidential information in an industrial or trade setting—the party claiming confidentiality must believe that release of the information would be injurious to him or of advantage to his rivals or others; the party claiming confidentiality must believe that the information is confidential, i.e. not already in the public domain; his belief under the two previous heads must be reasonable; and the information must be judged in the light of the usage and practices of the particular industry or trade concerned.

3–079   In *Lancashire Fires Ltd v S A Lyons & Co. Ltd*[23] (also a trade secret case) Carnwath J. noted the "subjective emphasis" of that approach and said that:

> "The subjective view of the owner cannot be decisive. There must be something which is not only objectively a trade secret, but something which was known, or ought to have been known, by both parties to be so."

3–080   Adapted for more general application, the following elements may be suggested:

---

[22] [1979] 1 Ch. 227 at 248.
[23] [1996] F.S.R. 629 at 646, 656.

(1) There must be some value to the party claiming confidentiality (not necessarily commercial) in the information being treated as confidential;
(2) The information must be such that a reasonable person in the position of the parties would regard it as confidential; and in considering reasonableness, usage and practices in the relevant sector (for example, industrial or professional) are to be taken into account.

These elements are expressed in positive terms. The courts have also identified particular factors which negate confidentiality, and these can be seen as instances where one or more of the positive elements is lacking.

Confidentiality and reasonableness

In *Dunford & Elliott v Johnson & Firth Brown*[24] Lord Denning M.R. held that the courts would recognise confidentiality only to the extent that it was reasonable to do so.   **3–081**

This principle has not been explicitly followed in later cases, but there is no doubt that the concept of what is reasonable has influenced the development of the law of confidentiality.   **3–082**

First, in *Coco v Clark*[25] itself Megarry J. pressed into service "that hard-worked creature, the reasonable man" in determining whether information should be regarded as confidential.   **3–083**

Secondly, in many cases the difficult question has been not whether there is any duty of confidence but what are its limits. In determining that question the court is bound to be influenced by consideration of what is reasonable, and there are plenty of examples among the cases.[26]   **3–084**

Necessity of identification of information claimed to be confidential

Information alleged to be confidential must be specific in the sense that it is clear and identifiable as confidential.[27] The problem arises especially with alleged trade secrets, where elements of the information for which protection is sought may be in the public domain or within a former employee's general expertise. In some cases there may be confidentiality about a system   **3–085**

---

[24] [1978] F.S.R. 143 at 148.
[25] [1978] F.S.R. 143 at 148.
[26] *Tournier v National Provincial and Union Bank* [1924] 1 K.B. 461; *Printers & Finishers Ltd v Holloway* [1965] R.P.C. 239 at 256; *Smith Kline & French Laboratories (Australia) Ltd v Secretary to the Department of Community Services and Health* (1991) 99 A.L.R. 679 at 691–692; *R. v Department of Health, Ex p. Source Informatics Ltd* [2001] Q.B. 424; *W v Egdell* [1990] 1 Ch. 359; *Hellewell v Chief Constable of Derbyshire* [1995] 1 W.L.R. 804 at 810.
[27] *Amway Corporation v Eurway International Ltd* [1974] R.P.C. 82 at 86–87; *Potters-Ballotini Ltd v Weston-Baker* [1977] R.P.C. 202 at 205–206; *O'Brien v Komesaroff* (1982) 150 C.L.R. 310 at 324–328; *Fraser v Thames Television Ltd* [1984] 1 Q.B. 44 at 63; and *De Maudsley v Palumbo* [1996] F.S.R. 447.

even if it is made up of parts which are familiar. In *Under Water Welders & Repairers Ltd v Street and Longthorne* Buckley J. said[28]:

> "The fact that all the individual units of equipment that are employed in a particular operation may be articles that can be obtained in the general market and the fact that systems are well known to those concerned in whatever sort of activity is involved, does not mean that there cannot be *some degree of confidentiality* about the way in which they are used to achieve a particular result." (Emphasis added.)

It is, however, for the claimant to establish with particularity what is alleged to be confidential.

3–086   Further, it is a cardinal rule that an injunction must be framed in such a way that the party affected can know with certainty what he is or is not allowed to do. In *Potters-Ballotini Ltd v Weston-Baker*,[29] *Lawrence David Ltd v Ashton*[30] and *CMI-Centres for Medical Innovation GmbH v Phytopharm Plc*[31] applications for interlocutory injunctions to restrain alleged misuse of confidential information, which was insufficiently defined, were refused for that reason.[32]

3–087   Those cases concerned alleged trade secrets, but the problem also arose in *Times Newspapers Ltd v MGN Ltd*,[33] in which an unsuccessful attempt was made to restrain the unauthorised, advance publication of extracts from Lady Thatcher's memoirs. Leggatt L.J. said:

> "It is a matter of regret that because the plaintiffs are constrained to concede that vital parts of the book should be excepted from the scope of any injunction, and because the drafting of such an exception could not, in my judgment, be satisfactorily achieved, as the plaintiffs' draft demonstrates, the continued pirating of passages from the book cannot be effectually restrained by the plaintiffs, whatever prospects they may enjoy of eventually recovering damages."

Trivial or useless information

3–088   The rule that confidentiality does not attach to trivial or useless information reflects the underlying rationale of the jurisdiction. The reasoning was expressed by Deane J. in *Moorgate Tobacco Co. Ltd v Philip Morris Ltd (No. 2)*[34] as follows:

---

[28] [1968] R.P.C. 498 at 506–507.
[29] [1977] R.P.C. 202 at 206.
[30] [1991] 1 All E.R. 385 at 393.
[31] [1999] F.S.R. 235.
[32] See also the Court of Appeal's decision in *FSS Travel and Leisure Systems Ltd v Johnson* [1999] F.S.R. 505, upholding Ronald Walker Q.C.'s refusal of a final injunction, on the grounds (among others) that the pleadings and evidence were insufficiently specific, precise and cogent.
[33] [1993] E.M.L.R. 443 at 448.
[34] (1984) 156 C.L.R. 414 at 438.

"Like most heads of exclusive equitable jurisdiction, its rational basis does not lie in proprietary right. It lies in the notion of an obligation of conscience arising from the circumstances in or through which the information was communicated or obtained. Relief under the jurisdiction is not available, however, unless it appears that the information in question has 'the necessary quality of confidence about it' (*per* Lord Greene M.R., *Saltman*[35]) and that it is significant, not necessarily in the sense of commercially valuable (see *Argyll v Argyll*[36]) but in the sense that the preservation of its confidentiality or secrecy is of substantial concern to the plaintiff."

In *Spycatcher*[37] Scott J. referred as an example to *McNicol v Sportsman's Book Stores*,[38] where the plaintiff was the originator of a betting system based on the age of the moon. Maugham J. refused an injunction to protect its alleged confidentiality. Scott J. said that: **3–089**

"The ground for the refusal was that the information was 'perfectly useless'."

In *Stephens v Avery*[39] the plaintiff revealed to a friend details of a lesbian relationship with a woman who was murdered. The friend passed the information to a newspaper, which published it. Sir Nicolas Browne-Wilkinson V.C. refused to strike out a claim against the confidant and the newspaper for damages for breach of confidence. One of the grounds unsuccessfully relied upon by the newspaper was that the information was mere gossip or "trivial tittle-tattle" outside the protection of the law.[40] Rejecting this argument, Sir Nicolas Browne-Wilkinson said[41]:   **3–090**

"As to the submission that there is no confidentiality in tittle-tattle and gossip, Mr. Wilson relied on a passage in the *Coco* case [1969] R.P.C. 41, 48, where Megarry, J. said:

' ... I doubt whether equity would intervene unless the circumstances are of sufficient gravity; equity ought not to be invoked merely to protect trivial tittle-tattle, however confidential.'

Since the *Coco* case was exclusively concerned with information which was of industrial value, those remarks were plainly obiter dicta. Moreover, I have the greatest doubt whether wholesale revelation of the sexual conduct of an individual can properly be described as 'trivial' tittle-tattle. Again, although it is true that the passage I have

---

[35] [1948] 65 R.P.C. 203 at 215.
[36] [1967] Ch. 302 at 329.
[37] [1990] 1 A.C. 109 at 149.
[38] (1930) McG.C.C. 116.
[39] [1988] 1 Ch. 449; followed by Jacob J. in *Barrymore v News Group Newspapers Ltd* [1997] F.S.R. 600.
[40] *ibid.* at 452.
[41] *ibid.* at 454.

quoted occurs in that part of the judgment which deals with the nature of information which can be protected, it is to be noted that the judge appeared to be considering when equity would give a remedy, not dealing with the fundamental nature of the legal right. If, as I think he was, Megarry J. was saying that the discretion to grant an injunction or to award damages would not be exercised in a case which was merely trivial, I agree. But the exercise of such a discretion can only be decided in the light of all the circumstances. Those cannot be known until there has been a trial."

Although Sir Nicolas Browne-Wilkinson V.C. saw the question of triviality as a factor going to the exercise of the court's discretion, rather than to the principle whether a duty of confidence was owed, in *Spycatcher* Lord Goff recognised it as a "limiting principle . . . that the duty of confidence applies neither to useless information, nor to trivia."[42]

3–091 If a matter is not such that the preservation of its confidentiality would be thought by a person of ordinary honesty and intelligence to be of any substantial concern to the plaintiff, there is sense in not attaching to it any duty of confidence.

Falsity of information

3–092 It has sometimes been argued that there can be no confidentiality in false information or, to put it more fully, that the publication of information said to be inaccurate cannot give rise to a claim for breach of confidentiality.[43] The argument is based on the distinction between defamation and breach of confidentiality referred to by Sir David Cairns in *Khashoggi v Smith*[44]:

> "It seems to me that there is a fundamental distinction between the two types of action, in that in the one case the plaintiff is saying 'Untrue and defamatory statements have been made about me,' and in the other case the plaintiff is saying 'Statements which are about to be published are statements about events which have happened and have been disclosed as a result of a breach of confidence.' "

However, a claimant might say with good cause "Statements which are about to be published are about a subject matter which ought properly to be treated as confidential and also contain inaccuracies". In such a case there is no just or logical reason why the inaccuracies should obliterate the confidential nature of the subject matter. If, for example, one party to a

---

[42] [1990] 1 A.C. 109 at 282. See also *McKennitt v Ash* [2005] EWHC 3003, Q.B., [2006] E.M.L.R. 10, discussed at para.7–035 below. The Court of Appeal gave permission to the defendant to appeal: [2006] EWCA Civ 778.
[43] See *Campbell v MGN Ltd* [2002] EWHC 499, Q.B. at para.55 (Morland J.) [2003] Q.B. 633 at paras 56–57, CA; *Interbrew v Financial Times Ltd* [2002] EWCA Civ 274; [2002] 2 Lloyd's Rep. 229 at para.38.
[44] (1980) 124 S.J. 149, cited by the Court of Appeal in *Lion Laboratories v Evans* [1985] 526 at 538 (Stephenson L.J.), 548 (O'Connor L.J.).

marriage proposed to publish what purports to be an intimate account of their sexual life, the other party ought to be able to apply for an order restraining the publication on the grounds of the confidentiality of the subject matter, regardless of the accuracy of the details. Or if a disgruntled former spy proposed to publish the alleged identities of other agents, the security service ought to be able to apply for an order restraining the publication without having to accept the accuracy of the identifications.

An account about a confidential subject may not be less injurious to the interests which are intended to be protected by its confidentiality because it contains falsehoods.   **3–093**

In *Cornelius v de Tarranto*[45] a psychiatrist was instructed for a fee to provide a medical report on the claimant for legal purposes. On ordinary principles the psychiatrist owed a contractual and equitable duty to the claimant not to make improper disclosure of the report. Without the claimant's consent, she disclosed her report to other medical staff. It contained some defamatory statements. The claimant sued the psychiatrist for defamation and breach of confidentiality. Morland J. dismissed the claim for defamation on grounds of justification but found for the claimant on the issue of breach of confidentiality. If, however, the defence of justification had failed, it would be odd to suppose that the defamatory nature of the report would have afforded a defence to the claim for breach of confidentiality, whether in contract or in equity, although it would have been necessary to avoid double counting in the assessment of damages.   **3–094**

It would also run counter to the object of confidentiality if a party had to disclose the extent to which he accepted the account of the other party on a confidential subject in order to be able to claim that the subject should be treated as confidential. This point was made by Eady J. in *McKennitt v Ash*[46]:   **3–095**

> "Although there is no claim for defamation or malicious falsehood, Ms McKennitt has indicated, in respect of certain parts of the evidence, that the account which Ms Ash has chosen to give is untrue, distorted or misleading. It is not in my judgment, however, permissible to respond by advancing the somewhat simplistic proposition that a reasonable expectation of protection, or a duty of confidence, as the case may be, *cannot* arise in relation to false allegations. As I observed in the case of *Beckham v Gibson*, 29 April 2005 (unreported), the protection of the law would be illusory if a claimant, in relation to a long and garbled story, was obliged to spell out which of the revelations are accepted as true, and which are said to be false or distorted: see also *W v Westminster City Council* [2005] EWHC 102; Q.B. Tugendhat J."

---

[45] [2002] E.M.L.R. 6.
[46] [2005] EWHC 3003, Q.B. at [78].

3–096   The European Court of Human Rights has gone further. In *Cumpana v Romania*[47] two journalists were convicted of criminal defamation after they published an article in virulent terms making false allegations of corruption against two public officials. The European Court rejected a complaint that their convictions violated their rights under Art.10,[48] holding that the protection of the reputation of those against whom the allegations had been made was "a right which, as an aspect of private life, is protected by Article 8 of the Convention".[49] In *Radio France v France*[50] the court reiterated that a person's right to a reputation is among the rights guaranteed by Art.8.

3–097   Where a publication goes unacceptably into a person's private life, and is also defamatory, Art.8 is breached in both respects. The wronged party is entitled to complain of one or other or both.

Intention to publish

3–098   In *Times Newspapers Ltd v MGN Ltd*[51] Sir Thomas Bingham M.R. expressed doubt whether the necessary quality of confidence could attach to Lady Thatcher's memoirs in circumstances in which the book was shortly due to be published, although he expressed no final view and regretted that because of the timescale the decision whether to grant an interlocutory injunction had had to be made after brief argument and without full time for reflection.

3–099   It is suggested that the fact that the plaintiffs intended to publish the material did not prevent it from having the quality of confidence prior to its intended publication. The fact that somebody intends to publish material may in some circumstances be inconsistent with an intention to regard it as confidential but that will by no means always be so.

3–100   Many examples could be given. A company may intend to apply for a patent. That involves publication of the secret. It would be surprising if an employee or other person to whom the details were imparted in confidence, or a third party who obtained them from such a person, could contend that the information lacked the quality of confidence because the company intended to publish it.

3–101   It would be surprising if details of the Government's budget proposals were held not to have the quality of confidence on the day before the budget, because they were due to be published next day.[52]

3–102   The same would apply to a company's yearly or half-yearly results in advance of publication.

---

[47] [2004] E.C.H.R. 692.
[48] The court considered that the convictions were sufficient to restore the balance between the various competing interests at stake and that sentences including imprisonment and a year's ban on working as journalists were manifestly excessive: paras 115–122, 129.
[49] *ibid.* at para.91.
[50] [2004] E.C.R. 127; (2005) 40 E.H.R.R. 706 at para.31.
[51] [1993] E.M.L.R. 443.
[52] Or take the D-day landing plans referred to by Bingham L.J. in *Spycatcher* in the Court of Appeal [1990] 1 A.C. 109 at 215. See para.3–111, below.

In *Khashoggi v Smith*[53] the Court of Appeal (Roskill L.J. and Sir David   **3–103**
Cairns) did not consider that that the plaintiff had lost her claimed right to
confidentiality because she had been negotiating with a newspaper for the
sale of her memoirs (although their observations were obiter because the
claim failed on other grounds). Sir David Cairns said:

> "It seems to me that a person may well be entitled, in an ordinary case,
> to say: 'I am willing for the details of my private life to be made known
> to the public by me in the form which I choose and for my financial
> benefit; but not for them to be published through information disclosed
> by my confidential servant in a form chosen by her and others and to
> the profit of her and others.' "

In *Shelley Films Ltd v Rex Features Ltd*[54] an injunction was granted to   **3–104**
restrain disclosure of details of a film costume prior to the film's release.
In *Creation Records Ltd v News Group Newspapers Ltd*[55] an injunction   **3–105**
was granted to restrain premature publication of photos of the design for an
album sleeve.

Public domain

The law regarding confidentiality and "public domain" began simply but   **3–106**
has become more complicated. In *Saltman*[56] Lord Greene M.R. said:

> "The information, to be confidential, must, I apprehend, apart from
> contract, have the necessary quality of confidence about it, namely it
> must not be something which is public property and public knowl-
> edge."

"Public domain" has come to be the expression most often used in this
context, but other phrases used in the cases include "common knowledge"[57]
and "information generally available to the public".[58]
In the *Spycatcher* case Lord Goff observed that the equitable duty of   **3–107**
confidentiality is subject to certain limiting principles. He continued:

> "The first limiting principle (which is rather an expression of the scope
> of the duty) is . . . that the principle of confidentiality only applies to
> information to the extent that it is confidential. In particular, once it has
> entered what is usually called the public domain (which means no more
> than that the information in question is so generally accessible that, in
> all the circumstances, it cannot be regarded as confidential) then, as a

---

[53] (1980) 124 S.J. 149.
[54] [1994] E.M.L.R. 134.
[55] [1997] E.M.L.R. 444.
[56] (1948) 65 R.P.C. 203 at 217.
[57] *Mustad & Son v Dosen* [1963] R.P.C. 41 at 43; *Coco v A N Clark (Engineering) Ltd* [1969]
R.P.C. 41 at 47.
[58] *Ackroyds (London) Ltd v Islington Plastics Ltd* [1962] R.P.C. 97 at 104.

general rule, the principle of confidentiality can have no application to it."[59]

3–108   Because there has been a misleading tendency at times to treat the question of public domain as if it involves a free standing rule to be mechanistically applied, three points are to be noted about the principle as set out in this passage. First, it is expressed as a general and not an absolute rule. This is reflected in the statement of the Court of Appeal in *Douglas v Hello! Ltd (No. 3)* that "In general, once information is in the public domain, it will no longer be confidential or entitled to the protection of the law of confidence, though this may not always be true".[60] Secondly, it is seen to be an aspect of the scope of the duty of confidentiality—or in other words a factor affecting the question whether a person's conscience ought to require him to treat information as confidential. Thirdly, the statement that the principle of confidentiality cannot generally apply to information so generally accessible that it cannot be regarded as confidential might be considered somewhat circular, but its value lies in the flexibility of the guidance which it provides. Read as a whole, the passage highlights that in each case the question for the court is whether the degree of accessibility of the information is such that, in all the circumstances, it would not be just to require the party against whom a duty of confidentiality is alleged to treat it as confidential.

3–109   It is relevant to consider why the fact of information being publicly accessible should affect that issue. The reasons correspond, negatively, with the positive elements of confidential information previously identified: that there is value to the party claiming confidentiality in the information being treated as confidential; and that a reasonable person in the position of the parties would regard the information as confidential.

3–110   The first reason is that the essence of the law of confidentiality is that it is designed to protect secrecy. The essence of a secret is that it is not publicly known. If information is known to the public at large, it would be idle (both in the sense of unreal and in the sense of purposeless) to seek to regard it as confidential.

3–111   Bingham L.J. gave a vivid illustration in the *Spycatcher*[61] case in the Court of Appeal:

> "Forty-four years ago there can have been few, if any, national secrets more confidential than the date of the planned invasion of France. Any Crown servant who divulged such information to an unauthorised recipient would plainly have been in flagrant breach of his duty. But it would be absurd to hold such a servant bound to treat the date of the invasion as confidential on or after (say) 9 June 1944 when the date had become known to the world. A purist might say that the Allies, as confiders and owners of the information, had by their own act

[59] [1990] 1 A.C. 109 at 282.
[60] [2005] EWCA Civ 595; [2006] Q.B. 125, at [105].
[61] [1990] 1 A.C. 109 at 215.

destroyed its confidentiality and so disabled themselves from enforcing the duty, but the common sense view is that the date, being public knowledge, could no longer be regarded as the subject of confidence."

In the same case Dillon L.J. said that it would be "futile and just plain silly" to maintain an injunction against further distribution of *Spycatcher* when it had been widely circulated in the English language throughout the world.[62]

The House of Lords upheld the Court of Appeal in concluding (by a **3–112** majority) that the extensiveness of the publication of *Spycatcher* abroad and the availability of copies in the UK had resulted in all possible damage being already done and all confidentiality in the subject matter effectively destroyed, so there was no purpose in preventing further publication.[63]

In less extreme cases there may be significant value to a person in being **3–113** able to claim confidentiality despite some loss or lack of secrecy. Cross J. said in *Franchi v Franchi*[64]:

"Clearly a claim that the disclosure of some information would be a breach of confidence is not defeated simply by proving that there are other people in the world who know the facts in question besides the man as to whom it is said that his disclosure would be a breach of confidence and those to whom he has disclosed them.

There appear to be no English cases on this branch of the law of trade secrets, but the plaintiffs referred me to the United States case of *Vulcan Detinning Co. v Assam* (1918) 185 N.Y. App. Div. 399 … where it was held that the fact that a German and a Dutch firm had complete knowledge of the process in question which one of the defendants (an employee of the plaintiffs) had disclosed to the other defendant was no bar to the plaintiff's success. If it is not impertinent for me to say so, that seems to me sound sense. It must be a question of degree depending on the particular case, but if relative secrecy remains, the plaintiff can still succeed."[65]

The question of confidentiality has sometimes arisen where the information relates to an event which happened in public or is accessible to the general public, although the degree of public knowledge about it is limited.

The Law Commission discussed the issue and posed an example in its **3–114** Working Paper on Breach of Confidence[66]:

---

[62] *ibid.* at 205.
[63] [1990] 1 A.C. 109 at 259–260, 265–267, 290–291, 293.
[64] [1967] R.P.C. 149 at 152–153.
[65] See also *Spycatcher* [1990] 1 A.C. 109 at 260, *per* Lord Keith; *Commonwealth of Australia v John Fairfax & Sons Ltd* (1980) 147 C.L.R. 39 at 54, *per* Mason J.; *Artedomus v Del Casale* [2006] N.S.W.S.C. 146 at paras 23–26, *per* Burchett A.J.
[66] No.58, 1974, at para.102.

"Much information which is technically available to the public is not generally known and may in fact be known only to a handful of people. For example, the back files of a local newspaper may, if properly and assiduously searched, yield a good deal of information not generally known about a person who spent his early life in the area—his family and educational background, his business connections, his political beliefs and his personal and social problems. Perhaps they show that he was at the centre of an unfortunate affair at his school, that he attempted to take his own life, that he took part in a political demonstration in favour of an unpopular cause, that he associated in his business or private life with someone later convicted of grave crimes against society or even that he 'helped the police' with their inquiries into an offence with which he was never charged. These facts will, of course, be known to and remembered by those who were directly involved, but if the publication took place a long time ago it is quite possible that nobody now knows or remembers them solely by reason of the publication in the local newspaper. If the person concerned subsequently discloses any of these facts in confidence to another in the course of a relationship in which absolute frankness is essential, is it right that the person who accepts the confidence should be able, solely on the ground that the facts are technically accessible to the public, to disclose them to others in breach of his duty of confidence?"

The confidant would surely owe a duty of confidentiality to the confider on grounds that the information was communicated in confidence as well as on the ground that he would be entitled to respect for his private life under Art.8.

3–115 In this context it is instructive to contrast the decisions of the Court of Appeal in *Woodward v Hutchings*[67] and *Schering Chemicals Ltd v Falkman Ltd*.[68]

3–116 In *Woodward v Hutchins* the Court of Appeal discharged an injunction against a former press relations agent to a group of singers who had embarked on the publication in the media of details of the group's lives, including what was described by Lord Denning M.R. as "a very unsavoury episode in a Jumbo Jet". The plaintiffs failed on two grounds.

3–117 First, it was held that since the group had retained the press agent "to have themselves presented to the public in a favourable light", they could not complain afterwards if he revealed unfavourable details, it being in the public interest that the truth should be known.

3–118 Secondly, it was held that the information was not confidential because it was in the public domain. Lord Denning said[69]:

"But what is confidential? As Bridge L.J. pointed out in the course of the argument, Mr Hutchins, as a press agent, might attend a dance

[67] [1977] 1 W.L.R. 760.
[68] [1982] 1 Q.B. 1.
[69] [1977] 1 W.L.R. 760 at 764.

which many others attended. Any incident which took place at the dance would be known to all present. The information would be in the public domain. There could be no objection to the incidents being made known generally. It would not be confidential information. So in this case the incident on the Jumbo Jet was in the public domain. It was known to all passengers on the flight. Likewise with several other incidents in the series."

But suppose instead that the defendant had been a solicitor, instructed by one or more of the group in connection with the incident in the aircraft. It is hard to conceive that the court would in that case have refused an injunction restraining him from selling the story to the media.[70]

In *Schering Chemicals Ltd v Falkman Ltd*[71] the plaintiffs manufactured a   **3–119** pregnancy testing drug marketed as "Primodos". An issue arose as to its safety and it was withdrawn from the market. Schering retained Falkman to give media and public relations training to Schering's executives in order to counteract bad publicity, and for this purpose they supplied to Falkman a large amount of information about the drug. Falkman retained for a daily fee the second defendant, Elstein, to give instruction to its staff, and he too was provided with information supplied by Schering. He subsequently, without Schering's permission, approached a television company and gave them information from which they made a documentary on the drug. It was contended on their behalf that the information on which the film was based was all available to the public. The Court of Appeal by a majority (Lord Denning M.R. dissenting) upheld an injunction against Elstein and the television company to prevent the broadcasting of the film.

Templeman L.J. said[72]:   **3–120**

> "In my judgment, when Mr Elstein agreed for reward to take part in the training course and received and absorbed information from Schering, he became under a duty not to use that information and impliedly promised Schering that he would not use that information for the very purpose which Schering sought to avoid, namely, bad publicity in the future, including publicity which Schering reasonably regarded as bad publicity."

He continued:

> "The information supplied by Schering to Mr. Elstein had already been published, but it included information which was damaging to Schering when it was first published and which could not be re-published without the risk of causing further damage to Schering."

---

[70] See the discussion of *Hilton v Barker Booth & Eastwood* [2005] UKHL 8, [2005] 1 W.L.R. 567 at para.3–132 below.
[71] [1982] 1 Q.B. 1.
[72] [1982] 1 Q.B. 1 at 37.

3–121   In both *Woodward v Hutchins* and *Schering Chemicals Ltd v Falkman Ltd* the defendants' professional skills were engaged to produce good publicity for the plaintiffs and were used by them to produce bad publicity. This was regarded as a reason for refusing an injunction in the former case; but for granting it in the latter case (where paradoxically, the public interest in knowing the truth about Primodos was far greater than any public interest in the private lives of a group of singers). Unless the engagement was in some way disreputable, it is suggested that the approach in *Schering Chemicals Ltd v Falkman Ltd* is to be preferred. But the more important difference is in their approach to the question of confidentiality and the public domain.

3–122   The simplest and most satisfactory explanation of *Woodward v Hutchins* is that there was nothing in the defendant's engagement which required him to regard as confidential the behaviour of the plaintiffs in a public place. If, on the other hand, the plaintiffs had consulted a solicitor about the incident in the aircraft, he would have been under a duty to use the information given to him for the purpose for which it was given and not otherwise.[73]

3–123   In *Schering Chemicals Ltd v Falkman Ltd* information was given to the defendants in confidence, and although such information might be obtained from other sources, it was nevertheless perceived by the plaintiffs (reasonably in the eyes of the court) that the defendants would do harm to the plaintiffs if the programme, compiled from information supplied in confidence, were broadcast on a major television network, using information supplied in confidence as a springboard.

3–124   In *Creation Records Ltd v News Group Newspapers Ltd*[74] Lloyd J. granted an injunction to prevent publication in poster form of photographs which the defendants had already published in three editions of *The Sun* (as the judge said "in no doubt millions of copies"), holding that the degree of publication was not a reason in itself for refusing to restrain a further publication of a different kind which the claimants reasonably believed would cause them further damage.[75] The decision was cited with implicit approval by the Court of Appeal in *Douglas v Hello! Ltd (No. 3)*.[76]

3–125   The possibility of further publication causing further damage is particularly likely to arise where the information is personal and the damage is to the person's feelings. In *Spycatcher*[77] Lord Keith envisaged the possibility of cases where, even in the light of widespread publication, a person might still be entitled to restrain further publication if it would cause them further damage, and he gave disclosure of marital secrets as an example. In

---

[73] See *Australian Football League v The Age Company Ltd* [2006] VSC 308, *per* Kellam J. at para.42. In *Campbell v Frisbee* [2002] EWCA Civ 1374 at [34] Lord Phillips M.R. commented, obiter, that Lightman J. might well be right to suggest that *Woodward v Hutchins* should no longer be applied.
[74] [1997] E.M.L.R. 444.
[75] See also *Mills v News Group Newspapers Ltd*, June 4, 2001, *per* Lawrence Collins J. at para.25. Contrast *Bunn v British Broadcasting Corporation* [1998] 3 All E.R. 552.
[76] [2005] EWCA Civ 595; [2006] Q.B. 125, at [105].
[77] [1990] 1 A.C. 109 at 260.

McKennitt v Ash[78] Eady J. commented on Lord Keith's remarks, observing that:

> "there are grounds for supposing that the protection of the law will not be withdrawn unless and until it is clear that a stage has been reached where there is no longer anything left to be protected. For example, it does not necessarily follow that because personal information has been revealed impermissibly to one set of newspapers, or to readers within one jurisdiction, there can be no further intrusion upon a person's privacy by further revelations. Fresh revelations to different groups of people can still cause distress and damage to an individual's emotional or mental well-being."

To summarise the discussion of the first reason identified for the accessibility of information being relevant to the issue whether a person may justly be required to treat it as confidential, it is a question of fact in each case whether the degree of public accessibility is such that it that it would be senseless to try to protect it as confidential. The distinction between *Spycatcher*, on the one hand, and *Schering Chemicals Ltd v Falkman Ltd* and *Creation Records Ltd v News Group Newspapers Ltd*, on the other hand, is that in the former the courts considered that further publication could do no further damage but in the latter they considered that it could do further damage.   **3–126**

The second reason is that the accessibility of information may affect whether a reasonable person in the position of the parties would regard it as confidential. The position of the parties, as well as the accessibility of the information, is important in this regard.   **3–127**

Accessibility may itself depend on the skills and knowledge of the particular defendant, which may therefore also be a relevant factor. Suppose, for example, that a company, C, consulted a solicitor, S, with a view to litigation on its behalf against an ex-employee, E, to restrain him from using certain technical know-how in his employment by another company. Suppose that another company in the industry, hearing of the dispute, approached S or an employee of S and offered him money to provide it with details of the same know-how. Suppose further that the technical know-how was not exclusive to C, and was capable of being acquired from other legitimate sources by a person with E's skills, but only by someone with his skills. E might well be entitled to regard the know-how as non-confidential, since he knows that he could acquire it by his own skills and knowledge from another public source, whereas S (or his employee) could say no such thing.   **3–128**

If E were obliged to continue to treat the information as confidential, it could inhibit his proper ability to develop and use his own skills, and might place him under a disadvantage compared with others in his sphere of employment. No such considerations would apply to S (or his employee).   **3–129**

---

[78] [2005] EWHC 3003, Q.B. at 80.

3–130   In each case the decision should accord with the usage and practices of the relevant industry or profession (factors which Megarry V.C. in *Thomas Marshall Ltd v Guinle*[79] regarded as pertinent to the question whether the information possessed the necessary quality of confidence) and the standards of the man of average intelligence and honesty (invoked by Cross J. in *Printers & Finishers Ltd v Holloway*[80]).

3–131   As Bankes L.J. said in *Tournier v National Provincial and Union Bank of England*[81]:

> "The privilege of non-disclosure to which a client or a customer is entitled may vary according to the exact nature of the relationship between the client or the customer and the person on whom the duty rests. It need not be the same in the case of the counsel, the solicitor, the doctor, and the banker, though the underlying principle may be the same."

Hilton v Barker Booth & Eastwood

3–132   More recently it has been suggested that solicitors may owe duties of confidentiality which do not form part of the ordinary concept of confidentiality and the law relating to it. In *Hilton v Barker Booth & Eastwood*[82] a firm of solicitors in breach of professional duty acted for both the claimant and another client, B, in a property development transaction. Unknown to the claimant, but known to the solicitors, B had recently been released from prison after serving a sentence for offences of fraudulent trading and obtaining credit while an undischarged bankrupt. It was held that their duty to the claimant required the solicitors to disclose these facts to him, and it was no excuse that in so doing they would have breached their duty to B. The solicitors through their own fault had placed themselves in a situation where they were bound to be in breach of their duty to one client or the other, whatever they did. The relevance of the case for present purposes is in the comments made, obiter, about the nature of the duty owed by the solicitors to B not to divulge his previous bankruptcy and criminal convictions.

3–133   Lord Scott[83] doubted whether "a matter of public record, such as a bankruptcy or a criminal conviction", could justify being described as confidential; and that the reason why it would have been a breach of the solicitors' duty to have disclosed those facts to the claimant was not that the information was confidential, but that they owed B a duty to do their best to further his interests in the proposed transaction and that disclosure of those facts would have frustrated it.

---

[79] [1979] 1 Ch. 227 at 248.
[80] [1965] R.P.C. 239 at 256.
[81] [1924] 1 K.B. 461 at 474.
[82] [2005] UKHL 8; [2005] 1 W.L.R. 567.
[83] *ibid.* at para.7. See also his decision, when Vice-Chancellor, in *Elliott v Chief Constable of Wiltshire, The Times*, December 5, 1996.

Lord Walker said[84]:   **3–134**

> "In my opinion the notion of confidentiality, as generally understood by
> lawyers, is not really relevant to the issues in this case. It is a solicitor's
> duty to act in his client's best interests and not to do anything likely to
> damage his client's interests, so far as this is consistent with the
> solicitor's professional duty. To disclose discreditable facts about a
> client, and to do so without the client's informed consent, is likely to be
> a breach of duty, even if the facts are in the public domain. Some of the
> references in the Court of Appeal judgments to confidential informa-
> tion must, I think, be understood in this looser sense."

These comments raise questions of substance and classification. The question of substance is whether and in what circumstances a person can be
under a duty to treat as confidential information about something which is
a matter of "public record".

Public record

The phrase "public record" is itself a loose expression. The Law Commis-   **3–135**
sion in its Working Paper on Breach of Confidence[85] proposed that the test
of public domain should be broader in the case of commercial than private
information and that in the case of private information it should be a
defence to an action for breach of confidence to prove that

> "1. the information can be ascertained by recourse to any register kept
>   in pursuance of any Act of Parliament which is open to inspection
>   by the public or to any other document which is required by the
>   law of any part of the United Kingdom to be open to inspection by
>   the public; or
> 2. the information was disclosed in the course of any proceedings,
>   judicial or otherwise, which the public were by the law of any part
>   of the United Kingdom entitled to attend."

However, there appears to have been an internal inconsistency in the
Working Paper (illustrative of the problem of hard rules in this area)
because in referring to the types of case where the Commission considered
that a person should be able to obtain damages for pecuniary loss resulting
from disclosure of private information, supplied in confidence, it stated[86]:

> "An example would be where the defendant publishes information in
> breach of confidence that the plaintiff is divorced in circumstances
> where the defendant knows or ought to know that, owing to the

---

[84] *ibid.* at para.34.
[85] No. 58, 1974, at para.103. (See more generally paras 94–105 *et seq.*)
[86] *ibid.* at para.63.

attitude of the plaintiff's employer, publication of this information will lead to the plaintiff's dismissal."

But pronouncement of a divorce would have been a judicial act done in open court.

3–136   In its final report[87] the Law Commission stated that, after consultation and reconsideration of the matter, it was departing from its provisional recommendation. It considered that it should be for the courts to decide in the circumstances of the individual case whether the information at the time of the alleged breach of confidence was "relatively secret"[88] or "available to the public",[89] and it did not think that it would be practical or desirable to impose a more rigid standard of what constitutes "the public domain" in respect of personal information than in respect of purely commercial information.

3–137   Since the Law Commission considered the matter, technological developments have led to changes in practice and in statutory provisions affecting the ways in which information is stored and used by public and private bodies. The Government has set for public bodies the aim of having an entirely electronic system of information storage. The electronic processing of personal data as part of a filing system (by public bodies or others) is subject to control under the Data Processing Act 1998. "Processing" of information or data for the purposes of the Act includes use or disclosure by transmission or otherwise making it available. The provisions of the Act are complex, reflecting the complexity of the European Directive[90] which it implements. The topic is discussed more fully in Chapter 8. The point of relevance for present purposes is that it is likely to be misleading and oversimplified to speak of personal data being a matter of public record (with the implication that the information is generally available), if the record is electronically maintained, because the criteria for permissible disclosure of personal data electronically stored as part of a filing system are intricate. Personal data are exempt from the non-disclosure provisions of the Act where the data consist of information which the data controller is obliged by or under any enactment to make available to the public[91] or the particular disclosure is required by any enactment, rule of law or order of the court,[92] but generally such data can only be disclosed without the consent of the person concerned where there is an identifiable public interest in doing so.[93]

3–138   Information about matters which are contained in a recorded form available to the public or have been stated in open court can vary in many respects. It may be known to many or to few or possibly only to the person

---

[87] Law Com. No.110 (Cmnd 8388), 1981, at para.6.69.
[88] *Franchi v Franchi* [1967] R.P.C. 149 at 152–3.
[89] *Ackroyds (London) Ltd v Islington Plastics Ltd* [1962] R.P.C. 97 at 104.
[90] Council Directive 95/46/EC.
[91] s.34.
[92] s.35.
[93] Schs 1–3 set out principles to be applied in processing personal data or sensitive personal data.

concerned. It may be fresh or stale. The subject matter may or may not affect the wider public. It may relate to misconduct, of which the person concerned may have been the perpetrator or the victim, or to misfortune.

A rule which provided that a person who confides information to another **3–139** about some matter which is contained in a recorded form technically available to the public, or has been stated in open court, can never be entitled to have the confidence respected, could produce surprising and unfair results.

Consider the following examples: **3–140**

1. A person is illegitimate and had an unhappy childhood, involving a sibling who committed suicide and a drunken, violent stepfather who used to beat his mother and himself. These facts have left emotional scars. He discloses them in confidence to a doctor or a counsellor or a close friend. No one else knows about them, although his illegitimacy could be deduced from his birth certificate, his sibling's suicide was the subject of a coroner's inquest and evidence was given about his stepfather's violence when the step-father was prosecuted for an assault.
2. A person was convicted as a student for possession of drugs. Years later he discloses it in a job application because he is required to state if he has ever had any criminal conviction. No one else knows about it.

In these circumstances a reasonable person would expect the information to be treated in confidence and the idea that the recipient could sell it to a newspaper would be shocking.

In *R. v Chief Constable of North Wales Police Ex p. AB*[94] the applicants, **3–141** a married couple ("AB" and "CD"), were released from prison after serving long sentences for sexual offences against children. They bought a caravan and moved onto a caravan site. The local police tried unsuccessfully to persuade them to leave and then informed the site owner of their records. The site owner ordered them to move on. The applicants sought judicial review by way of declarations that the decision to inform the site owner of their convictions was unlawful. Their grounds included breach of con-fidence and breach of their rights under Art.8.

The claim was rejected by the Divisional Court. Lord Bingham C.J.[95] **3–142** accepted the principle that when in the course of performing its public duties a public body comes into possession of information regarding a member of the public, being information not generally available and damaging to that member of the public if disclosed, the body ought not to disclose such information save for the purpose of and to the extent necessary for performance of its public duty or enabling some other public body to perform its duty. He stated that the principle rested in his view on

[94] [1999] Q.B. 396.
[95] *ibid.* at 409–410.

a fundamental rule of good public administration and not on the existence of a duty of confidence owed by the public body to the member of the public, but he added that "it might well be that such a duty of confidence might in certain circumstances arise". On the facts, the police had not acted in breach of that principle because they had legitimate ground for disclosing the information.

3–143   Buxton J. agreed that the police's knowledge that the applicants had committed serious crimes was not something that they were free to impart to others without restraint, but that the restraint was not based on the law of confidence. His reasoning was that the information did not come to the police through any relationship with AB and CD; was not imparted to them by AB and CD; and was not acquired by the police subject to any express obligation of confidence.[96]

3–144   He also said[97]:

> " . . . counsel for the Secretary of State and also, I think, counsel for the police authority were disposed to argue that issues of disclosure of confidential or private information could not arise in any event on the facts of this case, because the fact of AB and CD's convictions were by concession and self-evidently neither confidential nor private, and the identity of AB and CD and their presence on the caravan site was already known to the person to whom disclosure was made. I do not think that the matter can be turned away so easily. What in this case might at least be argued to have the basic attribute of inaccessibility (see *Gurry, Breach of Confidence* (1984), p.70, cited in *Attorney-General v Guardian Newspapers Ltd (No. 2)* [1990] 1 A.C. 109, 215) was the *conjunction* of those various facts. It was that conjunction that the police deliberately brought to the attention of the site owner, when otherwise he would not, or probably would not, have found it out. As I have said, I very much doubt whether the subject of even that conjunction of information can claim confidence in it, because none of that information has come into the possession of its holder in circumstances that impart an obligation of confidence. I do however consider that a wish that certain facts in one's past, however notorious at the time, should remain in that past is an aspect of the subject's private life sufficient at least potentially to raise questions under article 8 of the Convention . . . "

The decision of the Divisional Court was upheld by the Court of Appeal. The applicants did not pursue their arguments based on breach of confidence.

3–145   Although the Divisional Court did not consider that the police owed any duty of confidentiality to the applicants on the facts, neither Bingham C.J. nor Buxton J. excluded the possibility that information of the kind with

---

[96] *ibid.* at 414–415.
[97] *ibid.* at 415–416.

which the court was concerned could be imparted in circumstances which would give rise to a duty of confidentiality.

The passage from Buxton J.'s judgment set out above (and cited in part in the judgment of the Court of Appeal[98]) is significant for two other reasons. The first is his point about the conjunction of facts. As with trade secrets, so with personal information, individual pieces of a jigsaw may be accessible but the whole may not. The second is his anticipation of the potential effect of Art.8. His remarks pre-dated the incorporation of the Convention in domestic law by the Human Rights Act and were prescient. **3–146**

Under the species of action for breach of confidentiality based on a person's right to respect for his private life, injunctions were granted in *Venables v News Group Newspapers Ltd*[99] and *X (formerly Mary Bell) v O'Brien*[1] to prevent publication of the present names and addresses of the claimants, who had been convicted of murder or manslaughter when they were children and whose names the trial judge had in each case permitted to be published. **3–147**

These were exceptional cases, but if in an appropriate case the court may make an order to protect the identity of a person previously convicted in open court of a grave crime which has received national publicity, it is hard to see why a court should not be able to protect information which is not as a matter of practicality readily accessible and has been received in circumstances which a reasonable person would regard as confidential. **3–148**

In *Hilton v Barker Booth & Eastwood*[2] the House of Lords recognised that the defendant solicitors owed a duty to their client B not to disclose his past bankruptcy and criminal convictions to the claimant, but (obiter) treated the duty as unrelated to the ordinary law relating to confidentiality. If the law of confidentiality is circumscribed so that it cannot apply to information imparted in confidence about anything which has occurred in open court or is contained in a record theoretically available to the public, regardless of how secret or accessible it may be in practical terms, then the defendants' duty of non-disclosure could only be explained on some other basis. For the reasons discussed above, it is suggested that this is an over narrow view of the law. If not, it gives rise to difficult issues of classification. **3–149**

Where contracting parties are in a confidential relationship, it is common place for a court to imply a duty of confidentiality in relation to information about which there is relative secrecy. It is also established law[3] that there can be an express contractual duty to refrain from publicising information about which there is no element of secrecy.

The approach in *Hilton v Barker Booth & Eastwood* seems to involve a new classification of duty—an implied duty of non-disclosure of information said to lack the quality of inaccessibility which is necessary for a duty **3–150**

---

[98] [1999] Q.B. 396 at 425.
[99] [2001] Fam. 430.
[1] [2003] EWHC 1101.
[2] [2005] UKHL 8; [2005] 1 W.L.R. 567.
[3] *Att-Gen v Blake* [2001] 1 A.C. 268.

of confidentiality in the normal sense. The result of this approach would be a category of cases where there is a duty of confidentiality but not so described. The cases would be those where the duty to treat information as confidential is a consequence or part of a wider duty. But that is typical of a large number of confidential relationships, such as doctor–patient, employer–employee, banker–customer, trading partners and the like. Just as it has been said that the phrase "fiduciary duties" is a dangerous one, giving rise to a mistaken assumption that all fiduciaries owe the same duties in all circumstances, and that the extent and nature of the fiduciary duties owed in any particular case fall to be determined by reference to any underlying contractual relationship between the parties,[4] so the same may be said about duties of confidentiality. The precise scope of the duty of confidentiality in each case depends on the nature of the relationship and its underlying purpose. As the Law Commission observed in its Working Paper on Breach of Confidence,[5]

> "to compile an exhaustive list of such relationships would not be practicable, and, even if it were, the list would be of limited value because the extent of the obligation of confidence varies according to the exact nature of the relationship."

Conclusion on public record

3–151 It is suggested that whether information is, or was once upon a time, a matter of "public record" (whatever the meaning intended by that expression, as compared with the broader expression "public domain") is simply a factor in determining whether it is so generally accessible that it would not be just to require the party against whom a duty of confidentiality is alleged to treat it as confidential.

Misuse

3–152 It is an essential ingredient of the action for breach of confidence that confidential information has been or is threatened to be, misused. The principle is self-evident, but determining what is misuse can present difficult questions.

3–153   Misuse will typically take the form of disclosure to another, but it need not do so.[6] Where a duty of confidentiality exists, misuse need not be

---

[4] *Henderson v Merrett Syndicates Ltd* [1995] 2 A.C. 145 at 206 *per* Lord Browne-Wilkinson.

[5] (1974), Working Paper No. 58, p.14.

[6] *Prince Jefri Bolkiah v KPMG* [1999] 2 A.C. 222 at 235, where Lord Millett said in a case about a solicitor and a former client,

> "It [the duty] is not merely a duty not to communicate the information to a third party. It is a duty not to misuse it that is to say, without the consent of the former client to make any use of it or cause any use to be made of it by others otherwise than for his benefit.".

intentional in order to found liability.[7] This is not to be confused with the situation where the nature of the information and position of the parties are such that someone of ordinary intelligence and honesty in the shoes of the recipient would be likely to use the information, consciously or unconsciously, without any apprehension of being under restraint; in such a case the recipient's defence to an allegation of breach of confidence would not be that the alleged breach was unintentional, but that he owed no duty or only a qualified duty.[8] What constitutes misuse is necessarily dependent on the scope of the duty owed in the particular relationship.

Cross J.'s observation in *Printers & Finishers v Holloway*[9] that the law would defeat its own object if it sought to enforce in this field standards which would be rejected by the ordinary person is pertinent when considering questions of the scope of a duty of confidentiality and whether particular conduct constitutes misuse.

3–154

In *Smith Kline & French v Community Services*[10] a question arose as to the extent of the duty owed by a government department to a pharmaceutical company in relation to confidential information supplied for the purpose of obtaining approval of a drug. The court referred to Megarry J.'s suggested test in *Coco v Clark*[11] for determining whether a duty of confidence existed (whether a reasonable person in the shoes of the recipient would have realised that, on reasonable grounds, the information was being given to him in confidence) and continued[12]:

3–155

"However, this test does not give guidance as to the scope of an obligation of confidence, where one exists. Sometimes the obligation imposes no restriction on use of the information, as long as the confidee does not reveal it to third parties. In other circumstances, the confidee may not be entitled to use it except for some limited purpose. In considering these problems, and indeed the whole question, it is necessary not to lose sight of the basis of the obligation to respect confidences:

'It lies in the notion of an obligation of conscience arising from the circumstances in and through which the information was communicated or obtained.'

This is quoted from *Moorgate Tobacco Co. Ltd v Philip Morris Ltd (No. 2)* (1984) 156 C.L.R. 414 at 438, *per* Deane J., with whom the other members of the court agreed .... Similar expressions recur in other cases: see *Seager v Copydex Ltd* [1967] R.P.C. 349 at 368:

---

[7] *Seager v Copydex Ltd* [1967] 1 W.L.R. 923.
[8] *Printers & Finishers Ltd v Holloway* [1965] R.P.C. 239 at 256–257.
[9] [1965] R.P.C. 239 at 256.
[10] (1991) 28 F.C.R. 291.
[11] [1969] R.P.C. 41 at 48.
[12] *ibid.* at 303–304.

'The law on this subject ... depends on the broad principle of equity that he who has received information in confidence shall not take unfair advantage of it.'

To avoid taking unfair advantage of it does not necessarily mean that the confidee must not use it except for the confider's limited purpose. Whether one adopts the 'reasonable man' test suggested by Megarry J. or some other, there can be no breach of the equitable obligation unless the court concludes that a confidence reposed has been abused, that unconscientious use has been made of the information."

This passage was cited by Simon Brown L.J. in *R. v Department of Health, Ex p. Source Informatics Ltd.*[13] He applied the test whether a reasonable person's conscience would be troubled by the proposed use of the relevant information.[14]

Misuse and negligence

3–156   The Law Commission in its Report on Breach of Confidence[15] considered whether a person under an obligation of confidentiality could be liable if disclosure or use of a confidential document or information occurred, not through his direct disclosure or use, but through his failure to take reasonable care to prevent its disclosure or use by someone else.

3–157   A person may undoubtedly owe a contractual duty to take reasonable care to safeguard the confidentiality of a document or information entrusted to him,[16] but the Law Commission said that:

"There does not appear to be any clear answer in the present state of the law to the question whether... a person who is under a duty of confidence, but is not in any contractual relationship with the person to whom it is owed, can be liable for breach of confidence if the information to which the duty relates is disclosed or used owing to his negligence."

3–158   There is a distinction between an equitable duty of confidentiality and a duty to take care to prevent confidential information or documents from falling into the hands of someone else. The former is an obligation of conscience, which requires the recipient not to misuse the information or documents. The latter is a duty of a different character and is not an automatic concomitant of the former. In the absence of a relevant contract, it will arise only if there is a special relationship between the parties giving rise to a duty of care under the law of negligence.[17]

---

[13] [2001] Q.B. 424 at para.24.
[14] *ibid.* at para.31.
[15] Law Com. No.110, Cmnd. 8388 (1981), at para.4.14.
[16] In *Weld-Blundell v Stephens* [1919] 1 K.B. 520; [1920] A.C. 956, it was conceded that a firm of accountants owed a duty to take reasonable care of their client's documents as a bailee for reward: [1919] 1 K.B. at 523.
[17] *B v A County Council* [2006] EWCA Civ 1388.

The question of the existence of such a duty arose in *Swinney v Chief*   **3–159**
Constable of Northumbria.[18] An informant gave information to a police
officer about the identity of the driver of a vehicle which had hit and killed
another police officer. Details of the information and the informant's name
and address were recorded in a document which was stolen from a police
vehicle and came into the hands of the alleged driver. As a result, the
informant and her husband were threatened with violence and arson. They
sued the chief constable, alleging that they had suffered psychological
damage and economic loss because of failure by the police to take proper
care of the information. On an application to strike out the claim, the Court
of Appeal held that it was arguable that there was a special relationship
between the parties so as to give rise to a duty of care on the part of the
police.[19]

Misuse and detriment

The question has from time to time been raised whether misuse, actual or   **3–160**
threatened, must be detrimental in order to give rise to a cause of action for
breach of confidentiality.

In *Coco v A N Clark (Engineering) Ltd*[20] Megarry J. observed: **3–161**

> "Some of the statements of principle in the cases omit any mention of
> detriment; others include it. At first sight, it seems that detriment ought
> to be present if equity is to be induced to intervene; but I can conceive
> of cases where a plaintiff might have substantial motives for seeking the
> aid of equity and yet suffer nothing which could fairly be called
> detriment to him, as when the confidential information shows him in a
> favourable light but gravely injures some relation or friend of his whom
> he wishes to protect. The point does not arise for decision in this case,
> for detriment to the plaintiff plainly exists."

In the *Spycatcher* case[21] opinions were divided. Lord Keith[22] said:

> " . . . as a general rule, it is in the public interest that confidences should
> be respected, and the encouragement of such respect may in itself
> constitute a sufficient ground for recognising and enforcing the obliga-
> tion of confidence even where the confider can point to no specific
> detriment to himself . . . So I would think it a sufficient detriment to
> the confider that information given in confidence is to be disclosed to
> persons whom he would prefer not to know of it, even though the
> disclosure to him would not be harmful to him in any positive way. The

---

[18] [1997] Q.B. 464.
[19] At the trial before Jackson J. (April 21, 1999, unreported) it was conceded by the police that
they owed a duty of care to the informant, but the judge found that there was no negligence.
[20] [1969] R.P.C. 41 at 48.
[21] [1990] 1 A.C. 109.
[22] *ibid.* at 255–256.

position of the Crown, as representing the continuing government of the country may, however, be regarded as being special . . . . The Crown . . . as representing the nation as a whole, has no private life or personal feelings capable of being hurt by the disclosure of confidential information. In so far as the Crown acts to prevent such disclosure or to seek redress for it on confidentiality grounds, it must necessarily, in my opinion, be in a position to show that the disclosure is likely to damage or has damaged the public interest."

Lord Griffiths[23] considered that detriment, or potential detriment, to the confider must be established before a private individual was entitled to a remedy for breach of confidence, since the remedy was fashioned to protect the confider and not to punish the confidant, and therefore there was little point in extending it to a confider who did not need protection. Lord Goff[24] wished to keep the point open, but observed that it might depend on how wide a meaning could be given to the word "detriment".

3–162 In *Smith Kline & French Laboratories (Australia) Ltd v Department of Community Services*[25] Gummow J., after reviewing the authorities, noted that the issue remained open in Australia but expressed his view that:

"The basis of the equitable jurisdiction to protect obligations of confidence lies . . . in an obligation of conscience arising from the circumstances in or through which the information, the subject of the obligation, was communicated or obtained: *Moorgate Tobacco Co. Ltd v Philip Morris Ltd (No. 2)*[26] . . . . The obligation of conscience is to respect the confidence, not merely to refrain from causing detriment to the plaintiff. The plaintiff comes to equity to vindicate his right to observance of the obligation, not necessarily to recover loss or to restrain infliction of apprehended loss. To look into a related field, when has equity said that the only breaches of trust to be restrained are those that would prove detrimental to the beneficiaries?"

3–163 In *Rapid Metal Developments (Australia) Pty Ltd v Anderson Formrite Pty Ltd*,[27] Johnson J., sitting in the Supreme Court of Western Australia, followed Gummow J. in stating:

"In my view, the requirement for proof of detriment is inconsistent with the established notion that the basis for the exercise of equitable jurisdiction is to enforce the obligation of confidence."

It is suggested that the key, whether the case is approached in equity or in contract, lies in correctly identifying in each set of circumstances the nature of the obligation and the interest which it is intended to protect. This was

[23] *Att-Gen v Guardian Newspapers Ltd (No. 2)* [1990] 1 A.C. 109 at 270.
[24] *ibid.* at 281–282.
[25] [1990] F.S.R. 617 at 664.
[26] (1984) 156 C.L.R. 414 at 438.
[27] [2005] W.A.S.C. 255, at para.78.

the approach taken by Scott J. at first instance in the *Spycatcher* case. After citing *Moorgate Tobacco Co. Ltd v Philip Morris Ltd (No. 2)*[28] and *Commonwealth of Australia v John Fairfax & Sons Ltd*,[29] he said[30]:

> "The dicta in these two cases place the origin of the duty of confidence not in contract, express or implied, but in equity. But the ambit of the duty of confidence imposed by equity will depend, in my view, on the same type of judicial approach to the surrounding circumstances of the case as that adopted where an implicit term is treated as the basis of the duty. As long ago as 1893 the Court of Appeal concluded that there was no distinction between the duty of confidence placed on an agent by implied contract and that imposed on him by equity; see *Lamb v Evans* [1893] 1 Ch. 218."

In the case of private confidences, the confider may have an interest in the information being kept confidential, regardless of whether disclosure would be positively harmful to him, for reasons which may be perfectly understandable (and which would be understood by any reasonable person in the position of the confidant). If so, for the reasons suggested by Lord Keith in the *Spycatcher* case, that should be sufficient to found a cause of action; and the question whether unauthorised disclosure in such circumstances is considered to involve "detriment" is an exercise in semantics. If on the other hand the confider has no substantial interest in the information being kept confidential, it would follow that the information would not possess the necessary quality of confidence to found an obligation of confidentiality.[31]   **3–164**

In the case of public confidences, the interest intended to be protected is the public interest, and it is therefore logical that the jurisdiction should only come into play in circumstances where disclosure would be injurious to the public interest. It is for that reason that cases of public confidence involve what Lord Goff referred to in the *Spycatcher* case as the additional requirement of establishing that the public interest would be harmed by publication.[32] Conversely, it is misleading in such cases to speak of a public interest defence, since the injurious effect of publication on the public interest is an ingredient required to be established in order for the jurisdiction to arise.   **3–165**

Qualifications to a duty of confidentiality

In *Tournier v National Provincial and Union Bank*[33] the Court of Appeal held that the duty of confidence owed by a banker to his customer is   **3–166**

---

[28] (1984) 156 C.L.R. 414.
[29] (1980) 147 C.L.R. 39.
[30] [1990] 1 A.C. 109 at 147–148.
[31] *Moorgate Tobacco Co. Ltd v Philip Morris Ltd (No. 2)* (1984) 156 C.L.R. 414 at 438.
[32] [1990] 1 A.C. 109 at 283.
[33] [1924] 1 K.B. 461 at 473.

impliedly subject to qualifications, which Bankes L.J. said could not be exhaustively defined, but could be classified under four headings:

> (1) where disclosure was made with the express or implied consent of the customer;
> (2) where disclosure was made under compulsion of law;
> (3) where there was a duty to the public to disclose;
> (4) where the interests of the bank required disclosure.

Such factors are not unique to the relationship of banker and customer, but involve considerations of wider application. Although Bankes L.J. referred to the qualifications as implied qualifications of an implied contractual duty of secrecy, the underlying considerations are equally relevant to the parallel jurisdiction in equity. Bankes L.J. also observed that[34]:

> "The privilege of non-disclosure to which a client or customer is entitled may vary according to the exact nature of the relationship between the client or the customer and the person on whom the duty rests. It need not be the same in the case of the counsel, the solicitor, the doctor and the banker, though the underlying principle may be the same."

Express or implied consent

3–167   A person cannot be in breach of a duty of confidence to another by disclosure of information or material to which the other consents. Consent to disclosure may be express or implied, and general or limited. A person seeking life insurance, who gives information about his health to his insurance broker, impliedly consents to the broker passing on the information to the underwriter, but not to the press.

Disclosure required by law

3–168   The law cannot at the same time require a person to treat information as confidential and compel him to disclose it, and therefore disclosure required by law cannot be misuse.[35] Such requirement may arise in a variety of ways.

3–169   A number of statutory provisions require the disclosure of information otherwise confidential.[36] In litigation, a duty of confidence to another is generally no bar to disclosure, although the court in its discretion will only

---

[34] *ibid.* at 474.
[35] The subject of confidentiality and foreign law raises separate problems as to which see Ch. 10, below.
[36] In *Tournier v National Provincial & Union Bank* [1924] 1 K.B. 461 at 473 Bankes L.J. gave the example of the Bankers Books Evidence Act 1879.

compel the production of otherwise confidential documents if it considers it necessary to do so.[37] Nor is duty of confidence to another a ground for refusal by a witness to answer questions or produce documents if ordered to do so by a court or tribunal of competent jurisdiction, although again a court will require a witness to disclose otherwise confidential information only if disclosure is necessary for attainment of justice in the particular case.[38]

Duty to the public

Public interest as a justification for disclosure is an important topic on which much has been written. It is considered in Chapter 6.   **3–170**

Disclosure required in the interests of the confidant

Disclosure or use of confidential information will often be motivated by self-interest, without being in any sense necessary. A duty of confidentiality would be of little value if it could be easily trumped by the interests of the confidant. But there may be circumstances in which the confidant has a real need to be permitted to disclose or use information otherwise confidential and where the courts will not imply or impose an obligation preventing him from doing so. Brennan J. captured the flavour when he referred in *Esso Australia Resources Ltd v Plowman*[39] to cases "where disclosure of the material is fairly required for the protection of the party's legitimate interests". What is "fairly required" and what are "legitimate interests" will necessarily depend on the circumstances and the nature of the relationship between the confider and confidant.   **3–171**

One type of case which may be seen as falling within this category is that of the ex-employee who has learned confidential information during his employment, which has become inseparable from the general skill and knowledge that he needs to use for earning his living.   **3–172**

Another purpose for which it may be necessary for a party to refer to information otherwise confidential is in order to establish or protect his legal rights against other parties or to defend himself.   **3–173**

In *Hassneh Insurance v Mew*[40] Colman J. held that the implied contractual duty of confidence which arises between the parties to an arbitration agreement is subject to the qualification that it does not prevent   **3–174**

---

[37] *D. v N.S.P.C.C.* [1978] A.C. 171; *Science Research Council v Nasse* [1980] A.C. 1028; *British Steel Corporation v Granada Television Ltd* [1981] A.C. 1096.
[38] *Duchess of Kingston's Case* (1776) 20 St.Tr. 355 at 386–391; *Garner v Garner* (1920) 36 T.L.R. 196; *Att-Gen v Mulholland and Foster* [1963] 2 Q.B. 477; *Att-Gen v Clough* [1963] 1 Q.B. 773; *D v N.S.P.C.C.* [1978] A.C. 171 at 238 and 243; *British Steel Corporation v Granada Television Ltd* [1981] A.C. 1096; *Macmillan Inc. v Bishopsgate Investment Trust Plc* [1993] 1 W.L.R. 1372. See also Contempt of Court Act 1981, s.10.
[39] [1994–1995] 183 C.L.R. 10 at 36.
[40] [1993] 2 Ll.Rep. 243 at 249.

disclosure of the award "if it is reasonably necessary for the establishment or protection of an arbitrating party's legal rights *vis-à-vis* a third party". In so holding Colman J. drew on the judgments of the Court of Appeal in *Tournier*.[41]

3–175   In *Lillicrap v Nalder*[42] property developers sued their solicitors for negligently failing to advise them on rights of way affecting their title to property which they bought when the defendants were acting for them. Negligence was admitted, but the solicitors disputed the plaintiffs' claim that, if properly advised, they would not have entered into the transaction. They sought to allege that on previous occasions they had advised the plaintiffs on similar matters affecting other properties and that their advice had been ignored. On an interlocutory application the judge refused to allow the solicitors to refer in their pleadings to previous retainers, and ordered that they deliver up to the plaintiffs all confidential documents relating to those retainers and refrain from publishing them. He said:

> "The bringing of a claim for negligence in relation to a particular retainer will normally be a waiver of privilege and confidence for facts and documents relating to that retainer, but not without more for those relating to other discrete retainers."

The Court of Appeal agreed with that statement of principle, saying that the waiver could only extend to matters relevant to an issue in the proceedings. But, said Dillon L.J.[43]:

> "the waiver must go far enough, not merely to entitle the plaintiff to establish his cause of action, but to enable the defendant to establish a defence to the cause of action if he has one."

The Court of Appeal accordingly reversed the judge's decision. A confider cannot therefore rely on confidence to prevent the confidant from defending himself against subsequent attack by the confider.[44]

3–176   Suppose, however, that the attack had come from someone other than the confider. Suppose, for example, that criticism of a hospital consultant's treatment of a case (e.g. involving alleged euthanasia) by other members of staff led to his prosecution, or to professional disciplinary proceedings,[45] or to the health authority taking steps under his contract to suspend or dismiss him. Grave injustice might be done to the doctor if he were not free to

---

[41] [1924] 1 K.B. 461.
[42] [1993] 1 W.L.R. 94.
[43] [1993] 1 W.L.R. 94 at 99.
[44] The Court of Appeal gave further guidance in *Paragon Finance plc v Freshfields* [1999] 1 W.L.R. 1183 as to the scope of the waiver of privilege effected by a claim against one's former solicitors.
[45] In *Duncan v Medical Practitioners Disciplinary Committee* [1986] 1 N.Z.L.R. 513 (N.Z. High Court) and *R. v Institute of Chartered Accountants of England and Wales Ex p. Brindle* [1994] B.C.C. 297 at 312, *per* Hirst L.J., it was recognised that a professional person was entitled to use confidential information to defend himself against disciplinary charges.

disclose matters concerning the patient which he would otherwise be required to treat as confidential.

Another example would be that of a solicitor who (not uncommonly) **3–177** acted for a person buying a property with a mortgage loan and for the mortgagee. Suppose that the borrower defaulted and the mortgagee sued the solicitor, alleging that the affair had been a mortgage fraud and that the solicitor was a party to it. It might be important to the solicitor's defence to refer to otherwise confidential information concerning the transaction or other aspects of the purchaser's affairs or previous transactions. Here, however, the position is complicated by the absolute nature of the protection afforded by the courts to legal professional privilege. If the information was not merely confidential but privileged, it is clear from the House of Lords' observations in *Medcalf v Mardell*[46] that the lawyer would not be able to use it to protect his own interest (except with the consent of the person entitled to the benefit of the privilege).

Questions of privilege apart, it is suggested that the legitimate interests of **3–178** the confidant may in appropriate cases include disclosure to another party who has a legitimate interest in the matter, for example, disclosure by a wholly owned subsidiary to its holding company.[47]

A possible approach is to say that it is all a matter for the court's **3–179** discretion. In *Webster v James Chapman & Co.* Scott J. said[48]:

> "The court must, in each case where protection of confidential information is sought, balance on the one hand the legitimate interests of the plaintiff in seeking to keep the confidential information suppressed and on the other hand the legitimate interests of the defendant in seeking to make use of the information. There is never any question of an absolute right to have confidential information protected. The protection is the consequence of the balance to which I have referred coming down in favour of the plaintiff."

The decision whether to grant a particular form of equitable relief may involve an exercise in discretion. But an essential ingredient of the action for breach of confidence, before reaching any question of discretion, is that there must be actual or threatened misuse of confidential information. What constitutes misuse depends on the scope of the duty, which is not a matter of discretion but a matter of law, requiring analysis of the facts and application of principle.

In so far as a contractual duty is relied upon, determining its scope is a **3–180** matter of contractual analysis. In so far as an equitable duty is relied upon, there is force in the observation that:

---

[46] [2002] UKHL 27; [2003] 1 A.C. 120, at paras 23–24, *per* Lord Bingham, 30–31, *per* Lord Steyn, and 60–61, *per* Lord Hobhouse. See para.16–028 below.
[47] The distinction between parent companies and their subsidiaries from the point of view of confidentiality was emphasised by the Court of Appeal in *Bank of Tokyo Ltd v Karoon* [1987] A.C. 45.
[48] [1989] 3 All E.R. 939 at 945.

"equitable principles are best developed by reference to what conscionable behaviour demands of the defendant not by 'balancing' and then overriding those demands by reference to matters of social or political opinion."[49]

Preservation of confidentiality may affect the interests of the confider, the confidant and other people (including the public at large). There has been more discussion of the extent to which duties of confidence should be qualified so as to permit disclosure in cases of potential harm to others than in cases of potential harm to the confidant. But the judgment of Bankes L.J. in *Tournier v National Provincial and Union Bank*[50] illustrates that there is scope for the courts to recognise a qualification of a duty of confidence, not only where disclosure is necessary to prevent harm to others, but also where disclosure is necessary for the protection of the confidant.

Who may sue?

3–181   As a general principle, the person suing must be someone to whom the relevant duty of confidence is owed. In *Fraser v Evans*[51] the plaintiff prepared a confidential report for the Greek Government. A copy of the report was leaked to a newspaper and the plaintiff sought an injunction to prevent publication or use of its contents. It was held that the plaintiff had no standing to complain. Lord Denning M.R. said[52]:

"The jurisdiction is based not so much on property or on contract as on the duty to be of good faith. . . . But the party complaining must be the person who is entitled to the confidence and to have it respected. He must be a person to whom the duty of good faith is owed. . . . There is no doubt that Mr Fraser was himself under an obligation of confidence to the Greek Government. . . . The Greek Government entered into no contract with Mr Fraser to keep it secret. . . . They were the people to say aye or no whether it should be communicated elsewhere, or be published generally. It follows that they alone have any standing to complain if anyone obtains the information surreptitiously or proposes to publish it."

3–182   In *Broadmoor Special Hospital Authority v Robinson*[53] the defendant, who had been convicted of manslaughter and ordered to be detained in a secure hospital, wrote a book which included information about other inmates, their mental condition, treatment and progress in hospital. The hospital

---

[49] *Smith Kline & French Ltd v Department of Community Services* [1990] F.S.R. 617 at 663, *per* Gummow J.
[50] [1924] 1 K.B. 461.
[51] [1969] 1 Q.B. 349.
[52] *ibid.* at 361.
[53] [2000] Q.B. 775.

authority sought to prevent him from publishing it. The Court of Appeal held that it could not bring proceedings to protect other patients' rights to privacy or confidentiality.[54]

Since the European Court of Human Rights has held[55] that the obliga- **3–183** tions of the state under Art.8 may involve a positive obligation to adopt measures designed to secure respect for private life, it is arguable that a court could be acting in breach of the Convention if it refused on jurisdictional grounds to entertain proceedings begun by a hospital author- ity to safeguard respect for the private lives of its patients, whose privacy the authority would owe them a duty to protect.[56]

In *Green Corns Ltd v Claverley Group Ltd*[57] Tugendhat J. granted an **3–184** injunction to a children's home provider to restrain a newspaper from publishing the addresses of homes provided for troubled children in order to prevent the risk of serious harm to the children and carers occupying the addresses concerned.

In *A Local Authority v W*[58] Sir Mark Potter P. granted an injunction on **3–185** the application of a local authority to prevent the media from publishing information which would be likely to cause prejudice to the welfare of children who were the subject of care proceedings.

An interesting question is what happens when the right to use confidential **3–186** information, e.g. technical know-how, is shared or "assigned". It has been suggested that, if confidential information is not property, the "assignor" cannot pass to the "assignee" his personal right to have the information treated as confidential, and therefore the "assignee" cannot sue to enforce a duty of confidence,[59] but has at most a right to compel the "assignor" to take action.

In *Morison v Moat*[60] the defendant was held to owe a duty of confidence **3–187** to the plaintiff in respect of the recipe for "Morison's Universal Medicine", details of which were supplied by the plaintiff's father to the defendant's father. Turner V.C. stressed that:

> "what we have to deal with here is, not the right of the Plaintiffs against the world, but their right against the Defendant."[61]

---

[54] *ibid.* at paras 30 (Lord Woolf M.R.) and 54 (Waller L.J.).
[55] *Marckx v Belgium* (1979) 2 E.H.R.R. 330 at para.31; *X and Y v Netherlands* (1986) 8 E.H.R.R. 235 at para.23; *Stjerna v Finland* (1997) 24 E.H.R.R. 195 at para.38; *Von Hanover v Germany* (2005) 40 E.H.H.R. 1 at para.57.
[56] See *Mersey Care NHS Trust v Ackroyd* [2006] EWHC 17, QB, Tugendhat J., at para.96: "The hospital is not suing on behalf of any patient. It could not do that. But it is suing to safeguard the respect for the private lives of all its patients. It would be unlawful for the court to act in a way which would be incompatible with the rights of the patients at Ashworth."
[57] [2005] EWHC 958, Q.B.
[58] [2005] EWHC 1564, Fam.
[59] See the judgment of Hope J.A. in the New South Wales Court of Appeal in *Moorgate Tobacco Co. Ltd v Philip Morris Ltd* (1982) 64 F.L.R. 387 at 404. The point was not referred to in the judgment of Deane J. in the High Court of Australia (1984) 156 C.L.R. 414. In *Mid-City Skin Cancer & Laser Centre v Zahedi-Anarak* [2006] NSWSC 844, Campbell J. declined to follow the Court of Appeal's decision in *Moorgate*.
[60] (1851) 9 Hare 241; (affirmed (1852) 21 L.J. Chanc. (N.S.) 248).
[61] *ibid.* at 258.

He distinguished *Canham v Jones*[62] as a case (unlike *Morison v Moat*[63]) based on property and not confidence. The injunction against the defendant was therefore based not on an assignment of a proprietary right, but on the principle that the defendant owed a duty in conscience towards the plaintiff to respect the original confidence in which the information was supplied, although the plaintiff had not been the original confider of the information, but had himself been originally a confidant (from his father).

3–188   In *Gilbert v Star Newspaper Co. Ltd*[64] the plot of a Gilbert comic opera was leaked to the defendant newspaper, probably by a member of the cast or theatre employee whose contract was with the theatre manager. Gilbert brought a claim for an injunction to prevent further disclosure by the newspaper. As an indirect recipient of confidential information, with knowledge of its confidentiality, on ordinary principles the newspaper's source owed an equitable duty of confidentiality to Gilbert, but Chitty J. required the joinder as plaintiff of the theatre manager, and granted an interlocutory injunction to both Gilbert and the manager. The decision to grant an injunction to the manager necessarily implied that he too was owed a duty of confidentiality in respect of the libretto. In *Douglas v Hello! Ltd (No. 3)*[65] the Court of Appeal observed that:

> "This decision supports the proposition that, where the benefit of confidential information is shared between A and B, B can claim that disclosure of that information will constitute a breach of confidence owed to B."

3–189   In *Mustad & Son v Dosen*[66] the defendant was employed as a skilled mechanic by a firm which went into liquidation. His contract of employment contained a confidentiality clause. The plaintiffs paid the liquidator for the business, including the benefit of any trade secrets and pledges of confidentiality. The defendant went to work for new employers and in the course of his new employment gave them some information about the construction of a machine about which he had acquired in his previous employment. The plaintiffs applied for an injunction to restrain him from disclosing any further details. Lord Buckmaster observed that it was essential for the plaintiffs to prove that the defendant had obtained "special information" during his first employment which he was prevented from disclosing, and that he either had disclosed it or had threatened to do so. The claim failed for an injunction failed on the ground that by the time the case reached the House of Lords all the relevant information was in the public domain, but not on the ground that the defendant could not owe a duty of confidentiality to the plaintiffs.

---

[62] (1813) 2 V. & B. 218.
[63] (1851) 9 Hare 241; (affirmed (1852) 21 L.J. Chanc. (N.S.) 248).
[64] (1894) 11 T.L.R. 4.
[65] [2005] EWCA Civ 595; [2006] Q.B. 125, para.129.
[66] [1964] 1 W.L.R. 109n.

If therefore the original confider has passed confidential information to **3–190** another person, with the intention that the latter shall enjoy the benefit of it, that person may be entitled to prevent disclosure or misuse of the information by a third party on the principle of the duty of good faith referred to by Lord Denning in *Fraser v Evans*.[67]

The Law Commission[68] considered the effect of death on duties of confidentiality. By s.1(1) of the Law Reform (Miscellaneous Provisions) Act 1934 all causes of action, except for defamation, subsisting against or vested in any person on his death survive against or, as the case may be, for the benefit of the estate. But there may be situations falling outside the scope of that section, as illustrated by the following example from the Law Commission's Report[69]:

> " . . . there is the situation in which a person who has imparted information in confidence to another dies before any breach of confidence has taken place. His personal representatives will have a right of action for any subsequent breach only if the information is of a 'quasi proprietorial' character—such as information relating to 'know-how'—which can be regarded as an asset of the deceased person's estate. The personal representatives of a deceased patient cannot employ the action for breach of confidence to protect the relations or friends of the deceased from distress resulting from the doctor's disclosure of his deceased patient's confidences."

It is doubtful whether that would be a correct statement of law today. **3–191** "Quasi-proprietorial" is not a familiar term in the law of confidentiality and its meaning is unclear. If it is meant to include information which could be used for financial profit, it would include much beside technical know-how, for example, intimate confidences of a celebrity. If a doctor who treated a celebrity suffering from AIDS during his final illness were subsequently to sell to a newspaper intimate details which had been revealed to him by his former patient in confidence, and in the expectation that the doctor would continue to respect that confidence after the patient's death, it is likely that a court would regard the obligation of confidence as subsisting after his death[70]; and would grant to the personal representatives (depending on the circumstances) an injunction and/or an account of profits as the only effective means of enforcing the obligation.[71] In such a case it could not be said that the deceased would suffer detriment from the publication, but it would seem contrary to justice that the doctor should make a windfall from

---

[67] [1969] 1 Q.B. 349.
[68] *Breach of Confidence*, Law Com. No.110, Cmnd. 8388 (1981), paras 4.105–4.107.
[69] *ibid.*, para.4.107.
[70] See para.11–053, below.
[71] Compare *White v Jones* [1995] 2 A.C. 207 at 268 where the House of Lords held that a solicitor whose negligence in drawing a will led to the inability of an intended beneficiary to inherit as the testator had intended, was liable to the intended beneficiary, because otherwise there would be no effective means of enforcing the obligation owed by the solicitor to the deceased.

his breach of his obligation. Privilege may survive in favour of a deceased's estate[72] and it is hard to see why a court should not recognise the survival of an obligation of confidentiality. The period for which any duty of confidentiality could reasonably be expected to continue would depend on many circumstances, including the nature of the relationship, the nature of the information and any harm which might be caused to the deceased's estate or, possibly, those whom the deceased would reasonably have wished to protect, as well as any grounds for justifying disclosure.

[72] *Bullivant v Att-Gen for Victoria* [1901] A.C. 196.

CHAPTER 4

Duration of Confidentiality

General principle

In principle a duty of confidentiality should cease if the information loses **4–001** the quality of confidence, whether through passage of time, loss of secrecy or other change of circumstances. Most of the reported cases concern loss of secrecy.

Loss of secrecy

In 1928 the House of Lords held in *Mustad & Son v Dosen*[1] that an **4–002** injunction could not be granted to restrain misuse of confidential information about a "secret" process after the plaintiffs had applied for a patent for it, since by that publication, in the words of Lord Buckmaster, "The secret, as a secret, had ceased to exist".[2]

In later cases the courts have also considered whether publication by a **4–003** third party or by the defendant has the same effect as publication by the plaintiff.

---

[1] [1964] 1 W.L.R. 109.
[2] *ibid.* at 111.

Terrapin and the springboard theory

4-004   Because *Mustad* was not reported until 1964, it was not cited in *Terrapin Ltd v Builders' Supply Company (Hayes) Ltd*, decided by Roxburgh J. in 1959.[3] *Terrapin* is significant for the introduction of the so-called "springboard doctrine".

4-005   The defendants manufactured portable buildings to the plaintiffs' design. The plaintiffs disclosed to the defendants in confidence details of proposed modifications. Subsequently the defendants sold in competition with the plaintiffs a form of portable building containing many of the plaintiffs' revised features. It was argued for the defendants that the plaintiffs' conduct in selling buildings and publishing brochures which disclosed all their features discharged any obligation of confidentiality by the defendants, since the information could no longer be regarded as secret. Roxburgh J. rejected this argument. Founding on Lord Greene's judgment in *Saltman's* case, he said[4]:

> "As I understand it, the essence of this branch of the law, whatever the origin of it may be, is that a person who has obtained information in confidence is not allowed to use it as a spring-board for activities detrimental to the person who made the confidential communication, and spring-board it remains even when all the features have been published or can be ascertained by actual inspection by any member of the public. The brochures are certainly not equivalent to the publication of the plans, specifications, other technical information and know-how. The dismantling of a unit might enable a person to proceed without plans or specifications, or other technical information, but not, I think, without some of the know-how, and certainly not without taking the trouble to dismantle. I think it is broadly true to say that a member of the public to whom the confidential information had not been imparted would still have to prepare plans and specifications. He would probably have to construct a prototype, and he would certainly have to conduct tests. Therefore, the possessor of the confidential information still has a long start over any member of the public . . . It is, in my view, inherent in the principle upon which the *Saltman* case rests that the possessor of such information must be placed under a special disability in the field of competition in order to ensure that he does not get an unfair start . . . "

The *Mustad* and *Terrapin* debate

4-006   In *Peter Pan Manufacturing Corporation v Corsets Silhouette Ltd*[5] the relationship between the reasoning of Roxburgh J. in the *Terrapin* case and

---

[3] But not fully reported at first instance until [1967] R.P.C. 375, although the decision of the Court of Appeal was reported at [1960] R.P.C. 128.

[4] [1967] R.P.C. 375 at 391–392.

[5] [1963] R.P.C. 45; [1964] 1 W.L.R. 96. *Peter Pan* is interesting on a separate point for its recognition of an account of profits as a remedy available for breach of confidence.

of Lord Buckmaster in *Mustad's* case arose for consideration, but Penny-cuick J. did not find it necessary to decide the issue, which he referred to as one of considerable general importance and difficulty.

The point arose again in *Cranleigh Precision Engineering Ltd v Bryant*.[6] **4–007**
The defendant, as managing director of the plaintiffs, invented an above-ground swimming pool with two unique features. While still in the plaintiffs' employment, he learned of a Swiss patent for a similar pool but lacking the two special features. After leaving the plaintiffs' employment the defendant obtained an assignment of the Swiss patent. The plaintiffs brought two actions against him. In the first action, they obtained an injunction to restrain him from using the knowledge he had gained in confidence about the plaintiffs' product, in particular the two unique features. In the second action they claimed an injunction to prevent the defendant from using the information obtained by him about the Swiss patent and sought damages.

Roskill J. summarised the plaintiffs' arguments in the second action as follows:

" . . . it was not what appeared in [the Swiss patent] itself which was confidential. It was the knowledge of the possible effect to and upon the plaintiffs of the existence and publication of this specification which was confidential in the hands of the one person who was in a position to assess its true significance because of the knowledge which he, as the plaintiffs' managing director, possessed of all the facts of the plaintiffs' swimming pool and of their business connected therewith."[7]

The defendant argued that confidentiality ceased when information **4–008**
entered the public domain; that all confidentiality concerning the Swiss patent ended on its publication; and that in so far as *Terrapin* provided a precedent for injunctive relief after the supposed secret had ceased to be secret as a result of publication, it was inconsistent with *Mustad's* case.

Roskill J. found that the defendant acted in breach of his duty to the **4–009**
plaintiffs in concealing from them the information which he had learned about the Swiss patent and in taking no steps to protect the plaintiffs against its possible consequences; and that he acted in breach of confidence in using, after he left the plaintiffs, the information which he had acquired about the Swiss patent and its possible effect on the plaintiffs' business for his own advantage. He distinguished *Mustad's* case on the ground that in that case the plaintiffs had themselves been the publishers of the specification, whereas in the present case the publishers were the Swiss applicants. He accordingly followed *Terrapin* and granted an injunction and damages.

The reasoning of Roskill J. was criticised by the Law Commission in its Report on Breach of Confidence[8]:

---

[6] [1966] R.P.C. 81.
[7] At p.93.
[8] Law Com. No.110; Cmnd. 8388 (1981), at para.4.29.

"Notwithstanding the view of *Mustad* taken by Roskill J., however, it is doubtful whether an obligation of confidence, as distinguished from any express or implied contractual obligation which may exist between the parties, can persist after the information in question has reached the public domain, irrespective of the way in which it has come into the public domain. Suppose an inventor has given particulars of a certain device to a draughtsman who accepts an obligation in respect of that information. The draughtsman passes on that information to a third party, who knows that he is obtaining the information in breach of the draughtsman's obligation of confidence. Subsequently all the details of the device are independently published in a trade journal. Is the third party thereafter subject to indefinite restraint in making and marketing the device at a time when any of his trade rivals are free to exploit the information in the article?"

4–010 The Law Commission also referred to divergent opinions in the American courts between those which followed *"the Rule in Shellmar"*,[9] according to which a defendant could be enjoined in perpetuity from using what he had once misused, and those which followed *"the Rule in Conmar"*,[10] under which a defendant who had misused information might nevertheless legitimately use it once it had passed into the public domain. The Law Commission preferred the latter.

4–011 In *Speed Seal Products Ltd v Paddington*[11] the defendants were an engineer and a company under his control. He had formerly worked for the plaintiffs and been a member of their design committee. It was alleged that the committee designed a novel cam-operated coupling device, that the information about its design was confidential and that the defendants had wrongly used that information to market a rival product. The defendants applied to strike out the claim for injunctions on the ground that they had published the design in a brochure and in a European patent application, and that even if they had acted wrongly in doing so, they could be under no continuing duty of confidentiality. It was not in dispute for the purposes of the appeal that the alleged confidential information had been "published to the world", but the plaintiffs argued that a wrongdoer could not rely on his own wrongdoing and that an injunction could be granted under the springboard principle. The Court of Appeal refused to strike out the claim. Founding on the reasoning of Roskill J. in *Cranleigh Precision Engineering*,[12] they held that publication of confidential information by a third party does not necessarily release from his obligations a person who previously owed a duty of confidentiality. The defendants could be in no better position than if publication had been made by a third party. In considering the question of an injunction Fox L.J. said[13]:

[9] *Shellmar Products Co v Allen-Qualley Co* (1936) 87 F.2d 104.
[10] *Conmar Products Corporation v Universal Slide Fastener Co Inc* (1949) 172 F.2d 150.
[11] [1985] 1 W.L.R. 1327.
[12] [1966] R.P.C. 81.
[13] [1985] 1 W.L.R. 1327 at 1332.

"The purpose of an injunction is protection. Whether a plaintiff, in circumstances such as the present, needs protection might depend upon the state of the market. If, for example, the only traders seriously competing in the market are the plaintiff and the defendant (the latter being a person who, in breach of duty to the plaintiff, wrongfully published the information to the world) it may be a matter of continuing importance to the plaintiff that the defendant should not continue to get the benefit of the wrongdoing. If, on the other hand, the publication has produced a market with a large number of traders, the elimination of one trader (the defendant) might not be of consequence."

Spycatcher

Peter Wright, a former intelligence officer, in breach of his contract of service with the Crown and of the provisions of the Official Secrets Act 1911, contracted with Australian publishers for the publication of his memoirs of his service in MI5. The book was distributed world wide. The *Sunday Times* bought the serialisation rights and published the first instalment shortly before the book went on sale in the USA. The Attorney-General sought an injunction to restrain the *Sunday Times* from serialising further extracts. The House of Lords held unanimously that the *Sunday Times* had acted in breach of duty of confidence in publishing the first extract, but refused by a majority to grant an injunction to prevent further serialisation because the entire book was now in the public domain.[14]   **4–012**

In considering the position of the *Sunday Times*, the House also considered the position of Peter Wright, although he was not a party to the proceedings. It was necessary to do so, because the argument on behalf of the Crown was that an English court would grant an injunction against Peter Wright, on the ground that an obligation of confidence still attached to him, and that such duty continued to attach in conscience to third parties. This was described by Lord Goff as a "formidable argument"[15] and caused him to consider the premise on which it was based, *viz.* the continuing duty of confidence said to be owed by Peter Wright.   **4–013**

Lord Goff approached the issue from the starting point that a duty of confidence can only apply in respect of information which is confidential; from which the logical consequence should be that, if confidential information ceases to be confidential, the duty of confidence should end (as held in *Mustad*). Referring to *Cranleigh Precision Engineering* Lord Goff said[16]:   **4–014**

" . . . it seems to me that the true basis of the decision was that, in reliance on the well known judgment of Roxburgh J. in the 'springboard' case, *Terrapin Ltd v Builders' Supply Co. (Hayes) Ltd* [1967]

---

[14] *Att-Gen v Guardian Newspapers Ltd (No. 2)* [1990] 1 A.C. 109.
[15] *ibid.* at 285.
[16] *ibid.* at 285.

R.P.C. 375, the defendant was in breach of confidence in taking advantage of his own confidential relationship with the plaintiff company to discover what a third party had published and in making use, as soon as he left the employment of the plaintiff company, of information regarding the third party's patent which he had acquired in confidence."

4–015   Lord Goff did not consider that *Cranleigh Precision Engineering*[17] supported any general principle that, if it is a third party who puts the confidential information into the public domain, the confidant would not be released from his duty of confidence. He therefore disapproved the reasoning in *Speed Seal*.[18] Lord Goff reserved the question (since it had not been fully argued) whether some more limited obligation (analogous to the springboard doctrine) might nevertheless continue to rest on a confidant who, in breach of confidence, destroyed the confidential nature of the information entrusted to him, whilst he rejected the broader argument of the Crown that a confidant who publishes confidential information to the world can remain under a further obligation not to disclose it, simply because it was he who wrongly destroyed its confidentiality. This rejection of the Crown's main argument forms an essential part of the *ratio* of Lord Goff's speech, because, in Lord Goff's words, it enabled him to "consider the specific issues in the case unfettered by its otherwise considerable force".[19]

4–016   Lord Keith and Lord Brightman dealt with the matter more concisely. Lord Keith cited Lord Widgery's judgment in *Attorney-General v Jonathan Cape Ltd*,[20] in which he held that the confidential character of public confidences lapsed when publication would no longer do public harm. Lord Keith said that the question whether Mr Wright would be at liberty to publish *Spycatcher* in England did not arise for immediate consideration, but, since such publication would cause no further harm:

> " . . . the case for an injunction now against publication by or on behalf of Mr Wright would in my opinion rest upon the principle that he should not be permitted to take advantage of his own wrong-doing."[21]

Lord Brightman said[22]:

> "In my opinion the reason why the court would, or might, grant an injunction against Wright if he now brought himself within the jurisdiction and sought to publish *Spycatcher* here, is not that such an

---

[17] [1966] R.P.C. 81.
[18] [1985] 1 W.L.R. 1327.
[19] *Att-Gen v Guardian Newspapers Ltd (No. 2)* [1990] 1 A.C. 109 at 289.
[20] [1976] 1 Q.B. 752 at 771.
[21] [1990] 1 A.C. 109 at 259.
[22] *ibid.* at 266.

order would recognise a subsisting duty of confidence, but that it would impede the unjust enrichment of Wright, or preclude him from benefiting, tangibly or intangibly, from his own wrongdoing; or perhaps that the copyright of the work would in equity be vested in the Crown, as suggested by three of Your Lordships."

He added[23]:

"The Crown is only entitled to restrain the publication of intelligence information if such publication would be against the public interest, as it normally will be if theretofore undisclosed. But if the matter sought to be published is no longer secret, there is unlikely to be any damage to the public interest by re-printing what all the world has already had the opportunity to read. There is no possible damage to the public interest if Tom, Dick or Harry, or "The Sunday Times" reprints in whole or part what is already printed and available within the covers of *Spycatcher*. Therefore it seems to me that no injunction should be granted to restrain further serialisation."

A majority of the House therefore rejected the concept of a duty of confidentiality subsisting after the information had so lost the quality of confidence that further publication would do no harm, while leaving open the possibility of an injunction against repetition of disclosure by the wrongdoer, based not on a continuing duty but either on the desirability of preventing him from profiting from his past breach or on an application of the springboard principle.

Lord Griffiths, dissenting, considered that an injunction would have been **4–017** granted against Mr Wright on the basis of a continuing duty of confidence and ought to have been granted against the *Sunday Times*.

Lord Jauncey considered that an injunction would have been granted **4–018** against Peter Wright, and should have been granted also against the *Sunday Times* if to do so would have been effective to prevent further serialisation, but that the grant of such an injunction would be a vain act in circumstances in which that any other newspaper could publish whatever extracts it wished.

In *Attorney-General v Blake*[24] the proposition that a former member of **4–019** the security services, who had turned traitor, owed a continuing fiduciary duty not to publish information which had once been confidential, but had lost its confidentiality, was rejected by Sir Richard Scott V.C. and the Court of Appeal.[25] Lord Woolf M.R. stated that[26]:

"Equity . . . does not impose a duty to maintain the confidentiality of that which has ceased to be confidential."

[23] [1990] 1 A.C. 109 at 267.
[24] [1987] Ch. 84; [1988] Ch. 439; [2001] 1 A.C. 268.
[25] The argument was not pursued in the House of Lords.
[26] [1988] Ch. 439 at 453.

Injunction to prevent profit from past misconduct?

4–020   The concept of granting injunctive relief, not for the purpose of preventing a threatened breach of duty, but for the purpose of preventing a wrongdoer from profiting from past misconduct, presents problems. Since it is not based on any continuing duty of confidence, but on the broader principle that wrongdoers should not be allowed to take advantage of their wrongdoing, there would be no justification for limiting it to cases of breach of confidence; but it is unclear whether it would apply to all forms of civil liability, or only to deliberate acts, or to acts involving some form of moral obliquity (and, if so, how they are to be defined).

4–021   If an injunction could be granted on the broad principle that a wrongdoer should not be permitted to profit from his wrongdoing, an exceptionally strong case on the facts arose in *Kaye v Robertson*.[27] In that case a journalist entered without permission a hospital room where the plaintiff was recovering from brain injuries and took photographs of him without his fully informed consent. The defendants not only obtained the photographs by trespass, but their conduct towards the plaintiff was a "monstrous invasion of his privacy" (*per* Bingham L.J.[28]) committed for commercial gain. However, the Court of Appeal (Glidewell, Bingham and Leggatt L.JJ.) held that it had no power in law to grant an injunction prohibiting the defendants from publishing the photographs so as to prevent them from profiting from the taking of the photographs, i.e. from their own trespass, attractive though the argument might appear to be.[29]

4–022   In the *Spycatcher* case Lord Goff gave the example of convicted criminals being invited to sell their stories on release from prison.[30] He observed that this is highly offensive to many people; but doubted whether that fact provided an appropriate basis for defining the scope of a confidant's civil obligations at common law.

4–023   Further, if the object is to prevent commercial profiteering from past misconduct, why should injunctive relief be limited to the wrongdoer and not extend to those co-operating with him for commercial profit? If the *Sunday Times* was guilty of breach of confidence in publishing Peter Wright's first instalment, why should it not itself have been prohibited from publishing further extracts in order to prevent it too from continuing to exploit a prior wrong to which it had been party? Only one of their Lordships, Lord Griffiths, would have gone that far.[31]

---

[27] [1991] F.S.R. 62.

[28] *ibid*. at 70.

[29] *ibid*. at 69.

[30] [1990] 1 A.C. 109 at 289. It is not a novel practice. In 1874 the imposter in the *Titchborne* case, Arthur Orton (otherwise Thomas Castro, otherwise Sir Roger Titchborne, Bart.) was finally sent to prison for 14 years. On his release, encouraged by a newspaper, he published his story.

[31] See also the judgment of the European Court of Human Rights in *Observer and Guardian v United Kingdom* (1991) 14 E.H.R.R. 153 at 195–196 and *Sunday Times v United Kingdom (No. 2)* (1991) 14 E.H.R.R. 229 at 243–244, echoing Lord Oliver's objections in his dissenting speech in *Spycatcher (No. 1)* [1987] 1 W.L.R. 1248 at 1318.

Conclusions on springboard

It is noteworthy that the House of Lords expressed no disapproval of the **4–024** decision in *Cranleigh Precision Engineering*,[32] nor of the springboard doctrine stated in *Terrapin*.[33] On the contrary, Lord Goff impliedly considered both to be right, although in relation to the former only as he interpreted it, i.e. as a springboard case.

As the Law Commission argued in its report on Breach of Confidence,[34] **4–025** the springboard doctrine is not in total conflict with the principle that information cannot enjoy the protection of the action for breach of confidence once it has entered the public domain, but rather is a limited qualification of it. The object of the springboard doctrine is merely to ensure that the recipient of confidential information does not obtain an unfair start by misuse of information received in confidence. Subsequent decisions have confirmed that the protection given should be related to the unfair advantage which the defendant would otherwise obtain, and, accordingly, that an injunction should not normally extend beyond the period for which the unfair advantage is likely to continue.[35] In *Sun Valley Foods Ltd v Vincent*,[36] Jonathan Parker J. held that it was a further requirement for the grant of an injunction that, as at the date of the court's order, the unfair advantage should still exist and be continuing to have effect.

Although the springboard doctrine is in itself narrow, it can also be seen **4–026** as part of a wider principle. In *United States Surgical Corp v Hospital Products International Pty Ltd*[37] the New South Wales Court of Appeal held:

> "It is a principle applied in conformity with the more general principle that a person misusing confidential information must answer for his default according to his gain. A headstart may often be the gain in these cases. If it is the gain, damages will be assessed accordingly and any other relief, such as injunction, will be moulded. If it is not the gain the method of assessing damages or the appropriateness of some other remedy has to be considered in the light of what that gain is."

In the *Cranleigh Precision Engineering* case two features were partic- **4–027** ularly relevant in considering what fairness required. The first was that not

---

[32] [1966] R.P.C. 81.
[33] [1967] R.P.C. 375.
[34] Cmnd. 8388 (1981), para.4.31.
[35] *Potters-Ballotini Ltd v Weston-Baker* [1977] R.P.C. 202 at 206, *per* Lord Denning M.R. ("Although a man must not use such information as a springboard to get a start over others, nevertheless that springboard does not last for ever.") *Roger Bullivant Ltd v Ellis* [1987] F.S.R. 172 at 184, *per* Nourse L.J. ("All these observations support the view that the injunction should not normally extend beyond the period for which the unfair advantage may reasonably be expected to continue. That is in my judgment the period for which an injunction should normally be granted in springboard cases.")
[36] [2000] F.S.R. 825 at 834–837.
[37] [1983] 2 N.S.W.L.R. 157 at 233 (reversed in the High Court on other grounds (1984) 156 C.L.R. 41).

only did the defendant's knowledge of the third party's patent come to him in his capacity as the company's managing director from its patent agents, but he immediately realised its significance for the company from facts which were not in the public domain. The second is that, although he was under a duty to the company to bring his knowledge of the patent to the board's attention, he deliberately concealed it in order to make use of it to his advantage and against the interests of the company. Roskill J. emphasised these matters in his judgment. Typically cases of breach of confidence involve the passing by A to B of confidential information, which B wrongly divulges to C. *Cranleigh Precision Engineering* does not fall into that pattern, but is rather a case of an agent using his position as agent to acquire information which is pertinent to his principal's affairs and which is not known to his principal, and then using that information for his personal benefit without the principal's fully informed consent. This is a classic example of breach of fiduciary duty by an agent, for which the courts will grant an injunction, damages or an account of profits. It is analogous in its essential elements to *Phipps v Boardman*.[38]

Passage of time and change of circumstances

4-028 In *Attorney-General v Jonathan Cape Ltd*[39] Lord Widgery C.J. recognised in the case of public confidences that:

> "There must, however, be a limit in time after which the confidential character of the information, and the duty of the court to restrain publication, will lapse."

He added that:

> "It may, of course, be intensely difficult in a particular case, to say at what point the material loses its confidential character, on the ground that publication will no longer undermine the doctrine of Cabinet responsibility."

4-029 The principle that, on information losing its confidential character, the duty of confidence ceases must apply equally in the case of private confidences. In applying that principle, due attention must be paid in each case to the original purpose of the duty of confidence. In the case of private confidence, the duty exists "to protect the personal, private and proprietary interests of the citizen".[40] The duration of such duty will vary according to the nature of the information and the nature of the relationship.

[38] [1967] 2 A.C. 46. See para.2–039, above.
[39] [1976] 1 Q.B. 752 at 771.
[40] *Commonwealth of Australia v John Fairfax & Sons Ltd* (1980) 147 C.L.R. 39 at 51, *per* Mason J.

It may be difficult, as in the case of public confidences, to identify the **4–030** point at which such information loses its confidential character, and any statement of principle can only be expressed in general terms. The remarks which follow are intended merely to be illustrative.

The General Medical Council states in its advice to doctors that the **4–031** obligation to keep personal information confidential does not end with the patient's death.[41]

The implication of the G.M.C.'s advice is that it regards the duty to a **4–032** living patient as life long (subject to other qualifications, which are discussed in the chapter on medical confidence).

In the case of employees it is well recognised that termination of the **4–033** employment will bring to an end the duty of confidence in relation to some forms of information (that is, information which has become part of the employee's general skill and knowledge), but not in relation to the narrower band of information which may qualify for continued protection under the head of trade secrets.[42]

Trade secrets, too, may lose their confidentiality by other means than by **4–034** entering the public domain. In *Thomas Marshall Ltd v Guinle*[43] Sir Robert Megarry V.C. suggested, inter alia, that, for information to constitute a trade secret, the party claiming confidentiality must reasonably believe that the release of the information would be injurious to him or of advantage to his rivals or others. A trade secret may cease to have that quality, for example, through changes in the confider's business or through technological advances rendering the trade secret obsolescent.

Continuing contractual obligations

It is possible for a party to be subject to a contractual obligation not to **4–035** publish information even though it does not have or may have ceased to have the quality of confidentiality.[44]

Effect of a repudiatory breach of contract

In *Campbell v Frisbee*[45] the claimant applied for summary judgment for **4–036** breach of a confidentiality clause in a contract for the provision of management services. The defendant had supplied information about the

---

[41] *Confidentiality: protecting and providing information* (April 2004), at para.30; see the discussion at para.11–053 below.
[42] See Ch.14, below.
[43] [1979] 1 Ch. 227 at 248.
[44] *Att-Gen v Barker* [1990] 3 All E.R. 256 and *Att-Gen v Blake* [2001] 1 A.C. 268. See also the Law Commission's Report on Breach of Confidence, 1981 (Law Com. No.110, Cmnd. 8388) at para.4.29: " . . . it is doubtful whether an obligation of confidence, *as distinguished from any express or implied contractual obligation which may exist between the parties*, can persist after the information in question has reached the public domain, irrespective of the way in which it has come into the public domain". (Emphasis added.)
[45] [2002] EWCA Civ 1374.

claimant's sex life to a newspaper, contrary to the provisions of the confidentiality clause. The defendant argued that the clause was not binding because the claimant had acted in repudiatory breach of the contract. Lightman J. held:

> "In the case of a contract for services, there can be no conceivable basis for the suggestion that a repudiatory breach by the client entitles the independent contractor to a release from the obligations of confidentiality. It is plain beyond question that the obligation of confidence of e.g. a lawyer, doctor or security consultant survives acceptance by the service provider of the repudiation of his contract by the client. Indeed that is surely the premise on which the relationship between client and service provider is created. Likewise the law protects marital confidence notwithstanding repudiation of the marriage vows, adultery and divorce: none of these events operate to release the "innocent" spouse from the obligation to preserve these earlier confidences: *Argyll v Argyll* [1967] Ch. 302 at 332–3."

The Court of Appeal allowed an appeal by the defendant. Lord Phillips M.R. said[46]:

> "We do not believe that the effect on duties of confidence assumed under contract when the contract in question is wrongfully repudiated is clearly established. While we do not think that it is likely that Miss Frisbee will establish that Lightman J. erred in his conclusions in a manner detrimental to her case, it cannot be said that she has no reasonable prospect of success on the issue."

The issue remains open.

4–037   Lord Diplock's speech in *Photo Production Ltd v Securicor Transport Ltd*[47] is the leading modern authority on the effect of a repudiatory breach of contract (although he did not use that expression) on the innocent party's obligations. He held that it entitled the innocent party to elect to put an end to all primary obligations of both parties remaining unperformed (and to claim monetary compensation for loss caused by the guilty party's non-performance of its primary obligations). However, this general principle did not mean that the parties could not validly contract for what should happen in such a situation.

4–038   Arbitration or choice of forum clause are examples.[48] The validity of such a clause can be analysed on the basis that the arbitration is a collateral agreement or more simply it may be seen as a qualification to the general principle based on the parties' intention that the clause should apply in cases of alleged repudiatory breach of contract.

---

[46] [2002] EWCA Civ 1374 at [22].
[47] [1980] A.C. 827 at 848–850.
[48] *Heyman v Darwins Ltd* [1942] A.C. 356.

Clauses limiting liability for damages are another example. It is artificial   **4–039**
to try to analyse such a clause as a collateral contract. The true reason for
giving effect to such a clause even after a repudiatory breach is that to do so
gives effect to the parties' intention.

Arbitration, choice of forum and limitation of liability clauses have in   **4–040**
common that they can be described as ancillary rather than core contractual
terms, but so can a confidentiality clause. Whatever the main purpose of a
contract, a confidentiality clause is ancillary to it in that its purpose is to
protect a party who provides confidential information during a contract
against its use by the other party for other purposes. It is hard to see why a
confidentiality clause should not continue to be effective after a repudiatory
breach if on the proper construction of the contract that represents the
parties' intention. If, however, that view is wrong, or if the party claiming
confidentiality is unable to establish as a matter of construction that a
confidentiality clause was intended to have contractual effect after repudiation of the contract, it does not follow that the other party should cease to
be under an obligation of conscience. It is the receipt of confidential
information which gives rise to an obligation of confidentiality, whether
contractual or equitable, and there is no reason why an obligation of
conscience should necessarily cease just because the other party has
subsequently been guilty of a repudiatory breach of contract.

There may be particular circumstances in which it would be unfair to   **4–041**
hold the innocent party under a continuing obligation of confidentiality. For
example, if two parties agreed to carry out a joint venture, which one party
repudiated after disclosing confidential information relevant to the venture
to the other, the effect of the innocent party being required not to use the
information for purposes other than the joint venture could be to prevent
that party from attempting to carry out the venture on its own, and so leave
the field clear for the party in repudiation to do so. In such a case a
reasonable person would not regard it as fair for the innocent party to be
under a continuing obligation of confidentiality, but that would be because
on those facts it would result in an unjust disadvantage.

CHAPTER 5

Public Sector Confidentiality

5–001   The application of the doctrine of confidence to government secrets should not be confused with the doctrine of public interest immunity, which is part of the law of evidence.[1] Public interest immunity (or Crown privilege as it used to be known) has a long history. Under this doctrine, documents which would otherwise be disclosable in litigation may be immune from production if wider public interest so requires.

5–002   In *Conway v Rimmer*[2] the House of Lords adopted the principle expressed by Lord Reid:

> "I would therefore propose that the House ought now to decide that Courts have and are entitled to exercise a power and duty to hold a balance between the public interest, as expressed by a Minister, to withhold certain documents or other evidence, and the public interest in ensuring the proper administration of justice."

Lord Reid also observed that:

> "Virtually everyone agrees that Cabinet minutes and the like ought not to be disclosed until such time as they are only of historical interest."

5–003   Fortuitously, the first case in which the courts were asked to apply the equitable doctrine of confidentiality to the workings of Government in fact concerned the publication of details of cabinet discussions. In *Attorney-General v Jonathan Cape Ltd*[3] the Attorney-General sought an injunction restraining publication of Richard Crossman's *Diaries of a Cabinet Minister*. It was argued, unsuccessfully, by the defendants that the principle underlying such cases as *Prince Albert v Strange*,[4] *Saltman*[5] and *Argyll*[6] should be restricted to private relationships and not extend to Government secrets.

---

[1] *D v N.S.P.C.C.* [1978] A.C. 171 at 241, *per* Lord Simon. Public interest immunity is discussed in Ch.19, below.
[2] [1968] A.C. 910 at 952.
[3] [1976] 1 Q.B. 752.
[4] (1848) 1 Mac. & G. 25.
[5] (1948) 65 R.P.C. 203.
[6] [1967] Ch. 302.

Lord Widgery C.J. said[7]:

"I cannot see why the courts should be powerless to restrain the publication of public secrets, while enjoying the *Argyll* powers in regard to domestic secrets. Indeed, as already pointed out, the court must have power to deal with publication which threatens national security, and the difference between such a case and the present case is one of degree rather than kind. I conclude, therefore, that when a Cabinet Minister receives information in confidence the improper publication of such information can be restrained by the court, and his obligation is not merely to observe a gentleman's agreement to refrain from publication."

Lord Widgery went on to hold as a matter of principle that:

"The Attorney-General must show

(a) that ... publication would be a breach of confidence;
(b) that the public interest requires that the publication be restrained; and
(c) that there are no other facts of the public interest contradictory of and more compelling than that relied upon."

This required a balancing exercise. Lord Widgery refused an injunction because 10 years and three general elections had passed since the events described in the diaries, and he concluded after reading the book that:

"I cannot believe that the publication at this interval of anything in volume one would inhibit free discussion in the Cabinet of today, even though the individuals involved are the same, and the national problems have a distressing similarity with those of a decade ago."[8]

Lord Widgery's approach was followed by Mason J. in *Commonwealth of Australia v John Fairfax & Sons Ltd.*[9] He said:

"However, the plaintiff must show, not only that the information is confidential in quality and that it was imparted so as to import an obligation of confidence, but also that there will be 'an unauthorised use of that information to the detriment of the party communicating it' (*Coco v A. N. Clark (Engineers) Ltd*).[10] The question then, when the executive government seeks the protection given by equity, is: What detriment does it need to show?

[7] [1976] 1 Q.B. 752 at 769–770.
[8] *Att-Gen v Jonathan Cape Ltd* [1976] 1 Q.B. 752 at 771.
[9] [1969] R.P.C. 41 at 47.
[10] (1980) 147 C.L.R. 39 at 51–52.

The equitable principle has been fashioned to protect the personal, private and proprietary interests of the citizen, not to protect the very different interests of the executive government. It acts, or is supposed to act, not according to standards of private interest, but in the public interest. This is not to say that equity will not protect information in the hands of the government, but it is to say that when equity protects government information it will look at the matter through different spectacles.

It may be a sufficient detriment to the citizen that disclosure of information relating to his affairs will expose his actions to public discussion and criticism. But it can scarcely be a relevant detriment to the government that publication of material concerning its actions will merely expose it to public discussion and criticism. It is unacceptable in our democratic society that there should be a restraint on the publication of information relating to government when the only vice of that information is that it enables the public to discuss, review and criticise government action.

Accordingly, the court will determine the government's claim to confidentiality by reference to the public interest. Unless disclosure is likely to injure the public interest, it will not be protected."

5–006   This principle was approved and applied in the *Spycatcher* case.[11] In that case Peter Wright's book had been disseminated world wide to the extent of over a million copies and was freely available in the United Kingdom. There was therefore no longer a secret to protect, and any damage which might be caused had already been caused.

5–007   While the *Spycatcher* case was working its way through the English courts, *Lord Advocate v The Scotsman Publications Ltd*[12] was proceeding through the Scottish courts, reaching the House of Lords after the *Spycatcher* decision. The case concerned the memoirs of another former member of the security service, Anthony Cavendish. After permission to publish had been requested, and refused, he had 500 copies printed at his own expense. He provided 279 copies to private individuals, before giving an undertaking to the Crown not to distribute any further copies without advance notice. A copy came into the hands of *The Scotsman* newspaper, which published an article including some of the material.

5–008   The Government brought proceedings for an injunction to restrain further publication. They sought to distinguish *Spycatcher* on the grounds that Anthony Cavendish's memoirs, unlike Peter Wright's, were not in general circulation. It was conceded by the Government that the contents of the book did not include any material damaging to national security. But it was argued that publication was damaging, irrespective of the innocuous nature of the contents, because it would lower morale, encourage copy cats,

---

[11] [1990] 1 A.C. 109 at 258, *per* Lord Keith; 270, *per* Lord Griffiths and 283, *per* Lord Goff. See also para.4–012, above.
[12] [1990] 1 A.C. 812.

and cause foreign security powers to lose confidence in the ability of the British security and intelligence services to protect their own secrets.

The House of Lords held that the combination of circumstances (that the book did not contain any material damaging to national security and that publication on a limited scale had already taken place) meant that the Government had no arguable case that further publication would do any material damage to the public interest. The contents were not going to be harmful, and in so far as the fact of publication might be harmful, it had already happened. **5–009**

Lord Keith (with whose speech Lord Griffiths and Lord Goff agreed)[13] added: **5–010**

"It was argued for the appellant that the dismissal of this appeal would have the effect that any newspaper which received an unsolicited book of memoirs by a present or former member of the Security or Intelligence Service would be free to publish it. That is not so. If there had been no previous publication at all and no concession that the contents of the book were innocuous the newspaper would undoubtedly itself come under an obligation of confidence and be subject to restraint. If there had been a minor degree of prior publication, and no such concession it would be a matter for further investigation whether further publication would be prejudicial to the public interest, and interim interdict would normally be appropriate."

It is implicit that it would be for the Government to have to establish that further publication would be detrimental to the public interest, following the judgments of Mason J. in *Commonwealth of Australia v John Fairfax & Sons Ltd*[14] and of the House of Lords in the *Spycatcher* case.[15] **5–011**

In *Attorney-General v Blake*[16] the defendant was a former member of the intelligence service and Russian agent. He was caught and sent to prison, but escaped and fled to Moscow. Over 20 years later he wrote an autobiography. He had given a contractual undertaking not to divulge in press or book form, during or after his period of service, any official information gained by him as a result of his employment. At the time of the book's publication none of the information contained in it was secret and its disclosure was therefore harmless. The Attorney-General brought a claim to recover the proceeds of the publication. **5–012**

At the trial it was accepted on behalf of the Attorney-General that in writing the book Blake had not committed any breach of duty of confidence, but it was argued that he owed a continuing fiduciary duty not to use his position as a former public servant to generate a profit for himself. This argument was rejected by Scott V.C. and by the Court of Appeal. In the judgment of the Court of Appeal, given by Lord Woolf M.R., it was noted **5–013**

[13] [1990] 1 A.C. 812 at 822–823.
[14] (1980) 147 C.L.R. 39.
[15] [1990] 1 A.C. 109.
[16] [2001] 1 A.C. 268.

that Blake had committed a clear breach of contract in submitting the book for publication without clearance by the Government but that the Attorney-General had decided not to advance a claim to the profits of the book on that ground, while wishing to keep the point open for a higher court.[17] The claim was advanced in the House of Lords and succeeded. Most of the argument was about the availability of an account of profits as a remedy for breach of contract. The fact that publication was harmless to the public interest did not prevent the Government from succeeding in a claim for breach of contract. Lord Nicholls (with whom Lord Goff and Lord Browne-Wilkinson agreed) said[18]:

"The Crown had and has a legitimate interest in preventing Blake profiting from the disclosure of official information, whether classified or not, while a member of the service and thereafter. Neither he, nor any other member of the service, should have a financial incentive to break his undertaking."

There seems no reason to suppose that the principles relating to public sector confidentiality are limited to central government. They may equally apply, it is suggested, to local government.

5–014   The Cabinet Office's *Public Bodies 2005* recorded that:

"There were 910 public bodies sponsored by UK Government departments as at 31 March 2005. This figure is made up of 21 Public Corporations, the Bank of England, 26 NHS Bodies and 861 NDPBs [Non-Departmental Public Bodies]. The NDPB group is made up of 211 Executive NDPBs, 458 Advisory NDPBs, 42 Tribunal NDPBs (counted on the basis of tribunal systems rather than individual boards) and 151 Independent Monitoring Boards . . . "

Insofar as such bodies are carrying out functions comparable to those of government, comparable principles should apply to them.[19]

5–015   In *Esso Australia Resources Ltd v Plowman*[20] Mason C.J. (with whom Dawson and McHugh JJ. agreed) went further. The case arose from contracts for the supply of natural gas by oil companies to two public utilities. Disputes under the contracts were referred to arbitration. The oil companies wished to prevent commercially sensitive information from being disclosed outside the arbitration. Mason C.J. rejected the oil companies' argument that a duty of confidence was owed to them by virtue of the fact that information was provided in, and for the purposes of, the arbitration. He went on to suggest, *obiter*, that if such a duty were owed, the case should be viewed as one involving governmental secrets, rather than

---

[17] [1998] Ch. 439 at 455–456.
[18] [2001] 1 A.C. 268 at 287.
[19] *London Regional Transport v Mayor of London* [2001] EWCA Civ 1491 provides a good example on its facts, but the point was not raised. The case is discussed at para.6–053.
[20] [1994–1995] 183 C.L.R. 10.

personal or commercial secrets, and therefore it would have to be established that the public interest demanded non-disclosure. He explained his reasoning as follows[21]:

> "The approach outlined in John Fairfax[22] should be adopted when the information relates to statutory authorities or public utilities because, as Professor Finn notes,[23] in the public sector '[t]he need is for compelled openness, not for burgeoning secrecy.' The present case is a striking illustration of this principle. Why should the consumers and the public of Victoria be denied knowledge of what happens in these arbitrations, the outcome of which will affect, in all probability, the prices chargeable to consumers by the public utilities?"

Mason C.J.'s approach differed from that adopted by the majority of the **5–016** House of Lords in *British Steel Corporation v Granada Television Ltd*,[24] as he recognised. Moreover, whether or not the principles relating to public sector confidentiality should apply to a public utility seeking to enforce an obligation of confidentiality, it is difficult to see why such principles should apply where a commercial organisation seeks to enforce an obligation of confidentiality against a public utility in order to protect its commercial secrets. There is, it is suggested, a fallacy in viewing the information which the oil companies were seeking to protect as government secrets.

---

[21] [1994–1995] 183 C.L.R. 10 at 32.
[22] *Commonwealth of Australia v John Fairfax & Sons Ltd* (1980) 147 C.L.R. 39.
[23] Finn, "Confidentiality and the 'Public Interest' " (1984) 58 *Australian Law Journal* 497 at 505.
[24] [1981] A.C. 1096.

CHAPTER 6

Public Interest

6–001 There is a distinction between private and public sector confidentiality. Public interest is potentially relevant to both, but different principles are involved. Where confidentiality is invoked in support of Government, detriment to the public interest is an essential ingredient of the cause of action.[1] That topic is considered in Chapter 5.

6–002 In other cases, a duty of confidentiality may be negated or circumscribed by overriding public interest considerations. That topic is considered in the present chapter.

The defence of iniquity

6–003 The earliest manifestation of what has come to be referred to as the public interest defence was the so-called defence of iniquity, which owed its origin to the judgment of Sir William Page-Wood V.C. in *Gartside v Outram*.[2]

6–004 *Gartside v Outram* was reinterpreted, and the beginnings of a broader principle recognised, in *Weld-Blundell v Stephens*.[3] The plaintiff sent a letter to the defendant, an accountant, instructing him to investigate the affairs of a company, with which he had dealings, and making libellous statements about those responsible for running the company. The defendant's partner

---

[1] *Att-Gen v Jonathan Cape Ltd* [1976] 1 Q.B. 752; *Commonwealth of Australia v John Fairfax & Sons Ltd* (1980) 147 C.L.R. 39; *Att-Gen v Guardian Newspapers Ltd (No. 2)* [1990] 1 A.C. 109.

[2] (1857) 26 L.J.Ch. (N.S.) 113. See para.1–030 above.

[3] [1919] 1 K.B. 520, affirmed [1920] A.C. 956.

carelessly left the letter at the company's office. Libel actions were success-fully brought against the plaintiff by persons defamed in the letter (one of whom he described as "an ingenious thief"). The plaintiff sued the accountant for negligence.

The defendant argued that there was no duty of confidence in relation to 6–005 the letter, since the libels amounted to a malicious wrong. The argument failed. Warrington and Scrutton L.JJ. interpreted *Gartside v Outram* (questionably, perhaps) as a case in which the court had declined to exercise its equitable jurisdiction in favour of the plaintiffs and left them to their remedy at law. Bankes and Warrington L.JJ. considered that there could be circumstances in which the duty of confidence would be overridden by a duty to the public, and they drew a distinction between a document concerning a past crime and a crime in contemplation.

Scrutton L.J. said[4]: 6–006

> "Under the decision in *Reg. v Cox and Railton*,[5] when the accused has consulted his solicitor after the commission of a crime for the legitimate purpose of being defended the communication is privileged, the privilege being that of the client. If then the solicitor in breach of this confidence and privilege announced his intention of informing the prosecution of the contents of his client's communication, I cannot believe that the Court would not restrain him before communication or give damages against him for breach of his contract of employment after communication, even though those damages were based on his having provided evidence to prove the client guilty of a crime he had in fact committed. The reason would be that the public policy that crime should be punished would be outweighed by the public policy that accused persons should be properly defended, and contracts necessary for their defence observed. There is a public policy in not lightly interfering with freedom of contract: *per* Jessel M.R. in *Printing and Numerical Registering Co. v Sampson*."[6]

Scrutton L.J., however, was in a minority on the plaintiff's entitlement to damages, the majority (both in the Court of Appeal and in the House of Lords) holding that he was entitled to nominal damages only, since the damages which he had been ordered to pay in the libel actions were to be regarded as caused by his own wrongful acts.

In the House of Lords,[7] the defendant limited his argument to the latter 6–007 issue of causation, but Viscount Finlay commented:

> "It would be startling if it were the law that an agent who is negligent in the custody of a letter handed to him in confidence by his principal might plead in defence that the letter was libellous. There may, of

---

[4] [1919] 1 K.B. 520 at 544.
[5] (1884) 14 Q.B.D. 153 at 175.
[6] (1875) L.R. 19 Eq. 462 at 465.
[7] [1920] A.C. 956 at 965.

course, be cases in which some higher duty is involved. Danger to the State or public duty may supersede the duty of the agent to his principal. But nothing of that nature arises in this case."

6–008   In *Tournier v National Provincial and Union Bank of England*[8] the Court of Appeal had to consider what duty of confidentiality was owed by a bank to its customer. The Court (Bankes, Scrutton and Atkin L.JJ.) held that there was necessarily implied into the contract between them a duty of confidentiality, but subject to qualifications.

6–009   Bankes L.J. said[9]:

"On principle I think that the qualifications can be classified under four heads: (a) Where disclosure is under compulsion by law; (b) where there is a duty to the public to disclose; (c) where the interests of the bank require disclosure; (d) where the disclosure is made by the express or implied consent of the customer."

In relation to the second qualification Bankes L.J. said:

"Many instances of the second class might be given. They may be summed up in the language of Lord Finlay in *Weld-Blundell v Stephens*,[10] where he speaks of cases where a higher duty than the private duty is involved, as where 'danger to the State or public duty' may supersede the duty of the agent to his principal."

Scrutton and Atkin L.JJ.,[11] agreed that the term necessarily to be implied into the contract between a bank and its customer must be subject to qualifications, entitling the bank to make disclosure in certain circumstances, including for prevention of or protection against frauds or crimes.

The contractual analysis

6–010   The contractual analysis begun in *Weld-Blundell* and *Tournier* was further developed in *Initial Services Ltd v Putterill*.[12] The plaintiffs ran a laundry. The defendant, who had been their sales manager, resigned and took with him various documents which, according to him, were part of or related to a price fixing agreement entered into between the plaintiffs and other launderers, but not registered, contrary to the Restrictive Practices Act 1956. The defendant passed the documents to a newspaper, which published two articles on the subject. The plaintiffs sued the defendant for

---

[8] [1924] 1 K.B. 461.
[9] *ibid.* at 473.
[10] [1920] A.C. 956 at 965.
[11] [1924] 1 K.B. 46 at 480–481, 483–484 and 486.
[12] [1968] 1 Q.B. 396.

breach of an implied term of his contract of employment not to disclose to third parties confidential information relating to the plaintiffs obtained during his employment. The defendant alleged in his defence that the plaintiffs were part of a cartel conducting business in breach of statute, and he denied that his disclosure of their activities was in breach of the implied term of the contract relied on by the plaintiffs. The plaintiffs applied, unsuccessfully, to strike out the paragraphs of the defence containing the defendant's allegations as disclosing no defence.

Breach of the provisions of the Restrictive Practices Act was not a criminal offence, and it was argued by the plaintiffs that the relevant qualification to the implied duty of confidentiality owed by an employee was limited to crime or fraud. This argument was rejected. **6–011**

Lord Denning M.R. accepted that every contract of employment contained an implied obligation that the employee would not, during or after his employment, disclose information or documents received in confidence; but the obligation was subject to exceptions. As to the scope of the relevant exception, he said[13]: **6–012**

> "In *Weld-Blundell v Stephens*,[14] Bankes L.J. rather suggested that the exception is limited to the proposed or contemplated commission of a crime or a civil wrong. But I should have thought that was too limited. The exception should extend to crimes, frauds and misdeeds, both those actually committed as well as those in contemplation, provided always—and this is essential—that the disclosure is justified in the public interest. . . .
>
> The disclosure must, I should think, be to one who has a proper interest to receive the information. Thus it would be proper to disclose a crime to the police; or a breach of the Restrictive Trade Practices Act to the registrar. There may be cases where the misdeed is of such a character that the public interest may demand, or at least excuse, publication on a broader field, even to the press."

Salmon L.J. said[15]:

> "Suppose the servant had entered into a contract with the master not to disclose certain information, would that contract be enforceable or would it be illegal? To my mind that must depend on the circumstances of the particular case. Consider this case: the Restrictive Trade Practices Act, 1956, is an Act which certainly was very much concerned with the public interest. It imposed an obligation upon these plaintiffs to disclose to the registrar the agreements into which they had entered with their fellow launderers in relation to the supply of goods. That obligation was imposed in the public interest . . . .
>
> Suppose the master had said to the servant,

[13] [1968] 1 Q.B. 396 at 405–406.
[14] [1919] 1 K.B. 520 at 527.
[15] [1968] 1 Q.B. 396 at 409–410.

'We, of course, appreciate that these agreements into which we have entered ought in the public interest to be disclosed to the registrar, but we hope that the registrar will never find out about them. We propose to ignore our statutory obligation to disclose these agreements. You must agree with us that you will never make any disclosure about them to anyone.'

Suppose that the servant had agreed. I am by no means convinced that any court would do other than regard such an agreement as illegal on the ground that it was clearly contrary to the public interest. I do not think that the law would lend assistance to anyone who is proposing to commit and to continue to commit a clear breach of a statutory duty imposed upon him in the public interest."

Winn L.J. adopted the same approach, saying[16]:

"I agree with both of the judgments delivered by my Lords. I desire to say that for my own part my approach to this problem has been in substance identical with that of Salmon L.J. It seems to me that the proper function of an implied term of a contract is either to dot the i's and cross the t's of the express terms or to fill in some lacuna left by the contracting parties which must properly be filled by the implied term in order to give business efficacy, and produce the true intent of those contracting parties. As my Lord has said, the question whether or not a term properly to be implied in a contract is enforceable in law must be decided by asking whether it would have been enforced had it been an express term. I entirely agree, if I may respectfully say so, with that approach, which has been my own approach also to this problem."

To pose the question whether a term "properly to be implied" is enforceable may be said to be tortuous in that there cannot be "properly implied" into a contract a term which would be unenforceable; but the sense is clear, namely that the court should not imply a term requiring secrecy in circumstances where, if there were an express term to that effect, the court would refuse to enforce it as contrary to public policy.

6–013   The same analysis was advanced by Gummow J. in the Federal Court of Australia in *Corrs Pavey Whiting & Byrne v Collector of Customs*.[17] Referring to *Gartside v Outram*, he said that:

" . . . any court of law or equity would have been extremely unlikely to imply in a contract between master and servant an obligation that the servant's good faith to his master required him to keep secret details of his master's gross bad faith to his customers. Likewise, before any express contractual obligation of confidence is enforced at law or in equity the term relied on must be valid at law."

[16] [1968] 1 Q.B. 396 at 410–411.
[17] (1987) 74 A.L.R. 428 at 449.

He added[18] that where the plaintiff asserted a contractual right of confidence, the law of contract (supplemented by equitable defences where equitable relief was sought) sufficiently dealt with the matter. Where the plaintiff asserted an equitable duty of confidence, the principle applicable was no wider than that:

" . . . information will lack the necessary attribute of confidence if the subject matter is the existence or real likelihood of the existence of an iniquity in the sense of a crime, civil wrong or serious misdeed of public importance, and the confidence is relied upon to prevent disclosure to a third party with a real and direct interest in redressing such crime, wrong or misdeed."

In other words equity, following the law, would not impose an equitable obligation to do that which in contract would be unenforceable.

Misdeeds may include "anti-social" conduct in the sense of "activities   **6–014** which, whilst not in breach of the law, are seriously contrary to the public interest".[19] But that has to be judged according to generally accepted standards, as was emphasised by Sir Nicolas Browne-Wilkinson V.C. in *Stephens v Avery*[20] in relation to alleged sexual "wrongdoing":

"If it is right that there is now no generally accepted code of sexual morality applying to this case, it would be quite wrong in my judgment for any judge to apply his own personal moral views, however strongly held, in deciding the legal rights of the parties. The court's function is to apply the law, not personal prejudice. Only in a case where there is a generally accepted moral code can the court refuse to enforce rights in such a way as to offend that generally accepted code."

Serious harm to the public

The reasoning which applies in cases of serious misdeeds has been extended   **6–015** to cases where there is serious danger of harm, without misconduct necessarily being the cause, but differing views have been expressed about the scope of the principle involved.

In *Beloff v Pressdram Ltd*[21] Ungoed-Thomas J. said: **6–016**

"The defence of public interest clearly covers and, in the authorities does not extend beyond, disclosure, which . . . must be disclosure justified in the public interest, of matters carried out or contemplated, in breach of the country's security, or in breach of law, including statutory duty, fraud, or otherwise destructive of the country or its

[18] (1987) 74 A.L.R. 428 at 450.
[19] *Francome v Mirror Group Newspapers Ltd* [1984] 1 W.L.R. 892 at 895–896.
[20] [1988] 1 Ch. 449 at 454.
[21] [1973] 1 All E.R. 241 at 260.

people, including matters medically dangerous to the public; and doubtless other misdeeds of similar gravity."

6–017   In *Woodward v Hutchins*[22] Lord Denning M.R. took an altogether broader approach. He said,

> "There is no doubt whatever that this pop group sought publicity. They wanted to have themselves presented to the public in a favourable light so that audiences would come to hear them and support them . . . . If a group of this kind seek publicity which is to their advantage, it seems to me that they cannot complain if a servant or employee of theirs afterwards discloses the truth about them. If the image which they fostered was not a true image, it is in the public interest that it should be corrected. *In these cases of confidential information it is a case of balancing the public interest in maintaining the confidence against the public interest in knowing the truth.*" (Emphasis added.)

This approach did not involve considering the seriousness of the need for public disclosure but amounted to an unstructured balancing exercise. In effect, the court assumed a general discretion whether or not to enforce confidentiality. In that respect it went further than previous authorities and has not generally been supported by later authorities.

6–018   In *Lion Laboratories Ltd v Evans*[23] Griffiths L.J. said:

> "I am quite satisfied that the defence of public interest is now well established in actions for breach of confidence . . . .
>
>   I can see no sensible reason why this defence should be limited to cases in which there was been wrongdoing on the part of the plaintiffs. I believe that the so-called iniquity rule evolved because in most cases where the facts justified a publication in breach of confidence, it was because the plaintiff had behaved so disgracefully or criminally that it was judged in the public interest that his behaviour should be exposed. No doubt it is in such circumstances that the defence will usually arise, but it is not difficult to think of instances where, although there has been no wrongdoing on the part of the plaintiff, it may be vital in the public interest to publish a part of his confidential information."

6–019   In *Francome v Mirror Group Newspapers Ltd*[24] the Court of Appeal recognised that there may be public interest grounds for limited but not general disclosure. It upheld an interlocutory injunction restraining the defendants from general publication of tapped telephone conversations, which allegedly revealed breaches by a well-known jockey of the rules of racing and possibly the criminal law, but the court was willing for them to be disclosed to the Jockey Club and the police.

---

[22] [1977] 1 W.L.R. 760 at 763–764. See para.3–115, above.
[23] [1985] Q.B. 526 at 550.
[24] [1984] 1 W.L.R. 892.

Spycatcher

In the *Spycatcher* case, Lord Goff said[25]:   **6–020**

> " . . . although the basis of the law's protection of confidence is that there is a public interest that confidences should be preserved and protected by the law, nevertheless that public interest may be outweighed by some other countervailing public interest which favours disclosure. This limitation may apply, as the learned judge pointed out, to all types of confidential information. It is this limiting principle which may require a court to carry out a balancing operation, weighing the public interest in maintaining confidence against a countervailing public interest favouring disclosure.
>
> Embraced within this limiting principle is, of course, the so called defence of iniquity. In origin, this principle was narrowly stated, on the basis that a man cannot be made 'the confidant of a crime or a fraud': see *Gartside v Outram* (1857) L.J.Ch. 113 at 114, *per* Sir William Page Wood V.C. But it is now clear that *the principle extends to matters of which disclosure is required in the public interest*: see *Beloff v Pressdram Ltd* [1973] 1 All E.R. 241 at 260, *per* Ungoed-Thomas J., and *Lion Laboratories Ltd v Evans* [1985] Q.B. 526 at 550, *per* Griffiths L.J. It does not however follow that the public interest will in such cases *require* disclosure to the media, or to the public by the media. There are cases in which a more limited disclosure is all that is *required*: see *Francome v Mirror Group Newspapers Ltd* [1984] 1 W.L.R. 892. A classic example of a case where limited disclosure is *required* is a case of alleged iniquity in the Security Service. Here there are a number of avenues for proper complaint; these are set out in the judgment of Sir John Donaldson M.R." (Emphasis added.)

The limiting principle recognised by Lord Goff applies to matters of which disclosure is required in the public interest, but only to such form of disclosure as the public interest requires. The word "required" is instructive. It is not enough to show that disclosure would be interesting to the public. It has to be shown that disclosure is required to serve some important public interest, such as the interest in public safety, health, the exposure of serious wrongdoing, or the proper conduct of public affairs.

The limitation is consistent with the underlying notion of confidentiality   **6–021**
as an obligation of conscience in recognising that there may be circumstances in which a conscientious recipient of confidential information would reasonably consider it right as a responsible citizen to make some form of disclosure of the information.

Something may present a serious risk to the medical health of the public,   **6–022**
national security, the administration of justice or a matter of comparable public importance such that it may fairly be regarded as necessary in the

---

[25] [1990] 1 A.C. 109 at 282–283.

public interest that a person possessing such information should be free to disclose it to an appropriate third party, whether or not the matter involves individual wrongdoing (by the claimant or anyone else). As in the case of "iniquity", so also in the case of such information, it may be said that no court would imply a contractual obligation prohibiting such disclosure, or enforce an express contractual prohibition, and that such information would be regarded both at common law and in equity as lacking the necessary attribute of confidence to prevent such disclosure. It is perfectly possible to accommodate such an extension to *Gartside v Outram*[26] within the framework of the analysis favoured by Gummow J. in the *Corrs Pavey* case, and there are strong grounds to do so. It would be wholly unsatisfactory if, for example, a hospital doctor were prevented by his contract of employment from notifying the Department of Health of an imminent risk to public health detected by him in the course of his hospital duties, whether misconduct was involved or not.

6–023 That is very different from the approach adopted by the Court of Appeal in *Woodward v Hutchins*.[27] It could hardly be suggested that the group's desire to foster a good public image presented a danger to the public. Notwithstanding the absence of any such danger, the Court of Appeal considered that it was free to balance generally "the public interest in maintaining the confidence against the public interest in knowing the truth" and resolved in favour of the latter.

Application of the limiting principle

6–024 Lord Goff's statement of the limiting principle has been influential. In *Re A Company's Application*[28] Scott J. considered the scope of an employee's duty of confidentiality in the context of disclosure to an industry regulator. A company which carried on a business regulated under the Financial Services Act 1986 dismissed its compliance officer. In discussions about compensation for alleged unfair dismissal he mentioned that he intended to report the company to the financial services regulator, FIMBRA, for breach of the regulatory scheme introduced under the Act, and to the Inland Revenue for misfeasances by the company's directors.

6–025 The company applied for an injunction to restrain him from making use of any confidential documents or information relating to the company's affairs. The defendant volunteered an undertaking not to disclose his placing of information with FIMBRA or the Inland Revenue to other persons apart from his legal advisers. The issue was whether the defendant was to be restrained, pending trial, from making the threatened disclosures to FIMBRA and the Inland Revenue. The company argued that it was a case of naked blackmail. The defendant denied any blackmailing attempt.

[26] [1857] 26 L.J.Ch. (N.S.) 113.
[27] [1977] 1 W.L.R. 760.
[28] [1989] Ch. 477. For a review of the case, see Lomnicka, "The Employee Whistleblower and the Duty of Confidentiality" (1990) 106 L.Q.R. 42.

Scott J. refused to restrain the defendant from disclosing the matters in **6–026** question to FIMBRA or the Inland Revenue. He observed[29] that if there were any threat of general disclosure by the defendant of confidential information concerning the way in which the plaintiff carried on its business or the affairs of any of its clients, there could be no answer to a claim for an injunction, but that the question was whether an employee of a company carrying on the business of giving financial advice and of financial management to members of the public under the regulatory umbrella provided by FIMBRA owed a duty of confidentiality that extends to barring disclosure of information to FIMBRA.

He concluded[30]: **6–027**

> "I think it would be contrary to the public interest for employees of financial services companies who thought that they ought to place before FIMBRA information of possible breaches of the regulatory system, or information about possible fiscal irregularities before the Inland Revenue, to be inhibited from so doing . . . "

Scott J. also held that it was not for him to conduct a preliminary investigation into the merits of the allegations where the disclosure was proposed to be made to a body which itself had responsibility for investigating such matters.

The judge accepted that the company might be right in its assertion that **6–028** the proposed disclosure was a blackmailing ploy. But if the defendant owed no contractual duty not to disclose information to FIMBRA, malicious motivation could not make the proposed disclosure a breach of contract.

In *W v Egdell*[31] the plaintiff, a paranoid schizophrenic, shot and killed **6–029** five people and injured two others. He pleaded guilty to manslaughter on the ground of diminished responsibility and was ordered to be detained in a secure hospital. For the purpose of an application to a mental health review tribunal with a view towards his ultimate release, the plaintiff, through his solicitors, retained the defendant, a consultant psychiatrist, to report on his state of mental health. The defendant formed a more serious view of the plaintiff's condition than had been taken by the medical officer responsible for his treatment, and his report was adverse to the plaintiff's application. After considering the report, the plaintiff, through his solicitors, withdrew his application. The defendant was so concerned about the difference between his views and those formed by the medical officer that, without the plaintiff's consent, he forwarded a copy of his report to the assistant medical director at the hospital. The plaintiff brought an action against the defendant alleging breach of confidence. The claim failed before Scott J. and on appeal.

---

[29] [1989] Ch. 477 at 481.
[30] *ibid.* at 483.
[31] [1989] Ch. 359.

6–030   Scott J. sought to identify the scope of the relevant duty owed by the defendant to the plaintiff. He said[32]:

> "It is convenient for me first to ask myself what duty of confidence a court of equity ought to regard as imposed on Dr Egdell by the circumstances in which he obtained information from and about W. and prepared his report. It is in my judgment plain, and the contrary has not been suggested, that the circumstances did impose on Dr Egdell a duty of confidence. If, for instance, Dr Egdell had sold the contents of his report to a newspaper, I do not think any court of equity would hesitate for a moment before concluding that his conduct had been a breach of his duty of confidence. The question in the present case is not whether Dr Egdell was under a duty of confidence; he plainly was. The question is as to the breadth of that duty. Did the duty extend so as to bar disclosure of the report to the medical director of the hospital?"

He concluded[33]:

> "True it is that Dr. Egdell was engaged by W. He was the doctor of W.'s choice. Nonetheless, in my opinion, the duty he owed to W. was not his only duty. W. was not an ordinary member of the public. He was, consequent upon the killings he had perpetrated, held in a secure hospital subject to a regime whereby decisions concerning his future were to be taken by public authorities, the Home Secretary or the tribunal. W.'s own interests would not be the only nor the main criterion in the taking of those decisions. The safety of the public would be the main criterion. In my view, a doctor called upon, as Dr. Egdell was, to examine a patient such as W. owes a duty not only to his patient but also a duty to the public. His duty to the public would require him, in my opinion, to place before the proper authorities the result of his examination if, in his opinion, the public interest so required. This would be so, in my opinion, whether or not the patient instructed him not to do so."

6–031   In the Court of Appeal the plaintiff criticised the judge's approach for leaving the question whether disclosure was justified to the subjective judgment of the doctor. Bingham L.J. agreed with the criticism, but added that in judging whether the disclosure was justified in law the court would attach weight to the doctor's considered judgment.[34] In considering the public interest qualification to the duty of confidence owed to the plaintiff, Bingham L.J. stated that only the most compelling circumstances could justify a doctor in acting in a way which would injure the immediate

---

[32] [1989] Ch. 359 at 389.
[33] *ibid.* at 392.
[34] *ibid.* at 422.

interests of the patient, as the patient perceived them, without obtaining his consent, but he concluded[35]:

> "Where a man has committed multiple killings under the disability of serious mental illness, decisions which may lead directly or indirectly to his release from hospital should not be made unless a responsible authority is properly able to make an informed judgment that the risk of repetition is so small as to be acceptable. A consultant psychiatrist who becomes aware, even in the course of a confidential relationship, of information which leads him, in the exercise of what the court considers a sound professional judgment, to fear that such decisions may be made on the basis of inadequate information and with a real risk of consequent danger to the public is entitled to take such steps as are reasonable in all the circumstances to communicate the grounds of his concern to the responsible authorities."

Dr Egdell was clearly fearful of the risk to the public from the possible premature release into the community of a dangerous schizophrenic who had, according to his report, a seriously abnormal interest in the making of home made bombs. If the plaintiff had confided to the doctor that he planned to commit murder, no court would have held that there was an implied obligation on the part of the defendant to keep that information to himself, nor would it have upheld an express agreement to do so. Should different principles apply because the perceived danger to the public arose from illness? It would be surprising if any court had thought so. As Meagher Gummow and Lehane observe[36]: **6–032**

> "A contract not to disclose to the responsible authorities the continued murderous propensities of the plaintiff would have offended public policy: *A v Hayden*."[37]

As to the criticism made of Scott J.'s approach that it left the question whether disclosure was justified to the subjective judgment of the doctor (in saying that the doctor's "duty to the public would require him to place before the proper authorities the result of his examination if, in his opinion, the public interest so required"), a similar point arose in *Woolgar v Chief Constable of Sussex Police*.[38] A nurse who was the matron of a nursing home was arrested and interviewed by the police after the death of a patient. The police concluded that there was insufficient evidence to charge her with any offence. The health authority then referred the matter to the council which was the regulatory body for nursing. The nursing council asked the police for any relevant information. The police asked the nurse for her consent to disclosure of a transcript of her interview under caution, which **6–033**

---

[35] [1989] Ch. 359 at 423–424.
[36] *Equity: Doctrines and Remedies* (4th edn, 2002) at para.41–115.
[37] (1984) 156 C.L.R. 532.
[38] [2000] 1 W.L.R. 25.

she refused. On being told that the police solicitor would listen to the tape
and then decide whether it should be disclosed to the nursing council, the
nurse applied for an injunction to restrain the police from disclosing the
transcript on ground that it was confidential. Kennedy L.J. stated the issue
as follows[39]:

> "Undoubtedly when someone is arrested and interviewed by the police
> what he or she says, is confidential. Plainly it may be used in the course
> of a criminal trial if charges are brought arising out of that investiga-
> tion, but if it is not so used the person interviewed is entitled to believe
> that, generally speaking, his or her confidence will be respected. If
> authority be required for that proposition, it can be found in *Taylor v
> Director of the Serious Fraud Office* [1999] 2 A.C. 177, but, as all of
> the authorities cited to us indicate, there are exceptional circumstances
> which justify the disclosure by the police, otherwise than in the course
> of a criminal trial, of what has been said by a suspect during the course
> of an interview, in circumstances where the suspect, or former suspect,
> does not consent to such disclosure. The question which arises in this
> case is whether, if the regulatory body of the profession to which the
> suspect belongs is investigating serious allegations and makes a formal
> request to the police for disclosure of what was said in interview, the
> public interest in the proper working of the regulatory body is or may
> be such as to justify disclosure of the material sought. If the answer to
> that question is in the affirmative how, as a matter of procedure, should
> contentious issues in relation to disclosure be resolved?"

He concluded[40] that where a regulatory body operating in the field of public
health and safety seeks access to confidential material, which the police are
reasonably persuaded is relevant to the subject matter of an inquiry being
conducted by the regulatory body, a public interest is shown to exist which
entitles the police to release the material to the regulatory body on the basis
that, save insofar as it may be used by the regulatory body for its own
inquiry, the confidentiality which attaches to the material will be maintained. He added:

> "Even if there is no request from the regulatory body, it seems to me
> that if the police come into possession of confidential information
> which, in their reasonable view, in the interests of public health or
> safety, should be considered by a professional or regulatory body, then
> the police are free to pass that information to the relevant regulatory
> body for its consideration.
>
> Obviously in each case a balance has to be struck between competing
> public interests, and at least arguably in some cases the reasonableness
> of the police view may be open to challenge. If they refuse to disclose,

[39] [2000] 1 W.L.R. 25 at para.6.
[40] *ibid.* at para.9.

the regulatory body can, if aware of the existence of the information, make an appropriate application to the court. In order to safeguard the interests of the individual, it is, in my judgment, desirable that, where the police are minded to disclose, they should, as in this case, inform the person affected of what they propose to do in such time as to enable that person, if so advised, to seek assistance from the court. In some cases that may not be practicable or desirable, but in most cases that seems to me to be the course that should be followed. In any event, in my judgment, the primary decision as to disclosure should be made by the police who have the custody of the relevant material, and not by the court."

The patterns of thought involved in this approach contain a mixture of **6–034** private and public law. It was held that the police owed a legal duty of confidentiality to the nurse in relation to what she told them in her interview, subject to a qualification enabling the police to disclose the transcript to the nursing regulatory authority if it was reasonable to consider that it was in the interests of public health and safety to do so. But the court did not consider that it was for itself to decide whether disclosure should be made. Rather, this was a matter for the decision of the police, subject "arguably in some cases" to review in the way that a court may review the legality of a decision of a public body as a matter of public law. In this respect the court's approach differed from *W v Egdell,* where Bingham L.J. said[41]:

"Where, as here, the relationship between doctor and patient is contractual, the question is whether the doctor's disclosure is or is not a breach of contract. The answer to that question must turn not on what the doctor thinks but on what the court rules. But it does not follow that the doctor's conclusion is irrelevant. In making its ruling the court will give such weight to the considered judgment of a professional man as seems in all the circumstances to be appropriate."

While at a technical level the difference may be explained because there was no contract involved in *Woolgar v Chief Constable of Sussex Police,* nevertheless if the police owed the nurse an obligation of confidentiality the question whether there was a breach or threatened breach of that duty was one for the court.

In considering whether the interests of public health or safety should **6–035** permit a doctor or the police to disclose information given in circumstances importing an obligation of confidentiality, without the consent of the person to whom the obligation is owed, it does not seem satisfactory to draw a distinction according to whether there was an underlying contract. It is suggested that in either case it is for the court to rule on the legal criteria which govern the question whether and in what circumstances public

[41] [1990] 1 Ch. 359 at 422.

interest may justify disclosure. Within those criteria, a person should not be held to have acted unconscionably if their decision was reasonable.[42]

6–036   The suggestion that an unreasonable but honestly held belief that publication is justified should provide a defence to a claim for breach of confidence was rejected by the Court of Appeal in *Campbell v MGN Ltd*[43] and was not pursued on appeal to the House of Lords.

6–037   An applicant for an injunction to prevent a disclosure on grounds of confidentiality has to satisfy the court that there is a threatened breach of duty. In *Woolgar v Chief Constable of Sussex Police* the applicant was not in a position to do so (since the police solicitor had not listened to the tape or made a decision on the nursing council's request for disclosure) unless she could establish that disclosure would necessarily be wrongful. Having rejected that argument, it would have been premature for the court to rule whether a decision to disclose the nurse's interview would be justifiable, and it did not have the material on which to do so.

6–038   There is some uncertainty whether it may make a difference if the party claiming confidentiality is relying on an express term rather than on an implied term or an equitable obligation when considering the issue of public interest.

6–039   In *Initial Services Ltd v Putterill*[44] Salmon and Winn L.JJ. considered that the proper test in deciding if an implied contractual obligation or an equitable obligation of confidentiality arising from an employment contract extended to the disclosure in question was to ask whether an express term prohibiting the disclosure would have been contrary to public policy.

6–040   In *Spycatcher* Scott J. followed the same approach[45]:

> "The court would obviously never, by means of an implied term, impose on an ex-employee a duty which would have been unenforceable if it had been incorporated into an express term. But in deciding upon the ambit of the implied term the same considerations will, in my view, be relevant as would be relevant to an examination of whether an express term was enforceable."

6–041   In *Price Waterhouse v BCCI*[46] Millett J. arguably took a different approach. An inquiry into the supervision of BCCI under the Banking Act 1987 was set up under the Chairmanship of Bingham L.J. by the Treasury and the Bank of England. The inquiry had no statutory power to enforce the attendance of witnesses or to compel the production of documents, and the

---

[42] "It may be that that hard-worked creature, the reasonable man, may be pressed into service once more; for I do not see why he should not labour in equity as well as at law." *per* Megarry J. in *Coco v A.N. Clark (Engineers) Ltd* [1969] R.P.C. 41 at 48.

[43] [2002] EWCA Civ 1373; [2003] Q.B. 633, at [66]–[70].

[44] [1968] 1 Q.B. 368 at 409 *per* Salmon L.J. and 411 *per* Winn L.J.

[45] [1990] 1 A.C. 109 at 146.

[46] [1992] B.C.L.C. 583. The collapse of BCCI and subsequent litigation and inquiries gave rise to various confidentiality problems. See also *El Jawhary v BCCI* [1993] B.C.L.C. 396; *R. v Institute of Chartered Accountants of England and Wales Ex p. Brindle* [1994] B.C.C. 297; *Morris v Director of Serious Fraud Office* [1993] B.C.L.C. 580.

judge rejected the argument that the Bank of England could have required production of documents for the purposes of the inquiry under s.39 of the Banking Act (since that section empowered the Bank of England to require the production of documents only if necessary for the performance of its supervisory function, not for the purpose of enabling the inquiry to review its performance). The inquiry requested the accountants Price Waterhouse to submit evidence and produce documents.

The accountants performed various functions in relation to the bank, **6–042** including co-ordinating the worldwide audits of the companies in the group. They were concerned that most of the information in their possession was confidential to the bank, and that much of it was also covered by a duty of banking confidentiality owed by the bank to its customers, of which the accountants had notice. They sought a declaration that they were not precluded from supplying information or documents to the inquiry. There was unquestionably a relationship of confidentiality between the bank and its customers (of which the accountants had notice), and between the accountants and the bank, but the issue was whether the scope of the accountants' obligations to the bank and its customers was such as to preclude them from cooperating with the inquiry.

After citing passages from the speeches of Lord Griffiths and Lord Goff in the *Spycatcher* case[47] and from the judgment of Bankes L.J. in *Tournier*,[48] Millett J. said[49]:

> "In all the cases cited to me in which the public interest in favour of disclosure has prevailed, it has been the public interest in the detection or prevention of wrong-doing, or in preventing a miscarriage of justice, or in the maintenance of public safety. An express contractual undertaking not to make disclosure in such circumstances would be against public policy. However, if those who set up the inquiry had thought that the public interest required that all relevant material should be made available to it, they could have set it up under the Tribunal of Inquiries and Evidence Act 1921. No doubt there were good reasons for not doing so. But they were content to rely upon the voluntary submission of evidence by those willing to co-operate with the inquiry. Where the information is confidential, the choice whether to volunteer it ought prima facie in my view to rest with the person to whom the duty of confidence is owed, rather than with the person who owes it. An express contractual undertaking not to co-operate with the inquiry would not, I apprehend, be contrary to public policy. That, however, is not the test which has been laid down by the authorities. The duty of confidentiality, whether contractual or equitable, is subject to a limiting principle. It is subject to the right, not merely the duty, to disclose information where there is a higher public interest in disclosure than in maintaining confidentiality.

[47] [1990] 1 A.C. 109 at 268 and 282.
[48] [1924] 1 K.B. 461 at 472–473.
[49] [1992] B.C.L.C. 583 at 601.

> I have reached the conclusion that in the particular circumstances of
> the present case the public interest in favour of disclosure ought to
> prevail."

6–043   When the judge said that an express contractual undertaking not to help
the inquiry would not have been contrary to public policy, but that this was
not the test laid down by the authorities, it is unclear whether he meant: (a)
that even if there had been such an undertaking he would have made the
declaration sought, because he judged that there was a higher public interest
in disclosure, or (b) that although such an express undertaking would not
have been contrary to public policy, and therefore would have been
enforceable, that was irrelevant to the question whether the court should
imply or impose a contractual or equitable obligation precluding the
accountants from helping the inquiry. Either approach presents difficulties.

6–044   The difficulty with the first approach is that it is one matter to hold (as in
Initial Services Ltd v Putterill[50]) that public policy would require a court to
declare a term unenforceable because its enforcement would be contrary to
public policy; it is another matter to declare in advance, on grounds of
public interest, that a party is free not to comply with a contractual
undertaking, even though public policy does not require the undertaking to
be treated as unenforceable. The difficulty with the second approach is that
it is inconsistent with previous authorities.

6–045   The proceedings were most unusual in that the judge was being asked in
effect to give a negative declaration as to the accountants' obligations
towards the bank's customers (or possibly a dispensation from complying
with them), without having details of the information which might be
disclosed and without the customers having the opportunity to make
representations. Because all the parties to the action supported the relief
claimed, the judge did not have the benefit of contrary argument as to the
appropriateness of the declaration. It is suggested that it would be unsafe to
draw any general conclusions from the case.

6–046   In *Campbell v Frisbee*[51] Lord Phillips M.R. said:

> "We consider it arguable that a duty of confidentiality that has been
> expressly assumed under contract carries more weight, when balanced
> against the right of freedom of expression, than a duty of confidential-
> ity that is not buttressed by express agreement—contrast the observa-
> tions of Walker L.J. in *London Regional Transport v The Mayor of
> London* [2001] EWCA Civ 1491 at paragraph 46 with those of Lord
> Donaldson of Lymington M.R. in *Attorney-General v Barker* [1990] 3
> All E.R. 257 at p 260."

---

[50] [1968] 1 Q.B. 396.
[51] [2002] EWCA Civ 1374 at [22].

The court expressed no further view on the matter. The two cases mentioned by Lord Phillips shared the significant feature that they concerned publication of material which was not intrinsically confidential. Because of the lack of intrinsic confidentiality, no question of an implied contractual obligation not to publish the material could have arisen in either case. In each case the claimants' attempts to prevent publication were entirely dependent on express contractual undertakings.

Where information is of an intrinsically confidential nature, it is not easy **6–047** as a general proposition to see why in determining any limitation on the scope of the duty of confidentiality required by the public interest it should make a difference that there is an express confidentiality clause.

Article 10

Article 10 of the European Convention provides as follows: **6–048**

> "(1) Everyone has the right to freedom of expression. This right shall include freedom to hold opinions and to receive and impart information and ideas without interference by public authority and regardless of frontiers. This Article shall not prevent States from requiring the licensing of broadcasting, television or cinema enterprises.
>
> (2) The exercise of these freedoms, since it carries with it duties and responsibilities, may be subject to such formalities, conditions, restrictions or penalties as are prescribed by law and are necessary in a democratic society, in the interests of national security, territorial integrity or public safety, for the prevention of disorder or crime, for the protection of health or morals, for the protection of the reputation or rights of others, for preventing the disclosure of information received in confidence, or for maintaining the authority and impartiality of the judiciary."

Section 12 of the Human Rights Act 1998 prohibits a court from granting an injunction before trial which might affect the exercise of the Convention right to freedom of expression unless it is satisfied that the applicant is likely to establish that publication should not be allowed. In *Cream Holdings Ltd v Bannerjee*[52] the House of Lords held that the word likely should be interpreted with some flexibility and that the court should not make an interim restraint order unless satisfied that the applicant's prospects of success at the trial are sufficiently favourable to justify such an order being made in all the circumstances of the case.

In the *Spycatcher* case Lord Goff considered Art.10, although the **6–049** Convention had not yet been incorporated into domestic law. He said[53]:

[52] [2004] UKHL 44; [2005] 1 A.C. 253.
[53] [1990] 1 A.C. 109 at 283–284.

" . . . I can see no inconsistency between English law on this subject and article 10 of the European Convention on Human Rights. This is scarcely surprising, since we may pride ourselves on the fact that freedom of speech has existed in this country perhaps as long as, if not longer than, it has existed in any other country in the world . . . . The exercise of the right to freedom of expression under article 10 may be subject to restrictions (as are prescribed by law and are necessary in a democratic society) in relation to certain prescribed matters, which include 'the interests of national security' and 'preventing the disclosure of information received in confidence'. It is established in the jurisprudence of the European Court of Human Rights that the word 'necessary' in this context implies the existence of a pressing social need, and that interference with freedom of expression should be no more than is proportionate to the legitimate aim pursued. I have no reason to believe that English law, as applied in the courts, leads to any different conclusion."

Except in the area of privacy (discussed in Chapter 7), the incorporation of the Convention by the Human Rights Act 1998 has not led to a change of substance in the approach of the courts to issues of confidentiality and public interest, but in some cases the courts have used the language of Art.10 as reinforcement of the relevant principles.

6–050   In *R. v Department of Health Ex p. Source Infomatics Ltd*[54] arguments were based both on domestic jurisprudence and on Art.10. In his judgment (with which the other members of the court agreed) Simon Brown L.J. recognised

"the importance of confining any public interest defence in this area of the law within strict limits—lest, as Gummow J. put it at first instance in *Smith Kline and French Laboratories (Australia) Ltd v Department of Community Services and Health* [1990] F.S.R. 617, 663, it becomes 'not so much a rule of law as an invitation to judicial idiosyncrasy by deciding each case on an ad hoc basis as to whether, on the facts overall, it is better to respect or to override the obligation of confidence' ".

He also commented on the need to avoid a starting point of an overwide equitable obligation of confidence.

6–051   In *Imutran Ltd v Uncaged Campaigns Ltd*[55] the claimant was a pharmaceutical company engaged in research into organ transplantation. The research involved experiments on pigs. The work was subject to regulatory control by the Home Secretary under the Animals (Scientific Procedures) Act 1986 and by a section of the Department of Health called the Good Laboratory Practice Monitoring Authority (GLPMA). The defendants were

---

[54] [2001] Q.B. 424 at 444.
[55] [2001] 2 All E.R. 385.

a body which campaigned against animal experimentation and one of its directors. The defendants received a large number of leaked documents belonging to the claimant, which were obviously confidential. The defendants considered that they raised extremely serious questions about animal welfare and the public regulation of research. From the leaked documents they compiled a dossier, which was placed on websites, but the websites were soon closed down by the service providers. The dossier was also supplied to the Home Office, GLPMA and the RSPCA.

Sir Andrew Morritt V.C. granted the claimants' application for an **6–052** injunction to prevent its general publication pending trial, considering that they were likely to establish at the trial that publication of the leaked documents should not be allowed. The defendants relied on public interest and Art.10. The judge said[56]:

> "I have been referred to the well-known line of cases consisting of *Initial Services Ltd v Putterill* [1967] 3 All E.R. 145, [1968] 1 Q.B. 396, *Hubbard v Vosper* [1972] 1 All E.R. 1023, [1972] 2 Q.B. 84, *Francome v Mirror Group Newspapers Ltd* [1984] 2 All E.R. 408, [1984] 1 W.L.R. 892, *Lion Laboratories Ltd v Evans* [1984] 2 All E.R. 417, [1985] Q.B. 526, *Re a Company's application* [1989] 2 All E.R. 248, [1989] Ch. 477 and *A-G v Guardian Newspapers Ltd (No.2)* [1988] 3 All E.R. 545, [1990] 1 A.C. 109. Each of them demonstrates that the public interest in disclosure may outweigh the right of the plaintiff to protect his confidences. They demonstrate that the court will also consider how much disclosure the public interest requires; the fact that some disclosure may be required does not mean that disclosure to the whole world should be permitted.
>
> In addition the 1998 Act requires the court, as a public authority, to take into account the right of freedom of expression conferred by art 10 of the convention . . . .The effect of that article for present purposes is that any injunction, which by definition is a restriction on the exercise of the right to freedom of expression, must be justified as being no more than is necessary in a democratic society."

The judge was unimpressed by the argument that because the issue of animal welfare was of public importance the defendants should be able to make general disclosure of the documents. In considering what was necessary in a democratic society, he observed that Parliament had considered the issue of animal experimentation and laid down a licensing and inspection system. The form of the injunction meant that the defendants would be able to communicate the leaked information to the regulatory bodies denoted by Parliament as having responsibility in the field. The defendants had a democratic right to campaign for the abolition of animal experimentation but not with the claimants' confidential documents.

---

[56] [2001] 2 All E.R. 385 at paras 20–21.

6-053   In *London Regional Transport v Mayor of London*[57] the first claimant (LRT) was a public body established by the London Regional Transport Act 1984. The second claimant, London Underground Ltd (LUL), was a wholly owned subsidiary of LRT. The Greater London Authority Act 1999 provided for LRT to be replaced by a new statutory body, Transport for London (TfL), whose chairman would be the Mayor of London. LUL's functions were to be restricted to operating underground railway services, and the responsibilities for the infrastructure of the system were to be transferred to three newly created subsidiaries of LUL, whose shares were then to be sold to the private sector. In the transitional period the Mayor, LRT and TfL were under a statutory duty (by s.298(3) of the 1999 Act) to consult and cooperate with one another and to provide such information as might reasonably be required by one another for the purpose of discharging any of its functions. K was appointed as chairman of LRT and was also appointed by the Mayor as Commissioner of TfL. LUL had confidentiality agreements with all bidders. LUL supplied information about the bids to TfL under a confidentiality agreement which included the provision:

> "All information related to the review of bids . . . being undertaken by [K] . . . must be held in the strictest confidence and not used for any purpose other than for the purpose of enabling TfL and the Mayor to discharge their duties pursuant to Section 298(3) of the Greater London Authority Act 1999."

K on behalf of TfL commissioned a firm of accountants to report on the value for money exercise conducted by LUL and its advisers. The accountants were given access to the bids. Their report was highly critical. K wrote to the Prime Minister saying that in his opinion the public-private partnership project was not feasible. K was about to present the accountants' report to the board of LRT when he was removed from his chairmanship of LRT by the Secretary of State. On the following day the Mayor announced his intention of publishing the contents of the report. The claimants immediately applied for an injunction against TfL and the Mayor.

6-054   After a short injunction the defendants produced a redacted version of the report which excluded all sensitive price information. On a resumed hearing the judge did not accept that publication of the redacted version would cause significant harm to LRT, LUL, or successful or unsuccessful bidders and he refused to stop its publication. His decision was upheld on appeal.

6-055   The position was summarised by Sedley L.J.[58]:

> "The discharge of the injunction by Sullivan J. is justified on the straightforward ground that there is nothing of genuine commercial

[57] [2001] EWCA Civ 1491.
[58] *ibid.* at [53].

sensitivity in the redacted version of the Deloittes report and nothing therefore to justify the stifling of public information and debate by the enforcement of a bare contractual obligation of silence."

While the report had been written as a result of studying confidential bid information, it did not disclose any bid information which could be identified as confidential. The claim that its publication would be a misuse of confidential information therefore rested entirely on the terms of TfL's contractual undertaking. It is possible for parties to contract for non-disclosure of information even though the information in question is not intrinsically confidential,[59] but a contractual undertaking of that kind will not be enforced if to do so would be contrary to the public interest.

The claimants argued that the test was to be found in the passage from Lord Goff's speech in the *Spycatcher* case, where he referred to "matters of which disclosure is required in the public interest" in his summary of the public interest limitation on the principle of confidentiality.[60] However, Lord Goff was considering information which possessed the quality of confidentiality. He was not considering "a bare contractual obligation of silence".   **6–056**

There would also have been a strong case for saying that since the claimants were public bodies (and were not acting in support of any confidentiality of private bodies), it was incumbent on them to establish that publication would be harmful to the public interest, adopting the principles which apply to public sector confidentiality,[61] but this point does not appear to have been argued. The question whether the intended public-private partnership represented good value for money was obviously important to the population of London (if not beyond), and the accountants' report was capable of informing public debate on the issue. There was a strong public interest in its disclosure and no public interest in its non-disclosure.   **6–057**

In the Court of Appeal, Robert Walker L.J. dealt with the matter in terms of principles of confidentiality. Sedley L.J. agreed with his approach but added that the conclusion was reinforced by Art.10.[62] He went on to suggest that an Art.10 approach based on a test of proportionality might provide a more certain guide than the test of the reasonable recipient's conscience.   **6–058**

Article 10 requires any qualification preventing the disclosure of information received in confidence to be prescribed by law. In English law that prescription is to be found in the established principles of confidentiality, and it must be for the claimant in any case to bring the claim within those principles. In so far as the claim is based on the equitable doctrine of   **6–059**

---

[59] *Att-Gen v Blake* [2001] 1 A.C. 268.
[60] [1990] 1 A.C. 109 at 282–3.
[61] *Att-Gen v Jonathan Cape Ltd* [1976] 1 Q.B. 752; *Commonwealth of Australia v John Fairfax & Sons Ltd* (1980) 147 C.L.R. 39; *Att-Gen v Guardian Newspapers Ltd (No. 2)* [1990] 1 A.C. 109.
[62] [2001] EWCA Civ 1491 at [54]–[58].

confidentiality, it involves the conscience test. The principles include recognition that in some cases a duty of confidentiality may be negated or qualified by public interest. Proportionality in this context is an aspect of the relevant principles rather than a separate principle.

New Zealand

6–060   In New Zealand it has been held by the Court of Appeal that:

> "What has been called ever since *Gartside v Outram* (1856) 26 L.J.Ch. 113 the defence of iniquity is an instance, and probably the prime instance, of the principle that the law will not protect confidential information if the publication complained of is shown to be in the overriding public interest: see generally *Lion Laboratories Ltd v Evans* [1985] Q.B. 526; *Attorney-General for the United Kingdom v Wellington Newspapers Ltd* [1988] 1 N.Z.L.R. 129, at 176–177, 178; *Attorney-General v Observer Ltd* [1990] 1 A.C. 109, at 268–269 and at 282–283."[63]

Australia

6–061   Australian courts have generally preferred the narrower "public interest defence" enunciated in such cases as *Beloff v Pressdram Ltd*[64] to the broader version put forward by Lord Denning M.R. in *Woodward v Hutchins*,[65] but there have been different judicial views about the preferred approach.

6–062   In *Castrol Australia Pty Ltd v Emtech Associates Pty Ltd*[66] Rath J. observed that the public interest "exception" could not universally be extended to all crimes committed, as Bankes L.J. pointed out in *Weld-Blundell v Stephens*[67]; but that exclusion from protection of designs "to destroy the public welfare" expressed a concept authoritatively expressed by Viscount Finlay in the same case, when he referred to cases where some "higher duty is involved" and said that "danger to the state or public duty may supersede the duty of the agent to his principal".[68]

6–063   Rath J. also cited with agreement Ungoed-Thomas J.'s summary in *Beloff v Pressdram Ltd*[69] (approved by Lord Goff in *Spycatcher*[70]), saying that it expressed no more than a reasonable elaboration of Viscount Finlay's

---

[63] *European Pacific Banking Corp v Television New Zealand Ltd* [1994] 3 N.Z.L.R. 43 at 46.
[64] [1973] 1 All E.R. 241 at 260.
[65] [1977] 1 W.L.R. 760.
[66] (1980) 33 A.L.R. 31 at 54.
[67] [1919] 1 K.B. 520 at 527 and 528.
[68] [1920] A.C. 956 at 965.
[69] [1973] 1 All E.R. 241 at 260.
[70] [1990] 1 A.C. 109 at 282.

"higher duty" concept and was an acceptable statement of the law as to the defence of public interest in an action for breach of confidence. He added[71]:

"What is particularly important in Ungoed-Thomas J.'s formulation of principle is his emphasis on the gravity of the conduct that may give rise to the defence. If there is to be a defence labelled public interest, some such confinement of its vague boundaries is in my view essential."

Rath, J. declined to follow the broader test applied by Lord Denning M.R. in *Woodward v Hutchins*,[72] saying that[73]:

"If Lord Denning's quoted statement is taken literally the court will test the legitimacy of breach of confidence by its conception of the balance of public interest in the particular circumstances of the case."

He went on to say that the court[74]:

" . . . must have regard to matters of a more weighty and precise kind than a public interest in the truth being told . . . . In a sense [the plaintiffs'] image was a matter of 'public interest', but not in the sense that as a matter of public policy the defendants were entitled, or required, to break confidence."

In *Corrs Pavey Whiting & Byrne v Collector of Customs*[75] Gummow J.   **6–064** was also critical of *Woodward v Hutchins* and, like Rath J., rejected a broad "public interest defence". He considered that if there were some principle of general application inspired by *Gartside v Outram* it was no wider than that

"information will lack the necessary attribute of confidence if the subject matter is the existence or real likelihood of the existence of an iniquity in the sense of a crime, civil wrong or serious misdeed of public importance, and the confidence is relied upon to prevent disclosure to a third party with a real and direct interest in redressing such crime, wrong or misdeed."

Kirby P. took a broader approach in the *Spycatcher* litigation in Aus-   **6–065** tralia,[76] describing *Gartside v Outram* as

"an instance of the wider category of the public interest which may sometimes, even if rarely, outweigh the public interest in confidentiality

---

[71] (1980) 33 A.L.R. 31 at 55.
[72] [1977] 1 W.L.R. 760.
[73] (1980) 33 A.L.R. 31 at 56.
[74] *ibid.*
[75] (1987) 74 A.L.R. 428 at 445–450.
[76] *Att-Gen (UK) v Heinemann Publishers Australia Pty Ltd* (1987) 147 C.L.R. 39 at 57.

and secrecy: *cf.* Gibbs C.J. in *A v Hayden (No.2)* (1984) 156 C.L.R. 532 at 545 *et seq.*"

6–066　　In *Smith Klein & French Laboratories (Australia) Ltd v Department of Community Services*[77] Gummow J. drew a distinction between factors which may qualify a duty of confidentiality and the question of a public interest defence. A court of equity would not impute to a party an obligation which would restrict him in his performance of public responsibilities, but the question was what was the content of the obligation at its inception, rather than whether there was a public interest defence to a breach of obligation. He noted that this had been the approach of Scott J. at first instance in the *Spycatcher* case[78] (and, he might have added, in *In Re A Company's Application*[79] and *W v Egdell*[80]). As to the question of a public interest defence, he said:

> "My views upon the wisdom of adopting in Australia the English authorities in which the 'public interest' defence has been constructed in recent years from what may be thought inadequate historical and doctrinal materials, have been expressed in *Corrs Pavey Whiting & Byrne v Collection of Customs (Vic)* . . . , at 451–458. Those views are consistent with what was said by Rath J. in *Castrol Australia Pty Ltd v EmTech Associates Pty Ltd*, . . . , at 210–216 and by Hutley A.P. in *David Syme & Co. Ltd v General Motors-Holden's Ltd* [1984] 2 N.S.W.L.R., 294 at 305–306 . . .
>
> Further, I would accept the submissions by counsel for the applicants in the *SK&F* proceedings that (i) an examination of the recent English decisions shows that the so-called 'public interest' defence is not so much a rule of law as an invitation to judicial idiosyncrasy by deciding each case on an *ad hoc* basis as to whether, on the facts overall, it is better to respect or to override the obligation of confidence, and (ii) equitable principles are best developed by reference to what conscionable behaviour demands of the defendant not by 'balancing' and then overriding those demands by reference to matters of social or political opinion."

6–067　　In *Esso Australia Resources Ltd v Plowman*,[81] a case concerning arbitration proceedings, Brennan J. observed that in determining the scope of an implied obligation of confidentiality a party will not be taken to have intended that it would keep confidential documents or information when that party had an obligation, albeit not a legal obligation, to satisfy a public interest—more than mere curiosity—in knowing what was contained in the documents or information. Mason C.J. (with whom Dawson and McHugh

---

[77] [1990] F.S.R. 617 at 662–663.
[78] [1988] 3 All E.R. 545 at 582–584.
[79] [1989] Ch. 477 at 481.
[80] [1989] Ch. 359 at 389.
[81] [1994–1995] 183 C.L.R. 10.

JJ. concurred) said that the precise scope of the public interest exception to
a duty of confidentiality remained unclear.

In *Sullivan v Sclanders*[82] the Supreme Court of South Australia reviewed   **6–068**
the Australian authorities and preferred the approach of Gummow J. in
Corrs Pavey v Collector of Customs.[83] Gray J. said[84]:

> "Equitable principles are best developed by reference to what con-
> scionable behaviour demands of the defendant rather than by balanc-
> ing those demands with matters of public interest. This approach
> avoids the ad hoc judicial idiosyncracy associated with deciding
> whether, on the facts overall, it is better to respect or override the
> obligation of confidence."

In *AG Australia Holdings Ltd v Burton*[85] Campbell J. concluded, after a   **6–069**
lengthy review of the authorities, that the present status of a public interest
defence in Australia where the plaintiff relies on an equitable duty of
confidentiality is not clear. In that case the defendant was a former senior
employee of an insurance company which was the subject of a partially
successful hostile takeover. After the takeover the share price of the
company slumped as a result of disclosures that it was facing much heavier
losses than previously forecast. Proceedings for alleged deception were
brought on behalf of those shareholders who had rejected the bidder's offers
against various officers and professional advisers of the company. The
plaintiff's solicitors were provided with information by the defendant,
contrary to express confidentiality terms in his contract of employment.

It was argued that the clause was void or unenforceable on the ground   **6–070**
that it would interfere with the proper administration of justice. The judge
rejected the argument, observing that there was no authority to support the
proposition that an offence connected with interfering with the course of
justice is committed if an employer seeks to enforce a confidentiality clause
in a contract of employment with his employee (or former employee), by
preventing the employee from disclosing to a solicitor, out of court,
confidential information of the employer.[86] He accepted that public policy
would prevent the enforcement of the contract so as to make the defendant
keep quiet about the commission of a widespread and serious fraud, but the
evidence before him was not sufficient to establish that this was a case in
which that principle applied. The mere allegation of such iniquity by the
plaintiffs was not enough.[87]

---

[82] [2000] S.A.S.C. 273.
[83] (1987) 74 A.L.R. 428.
[84] [2000] S.A.S.C. 273 at para.45.
[85] [2002] N.S.W.S.C. 170 at para.177. See too *Australian Football League v The Age Company Ltd* [2006] VSC 308.
[86] *ibid.* at para.109.
[87] *ibid.* at paras 196–203.

Conclusions on public interest

6–071   In any country which professes the rule of law and places value on the rights
of individuals, those rights should not be lightly overridden in the name of
public interest. Courts should do so only with caution, taking care that they
act on clearly identified.

6–072   Whether English law recognises a "defence of public interest" as broad as
its critics have suggested is therefore a question of considerable importance.
The concept of such a broad defence appears to have originated in
Woodward v Hutchins,[88] which does suggest that it is for the court to decide
in each case on an ad hoc basis whether, on the facts, it is better to respect
or override the obligation of confidence; and the result in that case may well
be regarded as an instance of judicial idiosyncrasy. There are also dicta in
later cases which support the same general approach, but other authorities
suggest that the true principle is narrower.

6–073   Courts have sometimes referred to public interest as a factor negating or
circumscribing a duty of confidentiality and sometimes as a factor justifying
a breach of a duty of confidentiality. It is a limiting factor which may
operate as a defence because it may negate or circumscribe a duty of
confidentiality. This does not mean that the public interest factor must have
arisen at the inception of the duty, for, as Viscount Finlay said in *Weld-
Blundell v Stephens*,[89] "danger to the state or public duty may supersede the
duty of the agent to his principal".

6–074   No duty of confidentiality can be said to be absolute in all circumstances,
because it is always subject to the possibility that public interest may require
disclosure. However, the law of confidentiality is based on the recognition
that people who are entrusted with confidential information (or obtain it in
circumstances where they should regard it as confidential) ought as a
general principle to respect that confidentiality. That principle and the
ability to depend on it would be weakened if the public interest limitation
became too broad or, as has been said of some decisions, idiosyncratic in its
operation.

6–075   The Law Commission in its Working Paper on Breach of Confidence[90]
discussed the difficulties of trying to define the criteria:

> "Our provisional view is . . . that the range of circumstances in which
> the defence might properly be used is so wide and so variable that it is
> not practicable to define in general terms all the criteria to be used and
> that it would be misleading to single out particular issues (such as the
> existence of misconduct) for consideration. There is also a further
> point, which is perhaps even more important. The public interest is a
> developing concept which changes with the social attitudes of the
> times: many things are regarded as being in the public interest today
> which would not have been so regarded in the last century, or even

[88] [1977] 1 W.L.R. 760.
[89] [1920] A.C. 956 at 965.
[90] No.58, 1974, at para.93.

twenty years ago, and it would be unrealistic to suppose that the concept will not undergo further changes in the years ahead. If this fact is recognised, it seems to us that the only prudent course is to frame the defence in terms which are flexible enough to enable each case to be judged on its individual merits. There is, of course, a substantial public interest in the reservation of confidences and the task of the court would therefore be to balance this against the public interest in disclosing the information to which a confidence related. This is a function which the courts already discharge in other spheres: *Norwich Pharmacal Co v Customs and Excise Commissioners*[91] and *Alfred Crompton Amusement Machines Ltd v Customs and Excise Commissioners (No.2)*[92] are recent examples of cases in which the House of Lords considered the question of where the balance of the public interest lay in relation to a claim for an order of discovery."

Where public interest is relied on to justify disclosure of otherwise confidential information, the courts have drawn no distinction between the position in equity and in contract. In the case of an express contractual non-disclosure term the question is whether it is unenforceable as contrary to public policy. In cases of an alleged implied contractual obligation or an equitable obligation the question is as to the existence and scope of the obligation. The approach of the courts is the same in each case.[93]

Although each case has to be examined on its own facts, the following **6–076** general principles are suggested:

(1) Respect for confidentiality is itself a matter of public interest.

(2) To justify disclosure of otherwise confidential information on the grounds of public interest, it is not enough that it is interesting to the public.

(3) In broad summary, the disclosure must either relate to serious misconduct (actual or contemplated) or it must otherwise be important for safeguarding the public welfare in matters of health and safety, or of comparable public importance, that the information should be known by those to whom it is disclosed or proposed to be disclosed.

(4) (i) Even if the information meets that test, it does not necessarily follow that it would be proper for the defendant to disclose it.

(ii) The court must consider the relationship between the parties and the risks of harm which may be caused (or avoided) by permitting or prohibiting disclosure, both in the particular case and more generally. For example, if the law inhibits a doctor from disclosing information about a patient which

---

[91] [1974] A.C. 133.
[92] [1974] A.C. 405.
[93] *Price Waterhouse v BCCI* [1992] B.C.L.C. 583 suggests otherwise, but the observation was (arguably) obiter. The case is discussed at para.6–041, above.

may affect another person, it may lead to risk of avoidable injury or death; but if it permits a doctor to do so, it may impair a patient's willingness to confide in the doctor and receive treatment.

(5) Ultimately the court has to decide what is consciable or unconscionable, which will depend on its view of what would be acceptable to the community as a fair and proper standard of behaviour. This requires the court to make an evaluative judgment, but it does not have an unfettered discretion.

(6) In cases where the party claiming confidentiality is a branch of Government, or a body performing a governmental function, a separate principle applies. In such cases detriment to the public interest is an essential ingredient of the cause of action.

Some degree of unpredictability is inevitable, but the courts should avoid the charge of idiosyncrasy if the concept of public interest is approached in accordance with these principles.

Clean hands

6–077 The so-called "public interest" defence is not to be confused with the discretion of the court to refuse equitable relief in cases where the plaintiff is not seen to come with clean hands. That discretion applies as much to confidentiality cases as to any other.

6–078 A colourful illustration is provided by *McNicol v Sportsman's Book Stores*.[94] The plaintiff sold to subscribers a supposedly successful method of predicting horse-race winners by the age of the moon, on express terms that each purchaser would treat the information as private and confidential for his own personal use. The defendant intended to publish a review of results of using the system, without divulging its precise rules. The plaintiff's application for an injunction to restrain the defendant from doing so failed before Maugham J., among other reasons because he did not consider that the assistance of the court should be given to the plaintiff in circumstances in which:

> " . . . the poor people all over this country who are deceived into paying two guineas for this system are getting something which is perfectly worthless."[95]

6–079 Sometimes both concepts may be invoked in the same case, as, for example, in *Hubbard v Vosper*.[96] The defendant had been a member of the

---

[94] (1930) McG.C.C. 116.
[95] *ibid.* at 125. In *Spycatcher* [1990] 1 A.C. 109 at 149 Scott J. cited *McNicol* as a case where the information lacked the quality of confidence because it was trivial.
[96] [1972] 2 Q.B. 84.

Church of Scientology for 14 years. He attended a course, for which he paid a fee, and signed an undertaking not to divulge course materials to those not entitled to receive them. He later wrote a book criticising the teaching and practice of scientology. The Church (and its founders) sued the defendant, alleging breach of a contractual duty of confidence, and sought an interlocutory injunction restraining publication of his book.

Lord Denning M.R. considered that an injunction should be refused **6–080** because, on the material before the court, the courses appeared to contain such dangerous medical quackery that no confidence could be claimed to keep them secret.[97]

Megaw L.J. agreed with Lord Denning M.R., but he also referred to evidence that the plaintiffs sought to enforce secrecy on cult members by improper methods. He accepted the defendant's proposition[98]:

> "that there is here evidence that the plaintiffs are or have been protecting their secrets by deplorable means . . . and, that being so, they do not come with clean hands to this court in asking this court to protect these secrets by the equitable remedy of an injunction."

In *Church of Scientology v Kaufman*[99] Goff J. followed both approaches.

---

[97] *Hubbard v Vosper* [1972] 2 Q.B. 84 at 95–96.
[98] *ibid.* at 101.
[99] [1973] R.P.C. 627.

CHAPTER 7

Confidentiality and Privacy

7–001 English law now has a partial law of privacy. Its boundaries are uncertain and it is at a transitional stage. It has developed in a curious way involving a hybridisation of Art.8 of the European Convention and the cause of action for breach of confidence.

7–002 Articles 8 and 10 of the European Convention provide as follows:

> "*Article 8*
>
> (1) Everyone has the right to respect for his private and family life, his home and his correspondence.
>
> (2) There shall be no interference by a public authority with the exercise of this right except such as is in accordance with the law and is necessary in a democratic society in the interests of national security, public safety or the economic well-being of the country, for the prevention of disorder or crime, for the protection of health or morals, or for the protection of the rights and freedoms of others.

> *Article 10*
>
> (1) Everyone has the right to freedom of expression. This right shall include freedom to hold opinions and to receive and impart information and ideas without interference by public authority and regardless of frontiers. This Article shall not prevent States from requiring the licensing of broadcasting, television or cinema enterprises.

(2) The exercise of these freedoms, since it carries with it duties and responsibilities, may be subject to such formalities, conditions, restrictions or penalties as are prescribed by law and are necessary in a democratic society, in the interests of national security, territorial integrity or public safety, for the prevention of disorder or crime, for the protection of health or morals, for the protection of the reputation or rights of others, for preventing the disclosure of information received in confidence, or for maintaining the authority and impartiality of the judiciary."

Section 6 of the Human Rights Act 1998 provides that it is unlawful for a public authority to act in a way which is incompatible with a Convention right. A public authority includes a court.

Section 12 of the Act applies where a court is considering whether to **7–003** grant relief which might affect the exercise of a Convention right to freedom of expression. Section 12 (3) provides that there should be no pre-trial restraint on publication unless the court is satisfied that the applicant is likely to establish that publication should not be allowed. Section 12 (4) provides that:

"The court must have particular regard to the importance of the Convention right to freedom of expression and, where the proceedings relate to material which the respondent claims, or which appears to the court, to be journalistic, literary or artistic material (or to conduct connected with such material), to—
(a) the extent to which—
(i) the material has, or is about to, become available to the public; or
(ii) it is, or would be, in the public interest for the material to be published;
(b) any relevant privacy code."

Historical background: case law

Before the introduction of the Human Rights Act the courts held that the **7–004** development of rights of privacy was not a matter for the courts but for Parliament. In *Kaye v Robertson*[1] a journalist interviewed and took photographs of the plaintiff, a well-known actor, while he was in hospital suffering from severe brain injury and in no fit condition either to be interviewed or to give informed consent to be interviewed. The journalist ignored notices at the entrance to the hospital ward and on the plaintiff's door asking visitors to see a member of the medical staff before visiting. The Court of Appeal held with regret that in English law there was no right to privacy and therefore no right of action for breach of privacy.

[1] [1991] F.S.R. 62.

7–005   Leggatt L.J. said[2]:

> "This right has so long been disregarded here that it can be recognised now only by the legislature."

Bingham L.J. said[3]:

> "This case . . . highlights, yet again, the failure of both the common law of England and statute to protect in an effective way the personal privacy of individual citizens . . . . If ever a person has a right to be let alone by strangers with no public interest to pursue, it must surely be when he lies in hospital recovering from brain surgery and in no more than partial command of his faculties. It is this invasion of his privacy which underlies the plaintiff's complaint. Yet it alone, however gross, does not entitle him to relief in English law."

The court granted limited relief, under the tort of malicious falsehood, in the form of an injunction prohibiting the defendants from publishing an article which implied that the plaintiff had been interviewed and photographed with his consent. The court also held that it could not, as a matter of law, grant an injunction prohibiting the publication of the photographs so as to prevent the defendants from profiting from their own trespass.

7–006   *Kaye v Robertson* was followed by the House of Lords in *Wainwright v Home Office*.[4] Lord Hoffmann distinguished between privacy as a value underlying the existence of some legal right and privacy as a legal right in itself,[5] holding that any protection of privacy as such was a matter for Parliament.

7–007   At the same time there was a growing body of case law in which the law of confidentiality was used to protect aspects of privacy. It has long been accepted that the law of confidentiality may apply to information and materials of a personal and private nature. They may include etchings made in private[6] and photographs taken in private.[7] Such materials have about them "the necessary quality of confidence" (in the words of Lord Greene M.R. in *Saltman*[8]) to be capable of protection by an equitable obligation of confidence.

7–008   In *Argyll v Argyll*[9] an injunction was granted against the revelation of marital confidences. Commenting on that decision in *Spycatcher*,[10] Lord Keith said:

[2] [1991] F.S.R. 62 at 71.
[3] *ibid.* at 70.
[4] [2003] UKHL 53; [2004] 2 A.C. 406.
[5] *ibid.* at para.31.
[6] *Prince Albert v Strange* (1849) 2 De G. & S.M. 652.
[7] *Pollard v Photographic Company* (1889) 40 Ch.D. 345.
[8] (1948) 65 R.P.C. 203 at 215.
[9] [1967] Ch. 302.
[10] [1990] 1 A.C. 109 at 255.

"The right to personal privacy is clearly one which the law should in this field seek to protect."

When material has the necessary quality of confidence, equitable protection is not limited to cases in which it passes to a recipient under a consensual transaction, but is in principle available in cases in which the material is disclosed to the recipient under compulsion of law or is obtained by mistake known to the recipient or by improper means. If private photographs were accidentally delivered to the wrong house, the recipient who knew that they were not meant for him would be under an obligation of conscience not, for example, to sell them to a magazine, just as much as the recipient of a letter meant for somebody else and marked "Private and Confidential" would be constrained by an equitable obligation of confidence.[11]

In *Hellewell v Chief Constable of Derbyshire*[12] the plaintiff sued for **7–009** breach of confidence in relation to the use made by the police of a "mugshot" photograph of the plaintiff, taken while he was in police custody (acting under a code of practice issued by the Secretary of State under s.166 of the Police and Criminal Act 1984). The Chief Constable denied that the police owed any duty of confidence to the plaintiff in relation to the photograph. The judgment dealt with three connected issues: whether a photograph was capable of being the subject of a duty of confidence, whether the plaintiff was owed any such duty by the defendant, and what was the scope of the duty (although the judge also analysed the third issue in terms of the public interest defence).

In relation to the first matter Laws J. said[13]: **7–010**

"I entertain no doubt that disclosure of a photograph may, in some circumstances, be actionable as a breach of confidence. If a photographer is hired to take a photograph to be used only for certain purposes but uses it for an unauthorised purpose of his own, a claim may lie against him (*Pollard v Photographic Co.* (1888) 40 Ch.D. 345). That case concerned portrait photographs of a lady taken for her private use by a hired photographer who then used one of the pictures for a Christmas card which was put on sale in his shop. North J. upheld the plaintiff's claim, both in contract and breach of confidence. If someone with a telephoto lens were to take from a distance and with no authority a picture of another engaged in some private act, his subsequent disclosure of the photograph would, in my judgment, as surely amount to a breach of confidence as if he has found or stolen a letter or diary in which the act was recounted and proceeded to publish it. In such a case, the law would protect what might reasonably be

---

[11] *English & American Insurance v Herbert Smith* [1988] F.S.R. 232. *per* Sir Nicolas Browne-Wilkinson V.C.
[12] [1995] 1 W.L.R. 804.
[13] *ibid.* at 807.

called a right of privacy, although the name accorded to the cause of action would be breach of confidence."

As to the duty of the defendant, the judge held that the fact that the police took a photograph of the plaintiff, in custody and without freedom of choice, constrained them in the use to which they might lawfully put it. The circumstances in which they acted imposed a duty of confidence, breach of which would be actionable as a matter of private law. The scope of the duty was governed by what was reasonable.

7–011   There were therefore signs before the Human Rights Act of a broadening of the law of confidentiality in the area of privacy, but it was still necessary to show either that there was a breach of an underlying relationship of confidentiality or that the defendant had obtained the information in circumstances (in particular, by improper or surreptitious means, by accident or by legal compulsion) which gave rise to an equitable obligation of confidentiality.

Historical background: proposals for reform

7–012   The possibility of a statutory right of privacy was the subject of various reports by committees and various unsuccessful parliamentary bills.[14] The Report of the Law Commission in 1981 on Breach of Confidence[15] was an indirect sequel to the 1972 Report of the Younger Committee on Privacy. The Younger Committee rejected proposals that there should be a general remedy for the protection of privacy, but it recommended new remedies to cover certain specific ways in which privacy might be invaded and it drew attention to the action for breach of confidence, which it considered was potentially capable of affording greater protection to privacy than had hitherto been realised. The Committee also recommended that the action for breach of confidence should be referred to the Law Commission.

7–013   The Younger Committee was particularly concerned at the covert use of surveillance devices and recommended the creation of a criminal offence of surreptitious surveillance by means of a technical device, i.e. an electronic or optical extension of the human senses.[16] This recommendation was not implemented.

7–014   The Law Commission considered the same subject in the context of civil liability for breach of confidence and commented as follows[17]:

"To turn now to the principles which in our view should govern the imposition of an obligation of confidence upon someone who obtains information by means of a surveillance device, we believe that a

---

[14] Bills were introduced by Lord Mancroft in 1961, Alexander Lyon in 1967, Brian Walden in 1969, William Cash in 1987 and John Browne in 1989.
[15] Cmnd. 8388 (1981), para.1.2.
[16] Cmnd. 5012 (1972), paras 503 and 563.
[17] Cmnd. 8388 (1981), paras 6.37–6.38.

distinction must be made between (i) devices which are primarily designed *for the purpose of surveillance* and (ii) the wide range of devices which are not in themselves designed or adapted solely or primarily for that purpose, although they are *capable of being so used.* Examples of devices falling within the second category are ordinary binoculars, and an ordinary tape-recorder which may be used to record the conversation of participants at a meeting, either openly or secretly by hiding it under the table. There may be situations when surveillance devices of the latter kind are used to which those subject to that surveillance should not reasonably take exception, if they are or ought reasonably to be aware of it and if they could without undue inconvenience take precautions to avoid the surveillance in question. Thus, on the one hand, it may be thought that two people, who meet secretly in a secluded corner of a large railway station throughout which clear notices are displayed that television cameras are being used to detect criminal activities (such as malicious damage), cannot reasonably expect the fact of their meeting to be treated as confidential. On the other hand, it may well be that the use of an ordinary camera with a telephoto lens to obtain from the street a picture of a confidential document lying on a desk in a private house would go far beyond the reasonable expectations of the person who left it there, and that the taker of the picture should be subject to an obligation of confidence in respect of the information so obtained.

We can summarise our views on the use of surveillance devices as follows. We think that an obligation of confidence should cover information obtained by the use of *any* surveillance device, provided that such information would not have been acquired without the use of that device. However, in the case of devices which, though not designed or adapted primarily for surreptitious surveillance, enable information to be obtained which would not otherwise have been acquired, liability for the subsequent disclosure or use of that information should arise only if the person from whom the information has been obtained was not or ought not reasonably to have been aware of the use of the device, and ought not reasonably to have taken precautions to prevent the information from bring acquired in the way in question."

The Law Commission's draft Breach of Confidence Bill contained provisions to that effect,[18] but its recommendation that the law of breach of confidence should be made statutory was not adopted.

In 1989 the Government responded to a private member's bill, which **7–015** attracted wide support in the House of Commons, by appointing a committee under the chairmanship of David Calcutt Q.C. to consider the introduction of a statutory law of privacy. The Calcutt Report[19] concluded that it would be possible to create a statutory tort of infringement of

[18] Clause 5.
[19] *Report on Privacy and Related Matters* (1990) Cmnd. 1102, para.12.17.

privacy. It could specifically relate to publication of personal information (including photographs). Personal information could be defined in terms of an individual's personal life, that is to say, those aspects of life which reasonable members of society would respect as being such that an individual is ordinarily entitled to keep them to himself, whether or not they relate to his body or mind, to his home, to his family, to other personal relationships, or to his correspondence or other documents. The committee did not see advantage in laying down a more detailed statutory definition of personal information. It expressed serious reservations about a general defence labelled merely "public interest". It considered that some form of public interest defence would be necessary, but that it should be limited to cases where the defendant had reasonable grounds for believing that:

(a) publication of the personal information would contribute to the prevention, detection or exposure of any crime or other seriously anti-social conduct; or

(b) it would be necessary for the protection of public health or safety; or

(c) there would, but for the publication, be a real risk that the public, or some section of the public, would be materially misled by a statement previously made public by or on behalf of any individual whose privacy would otherwise be infringed.[20]

In 1993 Sir David Calcutt published a further report[21] recommending that the Government should give further consideration to the introduction of a statutory tort of invasion of privacy.

7–016   In 1995 the Government rejected proposals for a statutory right of privacy, but stated that the Lord Chancellor was reconsidering the Law Commission's recommendations concerning the introduction of legislation on breach of confidence.[22]

Human Rights Act 1998

7–017   The Human Rights Act presented a conundrum both because of the terms of Art.8 and because of the terms of s.6 of the Act. Article 8 recognises a right to respect for private life (in terms far more general than would be expected in a statute), but the direct obligations created by the Convention are obligations on the part of states. The Act makes it unlawful for any public authority to act in a way which is incompatible with the Convention, but it does not on its face create rights against private individuals or bodies. A direct interference by a public authority with a person's rights under Art.8 would undoubtedly be a statutory tort, but the controversial question which arose from the Act was whether the court as a public authority would be

[20] *Report on Privacy and Related Matters* (1990) Cmnd. 1102 at paras 12.22–12.23.
[21] *Review of Press Self-Regulation*, Cmnd. 2135.
[22] White Paper on *"Privacy and Media Intrusion"*, July 1995, Cmnd. 2918.

acting in a way which was incompatible with the Convention if it failed to recognise and enforce rights under Art.8 against private individuals or bodies. This question involved issues not only about the scope of the Act but about the scope of the Convention, that is to say whether and to what extent there may be a positive obligation on states to ensure that their laws protect people against infringement of Art.8 rights by other people (and not merely by the state itself).

The European Court of Human Rights had previously held that Art.8 **7–018** may require the adoption of measures to secure respect for private life between individuals.[22a] This principle was reiterated and developed in *Von Hannover v Germany*,[23] where the court said that:

> "although the object of Article 8 is essentially that of protecting the individual against arbitrary interference by public authorities, it does not merely compel the State to abstain from such interference: in addition to this primary negative undertaking, there may be positive obligations inherent in an effective respect for private or family life. These obligations may involve the adoption of measures designed to secure respect for private life even in the sphere of relations between individuals themselves. That also applies to the protection of a person's picture against abuse by others.
>
> The boundary between the State's positive and negative obligations in this respect does not lend itself to precise definition. The applicable principles are, nevertheless, similar. In both contexts regard must be had to the fair balance that must be struck between the competing interests of the individual and of the community as a whole; and in both contexts the State enjoys a certain margin of appreciation."

The courts have not in terms decided the question of the extent of the duty **7–019** imposed on courts by s.6 of the Human Rights Act, and in *Campbell v MGN Ltd*[24] Lord Nicholls said that it was unnecessary to do so. Instead they have finessed the question by holding that the law of confidentiality has absorbed the rights protected by Art.8 in regard to the use of information.

In *Venables and Thompson v News Group Newspapers Ltd*[25] Dame **7–020** Elizabeth Butler-Sloss P. granted injunctions against the whole world prohibiting publication of information about the appearance, whereabouts and new names of the claimants on their release from custody after they had served periods of detention for the murder of a small boy, which they had committed when they were aged 10. The President held that the law of confidentiality could cover the injunctions sought and that they were necessary to protect the claimants from the risk of death or serious injury. A similar injunction was granted in *X (formerly Mary Bell) v O'Brien*.[26]

[22a] *X and Y v Netherlands* (1986) 8 E.H.R.R. 235 at para.23; *Stjerna v Finland* (1997) 24 E.H.R.R. 195 at para.38; see also *Marckx v Belgium* (1979) 2 E.H.R.R. 330 at para.81.
[23] (2005) 40 E.H.R.R. 1 at para.57.
[24] [2004] UKHL 22; [2004] 2 A.C. 457 at para.18.
[25] [2001] Fam. 430.
[26] [2003] EWHC 1101.

7–021 In *A v B plc*[27]a footballer applied for an injunction to prevent a newspaper publishing lurid accounts by two women of brief affairs which he had with them after they had met in bars. The Court of Appeal held that it was able to achieve the objective of s.6 of the Human Rights Act by "absorbing the rights which articles 8 and 10 protect into the long-established action for breach of confidence."[28] There was therefore no need in the court's view to consider in relation to events after the Human Rights Act came into force "the vexed question of whether there is a separate action based upon a new tort involving the invasion of privacy".[29]

7–022 Adapting Lord Goff's statement of general principle in *Spycatcher*,[30] the court held that:

> "A duty of confidence will arise whenever the party subject to the duty is in a situation where he either knows or ought to know that the other person can reasonably expect his privacy to be protected."[31]

This test does not of itself help to determine the border between what is public and private.

7–023 On this issue the court observed that usually the question whether there was a private interest worthy of protection would be obvious; and that, if it was not obvious, an answer would often be unnecessary, because the weaker the claim for privacy the more likely it was to be outweighed by the right to freedom of expression.[32] It added:

> "The advantage of not having to distinguish between acts which are public and those which are private in a difficult case is made clear by what Gleeson CJ had to say on the subject in *Australian Broadcasting Corpn v Lenah Game Meats Pty Ltd* (2001) 185 A.L.R. 1. He explained the difficulty of distinguishing between public and private information when he said at p.13, para.42:
>
> > 'There is no bright line which can be drawn between what is private and what is not. Use of the term "public" is often a convenient method of contrast, but there is a large area in between what is necessarily public and what is necessarily private. An activity is not private simply because it is not done in public. It does not suffice to make an act private that, because it occurs on private property, it has such measure of protection from the public gaze as the characteristics of the property, the nature of the activity, the locality, and the disposition of the property owner combine to afford. Certain kinds of information about a person, such as information relating to

[27] [2002] EWCA Civ 337; [2003] Q.B. 195.
[28] *ibid.* at [4].
[29] *ibid.* at [11(vi)].
[30] [1990] 1 A.C. 109 at 281.
[31] [2003] Q.B. 195 at para.11(ix).
[32] *ibid.* at para.11(vii).

health, personal relationships, or finances, may be easy to identify as private; as may certain kinds of activity, which a reasonable person, applying contemporary standards of morals and behaviour, would understand to be meant to be unobserved. The requirement that disclosure or observation of information or conduct would be highly offensive to a reasonable person of ordinary sensibilities is in many circumstances a useful practical test of what is private.' "

The Court of Appeal rejected A's claim for an injunction, saying that:

"Relationships of the sort which A had with C and D are not the categories of relationships which the court should be astute to protect when the other parties to the relationships do not want them to remain confidential."[33]

In *Campbell v MGN Ltd*[34] a newspaper published reports and pictures of a famous fashion model attending meetings of a self-help group for drug addiction. She had previously courted media attention and had claimed untruthfully not to have a drug problem. She accepted that in those circumstances the newspaper was entitled to publish the fact that she was receiving treatment for drug addiction, but she claimed damages for breach of confidentiality in publishing the details of the meetings and the pictures, which had been taken covertly. She won her claim and was awarded £3,500 damages. The judgment was reversed by the Court of Appeal but reinstated by the House of Lords.

7–024

The decision of the House of Lords was by a majority of three to two, but there was agreement on the following principles:

7–025

(1) The action for breach of confidentiality now covers infringement of a person's right to respect for his private life under Art.8 where the infringement is in the form of disclosure of information (including pictures).

(2) The principles involved apply as much between individuals or between individuals and non-governmental bodies as they do between individuals and public authorities.

(3) Article 8 is engaged when the person publishing the information knows or ought to know that the other person can reasonably expect the information to be kept confidential because of its private nature.[35]

---

[33] [2003] Q.B. 195 at para.45.
[34] [2004] UKHL 22; [2004] 2 A.C. 457.
[35] This is a distillation of what was said by Lord Nicholls at [20]–[21], Lord Hope at [85] and Baroness Hale at [134].

Subsumed within this last proposition are two factors—that the information relates to a person's private life and that the person concerned has a reasonable expectation that it will therefore be kept confidential, as the person publishing it knows or should know.

(4) Where Arts 8 and 10 are both relevant, the court has to balance the competing considerations, neither being presumed to have priority over the other.

7–026   On the question how the courts should differentiate between what is private and what is public Lord Hope followed the approach of the Court of Appeal in *A v B plc*.[36] Echoing Gleeson C.J.'s test in *Australian Broadcasting Corpn v Lennah Game Meats Pty Ltd*, cited by the Court of Appeal in *A v B plc*, Lord Hope said that where the answer to the question whether the information was private or public was not obvious,

> "the broad test is whether disclosure of the information about the individual ("A") would give substantial offence to A, assuming that A was placed in similar circumstances and was a person of ordinary sensibilities."

Lord Nicholls and Baroness Hale took a different approach. Lord Nicholls considered that Gleeson C.J.'s "highly offensive" formula suggested an over-strict test of what was private and that it was liable to conflate the question what was private with issues which went to proportionality (the degree of intrusion into private life and the extent to which publication was a matter of proper public concern).[37] Baroness Hale considered that an objective reasonable expectation test was simpler and clearer than Gleeson C.J.'s formula, but she emphasised that the reasonable expectation of privacy test was merely a threshold test which brought into play issues of proportionality and the countervailing rights of others.[38]

7–027   Although at one level Lord Nicholls and Baroness Hale were agreed in trying to separate (a) the issue whether the claimant had a reasonable expectation of privacy and (b) issues of proportionality and countervailing interests, they disagreed about what fell within the first issue. Lord Nicholls considered that by repeatedly asserting in public that she did not use drugs Ms Campbell could no longer have a reasonable expectation that this aspect of her life should be kept private. Her claim therefore in his opinion failed at the first stage.[39] Baroness Hale considered that all the information about Ms Campbell's addiction and treatment was private, because it related to an important aspect of her physical and mental health, and confidential, because it had been received from an insider in breach of confidence.[40] Her

[36] [2004] UKHL 22; [2004] 2 A.C. 457 at [92]–[94].
[37] *ibid.* at [22].
[38] *ibid.* at [135]–[137].
[39] *ibid.* at [24]–[26].
[40] *ibid.* at [147].

public statements about drugs were relevant only to the second stage inquiry whether there was justification for publication of the information. The difference serves to demonstrate that behind the apparent simplicity of the "reasonable expectation" test lurk questions about the meaning of private life and the protection which the person concerned may legitimately expect.

In considering how far Art.8 protects a person against publication of   **7–028**
information about them or pictures of them, there are the following issues:

(1) What does Art.8 mean by "private life"?
(2) What does "respect" for private life require and how is it to be balanced against the interests either of other individuals or of the public in general?

The concept of private life in Article 8

The European Court of Human Rights has adopted a broad concept of   **7–029**
private life, based on the need to protect a person's autonomy and relationships with others from unjustifiable outside interference.

In *Niemietz v Germany*[41] a lawyer's offices were searched by police   **7–030**
looking for information about a suspect. In holding that the search violated Art.8, the Court said[42]:

> "The Court does not consider it possible or necessary to attempt an exhaustive definition of the notion of 'private life'. However, it would be too restrictive to limit the notion to an 'inner circle' in which an individual may choose to live his personal life as he chooses and to exclude entirely the outside world not encompassed within that circle. Respect for private life must also comprise to a certain degree the right to establish and develop relationships with other human beings.
>
> There appears, furthermore, to be no reason in principle why this understanding of the notion of 'private life' should be taken to exclude the activities of a professional or business nature since it is, after all, in the course of their working lives that the majority of people have a significant, if not the greatest opportunity of developing relationships with the outside world."

In *Bensaid v United Kingdom*[43] the Court said: **7–031**

> " 'Private life' is a broad term not susceptible to exhaustive definition. The Court has already held that elements such as gender identification, name and sexual orientation and sexual life are important elements of

---

[41] (1992) 16 E.H.R.R. 97.
[42] *ibid.* at para.29.
[43] (2001) 33 E.H.R.R. 208 at para.47.

the personal sphere protected by Article 8 . . . Mental health must also be regarded as a crucial part of private life associated with the aspect of moral integrity. Article 8 protects a right to identity and personal development, and the right to establish and develop relationships with other human beings and the outside world."

7–032   In *Von Hannover v Germany*[44] the German courts held that the claimant's private life was confined to what happened when she was in her home or some other secluded place out of the public eye. The European Court of Human Rights rejected this approach as too narrow. It held that the object of Art.8 is to protect the development of every human being's personality, which includes a social dimension.[45] It said:

"There is, therefore, a zone of interaction of a person with others, even in a public context, which may fall within the scope of 'private life'."[46]

The case concerned photos of the claimant in scenes from her daily life—on horseback, playing tennis, cycling, visiting a horse show, on a skiing holiday, at a beach club, leaving her house, in a restaurant and shopping. The court held that these were all activities of a purely private nature and therefore fell within the scope of her private life, even if they occurred in places which could not be described as secluded.

Respect for private life and justifiability of interference

7–033   Unauthorised disclosure or use of information about a person's private life will be a violation of Art.8 only if the following conditions are satisfied:

(1) it is sufficiently serious to cause substantial offence to a person of ordinary sensibilities; and

(2) there is no good and sufficient reason for it—"good" meaning a reason capable of justifying the interference, and "sufficient" meaning sufficient to outweigh the person's Art.8 rights on a balance of the legitimate competing interests.

Serious interference and the ordinary incidents of social living

7–034   Not every disclosure of information about a person's private or family life or home will necessarily cross the threshold of interfering with their rights under Art.8. The disclosure may be too limited or trivial.

---

[44] (2005) 40 E.H.R.R. 1.
[45] *ibid.* at paras 50, 69 and 74.
[46] *ibid.* at para.50.

In *McKennitt v Ash*[47] the claimant was a celebrated composer and   **7–035**
performer of folk music. The defendant was a close friend, who sometimes
worked with the claimant in connection with her business and on one
occasion accompanied her on a foreign tour under a contract containing a
confidentiality clause. They fell out, particularly over a property bought by
the defendant and her partner with the claimant's help. The dispute resulted
in High Court proceedings, which were settled privately through the
mechanism of a Tomlin order. The defendant then published a book entitled
"Travels with Loreena McKennitt: My life as a Friend". The claimant sued
for breach of privacy and confidentiality, relying both on the nature of their
confidential relationship and on Art.8.

Eady J. described some of the disclosures as anodyne and held that they   **7–036**
were insufficiently intimate or intrusive to require protection from disclosure. For example, he said about the description of a shopping trip[48]:

> "It is trivial and of no consequence, and unlike relatively trivial but
> intrusive descriptions of a person's home, there is no need for the law
> to step in and offer protection. Nor is it likely to cause significant
> distress or other harm to, say, a celebrity or anyone else, that a friend
> accompanied her on a shopping trip and managed to bargain with
> vendors to save money. It is anodyne and not such as to attract any
> obligation of confidence. I do not even need to ask whether there is any
> public interest—although, of course, there is not."

As indicated in that passage, the judge took a stricter view of descriptions   **7–037**
of the claimant's home. He held that even relatively trivial details would fall
within the protection of Art.8, because of the traditional sanctity accorded
to hearth and home, and he observed[49]:

> "To describe a person's home, the décor, the layout, the state of
> cleanliness, or how occupiers behave inside it, is generally regarded as
> unacceptable. To convey such details, without permission, to the
> general public is almost as objectionable as spying into the home with
> a long distance lens and publishing the resulting photographs."

The judge upheld complaints about disclosures regarding the claimant's
health, her relationship with her fiancé and her reaction to his death by
drowning.

He also upheld her complaint about disclosure of details regarding the   **7–038**
acquisition of the property which had led to previous litigation. He held that
she was entitled to expect that the arrangements by which she advanced
money to the defendant and her partner would be kept private, and that the
confidentiality had not been lost by proceedings which had resulted in a
private settlement.

---

[47] [2005] EWHC 3003, QB.
[48] *ibid.* at [139].
[49] *ibid.* at [135].

7–039   Although a person's private life is not confined to activities which take place in seclusion, the level of privacy which a person can reasonably expect to enjoy for private activities carried on in public surroundings will vary according to the nature of the activities and their context. A person is entitled to enjoy social relationships without undue outside interference, but not to protection from the ordinary incidents of social living.

7–040   A person, for example, who attends a sporting event could not complain if his face appears on television in a picture of the crowd. By contrast, in *Von Hannover v Germany* a photograph of the claimant visiting a horse show was held to infringe her right to respect for her private life, but that was in the context of her being targeted by paparazzi. The European Court of Human Rights observed that "photos appearing in the tabloid press are often taken in a climate of continual harassment that induces in the persons concerned a very strong sense of intrusion into their private life or even of persecution".[50] The court rejected the view that public figures are required to accept such intrusion as an ordinary part of daily life. It also stated[51]:

> "Furthermore, increased vigilance in protecting private life is necessary to contend with new communication technologies which make it possible to store and reproduce personal data. This also applies to the systematic taking of specific photos and their dissemination to a broad section of the public."

7–041   *Von Hannover v Germany* and *Campbell v MGN Ltd* both demonstrate the courts' sensitivity to the particularly intrusive effect which the use of cameras can have on a person's sense of privacy.[52] In *Campbell v MGN Ltd* Lord Hope addressed the difference between the ordinary incidents of social living and subjection to intrusive photography[53]:

> "The taking of photographs in a public street must, as Randerson J. said in *Hosking v Runting* [2003] 3 N.Z.L.R. 385, 415, para.138, be taken to be one of the ordinary incidents of living in a free community. The real issue is whether publicising the content of the photographs would be offensive: Gault and Blanchard JJ. in the Court of Appeal [2004] N.Z.C.A. 34, para.165 . . .
>
> Miss Campbell could not have complained if the photographs had been taken to show the scene in the street by a passer-by and later published simply as street scenes. But these were not just pictures of a street scene where she happened to be when the photographs were taken. They were taken deliberately, in secret and with a view to publication with the article. The zoom lens was directed at the doorway

---

[50] (2005) 40 E.H.R.R. 1 at para.59.
[51] *ibid.* at para.70.
[52] See also *D v L* [2003] EWCA Civ 1169; [2004] E.M.L.R. 1 at 10, where Waller L.J. said that a court may restrain the publication of an improperly obtained photograph even if the taker is free to describe the information which the photograph provides or if the information portrayed by the photograph is already in the public domain.
[53] [2004] 2 A.C. 457; [2004] UKHL 22 at paras 122–124.

of the place where the meeting had been taking place. The faces of others in the doorway were pixelated so as not to reveal their identity. Hers was not, the photographs were published and her privacy was invaded . . .

Any person in Miss Campbell's position, assuming her to be of ordinary sensibilities but assuming also that she had been photographed surreptitiously outside the place where she had been receiving treatment for drug addiction, would have known what they were and would have been distressed on seeing the photographs. She would have seen their publication, in conjunction with the article which revealed what she had been doing when she was photographed and other details about her engagement in the therapy, as a gross interference with her right to respect for her family life."

There is some difficulty in regarding the interference as happening only at the moment when an intrusive photograph is published. If a person is targeted by photographers when at home or involved in activities of a private nature, that in itself is an interference with their right to respect for their private life, which may cause a strong and legitimate sense of harassment. However, because of the way in which rights of privacy have been developed within the framework of confidentiality, the courts have not yet reached the stage of treating such interference as directly actionable. From the viewpoint of the mischief against which Art.8 is aimed, such a development seems natural, if not inevitable. **7–042**

Technological surveillance for security purposes in shops and other public places has become an ordinary incident of life in many situations, but that does not give the organisers carte blanche in the use made of the material recorded. *Peck v United Kingdom*[54] illustrates the distinction in this context between the ordinary incidents of social living and a serious interference with respect for a person's private life. Late one evening the claimant, who was suffering from depression, tried to commit suicide in the street by cutting his wrists with a kitchen knife. The incident was partially recorded on a CCTV system which had been installed by the local council and was linked to the police. Police officers came and took him to the police station, where he was detained under the Mental Health Act. He was later released without charge after examination and treatment by a doctor. The council released footage of the incident to the media, and pictures from which the claimant could be identified were shown in newspapers and on television. The European Court of Human Rights said[55]: **7–043**

"As a result, the relevant moment was viewed to an extent which far exceeded any exposure to a passer-by or to security observation and to a degree surpassing that which the applicant could possibly have foreseen . . .

[54] (2003) 36 E.H.R.R. 41.
[55] *ibid.* at paras 62–63.

Accordingly, the Court considers that the disclosure by the Council of the relevant footage constituted a serious interference with the applicant's respect for his private life."

7–044 In *Halford v United Kingdom*[56] the court was concerned with electronic surveillance of a different kind. Personal calls made by the claimant on her office telephone were covertly intercepted by her employer. The court held that calls made from business premises as well as from the home could be covered by the concept of private life. It rejected the argument that an employer was entitled to intercept calls made by an employee on a telephone provided by the employer as an ordinary incident of their relationship.

Justification for interference

7–045 An individual's interest in not having information about his private life published has to be set against the freedoms of others, particularly the right to freedom of expression under Art.10, and the interests of the general public.

7–046 It is necessary to distinguish between (a) cases where the person by or to whom the information is being disclosed has some personal interest in it, which may justify its disclosure independently of any wider public interest, and (b) cases where the information has nothing to do with the person disclosing it or the person to whom it is being disclosed, but public interest is advanced as justification for the disclosure.

Disclosure by or to someone with a personal interest in the disclosure being made

7–047 Freedom of expression includes the right of people not only to express their own views but to talk about their own experiences (regardless of any general public interest), provided that it does not involve breaking a trust or confidence.

7–048 In *McKennitt v Ash*[57] the defendant argued that she should be permitted to tell her own story. The argument was weakened by the description of the book on its cover as "a must for every Loreena McKennitt fan" and the judge's conclusion that much of its content would have been of no interest to anyone but for the fact that the claimant was its central character. It was not an autobiography in which disclosures about the claimant were merely incidental. In any case, as the judge observed[58]:

---

[56] (1997) 24 E.H.R.R. 523.
[57] [2005] EWHC 3003, QB.
[58] *ibid.* at [13].

"It does not follow, because one can reveal one's own private life, that one can also expose confidential matters in respect of which others are entitled to protection if their consent is not forthcoming."

The key issue is the extent to which the other person is entitled to protection. It has particular relevance in the context of "kiss and tell" stories, where there is seldom a public interest in publication, but the question is whether the teller is free to publish their own story. In *Barrymore v News Group Newspapers Ltd*[59] Jacob J. said that "when people kiss and later one of them tells, that second person is almost certainly breaking a confidential relationship", but in *A v B plc*[60] the Court of Appeal held that the court should not be astute to protect the confidentiality of a transient sexual relationship when the other party to the relationship does not want it to remain confidential.[61]

7–049

There is a considerable difficulty in trying to measure the degree of mutual commitment and expectation of confidentiality in such a personal area, especially when a court is having to consider the matter on an interlocutory application at short notice and on limited evidence. It is suggested that a person's right to respect for their private life under Art.8 should prima facie include their intimate physical relationships, but that is not to say that whenever sexual activity occurs there must be a relationship of a kind which would give rise to a legitimate mutual expectation of confidentiality.

7–050

In *Theakston v MGN Ltd* the claimant attempted to restrain publication by a newspaper of prostitutes' account of a visit by the claimant to a brothel and photographs of their activities. Ouseley J. refused to restrain publication of the story, saying[62]:

7–051

"I can see no reason why the question of confidentiality should be judged solely from the point of view of one participant in the activities and in the relationship, if it can be so called. The prostitutes clearly took a different view of what they had seen and done with the claimant. If a well known man has sexual relations with a prostitute in a brothel, the desire on his part to keep their actions and 'relationship' confidential and the desire on the part of the other to exploit their actions and relationship commercially are irreconcilable. There was no express stipulation for confidentiality... It is not inherent in the nature of a brothel that all or anything that transpires within it is confidential. The relationship between a prostitute in a brothel and the customer is not confidential of its nature and the fact that they participate in sexual activity does not in my judgment constitute a sufficient basis by itself for the attribution to the relationship, if such it be, of confidentiality."

[59] [1997] F.S.R. 600 at 603.
[60] [2002] EWCA Civ 337; [2003] Q.B. 195.
[61] *ibid.* at [43] and [45].
[62] *ibid.* at [64].

The judge did, however, grant an injunction against publication of the photographs because the publication of photographs of him taken without his consent could properly be seen as an intrusion into his personal and private life, and there was no public interest to justify their publication.[63]

7–052   In *Douglas v Hello! Ltd (No. 3)*[64] the Court of Appeal observed that to date the English courts appear to have taken a less generous view of the protection that an individual can reasonably expect in respect of his or her sexual activities than has the European Court of Human Rights.

7–053   The difference has been in the English and European courts' approach to the subject. In *A v B plc* the Court of Appeal approached the matter by considering whether morally the relationships between the applicant and those with whom he had brief affairs merited any or much protection. The court rejected as objectionable the view taken by the judge at first instance that in the context of modern sexual relations it should make no difference to a person's rights under Art.8 whether a relationship was within marriage or outside marriage. It held that there was a significant difference between the confidentiality which attaches to what is intended to be a permanent relationship and that which attaches to a more casual relationship. It did not go so far as to say that transient sexual relationships could never be entitled to any confidentiality, but it described them as being "at the outer limits of relationships which require the protection of the law".[65] The interest in freedom of speech was therefore much more likely to prevail, at least where one party did not want the relationship to remain confidential.

7–054   The approach of the European Court has been to regard sexual activities between consenting adults in private as ordinarily constituting a particularly intimate aspect of private life protected by Art.8.[66] The limits were explored in the contrasting cases of *Laskey, Jaggard and Brown v UK* and *ADT v UK*.

7–055   In *Laskey, Jaggard and Brown v UK* the applicants were members of a sado-masochistic group. They were convicted of offences of unlawful wounding or assault occasioning actual bodily harm under s.20 or s.47 of the Offences against the Person Act 1861, and their convictions were upheld by a majority of the House of Lords.[67] Their complaint that their convictions violated their right to respect for their private lives under Art.8 was rejected by the European Court. The court observed that not every sexual activity carried out behind closed doors necessarily fell within the scope of Art.8. It noted that in the applicants' case a considerable number of people were involved in the activities, which included recruitment of new people to the group, the provision of specially equipped chambers and the making of video recordings which were distributed to members of the group. The court said that in these particular circumstances it was open to question whether

---

[63] [2002] EWCA Civ 337; [2003] Q.B. 195 at paras 77–80.
[64] [2005] EWCA Civ 595; [2006] Q.B. 125 at [73].
[65] [2002] EWCA Civ 195; [2003] Q.B. 195 at [43(ii)] and [47].
[66] *Dudgeon v UK* (1981) 4 E.H.R.R. 149; *Norris v Ireland* [1988] E.C.H.R. 22; *Modinos v Cyprus* [1993] E.C.H.R. 19; *Laskey, Jaggard and Brown v UK* [1997] E.C.H.R. 4; (1997) 24 E.H.R.R. 39; *ADT v UK* [2000] E.C.H.R. 402; (2000) 31 E.H.R.R. 303.
[67] [1994] 1 A.C. 212.

their sexual activities fell entirely within the notion of private life,[68] but it proceeded on the basis that Art.8 was engaged since the Government had not disputed it. The Government relied, as justification for interfering with the applicants' private lives, on the qualification in Art.8(2) concerning the protection of health or morals. The court accepted that the interference was justifiable for the protection of health, because the evidence showed that there was risk of significant injury, and that on that ground there was no violation of Art.8. It made no decision on the question whether the interference was justifiable on the ground of protection of morals.[69]

In *ADT v UK* the applicant was convicted of an offence of gross **7–056** indecency. He and four others took part in group homosexual activities of a non-violent kind at his home, which were filmed. His complaint that his conviction violated his right to respect for his private life was upheld by the European Court. The Government argued (relying on what had been said in *Laskey, Jaggard and Brown v UK*) that his activities did not fall within Art.8 because of the filming and the number of people involved. The court rejected the argument, saying that the only matter which could cast doubt on whether Art.8 applied was the filming of the activities, but that the evidence did not suggest that there was any likelihood of the films being made public.[70] The court considered that the applicant's activities were genuinely private, and it held that only a narrow margin of appreciation should be afforded to national authorities in an area involving intimate aspects of private life.[71] It accepted that at some point sexual activities could be carried out in such a way that state interference could be justified, but in the absence of public health considerations there was no justification for interference in the applicant's case.

Since the court has held that the obligations of the state go beyond **7–057** refraining from interfering with a person's rights under Art.8 and may require domestic law positively to protect them, it can be only a matter of time before it is asked to consider a case of publication of a kiss and tell story about a celebrity.

There is an obvious difference between a person who goes to a brothel **7–058** and non-commercial sexual activities. In the case of the former, there is much force in Ouseley J.'s reasoning in *Theakston v MGN Ltd* and it may well be held that Art.8 is not engaged (in the absence of surreptitious photography or the like), regardless of any justification for disclosure. But in the case of genuinely private sexual activities between consenting partners, Art.8 is plainly engaged.

The wider the disclosure of such matters, the greater the interference with **7–059** the rights protected by Art.8 and the stronger the need for justification. The fact that one party is publicly well known should be irrelevant, unless there is a genuine public interest sufficiently strong to justify the particular degree of interference in a particularly intimate area.

---

[68] [1997] E.C.H.R. 4 at para.36.
[69] *ibid.* at paras 43–46, 51.
[70] [2000] E.C.H.R. 402 at para.25.
[71] *ibid.* at para.37.

7–060   The scale of disclosure (both the size or potential size of the audience and the extent of the details revealed) may be highly relevant not only to the question whether there has been prima facie interference with a person's rights under Art.8 but also to the question of justification. Disclosure of details of an affair to a friend, or to the other party's partner or employer, would involve different considerations in each case, and these would be significantly different from the considerations involved where a story is sold to a newspaper with a view to disclosure to those who have no personal connection with the parties involved.

7–061   Sharing life's experiences, romantic or otherwise, with friends and family is a normal part of social living, because people naturally look to those who are close to them for support and interest in each other's affairs. It falls within the "zone of interaction of a person with others" which Art.8 is intended to support.[72]

7–062   There may be other cases where someone to whom disclosure is made has a personal interest or involvement such that there could be no reasonable or legitimate expectation that the matter should be kept private from them. A person who deceives a partner by having an affair with someone else may hope and expect not to be caught out, but the courts are unlikely to regard it as a legitimate expectation meriting protection under Art.8 from disclosure to the other person concerned. Whether an employer or business partner would fall into the category of someone with such an interest or involvement that there could be no reasonable or legitimate expectation that the matter should be kept private from them would depend on the particular facts. For example, the partners in a medical practice would have a strong interest in knowing that one of them was having an affair with a patient, but not in knowing about the private life of a bookkeeper or receptionist.

Public interest

7–063 Cases in which public interest is advanced most commonly involve either public authorities or the media. The grounds available to public authorities are limited by Art.8(2). In cases involving the media, s.12(4) of the Human Rights Act requires the court to have particular regard not only to the importance of the Convention right to freedom of expression, but also to the extent to which it is or would be in the public interest for the material to be published and to any relevant privacy code. The codes of practice for journalists and broadcasters published by the Press Complaints Commission and Ofcom are considered in greater detail in Chapter 13.

7–064   The court is also prohibited by s.12(3) from restraining publication before trial unless satisfied that the applicant is likely to establish that publication should not be allowed. This provision was interpreted by the House of Lords in *Cream Holdings Ltd v Banerjee*[73] as having the effect that a court should not make an interim restraint order unless satisfied that

---

[72] See *Torbay Borough Council v News Group Newspapers* [2003] EWHC 2927, Fam; [2004] E.M.L.R. 18 at [35], *per* Munby J.
[73] [2004] UKHL 44; [2005] 1 A.C. 253.

the applicant's prospects of success at trial were sufficiently favourable to justify the order being made in the light of all the other circumstances; and that in general the court should be exceedingly slow to make such an order unless satisfied that the applicant would probably succeed at trial, although this was not a rigid test.

The European Court of Human Rights and domestic courts have **7–065** repeatedly emphasised the vital role of the press in a democratic society both as a watchdog and as a medium for public education and the dissemination of ideas. In *Von Hannover v Germany* the European Court of Human Rights held that the decisive factor in balancing the protection of private life against freedom of expression should lie in the contribution that the published photos and articles made to a debate of general interest.[74]

It said[75]: **7–066**

"The Court considers that a fundamental distinction needs to be made between reporting facts—even controversial ones—capable of contributing to a debate in democratic society relating to politicians in the exercise of their functions, for example, and reporting details of the private life of an individual who, moreover, as in this case, does not exercise official functions. While in the former case the press exercises its vital role of 'watchdog' in a democracy by contributing to imparting information and ideas on matters of public interest it does not do so in the latter case.

Similarly, although the public has a right to be informed, which is an essential right in a democratic society that, in certain special circumstances, can even extend to aspects of the private life of public figures, particularly where politicians are concerned, this is not the case here. The situation here does not come within the sphere of any political or public debate because the published photos and accompanying commentaries relate exclusively to details of the applicant's private life.

As in other similar cases it has examined, the Court considers that the publication of the photos and articles in question, of which the sole purpose was to satisfy the curiosity of a particular readership regarding the details of the applicant's private life, cannot be deemed to contribute to any debate of general interest to society despite the applicant being well known to the public."

The role of the press as a medium for public education may include **7–067** putting the record straight when a person has previously presented a false public picture. In *Campbell v MGN Ltd* the claimant's treatment for drug addiction would have been a private matter which the press had no right to publicise but for the fact that she had presented herself to the public as someone who was not involved in drugs. The mode of disclosure went beyond what a majority of the House of Lords considered to be justified

---

[74] (2005) 40 E.H.R.R. 1 at para.76.
[75] *ibid.* at paras 63–65.

because of the publication of photographs taken of her outside the place where she had been receiving treatment.

7–068 If a person has not set out to present a false picture, it is not part of the watchdog role of the press to seek to obtain information about their private life and then put it to them in order to place them in the dilemma of admitting it (thereby giving voluntary disclosure), refusing to comment (thereby seeming to be evasive) or denying it (thereby risking publication in order to rebut the denial).

7–069 Where the justification put forward for publication of personal information is not that the person concerned has made false factual statements but has been guilty of hypocrisy in advocating a set of standards and behaving differently, much will depend on the particular circumstances, including the person's role (for example, whether he holds or is a candidate for public office) and to what extent the conduct is truly hypocritical.

7–070 In *McKennitt v Ash*[76] the defendant sought to justify publication on the basis that the claimant's conduct belied the standards of behaviour set out on her website as her "compass points". These included a number of goals such as "Be compassionate and never forget how to love". The judge described them as a fragile peg on which to hang a public interest defence. The claimant recommended them as goals to which she and others could aspire, but had never claimed to have fulfilled them throughout her life. He observed that it could not be right that any person in the public eye who chose to share his or her aspirations with fans or the general public would immediately become vulnerable to having every detail in their private lives exposed to public scrutiny.

Public domain

7–071 This subject has been considered in Chapter 3. Publication of information which would otherwise be protected by Art.8 will only be justified on the ground that it is in the public domain if it has been so fully publicised that further publication could not reasonably be expected to cause damage or distress to the person concerned.

7–072 For example, in *Green Corns Ltd v Claverly Group Ltd*[77] a children's home provider applied for an injunction to restrain a local newspaper from publishing the addresses of homes provided for troubled children. The newspaper had published a number of articles reporting that homes had been bought by the claimants to house sex offenders and troubled teenagers in the local community and the addresses of the homes were included. Tugendhat J. rejected the argument that an injunction should be refused on the ground that the information was already in the public domain. He said[78]:

---

[76] [2005] EWHC 3003, QB; [2006] E.M.L.R. 10 at [98]–[100].
[77] [2005] EWHC 958, QB; [2005] E.M.L.R. 31.
[78] *ibid.* at [81].

"I conclude that the information as to the addresses which is sought to be restrained is not in the public domain to the extent, or in the sense, that republication could have no significant effect, or that the information is not eligible for protection at all. The information as to the addresses linked with information as to the business of the applicant and thus to the likely disabilities and other characteristics of the occupants of the addresses brings together matters which together amount to new information which was previously available to the public only in a limited and theoretical sense. Publication or republication risks causing serious harm to the children and carers who occupy, or are about to occupy, the addresses concerned."

In *Douglas v Hello! Ltd (No. 3)*[79] the Douglases contracted with OK! magazine to give it exclusive rights to publish photographs of their wedding. The Douglases were to control which photographs could be published, but they undertook to use their best endeavours to prevent any other media from having access to the wedding and to prevent any guests from taking photographs. Despite elaborate security arrangements, a paparazzo succeeded in gate crashing the event and took photographs which were sold to OK!'s rival Hello! The Douglases and the publishers of OK! sued the publishers of Hello! **7–073**

It was argued by Hello! that after the Douglases entered into their contract with OK! publication of other photographs of the event could not infringe their rights under Art.8, since they had chosen that the event should be publicised. The Court of Appeal rejected the argument, observing that it was wrong to suppose that a person who authorised the publication of selected personal photographs taken on a private occasion would not reasonably feel distress at the publication of unauthorised photographs taken on the same occasion.[80] **7–074**

The court also commented more generally on the propensity of unauthorised personal photographs to cause distress not only on publication but on re-publication[81]: **7–075**

"Once intimate personal information about a celebrity's private life has been widely published it may serve no useful purpose to prohibit further publication. The same will not necessarily be true of photographs. Insofar as a photograph does more than convey information and intrudes on privacy by enabling the individual to focus on intimate personal detail, there will be a fresh intrusion of privacy when each additional viewer sees the photograph and even when one who has seen a previous publication of the photograph is confronted with a fresh publication of it. To take an example, if a film star were photographed, with the aid of a telephoto lens, lying naked by her private swimming pool, we question whether widespread publication of the photograph

---

[79] [2005] EWCA 595; [2006] Q.B. 125.
[80] *ibid.* at [106]–[107].
[81] *ibid.* at [105].

by a popular newspaper would provide a defence to a legal challenge to repeated publication on the ground that the information was in the public domain."

The ultimate balancing exercise

7–076 In *Re S*[82] Lord Steyn (with whom the other members of the House of Lords agreed) reiterated that neither Art.8 nor Art.10 as such has priority over the other. When both are engaged, "an intense focus on the comparative importance of the specific rights being claimed in the individual case is necessary". The justifications for interfering with each right must be taken into account and an ultimate balancing exercise carried out.[83]

7–077 The case concerned an eight-year-old boy, who was the subject of care proceedings brought by his local authority. His mother faced trial for murder of his older brother by allegedly poisoning him with salt. The issue was whether an order should be made prohibiting the press from publishing the names or photographs of the mother or the deceased child so as to prevent avoidable distress to the boy from the publicity surrounding the trial. The court accepted that Art.8 was engaged and that the trial with its publicity was bound to be deeply painful for him, but in measuring the impact Lord Steyn observed that it was essentially indirect. There would be no reference at the trial to the boy, his private life or his upbringing. On the other hand, an injunction preventing the press from identifying the mother or the deceased child would be a direct interference with the freedom of the press to perform the important function of reporting criminal trials. The function is important because full contemporaneous reporting of criminal trials promotes public confidence in the administration of justice and the values of the rule of law. A report of the trial without revealing the identity of the defendant would be a "very much disembodied trial". The court concluded that the arguments under Art.8 were insufficient to outweigh the arguments under Art.10.

7–078 The case may be contrasted on its facts with *A Local Authority v W*,[84] where the issue was similar but the result was different. A mother of two small children was due to be sentenced for knowingly infecting the father of one of them with the HIV virus. The children were the subject of care proceedings. Sir Mark Potter P. granted an injunction on the application of the local authority to prevent the publication of the identities of the parents or any other information likely to lead to the identification of the children. Although the children were too young to be aware themselves of any publicity, the judge accepted that there was a serious risk of short term and long term prejudice to their welfare if their association with the parties involved in the criminal proceedings became known in the communities where they were living or where the local authority might seek to place them.

---

[82] [2004] UKHL 47; [2005] A.C. 593.
[83] *ibid.* at [17].
[84] [2005] EWHC 1564; [2006] 1 FLR 1, Fam. See Ch.21 for further discussion of *Re S* and *A Local Authority v W*.

Privacy and commercialism

Douglas v Hello! Ltd (No. 3) raised novel issues about personal privacy and commercial exploitation. The purpose of Art.8 is to protect a person from unwanted intrusion into his private life. A person may choose to reveal details about his private life, either in photographic form or otherwise, for commercial purposes. The Douglases did so by their contract with OK! The case raised questions about the extent to which (a) the Douglases and (b) OK! were entitled to use the law of confidentiality to protect their commercial interests. **7–079**

Lindsay J. awarded the Douglases £3,750 each for their personal distress and £7,000 jointly for the labour and expense in expediting their selection of photographs because of the impending publication by Hello!.[85] The Court of Appeal commented that this sum could only have reflected damage or the cost of mitigating damage to their commercial interest in the information about their wedding. He awarded £1,033,156 to OK! as damages for lost revenue resulting from Hello! spoiling OK!'s opportunity to exploit exclusive photographic coverage of the wedding. The basis of his reasoning was that the case was analogous to commercial confidence cases where it was common for the benefit of the confidentiality to be shared with another person who could thereafter enforce it. **7–080**

The Court of Appeal upheld the award in favour of the Douglases but reversed the decision in favour of OK! In relation to the Douglases's claim, the court acknowledged that recognition of the right of a celebrity to make money out of publicising private information about himself, including photographs taken on a private occasion, broke new ground and had echoes of the "image rights" recognised by French and German law, but it saw no reason in principle why equity should not protect the opportunity to profit from commercial information about oneself in the same circumstances that it protects the opportunity to profit from confidential information in the nature of a trade secret.[86] **7–081**

In relation to OK!'s claim, the court rejected the argument that there could be any proprietary interest in information about the wedding. The Douglases' right to protection depended not on any property right, but on the effect on the conscience of a third party's knowledge of the nature of the information and the circumstances in which it was obtained.[87] **7–082**

The court appears to have accepted the proposition that **7–083**

"where the benefit of confidential information is shared between A and B, B can claim that disclosure of that information will constitute a breach of duty of confidence owed to B."[88]

---

[85] [2005] EWCA 595; [2006] Q.B. 125, at [36].
[86] *ibid.* at [113].
[87] *ibid.* at [126]–[127].
[88] *ibid.* at [129].

However, it held that the contract between the Douglases and OK! had not purported to transfer to, or share with, OK! the right to use any photographic information about the wedding other than the approved photographs released to OK! by the Douglases for publication. Although the Douglases retained a residual right of privacy or confidentiality in those details of the wedding which were not portrayed by the official photographs released to OK!, it was the Douglases and not OK! who had the sole right to protect that area of privacy or confidentiality.[89] OK!'s claim therefore failed.

7–084   The terms of the contract provided that the Douglases would procure the taking of photographs of the wedding (described as the official photographs); that they would provide OK! with approved photographs selected from the official photographs; that OK! should have exclusive rights to publish the approved photographs for a period of nine months; and that the Douglases would use their best efforts to ensure that nobody else took photographs of the wedding.

7–085   The aim, in summary, was that OK! should have exclusive rights to publish photographs of the wedding for nine months, and that the published photographs should be only ones which the Douglases had approved. If the contract had been so expressed, it would appear from the Court of Appeal's reasoning that OK!'s claim would have succeeded. Its claim failed on what may seem rather narrow grounds based on the form of wording of the contract. The House of Lords has given permission to appeal.

7–086   The Court of Appeal's ruling that there is no proprietary interest in confidential information is welcome.[90] So too is its apparent approval of the proposition that if A passes confidential information to B, for B's sole or joint benefit, a third party may owe an equitable obligation of confidentiality to B (subject to the third party's state of knowledge). It is not difficult to envisage circumstances where it is just that this should be so, and there are precedents supporting the proposition. The Court of Appeal referred[91] to *Gilbert v Star Newspaper Ltd*[92] and *Mustad & Son v Dosen*[93] (which had been cited by Linday J.). An earlier example is *Morison v Moat*,[94] where the plaintiff's father provided details of "Morison's Universal Medicine" in confidence to the defendant's father. It was held that the plaintiff was entitled to prevent its use by the defendant, not on the ground of property but on the ground of an equitable obligation owed to the plaintiff.

7–087   The novel feature of *Douglas v Hello Ltd!* was that, leaving aside the personal distress to the Douglases from the publication of the unauthorised photographs (which the judge considered to be modest in that the damages awarded to them under that head were £3,750 each), the case was not about

[89] [2005] EWCA 595; [2006] Q.B. 125 at [131]–[136].
[90] The issue is considered in further detail in Ch.2.
[91] [2005] EWCA Civ 595; [2006] Q.B. 125 at [129]–[130].
[92] (1894) 11 T.L.R. 4.
[93] [1964] 1 W.L.R. 109n.
[94] (1851) 9 Hare 241.

the Douglases' enjoyment of personal privacy but about Hello!'s interference with the commercial exploitation of an event in their private lives which the Douglases had decided to commercialise in a particular way.

It is right that the law should protect a person from unwanted exposure **7–088** of his private life to the scrutiny of the general public. To that end, English law treats photographs of private activities as information protected by the law of confidentiality. The particular characteristic of photographs is, as the Court of Appeal put it,[95] that

> "They enable the person viewing the photograph to act as a spectator, in some circumstances voyeur would be the more appropriate noun, of whatever it is that the photograph depicts."

Applied to celebrities, that characteristic and the public appetite for it can create not only vulnerability to intrusive and unwanted publicity but also valuable commercial opportunities. *Douglas v Hello! Ltd (No. 3)* is authority that a person who chooses to allow disclosure to the general public of selected photographs of an otherwise private event, for commercial purposes, is entitled to rely on the law of confidentiality for protection against commercial damage resulting from unauthorised disclosure of improperly obtained similar material by another.

Privacy and companies

In *R v Broadcasting Standards Commission Ex p. BBC*[96] it was held that a **7–089** company could make a complaint under the Broadcasting Act 1996 of unwarranted infringement of its privacy, but that was because of the particular language of the statute and its underlying purpose. Commenting more generally, Lord Mustill observed[97] that an infringement of privacy is an affront to the personality in a sense which cannot be applied to an impersonal corporate body. Many things which could be presented by an individual as a breach of privacy could also amount to wrongs to a company, such as clandestine copying of documents, but when done to a company such conduct would lack the extra dimension of intrusion into the personal space of an individual. A company may have secrets, but that is different from the essentially human concept of privacy.

In *Australian Broadcasting Corporation v Lennah Game Meats Pty Ltd*[98] **7–090** the High Court of Australia considered, but did not need to decide, whether Australian law recognises a cause of action for breach of privacy and, if so, whether it may be available to a company.

---

[95] [2005] EWCA Civ 595; [2006] Q.B. 125 at [84].
[96] [2001] Q.B. 885.
[97] *ibid.* at paras 48–49.
[98] [2001] H.C.A. 63; 208 C.L.R. 199.

7–091   Gleeson C.J. observed[99] that he could see no reason why some internal corporate communications were any less private than those of a partnership or an individual; but that the foundation of much of what is protected, where rights of privacy are acknowledged, is human dignity.

7–092   Gaudron,[1] Gummow and Hayne JJ. examined the development of authority in the United States[2] and considered that any development in Australia of a tort of invasion of privacy should be for the benefit of natural, not artificial, persons.[3] Kirby J. was also doubtful whether a company was apt to enjoy any common law right to privacy, but refrained from expressing a final view.[4] Callinan J. was more favourable to the possibility that in some circumstances a company might be able to enjoy the same or similar rights to privacy as a natural person.[5]

7–093   The broad statements of the European Court of Human Rights about the object of Art.8 being to protect an individual's personal development and relationships with other human beings from unjustifiable outside interference are by their nature applicable only to human beings, not inanimate entities. However, in *Societe Colas Est v France*[6] the court upheld complaints by a number of companies under Art.8, stating that[7]:

> "Building on its dynamic interpretation of the Convention, the Court considers that the time has come to hold that in certain circumstances the rights guaranteed by Art.8 of the Convention may be construed as including the right to respect for a company's registered office, branches or other business premises (see, *mutatis mutandis, Niemietz*)."

The complaints arose from raids by Government officials of the applicants' offices, during which documents were seized. The raids were part of an investigation into suspected corruption in the construction industry. The purpose was to find evidence of unlawful agreements between public works contractors in the award of roadwork contracts. The court accepted that this was a legitimate purpose for interfering with the companies' right to respect for their premises, but it held that the circumstances and manner in which the raids were conducted made the interference disproportionate to the legitimate aims pursued. The seizure of the documents resulted in the companies being fined for breaches of competition law. The companies asked the court to award them reimbursement of the fines. It refused to do so, but awarded each company 5,000 euros as compensation for "non-pecuniary damage".

---

[99] [2001] H.C.A. 63; 208 C.L.R. 199 at para.43.
[1] *ibid.* at para.58.
[2] *ibid.* at para.120.
[3] *ibid.* at paras 130–132.
[4] *ibid.* at paras 190–191.
[5] *ibid.* at para.328.
[6] [2002] E.C.H.R. 421.
[7] *ibid.* at para.41.

It is not easy to understand what "non-pecuniary" damage the companies **7–094** suffered. The companies were entities with legal but not human personality, created for the economic purposes of the shareholders. The awards of damages seem more like fines, designed to mark the court's disapproval of what had happened, than true compensation for damage to the companies.

In its argument the French Government accepted that the inspection of **7–095** the companies' documents amounted to interference with their right to respect for their home ("domicile" in the French version of the Convention, which the court said has a broader connotation than "home"[8]). However, it submitted that, while juristic persons could enjoy similar rights under the Convention to those afforded to natural persons, they could not claim a right to protection of their business premises "with as much force" as an individual, and that the inspections had been carried out within the law.[9]

Possibly because of the French Government's concession, the judgment **7–096** does not attempt a detailed analysis of how the accordance of rights to a non-natural person under Art.8 fits with the purpose of the article, as explained by the court in other cases.

In the case of an individual, it might be argued that the rights protected **7–097** by Art.8 include a proprietorial dimension, because a person's home and his correspondence are forms of property in which he has an interest that he is entitled to enjoy, as well as being essential to his private life. But the heading to the Article is "Right to Respect for Private and Family Life", and it has been interpreted as having a very broad purpose based on the need of human beings for a zone of freedom from outside interference in which to be able to develop their personality and relationships with others. A home and the ability to correspond with others are especially important ingredients of this zone of freedom. Seen in this context, the protection given by Art.8 to a person's home and correspondence is merely a part (but an important part) of this freedom, and not a free standing right available to any legal entity (natural or artificial) in possession of premises or correspondence.

Property rights are protected elsewhere under the Convention. Article 1 **7–098** of the First Protocol provides that every *natural or legal* person is entitled to the peaceful enjoyment of his possessions. Possessions have been interpreted as including immovable and movable property, intellectual property, contractual rights and the goodwill of a business.[10]

In stating that the rights guaranteed by Art.8 may be construed as **7–099** including respect for a company's registered office or other business premises, the European Court of Human Rights cited its previous decision in *Niemietz v Germany*.[11] In that case the court held that a search of a lawyer's offices by police looking for information about the whereabouts of

[8] [2002] E.C.H.R. 421 at para.40.
[9] *ibid.* at paras 30 and 32.
[10] For further study of this subject, see Clayton & Tomlinson, *The Law of Human Rights* (Oxford University Press, 2000 and supplement), ch.18.
[11] (1992) 16 E.H.R.R. 97.

a criminal suspect violated Art.8, but its reasoning was that a individual's private life may include activities of a business or professional nature. The search of the lawyer's offices was therefore an intrusion into his private life. If anything, the reasoning in that case would tend to negate the extension of rights under Art.8 to an inanimate entity, because the court approached the construction of the article from the standpoint that respect for private life is about the right of an individual to live his personal life as he chooses, and that this must comprise the right to establish and develop relationships with other human beings.

7–100   It remains to be seen how the court will approach claims by companies under Art.8 in future cases, but the outcome is unlikely to make a difference to the English law of confidentiality, since the law already protects companies against the obtaining of confidential information by improper means.[12]

---

[12] *Shelley Films Ltd v Rex Features Ltd* [1994] E.M.L.R. 134; *Creation Records Ltd v News Group Newspapers Ltd* [1997] E.M.L.R. 444.

CHAPTER 8

Data Protection and Freedom of Information

The DPA and the FOIA: Introduction

Data Protection

The statutory development of data protection legislation in the United Kingdom, as elsewhere, has been a response to the rapid technological advances made in the last quarter of the 20th century and subsequently—in particular, in the field of computers.   **8–001**

On January 28, 1981, the member states of the Council of Europe signed the Convention for the Protection of Individuals with regard to Automatic Processing of Personal Data. The Data Protection Act 1984, since repealed, reflected the provisions of the Convention.   **8–002**

The present United Kingdom legislation, in particular the Data Protection Act 1998 ("DPA"), is a consequence of Directive 95/46/EC, on the protection of individuals with regard to the processing of personal data and on the free movement of such data, which was authorised by the European Parliament and Council on October 24, 1995. The DPA came into force on March 1, 2000, but contains extensive transitional provisions.   **8–003**

Freedom of information

While complementing the DPA in a number of respects, the Freedom of Information Act 2000 ("the FOIA") has rather different origins. Its legislative history dates back to the Government's white paper in December 1997, entitled "Your right to know", which set out the Government's proposals for a Freedom of Information Act. The Government expressed its intention to promote openness in government and referred to the similar measures already in existence in a number of other countries (including the   **8–004**

USA, Canada, Australia, New Zealand, Sweden, France and the Netherlands).

8–005   The FOIA received royal assent in November 2000, but the Act did not come into force for most substantive purposes until January 1, 2005. In order to avoid overlap with the DPA, s.40 of the FOIA ensures that all requests by a data subject for access to personal data relating to him fall under the subject access provisions of the DPA, by expressly exempting such information from the FOIA regime.

8–006   The DPA and the FOIA together represent a considerable accretion to the law of confidentiality in the United Kingdom. A full examination of the two Acts is beyond the scope of this work and the reader is referred to the textbooks that address them specifically.[1] There follows merely an outline introduction to the structure of the Acts.

The Information Commissioner

8–007   The Data Protection Act 1984 established a Data Protection Registrar, whose title was changed, under the DPA, to Data Protection Commissioner. With effect from January 30, 2001, the Data Protection Commissioner took over responsibility also for the FOIA and his title changed again, to Information Commissioner. As well as the DPA and the FOIA, the Information Commissioner also enforces and oversees the Privacy and Electronic Communications (EC Directive) Regulations 2003[2] and the Environmental Information Regulations 2004.[3]

8–008   The powers of the Information Commissioner include the service of enforcement notices, where there has been a breach of the data protection principles,[4] the service of information notices, by which information relating to compliance can be required,[5] and the prosecution of those who commit criminal offences under the DPA.[6] Under the FOIA, the Information Commissioner is empowered to issue decision notices (having investigated a complaint against a public authority)[7] and enforcement notices,[8] requiring a public authority to address its failure to comply with Pt 1 of the FOIA.

---

[1] See, for example: Boardman, Gaskill & Grant's *Encyclopedia of Data Protection and Privacy* (loose-leaf, Sweet & Maxwell) Peter Carey's *Data Protection* (2nd edn, 2004, OUP) and Carey and Turle's *Freedom of Information Handbook* (2006, the Law Society).

[2] These make further provision in relation to such matters as the use of "cookies", the processing of "traffic data" (i.e. information relating to electronic communications), itemised telephone bills, the identification of incoming/outgoing calls or the geographical location of mobile telephones, subscriber directories, the use of automated calling systems, and telephone or electronic marketing.

[3] These provide a parallel freedom of information regime for environmental information, which is accordingly exempted from the scope of the FOIA (s.39).

[4] See s.40 of the DPA.

[5] See s.43 of the DPA.

[6] See s.60 of the DPA.

[7] See s.50 of the FOIA.

[8] See s.52 of the FOIA.

Appeals from the Information Commissioner's notices are heard by the Information Tribunal (formerly, the Data Protection Tribunal).

The Information Commissioner's statutory functions include the dissem- **8–009** ination of information about the operation of the DPA and the FOIA.[9] Guidance is to be found on the web-site of the Commissioner's Office, as well as copies of the Commissioner's decisions.

The DPA

The DPA is a complex statute and its drafting has not escaped judicial **8–010** criticism.[10] In *Campbell v MGN Ltd*,[11] the Court of Appeal said:

> "In interpreting the Act it is appropriate to look to the Directive for assistance. The Act should, if possible, be interpreted in a manner that is consistent with the Directive. Furthermore, because the Act has, in large measure, adopted the wording of the Directive, it is not appropriate to look for the precision in the use of language that is usually to be expected from the parliamentary draftsman. A purposive approach to making sense of the provisions is called for."

The DPA governs the *processing* of *personal data*, but there has been surprising difficulty in identifying the scope even of these central concepts.

Processing

"Processing" is defined in s.1 in the widest terms, which are likely to **8–011** encompass most forms of use, whether automatic or manual.[12] It may include both the obtaining and the publication of data, although, as the Court of Appeal said in *Campbell v MGN Ltd*[13]:

> "It would conflict with the overall nature and object of the Directive and the Act to seek to apply their provisions to the acts of those who

[9] See s.51 of the DPA and s.47 of the FOIA.
[10] The Court of Appeal in *Campbell v MGN Ltd* [2003] EWCA Civ 1373; [2003] Q.B. 633 described it at para.72 as a "cumbersome and inelegant piece of legislation".
[11] [2003] EWCA Civ 1373; [2003] Q.B. 633, at [96]. (The DPA did not receive separate consideration by the House of Lords.)
[12] If linked to automatic processing: *Johnson v The Medical Defence Union Ltd* [2006] EWHC 321, Ch (Rimer J.), at [86]–[97], citing the Court of Appeal's judgment in *Campbell v MGN Ltd* [2003] Q.B. 633, at paras 101–103. See also *Lindqvist v Kammaraklagaren* European Court of Justice C-101/01, November 6, 2003.
[13] At para.102.

distribute and make available to the public the product of prior data processing in which they have not been concerned."

Data

8–012 The courts have sought to set limits to the scope of the DPA by careful scrutiny both of what constitutes "data" and of what data is "personal". "Data" is defined in s.1 as:

"... information which—

    (a) is being processed by means of equipment operating automatically in response to instructions given for that purpose,

    (b) is recorded with the intention that it should be processed by means of such equipment,

    (c) is recorded as part of a relevant filing system or with the intention that it should form part of a relevant filing system,

    (d) does not fall within paragraph (a), (b) or (c) but forms part of an accessible record as defined by section 68[14]; or

    (e) is recorded information held by a public authority and does not fall within paragraphs (a) to (d)."

8–013 *Durant v Financial Services Authority*[15] concerned the extent of the rights of an individual, who had brought unsuccessful proceedings against his bank, to gain access under s.7 to information about him that was held by the Financial Services Authority in its capacity as the bank's regulator. The Court of Appeal considered a number of issues relating to the construction of the DPA, including the question whether the FSA's manual files fell within the scope of para.(c) of the DPA's definition of "data". The DPA's definition of "a relevant filing system"[16] is:

"any set of information relating to individuals to the extent that, although the information is not processed by means of equipment operating automatically in response to instructions given for that purpose, the set is structured, either by reference to individuals or by reference to criteria relating to individuals, in such a way that specific information relating to a particular individual is readily accessible."

8–014 Auld L.J., who gave the leading judgment, observed[17] that:

"It is clear from those provisions that the intention is to provide, as

---

[14] As defined at s.68 and in Schs 11 and 12, "accessible records" include health records, educational records and local authority housing and social services records.
[15] [2003] EWCA Civ 1746; [2004] F.S.R. 28.
[16] At s.1.
[17] At para.34.

near as possible, the same standard or sophistication of accessibility to personal data in manual filing systems as to computerised records."

Auld L.J. considered that any wider approach would be impractical and unfair to data controllers:

"To leave it to the searcher to leaf through files, possibly at great length and cost, and fruitlessly, to see whether it or they contain information relating to the person requesting information and whether that information is data within the Act bears . . . no resemblance to a computerised search."[18]

He concluded[19] that "a relevant filing system" was one:

"(1) in which the files forming part of it are structured or referenced in such a way as clearly to indicate at the outset of the search whether specific information capable of amounting to personal data of an individual . . . is held within the system and, if so, in which file or files it is held; and (2) which has, as part of its own structure or referencing mechanism, a sufficiently sophisticated and detailed means of readily indicating whether and where in an individual file or files specific criteria or information about the applicant can be readily located."

By virtue of paragraph (e) of the DPA's definition of "data",[20] this significant limitation in respect of information stored manually no longer applies to information held by public authorities. However, protection for public authorities is achieved instead by s.33A, which provides exemptions for manual data held by public authorities. Moreover, s.9A now provides that a public authority is not obliged to comply with a data subject's request for access to "unstructured personal data" (as defined in s.9A), unless the request contains a description of the data; and even then the authority is not obliged to comply if the cost of compliance exceeds either £450 or £600.[21]

Personal data

In *Durant v Financial Services Authority* the Court of Appeal also adopted a restrictive approach to the meaning of *personal* data. Section 1 defines personal data as: **8–015**

---

[18] at para.48.
[19] At para.50.
[20] Introduced by amendment with effect from January 1, 2005.
[21] Para.3 of the Freedom of Information and Data Protection (Appropriate Limit and Fees) Regulations, 2004 (SI 2004/3244).

" . . . data which relates to a living individual who can be identified —

(a) from those data, or
(b) from those data and other information which is in the possession of, or is likely to come into the possession of, the data controller,

and includes any expression of opinion about the individual and any indication of the intentions of the data controller or any other person in respect of the individual."

8–016   Observing that the ultimate purpose of an individual's right to have access to information in the form of "personal data" was the protection of privacy, Auld L.J. rejected the suggestion that all information retrieved from a computer search against an individual's name or unique identifier was personal data within the DPA. He concluded[22]:

"It seems to me that there are two notions that may be of assistance. The first is whether the information is biographical in a significant sense, that is, going beyond the recording of the putative data subject's involvement in a matter or an event that has no personal connotations, a life event in respect of which his privacy could not be said to be compromised. The second is one of focus. The information should have the putative data subject as its focus rather than some other person with whom he may have been involved or some transaction or event in which he may have figured or have had an interest, for example, as in this case, an investigation into some other person's or body's conduct that he may have instigated. In short, it is information that affects his privacy, whether in his personal or family life, business or professional capacity."

The Court of Appeal's tethering of the meaning of personal data to the concept of privacy is valuable, but does not resolve all problems in this area. A possible difficulty in applying the second notion referred to by the Court—that of focus—is that (since the DPA relates not to documents but to information) much information is likely to be composite and capable of being broken down into more specific items of information. For example, the fact that 100 named individuals attended a meeting includes within it at least 100 further separate pieces of information, namely that X attended the meeting, that Y attended the meeting, that Z attended the meeting, etc. The overall list of attendance at the meeting may not be information that has X as its focus, but it is less easy to say that the specific information that X attended the meeting clearly does not have X as its focus.

---

[22] At para.28.

Sensitive personal data

Sensitive personal data attract a higher level of protection. Section 2 defines **8–017** sensitive personal data as data consisting of information as to

(a) the racial or ethnic origin of the data subject,
(b) his political opinions,
(c) his religious beliefs or other beliefs of a similar nature,
(d) whether he is a member of a trade union,
(e) his physical or mental health or condition,
(f) his sexual life,
(g) the commission or alleged commission by him of any offence, or
(h) any proceedings for any offence committed or alleged to have been committed by him, the disposal of such proceedings or the sentence of any court in any such proceedings.

The data protection principles

The DPA imposes duties on a data controller[23] and gives rights to an **8–018** individual who is the subject of personal data. Section 17 prohibits the processing of computerised data[24] except by registered data controllers and ss.18 to 20 contain further provisions relating to registration.[25]

Section 4 requires all data controllers to comply with the DPA's data **8–019** protection principles. These are set out in Pt I of Sch.1[26]:

"1. Personal data shall be processed fairly and lawfully and, in particular, shall not be processed unless—

(a) at least one of the conditions in Schedule 2 is met, and
(b) in the case of sensitive personal data, at least one of the conditions in Schedule 3 is also met.

2. Personal data shall be obtained only for one or more specified and lawful purposes, and shall not be further processed in any manner incompatible with that purpose or those purposes.

3. Personal data shall be adequate, relevant and not excessive in relation to the purpose or purposes for which they are processed.

4. Personal data shall be accurate and, where necessary, kept up to date.

5. Personal data processed for any purpose or purposes shall not be kept for longer than is necessary for that purpose or those purposes.

---

[23] I.e., "any person who (either alone or jointly or in common with other persons) determines the purposes for which and the manner in which any personal data are, or are to be, processed": s.1 of the DPA.
[24] I.e., data falling within paragraphs (a) or (b) of the definition of data in s.1 of the DPA.
[25] See also the Data Protection (Notification and Notification Fees) Regulations 2000 (SI 2000/188).
[26] As elaborated upon in Pt II of Sch.1.

6. Personal data shall be processed in accordance with the rights of data subjects under this Act.

7. Appropriate technical and organisational measures shall be taken against unauthorised or unlawful processing of personal data and against accidental loss or destruction of, or damage to, personal data.

8. Personal data shall not be transferred to a country or territory outside the European Economic Area unless that country or territory ensures an adequate level of protection for the rights and freedoms of data subjects in relation to the processing of personal data."

Schedules 2 and 3 set out detailed conditions relevant for the purpose of the first data protection principle. By way of example, the first condition in Sch.2 (relating to the processing of personal data) is that the data subject has given his consent to the processing, while the first condition in Sch.3 (relating to the processing of sensitive personal data) is that the data subject has given his *explicit* consent to the processing of the personal data.

Data subject rights

8–020   The rights of data subjects under the DPA include the following:

(1) Under s.7, a right of access to personal data.

(2) Under s.10, a right to prevent processing that is likely to cause damage or distress, if the damage or distress is "unwarranted".

(3) Under s.11, a right to prevent processing for the purposes of direct marketing.

(4) Under s.12, a right to restrain the automated taking of decisions that significantly affect the individual, for example in relation to his performance at work, his creditworthiness, his reliability, or his conduct.

(5) Under s.14, a right to apply to the court for an order to rectify, block, erase, or destroy inaccurate personal data relating to the applicant (and any expression of opinion based on that data).[27]

Of these rights, the first is probably the one to which appeal is most often made. Under subs.7(1),[28] an individual is entitled:

"(a) to be informed by any data controller whether personal data of which that individual is the data subject are being processed by or on behalf of that data controller,

(b) if that is the case, to be given by the data controller a description of—

---

[27] See also s.14A, in force only until October 23, 2007.

[28] Upon payment of any proper fee required, in accordance with the Data Protection (Subject Access) (Fees and Miscellaneous Provisions) Regulations 2000 (SI 2000/191) (as amended).

(i) the personal data of which that individual is the data subject,

(ii) the purposes for which they are being or are to be processed, and

(iii) the recipients or classes of recipients to whom they are or may be disclosed,

(c) to have communicated to him in an intelligible form—

(i) the information constituting any personal data of which that individual is the data subject, and

(ii) any information available to the data controller as to the source of those data, and

(d) where the processing by automatic means of personal data of which that individual is the data subject for the purpose of evaluating matters relating to him such as, for example, his performance at work, his creditworthiness, his reliability or his conduct, has constituted or is likely to constitute the sole basis for any decision significantly affecting him, to be informed by the data controller of the logic involved in that decision-taking."

Further effect is given to the rights of data subjects by s.13 of the DPA, which provides a right to compensation for damage or distress caused by contravention of a requirement of the DPA, subject to a defence that the defendant took reasonable care to comply with the requirement. In *Johnson v Medical Defence Union*,[29] Rimer J. held that s.13 did not permit recovery of damages for loss of reputation.

Exemptions

The DPA contains a large number of exemptions for specified categories of **8–021** information from some or all of the data protection principles or provisions of the DPA.[30] Some of these are couched in terms of considerable complexity. One of the most briefly expressed and (as it affects the scope of the Act) most significant of the exemptions is that provided by s.36:

"Personal data processed by an individual only for the purposes of that individual's personal, family or household affairs (including recreational purposes) are exempt from the data protection principles and the provisions of Parts I and II."

Other exemptions relate to national security (s.28), crime and taxation **8–022** (s.29), health, education and social work (s.30), regulatory activity (s.31), journalism, literature and art (s.32), research, history and statistics (s.33), information available to the public by or under an enactment (s.34),

[29] [2006] EWHC 321, Ch, at [218].
[30] Categorised as "subject information provisions" and "non-disclosure provisions", as defined at s.27.

disclosures required by law or made in connection with legal proceedings (s.35), Parliamentary privilege (s.35A), confidential references (para.1 of Sch.7), the armed forces (para.2 of Sch.7), judicial appointments and honours (para.3 of Sch.7), Crown employment and Crown or Ministerial appointments (para.4 of Sch.7), management forecasts (para.5 of Sch.7), corporate finance (para.6 of Sch.7), negotiations (para.7 of Sch.7), examination marks (para.8 of Sch.7), examination scripts (para.9 of Sch.7), legal professional privilege (para.10 of Sch.7) and self-incrimination (para.11 of Sch.7).

8–023   Moreover, under s.38, the Secretary of State has the power to make further exemption orders. Part II of the Data Protection (Miscellaneous Subject Access Exemptions) Order 2000[31] exempts information, the disclosure of which is prohibited or restricted by ss.31 and 33 of the Human Fertilisation and Embryology Act 1990 (Pt I of the Schedule to the Order), and adoption records, statements of special education needs and parental order records and reports (Pt II of the Schedule to the Order).

Public interest

8–024   Section 32 largely excludes from the data protection principles the processing of personal data with a view to the publication of journalistic, literary or artistic material, where the data controller reasonably believes that publication would be in the public interest, having regard in particular to the special importance of the public interest in freedom of expression.

8–025   The Data Protection (Processing of Sensitive Personal Data) Order 2000[32] lists a number of circumstances in which sensitive personal data may be processed in the public interest. The provisions are complex.

Offences

8–026   The DPA creates a number of criminal offences, punishable by fine. Among the relevant sections are s.21 (registration-related offences) and s.47 (offences in relation to enforcement notices or information notices). Section 55 creates offences in relation to the unlawful obtaining or disclosure of personal data. Under subs.55(1):

> "A person must not knowingly or recklessly, without the consent of the data controller—
>
> (a) obtain or disclose personal data or the information contained in personal data, or
>
> (b) procure the disclosure to another person of the information contained in personal data."

---

[31] SI 2000/419.
[32] SI 2000/417. Further circumstances are listed in subsequent orders (SI 2002/2905 and SI 2006/2068).

The effect of this prohibition is mitigated under subs.55(2) by disapplying subs.55(1) to:

" . . . a person who shows—

(a) that the obtaining, disclosing or procuring—

    (i) was necessary for the purpose of preventing or detecting crime,

    (ii) was required or authorised by or under any enactment, by any rule of law or by the order of a court,

(b) that he acted in the reasonable belief that he had in law the right to obtain or disclose the data or information or, as the case may be, to procure the disclosure of the information to the other person,

(c) that he acted in the reasonable belief that he would have had the consent of the data controller if the data controller had known of the obtaining, disclosing or procuring and the circumstances of it, or

(d) that in the particular circumstances the obtaining, disclosing or procuring was justified as being in the public interest."

The FOIA

Subsection 1(1) of the FOIA provides that: **8–027**

"Any person making a request for information to a public authority is entitled—

(a) to be informed in writing by the public authority whether it holds information of the description specified in the request, and

(b) if that is the case, to have that information communicated to him."

Public authorities are defined in s.3. Their ranks may be augmented or reduced by statutory instrument.[33] Sections 8 to 17 are largely procedural, providing for the manner in which requests must be made and answered. Of particular significance, s.14 provides that a public authority is not obliged to comply with vexatious or (until a reasonable interval has elapsed) repeated requests. Section 19 requires public authorities to maintain publication schemes, setting out what classes of information they intend to publish, how they intend to publish them and whether they intend to make them available to the public free of charge.

---

[33] See SI 2002/2623, SI 2003/1882, SI 2003/1883, SI 2004/938, SI 2004/1641, SI 2004/1870, SI 2005/3593 and SI 2005/3594.

8–028   Part II of the FOIA contains numerous total or partial exemptions, including exemptions for:

- information accessible by other means (s.21),
- information intended for future publication (s.22),
- information supplied by or relating to "security" organisations, such as MI5, MI6, GCHQ, special forces, etc. (s.23),
- information the exemption of which is required for the purpose of safeguarding national security (s.24),
- information the disclosure of which would be likely to prejudice defence or the operation of the armed forces, or forces cooperating with the armed forces (s.26),
- information the disclosure of which would be likely to prejudice international relations (s.27), or relations between the devolved government administrations of Scotland, Northern Ireland and Wales and/or the United Kingdom government (s.28),
- information the disclosure of which would be likely to prejudice the economy (s.29),
- information relating to certain investigations and proceedings conducted by public authorities (s.30),
- information the disclosure of which would be likely to prejudice various law enforcement matters, such as the prevention or detection of crime, or the administration of justice (s.31),
- information in court records, etc. (s.32),
- information held by public auditors (s.33),
- information bearing on the formulation of government policy (s.35),
- information the disclosure of which would be likely to prejudice the effective conduct of public affairs, by (for example) inhibiting the free and frank provision of advice, or the free and frank exchange of views for the purposes of deliberation (s.36),
- information relating to communications with members of the Royal Family or the honours system (s.37) and
- information the disclosure of which would be likely to endanger the health or safety of an individual (s.38).

Sections 39 and 40 (in broad terms) exempt information available under the Environmental Information Regulations 2004 or the DPA.

8–029   Section 41 provides a significant and wide-ranging exemption for information if:

> "(a) it was obtained by the public authority from any other person (including another public authority), and
> (b) the disclosure of the information to the public (otherwise than under this Act) by the public authority holding it would constitute a breach of confidence actionable by that or any other person."

Section 42 exempts legally privileged information. Section 43 exempts trade secrets and information the disclosure of which would be likely to prejudice the commercial interests of any person (including the authority holding it). Finally, under s.44, information is exempted if its disclosure is prohibited by or under any enactment, is incompatible with any Community obligation, or would constitute or be punishable as a contempt of court.

Part IV of the FOIA deals with enforcement. Section 56 provides that the **8–030** FOIA does not confer any right of action in civil proceedings in respect of any failure to comply with any duty imposed by or under the Act. However, s.54 provides that a public authority that fails to comply with the Information Commissioner's notices may be dealt with by the High Court as if it had committed a contempt of court.[34]

Part V covers appeals from the Information Commissioner's notices and **8–031** decisions, while Pt VI contains provisions relating specifically to historical and public records.

The DPA and the FOIA in confidentiality cases

To date, the impact of the DPA and the FOIA in cases relating to the general **8–032** law of confidentiality has been limited. In the case of the FOIA this is unsurprising, given the recent date on which it came into force, the restricted field of its operation and the lack of any entitlement to compensation for contravention of its provisions.

The absence so far of much detailed high-level judicial consideration of **8–033** the DPA may be due to a combination of two factors: the availability of remedies for breach of confidence at common law and in equity, as extended under human rights jurisprudence,[35] and the daunting complexity of the DPA. Where, for example, issues of public interest are raised, the parties may well surmise that the court is likely to arrive at the same result whether by applying Art.8 principles or by following the more tortuous routes of the DPA and the regulations made under it. Thus, in the House of Lords in *Campbell v MGN Ltd*,[36] the parties simply agreed that Naomi Campbell's claim under the DPA stood or fell with the outcome of the main claim.

---

[34] See also s.77, which creates a specific offence of altering, defacing, blocking, erasing, destroying, or concealing, any record held by a public authority with the intention of preventing the disclosure of information to which the applicant would have been entitled.
[35] In *Douglas v Hello! Ltd* [2003] EWHC 786, Ch; [2003] 3 All E.R. 996, at [230]–[239], Lindsay J. found that there was a breach of the DPA but that this did not provide a separate route to the recovery of damages beyond those to which the claimants were entitled for breach of confidentiality. No point was raised under the DPA when the case went to appeal.
[36] [2004] UKHL 22; [2004] 2 A.C. 457. See [32] and [130].

CHAPTER 9

Remedies

Injunction

9–001 A final injunction may be granted to a successful claimant in an action for breach of confidence (whether arising in contract or from an equitable obligation of confidence) or for inducement of breach of contract, in order to prevent continuation of the wrongful conduct. It may also be granted, *quia timet*, to prevent threatened breach of confidence. In all such cases the court has a discretion whether to grant an injunction and, if so, on what terms and for what period. The question of duration arises particularly in "springboard" cases,[1] where the injunction should not normally extend beyond the period for which unfair advantage may reasonably be expected to continue.[2]

9–002 The Human Rights Act 1998, s.12, requires the court to have particular regard to the importance of the right to freedom of expression under Art.10 of the European Convention in considering whether to grant relief which might affect the exercise of that right.[3]

9–003 An interim injunction may be granted on the principles set out in *American Cyanamid v Ethicon*,[4] except in a case where Art.10 may be engaged. In those circumstances s.12 (3) provides that no such relief may be granted unless the court is satisfied that the applicant is likely to establish at the trial that publication should not be allowed. This provision has been

---

[1] See Ch.4, above.
[2] *Potters-Ballotini Ltd v Weston-Baker* [1977] R.P.C. 202 at 206; *Roger Bullivant Ltd v Ellis* [1987] F.S.R. 172 at 183–184; *Sun Valley Foods Ltd v Vincent* [2000] F.S.R. 825.
[3] See paras 6–048 above and 13–010 below.
[4] [1975] A.C. 396.

construed by the House of Lords as meaning that the court should not make an interim restraint order unless satisfied that the applicant's prospects of success at trial are sufficiently favourable to justify the order being made in all the circumstances; and that generally this will require the applicant to satisfy the court that it would probably find that publication should not be allowed, but that there could be circumstances in which a lesser degree of likelihood would be sufficient.[5]

Independently of Convention considerations, where the period for which interlocutory relief is sought would be likely to expire before the trial, it is proper for the court to take into account the claimant's prospects of success at trial.[6]   **9–004**

Any injunction must be framed in terms sufficiently specific to leave no uncertainty what the affected person is or is not allowed to do.[7] In *Times Newspaper Ltd v MGN Ltd*,[8] the Court of Appeal held that no injunction could be granted to prevent premature publication of a pirated version of Lady Thatcher's memoirs, because the plaintiffs had to concede that vital parts of the book would have to be excepted from the scope of any injunction and the drafting of such an exception could not be satisfactorily achieved.   **9–005**

Universal Thermosensor Ltd v Hibben[9] provides salutary warning against obtaining an interlocutory injunction in too wide terms. In that case the plaintiff succeeding in establishing breach of duty of confidence, but, having obtained an interlocutory injunction in excessively wide terms which led to the collapse of the defendants' business, it had to pay damages to the defendants on its cross undertaking. Sir Donald Nicholls V.C. recognised that he had a discretion not to enforce the undertaking, and also found that the defendants had acted dishonestly, but he rejected the plaintiff's argument that the undertaking should for that reason not be enforced. He said[10]:   **9–006**

> "Punishment of the defendants is not my function. If the defendants have suffered material loss by reason of excessive width in the terms of the injunction sought and obtained by the plaintiff in July 1990, in my view they are entitled to look to the plaintiff for damages pursuant to its undertaking. Plaintiffs, and those who advise them, know or ought to know that there is a risk in obtaining interlocutory injunctive relief: the risk is that the plaintiff may have to pay compensation to the defendant if it turns out at the trial that, having regard to the facts and

---

[5] *Cream Holdings Ltd v Banerjee* [2004] UKHL 44; [2005] 1 A.C. 253.
[6] *Lansing Linde v Kerr* [1991] 1 All E.R. 418; *Sun Valley Foods Ltd v Vincent* [2000] F.S.R. 825.
[7] *Potters-Ballotini Ltd v Weston-Baker* [1977] R.P.C. 202; *Lawrence David Ltd v Ashton* [1991] 1 All E.R. 385; *PSM International plc v Whitehouse* [1992] 1 I.R.L.R. 279; *Times Newspaper Ltd v MGN Ltd* [1993] E.M.L.R. 442; *CMI-Centres for Medical Innovation GmbH v Phytopharm plc* [1999] F.S.R. 235; *Att-Gen v Punch Ltd* [2002] UKHL 50; [2003] 1 A.C. 1046, especially *per* Lord Nicholls at paras 33–37 and *per* Lord Hope at para.111.
[8] [1993] E.M.L.R. 443.
[9] [1992] 1 W.L.R. 840.
[10] *ibid.* at 858.

law as established at the trial, the effect of the injunction was to restrain a defendant from activities which it ought to have been at liberty to pursue."

Destruction or delivery up

9–007 The court has power to order delivery up or destruction of material containing confidential information or derived from misuse of confidential information, unless possibly the material has substantial intrinsic value independently of the misuse of confidential information.

9–008 In *Prince Albert v Strange* the defendant opposed an order for delivery up or destruction of the catalogues and the impressions of the royal etchings which were in his possession. Knight-Bruce V.C. said[11]:

> "It is then said that neither the copies of the catalogue, nor the impressions that have been taken, can be delivered, or be directed to be delivered up, inasmuch as the Defendant contends that he is entitled to the property in the materials on which they are printed. With regard to catalogues, no such question, I think, arises. They must be either cancelled or destroyed; and without destruction they can hardly be cancelled. With regard to the impressions, it might possibly be right to attend to the Defendant's claim, had the impressions been upon a material of intrinsic value—upon a material not substantially worthless, except for the impressions which, by the wrongful act of the Defendants, have been placed there. That case, however, does not arise. The material here is substantially worthless, except for that in which the Defendant has no property. There consequently can be no reason why the effectual destruction of subject should not be directed by the Court."

This passage was cited and applied by Dunn J. in *Franklin v Giddins*, where he ordered the delivery up for destruction of fruit trees propagated by the defendant from budwood cuttings stolen from the plaintiff's orchard.[12]

9–009 The court's power is discretionary. In *Saltman*, where the defendants misused confidential drawings of tools for the manufacture of leather punches, the report records that[13]:

> "In the course of the discussion as to the relief to be given to the Plaintiffs, their Lordships expressed reluctance to make any order which would involve the destruction or sterilisation of tools which would serve a useful purpose, since under Lord Cairns's Act the Court

---

[11] (1849) 2 De G. & S.M. 652 at 716. The point does not appear to have been argued on the defendant's appeal before Cottenham L.C.
[12] [1978] Qd.R. 72 at 81–83. See para.3–034, above.
[13] (1948) 65 R.P.C. 203 at 219.

could award damages, to cover both past and future acts, in lieu of an injunction."

The order finally agreed was that the defendants should deliver up the drawings, and that there should be an inquiry as to the damages suffered by the plaintiffs by reason of the defendants' conduct in using the drawings for the construction of leather punches for sale on their own account.

Where the successful plaintiff seeks an order for delivery up of material **9–010** containing confidential information it will usually be granted, especially if the defendant cannot be relied on to destroy it.[14] In *Robb v Green,*[15] for example, the defendant was ordered to deliver up for destruction a customer list which he had surreptitiously copied while employed by the plaintiff, and an injunction was granted restraining him from making use of the information so obtained.[16]

In *AG Australia Holdings Ltd v Burton*[17] a former employee of a **9–011** company involved in litigation gave confidential information to solicitors acting for the opposing party. The court ordered that materials, including draft witness statements or affidavits, relating to the disclosures made by the employee should be placed in store in sealed containers marked with notices that they were not to be opened without permission of the court.

Account of profits

Account of profits is an established form of equitable relief. In the **9–012** *Spycatcher* case the *Sunday Times* was held liable to account to the Crown for profits from its breach of duty of confidence in publishing material from Mr Wright's memoirs, before the information had entered the public domain, knowing that Mr Wright was acting in breach of duty of confidence in disclosing the information. Lord Keith said[18]:

"An account of profits made through breach of confidence is a recognised form of remedy available to a claimant (*Peter Pan Manufacturing Corporation v Corsets Silhouette Ltd* [1964] 1 W.L.R. 96; *cf. Reading v Attorney-General* [1951] A.C. 507). In cases where the information disclosed is of a commercial character an account of profits may provide some compensation to the claimant for loss which he has suffered through the disclosure, but damages are the main remedy for such loss. The remedy is, in my opinion, more satisfactorily to be attributed to the principle that no one should be permitted to gain from his own wrongdoing. Its availability may also, in general, serve a

[14] *Industrial Furnaces Ltd v Reaves* [1970] R.P.C. 605 at 627.
[15] [1895] 2 Q.B. 315.
[16] See also *Reid & Sigrist Ltd v Moss* [1932] 49 R.P.C. 461; and *Peter Pan Manufacturing Corporation v Corsets Silhouette Ltd* [1964] 1 W.L.R. 96.
[17] [2002] N.S.W.S.C. 170.
[18] [1990] 1 A.C. 109 at 262.

useful purpose in lessening the temptation for recipients of confidential information to misuse it for financial gain. In the present case 'The Sunday Times' did misuse confidential information and it would be naive to suppose that the prospect of financial gain was not one of the reasons why it did so. I can perceive no good ground why the remedy should not be made available to the Crown in the circumstances of this case, and I would therefore hold the Crown entitled to an account of profits in respect of the publication on 12 July, 1987."

Lord Goff expressed reservations about a general statement that a man is not to be allowed to profit from his own wrong and preferred to place the remedy of an account on a restitutionary basis. He said,[19]

"The statement that a man shall not be allowed to profit from his own wrong is in very general terms, and does not of itself provide any sure guidance to the solution of a problem in any particular case. That there are groups of cases in which a man is not allowed to profit from his own wrong, is certainly true. An important section of the law of restitution is concerned with cases in which a defendant is required to make restitution in respect of benefits acquired through his own wrongful act—notably cases of waiver of tort; of benefits acquired by certain criminal acts; of benefits acquired by certain criminal acts; of benefits acquired in breach of a fiduciary relationship; and, of course, of benefits acquired in breach of confidence. The plaintiff's claim to restitution is usually enforced by an account of profits made by the defendant through his wrong at the plaintiff's expense. This remedy of an account is alternative to the remedy of damages, which in cases of breach of confidence is now available, despite the equitable nature of the wrong, through a beneficent interpretation of the Chancery Amendment Act 1858 (Lord Cairns' Act), and which by reason of the difficulties attending the taking of an account is often regarded as a more satisfactory remedy, at least in cases where the confidential information is of a commercial nature, and quantifiable damage may therefore have been suffered."

The rule that the remedy of an account is an alternative remedy to damages was historically explained on the basis that by seeking an account the plaintiff adopted the defendant's acts,[20] and he therefore could not claim both. A better explanation is that both are forms of compensation for wrongful conduct at the plaintiff's expense and that to allow both would lead to over-compensation.

9–013   In *Attorney-General v Blake*[21] Lord Nicholls said that if the information disclosed by the former intelligence officer had still been confidential at the

---

[19] [1990] 1 A.C. 109 at 286.
[20] *Sutherland Publishing Co Ltd v Caxton Publishing Co Ltd* [1936] Ch. 323 at 336.
[21] [2001] 1 A.C. 268 at 287.

time of his book's publication, an account of profits would have been ordered "almost as a matter of course".

The distinctive features of the case were that the loss of confidentiality **9–014** was largely a result of his own past treachery, of which the book was an autobiographical account, and that he was in breach of contract in publishing the book even though its contents were no longer confidential. The House of Lords held that an account of profits was an appropriate remedy for the breach of contract. It recognised that for a breach of contract the remedies normally appropriate are damages for the loss suffered by the innocent party, an injunction or specific performance. But Lord Nicholls observed[22]:

> "Sometimes the injured party is given the choice: either compensatory damages or an account of the wrongdoer's profits. Breach of confidence is an instance of this. If confidential information is wrongfully divulged in breach of a non-disclosure agreement, it would be nothing short of sophistry to say that an account of profits may be ordered in respect of the equitable wrong but not in respect of the breach of contract which governs the relationship between the parties. With the established authorities going thus far, I consider that it would be only a small step for the law to recognise openly that, exceptionally, an account of profits may be the most appropriate remedy for breach of contract."

An account may be combined with other remedies apart from damages. In *Peter Pan Manufacturing Corporation v Corsets Silhouette Ltd*,[23] where the defendants misused confidential design information to produce two styles of bra, Pennycuick J. granted an injunction restraining the defendants from manufacturing, using or distributing those styles, an order for destruction or delivery up of existing stocks and an account of profits made from those styles.

Constructive trust

In some jurisdictions (notably Australia, Canada and the USA) the courts **9–015** have developed the concept of a constructive trust as a discretionary remedy. The difference between an "institutional" and a "remedial" constructive trust is that the former arises by operation of law as from the date of the circumstances which give rise to it, and the function of the court is merely to declare that it has arisen; the latter arises when the court decides that it is the most appropriate remedy for unconscionable behaviour.[24]

---

[22] [1990] 1 A.C. 109 at 285.
[23] [1964] 1 W.L.R. 96.
[24] *Westdeutsche Bank v Islington London Borough Council* [1996] A.C. 669 at 714–715 (Lord Browne-Wilkinson).

9–016   In *Beatty v Guggenheim Exploration Co*[25] Cardozo J. said:

> "A court of equity in decreeing a constructive trust is bound by no unyielding formula. The equity of the transaction must shape the measure of relief."

9–017   In *U.S. Surgical Corporation v Hospital Products International Pty Ltd*[26] the defendants, who were exclusive distributors in Australia of surgical stapling instruments manufactured by the plaintiffs, marketed their own similar product in circumstances which were found by the trial judge, McLelland J., to amount to a breach of a fiduciary duty owed to the plaintiffs. The plaintiffs sought relief on the basis of a constructive trust over the defendants' assets. McLelland, J. said[27]:

> "Liability for breaches of equitable obligations may be of either a restitutionary or a compensatory nature. Restitutionary relief may be given by way of the imposition of a constructive trust over specific property (specific restitution) or by an accounting for profits. The imposition of a liability to acount for profits is essentially a personal rather than a proprietary remedy, but it may in some cases be appropriate to impose an equitable lien over specific property by way of security for such accounting. In the area of relief against what used to be called equitable fraud, of which profiting from a fiduciary position is one example, the precise form of relief must be moulded to satisfy the demands of justice and good conscience in the particular case: 'the court must look at the circumstances in each case to decide in what way the equity can be satisfied' (*Chalmers v Pardoe* [1963] 1 W.L.R. 677 at 682; [1963] 3 All E.R. 552 at 555; 'the equity of the transaction must shape the measure of the relief': *Beatty v Guggenheim Exploration Co.* 122 N.E. 378 [1919], at 381; 225 N.Y. 380, at 389)."

He held that the assets of the defendants' manufacturing business were not property the obtaining or pursuing of which was or ought to have been an incident of the defendants' fiduciary duty, and therefore it would not be right to impose a constructive trust over those assets in favour of the plaintiffs. Instead he ordered an account of profits from sales of the defendants' rival products. He also directed that the defendants' liability to account should be secured by an equitable lien over the defendants' assets,

---

[25] (1919) 225 N.Y. 380 at 389, cited by Mason J. in *Hospital Products Ltd v U.S. Surgical Corp.* (1984) 156 C.L.R. 41 at 108. See also *Snepp v United States* (1980) 444 U.S. 507, in which the Supreme Court of the United States imposed a constructive trust on the proceeds of sale of a book written by a former CIA agent and—in breach of an express contractual obligation—not submitted for pre-publication review.

[26] [1982] 2 N.S.W.L.R. 766, reversed in the High Court on the ground that no fiduciary relationship existed between the parties ((1984) 156 C.L.R. 41).

[27] [1982] 2 N.S.W.L.R. 766 at 812–813.

holding that the imposition of such a lien was a matter within the discretion of the court.[28]

In *Muschinski v Dodds*[29] a constructive trust was imposed from the date of the court's order by a majority of the High Court of Australia (Gibbs C.J., Deane and Mason JJ.).[30]   **9–018**

In *LAC Minerals Ltd v International Corona Resources Ltd*[31] the defendant acquired mining rights through misuse of information given to it in confidence by the plaintiff, which would otherwise have obtained the mining rights and developed the mine for itself. The trial judge declared that the defendant held the property on trust for the plaintiff, and he ordered it to deliver up the property on being compensated for the value of improvements it had made to the property in developing the mine. The order was upheld (by a majority) by the Supreme Court of Canada. La Forest J. said[32]:   **9–019**

> "The issue then is this. If it is established that one party (here LAC) has been enriched by the acquisition of an asset, the Williams property, that would have, but for the actions of that party, been acquired by the plaintiff (here Corona) and if the acquisition of that asset amounts to a breach of duty to the plaintiff, here either a breach of fiduciary obligation or a breach of a duty of confidence, what remedy is available to the party deprived of the benefit? In my view the constructive trust is one available remedy, and in this case it is the only appropriate remedy.
>
> In my view the facts present in this case make out a restitutionary claim, or what is the same thing, a claim for unjust enrichment. When one talks of restitution, one normally talks of giving back to someone something that has been taken from them (a restitutionary proprietary award), or its equivalent value (a personal restitutionary award). As the Court of Appeal noted in this case, Corona never in fact owned the Williams property, and so it cannot be 'given back' to them. However, there are concurrent findings below that, but for its interception by LAC, Corona would have acquired the property. In *Air Canada v British Columbia* (judgment pronounced May 4, 1989 [now reported at 59 D.L.R. (4th) 161 at pp.193–194, B.C.L.R. (2d) 145; [1989] 4 W.W.R. 97]), I said that the function of the law of restitution 'is to ensure that where a plaintiff has been deprived of wealth that is either in his possession *or would have accrued for his benefit*, it is restored to him. The measure of restitutionary recovery is the gain the [defendant] made at the [plaintiff's] expense.' In my view the fact that Corona never owned the property should not preclude it from the pursuing [of] a

---

[28] Citing Goff and Jones, *The Law of Restitution* (2nd edn, 1978), pp.47, 48 and 61, but see now Goff and Jones (6th edn, 2002), chs 33 and 34.

[29] (1985) 160 C.L.R. 583 at 615, 623.

[30] See also *Giumelli v Giumelli* [1999] H.C.A. 10; (1999) 196 C.L.R. 101, where the court said that a constructive trust should not be imposed if there is an adequate alternative remedy.

[31] [1990] F.S.R. 441; (1989) 61 D.L.R. (4th) 14. See para.2–091, above.

[32] [1990] F.S.R. 441 at 469.

restitutionary claim: see Birks, *An Introduction to the Law of Restitution* (1985), at pp.133–139. LAC has therefore been enriched at the expense of Corona."

The minority would have awarded damages as the appropriate remedy. English law has not so far generally adopted the concept of a remedial constructive trust.[33]

9–020   *Phipps v Boardman*[34] was a case of misuse of information by a fiduciary. The defendants bought shares in a company in which a trust had a substantial holding. They used their own money to buy the shares, but they were held to be in breach of fiduciary duty because they gained the opportunity to make the purchase from information acquired as agents of the trustees and they acted without full disclosure to the trustees. Wilberforce J. made an order declaring that they held the shares as constructive trustees, and his judgment was upheld by the House of Lords.[35]

9–021   In the *Spycatcher* case Dillon L.J. said[36]:

> "It has seemed to me throughout the hearing of this appeal that there could have been strong arguments for saying that, as Mr Wright wrote and published *Spycatcher* in breach of his duty of secrecy to the Crown and was only able to do so by the misuse of secret information which had come to him in the course of his employment as an officer in the Security Service of the Crown, the copyright in *Spycatcher* belongs in equity to the Crown and is held on constructive trust for the Crown with whatever consequences may follow from that."

The point was not argued by the Crown, but in the House of Lords a majority commented on it in terms suggesting that it might well be right.[37] None of the judges who referred to the point suggested that it would depend on the information being classified as property.

9–022   The House of Lords held in that case that the Sunday Times was liable to account to the Crown for profits from its breach of confidence in publishing information which it knew had been supplied to it by Mr Wright in breach of his duty of confidence. He was also a fiduciary, but none of the judgments suggest that the remedy of an account against the Sunday Times was dependent on that additional factor. The Crown did not argue (and would not have gained from arguing) that the Sunday Times was a constructive trustee of its profits, but Goff and Jones's commentary on the case includes the suggestion that "in principle, a third party who instigates, or [sci. knowingly] participates in, a breach of trust should be deemed to be liable

---

[33] *Metall und Rohstoff AG v Donaldson Lufkin & Jenrette Inc* [1990] 1 Q.B. 391 at 478–480; *Westdeutsche Bank v Islington London Borough Council* [1996] A.C. 669 at 714–715; *Re Polly Peck International plc (No.2)* [1998] 3 All E.R. 812 at 823–825.

[34] [1967] 2 A.C. 46.

[35] See para.2–039, above.

[36] [1990] 1 A.C. 109 at 211.

[37] *ibid.* at 263 (Lord Keith), 275–276 (Lord Griffiths), 288 (Lord Goff).

as if he were a trustee of any benefits directly or indirectly thereby gained".[38]

As a matter of justice, it is an attractive proposition. The same might also **9–023** be argued in the case of a person who knowingly misuses confidential information, or who instigates or knowingly participates in the misuse of confidential information. The latter proposition was accepted by Chadwick J but rejected by the Court of Appeal in *Satnam Investments Ltd v Dunlop Heywood & Co. Ltd.*[39]

Satnam had an option to buy a site with development potential but the **9–024** option could be terminated if it went into receivership, which it did. A surveyor who had been acting for Satnam disclosed to a rival company, M Ltd, that Satnam had an interest in the site, that it had gone into receivership and that the local planning authority was well disposed to development of the site. M Ltd bought the site. Chadwick J. found (and these findings were upheld by the Court of Appeal) that the surveyors acted in breach of their duty of confidentiality to Satnam as a fiduciary and that M Ltd knew this at the time of the disclosure. He held that Satnam lost its opportunity to acquire the site because of M Ltd's breach of duty and he declared that the site was held by M Ltd on trust for Satnam.

The Court of Appeal reversed his judgment for essentially three reasons. **9–025** First, they found as a fact that the disclosure did not cause M Ltd to act in any way differently from the way in which it would have acted without the disclosure, because it would in any event have learned the facts disclosed to it within two weeks, well before it made an approach to the site owners. Secondly, it held that although M Ltd knew of the surveyors' breach of duty in making the disclosure it did not participate in it. Thirdly, it held that M Ltd could only be constructive trustees of the site if it was trust property or trust property could be traced into it.

The first reason presents no legal difficulty. If the disclosure made no **9–026** material difference to M Ltd's behaviour, its acquisition of the site cannot be said to have been a benefit resulting from the disclosure. The second and third reasons are more difficult. The second reason could be explained as a corollary of the first (ie that M Ltd cannot be said to have participated in the surveyors' breach of duty if it neither solicited the breach of duty nor acted in any different way because of it), but that is not how it was expressed. The court held that the allegation that M Ltd had unconscionably used and taken advantage of the information could not be treated as one of dishonesty, and that dishonesty was required. But unconscionable (i.e. knowing) misuse of information supplied in breach of a duty by the surveyors should be enough to put M Ltd in the same position as the surveyors. The third reason involves a narrow approach. On this approach the suggestion canvassed by several judges in *Spyycatcher* that Mr Wright held the copyright in his book on constructive trust for the Crown would be unsustainable, except on the notion (not advanced in *Spycatcher* and now

---

[38] *The Law of Restitution* (6th edn, 2002), para.33-033.
[39] [1999] 3 All E.R. 652.

discredited) that the information disclosed by him was property owned by the Crown.[40]

9–027   If an account of profits may be ordered against a person who has misused confidential information, it is hard to see in principle why a court should not have jurisdiction to decree a constructive trust where property represents the profit, but on the present authorities it is uncertain in what circumstances misuse of confidential information may give rise to a constructive trust.

Damages

9–028   Damages are available at common law for breach of a contractual duty of confidence or inducement of breach of contract. Under the jurisdiction derived from Lord Cairns' Act 1858 (now contained in s.50 of the Supreme Court Act 1981) the court has a discretionary jurisdiction to award damages in addition to or in substitution for an injunction.

9–029   In *Malone v Metropolitan Police Commissioner*[41] Sir Robert Megarry V.C. said in relation to the right of confidentiality:

> "This is an equitable right which is still in course of development, and is usually protected by the grant of an injunction to prevent disclosure of the confidence. Under Lord Cairns' Act 1858 damages may be granted in substitution for an injunction; yet if there is no case for the grant of an injunction, as when the disclosure has already been made, the unsatisfactory result seems to be that no damages can be awarded under this head: see *Proctor v Bayley* (1889) 42 Ch.D. 390. In such a case, where there is no breach of contract or other orthodox foundation for damages at common law, it seems doubtful whether there is any right to damages, as distinct from an account of profits."

The Law Commission said in its Report on Breach of Confidence[42] that, so far as the repetition of a past, or anticipation of a future, breach of confidence is concerned, the courts have been empowered since Lord Cairns' Act to award damages in addition to or in substitution for an injunction. Lord Goff also referred in the *Spycatcher* case, in the passage cited above,[43] to damages being available under the Act for breach of an equitable duty of confidence.[44]

9–030   A more problematical question is the availability of damages in the situation instanced by Megarry V.C. where there is no case for the grant of

---

[40] For further criticisms of the Court of Appeal's decision, see Goff and Jones, *The Law of Restitution* (6th edn, 2002) at paras 33-019—33-020.
[41] [1979] 1 Ch. 344 at 360.
[42] Law Com. No.110, Cmnd. 8388 (1981), para.4.73.
[43] See paras 2–074 and 9–012.
[44] The same approach was taken by the Full Court of the Victorian Supreme Court in *Talbot v General Television Corporation Pty Ltd* [1981] R.P.C. 1; [1980] V.R. 224.

an injunction. This is considered in Chapter 2, dealing with the foundation[45] of the courts' jurisdiction in relation to breach of confidence. It is suggested that, quite apart from Lord Cairns' Act, compensation in equity (also known as equitable damages) may be awarded generally for breach of an equitable duty of confidence, just as for breach of duty by a fiduciary; and that the same compensatory principles underlie compensation or damages in equity as underlie damages at common law.[46] If this is correct, damages are available for breach of duty of confidence, whether in contract or in equity. These may in an appropriate case include loss of anticipated profits or "expectation damages".

In *United Scientific Holdings Ltd v Burnley Borough Council*[47] Lord Diplock said:

9–031

> "Your Lordships have been referred to the vivid phrase traceable to the first edition of *Ashburner, Principles of Equity* where, in speaking in 1902 of the effect of the Supreme Court of Judicature Act he says (p.23) 'the two streams of jurisdiction' (sc. law and equity) — 'though they run in the same channel, run side by side and do not mingle their waters.' My Lords, by 1977 this metaphor has in my view become both mischievous and deceptive. The innate conservatism of English lawyers may have made them slow to recognise that by the Supreme Court of Judicature Act 1873 the two systems of substantive and adjectival law formerly administered by courts of law and Courts of Chancery (as well as those administered by courts of admiralty, probate and matrimonial causes), were fused. As at the confluence of the Rhone and Saône, it may be possible for a short distance to discern the source from which each part of the combined stream came, but there comes a point at which this ceases to be possible. If Professor Ashburner's fluvial metaphor is to be retained at all, the waters of the confluent streams of law and equity have surely mingled now."

Lords Simon and Fraser made similar observations.[48]

In *Henderson v Merrett Syndicates Ltd*,[49] Lord Browne-Wilkinson, dealing with the relationship of law and equity in a different context, warned of the need to ensure that the law did not "become again manacled by 'clanking chains'[50] this time represented by causes, rather than forms of action". Similarly it may be thought anachronistic today that the court's power to award damages for breach of confidence should differ according

9–032

---

[45] Where alternatives including a tortious theory of liability are discussed.
[46] *Royal Bank of Brunei v Tan* [1995] 2 A.C. 378. See the discussion by the Supreme Court of Canada in *Cadbury Schweppes Inc v FBI Foods Ltd* (1999) 167 D.L.R. (4th) 577, at paras 55–61.
[47] [1978] A.C. 904 at 924.
[48] *ibid.* at 944 and 957.
[49] [1995] 2 A.C. 145 at 206.
[50] *United Australia Ltd v Barclays Bank Ltd* [1941] A.C. 1 at 29, *per* Lord Atkin. "When these ghosts of the past stand in the path of justice clanking their mediaeval chains the proper course for the judge is to pass through them undeterred".

to whether the cause of action lies in contract or in an equitable obligation of confidence.

9–033   In *Indata Equipment Supplies Ltd v ACL Ltd*[51] a financial broker agreed to arrange finance for a company which wanted to buy a new fleet of cars. The structure of the transaction was that the broker would buy the fleet from the manufacturer and sell it to a finance company, which would supply the fleet to the end user under a financial lease. The broker approached a finance company and gave it details of the end user's financial requirements, the price which the broker was paying to the supplier and its profit margin. Armed with this information, the finance company approached the end user with an offer of better terms by cutting out the broker. The end user accepted the offer. The Court of Appeal held that (1) the finance company acted in breach of an equitable obligation of confidentiality to the broker; (2) the broker was entitled to damages; and (3) the correct measure of damages was "on the tortious basis, ie such sum as would have put the plaintiff into the position it would have been in had it not been for the tort or breach of confidence".[52] Two members of the court considered that the finance company committed the tort of unlawful interference with the broker's business, as well as breach of an equitable obligation, but the case shows that the court considered that the measure of compensation for breach of the equitable obligation of confidence was the same as for tort.

9–034   Where confidential information of a commercial nature has been misused, damages may be assessed by reference to its commercial value.[53] The practical difficulties that may arise in relation to the valuation exercise were discussed in some detail by the Court of Appeal in *Gorne v Scales*.[54] This approach is less likely to be justified in cases involving a domestic context. In *Douglas v Hello! Ltd (No. 3)*,[55] the Court of Appeal upheld Lindsay J.'s refusal to award the Douglases damages equivalent to the notional licence fee that they would have charged Hello! to permit them to publish unauthorised photographs. The Court of Appeal made particular reference to the fact that, having sold the exclusive rights to publish photographs to OK!, the Douglases would not have been in a position to grant a licence to Hello!, but also observed[56]:

> " . . . the whole basis of their . . . complaint about Hello!'s publication of the unauthorised photographs is upset and affront at invasion of privacy, not loss of the opportunity to earn money . . . the Douglases would never have agreed to any of the unauthorised photographs being published."

---

[51] [1998] 1 B.C.L.C. 412.
[52] *ibid.* at 425–427.
[53] *Seager v Copydex (No.2)* [1969] 1 W.L.R. 809 at 813 *per* Lord Denning M.R.
[54] [2006] EWCA Civ 311.
[55] [2005] EWCA Civ 595; [2006] Q.B. 125, at [243]–[249].
[56] At [246].

Where misuse of confidential information relates to personal matters, damages can be awarded for mental stress or injury to feelings as well as for economic loss.

Although damages cannot ordinarily be recovered for injury to reputation **9–035** or feelings,[57] there are exceptions. Defamation has always been an exception, because injury to reputation is the essence of the wrong. The courts have also made an exception in cases of contract where the subject matter of the contract is the provision of pleasure[58] or protection from distress,[59] as distinct from other contracts where mental distress is a foreseeable consequence of breach.[60] It is right that there should be a similar exception in the case of misuse of confidential information relating to personal matters, because here the law is intended to protect personal feelings.

In *Williams v Settle*[61] the defendant, a professional photographer, was **9–036** employed to take photographs of the plaintiff's wedding. The copyright in the photographs vested in the plaintiff. Two years later the plaintiff's father-in-law was murdered. The defendant sold some of the photographs to the press, one of which, showing a wedding group, was published prominently in national newspapers. The trial judge awarded damages of £1,000, and this was upheld by the Court of Appeal.

In *Cornelius v de Taranto*[62] Morland J. awarded damages for distress **9–037** caused by a doctor wrongly disclosing a medical report on her to other medical staff.

In *Campbell v MGN Ltd*[63] the claimant was awarded damages for **9–038** distress caused by the publication of an article with photographs showing her leaving therapy session for drug addicts.

In *Douglas v Hello! Ltd*[64] the Court of Appeal upheld an award of **9–039** damages for personal distress and economic loss resulting from the publication of surreptitiously taken photographs of the claimants' wedding.

Section 7 of the Human Rights Act 1998 provides a right of action for a **9–040** person who claims that a public authority has acted in a way which is incompatible with his Convention rights. Under s.8, the court is empowered to award damages if such an award is necessary to afford just satisfaction to the person in whose favour it is made.[65]

The Court of Appeal of New Zealand has expressed the view in **9–041** *Aquaculture Corporation v New Zealand Green Mussel Co. Ltd*[66] that there is no reason in principle why exemplary damages should not be

---

[57] *Addis v Gramophone Co. Ltd* [1909] A.C. 488.
[58] *Jarvis v Swan Tours Ltd* [1973] Q.B. 233.
[59] *Heywood v Wellers* [1976] Q.B. 446.
[60] *Bliss v South East Thames Regional Health Authority* [1987] I.C.R. 700 at 718; *Hayes v Dodd* [1990] 2 All E.R. 815 at 826; *Watts v Morrow* [1991] 1 W.L.R. 1421 at 1439.
[61] [1960] 1 W.L.R. 1072.
[62] [2001] E.M.L.R. 12. The defendant's appeal on liability failed: [2001] EWCA Civ 1511; [2002] E.M.L.R. 6.
[63] [2004] UKHL 22; [2004] 2 A.C. 457 .
[64] [2005] EWCA Civ 595; [2006] Q.B. 125.
[65] See the Court of Appeal: guidance in *Anufrijera v Southwark LBC* [2003] EWCA Civ 1406; [2004] Q.B. 1124.
[66] [1990] 3 N.Z.L.R. 299 at 301.

awarded for actionable breach of confidence in a case where a compensatory award would not adequately reflect the gravity of the defendant's conduct, but there is a lack of English authority on the subject.

9–042 The law as to exemplary or punitive damages is now that laid down by the House of Lords in *Rookes v Barnard*.[67] The situations in which such damages may be awarded include conduct calculated to give the defendant a profit likely to exceed the compensation payable to the plaintiff.

9–043 The type of case most likely to give rise to a claim for exemplary damages would be where confidential information of a personal nature is leaked to, or surreptitiously obtained by, the media and published in disregard of the rights of the person concerned under Art.8. However, the imposition of a liability on the defendant which was not based on an assessment either of the damage to the claimant or of the profit to the defendant (through the taking of an account) would be liable to involve a disproportionate balance between Arts 8 and 10, and would almost certainly do so unless the court was satisfied, for example, that there had been a wilful disregard of any relevant journalistic code of practice.[68]

Declaration

9–044 The court has a discretionary power to grant declaratory relief, and this may be an appropriate way of determining questions of confidentiality.[69] Such relief is normally sought by a person complaining of breach of confidence. However there is no reason in principle why a person who is threatened with proceedings for breach of confidence if he makes use of information alleged to be confidential should not bring proceedings for a declaration of non-confidentiality, just as a party threatened, for example, with an action for passing off may seek a declaration of non-liability.[70] In *Price Waterhouse v BCCI Holdings (Luxembourg) SA*[71] the plaintiffs applied for, and were granted, a declaration that they were not precluded by confidence owed to the defendant or its customers from supplying information and documents to an inquiry into the supervision of BCCI, although it is doubted whether the court was right to do so without the customers being represented.

Search order

9–045 *Anton Piller KG v Manufacturing Processes Ltd*[72] was an action for infringement of copyright and misuse of confidential information. The

[67] [1964] A.C. 1129 at 1226–1227.
[68] See *Steel and Morris v United Kingdom* (2005) 41 E.H.R.R. 403 at paras 96 to 98; *Jameel v Wall Street Journal Europe Sprl* [2006] UKHL 44; [2006] 3 W.L.R. 642, especially *per* Lord Bingham at [18] and [19].
[69] See, for example, *Malone v Metropolitan Police Commissioner* [1979] 1 Ch. 344 and *Hellewell v Chief Constable of Derbyshire* [1995] 1 W.L.R. 804.
[70] Compare *Bulmer Ltd v Bollinger S.A.* [1974] Ch. 401; [1978] R.P.C. 79.
[71] [1992] B.C.L.C. 583. See para.6–041, above.
[72] [1976] Ch. 55.

action began with orders made *ex parte*, authorising the plaintiffs to inspect the defendants' premises and seize relevant documents. The procedure was approved by the Court of Appeal, with the warning that such an order was only to be made where it was essential so that justice could be done between the parties and when, if the defendant were forewarned, there would be grave danger that vital evidence would be destroyed or hidden.

Concern that such orders were being made too readily, and executed in a way which amounted to abuse, led to stricter controls being imposed by the courts: see *Columbia Picture Industries Inc. v Robinson*[73] per Scott J.; *Lock International plc v Beswick*[74] per Hoffmann J.; and *Universal Thermosensors Ltd v Hibben*[75] per Nicholls V.C. **9–046**

In *Universal Thermosensors Ltd v Hibben*, Nicholls V.C. commented that the case illustrated both the virtues and the vices of Anton Piller orders. The plaintiff was enabled to recover stolen documents containing confidential information, which the judge considered would in all probability otherwise have been destroyed; but this result was achieved at a high price. Irregularities in the execution of the order led to claims against the plaintiff and the plaintiff's solicitors which were settled during the trial. The jurisdiction of the High Court to make such orders, now called search orders, was put on a statutory basis by the Civil Procedure Act 1997, s.7.[76] **9–047**

A search order remains a valuable weapon, but one which requires the utmost care by the court and by the claimant both in making the application and in executing any order. The fact that such applications are usually made in a hurry makes it all the more important for the claimant to take care to ensure that all relevant matters are drawn to the attention of the court. **9–048**

Action for discovery

A person whose confidence has been breached, but who does not know who was responsible, may be able to bring an action against a recipient of the confidential information to compel him to disclose the identity of the informer. This form of action is derived from the ancient bill of discovery in equity, which was given new life by the decision of the House of Lords in *Norwich Pharmacal Co. v Customs and Excise Commissioners*[77] and applied by the House of Lords in *British Steel Corporation v Granada Television Ltd*.[78] In the latter case the action was brought to compel the disclosure of the source of confidential documents which had been leaked to Granada and used in a television programme. Granada relied on its own obligation of confidentiality to its source, whose identity it had promised not to reveal. The House of Lords ordered disclosure, but recognised that **9–049**

---

[73] [1987] Ch. 38.
[74] [1989] 1 W.L.R. 1268.
[75] [1992] F.S.R. 361.
[76] The procedure for making an application and a draft form of order are set out in a practice direction on interim injunctions which supplements CPR Pt 25.
[77] [1974] A.C. 133.
[78] [1981] A.C. 1096 at 1171.

the remedy of an action for discovery, being equitable, was discretionary,[79] and that the court ought not to compel confidence bona fide given to be breached unless necessary in the interests of justice.[80]

9–050   The subject of disclosure of journalistic sources is discussed in Chapter 13.

Delay

9–051   In accordance with ordinary principles of equity, a person seeking equitable relief against breach of confidence will risk refusal if he fails to act with reasonable promptness once he knows of the breach. He cannot, for example, stand by while the party in breach exploits the information and then claim an account of profits. For actions based on breach of contract the limitation period is six years, subject to the provisions of s.32 of the Limitation Act 1980 relating to fraud, concealment or mistake.

---

[79] *British Steel Corporation v Granada Television Ltd* [1981] A.C. 1096 at 1174, *per* Lord Wilberforce.
[80] *Science Research Council v Nasse* [1980] A.C. 1028.

CHAPTER 10

Confidentiality and Foreign Law

A conflict of laws problem arises if the law of one country is invoked to **10–001** obtain disclosure of documents or information within the jurisdiction of another, *a fortiori* if such disclosure would be contrary to the law of the country in whose jurisdiction they are.

There is generally accepted and well founded dislike of laws which have **10–002** extra-territorial effect, both on grounds of respect for the jurisdiction of other countries and to avoid injustice in the form of a party being subject to mutually contradictory edicts. The risk is particularly great for companies, like banks, operating across frontiers. But there is another side to the picture. Neill L.J. observed in *Derby & Co Ltd v Weldon (Nos 3 & 4)*[1] that "assets, like the Cheshire cat, may disappear unexpectedly", and that modern technology and the ingenuity of its beneficiaries can make assets depart at a speed which would make the disappearance of the Cheshire cat look sluggish.

There may therefore be cases in which strict adherence by the courts to **10–003** the principle of territoriality may play into the hands of fraudsters. The authorities may be divided into three groups:

(1) cases where English courts are asked to make an order requiring production of documents of a confidential nature which are outside the jurisdiction;

(2) cases where foreign courts make an order requiring production of documents of a confidential nature which are within the United Kingdom;

(3) cases where English courts or regulatory authorities are asked to assist the courts or regulatory authorities of another country.

---

[1] [1990] Ch. 65 at 95.

Cases where English courts are asked to order production of confidential documents outside the jurisdiction

10–004   It is necessary to distinguish between:

(1) cases where the person against whom the order is sought is a party to litigation in the United Kingdom[2] (otherwise than merely for the purpose of obtaining disclosure of information under the *Norwich Pharmacal*[3] procedure); and

(2) cases where the person against whom the order is sought is not a party to the litigation or has been joined in an action only for the purpose of obtaining disclosure of information.

In the former class the ordinary rules of disclosure make no distinction between documents inside and outside the jurisdiction, so long as they are within the possession, custody or power of the party from whom disclosure is sought. This involves no breach of comity, because disclosure in the ordinary course of litigation is a matter of procedure, not substance, and the principle that procedure is governed by the *lex fori* is of general application and universally admitted.[4]

10–005   In cases where the party against whom a production order is sought is not a party to the action, or has been joined for the purpose of discovery, an order for production is not merely an incidental matter of procedure but is the substance of the relief sought. In *R. v Grossman*[5] an order was made, *ex parte*, against Barclays Bank Ltd at its London head office requiring it to allow the Inland Revenue to inspect and take copies of its books relating to the account of an Isle of Man company at its Isle of Man branch, under s.7 of the Bankers' Books Evidence Act 1879. The order was set aside by the Court of Appeal. Lord Denning M.R. said[6]:

"I think that the branch of Barclays Bank in Douglas, Isle of Man, should be considered in the same way as a branch of the Bank of Ireland or an American Bank, or any other bank in the Isle of Man which is not subject to our jurisdiction. The branch of Barclays Bank in Douglas, Isle of Man, should be considered as a different entity

---

[2] This category also includes cases in which an application for pre-action disclosure is made against a person *likely* to be made a party to litigation in the United Kingdom: see *Mitsui & Co Ltd v Nexen Petroleum UK Ltd* [2005] EWHC 625, Ch; [2005] 3 All E.R. 511, *per* Lightman J. at paras 30–32.

[3] *Norwich Pharmacal Co v Customs & Excise Commissioners* [1974] A.C. 133.

[4] Dicey, Morris & Collins, *The Conflict of Laws* (14th edn, 2006), p.177, citing *Ailes* (1941) 39 Mich.L.Rev. 392; *The Consul Corfitzon* [1917] A.C. 550 at 555–556; *MacKinnon v Donaldson, Lufkin & Jenrette Corp* [1986] 1 Ch. 483 at 494–495, *per* Hoffmann J.,"I am not concerned with the discovery required by R.S.C., Ord. 24 from ordinary parties to English litigation who happen to be foreigners. If you join the game you must play according to the local rules. This applies not only to plaintiffs but also to defendants who give notice of intention to defend".

[5] (1981) 73 Cr.App.R. 302.

[6] *ibid.* at 307.

separate from the head office in London. It is subject to the laws and regulations of the Isle of Man. It is licensed by the Isle of Man government. It has its customers there who are subject to the Manx laws. It seems to me that the court here ought not in its discretion to make an order against the head office here in respect of the books of the branch in the Isle of Man in regard to the customers of that branch. It would not be right to compel the branch—or its customers—to open their books or to reveal their confidences in support of legal proceedings in Wales. Any order in respect of the production of the books ought to be made by the courts of the Isle of Man—if they will make such an order. It ought not to be made by these courts. Otherwise there would be danger of a conflict of jurisdictions between the High Court here and the courts of the Isle of Man. That is a conflict which we must always avoid."

In *MacKinnon v Donaldson, Lufkin and Jenrette Securities Corporation*[7] the plaintiff in an action involving allegations of international fraud obtained an order *ex parte* under the Bankers' Books Evidence Act requiring an American bank, which was not a party to the action, to produce books held at its head office in New York relating to one of the defendants, a defunct Bahamian company. The plaintiff also issued a *supoena duces tecum* against an officer of the bank at its London office. Hoffmann J. set aside both orders. **10–006**

The plaintiff attempted to distinguish *Grossman* on the ground that in that case the Isle of Man court had previously refused a similar application and had granted an injunction restraining the bank from disclosing the information. It was also argued that the American bank, by carrying on business in London, had submitted to the jurisdiction of the English court and should be required to comply with the *subpoena* unless production would be unlawful by the law of the place where the documents were kept. **10–007**

Hoffmann J. rejected that argument. He said[8]: **10–008**

"I think that this argument confuses personal jurisdiction, i.e. who can be brought before the court, with subject matter jurisdiction, i.e. to what extent the court can claim to regulate the conduct of those persons. It does not follow from the fact that a person is within the jurisdiction and liable to be served with process that there is no territorial limit to the matters upon which the court may properly apply its own rules or the things which it can order such a person to do. As Dr Mann observed in a leading article "The Doctrine of Jurisdiction in International Law", (1964) 111 *Recueil de cours* 146,

---

[7] [1986] 1 Ch. 482.
[8] *ibid.* at 493.

'The mere fact that a state's judicial or administrative agencies are internationally entitled to subject a person to their personal or "curial" jurisdiction does not by any means permit them to regulate by their orders such person's conduct abroad. This they may do only if the state of the forum also had substantive jurisdiction to regulate conduct in the manner defined in the order. In other words, for the purpose of justifying, even in the territory of the forum, the international validity of an order, not only its making, but also its content must be authorised by substantive rules of legislative jurisdiction.'

See also by the same author "The Doctrine of International Jurisdiction Revisited after Twenty Years" (1984) 196 *Recueil des cours* 9, 19.

The content of the subpoena and order is to require the production by a non-party of documents outside the jurisdiction concerning business which it has transacted outside the jurisdiction. In principle and on authority it seems to me that the court should not, save in exceptional circumstances, impose such a requirement upon a foreigner, and, in particular, upon a foreign bank. The principle is that a state should refrain from demanding obedience to its sovereign authority by foreigners in respect of their conduct outside the jurisdiction."

The plaintiff also attempted to distinguish *Grossman* by arguing that he would be entitled to join the bank as a defendant under *Norwich Pharmacal*[9] and *Bankers Trust Co v Shapira*[10] and that the case should not therefore be regarded as an attempt to enforce discovery against a non-party.

10–009   Hoffmann J. rejected that distinction, holding that for jurisdictional purposes such cases were much more akin to a *subpoena* directed to a witness than to discovery required of an ordinary defendant, and that the court should recognise the same international jurisdictional limits in such cases as in cases of a *subpoena duces tecum* or an order under the Bankers' Books Evidence Act 1879. He accordingly held, following *Grossman*, that an order for production of documents held at a bank's foreign branch or head office should not be made save in very exceptional circumstances. He also expressed the opinion that, where alternative procedures were available (as by way of letters rogatory), an infringement of sovereignty could seldom be justified except perhaps on the grounds of urgent necessity relied upon by Templeman J. in *London and County Securities Ltd v Caplan*.[11]

10–010   In *Re Mid East Trading Ltd*[12] the Court of Appeal held that, since the courts had been given the power to wind up overseas companies under s.221 of the Insolvency Act 1986, the legislature must be taken to have intended the courts in appropriate circumstances to make such assertion of

---

[9] [1974] A.C. 133.
[10] [1980] 1 W.L.R. 1274.
[11] Unreported, May 26, 1978.
[12] [1998] 1 All E.R. 577 at 592–593.

sovereignty as might be required in making an order under s.236 of the Act to produce documents situated abroad. Where compliance with such an order would or might expose the respondent to civil claims or criminal penalties in the jurisdiction in which the documents were situated, that would be an important factor, to be weighted with others; but there was no special hurdle of "exceptional circumstances" to be overcome by the applicant.

Cases where foreign courts have ordered production of confidential documents within the United Kingdom

The same reasoning applies in reverse in cases of orders by foreign courts for production of confidential documents in the United Kingdom. In *X AG v A Bank*[13] a *subpoena* was issued in the United States District Court for the Southern District of New York against an American bank requiring it to produce documents relating to accounts maintained at its London branch by X, a Swiss corporation with no business in the United States, and Y, a subsidiary of X which was also incorporated in Switzerland, but had a major office in New York. The *subpoena* was returnable before a federal grand jury investigating alleged tax evasion. The bank declared its intention to comply with the *subpoena*. X and Y obtained an injunction in the English High Court restraining the bank from doing so on the ground that it would be in breach of duty of confidence. An order was then made by the New York District Court, *ex parte* and *in camera*, requiring the bank to comply with the *subpoena*. The bank applied to set aside the High Court injunction. Leggatt J. refused to do so.   **10–011**

Since the injunction was interlocutory, Leggatt J. decided the matter on *American Cyanamid* principles and did not have to reach a final determination of the points of law raised. However, he referred to the order enforcing the *subpoena* as "the exercise by the United States court in London of powers which, by English standards, would be regarded as excessive"[14] and stated that in relation to the merits he was firmly on the side of the plaintiffs.   **10–012**

After referring to the qualifications to the duty of banking confidentiality recognised in *Tournier v National Provincial and Union Bank of England*,[15] the first being where disclosure is by compulsion of law, the judge observed that to apply foreign law in relation to banking business conducted in the City of London would be "to allow a fairly large cuckoo in the domestic nest".[16]   **10–013**

It was also argued by the bank that an English court would not enforce a contract if performance required the doing of an act which violates the law   **10–014**

---

[13] [1983] 2 All E.R. 464.
[14] Cited by Hoffmann J. in *Mackinnon v Donaldson, Lufkin & Jenrette Corp* [1986] 1 Ch. 482 at 494.
[15] [1924] 1 K.B. 461 at 473.
[16] [1983] 2 All E.R. 464 at 478.

of the place of performance (*Ralli Bros v Compania Naviera a Sota y Aznar*[17]), and therefore the contract was unenforceable in so far as it sought to require confidentiality in New York.

10–015   If, following the approach in *Grossman*, a bank's London and overseas branches are to be regarded as separate entities, the performance which the English order was seeking to enforce was performance in England. Disclosure in New York could only happen if the London branch breached its duty of confidentiality in London by disclosure of documents to its New York branch for production in New York. The fact that a consequence of the contract being performed in its place of performance (England) was that the documents would not reach New York did not make the English order an extra-territorial order.[18]

10–016   Legatt J. rejected the argument that to continue the injunction would be to enforce a contract in a manner contrary to the law of the place of performance on a different ground, that the *subpoena* and order made without argument on the merits were not to be equated with legislation or a final judgment, and could not be said to have rendered the keeping of secrecy by the bank illegal, particularly since the evidence suggested the bank was most unlikely in the circumstances to be held in contempt by the New York court.

10–017   In *A v B Bank*[19] Morland J. made an order both restraining the defendant bank from delivering up to a grand jury in New York any documents held at their London branch relating to the plaintiffs' accounts, and also requiring the bank to return to their London branch any documents already removed from the jurisdiction in connection with the grand jury *subpoena*. By contrast, in *Pharaon v BCCI SA*[20] Price Waterhouse sought the permission of the court to comply with a subpoena issued in New York that required it to produce documents relating to BCCI's activities in the United States. Rattee J. held that the public interest in making documents available in US proceedings that arose out of alleged fraud on the part of BCCI outweighed the public interest in upholding the duty of confidentiality owed by Price Waterhouse to BCCI, its customers and its shareholders.

Assistance by English courts or regulatory authorities to foreign courts or regulatory authorities

10–018   The United Kingdom is a party to the Hague Convention on the *Taking of Evidence Abroad in Civil and Commercial Matters* (1970)[21] and to a

---

[17] [1920] 2 K.B. 287.

[18] Nor would an order requiring an English company to bring back documents relating to a domestic subject matter, which it had sent out of the jurisdiction (as in *Director of Public Prosecutions v Channel Four Television* [1993] 2 All E.R. 517), be regarded as assuming extra-territorial subject matter jurisdiction.

[19] Unreported, August 13, 1990. The order is recited in the later judgment of Hirst J. reported at [1993] Q.B. 311.

[20] [1998] 4 All E.R. 455.

[21] Cmnd. 3991 (1970). The Convention came into force in the United Kingdom on September 14, 1976.

number of bilateral civil procedure conventions. English courts have jurisdiction to assist in obtaining evidence for foreign courts or tribunals under the Evidence (Proceedings in Other Jurisdictions) Act 1975 and CPR Pt 34.

The question of confidentiality arose in *Re State of Norway's Application*.[22] Norwegian proceedings involved an issue whether a deceased tax payer was the settlor of a trust. On the request of the Norwegian court an order was made by the English court for examination of two directors of the trust's London bank on a number of matters including the identity of the settlor. The Court of Appeal[23] held, by a majority, that the order should be set aside on the grounds that its terms were too wide and that the directors should not be required to disclose banking confidences, which might affect unknown people, in a case where there was no allegation of fraud or crime.

10–019

On a second request by the Norwegian court, in more limited terms, a further order was made and was upheld by the judge, with the qualification that the witnesses were not to be asked the identity of the settlor unless either of them first gave evidence that the settlor was the agent or nominee of the deceased tax payer. The judge's order was reversed by the Court of Appeal on a point of jurisdiction but restored by the House of Lords. On the issue of confidentiality, Woolf L.J. said[24] that in deciding whether to assist in obtaining the evidence requested in the proceedings, where a question of confidentiality arose, the English court should adopt the same approach as if the proceedings were taking place before the English court. That required a balancing exercise which the judge had properly performed. The judge's approach was approved in the House of Lords by Lord Goff, with whom the other members of the appellate committee agreed.[25]

10–020

In relation to criminal law the United Kingdom is a party to various conventions, including the Convention on Mutual Assistance in Criminal Matters (2000). The Criminal Justice (International Co-operation) Act 2003, s.16, provides that the powers of entry, search and seizure under the Police and Criminal Evidence Act 1984 are extended to enable evidence to be obtained at the request of bodies including a foreign court or prosecuting authority, or the International Criminal Police Organisation, in cases which would be serious arrestable offences if they occurred in the United Kingdom, and s.19 provides for seized evidence to be sent directly to the requesting authority. Other provisions of the Act include measures, subject to judicial authorisation, for the monitoring of bank accounts and supply of banking information to assist foreign authorities investigating serious criminal offences.[26]

10–021

---

[22] [1990] 1 A.C. 723.
[23] [1987] 1 Q.B. 433.
[24] [1990] 1 A.C. 723 at 782.
[25] See *USA v Philip Morris Inc* [2004] EWCA Civ 330, in which, notwithstanding possible issues of legal professional privilege, the Court of Appeal acceded to a letter of request seeking the examination of a lawyer who had previously acted for the appellant tobacco company, which was now a defendant to proceedings in the United States.
[26] See ss.32–46.

10–022   A regulatory body which has power to require disclosure of confidential material may also have a right to disclose it to a foreign counterpart. In *A v B Bank*,[27] after the U.S. Federal Reserve Board had failed to secure the documents which it wanted from the defendant bank by grand jury *subpoena* (because the bank was restrained from disclosing them by injunction), it approached the Bank of England with information which caused the latter to serve a notice on the defendant bank, under s.39 of the Banking Act 1987, requiring production of documents relating to the plaintiffs' accounts. Section 82 of the Act placed restrictions on the Bank of England's power to disclose information which it obtained under the Act about a person's affairs to another person; but, by s.84, those restrictions did not preclude it from disclosing such information for the purpose of assisting an authority with corresponding functions in another country. So there was nothing to prevent the Bank of England from supplying the documents to the Federal Reserve Board.

10–023   Hirst J. rejected the plaintiffs' argument that the injunction previously granted by Morland J. precluded the defendant bank from complying with the Bank of England's notice. He also rejected the allegation that the notice was invalid because the Bank of England was acting for a collateral purpose, as an evidence gathering agency for a foreign supervisory body. His judgment suggests that the courts will incline to a broad view of a supervisory authority's functions in matters involving international co-operation. He said[28]:

> "[Counsel for the plaintiffs] seeks in effect to draw a line down the centre of the Atlantic, and to suggest that in some way the supervisory operations of the Federal Reserve Board and those of the Bank of England are separate and unconnected. In fact, in the world of international banking today, supervisory authorities in various countries can, should, and no doubt do regularly co-operate on matters of mutual supervisory concern as sections 84(6) and 86 confirm."

[27] [1993] Q.B. 311. See para.10–017, below.
[28] *ibid.* at 327.

PART 2

Particular Relationships

A list of all relationships, occupations and positions, likely to give rise to duties of confidence—if it were possible to compile—would be very long. It would include agents, trustees, partners and employees; professional people; holders of public and private offices; personal relationships, such as husband and wife; counsellors and mediators; and many others.

In this part of the book a small number are considered in further detail: medical advisers; bankers; broadcasters and journalists; employees; teachers, clergy, counsellors and mediators; and lawyers. They have been chosen either because there are important authorities relating to them, or because they are of particular interest, or for both reasons.

CHAPTER 11

Medical advisers[1]

The modern version of the Hippocratic Oath introduced by the World **11–001**
Medical Association as the Declaration of Geneva (as amended at Sydney in
1968) includes the statement:

> "I will respect the secrets which are confided in me, even after the
> patient has died."

There is no doubt that the relationship of doctor[2] and patient carries with
it a legal obligation of confidence in respect of confidential information
concerning the patient gained by the doctor in his professional capacity,[3]
whether directly from the patient or, for example, from medical records.
The scope of the duty can present particularly difficult questions.

A wide array of published guidance now exists to assist health profession- **11–002**
als in the assessment and performance of the duties of confidentiality owed
by them to patients and others, including (for example):

(1) The General Medical Council's *Confidentiality: Protecting and
Providing Information* (April 2004);

---

[1] On confidentiality and the medical profession, see Grubb, *The Principles of Medical Law*
(2nd edn, 2004), pp.554–638 and Mason and McCall Smith, *Law and Medical Ethics* (7th
edn, 2005), pp.253–294.
[2] This chapter concentrates on doctors, but duties of confidentiality are owed by all concerned
in advising and treating patients.
[3] *Hunter v Mann* [1974] Q.B. 767 at 772. *W v Egdell* [1990] Ch. 359.

(2) The Department of Health's *NHS Code of Practice: Confidentiality* (November 2003);

(3) The Department of Health's *Protecting and using patient information: a manual for Caldicott Guardians* (March 1999);

(4) The Royal College of Nursing's *Guidance for Occupational Health Nurses: Confidentiality* (2005);

(5) The Royal College of Pychiatrists and the Princess Royal Trust for Carers' *Carers and confidentiality in mental health: Issues involved in information-sharing* (August 2004);

(6) The Royal College of Paediatrics and Child Health's *Responsibilities of Doctors in Child Protection Cases with regard to Confidentiality* (February 2004);

(7) The General Dental Council's *Principles of Patient Confidentiality* (May 2005);

(8) The British Psychological Society (Division of Clinical Psychology)'s *Professional Practice Guidelines* 1995, s.6 (*Confidentiality*).

11–003   Although a patient may be the most obvious, he or she is not the only person entitled to assert the confidentiality of medical information. Health organisations and individual health professionals may also have independent rights of confidentiality.

In *Ashworth Hospital Authority v MGN Ltd*[4] the health organisation responsible for Ashworth Security Hospital obtained an order requiring the defendant newspaper publisher to disclose the identity of the source of confidential information that the *Daily Mirror* had obtained in relation to the medical records of Ian Brady, the notorious "Moors murderer". In the Court of Appeal, Lord Phillips M.R. said[5]:

> "Though they were personal to Brady, I consider that Ashworth had a clear independent interest in retaining their confidentiality. The Department of Health published, on 7 March 1996, Guidance on the Protection and Use of Patient Information. This includes the following guidance under the heading, 'Who has a duty of confidence?': Everyone working for or with the NHS who records, handles, stores, or otherwise comes across information has a personal common law duty of confidence to patients *and to his or her employer.*" [Emphasis added by Lord Phillips]

The *Daily Mirror*'s source, disclosed after the decision of the House of Lords, turned out to be an intermediary journalist, Mr Robin Ackroyd. A subsequent action, brought to require him in turn to reveal his own source,

---

[4] [2002] UKHL 29; [2001] 1 W.L.R. 515, CA; [2002] 1 W.L.R. 2033, HL.
[5] At para.52.

failed before Tugendhat J.[6] However, Tugendhat J. confirmed the hospital's standing to seek protection for the relevant information, saying[7]:

> "Ian Brady is the subject of that information. A patient has a right to disclose to the public at large information that he has previously given in confidence to a doctor. He also has certain rights of access to information recorded about him by the doctor or hospital. But he does not have an unrestricted right to seize the records kept by the doctor or hospital and publish them to the world. Nor would he have an unrestricted right to authorise any doctor or nurse to disclose the contents of those records. The hospital, as the body responsible for keeping and controlling those records, and other individuals referred to in them, have rights and responsibilities in respect of the information contained in those records."

A doctor may wish, or feel that he may be under a duty, to disclose **11–004** information about a patient for a wide variety of purposes. They include:

(1) diagnosis, advice and treatment;
(2) clinical audit and regulation;
(3) advancement of medicine;
(4) protection of others;
(5) protection of himself;
(6) management and record keeping;
(7) compliance with a requirement of law.

He is plainly at liberty to disclose information if required by law or with consent properly given.

Consent may be express or implied. Whether it is to be implied will **11–005** depend on the nature and purpose of the disclosure. But there may be situations in which, for one reason or another, the doctor acts deliberately without consent.

Difficulties may also arise in relation to minors or persons under a **11–006** disability and disclosures within the family. Medical confidence is one incident of the relationship between the doctor and his patient and exists for the benefit of the patient. It is not absolute, not only because it would defeat the object for which it exists if it precluded the doctor from making disclosure in circumstances where, in the exercise of a proper professional judgment, he considered it in the patient's best interests to do so, but also because its preservation could in some circumstances be harmful for other reasons.

---

[6] *Mersey Care NHS Trust v Ackroyd* [2006] EWHC 107, QB.
[7] At [94].

11–007   The fullest judicial statement is to be found in *Duncan v Medical Practitioner's Disciplinary Committee*, where Jeffries J. attempted to summarise both the principle of medical confidence and certain qualifications. He said[8]:

> "The Court now addresses directly what is medical confidence? It is not difficult to grasp the broad concept of professional confidence for it is fundamental to the relationship of a professional man with a lay person. On a strict analysis of legal relationships, it is probably contractually based, as several cases have suggested . . . .
>
> Without trust [the doctor/patient relationship] would not function properly so as to allow freedom for the patient to disclose all manner of confidences and secrets in the practical certainty that they would repose with the doctor. There rests with a doctor a strong ethical obligation to observe a strict confidentiality by holding inviolate the confidences and secrets he receives in the course of his professional ministerings. If he adheres to that ethical principle then the full scope of his ability to administer medical assistance to his patient will develop.
>
> The foregoing embodies the principle of medical confidence, but it cannot be left there without identifying the existence of qualifications and modifications for I have described, not defined exhaustively the concept. Confidentiality is not breached by private discussions with colleagues in pursuance of treatment, but this may require full disclosure and consent. The confidentiality may be waived by the patient. The doctor may be required by law to disclose. A doctor may be in a group practice where common filing systems are used. Staff who have access to information must be impressed with the requirement of confidence. Limited information to some outside agencies may be made available by a doctor from his files for statistical, accounting, data processing or other legitimate purposes. A doctor may be treating more than one person that requires, or mandates, exchange of information, but here caution and prudence must be carefully observed and consents obtained. As this very case demonstrates a doctor may reveal confidences and secrets if he is required to defend himself, or others, against accusations of wrongful conduct. There may be occasions, they are fortunately rare, when a doctor receives information involving a patient that another's life is immediately endangered and urgent action is required. The doctor must then exercise his professional judgment based upon the circumstances, and if he fairly and reasonably believes such a danger exists then he must act unhesitatingly to prevent injury or loss of life even if there is to be a breach of confidentiality. If his actions later are to be scrutinised as to their correctness, he can be confident any official inquiry will be by people sympathetic about the predicament he faced. However, that qualification cannot be advanced

[8] [1986] 1 N.Z.L.R. 513 at 520, N.Z. High Court.

so as to attenuate, or undermine, the immeasurably valuable concept of medical confidence. If it were applied in that way it would be misapplied, in my view, because it would be extravagant with what is essentially a qualification to the principle. Some might say that is line-drawing and if they do then so be it. The line-drawing is not arbitrary but based upon reason and experience, and is the exercise of pro-fessional judgment which is part of daily practice for a doctor. The foregoing, either in the description or the qualifications, is not advanced as anything but an outline."

Anonymisation

Problems relating to patients' consent or to disclosure without such consent **11–008** need not arise if the information is disclosed in such a manner as to ensure that the patients to whom it relates cannot be identified.

In *R. v Department of Health, Ex p. Source Informatics Ltd*,[9] the Court **11–009** of Appeal held that the applicant company committed no breach of confidence in purchasing information from the computerised prescription records of pharmacists and passing that information on to pharmaceutical companies, which used it for marketing purposes. Crucially, the informa-tion provided by the applicant was in anonymised form. Giving the only judgment, Simon Brown L.J. agreed[10] with submissions, advanced on behalf of the General Medical Council, that patients could not be taken to have impliedly consented to the use made by the applicant of information relating to them. Nevertheless, he concluded:

"The concern of the law here is to protect the confider's personal privacy. That and that alone is the right at issue in this case. The patient has no proprietorial claim to the prescription form or to the informa-tion it contains. Of course he can bestow or withhold his custom as he pleases . . . But that gives the patient no property in the information and no right to control its use provided only and always that his privacy is not put at risk."[11]

Annex B of the Department of Health's *NHS Code of Practice: Confiden-* **11–010** *tiality*[12] states that, once information is effectively anonymised, it is no longer confidential, but warns:

"Effective anonymisation generally requires more than just the removal of name and address. Full postcode can identify individuals, NHS Number can be a strong identifier and other information, e.g. date of

[9] [2001] Q.B. 424.
[10] At para.51.
[11] At para.34.
[12] November 2003, at p.29

birth, can also serve as an identifier, particularly if looked at in combination with other data items."

The General Medical Council goes further, advising that, in view of the difficulty in anonymising case studies fully,

" . . . you must obtain express consent from patients before publishing personal information about them as individuals in media to which the public has access, for example in journals or text books, whether or not you believe the patient can be identified."[13]

This guidance may well be sensible from a practical and professional standpoint, but it does not undermine the Court of Appeal's decision about the effect in law of anonymisation.

Diagnosis, advice and treatment

11–011   In *Sidaway v Board of Governors of the Bethlem Royal Hospital and the Maudsley Hospital*[14] the plaintiff underwent an elective operation which carried a very small risk of damage to the spinal column. This occurred. The surgeon had not advised her of the risk. The judge found that in refraining from doing so he was following a practice which would have been accepted as proper by a responsible body of skilled and experienced neuro-surgeons, and, applying the test formulated in *Bolam v Friern Barnet Management Committee*,[15] he held that the surgeon was not liable. His judgment was upheld by the House of Lords.

11–012   It was argued by the plaintiff that the surgeon's failure to inform should be regarded as a breach of duty, independently of any medical opinion or practice. The House of Lords preferred to view the matter in the context of the doctor's professional duty to his patient. Lord Bridge said that a doctor's professional functions may broadly be divided into three phases: diagnosis, advice and treatment, each requiring the exercise of professional judgment. He also said,[16]

"A very wide variety of factors must enter into a doctor's clinical judgment not only as to what treatment is appropriate for a particular patient, but also as to how best to communicate to the patient the significant factors necessary to enable the patient to make an informed decision whether to undergo the treatment. He may take the view, certainly with some patients, that the very fact of his volunteering, without being asked, information of some remote risk in the treatment

[13] *Confidentiality: Protecting and Providing Information/Frequently Asked* (answers to frequently asked questions, published on the GMC's web-site)
[14] [1985] A.C. 871.
[15] [1957] 1 W.L.R. 582.
[16] [1985] A.C. 871.

proposed, even though he described it as remote, may lead to that risk assuming an undue significance in the patient's calculations."

For purposes of diagnosis, advice or treatment, a doctor might wish to discuss a patient's case with colleagues or to have tests done. Investigative procedures involving the taking of samples or invasive techniques clearly require the patient's consent, whether they are performed for the purpose of routine screening (as in pregnancy) or for the more specific purpose of differential diagnosis.   **11–013**

A more difficult question is to what extent the patient's explicit consent is needed for a sample to be tested in a particular way which the patient may not appreciate is intended. A doctor might not wish to go into the precise forms of testing with his patient in advance, for reasons similar to those referred to by Lord Bridge, i.e. to avoid causing possibly undue alarm.   **11–014**

It is suggested that, in general, a patient who consults a doctor impliedly consents to the doctor disclosing such information about the patient to other appropriately skilled staff (whether by sending a sample for analysis or otherwise) as may be necessary to enable the doctor to decide how best to perform the three phases of diagnosis, advice and treatment. But that is a general, not a universal, proposition. It may be displaced by other considerations.   **11–015**

The scope of any implied consent may vary according to the purpose for which the doctor is consulted. For example, a doctor instructed to provide a medico-legal report for the purpose of possible legal proceedings may commit a breach of confidence if he or she discloses the report for therapeutic purposes, without the client's express consent, to the client's general practitioner, or to other medical practitioners.[17]   **11–016**

Special considerations also apply in relation to testing for serious communicable diseases. For example, there has been particular controversy in relation to HIV testing.[18] Performing a venepuncture without consent would be an assault. But, assuming that consent is given for the procedure, the question arises whether sending a sample for HIV testing without informing the patient of the proposed nature of the test would involve a breach of the doctor's duty towards his patient.   **11–017**

The GMC's guidance on this subject[19] is explicit. It advises that consent must be obtained from patients before testing for a serious communicable disease, except in rare specified circumstances. It also observes: **11–018**

"Some conditions, such as HIV, have serious social and financial, as well as medical, implications. In such cases you must make sure that the

---

[17] *Cornelius v de Taranto* [2001] E.M.L.R. 12, Morland J.; largely upheld by the Court of Appeal [2001] EWCA Civ 1511; [2002] E.M.L.R. 6, CA.
[18] See the discussion in Mason and McCall Smith, *Law and Medical Ethics* (7th edn, 2005), pp.386–393.
[19] *Serious Communicable Diseases* (October 1997).

patient is given appropriate information about the implications of the test, and appropriate time to consider and discuss them."[20]

It would be difficult for a doctor who ignored that advice to rely on a defence of implied consent to a claim by the patient for breach of confidence in using his specimen for HIV testing without his actual consent.

11–019   Even where a patient's consent to disclosure for the purposes of diagnosis, advice, or treatment can be implied, it is good practice to inform the patient expressly that such disclosure is possible. The GMC's advice is that:

> "Most people understand and accept that information must be shared within the health care team in order to provide their care. You should make sure that patients are aware that personal information about them will be shared within the health care team, unless they object, and of the reasons for this . . . "

Clinical audit and regulation

11–020   Doctors are professionally obliged to participate in clinical audit and to comply with the regulatory requirements of the General Medical Council. Although it is for the courts, not a professional body, to determine the scope of a doctor's duty of confidentiality, in doing so the courts will have close regard to any professional guidance or requirements promulgated by a responsible professional or regulatory body. A court would be likely to conclude that a doctor's duty of confidentiality would be qualified so as to permit him to participate properly in clinical audit or to comply with reasonable requirements of the General Medical Council, provided that steps are taken (by way of anonymisation or otherwise) to ensure that the confidential information thereby disclosed is reduced to the minimum level that is consonant with the doctor's professional obligations. Again, however, it is good practice to ensure that patients are properly informed in relation to any disclosures to be made.[21]

11–021   The General Medical Council has statutory powers under s.35A of the Medical Act 1983 to require a practitioner or any other person to supply information or produce documentation which appears relevant to the discharge of its functions in respect of professional conduct, professional performance or fitness to practise.

11–022   In *A Health Authority v X*,[22] the Court of Appeal considered the circumstances in which a doctor should comply with a health authority's request for patient records, made pursuant to para.36(6) of Sch.2 to the

---

[20] See also the Department of Health's *Guidelines for pre-test discussion on HIV testing* (PL CO (96)1, March 1996).
[21] GMC, *Confidentiality: Protecting and Providing Information* (April 2004), at paras 13 and 21.
[22] [2001] EWCA Civ 2014; [2002] 2 All E.R. 780.

National Health Service (General Medical Services) Regulations 1992.[23] At first instance, Munby J. had said[24]:

> "Now of course in the final analysis Dr X's ultimate obligation is to comply with whatever order the court may make. But prior to that point being reached his duty, like that of any other professional or other person who owes a duty of confidentiality to his patient or client, is to assert that confidentiality in answer to any claim by a third party for disclosure and to put before the court every argument that can properly be put against disclosure. All the more so when, as in the present case, he knows, because he has asked, that his patient or client is refusing to consent to disclosure."

On appeal, it was argued by the health authority that a doctor's duty was rather to comply with a para.36(6) request unless he had reason to doubt the health authority's right to make it. Giving the only judgment, Thorpe L.J. emphasised that the Court of Appeal's decision should not be construed or used as laying down any general propositions beyond the context of Children Act proceedings and their aftermath, but said[25]:

> "However I would add that I am not persuaded that Munby J. overstated the doctor's duty to his patient."

Leaving aside the provisions of the Family Proceedings Rules 1991 that were engaged in *A Health Authority v X*, Munby J.'s *dictum* may be very relevant to the question whether a doctor has acted properly in disclosing confidential information to a third party (such as a Primary Care Trust). He ought not to make such disclosure without considering the interests of the patient or client, and, if he is uncertain whether the patient or client might legitimately object to the disclosure, he would be well advised to insist upon an order of the court.

Advancement of medicine

In *W v Egdell* Bingham L.J. said[26]:   11–023

> "It has never been doubted that the circumstances here were such as to impose on Dr Edgell a duty of confidence owed to W. He could not lawfully sell the contents of his report to a newspaper, as the judge held . . . . Nor could he, without a breach of the law as well as professional etiquette, discuss the case in a learned article or in his

---

[23] Since repealed. See now Pt 5 of Sch.6 to the National Health Service (General Medical Services Contracts) Regulations 2004.
[24] See para.7 of the report.
[25] At para.25.
[26] [1990] 1 Ch. 359 at 419.

memoirs or in gossiping with friends, unless he took appropriate steps to conceal the identity of W."

The same principle must apply to the use of patient information for medical research unless with the patient's consent.

11–024   The Health Service (Control of Patient Information) Regulations 2002 (made pursuant to s.60 of the Health and Social Care Act 2001) provide for the processing of confidential patient information for purposes related either to the diagnosis or treatment of neoplasia (reg.2), or to communicable disease and other risks to public health (reg.3). Under reg.4, the processing of information in accordance with the Regulations is deemed to be lawful, notwithstanding any obligation of confidentiality that may exist. Regulation 7 imposes a number of obligations on the possessors of confidential patient information, including an obligation to anonymise such information, so far as it is practical to do so.

Protection of others

11–025   It is clear from *W v Egdell*[27] that disclosure of information about a patient, even contrary to his wishes and contrary to his interests, may be lawful for the protection of others potentially at risk. It is equally clear that the risk must be grave. Reference was made both by the trial judge and in the judgments of Sir Stephen Brown P. and Bingham L.J. (with which the third member of the court agreed) to the advice at that time published by the GMC that:

> "Rarely, disclosure may be justified on the ground that it is in the public interest which, in certain circumstances such as, for example, investigation by the police of a grave or very serious crime, might override the doctor's duty to maintain his patient's confidence."

11–026   The Department of Health's *NHS Code of Practice: Confidentiality*[28] addresses directly one of the difficult questions to which this guidance[29] gives rise:

> "The definition of serious crime is not entirely clear. Murder, manslaughter, rape treason, kidnapping, child abuse or other cases where individuals have suffered serious harm may all warrant breaching confidentiality. Serious harm to the security of the state or to public order and crimes that involve substantial financial gain or loss will also generally fall within this category. In contrast, theft, fraud or damage to

---

[27] [1990] 1 Ch. 359.
[28] Annex B, Figure 7.
[29] For the GMC's current guidance, see paras 22–27 of *Confidentiality: Protecting and Providing Information* (2004).

property where loss or damage is less substantial would generally not warrant breach of confidence."

The General Medical Council's *Reporting Gun Shot Wounds Guidance for Doctors in Accident and Emergency Departments*[30] is undoubtedly correct in its advice that the police should be told whenever a person has arrived at a hospital with a gun shot wound.

American courts have gone further. In *Tarasoff v Regents of the University of California*[31] the parents of a girl killed by a man, who two months earlier told a psychologist employed at the university of his intention to kill her, were held to have an arguable claim against the university authorities for negligent failure to warn the deceased of the danger, although they did warn the police. It is unlikely that an English court would entertain such a claim.[32]   **11–027**

It is not only violent criminals who may present a serious risk to the life or health of others. A motorist who suffers from blackouts obviously ought not to drive and is under a duty to inform the licensing authority of his disability. What is the position of his doctor if he advises the patient of his duty, but the patient ignores his advice and continues to drive? A motorist who drives in disregard of a serious disability is an obvious danger to the life of others, and it would be surprising if the doctor's duty of confidentiality extended to keeping secret the fact that he was doing so.   **11–028**

A controversial question is whether a specialist who diagnoses a serious communicable disease is at liberty to inform other health care professionals, who are or may be involved in the patient's care, and the patient's spouse or other sexual partner.   **11–029**

The GMC's Guidance on Serious Communicable Diseases (October 1997) recommends that the patient should be encouraged to give his consent to such disclosure, but advises that in the last resort it would not be improper to make such disclosure, without the patient's consent, where the doctor judges that such disclosure is necessary to protect others from the risk of death or serious harm.[33]   **11–030**

This advice is consistent with the principle that a doctor's duty of confidentiality is subject to the qualification that a doctor who learns in his professional capacity of matters which cause serious risk to others is not prevented from making such disclosure as may be necessary to safeguard those at risk, and it is likely that a court would support it. A person who knows that he is infected with a serious sexually transmissible disease and recklessly passes it to another person by sexual activity, without disclosing his condition to the other person, is guilty of a serious criminal offence.[34]   **11–031**

---

[30] September 2003.
[31] (1976) Sup., 131 Cal. Rptr. 14.
[32] See *Hill v Chief Constable of West Yorkshire* [1989] A.C. 53; *Palmer v Tees Health Authority* [2000] P.N.L.R. 87.
[33] Paras 18–23.
[34] Contrary to the Offences against the Person Act, 1861, s.20: see *R. v Dica* [2004] EWCA Crim 1103; [2004] Q.B. 1257; *R. v Konzani* [2005] EWCA Crim 706; [2005] 2 Cr. App. R. 198.

11–032　　In *X v Y*[35] the plaintiff health authority obtained injunctions against a newspaper reporter and the publishers of a newspaper, restraining publication of information about two doctors in general practice suffering from AIDS, which was supplied to the reporter by an employee or employees of the health authority from access to hospital records. Both doctors had sought medical advice and were being properly and effectively counselled. The judge found that the small theoretical risk of their infecting a patient was, in practice, removed by counselling. The sole justification sought to be advanced by the defendants for publication was not that it was necessary to protect individuals at risk, but that the subject was one of public interest and that publication would contribute to public debate. This was no defence.

Self-protection

11–033　　If a patient sues a doctor or makes a complaint about him, for example, to the Health Services Commissioner or the GMC, he would no doubt be taken to waive confidentiality to the extent necessary to enable the doctor to defend himself.[36]

11–034　　A doctor might have equal need to use information gained about a patient in his professional capacity for the protection of his own position in circumstances not resulting from a complaint by a patient, but, for example, from allegations by other staff. Just as the Court of Appeal has recognised an implied qualification of the implied duty of confidence owed by a banker to his customer where disclosure is required in the interests of the banker,[37] it would be surprising if there was no similar qualification in the case of a doctor and if he had to rely simply on a discretion of the court to enable him to safeguard his own professional position.[38]

Management and record keeping

11–035　　General practitioners and hospitals have to maintain computerised and other records. The storing of information, whether manually or on computer, to which as a matter of practical reality others may have access involves actual or potential loss of secrecy. Moreover information may be stored not merely for medical but for management purposes, e.g. in the case of a private hospital patient so that the accounting department bills the patient correctly. The legal justification may be put in alternative ways.

---

[35] [1988] 2 All E.R. 648.
[36] Compare *Paragon Finance plc v Freshfields* [1999] 1 W.L.R. 1183 (claim against solicitor). As to the limits on such waiver, see *Kadian v Richards* [2004] N.S.W.S.C. 382 (Campbell J.).
[37] *Tournier v National Provincial and Union Bank of England* [1924] 1 K.B. 461.
[38] See *Duncan v Medical Practitioner's Disciplinary Committee* [1986] 1 N.Z.L.R. 513, *per* Jeffries J. ("As this very case demonstrates a doctor may reveal confidences and secrets if he is required to defend himself, or others, against accusations of wrongful conduct".)

Since no medical practice or hospital could operate properly or efficiently without maintaining medical records, it may be said that the patient impliedly consents to it. Alternatively it may be said that the keeping of records is in part for the purpose of the patient's present or future treatment and in part for the protection of the doctor's or hospital's proper interests, and therefore does not in itself infringe upon any duty of confidentiality to the patient. Infringement will occur if records are leaked for other purposes, for example, by disclosure to the press (as in *X v Y*[39] or the *Ashworth Hospital* case[40]).

The European Court of Human Rights has emphasised the importance of **11–036** protecting the confidentiality of a person's medical data.[41] In *Z v Finland*[42] the court said:

> " . . . the protection of personal data, not least medical data, is of fundamental importance to a person's enjoyment of his or her right to respect for private and family life as guaranteed by Article 8 of the Convention. Respecting the confidentiality of health data is a vital principle in the legal systems of all Contracting Parties to the Convention. It is crucial not only to respect the sense of privacy of a patient but also to preserve his or her confidence in the medical profession and health services in general. Without such protection, those in need of medical assistance may be deterred from revealing such information of a personal and even intimate nature as may be necessary in order to receive appropriate treatment and, even, from seeking such assistance, thereby endangering their own health, and, in the case of transmissible diseases, that of the community."

The Data Protection Act 1998 imposes obligations on health organisa- **11–037** tions and health professionals in relation to the processing (which includes holding) of personal data,[43] as do the Health Service (Control of Patient Information) Regulations 2002.[44] A patient who is concerned what may be in his medical records has a right of access to them, subject to certain exceptions, under the Data Protection Act 1998. Special exceptions in the case of personal data consisting of information as to the physical or mental health or condition of the data subject were created by the Data Protection (Subject Access Modification) (Health) Order 2000.

For some limited purposes (for example, in relation to deceased patients) **11–038** the Access to Health Records Act 1990 also continues to be relevant, as does the Access to Medical Reports Act 1988 (in relation to medical reports for employment or insurance purposes).

---

[39] [1988] 2 All E.R. 648.
[40] See para.11–003 above.
[41] *Z v Finland* (1997) 25 E.H.R.R. 371; *MS v Sweden* (1997) 28 E.H.R.R. 313.
[42] *ibid* at para.95.
[43] See Ch.8 above.
[44] See para.11–024 above.

Disclosure required by law

11–039 A number of statutory provisions compel disclosure of otherwise confidential information and material. Some apply specifically to doctors;
others apply more generally but would include doctors. The General
Medical Council maintains a list of such provisions on its web-site.[45] The
following are examples:

(1) Road Traffic Act 1988, s.172.
    Under this section any person may be required to give informa-
    tion which may lead to the identification of a driver alleged to be
    guilty of certain offences. In *Hunter v Mann*[46] a doctor who
    refused to give such information under the equivalent section of
    the previous Act on grounds of confidentiality was held by the
    Divisional Court to have been rightly convicted.
(2) Abortion Act 1967 and Abortion Regulations 1991 (SI
    1991/499).
    Any practitioner terminating a pregnancy is required to provide
    specified information to the Chief Medical Officer.
(3) Police and Criminal Evidence Act 1984, ss.8 to 12.
    Medical records are excluded from powers of search under a
    magistrates' warrant, but a constable may obtain access to such
    records for the purposes of a criminal investigation by order of a
    circuit judge.
(4) Public Health (Control of Diseases) Act 1984 and Public Health
    (Infectious Diseases) Regulations 1988 (SI 1988/1546).
    These require a doctor to notify actual or suspected cases of
    patients suffering various forms of infectious disease to the proper
    officer of the local authority.
(5) Reporting of Injuries, Diseases and Dangerous Occurrences Reg-
    ulations 1995 (SI 1995/3163).
    These require notification of industrial accidents and diseases.
(6) A doctor may also be required as a witness to answer questions
    about matters learned confidentially in his professional
    capacity.[47]

Children

11–040 The relationship and rights of parent and child in connection with medical
treatment and advice, and the duties of the doctor, were considered by the

---

[45] *Confidentiality: Protecting and Providing Information/Frequently Asked* (answers to frequently asked questions)
[46] [1974] Q.B. 767.
[47] *Duchess of Kingston's Case* (1776) State Trials 355 at 571–572; see also at 586–591; *Garner
v Garner* (1920) 36 T.L.R. 196.

House of Lords in *Gillick v West Norfolk Area Health Authority*.[48] The Department of Health and Social Services issued to health authorities a memorandum of guidance on family planning services, including a section on contraceptive advice and treatment for young people. It recommended that clinics should be available for people of all ages; that if a girl under 16 wanted contraception the doctor should do his best to persuade her to inform her parents or guardian; but that if she refused, the doctor might exceptionally, in the exercise of his clinical judgment, prescribe contraceptive treatment, without parental knowledge or consent; and the document referred to the doctor's duty of confidentiality to patients, including those under 16.

The Court of Appeal declared that the advice was unlawful, but the House of Lords (by a majority) reversed the decision. The central reasoning of the majority was that parental rights existed only for the benefit of the child and diminished gradually as the child acquires the ability to make decisions for himself. The pace of that development will vary from child to child. Lord Scarman said[49]: **11–041**

"The law relating to parent and child is concerned with the problems of the growth and maturity of the human personality. If the law should impose upon the process of 'growing-up' fixed limits where nature knows only a continuous process, the price would be artificiality and a lack of realism in an area where the law must be sensitive to human development and social change."

It was held that the parental right to decide whether or not a child under 16 should have medical treatment terminates if and when the child has sufficient understanding and intelligence to enable him or her to understand fully what is involved.

The doctor's duty is to act in accordance with what he believes to be in the patient's best interest. That duty involves satisfying himself whether the patient has a sufficiently mature understanding to have the capacity to consent to the treatment in question. In assessing whether the patient has such capacity and what is in his or her best interests, the doctor must exercise his professional judgment. **11–042**

The same considerations must govern the doctor's approach to the question of confidentiality. The doctor stands in a confidential relationship to every patient of whatever age including a baby,[50] but the purpose of the relationship is the welfare of the patient. Information relevant to matters within the parent's responsibility for decision-making can and should ordinarily be disclosed to the parent in the child's interests, and to do so would not involve a breach of duty. **11–043**

---

[48] [1986] A.C. 112.
[49] *ibid.* at 186.
[50] *Re C (A Minor) (Wardship: Medical Treatment) (No.2)* [1990] Fam 39. See also *Re Z (A Minor) (Identification Restrictions on Publication)* [1997] Fam. 1.

11–044   The House of Lords' decision in *Gillick* was considered and applied in *R. (Axon) v Secretary of State for Health*[51] by Silber J., who upheld the lawfulness of guidance issued by the Department of Health in relation to the provision of advice and treatment to children on contraception and sexual and reproductive health. Silber J. provided guidelines as to the circumstances in which a medical professional is entitled to provide medical advice and treatment on sexual matters without the knowledge or consent of parents.

11–045   Whatever the age of the child, special considerations would arise if the doctor had reason to believe that the parent was abusing the child, or neglecting the child, or that disclosure to the parent would for some reason be harmful to the child. In those cases it might be the doctor's duty not to inform the parent but, for example, to inform the police or the social services department. Paragraph 29 of the GMC's *Confidentiality: Protecting and Providing Information* warns that:

> "If you believe a patient to be a victim of neglect or physical, sexual or emotional abuse and that the patient cannot give or withhold consent to disclosure, you must give information promptly to an appropriate responsible person or statutory agency, where you believe that the disclosure is in the patient's best interests . . . "

11–046   In matters where the doctor is satisfied that the patient has sufficient responsibility to make his or her own judgment, the doctor should respect the patient's confidentiality and should accordingly not disclose information to the patient's parent against the patient's wishes, save in the most exceptional circumstances.[52]

11–047   Because development is a continuous process, there may be grey areas in which the doctor can only be guided by his professional judgment in considering whether the interests of the patient require that information should or should not be disclosed.

Persons under a disability

11–048   The relationship between persons suffering from disability through age, illness or accident, and those who care for them will obviously vary according to the nature and extent of the disability, but the same general principles must apply in relation to invalid and carer as in relation to minor and parent or guardian.[53]

11–049   In *R. (S) v Plymouth City Council*,[54] the respondent local authority had made a guardianship order in respect of the claimant, an adult with mental difficulties. The claimant's mother, his nearest relative, sought disclosure of

---

[51] [2006] EWHC 37; [2006] H.R.L.R. 12.
[52] See para.11–050, below.
[53] See *E v Channel Four Television Corporation* [2005] EWHC 1144 (Fam); [2005] E.M.L.R. 30, *per* Munby J. at paras 115–120.
[54] [2002] EWCA Civ 388; [2002] 1 W.L.R. 2583.

the material on which the guardianship order had been made, for the purpose of applying for discharge of the guardianship order. The Court of Appeal recognised that the claimant had an interest, independent of his mother, in protecting the confidentiality of personal information about himself, but concluded that:

" . . . both at common law and under the Human Rights Act 1998, a balance must be struck between the public and private interests in maintaining the confidentiality of this information and the public and private interests in permitting, indeed requiring, its disclosure for certain purposes."

The Court of Appeal took into account the mother's Art.6 and Art.8 rights and observed that there was no suggestion that the claimant had any objection to his mother and her advisers being properly informed about his health and welfare. By a majority (Hale L.J. and Clarke L.J., with Kennedy L.J. dissenting as to where the balance lay), the court held that the claimant's mother was entitled to the disclosure sought by her.

Disclosure to a relative

Aside from patients of limited capacity, disclosure of information gained by the doctor in his professional capacity should in normal circumstances only be made to another member of the patient's family with the patient's express or implied consent. But there may be cases where a doctor believes that it would be in the patient's interests, for example, to inform the patient's husband or wife of something unknown to the patient. It is likely that the courts would regard that as a matter for the doctor's professional judgment, and would not hold him to be in breach of duty to the patient provided that he acted in what he reasonably believed to be in the patient's best interest, with the purpose of avoiding serious harm to the patient. The principle is not confined to disclosure within the circle of the patient's family, but that is where it is most likely to apply. **11–050**

The circumstances would have to be still more exceptional to justify a doctor disclosing confidential information about a patient from concern for his best medical interests but contrary to the patient's express wishes. However, it is difficult to say that this could never be justified. **11–051**

In *Weld-Blundell v Stephens*[55] Bankes L.J. took the example of a patient informing his doctor that he intended to commit suicide at a particular place and time, and he implied that a contract to keep that communication secret would be an illegal contract. Attempted suicide was then a criminal offence, and a different justification would now be required for the doctor to warn others if forbidden by the patient to do so, although it is still an offence to assist in another's suicide. Suppose that the patient was suffering from **11–052**

[55] [1919] 1 K.B. 520 at 527.

clinical depression. The doctor might well feel that it was his duty to warn someone close to the patient in order to try to avert the possibility of suicide. It is suggested that a court would be unlikely to hold that the doctor's duty of confidentiality extended to prevent him from taking what he believed to be necessary action for the purpose of saving the patient's life.

The dead

11–053   The ethical obligation recognised in the Declaration of Geneva ("I will respect the secrets which are confided in me, even after the patient has died") is repeated in *Confidentiality: Protecting and Providing Information* at para.30:

> "You still have an obligation to keep personal information confidential after a patient dies. The extent to which confidential information may be disclosed after a patient's death will depend on the circumstances . . . "

Equity may impose a duty of confidentiality towards another after the death of the original confider.[56] The question is not one of property (whether a cause of action owned by the deceased has been assigned) but of conscience.

11–054   It is open to the courts to regard divulgence by a doctor of information supplied in confidence by a patient who has since died as being unconscionable as well as unprofessional. If so, there is no reason in principle why equity should not regard the doctor as owing a duty of confidence to the deceased's estate, consonant with the maxim that equity will not suffer a wrong to be without a remedy.

11–055   It is possible also that a doctor might owe a duty in conscience towards others. A patient might disclose to his doctor information about X, another member of his family (who might or might not also be his patient), publication of which would be damaging or embarrassing to X, in the understandable belief that there was no risk to X of the doctor making the information public. It would be most unsatisfactory if, on the patient being killed the next day, the doctor became free to make disclosure.

11–056   If the doctor knew that the patient was concerned for X and did not want the information to get out for X's sake, it would be open to a court to hold that publication by the doctor on the patient's death would be unconscionable conduct towards X. *White v Jones*,[57] although not a case on confidentiality, nevertheless provides an interesting parallel. If under concepts derived

---

[56] *Morison v Moat* (1851) 9 Hare 241; affirmed (1852) 21 L.J. Chanc. 248.
[57] [1995] 2 A.C. 207.

from *Nocton v Lord Ashburton*[58] a solicitor may owe a duty in respect of the economic well being of his client's surviving intended beneficiary,[59] so should the doctor's conscience move him to continue to respect his former patient's confidence on behalf of X.

In *Plon v France*[60] the European Court of Human Rights considered the question whether publishers should be permitted to distribute a book by President Mitterand's doctor entitled "Le Grand Secret". Mitterand was diagnosed with cancer in 1981, only a matter of months after beginning the first of his two seven-year terms as president of France. The public was not officially informed until 1994. The book went into the details of his health and treatment, and the steps taken by the president and his medical team to keep the truth from the public. Mitterand died on January 8, 1996. Two days later *Le Monde* published an article saying that he had been suffering from cancer from the beginning of his first term, and soon afterwards Mitterand's brother complained publicly that he had not received proper treatment. These matters generated wide public interest. Publication of the book was planned for January 17 and 40,000 copies were distributed, but on the same day the Paris Tribunal de Grande Instance granted an interlocutory injunction on the application of Mitterand's widow and children to restrain further distribution pending a full hearing. Between the interlocutory and the full hearing the doctor was prosecuted for a criminal offence of breaking a professional confidence, convicted and sentenced to a suspended term of imprisonment and a fine. In October 1996, on the full hearing of the civil action, the court awarded damages to Mitterand's widow and children and ordered that the ban on distribution of the book should remain in force indefinitely. The ban was upheld by the French courts on appeal.

11–057

The European Court of Human Rights distinguished between the interim and the final injunction, observing that a need to interfere with freedom of expression may be present initially but subsequently cease to exist.[61] It concluded that the interim injunction did not violate Art.10. It was imposed for a limited period (until the full hearing) at a time of great grief to Mitterand's family, which could only have been intensified by publication so soon after his death.[62] But as his death became more remote, this factor became less important. The more time elapsed, the more the public interest in discussion of the history of Mitterand's two terms of office prevailed over protecting the president's right to medical confidence. This did not mean that the requirements of historical debate may release doctors from a duty of medical confidentiality save in strictly exceptional circumstances. But by the time of the final order, not only had 40,000 copies been sold but there had been discussion on the internet and considerable media comment, as a

11–058

---

[58] [1914] A.C. 932.
[59] *White v Jones* [1995] 2 A.C. 207 at 270–272 and 275–276, *per* Lord Browne-Wilkinson.
[60] [2004] E.C.H.R. 200.
[61] *ibid.* at para.45.
[62] *ibid.* at para.47.

result of which the book was to a large extent no longer confidential in practice. The doctor had also been subject to criminal sanctions.[63] Taking all these factors into account, the court concluded that at the time of the final order there was not a pressing social need for a permanent ban.[64]

[63] [2004] E.C.H.R. 200 at para.53.
[64] *ibid.* at para.55.

CHAPTER 12

Bankers

Tournier v National Provincial and Union Bank of England[1]

Tournier is the leading authority on the duty of confidence owed by a bank   **12–001**
to its customer. The Court of Appeal held that a bank owes to its customer
an implied contractual duty to keep his affairs secret, but that the duty is
qualified. The duty arises at the commencement of the relationship and
continues after the customer has closed his account in relation to information gained during the period of the account. It covers information about
the customer's affairs gained by virtue of the banking relationship and is not
limited to information from or about the account itself.[2] The duty may
prevent a bank from communicating information to other companies in the
same group, including its own direct subsidiaries.[3]

The appeal in *Tournier* arose from a jury trial, in which the judge had   **12–002**
directed the jury that disclosure of the state of a customer's account by a
banker to a third party was not a breach of contract if made "justifiably, that
is to say, if, under the circumstances of the particular case, it was reasonable
and proper that he should make the communication". This was held to be
an inadequate explanation of a difficult area of law. Atkin L.J. commented
that[4]:

> " . . . to leave to the jury what is 'justifiable' or 'proper' is merely to tell
> them that the bank may not divulge information except on occasions
> when they may divulge it, and that of what those occasions are the jury

[1] [1924] 1 K.B. 461.
[2] See also *Barclays Bank plc v Taylor* [1989] 1 W.L.R. 1066 at 1070 *per* Lord Donaldson
M.R., "The banker-customer relationship imposes upon the bank a duty of confidentiality in
relation to information concerning its customer and his affairs which it acquires in the
character of his banker".
[3] *Bank of Tokyo Ltd v Karoon: (Note)* [1987] A.C. 45, CA.
[4] *Tournier v National Provincial and Union Bank of England* [1924] 1 K.B. 461 at 485.

are the judges. This appears to me to treat as fact what is matter of law . . . ."

The fullest judgment on the qualifications to the implied obligation of secrecy is that of Bankes L.J. who said[5]:

"At the present day I think it may be asserted with confidence that the duty is a legal one arising out of contract, and that the duty is not absolute but qualified. It is not possible to frame any exhaustive definition of the duty. The most that can be done is to classify the qualification, and to indicate its limits. . . .

On principle I think that the qualifications can be classified under four heads: (a) Where disclosure is under compulsion by law; (b) where there is a duty to the public to disclose; (c) where the interests of the bank require disclosure; (d) where the disclosure is made by the express or implied consent of the customer."

These four qualifications are reflected in para.11 of the Banking Code[6] and para.11 of the Business Banking Code.[7] They were reaffirmed by the Court of Appeal in *Barclays Bank plc v Taylor*.[8]

12–003 The true effect of the qualifications is not to excuse a breach of duty, but to identify certain limits to the duty itself. In this regard the judgment of Lord Donaldson M.R. in *Barclays Bank plc v Taylor* is to be preferred to that of Croom-Johnson L.J. Lord Donaldson M.R. said[9]:

"The duty to maintain confidentiality is not all-embracing, subject to exceptions. It does not exist in four exceptional circumstances . . . ."

Croom-Johnson L.J. said[10]:

"Faced with those order [under section 9 of the Police and Criminal Evidence Act 1984], the banks complied with them, thereby necessarily breaching the duties of confidence which they owed to Mr and Mrs Taylor.

The four circumstances in which a banker is justified in breaking that duty are set out in *Tournier v National Provincial and Union Bank of England* [1924] 1 K.B. 461, 473 in the judgment of Bankes, L.J. The first is 'disclosure . . . under compulsion by law'. That means that, in complying with the orders under section 9, the banks were not in breach of that implied term in their contracts with Mr Taylor."

---

[5] *Tournier v National Provincial and Union Bank of England* [1924] 1 K.B. 461 at 471–472 and 473.

[6] (March 1, 2005), issued by the British Bankers' Association, the Building Societies Association and APACS (the UK payments association).

[7] (March 1, 2005), issued by the British Bankers' Association and APACS.

[8] [1989] 1 W.L.R. 1066 at 1070, *per* Lord Donaldson M.R.

[9] *ibid.* at 1074.

[10] *ibid.* at 1075.

It is contradictory to speak of the banks "necessarily breaching their duty of confidence" owed to the customer, and at the same time to say that "the banks were not in breach of that implied term of their contracts".

In *El Jawhary v BCCI*[11] Sir Donald Nicholls V.C. followed the approach taken by Lord Donaldson, saying:

> "Where the case is within one of the qualifications to the duty of confidence, the duty, ex hypothesi, does not exist . . . ."

12–004

In *Barclays Bank plc v Taylor* it was argued by the customer that a bank served with notice of an application for an order under the Police and Criminal Evidence Act, requiring disclosure of documents relating to his affairs, owed him a duty to resist the application and to inform him. The court held that the contract between banker and customer did not contain any such implied duty on the part of the bank; and that, once an order valid on its face was made, the bank was obliged to comply with it.

12–005

The same principle applies after disclosure as before it. In *El Jawhary v BCCI* Sir Donald Nicholls V.C. held that, where a bank disclosed information to a third party in circumstances within one of the qualifications to the duty of confidence, there was no basis for implying an obligation on the bank to tell the customer what it had done.

12–006

In *Robertson v Canadian Imperial Bank of Commerce*[12] a *subpoena* was served on a bank requiring it to give evidence and produce bank statements in an action to which the customer was not a party. The bank manager, having tried unsuccessfully to contact the customer before complying with the *subpoena*, produced the bank statements and gave evidence as required, without protest and without informing the court that he had been unable to contact the customer. The customer sued the bank, alleging breach of confidence in disclosing the information without having first consulted the client or voiced objection. At first instance the judge found that the defendant had breached its duty, but that the action failed because the bank manager's evidence, including the production of the information, was covered by absolute privilege.

12–007

The Privy Council held that the first of the *Tournier* qualifications applied (disclosure under compulsion by law), so that there was no duty, and expressed no opinion whether the bank, if it had been in breach of duty, would have been protected by the absolute immunity which attaches to the testimony of witnesses.

12–008

In concluding that the first of the *Tournier* qualifications applied, the Board left unanswered a number of questions. Lord Nolan said that the Board had much sympathy with the argument by the customer that he should have been notified of the issue of the *subpoena*. He added[13]:

12–009

---

[11] [1993] B.C.L.C. 396 at 400.
[12] [1994] 1 W.L.R. 1493.
[13] *ibid.* at 1498.

"In the ordinary way a customer in good standing could reasonably expect, *if only as a matter of courtesy and good business practice*, to be told by his bank that a subpoena had been received . . . . Their Lordships accept that the bank was compelled by law to produce the bank statement to the court, but it was under no compulsion to withhold knowledge of the subpoena from the customer." (Emphasis added.)

Although observing that there was no compulsion to withhold knowledge, the Board refrained from holding that there was a duty to inform. Lord Nolan recognised that it would be difficult to formulate the terms of any duty to be implied, and that it could not go beyond a duty to use best endeavours, in which case on the judge's findings there had been no breach.

12–010   On the question of the bank's failure to object to production, Lord Nolan said that there was no head of privilege which the customer, or the bank, could have claimed, and that it would be difficult to formulate the terms of any contractual duty to inform the court that the bank was producing the bank statement without the customer's consent. In any event, the customer had not established that the bank's omission to do so had caused him any loss, but Lord Nolan added[14]:

"Their Lordships would not exclude the possibility that a particular banker/customer relationship would include some such implied term or duty of care as that for which the customer has contended, and that damages might be recoverable as a result of its breach by the bank concerned, but this is not such a case."

There is no reason to differentiate between a bank given notice of an intention to apply for an order for discovery[15] and a bank served with a *subpoena*. *Barclays Bank plc v Taylor* was cited in argument in *Robertson*.[16] but regrettably is not referred to in the judgment. The judgment of the Privy Council leaves open the question whether a bank served with notice requiring production of documents owes any, and if so what, duty to try to inform the customer, or to object to the order (if there are potential grounds for objection), or to inform the court of the absence of the customer's consent.

12–011   In *Tournier* Atkin L.J. emphasised that it would not be right to imply an obligation of secrecy into the contract between a bank and its customer merely because it would be a reasonable term to include, but only if it was a necessary term; and that, whilst it was necessary to imply some term, there must be "important limitations" to the term required to be implied, one

---

[14] [1994] 1 W.L.R. 1493 at 1500.
[15] *Barclays Bank v Taylor* [1989] 1 W.L.R. 1066.
[16] [1994] 1 W.L.R. 1493.

being that it was "plain that there is no privilege from disclosure enforced in the course of legal proceedings".[17]

12–012 That limitation plainly applies to documents produced under *subpoena* or other compulsory process. That being so, as Lord Donaldson M.R. said in *Barclays Bank plc v Taylor*[18]:

> "The real question is whether, in order to give business efficacy to the relationship of banker and customer, there must be an implied obligation to contest a section 9 application or to probe it or to inform its customer."

It may be that a customer in good standing would reasonably expect, "as a matter of courtesy and good business practice", to be informed by the bank of any notice requiring it to produce documents regarding the customer's affairs. Courtesy and good business practice are no doubt the basis on which many commercial relationships are expected to be conducted, and in fact conducted, but they are not the basis for the imposition of an implied term. Although a customer might be displeased at his bank complying with an order for discovery without informing him or seeking to oppose the order, it is difficult to see how a term requiring the bank to do so could be said to be necessary. Moreover the difficulty which the Privy Council recognised about any attempt to formulate such an implied contractual term is argument against it.

Compulsion by law

12–013 Apart from obligations of disclosure which are of general application (e.g. to answer questions in the witness box[19]), compulsion may arise in various ways particularly relevant to banks. They include the following,[20]

(1) *Bankers' Books Evidence Act 1879*, under which orders for inspection may be made in civil or criminal proceedings.

(2) *Taxes Acts.* Banks may be compelled to disclose certain information to the Inland Revenue under the Taxes Management Act 1970, s.24 or the Income and Corporation Taxes Act 1988, s.745.

(3) *The Proceeds of Crime Act 2002.* Section 328 creates an offence of entering into or becoming concerned in defined arrangements relating to criminal property.[21] Section 330 creates an offence for

---

[17] [1924] 1 K.B. at 483 and 486.
[18] [1989] 1 W.L.R. at 1074.
[19] *Loyd v Freshfield* (1826) 2 Car. & P. 325 at 329; *Parry-Jones v Law Society* [1969] 1 Ch. 1 at 9; *Robertson v Canadian Imperial Bank of Commerce* [1994] 1 W.L.R. 1493.
[20] See Paget, *Law of Banking* (12th edn, 2002).
[21] The risk to bank customers of an injustice caused by the operation of s.328 was identified by Laddie J. in *Squirrell Ltd v National Westminster Bank plc* [2005] EWHC 664; [2006] 1 W.L.R. 637, at [7].

bankers and others in the regulated sector of failing to disclose their knowledge or suspicions of money laundering activities. Section 333 creates a "tipping off" offence of making a disclosure prejudicial to money laundering investigations.

(4) *Insolvency Act 1986*. A bank may be compelled to disclose information about the affairs of insolvent customers under ss.236 (companies) and 366 (individuals).

(5) *Financial Services and Markets Act 2000*. Sections 146 and 147 of the Act empower the Financial Services Authority to make rules about, respectively, money laundering and the disclosure and use of information held by an authorised person. Rules under these sections appear in the Financial Service Authority's handbook. Part 11 of the Act contains a number of further provisions in relation to the Financial Service Authority's information gathering powers (see especially s.175(5)).

(6) *Companies Act 1985*. Inspectors appointed under the Act may require a bank to disclose information or produce documents relating to the affairs of a customer, where the customer is the company under investigation, or where the requirement is authorised by the Secretary of State, or where the bank is itself under investigation: s.452(1A), (1B).

(7) *Police and Criminal Evidence Act 1984*. Under s.9 and Sch.1, a bank may be ordered to produce documents for the purposes of a criminal investigation, as illustrated by *Barclays Bank plc v Taylor*.[22] The Terrorism Act 2000 and the Serious Organised Crime and Police Act 2005 also contain disclosure provisions relating to their subject-matter.

(9) Disclosure orders may be made in support of a tracing claim in equity, or in support of a freezing injunction, requiring a bank to disclose information relating to its customer.[23]

Confidentiality and foreign law is considered in Chapter 10.

Duty to the public

12–014   In *Tournier* Banks L.J. said[24]:

"Many instances . . . might be given. They may be summed up in the language of Lord Finlay in *Weld-Blundell v Stephens*,[25] where he speaks of cases where a higher duty than the private duty is involved,

---

[22] [1989] 1 W.L.R. 1066.
[23] *A v C (Note)* [1981] Q.B. 956; *Banker's Trust Co v Shapira* [1980] 1 W.L.R. 1274; *A.J. Bekhor & Co Ltd v Bilton* [1981] Q.B. 923.
[24] [1924] 1 K.B. 461 at 473.
[25] [1920] A.C. 956 at 965.

as where 'danger to the State or public duty may supercede the duty of the agent to his principal'."

Scrutton L.J. thought it clear that the bank might disclose the customer's account and affairs to prevent fraud or crimes.[26]

Atkin L.J. also thought it safe to say that the bank's obligation was subject to the qualification that it had the right to disclose information relating to its customer's affairs when and to the extent to which it was reasonably necessary for protecting the bank, or other interested persons, or the public, against fraud or crime.[27]   **12–015**

In *Price Waterhouse v B.C.C.I.*[28] Millett J. had to consider banking confidence at one remove. The issue was whether Price Waterhouse was at liberty to disclose information, obtained in the course of acting for B.C.C.I. as auditors and professional advisers, to an inquiry set up by the Government and the Bank of England, under the chairmanship of Bingham L.J., to investigate the supervision of B.C.C.I. under the Banking Act and to make recommendations.   **12–016**

On the subject of banking confidentiality and public duty of disclosure, Millett J. said that[29]:   **12–017**

" . . . there seems no reason to doubt the general correctness of the statement in Paget's *Law of Banking* (10th edn, 1989) p.256, based on a remark of Bankes L.J. in the *Tournier* case [1924] 1 K.B. 461 at 474 . . . that

'The giving of information to the police, for instance in regard to a customer suspected of a crime would be unwarranted.' "

What Bankes L.J. said in *Tournier* was[30]:

"I cannot think that the duty of non-disclosure is confined to information derived from the customer himself or from his account. To take a simple illustration. A police officer goes to a banker to make an inquiry about a customer of the bank. He goes to the bank, because he knows that the person about whom he wants information is a customer of the bank. The police officer is asked why he wants the information. He replies, because the customer is charged with a series of frauds. Is the banker entitled to publish *that* information? Surely not. He acquired the information in his character of banker." (Emphasis added.)

The point which Bankes L.J. was making was that in his simple illustration the banker would not be entitled to publish to the world the information which he gained about his customer *from* the police that the customer was

---

[26] [1924] 1 K.B. 461 at 481.
[27] *Tournier v National Provincial and Union Bank of England* 1 K.B. 461 at 486.
[28] [1992] B.C.L.C. 583. For a fuller discussion, see paras 6–041 to 6–045, above.
[29] *ibid.* 583 at 598.
[30] [1924] 1 K.B. 461 at 474.

charged with a number of frauds, because he acquired that information "in his character of banker" (albeit not from the customer himself). Bankes L.J. was not there addressing the scope of the public duty qualification and whether the banker would be entitled to assist the police.

12–018   An express undertaking by a bank to a customer to keep secret the fact that the customer was presently engaged, or intending to engage, in a criminal or fraudulent course of conduct would be unenforceable as contrary to public policy; and a bank would not be under an implied obligation to keep such information secret (see the judgments of Scrutton and Atkin L.JJ. in *Tournier* referred to above).[31] The situation may be very different where a customer discloses the commission of a past offence. In *Weld-Blundell v Stephens*[32] the Court of Appeal drew a strong distinction between confiding in a professional man an intention to commit a crime and confessing a past crime, and between voluntary disclosure and disclosure under process of law. However, recent statutory interventions, such as the Proceeds of Crime Act 2002,[33] have significantly eroded this distinction—certainly in cases where previous criminal conduct has not yet come to the attention of the proper authorities.

12–019   The subject of public interest is considered further in Chapter 6.

Interest of the bank

12–020   In *Tournier* Bankes and Scrutton L.JJ. instanced disclosure in collecting or suing for an overdraft.[34] Atkin L.J. referred to the bank having the right to disclose information when, and to the extent to which, it is reasonably necessary for the protection of the bank's interests, either as against its customer or as against third parties in respect of transactions of the bank for or with its customer.[35]

12–021   In *Sunderland v Barclays Bank Ltd*[36] the defendants dishonoured a cheque drawn by the plaintiff in favour of her dressmaker at a time when her account was overdrawn. The bank manager's real reason was not the fact of the account being overdrawn, but that most of the cheques drawn on it had been to bookmakers. The plaintiff complained about the return of the cheque to her husband, who spoke to the bank manager. He told the plaintiff's husband about the cheques to the bookmakers. The plaintiff sued for breach of duty of confidence. Du Parcq L.J. dismissed her claim, holding that when the bank received an implied demand for an explanation of its apparent discourtesy in dishonouring the cheque, it was entitled in its own interests to explain the circumstances.

[31] [1924] 1 K.B. 461 at 481 and 486. See also *Gartside v Outram* [1857] 26 L.J.Ch. (N.S.) 113; *Initial Services Ltd v Patterill* [1968] 1 Q.B. 396; *Canadian Imperial Bank of Commerce v Sayani* (1993) 83 B.C.L.R. (2d) 167, Court of Appeal of British Columbia.
[32] [1919] 1 K.B. 521 at 527, *per* Bankes L.J. and 544–545, *per* Scrutton L.J.
[33] See para.12–013 above.
[34] [1924] 1 K.B. 461, at 473 and 481.
[35] *ibid.* at 486.
[36] *The Times*, November 24, 1938, 5 Legal Decisions Affecting Bankers 163.

Consent

In *Sunderland v Barclays Bank Ltd*, Du Parcq L.J. also held that there was **12–022** implied consent to disclosure in that when the plaintiff's husband took over the conduct of the matter of the dishonoured cheque, the plaintiff impliedly consented to the bank giving him the explanation.

Lee Gleeson Pty Ltd v Sterling Estates Pty Ltd[37] provides another **12–023** example of implied consent. A builder entered into a contract with a site owner for the development of a site. The owner ran into financial difficulties and the builder stopped work for non-payment. Negotiations took place involving the builder, owner and owner's bank. The builder and the owner came to an arrangement for the builder to complete the work and for the owner to pay by staged instalments. At the owner's request, the bank wrote to the builder confirming that the owner had authorised the bank to make payments in accordance with the arrangement. The owner subsequently countermanded the bank's instructions. The bank did not inform the owner. The owner sued the bank under an Australian statutory provision relating to misleading or deceptive conduct in trade or commerce.

The bank contended that it could not have informed the builder of the **12–024** revocation of the owner's instructions without placing itself in breach of confidence to its customer. Brownie J. rejected the bank's argument, holding that by authorising the bank to write to the builder, making a statement as to its authority to make payments to the builder, the customer impliedly authorised the bank to inform the owner of the change to those instructions.

In *Turner v Royal Bank of Scotland plc*,[38] the defendant bank answered **12–025** third party status enquiries in relation to its customer, without informing its customer that it was doing so. The bank argued that its approach had been in accordance with universal banking practice and that its customer had impliedly consented to such disclosures being made. The Court of Appeal rejected the bank's argument, observing that the evidence suggested that the bank had deliberately withheld knowledge of its practice from its customers.

Since the events to which *Turner* related, the Banking Code has intro- **12–026** duced a requirement (at para.11.2) that written permission should be sought before any banker's reference is given.

---

[37] [1992] 1 Bank L.R. 342 (New South Wales Supreme Court).
[38] [1999] Lloyd's Rep. Bank. 231.

CHAPTER 13

Broadcasters and Journalists

13–001   The law of confidentiality affects the media in two separate ways—(1) in limiting their freedom to publish, and (2) in providing qualified protection against disclosure of sources.

Freedom to publish

13–002   There are innumerable dicta which emphasise the importance in a democracy of a free press, but also that it must operate within the rule of law.[1] The principles of the law of confidentiality therefore apply to the press as they apply to others, but with recognition of the particular role of the press.[2] Many of the most important recent cases in which the general law of confidence has been developed have required the courts to assess rights of confidentiality or privacy in the context of publication in the media.

13–003   Since the introduction of the Human Rights Act 1998 and the statutory incorporation of Arts 8 and 10 of the European Convention into English domestic law, the decisions of the European Court of Human Rights on issues of press freedom have become increasingly important in the English courts.

---

[1] e.g. *British Steel Corporation v Granada Television* [1981] A.C. 1096 at 1168 *per* Lord Wilberforce,"First, there were appeals, made in vigorous tones to such broad principles as the freedom of the press, the right to a free flow of information, the public's right to know. In Granada's printed case we find quotations from pronouncements of Sheridan in Parliament and from declarations of eminent judges in cases where the freedom of the press might be involved. I too would be glad to be counted among those whose voice was raised in favour of this great national possession—a free press: who indeed would not? . . . Freedom of the press imports, generally, freedom to publish without pre-censorship, subject always to the laws relating to libel, official secrets, sedition and other recognised inhibitions".

[2] *Francome v Mirror Group Newspapers Ltd* [1984] 1 W.L.R. 892.

Relationship between Article 10 and rights of confidentiality

Article 10, containing the right to freedom of expression, is expressly **13–004**
subject to such restrictions as are prescribed by law and necessary in a
democratic society (in the well established sense of involving a pressing
social need) for, among other things, preventing the disclosure of information received in confidence. In cases where the claim for confidentiality is
based on a contractual or equitable obligation of confidentiality, rather than
Art.8 (i.e. breach of privacy), English law starts with the broad principle
(summarised by Lord Goff in *Spycatcher*[3]) that such a duty arises where
confidential information comes to a person's knowledge in circumstances
where he has notice that it is confidential, but it recognises that confidentiality may in certain circumstances be negated by public interest. Lord Goff
also observed that he could see no inconsistency on this subject between
English law on this subject and Art.10,[4] and the incorporation of Art.10 has
not changed the substantive law in this area. The scope of the public interest
defence is discussed in detail in Chapter 6.

Where a claim is based on Art.8, the interplay between that article and **13–005**
Art.10 is discussed more fully in Chapter 7. Neither article has predom-
inance over the other and the court must examine the comparative
importance of the factors supporting the rights claimed in the particular
circumstances of the case.

Article 10 and its application to different kinds of information

Article 10 states that everyone has the right to freedom of expression, but **13–006**
the European Court of Human Rights has emphasised its particular
importance in relation to the press. In *Von Hannover v Germany*,[5] Princess
Caroline of Monaco complained of the failure of the German courts to
protect her from the publication of photographs taken of her acting in a
private capacity, though in public locations. Referring to previous similar
expressions of principle, the Court observed:

> " . . . freedom of expression constitutes one of the essential foundations
> of a democratic society . . . In that connection the press plays an
> essential role in a democratic society. Although it must not overstep
> certain bounds, in particular in respect of the reputation and rights of
> others, its duty is nevertheless to impart—in a manner consistent with
> its obligations and responsibilities—information and ideas on all
> matters of public interest."[6]

---

[3] [1990] 1 A.C. 109 at 281.
[4] *ibid.* at 283–284.
[5] [2005] 40 E.H.R.R. 1.
[6] *Von Hannover v Germany* (2005) 40 E.H.R.R. 1, at para.58. See also *Reynolds v Times Newspapers Ltd* [2001] 2 A.C. 127, *per* Lord Nicholls at 200.

However, the Court considered that the importance to be attached to the press's freedom of expression varied in accordance with the nature of the information that it sought to convey. Where the sole purpose of publication was to satisfy the curiosity of a particular readership regarding the details of a person's private life, "freedom of expression calls for a narrower interpretation".[7] Finding in favour of Princess Caroline, the Court concluded:

> " . . . the decisive factor in balancing the protection of private life against freedom of expression should lie in the contribution that the published photos and articles make to a debate of general interest. It is clear in the instant case that they made no such contribution since the applicant exercises no official function and the photos and articles related exclusively to details of her private life."[8]

13–007   The importance of information may lie in a variety of different spheres. It is possible that at least a partial and informal hierarchy of types of media publication will emerge from judicial decisions. In *Campbell v MGN Ltd*,[9] Baroness Hale said:

> "There are undoubtedly different types of speech, just as there are different types of private information, some of which are more deserving of protection in a democratic society than others. Top of the list is political speech. The free exchange of information and ideas on matters relevant to the organisation of the economic, social and political life of the country is crucial to any democracy. Without this, it can scarcely be called a democracy at all. This includes revealing information about public figures, especially those in elective office, which would otherwise be private but is relevant to their participation in public life. Intellectual and educational speech and expression are also important in a democracy, not least because they enable the development of individuals' potential to play a full part in society and in our democratic life. Artistic speech and expression is important for similar reasons, in fostering both individual originality and creativity and the free-thinking and dynamic society we so much value."

13–008   The courts recognise that even responsible journalism of real value may well require a degree of colour if it is to reach an audience of any size. Thus, in *Von Hannover*, the court accepted that:

> "Journalistic freedom also covers possible recourse to a degree of exaggeration, or even provocation."[10]

---

[7] At para.66.
[8] At para.76.
[9] [2004] UKHL 22; [2004] 2 A.C. 457, at [148]. See also *per* Lord Hope, at [117].
[10] At [58].

Similarly, in *Campbell v MGN Ltd*,[11] Lord Hope (although finding in **13–009** favour of the appellant claimant) observed:

> "There is no doubt that the presentation of the material that it was legitimate to convey to the public in this case without breaching the duty of confidence was a matter for the journalists. The choice of language used to convey information and ideas, and decisions as to whether or not to accompany the printed word by the use of photographs, are pre-eminently editorial matters with which the court will not interfere. The respondents are also entitled to claim that they should be accorded a reasonable margin of appreciation in taking decisions as to what details needed to be included in the article to give it credibility. This is an essential part of the journalistic exercise."

Statutory restriction on grant of injunctions and relevance of privacy codes

Section 12 of the Human Rights Act 1998 makes special provision for **13–010** circumstances in which a court is considering whether to grant any relief which, if granted, might affect the exercise of the Convention right to freedom of expression (pre-eminently, injunctive relief restraining publication). Of particular significance to the media are subss.(3) and (4):

> "(3) No such relief is to be granted to as to restrain publication before trial unless the court is satisfied that the applicant is likely to establish that publication should not be allowed.
>
> (4) The court must have particular regard to the importance of the Convention right to freedom of expression and, where the proceedings relate to material which the respondent claims, or which appears to the court, to be journalistic, literary or artistic material (or to conduct connected with such material), to—
>
> (a) the extent to which—
>
>> (i) the material has, or is about to, become available to the public; or
>> (ii) it is, or would be, in the public interest for the material to be published;
>
> (b) any relevant privacy code."

The Press Complaints Commission's Code of Practice and Ofcom's Broadcasting Code are each a "relevant privacy code" for the purposes of s.12(4)(b). They contain provisions dealing expressly with a number of specific matters as well as provisions of more general application.

Clause 3 of the PCC Code provides: **13–011**

---

[11] At [112].

"**Privacy**

(i) Everyone is entitled to respect for his or her private and family life, home, health and correspondence, including digital communications. Editors will be expected to justify intrusions into any individual's private life without consent.
(ii) It is unacceptable to photograph individuals in private places without their consent.

Note—Private places are public or private property where there is a reasonable expectation of privacy."

Clause 10 of the Code provides:

"**Clandestine devices and subterfuge**

(i) The press must not seek to obtain or publish material acquired by using hidden cameras or clandestine listening devices; or by intercepting private or mobile telephone calls, messages or emails; or by the unauthorised removal of documents or photographs.
(ii) Engaging in misrepresentation or subterfude can generally be justified only in the public interest and then only when the material cannot be obtained by other means."

Both of these clauses (and some others) are expressly made subject to the following paragraph:

"**The public interest**

There may be exceptions to the clauses . . . where they can be demonstrated to be in the public interest.
   1. The public interest includes, but is not confined to:

(i) Detecting or exposing crime or serious impropriety.
(ii) Protecting public health and safety.
(iii) Preventing the public from being misled by an action or statement of an individual or organisation.

   2. There is a public interest in freedom of expression itself.
   3. Whenever the public interest is invoked, the PCC will require editors to demonstrate fully how the public interest was served.
   4. The PCC will consider the extent to which material is already in the public domain, or will become so.
   5. In cases involving children under 16, editors must demonstrate an exceptional public interest to over-ride the normally paramount interest of the child".

13–012   Ofcom, a statutory broadcasting watchdog,[12] is required to secure in carrying out all its functions

---

[12] For its responsibilities see, in particular, the Broadcasting Act 1996 (as amended), ss.107(1) and 130, and the Communications Act 2003, s.3.

"the application, in the case of all television and radio services, of standards that provide adequate protection of all members of the public and all other persons from . . . unwarranted infringements of privacy resulting from activities carried on for the purpose of such services".[13]

Ofcom's Broadcasting Code covers privacy in s.8. This begins with the following general rule:

"8.1 Any infringement of privacy in programmes, or in connection with obtaining material included in programmes, must be warranted.

Meaning of 'warranted':

In this section 'warranted' has a particular meaning. It means that where the broadcasters wish to justify an infringement of privacy as warranted, they should be able to demonstrate why in the particular circumstances of the case, it is warranted. If the reason is that it is in the public interest, then the broadcaster should be able to demonstrate that the public interest outweighs the right to privacy. Examples of public interest would include revealing or detecting crime, protecting public health or safety, exposing misleading claims made by individuals or organisations or disclosing incompetence that affects the public."

Paragraphs 8.2–8.22 contain more detailed provisions about particular practices including "doorstepping" and surreptitious filming or recording.

Such codes are not to regarded simply as weapons in the hands of a publisher resisting an injunction application, since breaches may result in considerations of privacy outweighing a publisher's entitlement to freedom of speech.[14] In *A v B plc*[15] the Court of Appeal gave general guidance as to the manner in which such codes, and other relevant considerations, should be taken into account on the hearing of applications for interim injunctions restraining publication.

13–013

Disclosure of sources

A journalist who receives information from an informant in confidence will on ordinary principles owe an obligation of confidence to the informant not to reveal his identity; but that duty, like any other duty of confidence, is subject to qualifications, in particular where disclosure is required by law. Such disclosure may be required by statute.

13–014

The Police and Criminal Evidence Act 1984, for example, contains special provisions under which an order may be made by a circuit judge for

13–015

---

[13] Communications Act, 2003, s.3(2)(f).
[14] *Douglas v Hello! Ltd* [2001] Q.B. 967, *per* Brooke L.J. at para.94.
[15] [2002] EWCA Civ 337; [2003] Q.B. 195.

journalistic material held in confidence to be produced to the police in cases where they are investigating a serious offence, subject to various conditions.[16] Similarly, the Terrorism Act 2000 and the Serious Organised Crime and Police Act 2005 contain disclosure provisions relating to their subject-matter.

13–016　　At common law a journalist could be compelled to disclose otherwise confidential information, including his sources, if required to do so in the witness box or by an action for discovery,[17] although the court would only order such disclosure if it considered it necessary. The courts' approach to such actions is now guided by a combination of statute and European human rights jurisprudence.

13–017　　Section 10 of the Contempt of Court Act 1981 provides:

> "No court may require a person to disclose, nor is any person guilty of contempt of court for refusing to disclose, the source of information contained in a publication for which he is responsible, unless it be established to the satisfaction of the court that disclosure is necessary in the interests of justice or national security or for the prevention of disorder or crime."

Since the European Convention was incorporated into English domestic law by the Human Rights Act 1998, the leading authority on the protection of journalistic sources has been the House of Lords' decision in *Ashworth Hospital Authority v MGN Ltd*,[18] in which Lord Woolf C.J. (who gave the leading speech) observed[19] that:

> " . . . there can be no doubt now that both section 10 and article 10 have a common purpose in seeking to enhance the freedom of the press by protecting journalistic sources."

Among the patients at Ashworth, a secure mental hospital, was the Moors murderer, Ian Brady. The *Daily Mirror* obtained and published confidential information from Ashworth's medical records relating to Brady. The journalist concerned, Mr Gary Jones, stated that he did not know the identity of the original source of the leaked information and declined to identify his intermediary source. The House of Lords upheld an order requiring him to name the intermediary source.

13–018　　Lord Woolf cited the observations of the European Court of Human Rights in *Goodwin v United Kingdom*[20]:

---

[16] PACE 1984, s.9 and Sch.1.
[17] *Att-Gen v Clough* [1963] 1 Q.B. 773; *Att-Gen v Foster and Mulholland* [1963] 2 Q.B. 477; *British Steel Corporation v Granada Television Ltd* [1981] A.C. 1096; *Att-Gen v Lundin* (1982) 75 Cr. App. R. 90.
[18] [2002] UKHL 29; [2002] 1 W.L.R. 2033.
[19] At [38].
[20] (1996) 22 E.H.R.R. 123.

"The court recalls that freedom of expression constitutes one of the essential foundations of a democratic society and that the safeguards to be afforded to the press are of particular importance. Protection of journalistic sources is one of the basic conditions for press freedom, as is reflected in the laws and the professional codes of conduct in a number of contracting states and is affirmed in several international instruments on journalistic freedoms. Without such protection, sources may be deterred from assisting the press in informing the public on matters of public interest. As a result the vital public watchdog role of the press may be undermined and the ability of the press to provide accurate and reliable information may be adversely affected. Having regard to the importance of the protection of journalistic sources for press freedom in a democratic society and the potentially chilling effect an order of source disclosure has on the exercise of that freedom, such a measure cannot be compatible with article 10 of the Convention unless it is justified by an overriding requirement in the public interest."

Turning to the disclosure order made below, Lord Woolf said[21]:

"However, the protection is not unqualified. Both section 10 and article 10 recognise this. This leads to the difficult issue at the heart of this appeal, namely whether the disclosure ordered was necessary and not disproportionate. The requirements of necessity and proportionality are here separate concepts which substantially cover the same area . . . I find no difficulty in accepting the approach that the European Court emphasised . . . that (i) 'As a matter of general principle, the "necessity" for any restriction of freedom of expression must be convincingly established' and (ii) 'limitations on the confidentiality of journalistic sources call for the most careful scrutiny by the court'.

Furthermore . . . any restriction on the otherwise unqualified right to freedom of expression must meet two further requirements. First, the exercise of the jurisdiction because of article 10(2) should meet a 'pressing social need' and secondly the restriction should be proportionate to a legitimate aim which is being pursued."

Lord Woolf concluded[22] that the care of patients at Ashworth was fraught with difficulty and danger, that the disclosure of the patients' records increased that difficulty and danger and that, to deter the same or similar wrongdoing in the future, it was essential that the source should be identified and punished: that was what had made the orders to disclose necessary and proportionate and justified.

On the day after the House of Lords' decision, another journalist, Robin Ackroyd, identified himself as the intermediary source between the original **13–019**

[21] At [61]–[62].
[22] At [66].

source and the Daily Mirror. Ashworth's successor authority, the Mersey Care NHS Trust, commenced proceedings against him in turn, seeking disclosure of the identity of the original source. The Trust obtained summary judgment at first instance, but the Court of Appeal allowed Mr Ackroyd's appeal.[23]

13–020   The proceedings eventually came on for trial in January 2006 and, on February 7, 2006, Tugendhat J. dismissed the Trust's application for *Norwich Pharmacal* relief.[24] Having set out the facts and having conducted a detailed review of the law, the judge emphasised that he had followed the House of Lords on all points of law, but pointed out that the facts were in some instances were not as had been supposed in the proceedings against MGN. (For example, it was no longer contended that the original source had received payment for his information.) In other instances, the circumstances had changed since the House of Lords' decision. He concluded that it had not been established that there was a "pressing social need" that the original source should be identified.

"Necessary"

13–021   The introduction of the Human Rights Act 1998 and Art.10 have broadened the scope of the court's enquiry in relation to s.10 of the Contempt of Court Act 1981. To the extent that s.10 is still of independent significance, it is clearly to be construed so as to accord with the requirements of Art.10. Thus, in *Mersey Care NHS Trust v Ackroyd (No. 2)*,[25] Tugendhat J. observed that there had been a number of attempts to define the word "necessary" in s.10,[26] before adopting the test of necessity employed by Lord Bingham in relation to Art.10(2) in *R. v Shayler*[27]:

> " 'Necessary' has been strongly interpreted: it is not synonymous with 'indispensable', neither has it the flexibility of such expressions as 'admissible', 'ordinary', 'useful', 'reasonable', or 'desirable' . . . One must consider whether the interference complained of corresponded to a pressing social need, whether it was proportionate to the legitimate aim pursued and whether the reasons given by the national authority to justify it are relevant and sufficient under article 10(2) . . . "

13–022   In *John v Express Newspapers*[28] the Court of Appeal emphasised the practical evidential burden imposed by the test of necessity, citing an earlier dictum of Lindsay J. in *Saunders v Punch Ltd*[29]:

---

[23] *Mersey Care NHS Trust v Ackroyd* [2003] EWCA Civ 663; [2003] F.S.R. 820.
[24] *Mersey Care NHS Trust v Ackroyd (No.2)* [2006] EWHC 107, QB; [2006] E.M.L.R. 12.
[25] At [84].
[26] The leading authority prior to the introduction of the Human Rights Act 1998 was the House of Lords' decision in *Re an Inquiry under the Company Securities (Insider Dealing) Act 1985* [1988] A.C. 660.
[27] [2002] UKHL 11; [2003] 1 A.C. 247 at para.23.
[28] [2000] 1 W.L.R. 1931.
[29] [1998] 1 W.L.R. 986 at 997.

"To an extent, whether disclosure of a source is 'necessary' in the interests of justice can depend on whether the person seeking disclosure has made any attempt other than by applying to the court to find the source for himself and whether any such attempts, were they to be made, would have had any real prospects of making the compulsion of a court order unnecessary. I do not say that the making of such attempts is a necessary precondition of the court's assistance, but its absence can be a powerful, even a decisive, factor against the intervention of the court . . . "

The Court of Appeal agreed, adding[30]:

"Before the courts require journalists to break what a journalist regards as a most important professional obligation to protect a source, the minimum requirement is that other avenues should be explored. It cannot be assumed that it will not be possible either to find the culprit or, at least, to narrow down the number of persons who could have been responsible."

"The interests of justice"

On the other hand, the courts have adopted a broad view of the meaning of "the interests of justice" in s.10. In *Secretary of State for Defence v Guardian Newspapers Ltd*[31] Lord Diplock had interpreted the "interests of justice" exception narrowly as being used "in the technical sense of the administration of justice in the course of legal proceedings in a court of law or . . . before a tribunal or body exercising the judicial power of the state". Rose J. followed that interpretation in refusing to order disclosure of a newpaper's source in *X v Y*.[32]   **13–023**

However, in *X Ltd v Morgan-Grampian (Publishers) Ltd* it was held that Lord Diplock's dictum was too narrow, and that it is "in the interests of justice", within the meaning of s.10:   **13–024**

"that persons should be enabled to exercise important legal rights and to protect themselves from serious legal wrongs whether or not resort to legal proceedings in a court of law will be necessary to obtain these objectives."[33]

Lord Bridge added, as an "obvious" example, that if an employer of a large staff was suffering grave damage from the activities of an unidentified disloyal servant, it was in the interests of justice that he should be able to identify him in order to terminate his contract of employment, notwithstanding that no legal proceedings might be necessary to achieve that end.

[30] [1998] 1 W.L.R. 986 at para.27.
[31] [1985] A.C. 339 at 350.
[32] [1988] 2 All E.R. 648.
[33] [1991] 1 A.C. 1 at 43.

13–025   The breadth of "the interests of justice" was further emphasised by the Court of Appeal in *John v Express Newspapers*.[34] The defendant had obtained a copy of draft legal advice prepared by barristers instructed by or on behalf of the claimants. Although declining to make an order for disclosure of the defendant's source, the Court of Appeal rejected the defendant's submission that the interests of justice were to be assessed by reference only to the personal interest of the litigants involved:

> "Mr Beloff argued that section 10 should not be interpreted so as to protect a wide class such as lawyers and clients as a whole . . . However, this is precisely what section 10 can protect. The authorities make it clear that a broad approach should be taken to what is meant by the interests of justice in section 10. The need for clients to be able to consult their lawyers with assurance that they can do so without risk of their confidence being betrayed is of general importance."

13–026   In *Interbrew SA v Financial Times Ltd*[35] Sedley L.J. (with whom the other two members of the Court of Appeal agreed) warned that the courts should be cautious before allowing a journalist's statutory privilege to be abrogated for a reason unconnected with the applicant's initial right to disclosure. He suggested[36]:

> "The solution, in my view, is in the pivotal word 'necessary'. Read, as it must now be read, in the light of the Convention and its jurisprudence, it requires close regard to be had to the relationship between the mischief and the measure. If the mischief is a civil wrong, the measure which needs to be justified as relevant and proportionate is one which will right the wrong."

The nature of the source and the information revealed

13–027   In *Camelot Group plc v Centaur Ltd*[37] a copy of the claimant's draft preliminary financial statement was leaked and published about a week before the preliminary financial statement was due to be published. The Court of Appeal upheld an order which effectively required the defendant publisher to reveal its source. Schiemann L.J. said[38]:

> "There is a public interest in protecting sources. But it is relevant to ask 'what is the public interest in protecting from disclosure persons in the position of the source in the present case?' Is it in the public interest for people in his position to disclose this type of information? Embargoes on the disclosure of information for a temporary period are a common and useful feature of contemporary life. It does not seem to me that if

[34] [2000] 1 W.L.R. 1931 at para.17.
[35] [2002] EWCA Civ 274; [2002] 2 Lloyd's Rep. 229.
[36] At [49].
[37] [1999] Q.B. 124.
[38] At p.138.

people in the position of the present source experience the chilling effect referred to by the European Court of Human Rights the public will be deprived of anything which it is valuable for the public to have."

However, in *Ashworth Hospital Authority v MGN Ltd*[39] Lord Woolf C.J. expressly approved the judgment below of Laws L.J., which contained the following passage[40]:

"It is in my judgment of the first importance to recognise that the potential vice—the 'chilling effect'—of court orders requiring the disclosure of press sources is in no way lessened, and certainly not abrogated, simply because the case is one in which the information actually published is of no legitimate, objective public interest. Nor is it to the least degree lessened or abrogated by the fact (where it is so) that the source is a disloyal and greedy individual, prepared for money to betray his employer's confidences. The public interest in the non-disclosure of press sources is constant, whatever the merits of the particular publication, and the particular source . . . In my judgment, the true position is that it is always prima facie . . . contrary to the public interest that press sources should be disclosed; and in any given case the debate which follows will be conducted upon the question whether there is an overriding public interest, amounting to a pressing social need, to which the need to keep press sources confidential should give way."

Inevitably the relative importance attached to the public interest in the protection of sources may vary in accordance with the circumstances of the particular case. Whistle-blowers disclosing matters of genuine public concern to reputable media organisations are unlikely to be deterred by court decisions that treat the leaking of gossip for venal purposes as disclosures attracting a lower level of protection. The decision of the European Court of Human Rights in *Von Hannover v Germany*[41] demonstrates that it is possible for the courts to differentiate between types of utterance without abandoning the general principle that freedom of speech is an important right that the courts must uphold. As Lord Steyn said in *R. v Home Secretary, Ex p. Simms*[42]: **13–028**

"The value of free speech in a particular case must be measured in specifics. Not all types of speech have an equal value."

There are conflicting indications in the authorities about the relevance of the motive or purpose of the source. In *Interbrew SA v Financial Times* **13–029**

---

[39] [2002] 1 W.L.R. 2033 at para.66.
[30] [2001] 1 W.L.R. 515 at para.101.
[41] (2005) 40 E.H.R.R. 1.
[42] [2002] A.C. 115 at 127.

Ltd[43] Sedley L.J. interpreted the passage from Laws L.J.'s judgment in *Ashworth Hospital Authority v MGN Ltd*, set out above, as meaning that the source's motive ought to be ignored. Sedley L.J. considered that a distinction should be drawn between a source's motive and his purpose: the former was irrelevant to the legal issues, but the latter was likely to be highly material. But it is a difficult distinction to draw, whether at a theoretical or a practical level. Consider, for example, the fact of a payment to the source. Sedley L.J. would appear to regard whether the source acted for profit or for spite as simply a matter of motive, and therefore legally irrelevant.[44] However, in *Ashworth Hospital Authority v MGN Ltd* Lord Woolf regarded the fact (as the evidence then suggested) that the source had been paid as a relevant matter. He said that "the disclosure was made worse because it was purchased by a cash payment".[45] Conversely, the absence of payment was held to be relevant in *Mersey Care NHS Trust v Ackroyd*, at both interim and final stages.[46]

13–030   In a case where a source has disclosed confidential information to a journalist and disclosure of the source's identity is sought on *Norwich Pharmacal* grounds, a distinction needs to be drawn between the questions whether publication was justified on public interest grounds and, if not, whether disclosure of the source's identity should be ordered. The motive or purpose of the source will seldom be relevant to the first question, but may be very relevant to the second. A particular reason for its relevance to the second is that the purpose of *Norwich Pharmacal* relief includes, in an appropriate case, enabling the claimant to protect himself from future wrongdoing by the source. In assessing the risk of future wrongdoing, the source's apparent motive for his past conduct may have obvious significance.

---

[43] [2002] EWCA Civ 274; [2002] 2 Lloyd's Rep. 229 at [53].
[44] *ibid.* at [66]: "What matters in my judgment is the Source's evident purpose. It was on any view a maleficent one, calculated to do harm *whether for profit or for spite* . . . " (emphasis added).
[45] [2002] UKHL 29; [2002] 1 W.L.R. 2033 at [66].
[46] [2003] EWCA Civ 663; [2003] F.S.R. 820, CA, e.g. at para.46, and [2006] EWHC 107, QB, e.g. at [196].

CHAPTER 14

Employees

Contract

The relationship between an employer and employee is contractual and, **14–001** while the existence of a contract does not prevent concurrent application of the equitable doctrine of confidence,[1] the scope of the employee's duty of confidence is governed by the contract,[2] whether express or implied, for as long as the parties remain bound by the contract.[3]

Although the function of implied terms is to "dot the i's and cross the t's **14–002** of the express terms or to fill in some lacuna left by the contracting parties which must properly be filled by the implied term in order to give business efficacy",[4] it is convenient for present purposes to consider first what obligation of confidentiality the court will imply into a contract of employment before considering express terms.

Implied obligation during employment

The court will imply into any contract of employment a general obliga- **14–003** tion on the part of the employee not to use or disclose confidential information or materials acquired in his capacity as an employee, except for the purposes of his employment.

[1] *Lamb v Evans* [1893] 1 Ch. 218; *Printers & Finishers Ltd v Holloway* [1965] R.P.C. 239; *Thomas Marshall (Exports) Ltd v Guinle* [1979] 1 Ch. 227.
[2] *Robb v Green* [1895] 2 Q.B. 315; *Faccenda Chicken Ltd v Fowler* [1987] 1 Ch. 117 at 135.
[3] The special position which arises after termination by repudiatory breach is considered at para.14–028 below.
[4] *Initial Services Ltd v Putterill* [1968] 1 Q.B. 396 at 411.

14–004   This principle goes back at least to *Tipping v Clarke*, in which Sir James Wigram V.C. said[5]:

> " . . . it is clear that every clerk employed in a merchant's counting-house is under an implied contract that he will not make public that which he learns in the execution of his duty as clerk."

Wigram V.C's words were quoted with express approval by Lord Cottenham L.C. in *Prince Albert v Strange*[6] and the principle has been applied in many subsequent cases.[7]

14–005   The obligation is subject to usual qualifications, for example, where disclosure is required by law or in cases of serious wrongdoing.[8] The Public Interest Disclosure Act 1998 (amending the Employment Rights Act 1996) defines certain disclosures made in the public interest as protected disclosures and provides that employers should not subject their employees, in particular, to any detriment for making a protected disclosure. An employee whose rights in this respect are infringed may bring a claim before an employment tribunal. Section 43J of the Employment Rights Act 1996 provides that any provision in an agreement between employer and employee which purports to preclude the employee from making a protected disclosure is to that extent void.

Implied obligation after termination

14–006   The scope of an employee's obligation of confidence after termination of his employment is more difficult. In *Lamb v Evans*[9] it was suggested that the duty was limited to not using materials acquired in the course of his employment and did not prevent him from using his knowledge.

14–007   Subsequent authorities have made it clear that the duty is not so confined. In *Printers & Finishers Ltd v Holloway*[10] Cross J. said:

> "The mere fact that the confidential information is not embodied in a document but is carried away by the employee in his head is not, of course of itself a reason against the granting of an injunction to prevent its use or disclosure by him. If the information in question can fairly be regarded as a separate part of the employee's stock of knowledge which a man of ordinary honesty and intelligence would recognise to be the property of his old employer, and not his own to do as he likes with, then the court, if it thinks that there is a danger of the information

---

[5] (1843) 2 Hare 383 at 393.
[6] (1849) 1 Mac. & G. 25 at 45.
[7] *Merryweather v Moore* [1892] 2 Ch. 518; *Robb v Green* [1895] 2 Q.B. 315; *Reid & Sigrist Ltd v Moss* (1932) 49 R.P.C. 461.
[8] *Gartside v Outram* (1857) 26 L.J.Ch. (N.S.) 113; *Initial Services Ltd v Putterill* [1968] 1 Q.B. 396; *In re a Company's Application* [1989] 1 Ch. 477; see also Ch.6.
[9] [1893] 1 Ch. 218 at 236; see para.1–033, above.
[10] [1965] R.P.C. 239 at 255.

being used or disclosed by the ex-employee to the detriment of the old employer, will do what it can to prevent that result by granting an injunction. Thus an ex-employee will be restrained from using or disclosing a chemical formula or a list of customers which he has committed to memory."[11]

Customer lists have presented particular difficulties, to which further reference is made below.

The reference to the information being "a separate part of the employee's stock of knowledge" is important and echoes what was said by the House of Lords in *Herbert Morris Ltd v Saxelby*,[12] the fundamental principle of which is that a person is not to be fettered from making proper use of his skills, both for his own benefit and for that of the public. **14–008**

In so far as knowledge gained in confidence has become part of the employee's general skill and knowledge, he owes no duty after the termination of his employment to refrain from using it in other employment. Such knowledge is to be distinguished from the type of information referred to by Cross J. in the passage cited above, i.e. trade secrets and the like. **14–009**

The distinction between knowledge which is, and knowledge which is not, to be regarded as part of an ex-employee's general skill and knowledge has been a fruitful source of litigation, and drawing the line can be difficult.[13] **14–010**

In *Faccenda Chicken Ltd v Fowler*[14] the plaintiffs bred and sold chickens. The defendant, during his employment as their sales manager, introduced an operation of selling freshly killed chickens from refrigerated vans. He left their employment to set up a similar business of his own in the same area, and several of the plaintiffs' van salesmen went to work for him. The plaintiffs claimed an injunction and damages for misuse of confidential "sales information", including the names and addresses of customers, their usual requirements, the prices charged to them, and the van salesmen's delivery routes. **14–011**

Goulding J. found that the information came into the category of confidential information which the defendant was required to use only for the plaintiffs' benefit while he remained in their employment, but which became part of his general skill and knowledge, so that he was permitted to use it after the end of the contract for his own benefit in competition with **14–012**

---

[11] See also *Johnson & Bloy (Holdings) Ltd v Wolstenholme Rink plc* [1987] I.R.L.R. 499 at 502, *per* Parker L.J., "Somebody may hit upon the combination of two ingredients after many years of research, which produce an immensely valuable result wholly unknown to anybody else. An employee would have no difficulty in holding that knowledge in his head and inevitably carrying it away with him. But it cannot . . . be regarded as part of the ordinary skill and experience of the particular employee. It is a secret, whether or not it is carried away in his head . . . ."

[12] [1916] A.C. 688.

[13] For examples, see Brearley and Bloch, *Employment Covenants and Confidential Information* (2nd edition, 1999), pp.101–105; *Co-ordinated Industries Pty Ltd v Elliott* (1998) 43 N.S.W.L.R. 282.

[14] [1987] 1 Ch. 117 at 137–138.

the plaintiffs. The Court of Appeal agreed. Neill L.J., delivering the judgment of the Court, said:

> "In our judgment the information will only be protected [after the employment has ceased] if it can properly be classed as a trade secret or as material which, while not properly to be described as a trade secret, is in all the circumstances of such a highly confidential nature as to require the same protection as a trade secret eo nomine . . . It is clearly impossible to provide a list of matters which will qualify as a trade secret or their equivalent. Secret processes of manufacture provide obvious examples, but innumerable other pieces of information are *capable* of being trade secrets, though the secrecy of some information may be only short-lived."

There is no universal formula for determining what is a trade secret or item of equivalent confidentiality. In *PSM International plc v Whitehouse*[15] Lloyd L.J. described it as a question of degree. In *Lansing Linde Ltd v Kerr*[16] Staughton L.J. considered that "trade secret" embraced information used in a trade, restricted in its dissemination, and the disclosure of which would be liable to cause real or significant harm to the party claiming confidentiality. That is very close to Sir Robert Megarry, V.C.'s criteria in *Thomas Marshall Ltd v Guinle*[17] for identifying information protectable during a contract of employment.

14–013   In *Faccenda Chicken* itself,[18] the Court of Appeal identified four factors that were relevant to whether confidential information amounted to a trade secret: the nature of the employment, the nature of the information, the extent to which the employer impressed the information's confidentiality upon the employee and the ease with which the information could be isolated from other information that the ex-employee was free to use.[19] In *FSS Travel & Leisure Systems Ltd v Johnson*,[20] the Court of Appeal also referred to the extent of use in the public domain and the damage likely to be caused by the use and disclosure of the information in competition with the employer.

14–014   Since the underlying reason for a distinction being drawn between the duty of confidentiality owed during a contract of employment, and the duty which continues to subsist after it, is that the ex-employee should not be prevented from using his general skill and knowledge in subsequent employment, it is suggested that this should guide the court in deciding whether the post-termination duty extends to a particular piece of information. If the effect of holding that it does would be to put an unreasonable restriction on the ex-employee's ability to find or carry out work in the

---

[15] [1992] I.R.L.R. 279 at 282.
[16] [1991] 1 W.L.R. 251.
[17] [1979] 1 Ch. 227.
[18] At 137–138.
[19] For an example of the application of these factors, see the Court of Appeal's decision in *A.T. Poeton (Gloucester Plating) Ltd v Horton* [2001] FSR 169 at 185–186.
[20] [1999] F.S.R. 505 at 512.

sector in which he is skilled, the duty should not extend to it. If it would not, there is no reason why the duty of confidentiality should not continue to apply.

If the answer is doubtful, the issue should be resolved in favour of the ex-employee for reasons given by Scott J. in *Balston Ltd v Headline Filters Ltd*[21] and echoed by Mummery J. in *Ixora Trading Inc. v Jones*[22]: **14–015**

> "Technologically based industries abound. All have what they regard as secrets. Employees, particularly those employed on the scientific or technical side of the manufacturing business, necessarily acquire knowledge of the relevant technology. They become associated with technological advances and innovations. Their experience, built up during their years of employment, naturally equips them to be dangerous competitors if and when their employment ceases. The use of confidential information restrictions in order to fetter the ability of these employees to use their skills and experience after determination of their employment to compete with their ex-employer is, in my view, potentially harmful. It would be capable of imposing a new form of servitude or serfdom, to use Cumming-Bruce L.J.'s words on technologically qualified employees. It would render them unable in practice to leave their employment for want of an ability to use their skills and experience after leaving. Employers who want to impose fetters of this sort on their employees ought in my view to be expected to do so by express covenant. The reasonableness of the covenant can then be subjected to the rigorous attention to which all employee covenants in restraint of trade are subject. In the absence of an express covenant, the ability of an ex-employee to compete can be restricted by means of an implied term against use or disclosure of trade secrets. But the case must, in my view, be a clear one. An employee does not have the chance to reject an implied term. It is formulated and imposed on him subsequently to his initial entry into employment. To fetter his freedom to compete by means of an implied term can only be justified, in my view, by a very clear case."

In *Faccenda Chicken Ltd v Fowler*,[23] the Court of Appeal appeared to suggest that it was not possible for employers, by means of an express restrictive covenant, to protect confidential information after termination of the employment relationship, unless the information was equivalent to a trade secret. Subsequent decisions[24] indicate that the difficulty identified by the Court of Appeal does not prevent employers from protecting such information by means of restrictive non-compete covenants, so long as such covenants are limited so as not to constitute an unreasonable restraint on

---

[21] [1987] F.S.R. 330 at 351.
[22] [1990] 1 F.S.R. 251 at 261.
[23] [1987] Ch. 117 at 137.
[24] See, for example, *Lancashire Fires Ltd v S.A. Lyons & Company Ltd* [1996] F.S.R. 629 at 666–667.

trade. However, the fact that such covenants *do* amount to an unreasonable restraint on trade unless strictly limited (for example, in relation to duration) is consistent with the approach suggested above.

Customer lists

14–016 In the absence of a valid, express covenant to the contrary, an ex-employee may ordinarily solicit business from customers of his former employer after his employment has ended. He will, however, be in breach of duty to his employer if he solicits the employer's customers before the end of his employment with a view to obtaining their future business.[25]

14–017 The employee will also be in breach of duty if, during his employment, he copies his employer's customer list with a view to using it to compete against the employer later. In *Robb v Green*[26] an order was made in those circumstances against the ex-employee requiring him to deliver up the list for destruction and restraining him from making use of the information obtained by copying it. The same principle would apply if the employee had instead committed the list to his memory.[27]

14–018 In *N P Generations Pty Ltd v Fenely*,[28] the defendant ex-employee of an estate agency was required by the Supreme Court of South Australia to deliver up her address book, which had been copied in part from her former employer's customer list, but was permitted to retain her diary (which contained confidential information appearing also in the customer list, but had not been copied from the customer list).

14–019 The injunction granted in *Robb v Green* did not prohibit the defendant from sending out circulars to customers whose names he could remember apart from having copied the plaintiff's list. Maugham L.J. noted this point in *Wessex Dairies Ltd v Smith* adding[29]:

> "It follows, in my opinion, that the servant may, while in the employment of the master, be as agreeable, attentive and skilful as it is in his power to be to others with the ultimate view of obtaining the customers' friendly feelings when he calls upon them if and when he sets up business for himself."

14–020 In *Roger Bullivant Ltd v Ellis*[30] Nourse L.J. also noted the point that the injunction in *Robb v Green* did not prevent the defendant from contracting with any of the plaintiff's customers if he was able to do so without using the information which he had unlawfully acquired, and he commented that the form of order made in that case might not be satisfactory in relation to

[25] *Wessex Dairies Ltd v Smith* [1935] 2 K.B. 80.
[26] [1895] 2 Q.B. 315.
[27] *Printers & Finishers Ltd v Holloway* [1965] R.P.C. 239 at 255.
[28] (2001) 80 S.A.S.R. 151
[29] [1935] 2 K.B. 80 at 89.
[30] [1987] F.S.R. 172 at 182–183.

names of customers, because it might be difficult to know whether it had been breached. In those circumstances it was legitimate for the court to grant instead a springboard injunction, restraining the ex-employee from dealing with any customers on the list whom he had approached while the list was in his possession, provided that the term of the injunction was no longer than the period for which he was likely to obtain an unfair advantage from use of the list.

In *SJB Stephenson Ltd v Mandy*[31] the defendant was a senior employee of **14–021** a firm of insurance brokers until he left to join a competitor. His contract contained an express confidentiality clause prohibiting him from disclosing to any person any information in relation to the affairs of any client except in the course of his duties. Bell J. held that on the facts of the case the names of the firm's clients, the details of the cover arranged for them, the renewal dates, premiums charged and brokerage earned were protectable and that the covenant was not in unreasonable restraint of trade. It did not matter that the defendant had not deliberately memorised them. Bell J. indicated that he would grant an injunction to enforce the covenant indefinitely.[32] There was also an express post-contractual covenant against solicitation of the firm's clients, but this was limited to 12 months. The defendant was found to be in breach of both the confidentiality and the non-solicitation clause. In assessing damages the judge (a) did not differentiate between the different breaches and (b) acknowledged that the defendant would be free to solicit former clients for the second year's renewals of business.[33] It would seem hard to justify a clause, or an injunction, having the effect of preventing the defendant indefinitely from disclosing the names of the firm's clients, or information about the details of their cover, renewal dates, premium rates and brokerage, the relevance of which was time limited. The confidentiality clause might, however, be justified on the basis that it was intended to protect information only for as long as the requirements of confidentiality continued, and that in relation to details of clients and their contracts that period (adopting the approach of Nourse L.J. in *Roger Bullivant v Ellis*) would be no longer than the period during which disclosure would be likely to give an unfair advantage to a competitor. The real mischief in such a case is the employee leaving and immediately giving to his new employer all the details he knows about his previous employer's clients and their contracts.

Use of confidential information after termination for purposes other than use of the ex-employee's skills

It is one thing for the implied obligation of confidentiality to be qualified **14–022** so as not to impede an ex-employee's proper use of his general skill and knowledge in subsequent employment, whether for himself or others. It is a different matter for him to disclose such information for other purposes.

14–023 In *Mainmet Holdings plc v Austin*[34] the plaintiffs specialised in heating systems. The defendant was their former managing director. After his departure he sent to customers copies of internal reports about defects in the customers' systems, including one by himself marked "highly confidential". On an application for an interlocutory injunction it was held that there was no serious issue to be tried on the question of breach of confidence, because the reports did not come into the category of trade secrets or information of equivalent confidentiality, and therefore the defendant owed no continuing duty in respect of them.

14–024 It is suggested that the judge misdirected himself. Although the reports were not trade secrets, there was a strong prima facie case that they were confidential; they could not be regarded as part of the defendant's general skill and knowledge of the business of heating systems; nor was he attempting to use them as such. His use was conceded on the application to have been malicious.

Express terms

14–025 A contract may restrict a former employee from divulging information gained by him as a result of his employment even if the information is not confidential, provided that the clause would not prevent him from making proper use of his skills or otherwise amount to an unreasonable restraint on trade or would be otherwise unlawful.[35]

14–026 The courts have on occasion enjoined employers seeking to protect confidential information after the end of the employment relationship to insert express clauses in their employment contracts. Thus Cross J. said in *Printers & Finishers Ltd v Holloway*[36]:

> "If the managing director is right in thinking that there are features in the plaintiffs' process which can fairly be regarded as trade secrets and which their employees will inevitably carry away with them in their heads, then the proper way for the plaintiffs to protect themselves would be by exacting covenants from their employees restricting their field of activity after they have left their employment not by asking the court to extend the general equitable doctrine to prevent breaking confidence beyond all reasonable bounds."

In particular, an express term may be effective to *identify* what is, properly, regarded as confidential information or information falling in the narrower category of a trade secret or the equivalent. It is well established that for information to be treated as confidential or a trade secret it must be defined

---

[34] [1991] F.S.R. 538.
[35] For an example, see *Att-Gen v Blake* [2001] 1 A.C. 268. See also Ch.3.
[36] [1965] 1 W.L.R. 1 at 6.

with sufficient precision,[37] and an express contractual term may have that effect. The fact that the contract specifies that certain information is to be treated as a trade secret and kept confidential after the end of the employment does not compel a court to recognise it as such, for unreasonable restraints of trade cannot gain validity by being dressed up as clauses protecting trade secrets, if they are not.[38] But the terms of the contract may be a relevant factor in considering whether the man of ordinary honesty and intelligence, referred to by Cross J. in *Printers & Finishers Ltd v Holloway*, would think he was doing anything wrong in using some piece of information gained during his previous employment.

So, for example, in *United Sterling Corporation Ltd v Felton and*   **14–027**
Mannion[39] Brightman J. said:

> "In my judgment there is no evidence that Mr Mannion was given any special information which he ought to have regarded as a separate part of his stock of knowledge of polystyrene plants, information which an honest and intelligent man would have recognised as the property of the employer and not of the employee. There is no evidence that anything was expressly disclosed to Mr Mannion in confidence. He was never asked to sign any restrictive covenant. There is no evidence that he has done more during the years of his employment than add to his general stock of knowledge and experience of polystyrene plants in the ordinary way that any intelligent employee would naturally do. I see no basis for suggesting that Mr Mannion's conscience was affected during the period of his employment so as to place him under an obligation not to make use of that which he inevitably learned during his years with the plaintiff company."

Termination as a result of repudiatory breach

Where termination of employment occurs as a result of repudiatory breach   **14–028**
by the employer, typically by wrongful summary dismissal, the employee is relieved from further performance of his own contractual obligations, including restrictive post-employment covenants.[40] But the bringing to an end of all primary contractual obligations may leave the parties in a relationship in which duties are owed by operation of law.[41] It is suggested,

---

[37] See para.3–085 above.
[38] *Balston Ltd v Headline Filters Ltd* [1987] F.S.R. 330 at 351. Nor is it necessarily incumbent on an employer to point out the precise limits of what it seeks to protect as confidential information: *Lancashire Fires Ltd v Lyons & Co Ltd* [1996] F.S.R. 629 at 673–674.
[39] [1974] R.P.C. 162 at 173. See also *A.T. Poeton Ltd v Horton* [2001] F.S.R. 169 at 186.
[40] *General Billposting Co Ltd v Atkinson* [1909] A.C. 118.
[41] In *Photo Production Ltd v Securicor Transport Ltd* [1980] A.C. 827 at 850, Lord Diplock gave the example of bailor and bailee.

therefore, that while termination of employment through wrongful repudiation by the employer[42] brings to an end any contractual obligation of confidence owed by the employee to the employer, it does not ipso facto bring to an end the employee's equitable duty in respect of trade secrets or information of equivalent confidentiality.[43]

Employer's obligation

14–029   An employer or prospective employer may also owe a duty of confidence to an employee or prospective employee. In *Smith, Kline & French Laboratories (Australia) Ltd v Department of Community Services*[44] the court observed:

> "Confidential information is commonly supplied without payment: for example, by a prospective employee (or his referee) to support an application for employment. The understanding ordinarily would be that the prospective employer would not disclose the information to any third party; but it would hardly be expected that its use would necessarily be confined to the employment application itself. If that application were successful, the employee would not act on the assumption that material in the relevant file would be destroyed. He would surely be inclined to assume that it might be resorted to later to assist the employer in making decisions relevant to the employee—for example, as to whether the employee (rather than another) should be promoted, or dismissed."

Where the information is supplied by the prospective employee in response to an advertisement or request by the prospective employer, the obligation of confidence could be regarded as arising under an implied contract, the consideration for which would be the provision of the information,[45] or in equity. Such a duty would be owed to the prospective employee in respect of any information of a confidential nature concerning himself, whether it came from the prospective employee personally or from the referee acting on his request. An additional duty of confidence might be owed to the referee if the reference contained matters of a confidential nature relating to the referee. If the information was unsolicited, it is suggested that there would still be an equitable obligation of confidence.

---

[42] An employee cannot bring to an end his own contractual obligation by wrongful repudiation if not accepted by the employer: *Thomas Marshall Ltd v Guinle* [1979] Ch. 227, approved in *Gunton v Richmond Borough Council* [1981] Ch. 448.

[43] In *Campbell v Frisbee* [2002] EWCA Civ 1374, the Court of Appeal observed (at [22]) that "We do not believe that the effect on duties of confidence assumed under contract when the contract in question is wrongfully repudiated is clearly established". See Ch.4 for a fuller discussion.

[44] (1991) 28 F.C.R. 291 at 303, Full Court of the Federal Court of Australia.

[45] *Mechanical and General Inventions Co v Austin* [1935] A.C. 346 at 370.

On the formation of a contract of employment, the nature of the **14–030** relationship would change, but the employer would continue to owe a duty of confidentiality to the employee, whether under an implied term of the contract or in equity, in respect of personal information about the employee gained by the employer in that capacity, subject to usual qualifications.[46]

The obligation not to disclose personal information about an employee to **14–031** a third party without his consent will ordinarily continue after the employment has ended. An ex-employer who is asked for information about a former employee by a prospective employer should therefore be cautious. It is suggested that he would be free to express his views about the qualities of the former employee, because that would be a matter of his own opinion, but that he would not be free to divulge facts which would fairly be regarded as personal to the former employee, for example, his health record.

In *Prout v British Gas plc*[47] the defendants operated a scheme for **14–032** employees to make suggestions, promising confidentiality so long as the employee wished and that his interests would be protected if his suggestion was worth patenting. The plaintiff suggested a form of bracket designed to prevent warning lamps being vandalised. The defendants indicated that they were not interested in it, and the plaintiff then applied for a patent himself. He subsequently sued for breach of confidence and patent infringement. The claim for breach of confidence was put forward on alternative bases of breach of contract or of an equitable obligation. It was held that the plaintiff was entitled to succeed on either ground, and that the duty of confidence continued until the publication of the patent application, when the plaintiff thereby voluntarily put his invention in the possession of the public. The court directed an inquiry as to damages or an account of profits, at the plaintiff's option.

---

[46] An obvious example would be an employer's obligation to supply details of an employee's earnings to the Inland Revenue.
[47] [1992] F.S.R. 478.

CHAPTER 15

Teachers, Clergy, Counsellors and Mediators

TEACHERS

15–001 Schools keep records on every pupil's academic achievements, other skills and abilities and progress at school.[1] Such records, like medical records or the records kept on an employee by an employer, are confidential, but may be used for the purpose of the pupil's welfare, for example, in assisting a child care officer to prepare a report for a court. There would also be no objection to their use for preparing references or reports to a prospective employer, or university, or another school, that are provided with the consent of the pupil, or his parents on his behalf: in such cases, consent to the use of the information would be implied.

15–002 A teacher may also learn confidential information about a child or his family from the child, or from other sources. A teacher has a quasi-parental responsibility for a child in his care and owes a duty to the child to keep such information confidential, except in so far as to do so would conflict with his proper appreciation of the child's best interests. Here the position of a teacher *vis-à-vis* the pupil and the pupil's parents is similar to that of a doctor and can present similar difficulties, for example in relation to issues affecting a pupil's sexual health.[2]

15–003 Education should be a shared responsibility between teacher, parent and pupil. Ordinarily it would be in the pupil's interest that a teacher should feel

---

[1] Schools maintained by a local education authority and special schools are required to keep and update such records under the Education (Pupil Information) (England) Regulations 2005 (SI 2005/1437). The parents have a right to disclosure under para.5 of the Regulations, while the pupil has subject access rights under the Data Protection Act 1998 (subject to the Data Protection (Subject Access Modification) (Education) Order 2000).

[2] See paras 11–040—11–047 above. The Department for Education and Skills has produced Sex and Relationship Education Guidance for Head Teachers, Teachers & School Governors (July 2000), which contains advice as to confidentiality issues.

free to discuss matters concerning the pupil with the pupil's parents. But there are situations where that will not be so.

One example is where an older pupil confides in a teacher about matters **15–004** which he or she does not want his or her parents to know, in which case the teacher must respect that confidence unless he has good reason to believe that it would be damaging to the pupil to do so.

Another is where a teacher makes a promise of confidentiality to a pupil. **15–005** It may be necessary in the interests of the pupil that the teacher should break that promise, but he should do so only if satisfied for good reasons that it is.

There is also the difficult area of suspected child abuse. A teacher is not **15–006** required to act as a detective, nor is he qualified to make medical judgments about the cause of injuries. Reporting a case of suspected child abuse, which turns out to be unfounded, may cause immense distress. Nevertheless where a teacher is in possession of information from which he has real ground to suppose that a child is the subject of abuse, his paramount concern must be the interests of the child, and he will not be in breach of any duty of confidentiality if he reports his concern to an appropriate responsible person or authority such as the local authority's social services department.

CLERGY

The ecclesiastical law of the Church of England requires a minister not to **15–007** reveal or make known to any person any crime or offence revealed to him by confession "except they be such crimes as by the laws of this realm his own life may be called into question for concealing the same".[3]

The modern position in civil law was stated by Lord Denning M.R. in **15–008** *Attorney-General v Mulholland and Foster*[4] as follows:

> "The only profession I know which is given a privilege from disclosing information to a court of law is the legal profession, and then it is not the privilege of the lawyer but of his client.
>
> Take the clergyman, the banker or the medical man. None of these is entitled to refuse to answer when directed to by a judge. Let me not be mistaken. The judge will respect the confidence which each member of these honourable professions receives in the course of it and will not direct him to answer unless not only it is relevant but also it is a proper and, indeed, necessary question in the course of justice to be put and answered."

[3] *Canons Ecclesiastical* (1603), Canon 113 proviso, which remains unrepealed. *Halsbury's Laws of England* (4th edn), *Ecclesiastical Law*, para.308, fn.1. See also s.7 of *Guidelines for the Professional Conduct of the Clergy* (2003), produced by the Convocations of Canterbury and York.

[4] [1963] 2 Q.B. 477 at 489.

This passage was approved by the House of Lords in *British Steel Corporation v Granada Television Ltd.*[5] The same principles will apply also to ministers of other denominations and other religions.

15–009   The doctor with his medical responsibility and the clergyman with his pastoral responsibility are each concerned for the personal welfare of those to whom they minister, and should owe similar obligations of confidentiality to those under their care.

15–010   By the same reasoning the clergyman's duty of confidence should be subject to similar qualifications as obtain in the case of a doctor,[6] that is, not only where disclosure is required by law, but also where he reasonably believes disclosure to be necessary to prevent serious harm to others; or (exceptionally) for the protection of the person concerned (e.g. a seriously disturbed parishioner who may be in need of medical attention); or to enable the clergyman to protect himself against accusations of misconduct.

COUNSELLORS

15–011   There are many forms of counselling. Much important help is provided by voluntary organisations. Some, like the Samaritans, cope with emergencies. Other specialise in particular areas such as marriage breakdown. Within the state system counselling is provided by probation officers, social workers[7] and many others.

15–012   Those who provide such services, whether voluntarily or otherwise, clearly do so on a tacit assumption of confidentiality, and therefore owe an obligation of confidence to those who consult them, subject to the same general qualifications as apply to doctors or clergymen. In some cases the obligation may also be limited by particular public duties. Probation officers, for example, are responsible for providing reports to courts and for supervising the performance of court orders. Any duty of confidentiality owed by them in private law must therefore be subject to their duty in public law to the court. The same must apply to social workers when acting under the control of the court, for example, in wardship or adoption proceedings.[8]

MEDIATORS

15–013   Counselling, conciliation and mediation shade into each other, and the terms are sometimes used without discrimination, although they can take

---

[5] [1981] A.C. 1096. Lord Wilberforce (with whom Lord Russell agreed) described it at 1169–1170 as a "classic passage". Viscount Dilhorne cited it at 1181. Lord Fraser referred to it at 1196.

[6] See Ch.11.

[7] Guidance to social workers is included in the British Association of Social Workers' *Code of Ethics for Social Work* (2002).

[8] See Ch.21, below.

very different forms.[9] Mediation as a means of alternative dispute resolution may vary in its degree of formality.

The most formal type of alternative dispute resolution is arbitration, **15–014** although there is an important difference between an arbitrator, who makes a decision and a mediator, who tries to help the parties to reach an agreement.

In *Dolling-Baker v Merrett*[10] it was held that parties to an arbitration **15–015** agreement are under an implied obligation not to disclose or to use for any other purpose documents prepared for or disclosed in the arbitration, or to disclose in any way any evidence given in the arbitration, except with the consent of the other party or leave of the Court.[11]

The same logic, whether in support of an implied contractual term or an **15–016** equitable obligation, must apply as much, if not more strongly, in the case of mediation. For it would destroy the basis of mediation if, in the case of the mediation failing, either party could publicise matters which had passed between themselves or between either of them and the mediator for the purposes of mediation. An obligation of confidence would also be owed to both parties by the mediator.

In the case of *Theodoropoulas v Theodoropoulas*,[12] it was held that, **15–017** where a husband and wife were trying to effect a reconciliation in the presence of a conciliator, neither of the parties, nor the conciliator, could give evidence of the conversation in subsequent divorce proceedings without the consent of the other party. Simon P. said[13]:

> "No doubt, when a probation officer or an SSAFA representative or a clergyman is approached, the court will readily infer that the parties have gone to him with a view to reconciliation and on the tacit understanding that nothing said should afterwards be used against them; but, equally, where it is proved that any private individual is enlisted specifically as a conciliator, in my judgment the law will aid his or her efforts by guaranteeing that any admissions or disclosures by the parties are privileged in subsequent matrimonial litigation."

In *Re D*[14] the Court of Appeal held that in proceedings made under the **15–018** Children Act 1989 statements made by a party in the course of meetings held for the purposes of reconciliation, mediation or conciliation were privileged from production, by analogy with "without prejudice" correspondence, except if a statement was made clearly indicating that the maker had in the past caused or was likely in the future to cause serious harm to the well-being of a child. However, the court emphasised that it was concerned in that case only with a question of admissibility of evidence, and

---

[9] For a discussion of the differences in the context of divorce, see the Law Commission, "The Ground for Divorce", 1990.

[10] [1990] 1 W.L.R. 1205 at 1213, *per* Parker L.J.

[11] For a fuller discussion, see Ch.22.

[12] [1964] P. 311.

[13] *Theodoropoulas v Theodoropoulas* [1964] P. 311 at 313–314.

[14] *Re D (Minors) (Conciliation: Disclosure of Information)* [1993] Fam. 231.

not with duties of confidence. The without prejudice status of mediation was again upheld (in the context of costs arguments) by the Court of Appeal in *Reed Executive Plc v Reed Business Information Ltd.*[15]

15–019   In order that the parties should know where they stand, it is preferable that any formal mediation agreement should contain a confidentiality clause. CEDR Centre for Dispute Resolution's Model Mediation Procedure and Agreement (9th edn) provides:

> "16 Every person involved in the Mediation will keep confidential and not use for any collateral or ulterior purpose all information (whether given orally, in writing or otherwise) arising out of, or in connection with, the Mediation, including the fact of any settlement and its terms, save for the fact that the mediation is to take place or has taken place.
>
> 17 All information (whether oral, in writing or otherwise) arising out of, or in connection with, the Mediation will be without prejudice, privileged and not admissible as evidence or disclosable in any current or subsequent litigation or other proceedings whatsoever. This does not apply to any information, which would in any event have been admissible or disclosable in any such proceedings.
>
> 18 The Mediator will not disclose to any other Party any information given to him by a Party in confidence without the express consent of that Party.
>
> 19 Paragraphs 16—18 shall not apply if, and to the extent that:
>
> - all Parties consent to the disclosure; or
> - the Mediator is required under the general law to make disclosure; or
> - the Mediator reasonably considers that there is a serious risk of significant harm to the life or safety of any person if the information in question is not disclosed; or
> - the Mediator reasonably considers that there is a serious risk of his/her being subject to criminal proceedings unless the information in question is disclosed.
>
> 20 None of the Parties to the Mediation Agreement will call the Mediator... as a witness, consultant, arbitrator or expert in any litigation or other proceedings whatsoever arising from, or in connection with, the matters in issue in the Mediation. The Mediator... will not voluntarily act in any such capacity without the written agreement of all the Parties."

---

[15] [2004] EWCA Civ 887; [2004] 1 W.L.R. 3026.

CHAPTER 16

Lawyers

Even before any broad development of the law of confidence, it was **16–001**
recognised that the relationship between a lawyer and his clients imported
obligations of confidentiality. In *Taylor v Blacklow*,[1] for example, Gaselee J.
said that:

" . . . the first duty of an attorney is to keep the secrets of his client.
Authority is not wanted to establish that proposition . . . ."

The duty of confidence owed by a solicitor or barrister to his client is **16–002**
governed by the same general principles of law as apply to any other
professional person, but there are special features which affect lawyers
because of the central role performed by lawyers in the administration of
justice. In the case of a solicitor the duty will arise both by contract and
under the equitable doctrine of confidence; in the case of the barrister
(unless he is instructed by direct access) the duty is equitable.[2] An
individual's communications with his lawyers now also attract the courts'
protection under Art.8 of the European Convention on Human Rights.[3]

The duty owed by a lawyer to his client will extend to all confidential **16–003**
information obtained in that capacity during the period of his retainer,
irrespective of its source.[4] A client may consent either expressly or impliedly

---

[1] (1836) 3 Bing. (N.C.) 235.
[2] For the rules of professional conduct, see Rule 16E of the Solicitors' Practice Rules
1990—together with the explanatory notes contained in the Law Society's *Confidentiality and
Disclosure Guidance* (April 2006)—and the "Code of Conduct of the Bar of England and
Wales", paras 603(f), 608(b) and 702.
[3] *Foxley v United Kingdom* (2001) EHRR 637. See Ch.7 above.
[4] See para.3 of the Law Society's *Confidentiality and Disclosure Guidance* (April 2006). For
discussion of what constitutes confidential information (including comments in relation to
solicitors in *Hilton v BarkerBooth & Eastwood* [2005] UKHL 8; [2005] 1 W.L.R. 567) see
Ch.3.

to his lawyer's disclosure of confidential information.[5] However, it does not follow from the fact that two solicitors are retained by a single client in relation to different retainers that the client consents to the communication of confidential information between them.[6]

16–004   Although a lawyer's duty of confidentiality is ordinarily owed to his client, such a duty may also be owed to a third person. With his client's consent, a barrister, for example, may agree to receive information from his opponent on a "counsel only" basis, in which case he would owe a duty of confidence not to disclose it to anyone else without his opponent's consent.

Continuing duty after termination of retainer

16–005   Unlike the fiduciary duty of loyalty owed by a lawyer to an existing client, the lawyer's duty of confidentiality survives the end of his retainer. In *Wilson v Rastall*[7] (a case on privilege) Buller J., referring to a decision by him in an earlier case, said:

> " . . . I thought that the privilege of not being examined to such points was the privilege of the party, and not of the attorney: and that the privilege never ceased at any period of time. In such a case it is not sufficient to say that the cause is at an end; the mouth of such a person is shut for ever."

"For ever" may be an overstatement, for information can lose the quality of confidence, but the duty of confidence will continue for as long as the information retains that quality.

16–006   In *Prince Jefri Bolkiah v KPMG*[8] the plaintiff, a brother of the Sultan of Brunei, had retained the defendant accountants to provide forensic accountancy services in litigation relating to his financial affairs. Some time after that retainer had ended, the government of Brunei set up an investigation into aspects of Prince Jefri's former chairmanship of the Brunei Investment Agency. He obtained an interlocutory injunction restraining KPMG from acting for the Agency in the investigation. The injunction was discharged by the Court of Appeal, but reinstated by the House of Lords.

16–007   The leading speech was given by Lord Millett. He cited the earlier decision of the Court of Appeal in *Rakusen v Ellis, Munday & Clarke*[9] as authority for two propositions:

---

[5] See *TSB Bank plc v Robert Irving & Burns* [1999] Lloyd's Rep. (PN) 956.
[6] *Marsh v Sofaer* [2003] EWHC 3334, Ch; (2004) P.N.L.R. 24, *per* Sir Andrew Morritt V.C. at [46].
[7] (1792) 4 T.R. 753 at 759. Cited by Lord Taylor C.J. in *R. v Derbyshire Magistrates Court Ex p. B* [1996] A.C. 487 at 504.
[8] [1999] 2 A.C. 222.
[9] [1912] 1 Ch. 831.

"(i) that there is no absolute rule of law in England that a solicitor may not act in litigation against a former client; and (ii) that the solicitor may be restrained from acting if such a restriction is necessary to avoid a significant risk of the disclosure or misuse of confidential information belonging to the former client."[10]

Comparing the position of accountants and solicitors, he added:

"The duties of an accountant cannot be greater than those of a solicitor, and may be less, for information relating to his client's affairs which is in the possession of a solicitor is usually privileged as well as confidential. In the present case, however, some of the information obtained by KPMG is likely to have attracted litigation privilege, though not solicitor-client privilege, and it is conceded by KPMG that an accountant who provides litigation support services of the kind which they provided to Prince Jefri must be treated for present purposes in the same way as a solicitor."

Lord Millett held that, once the fiduciary relationship between solicitor and client had ended with the termination of the retainer, the court's jurisdiction to restrain the solicitor from acting against his former client could not be based on any conflict of interests, since the solicitor's only continuing duty was to preserve the confidentiality of information imparted during the retainer. Accordingly, a plaintiff seeking to restrain his former solicitor from acting for another client must show that the solicitor was in possession of relevant confidential information relating to his affairs.[11]

In relation to the extent of the solicitor's duty of confidentiality he observed[12]:

16–008

"Whether founded on contract or equity, the duty to preserve confidentiality is unqualified. It is a duty to keep the information confidential, not merely to take all reasonable steps to do so. Moreover, it is not merely a duty not to communicate the information to a third party. It is a duty not to misuse it, that is to say, without the consent of the former client to make any use of it or to cause any use to be made of it by others otherwise than for his benefit. The former client cannot be protected completely from accidental or inadvertent disclosure. But he is entitled to prevent his former solicitor from exposing him to any avoidable risk; and this includes the increased risk of the use of the information to his prejudice arising from the acceptance of instructions

---

[10] At 234.

[11] Their Lordships did not deal expressly with the court's inherent jurisdiction to supervise the conduct of its officers. The existence of the jurisdiction (in the context of an application to prevent a lawyer from acting in litigation) was confirmed by the Court of Appeal in *Geveran Trading Co Ltd v Skjevesland* [2002] EWCA Civ 1567; [2003] 1 W.L.R. 912, at [38]. See also the detailed analysis by Brereton J. in the Supreme Court of New South Wales in *Kallanicos v Hunt* [2005] N.S.W.S.C. 1181.

[12] At 235–236.

to act for another client with an adverse interest in a matter to which the information is or may be relevant."

Discussing the degree of risk of misuse necessary to justify the court's interference, Lord Millett said:

"Many different tests have been proposed in the authorities. These include the avoidance of 'an appreciable risk' or 'an acceptable risk.' I regard such expressions as unhelpful: the former because it is ambiguous, the latter because it is uninformative. I prefer simply to say that the court should intervene unless it is satisfied that there is no risk of disclosure.[13] It goes without saying that the risk must be a real one, and not merely fanciful or theoretical. But it need not be substantial."

Lord Millett treated the possible efficacy of "Chinese walls" within firms with considerable caution[14]:

"There is no rule of law that Chinese walls or other arrangements of a similar kind are insufficient to eliminate the risk. But the starting point must be that, unless special measures are taken, information moves within a firm. In *MacDonald Estate v Martin*, 77 D.L.R. (4th) 249, 269 Sopinka J. said that the court should restrain the firm from acting for the second client 'unless satisfied on the basis of clear and convincing evidence that all reasonable measures have been taken to ensure that no disclosure will occur.' With the substitution of the word 'effective' for the words 'all reasonable' I would respectfully adopt that formulation."

16–009   *Bolkiah* has been applied in a number of subsequent decisions.[15] The courts have frequently addressed, in particular, the adequacy of arrangements made by firms to prevent the free internal flow of confidential information. In *Koch Shipping Inc v Richards Butler*,[16] the Court of Appeal emphasised that all such cases depend on their own facts. However, Tuckey L.J., observed[17]:

"In these days of professional and client mobility it is of course important that client confidentiality should be preserved. Each case

[13] It is not often that damages will be an adequate remedy. See, for example, *National Westminster Bank plc v Bonas* [2003] EWHC 1821, Ch, *per* Lindsay J. at [131(viii)].
[14] At 237–238.
[15] See, for example, *Young v Robson Rhodes* [1999] 3 All E.R. 524 (Laddie J.); *Halewood International Ltd v Addleshaws Booth & Co* [2000] Lloyd's Rep. (PN) 298 (Neuberger J.); *In the matter of a Firm of Solicitors* [2000] 1 Lloyd's Rep. 31 (Timothy Walker J.); *Ball v Druces & Atlee* [2002] P.N.L.R. 23 (Burton J.); *Bodle v Coutts & Co* [2003] EWHC 1865, Ch (Peter Smith J.); *Marks & Spencer Group plc v Freshfields Bruckhaus Deringer* [2004] EWCA Civ 741; *GUS Consulting GmbH v Leboeuf Lamb Greene & Macrae* [2006] EWCA Civ 683; (2006) P.N.L.R. 32.
[16] [2002] EWCA Civ 1280; [2002] 2 All E.R. (Comm) 957.
[17] At [53].

must depend on its own facts. But I think there is a danger inherent in the intensity of the adversarial process of courts being persuaded that a risk exists when, if one stands back a little, that risk is no more than fanciful or theoretical. I advocate a robust view with this in mind, so as to ensure that the line is sensibly drawn."

Rule 16E(4) of the Solicitors' Practice Rules 1990 (made on April 25, **16–010** 2006) provides that:

"If you hold, or if your practice holds, confidential information in relation to a client or former client, you must not risk breaching confidentiality by acting, or continuing to act, for another client on a matter where:

> (i) that information might reasonably be expected to be material; and
>
> (ii) *that client has an interest adverse to the first-mentioned client or former client* except where proper arrangements can be made to protect that information . . . " [Emphasis added]

The absence of an obvious conflict between the interests of a new client and the interests of a former client may be relevant to the question whether, as a matter of fact, there is a real risk of disclosure or misuse of the former client's confidential information, and to the nature and extent of the arrangements necessary to guard against that risk. But the existence of an "adverse" interest forms no part of Lord Millett's reasoning in *Bolkiah* and is not a necessary condition for the application of the principles established in that case.

Legal professional privilege

When considering the duties of a lawyer to his client, a practical distinction **16–011** between the limits of confidence and the limits of privilege is often difficult to draw. (The subject here discussed is the duty of a lawyer to his client, as opposed to the difficult subject of the relationship of privilege and confidentiality as between a client and another party, about which see Chapter 18.) For confidentiality is a pre-requisite of legal professional privilege; and, conversely, if information is recognised to be privileged, the decision whether to disclose it belongs to the client and not to the lawyer. Legal professional privilege is no longer merely a procedural or evidential rule applicable only in the context of litigation. As Lord Hoffmann said in *R. (Morgan Grenfell Ltd) v Special Commissioner of Income Tax*[18]:

---

[18] [2002] UKHL 21; [2003] 1 A.C. 563 at [30].

"It is not the case that LPP does no more than entitle the client to require his lawyer to withhold privileged documents in judicial or quasi-judicial proceedings, leaving the question of whether he may disclose them on other occasions to the implied duty of confidence. The policy of LPP requires that the client should be secure in the knowledge that protected documents and information will not be disclosed at all."

16–012   This is consistent with the approach taken, for example, by Scrutton L.J. in *Weld-Blundell v Stephen*,[19] where he said:

"But take the case of a solicitor. Under the decision in *Reg. v Cox and Railton*[20] when the accused has consulted his solicitor after the commission of a crime for the legitimate purpose of being defended the communication is *privileged*, the *privilege* being that of the client. If then the solicitor in breach of this *confidence and privilege* announced his intention of informing the prosecution of the contents of his client's communication, I cannot believe that the Court would not restrain him before communication or give damages against him for breach of his contract of employment after communication . . . ." (Emphasis added.)

There are, however, limits to the circumstances in which legal professional privilege attaches. The information must itself be confidential. So, for example, legal professional privilege cannot attach to extracts from public records made by a solicitor for the purposes of a defence, nor to communications with an opposing party,[21] nor to copies of documents which were not brought into existence in circumstances covered by legal professional privilege even where the copies were obtained for the purposes of litigation.[22]

16–013   The scope and depth of legal professional privilege are further considered at Chapter 18 below.

Crime or fraud

16–014   Privilege does not attach to communications between a client and legal adviser, or documents brought into existence, as a step in a criminal or fraudulent enterprise, or for the purpose of stifling or covering up a crime or fraud, whether the legal adviser is himself a party to the plot or innocent,[23]

[19] [1919] 1 K.B. 520 at 544–545.
[20] (1884) 14 Q.B.D. 153 at 175.
[21] *Lyell v Kennedy (No.3)* (1884) 27 Ch.D. 1.
[22] *Ventouris v Mountain* [1991] 1 W.L.R. 607.
[23] *R. v Cox and Railton* (1884) 14 Q.B.D. 153; *Bullivant v Att-Gen for Victoria* [1901] A.C. 196 at 201, *per* Lord Halsbury; 206, *per* Lord Lindley; *O'Rourke v Darbishire* [1920] A.C. 581; *Gamlen Chemical Co (UK) Ltd v Rochem*, unreported, December 7, 1979, CA (Civil Division) Transcript No.777 of 1979; *Finers v Miro* [1991] 1 W.L.R. 35.

for, as Stephen J. said in *R. v Cox and Railton*,[24] a communication in furtherance of a criminal purpose does not "come into the ordinary scope of professional employment" and "the protection of such communications cannot possibly be otherwise than injurious to the interests of justice".

In *Bullivant v Attorney-General for Victoria*, Lord Halsbury L.C. said[25]:

> " . . . for the perfect administration of justice and for the protection of confidence which exists between a solicitor and his client, it has been established as a principle of public policy that those confidential communications shall not be subject to production. But to that, of course, this limitation has been put, that no court can be called upon to protect communications which are in themselves part of a criminal or unlawful proceeding."

16–015

A solicitor is not prevented by any duty of confidence from making appropriate disclosure of information that falls within the "crime or fraud" exception to legal professional privilege. The same factors that have deprived the information of its privileged status will serve also to undermine its confidentiality. However, a serious problem for an honest solicitor arises when the facts are not clear. Drawing a line between proper defence of a client and improper concealment of wrongdoing may be difficult. So is the position of a solicitor who begins to suspect that a transaction in which he has been retained involves fraud. Terminating his retainer may be a solution in some cases, but not in others, particularly where the solicitor is in possession of funds which may represent the proceeds of fraud. This problem arose in *Finers v Miro*.[26] The plaintiffs had acted for the defendant in setting up a complex corporate scheme to hold assets on his behalf. Secrecy was a primary aim of the scheme. Subsequently, reasonable grounds arose for suspicion that many of the assets represented the proceeds of fraud carried out on an insurance company, now in liquidation.

The solicitors were in a dilemma what to do and concerned that they might be liable as constructive trustees of the assets held under their control. They accordingly applied to the court, by an originating summons under Ord.85 of the Rules of the Supreme Court, for directions in relation to the assets. The Court of Appeal held that the insurance company's liquidator should be given notice of the solicitors' application, notwithstanding the defendant's contention that such notice would constitute a breach of the legal professional privilege to which he was entitled. Dillon L.J. said[27]:

16–016

> "It was urged for the defendant that the advice obtained by the defendant from Mr Stein [a partner in the firm of solicitors] was not advice on how to commit a fraud but advice after the fraud, if there was

---

[24] (1884) 14 Q.B.D. 153 at 167.
[25] [1901] A.C. 196 at 201.
[26] [1991] 1 W.L.R. 35.
[27] *ibid.* at 40.

one, had been committed. I note, however, that in *O'Rourke v Darbishire*[28] Lord Sumner refers, at p.613, to a party consulting a solicitor 'in order to learn how to plan, execute, or stifle an actual fraud'. The privilege cannot, in my judgment, apply if the solicitor is consulted—even though he does not realise this and is himself acting innocently—to cover up or stifle a fraud."

But how well established must a client's wrongdoing be in order to absolve a lawyer of his prima facie duty of confidence? In *Finers*, Dillon L.J. continued:

> "On the material before us I conclude that *it does seem probable* that the defendant may have consulted Mr Stein for the purpose of being guided and helped, albeit unwittingly on the part of Mr Stein, in covering up or stifling *a fraud on the insurance company of which there is a prima facie case resting on solid grounds*."[29] (Emphasis added.)

16–017 Sections 327 to 329 of the Proceeds of Crime Act 2002[30] create a variety of offences based on one form or another of involvement in dealings with "criminal property"—broadly speaking, property that is both the proceeds of crime and known or suspected by the offender to be the proceeds of crime. No offence is committed if disclosure is made to a specified individual in accordance with the provisions of s.338 of the Act.

16–018 In *Bowman v Fels*,[31] the solicitors acting for the claimant in civil litigation that related to the beneficial interests in a residential property came to suspect that the defendant had accounted fraudulently to the Inland Revenue and to Customs and Excise for certain works carried out at the property. They believed that they were obliged by s.328 of the Act to notify the National Criminal Intelligence Service of their suspicions and their notification effectively derailed the progress of the litigation. The Court of Appeal held that the ordinary conduct of litigation by lawyers did not engage ss.327 to 329 of the Act. The Court went on to hold obiter that ss.327 to 329 did not override legal professional privilege, nor the restrictions imposed on parties to whom disclosure is made during the course of litigation.[32]

16–019 Sections 327 to 329 do not themselves impose an obligation to disclose information: rather, disclosure under s.338 operates as a defence against what might otherwise be an offence under ss.327 to 329. The Court of Appeal did not state expressly whether its conclusion that ss.327 to 329 did not override legal professional privilege had the consequence (a) that no

---

[28] [1920] A.C. 581.
[29] A test derived from an amalgam of what was said by Lord Wrenbury in *O'Rourke v Derbyshire* [1920] A.C. 581 at 632–644 and by Templeman L.J. in *Gamlen Chemical Co (UK) Ltd v Rochem Ltd*. In relation to litigation privilege, see also *Kuwait Airways Corp v Iraqi Airways Co* [2005] EWCA Civ 286.
[30] Further secondary offences are created under the Money Laundering Regulations 2003.
[31] [2005] EWCA Civ 226; [2005] 1 W.L.R. 3083.
[32] At paras 85–91 of the judgment.

offence is committed—under those sections, at least—by a lawyer who continues to act in circumstances where his suspicions of money laundering remain unreported because of legal professional privilege, or (b) that legal professional privilege merely prevents a lawyer from making a disclosure under s.338 and thereby deprives the lawyer of the defence that a disclosure under s.338 would have provided. Advice subsequently issued by the Law Society[33] appears to proceed on the latter basis and this is at first sight more congruent with the structure of the statutory provisions. However, the terms of the Court of Appeal's judgment in *Bowman v Fels* lend some support to the former possibility (by appearing to suggest that, even if ss.327 to 329 were applicable to the conduct of litigation, a lawyer could continue to act, notwithstanding his suspicions).

Section 330 of the Act creates a further offence if someone carrying out **16–020** business in the regulated sector (as defined in Sch.9 of the Act) fails to disclose information causing him to suspect that another person is engaged in money laundering. Section 330(6)(b) creates an exception for legal advisers to whom information has been communicated in "privileged circumstances" (as defined at s.330(10) of the Act). Section 330(11) provides that privileged circumstances do not extend to "information or other matter which is communicated or given with the intention of furthering a criminal purpose".

Section 331 of the Act, which makes it an offence to "tip off" a client, **16–021** contains a similar defence in relation (broadly) to legally privileged advice. Again, disclosures "made with the intention of furthering a criminal purpose" are expressly excluded.

In *Bowman v Fels*, the Court of Appeal observed[34] (without deciding the **16–022** issue) that s.330(11) of the Act might arguably be applicable only where the lawyer is *aware* of the intention to further a criminal purpose. That leaves open the question by what standard a lawyer who discloses prima facie privileged information on the basis of the "crime or fraud" exception (whether common law or statutory) is to be judged, if the suspected crime or fraud proves to be illusory. If the test for the exception is that outlined by Dillon L.J. in *Finers v Miro*, it is suggested that the touchstone of liability, so far as the lawyer is concerned, should nevertheless be reasonableness. A solicitor who reasonably believes that the "crime or fraud" exception to privilege is applicable should not subsequently be held liable to his client if he makes such limited disclosure as would be required of him if the exception were established in fact.[35]

A solicitor's position may be made more difficult if his duty of confidence **16–023** to one client appears to conflict with his duty of disclosure to another. Suppose that a solicitor, acting for both prospective mortgagor and prospective mortgagee, discovers information that leads him to suspect that the

---

[33] Published in September 2005 under the title "Bowman v Fels", as an annex to its money laundering guidance booklet dated January 2004; see para.7.12.
[34] At para.94.
[35] See Ch.6 above, in relation to the public interest defence.

mortgagor is planning to defraud the mortgagee and that he, the solicitor, is to be the mortgagor's unwitting tool in this fraud.

16–024   If the solicitor's suspicion remains merely an unsubstantiated suspicion, it is open to him simply to decline to act further in the transaction. If it seems to him probable, however, that the purpose of his retainer is the furtherance of a fraud of which "there is a prima facie case on solid grounds", the question arises (a) whether there is any duty to the mortgagor which prevents the solicitor from informing the mortgagee of the fraud, and indeed (b) whether it is not the solicitor's *duty* to inform the mortgagee.

16–025   In *Mortgage Express Ltd v Bowerman & Partners*[36] the Court of Appeal held that where a solicitor acting for both borrower and mortgagee in a property purchase discovered, on investigating title, information about recent prior sales, which might have caused the mortgagee to suspect that the valuation with which he had been provided was excessive, the solicitor owed a duty to disclose that information to the mortgagee as well as to the borrower.

16–026   Sir Thomas Bingham M.R. stressed that it was not a case in which a solicitor acting for two parties received information confidential to one of them. He observed, *obiter*, that in such a case it might be necessary for the solicitor to obtain the consent of the client whose information it was to disclose it to the other, and that if consent were refused the solicitor might be obliged to cease to act for that other party or both.

16–027   In *Darlington Building Society v O'Rourke James Scourfield & McCarthy*,[37] the Court of Appeal, in the context of an unsuccessful application to amend a statement of claim, again considered the scope of a conveyancing solicitor's duties to lender and borrower. The defendant solicitors had acted for borrowers, to whom near-simultaneous loans had been made by the two plaintiff lenders. Each of the plaintiffs, for whom the defendants had also acted, remained ignorant of the involvement of the other, allegedly as a result of misrepresentation on the part of the borrowers. The plaintiffs wished to pursue a claim that the defendants should have disclosed the true position to both of them. Giving the only substantive judgment, Sir Iain Glidewell said[38]:

> " . . . in order to succeed in this action each of the plaintiffs must prove that the information which the defendants obtained and which the plaintiffs alleged should have been disclosed to them respectively was not confidential. Since *prima facie* information obtained whilst the solicitor is dealing with another transaction between his borrower client and another building society *is* confidential, the plaintiff thus has to prove that such information discloses or arises out of facts which tend to show fraud by the borrower. Clearly in order to be required to disclose that information the solicitor has to know of or at least to have strong evidence of such fraud from the facts he knows."

[36] [1996] 2 All E.R. 836.
[37] [1999] 1 Lloyd's Rep. (PN) 33.
[38] At 37.

Use of information in defence of the lawyer's own interests

It is clear from the House of Lords' decision in *Medcalf v Mardell*[39] that a **16–028** lawyer is not entitled to reveal confidential information in order to oppose the making of a wasted costs order against him pursuant to s.51(6) of the Supreme Court Act 1981 and CPR 48.7. It is apparent that this restriction cannot be ascribed simply to equitable principles of confidence, since professional persons are entitled in general to use information imparted to them confidentially, if it is reasonably necessary for them to do so in protection of their own legitimate interests.[40]

Rather, the restriction arises as a result of the privileged nature of the **16–029** information. Since orders for costs are within the discretion of the court, the court is unusually well placed to avoid any injustice in considering a wasted costs application by making proper allowance for this restriction upon respondent lawyers. In *Medcalf v Mardell*,[41] the House of Lords allowed an appeal brought by barristers against whom a wasted costs order had been made, on the basis that they had advanced allegations of fraud without reasonably credible material. Lord Bingham cited a well-known passage from the Court of Appeal's decision in *Ridehalgh v Horsefield*[42]:

> "The respondent lawyers are in a different position. The privilege is not theirs to waive. In the usual case where a waiver would not benefit their client they will be slow to advise the client to waive his privilege, and they may well feel bound to advise that the client should take independent advice before doing so. The client may be unwilling to do that, and may be unwilling to waive if he does. So the respondent lawyers may find themselves at a grave disadvantage in defending their conduct of proceedings, unable to reveal what advice and warnings they gave, what instructions they received. In some cases this potential source of injustice may be mitigated by reference to the taxing master, where different rules apply, but only in a small minority of cases can this procedure be appropriate. Judges who are invited to make or contemplate making a wasted costs order must make full allowance for the inability of respondent lawyers to tell the whole story. Where there is room for doubt, the respondent lawyers are entitled to the benefit of it. It is again only when, with all allowances made, a lawyer's conduct of proceedings is quite plainly unjustifiable that it can be appropriate to make a wasted costs order."

Lord Bingham said that he did not regard this passage as inaccurate or misleading, but he considered that it should be strengthened because only

---

[39] [2002] UKHL 27; [2003] 1 A.C. 120.
[40] *Tournier v National Provincial and Union Bank of England* [1924] 1 K.B. 461 (bankers); *Duncan v Medical Practitioner's Disciplinary Committee* [1986] 1 N.Z.L.R. 513 (doctors); *R. v Institute of Chartered Accountants of England and Wales Ex p. Brindle* [1994] B.C.C. 297 at 312 (accountants).
[41] At para.23.
[42] [1994] Ch. 205 at 237.

rarely will a court be able to make "full allowance" for the inability of the practitioner to tell the full story or be sure that nothing could be said by the practitioner which might influence the exercise of the court's discretion. He added:

> "Where a wasted costs order is sought against a practitioner precluded by legal professional privilege from giving his full answer to the application, the court should not make an order unless, proceeding with extreme care, it is (a) satisfied that there is nothing the practitioner could say, if unconstrained, to resist the order and (b) that it is in all the circumstances fair to make the order."

16–030　　The question arises whether this restriction upon lawyers opposing wasted costs applications extends to lawyers facing other civil claims or criminal sanctions. The Law Society's "Confidentiality and Disclosure Guidance"[43] states that:

> "You may reveal confidential information concerning the client to the extent that it is reasonably necessary to establish a defence to a criminal charge or civil claim by your client against you, or where your conduct is under investigation by the Law Society, or under consideration by the Solicitors Disciplinary Tribunal."

16–031　　If the proceedings have been brought, or have resulted from a complaint, by the client, clearly the client cannot assert privilege to prevent the solicitor from deploying previously confidential material to the extent reasonably necessary to defend himself.[44] If the proceedings have been brought by somebody else,[45] the problem is more difficult.

16–032　　In *R. v Derby Magistrates' Court Ex p. B*[46] Lord Taylor C.J. said that:

> " . . . no exception should be made to the absolute nature of legal professional privilege, once established . . . "

The decision in *R. v Derby Magistrates' Court Ex p. B*[47] appears to pre-empt any possibility that a solicitor facing a civil claim by a third party should be entitled to disclose his client's privileged information in his own defence. Indeed, if a solicitor were able to use any privileged material that *assisted* his case, it is not easy to see why, in principle, the third party claimant should be denied access to privileged material that *damaged* it.

---

[43] (2006), at para.19.
[44] *Paragon Finance plc v Freshfields* [1999] 1 W.L.R. 1183.
[45] See the example at para.16–023, above, of a claim by a mortgage lender. If the loan was fraudulent, no question of privilege would arise, but it might be the defendant's case that the loan was *not* fraudulent and he might need to disclose confidential documents with a view to establishing the innocence of the transaction and his own innocence.
[46] [1996] A.C. 487 at 508–509.
[47] See the discussion in Ch.18 below.

Again, on the basis of *R. v Derby Magistrates' Court Ex p. B*, if the **16–033** information given to a solicitor was originally privileged, and if there has been no express or implied waiver of privilege by the client, it is difficult to see how the solicitor may use such information to defend himself even against a criminal charge.[48] It may be that if the solicitor could show to the court with jurisdiction over the criminal proceedings that the effect of his inability to use the information would be seriously to impede his ability to defend himself, the court would have an inherent jurisdiction to stay the criminal proceedings, but even that solution may present difficulties, if it would be likely to involve the solicitor revealing to the court that which, *ex hypothesi*, he is not authorised to reveal.

The professional regulation of lawyers raises similar issues. Often the **16–034** regulator's involvement will arise from a complaint by the lawyer's client. In those circumstances the client, by making his complaint, will inevitably waive privilege to the limited extent necessary to dispose of his complaint fairly and properly. But what if a complaint is made, not by a lawyer's client, but by a third party, or if an investigation arises from the regulator's own motion?

In *Parry-Jones v Law Society*,[49] a solicitor sought to prevent the Law **16–035** Society, acting in its regulatory capacity, from gaining access to documents in respect of which his clients could assert legal professional privilege. The Court of Appeal dismissed his claim. Lord Denning M.R. held that the Law Society's statutory powers of investigation[50] overrode any privilege or confidence that might otherwise subsist between solicitor and client. Agreeing, Diplock L.J. expressed the view that privilege was in fact irrelevant when one was not concerned with judicial or quasi-judicial proceedings, because privilege was a right to withhold from a court, or a tribunal exercising judicial functions, material which would otherwise be admissible in evidence. Salmon L.J. agreed with both judgments.

In *R. (Morgan Grenfell) v Special Commissioner of Income Tax*[51] Lord **16–036** Hoffmann reviewed (obiter) the decision in *Parry-Jones v Law Society*. He rejected the view expressed by Diplock L.J. that the impact of privilege was confined to judicial, or quasi-judicial, proceedings:

> "The policy of LPP requires that the client should be secure in the knowledge that protected documents and information will not be disclosed at all."

However, approving the result in *Parry-Jones v Law Society*, he continued:

> " . . . I think that the true justification for the decision was not that Mr Parry-Jones's clients had no LPP, or that their LPP had been overridden

---

[48] *Pace* the view expressed at para.19 of the Law Society's *Confidentiality and Disclosure Guidance* (2006).
[49] [1969] 1 Ch. 1.
[50] Under rules made pursuant to s.29 of the Solicitors Act 1957.
[51] [2002] UKHL 21; [2003] 1 A.C. 563 at [26]–[33].

by the Law Society's rules, but that the clients' LPP was not being infringed. The Law Society were not entitled to use information disclosed by the solicitor for any purpose other than the investigation. Otherwise the confidentiality of the clients had to be maintained. In my opinion, this limited disclosure did not breach the clients' LPP or, to the extent that it technically did, was authorised by the Law Society's statutory powers. It does not seem to me to fall within the same principle as a case in which disclosure is sought for a use which involves the information being made public or used against the person entitled to the privilege."

The other members of the Judicial Committee agreed with Lord Hoffmann's speech. Although the result may be considered satisfactory, the passage has its difficulties. If the policy of legal professional privilege is as summarised by Lord Hoffmann, it is not readily apparent why disclosure to regulators without the client's consent would not amount to a breach of privilege. The distinction apparently drawn by Lord Hoffmann between (a) the Law Society's rules "overriding" privilege and (b) the Law Society's statutory powers "authorising" disclosure is also unclear.

16–037   Insofar as solicitors are concerned, s.31(1) of the Solicitors Act 1974 (as amended by the Access to Justice Act 1999), provides that:

" . . . the Council [of the Law Society] may, if they think fit, make rules, with the concurrence of the Master of the Rolls, for regulating in respect of any matter the professional practice, conduct and discipline of solicitors and for empowering the Society to take such action as may be appropriate to enable the Society to ascertain whether or not the provisions of rules made, or of any code or guidance issued, by the Council are being complied with."

It is suggested that there is necessarily implied in this provision a power on the part of the Council to make rules permitting an invasion of legal professional privilege to the limited extent necessary to ensure that the Law Society's regulatory functions are properly performed. In contrast with other, non-legal professions, the supervision of solicitors would become effectively impossible without such a power.

16–038   As for barristers, s.27 of the Courts and Legal Services Act 1990 provides that persons shall have a right of audience only where the right has been granted by an authorised body whose qualification requirements and rules of conduct have been approved in relation to that right. The Bar Council is one such authorised body. However, it cannot easily be argued that the Bar Council has implied statutory authority to override privilege. Unless full effect is given to Lord Hoffmann's explanation in *R. (Morgan Grenfell Ltd) v Special Income Commissioner* of *Parry-Jones v Law Society*, it therefore seems that disciplinary proceedings against barristers must be carried out subject to the same restrictions in relation to legal professional privilege as have been held to apply to wasted costs applications.

Disclosure required by law

A lawyer who discloses confidential information under compulsion of law **16–039** commits no breach of confidence. In *Parry-Jones v Law Society*,[52] Diplock L.J. said of a solicitor's contractual duty of confidence:

> "Such a duty exists not only between solicitor and client, but, for example, between banker and customer, doctor and patient and accountant and client. Such a duty of confidence is subject to, and overridden by, the duty of any party to that contract to comply with the law of the land."

A lawyer's obligation to refuse disclosure of material that is not only **16–040** confidential but also privileged (and his client's entitlement to assert privilege) is also subject to and may be overridden by statute. However, in *R. (Morgan Grenfell Ltd) v Special Commissioner of Income Tax*,[53] Lord Hoffmann observed that

> "Two of the principles relevant to construction are not in dispute. First, LPP is a fundamental human right long established in the common law... Secondly, the courts will ordinarily construe general words in a statute, although literally capable of having some startling or unreasonable consequence, such as overriding fundamental human rights, as not having been intended to do so. An intention to override such rights must be expressly stated or appear by necessary implication."

Bowman v Fels[54] demonstrates that the burden on a person seeking to argue that legislation impliedly overrides a right of privilege is a heavy one.

Children

In *Ramsbotham v Senior*,[55] Malins V.C. said: **16–041**

> " . . . no person, be he solicitor or not, can have any privilege whatever in doing, or abstaining from doing, that which has the effect of concealing the residence of a ward of this Court, and thereby preventing the Court exercising its due control over the ward."

In that case the mother of wards of court had absconded with them and her solicitor was ordered to produce envelopes of letters which he had received

[52] [1969] 1 Ch. 1 at 9.
[53] [2003] UKHL 21; [2003] 1 A.C. at [7] and [8].
[54] [2005] EWCA Civ 226; [2005] 1 W.L.R. 3083. See the discussion at para.16–018 above.
[55] (1869) L.R. 8 Eq. 575.

from her, with the object of discovering her residence from the postmarks. She was in grave, continuing contempt of court and therefore had no privilege in concealing her whereabouts from the court; and since she had no privilege in keeping the information confidential, the solicitor had none to protect.

16–042 In *Re L*[56] the House of Lords, by a majority of three to two, held that in care proceedings under the Children Act 1989 privilege did not attach to an expert's report, which was obtained by a party under an order of the court giving leave to the expert to study the court papers. The parents were drug addicts. The child became ill after ingestion of methadone. An order was made giving leave to disclose the court papers to a medical expert and requiring his report to be filed. The mother's solicitors instructed a chemical pathologist, whose report cast doubt on the mother's explanation of the incident. The judge ordered disclosure of the report to the police.

16–043 The mother appealed against the order, arguing that the report was the subject of legal professional privilege and that the court ought not to have made an order compelling its disclosure to other parties either at the time of the original order requiring the report to be filed or at the time of the order under appeal.

16–044 Lord Jauncey, delivering the opinion of the majority, distinguished *R. v Derby Magistrates Court Ex p. B*[57] on two grounds: care proceedings were of a special non-adversarial nature unlike ordinary litigation, and the expert's report was not a communication between solicitor and client but a report by a third party prepared on the instructions of the client for the purposes of the proceedings. He concluded that care proceedings were:

> "so far removed from normal actions that litigation privilege has no place in relation to reports obtained by a party thereto which could not have been prepared without the leave of the court to disclose documents already filed or to examine the child."

It followed that the question of the court's power to impose a disclosure condition when giving leave for the court papers to be shown to an expert did not arise, because in the absence of privilege the report would be disclosable to other parties to the proceedings in any event.

16–045 The House of Lords did not go so far as to hold that no legal professional privilege arose in care proceedings. On the contrary, Lord Jauncey not only distinguished the expert's report under consideration from communications between solicitor and client, but he said that his view that litigation privilege never arose in relation to the expert's report did not affect privilege arising between solicitor and client.

16–046 In *Vernon v Bosley (No. 2)*,[58] Thorpe L.J. dismissed as "little short of absurd" the submission that privilege would attach in circumstances where the court's leave should have been, but had not been, secured before the

---

[56] [1997] A.C. 16.
[57] [1995] 3 W.L.R. 681.
[58] [1999] Q.B. 18 at 61–62.

evidence was obtained. The Court of Appeal held also that the *ratio* in *Re L* was not confined to public law proceedings, but extended also to private law proceedings that were not adversarial but quasi-inquisitorial. However, it is uncertain whether privilege would attach to a report by an expert, a statement from a witness, or other communications between a solicitor and a third party for the purpose of proceedings, made without need for leave of the court to examine court documents or to examine the child.

Behind this issue lies the unresolved question whether a party to care proceedings is under a duty of disclosure of matters adverse to his or her case.[59] In *Essex County Council v R*.[60] Thorpe J. after holding that the court, when considering the welfare of the child, has power to override legal professional privilege, continued:

16–047

> "For my part, I would wish to see case law go yet further and to make it plain that the legal representatives in possession of such material relevant to determination but contrary to the interests of their client, not only are unable to resist disclosure by reliance on legal professional privilege, but have a positive duty to disclose to the other parties and to the court."

In *Oxfordshire County Council v P*[61] Ward J. said:

16–048

> "In all cases where the welfare of children is the court's paramount consideration, there is a duty on all parties to make full and frank disclosure of all matters material to welfare whether those matters are favourable to or adverse to their own particular case."

In *Re L* Lord Jauncey cited the passages above[62] and said that he preferred to wait until the point arose directly for decision before determining whether such a duty exists and if so what is its scope.

The premise to Thorpe J.'s approach in *Essex County Council v R*. (that the court has power to override legal professional privilege when considering the welfare of a child) is not consistent with the reasoning of the House of Lords in *R. v Derby Magistrates Court Ex p. B*, as to the absolute nature of legal professional privilege when established, or in *Re L*, which was based on the view that legal professional privilege never arose in relation to the expert's report rather than that it could be overridden.

16–049

If there is a duty on a party to care proceedings to disclose all material matters, whether favourable or adverse to their case, it must follow that they would have no privilege to withhold from other parties or the court any

16–050

[59] It is well established that local authorities are under such a duty in care proceedings: *R. v Hampshire County Council* [1990] 2 Q.B. 71.
[60] [1994] Fam. 167 at 168.
[61] [1995] Fam. 161 at 166.
[62] See also para.4 of *Practice Direction (Family Proceedings: Case Management)* [1995] 1 W.L.R. 332: "It is a duty owed to the court both by the parties and by their legal representatives to give full and frank disclosure in ancillary relief applications and also in all matters in respect of children".

relevant evidence obtained by their solicitor on their behalf. If on the other hand they are under no such duty, it is suggested that there is no good reason to deny them the right to claim privilege in respect of such material obtained by their solicitor on their behalf.

PART 3

Confidentiality and the Legal Process

Confidentiality is not in itself a bar to disclosure of information or documents in legal proceedings. Nevertheless there are a number of rules and practices by which the courts accord a greater or lesser degree of protection to confidential information, or certain kinds of confidential information, either by excluding it altogether, or by restricting the manner in which it is disclosed, or by restricting the use thereafter made of it. This part of the book looks at these rules and their relationship with principles of confidentiality.

CHAPTER 17

General Principle and Exceptions

The general principle

Generally speaking, confidentiality is not a bar to disclosure of documents **17–001** or information in the process of litigation, but the court will only compel such disclosure if it considers it necessary for the fair disposal of the case. This principle was recognised by the House of Lords in a trio of cases: *D v National Society for the Prevention of Cruelty to Children*,[1] *Science Research Council v Nassé*[2] and *British Steel Corporation v Granada Television Ltd.*[3]

In *Three Rivers District Council v The Governor and Company of the* **17–002** *Bank of England*,[4] Tomlinson J. suggested that, in view of the threshold requirement of necessity, Art.8 rights of privacy did not call for separate treatment in the courts' application of the general principle. However, where the documents of which disclosure are sought contain personal medical details relating to a non-party, the courts have approached the issue of disclosure with particular circumspection, attaching importance to Art.8. In *A v X & B*[5] Morland J. said that "only in a very exceptional factual situation would a court be justified in civil proceedings in ordering disclosure of a non-party's confidential medical data." In *R(TB) v Stafford Combined Court*[6] it was held that the complainant in a criminal case ought

[1] [1978] A.C. 171.
[2] [1980] A.C. 1028.
[3] [1981] A.C. 1096.
[4] [2002] EWHC 2309 (Comm), November 8, 2002, at [5]. See also *MS v Sweden* (1997) 28 E.H.R.R. 313.
[5] [2004] EWHC 447, QB.
[6] [2006] EWHC 1645 (Admin).

to have been given notice of an application made by the defendant for disclosure of her medical records, because her rights under Art.8 carried with them the procedural right to make representations to the court considering the application.

17–003   If a litigant wishes to withhold production of a relevant document on grounds of confidentiality, he should include it in his list of documents but object to its production. The court is entitled to inspect the document when considering whether to order production and, in some circumstances, *should* inspect the document before dismissing an application for disclosure.[7]

17–004   Under the CPR, the courts' powers to order disclosure from likely parties prior to the commencement of proceedings (CPR 31.16) or from non-parties (CPR 31.17) are broader than they were previously. These powers are discretionary but, where the court has jurisdiction to exercise them, it is suggested that the general principle set out above remains applicable: when a non-party's rights of confidentiality are in issue, there is little reason why the question whether disclosure is to be effected by a party to the litigation or by the non-party himself should be determinative of an application's success.

Exceptions

17–005   The principle that information necessary for the fair disposal of disputes should be disclosed, even if it is confidential, is subject to statutory and common law exceptions.

Statutory and regulatory exceptions

17–006   Various statutes and regulations which give powers to obtain information of a confidential information also impose restrictions on the disclosure of such information.[8] In such cases the recipient cannot be compelled by *subpoena* to make disclosure which is prohibited by statute.

Common law exceptions

17–007   The general principle does not apply in cases of:

> (1) "without prejudice" communications and communications to mediators and conciliators;

---

[7] *Wallace Smith Trust Co v Deloitte Haskins & Sells* [1997] 1 W.L.R. 257, *per* Neill L.J. at 267.

[8] For example, the Financial Services and Markets Act 2000 (Disclosure of Confidential Information) Regulations 2001 and the Financial Services and Markets Act 2000 (Confidential Information) (Bank of England) Order 2001.

(2) legal professional privilege; or

(3) public interest immunity,

the rationale being that the public interest in maintaining secrecy in such cases outweighs the general principle in favour of disclosure.[9]

"WITHOUT PREJUDICE" COMMUNICATIONS AND COMMUNICATIONS TO MEDIATORS AND CONCILIATORS

"Without prejudice" communications

Negotiations genuinely aimed at a settlement are inadmissible in evidence, not only in the litigation in the course of which they take place, but also in any subsequent litigation connected with the same subject-matter. Moreover, such negotiations are not disclosable to third parties—nor indeed apparently to the negotiators themselves (though the point may only be of theoretical importance).[10]   **17–008**

In the leading case of *Rush & Tompkins Ltd v Greater London Council*,[11] Lord Griffiths cited with approval the words of Oliver L.J. in *Cutts v Head*[12]:   **17–009**

> "That the rule rests, at least in part, upon public policy is clear from many authorities, and the convenient starting point of the inquiry is the nature of the underlying policy. It is that parties should be encouraged so far as possible to settle their disputes without resort to litigation and should not be discouraged by the knowledge that anything that is said in the course of such negotiations (and that includes, of course, as much the failure to reply to an offer as an actual reply) may be used to their prejudice in the course of the proceedings. They should, as it was expressed by Clauson J. in *Scott Paper Co. v Drayton Paper Works Ltd* (1927) 44 R.P.C. 151, 156, be encouraged fully and frankly to put their cards on the table . . . . The public policy justification, in truth, essentially rests on the desirability of preventing statements or offers made in the course of negotiations for settlement being brought before the court of trial as admissions on the question of liability."

---

[9] Privilege against self-incrimination is omitted. Although one of the factors underlying the existence of the privilege is personal privacy (*per* Lord Mustill in *R. v Directors of Serious Fraud Office Ex p. Smith* [1993] A.C. 1 at 31), it is unconnected with the general law of confidentiality which is the subject of this book.
[10] *Rush & Tompkins Ltd v Greater London Council* [1989] 1 A.C. 1280 at 1301 and 1304A.
[11] [1989] 1 A.C. 1280 at 1299.
[12] [1984] Ch. 290 at 306.

17–010   In *Cutts v Head*[13] Oliver L.J. took the view that this public policy justification came to an end once the trial of the issues in the action had taken place, and that the rationale of protection thereafter must therefore be "an implied agreement imported from the marking of a letter 'without prejudice' that it shall not be referred to at all".

17–011   This part of his judgment was not cited by the House of Lords in *Rush & Tompkins Ltd* and his premise was indeed contradicted in the speech of Lord Griffiths.[14] Nevertheless, the Court of Appeal has since confirmed that the rule is not based solely on public policy. In *Unilever plc v The Procter & Gamble Co.*,[15] Robert Walker L.J., who gave the leading judgment, said:

> "Its other basis or foundation is in the express or implied agreement of the parties themselves that communications in the course of their negotiations should not be admissible in evidence if, despite the negotiations, a contested hearing ensues."

Indeed the "without prejudice" rule, to the extent that it prevents the parties from adducing evidence that might be relevant to the determination of *costs*, is based solely on this alternative basis, since the exclusion of such evidence does not promote the policy of encouraging settlements.[16]

17–012   A person participating in "without prejudice" negotiations therefore owes to his opponent a private law duty of confidentiality, and this must be so whether or not the document is formally marked "without prejudice", although the duty will be subject to qualifications.

17–013   A publicly funded litigant, for example, may owe a duty to the Legal Services Commission to disclose a "without prejudice" offer made by the opposing party, which might cause the Legal Services Commission to consider whether public funding should be continued in the event of the offer being refused.

17–014   Similarly, a company being supported in litigation by its bank may wish, or feel under an obligation, to disclose to the bank a settlement offer which it has received (or made). Its auditors may also need to know the state of outstanding litigation for the purpose of reporting on the company's accounts pursuant to the statutory requirements of the Companies Act 1985.

17–015   In *Unilever plc v The Procter & Gamble Co.*, Robert Walker L.J. categorised a number of circumstances in which—and purposes for which—"without prejudice" communications may be admissible in evidence. A private law duty of confidence arising from the "without prejudice" nature of communications will not usually prevent a party from adducing such communications in those circumstances and for those purposes. However, if

---

[13] [1984] Ch. 290 at 307.
[14] [1989] 1 A.C. 1280 at 1300–1301.
[15] [2000] 1 W.L.R. 2436 at 2442.
[16] See *Reed Executive Plc v Reed Business Information Ltd* [2004] EWCA Civ 887; [2004] 1 W.L.R. 3026, *per* Jacob L.J. at paras 24 and 25.

no duty of confidentiality were owed at all, a party to "without prejudice" negotiations would be at liberty to publicise them at large. This would be inimical to the object of such negotiations and contrary to the assumption on which they are ordinarily conducted.

Statements to mediators and conciliators[17]

Mediation and other forms of alternative dispute resolution have assumed unprecedented importance within the court system since the Woolf reforms of civil procedure. Formal mediations are generally preceded by written mediation agreements between the parties that set out expressly the confidential and "without prejudice" nature of the process. However, even in the absence of such an express agreement, the process will be protected by the "without prejudice" rule set out above. **17–016**

In matrimonial cases privilege has been held to extend to statements made by the parties with the aim of effecting a reconciliation. The privilege covers both communications between the parties themselves, or their agents, and also communications to any private individual specifically enlisted as a conciliator. The earlier authorities were reviewed in *Theodoropoulas v Theodoropoulas*[18] by Sir Jocelyn Simon P. **17–017**

Similarly, in *Re D (Minors) (Conciliation: Disclosure of Information)*,[19] the Court of Appeal held that in proceedings under the Children Act 1989 privilege analogous to "without prejudice" privilege applied to prevent evidence being given of a statement made by a party in the course of meetings held or communications made for the purpose of conciliation (except in the very unusual case where a statement is made clearly indicating that the maker has in the past caused or is likely in the future to cause serious harm to the well-being of a child). **17–018**

Legal professional privilege and public interest immunity

These subjects are considered in the following chapters. **17–019**

---

[17] See also paras 15–013—15–019, above.
[18] [1964] P. 311.
[19] [1993] Fam. 231 at 241. See also *D v N.S.P.C.C.* [1978] A.C. 171, *per* Lord Hailsham at 226 and *per* Lord Simon at 237.

CHAPTER 18

Legal Professional Privilege and Confidence

Origins and basis of legal professional confidence

18–001 Communications between a person and his legal adviser, or (once litigation is contemplated or pending) between either of them and a third party, are protected from disclosure if they were created for the purposes (broadly interpreted) of legal advice.[1] The duty of confidence owed by a lawyer to his client has been discussed in more detail in Chapter 16, and the subject of legal professional privilege has been considered in that context.

18–002 Legal professional privilege, as it is now called, has its origins in the concept of confidence. At first its rationale was the protection of the honour of the professional man, but this approach was eventually rejected by the courts. As Lord Simon said in *D v N.S.P.C.C.*[2]:

> "A man of honour would not betray a confidence, and the judges as men of honour themselves would not require him to. Thus originally legal professional privilege was that of the legal adviser, not the client. (For the foregoing, see *Wigmore, Evidence*, secs. 2286, 2290.) But, with the decline in the ethos engendering the rule, the law moved decisively away from it. The turning point was the *Duchess of*

---

[1] This statement is deliberately general. Fuller treatment of the sub-divisions of legal professional privilege into "legal advice privilege" and "litigation privilege" is outside the scope of this book. See Passmore's *Privilege* (2nd edn, 2006) and *The Law of Privilege* (edn Thanki, 2006). Qualifications to the general principle have been considered in the context of qualifications to the lawyer's duty of confidence to his client in Chap.16, above.

[2] [1978] A.C. 171, at 238.

Kingston's Case (1776) 20 State Tr. 355 at 386–391, where both the duchess's surgeon and a personal friend, Lord Barrington, were compelled to give evidence in breach of confidence."

In the case of legal advisers, however, the courts, under their inherent jurisdiction to control their own rules of procedure and evidence, developed the special doctrine of legal professional privilege. The foundation of the modern doctrine of legal privilege was summarised by Sir George Jessel M.R. in *Anderson v Bank of British Columbia*[3]:

18–003

"The object and meaning of the rule is this: that as, by reason of the complexity and difficulty of our law, litigation can only be conducted by professional men, it is absolutely necessary that a man, in order to prosecute his rights or to defend himself from an improper claim, should have recourse to the assistance of professional lawyers, and it being so absolutely necessary, it is equally necessary, to use a vulgar phrase, that he should be able to make a clean breast of it to the gentleman whom he consults with a view to the prosecution of his claim, or the substantiating his defence against the claim of others; that he should be able to place unrestricted and unbounded confidence in the professional agent, and that the communications he so makes to him should be kept secret, unless with his consent (for it is his privilege, and not the privilege of the confidential agent), that he should be enabled properly to conduct his litigation."

The scope and depth of the protection afforded by privilege

It is a prerequisite of legal professional privilege that the information for which privilege is claimed is confidential.[4] The scope of legal advice privilege extends beyond documents conveying advice or requests for advice. In *Balabel v Air India*,[5] Taylor L.J. said:

18–004

"There will be a continuum of communication and meetings between the solicitor and client. The negotiations for a lease such as occurred in the present case are only one example. Where information is passed by the solicitor or client to the other as part of the continuum aimed at keeping both informed so that advice may be sought and given as required, privilege will attach."

Moreover,

---

[3] (1876) 2 Ch. D. 644 at 649.
[4] *Kennedy v Lyall* (1881) 23 Ch. D. 387 at 404–405, *per* Cotton L.J.
[5] [1988] Ch. 317 at 330.

> "Legal advice is not confined to telling the client the law; it must include advice as to what should prudently and sensibly be done in the relevant legal context."[6]

18–005   In *R. v Derbyshire Magistrates Court Ex p. B*[7] Lord Taylor C.J. described legal professional privilege as much more than an ordinary rule of evidence, but as a fundamental condition on which the administration of justice as a whole rests. This view has since been reasserted in a string of decisions at the highest level: *Medcalf v Mardell*,[8] *R (Morgan Grenfell) v Special Commissioner of Income Tax*,[9] *B v Auckland District Law Society*[10] and *Three Rivers District Council v Bank of England*.[11]

18–006   The House of Lords and the High Court of Australia have stated in the similar cases of *R. v Derby Magistrates' Court Ex p. B*[12] and *Carter v Managing Partner, Northmore, Hale, Davy & Leake*[13] that, where legal professional privilege applies, its nature is absolute and the court has no discretion whether to enforce it. In each case a defendant in criminal proceedings sought to compel production by witnesses of documents which had been brought into existence by legal practitioners for the purpose of giving confidential legal advice. The defendant was charged in one case with murder and in the other with conspiracy to defraud. Each asserted that the documents sought were likely to assist him in his defence. It was held in each case that production could not be ordered for essentially the same reasons, namely that legal professional privilege was a fundamental principle of the administration of justice, for the purpose of enabling a person to seek and obtain legal advice in confidence, and that where such privilege attached, no exception to it should be permitted (unless compelled by statute).

18–007   In *R. v Derby Magistrates' Court Ex p. B* the magistrate, following a decision of the Court of Appeal[14] which the House of Lords overruled, had directed himself that he must balance the public interest which protects confidential communications between a solicitor and his client against the public interest in securing that all relevant and admissible evidence was made available to the defence, and had concluded that the balance came down firmly in favour of production. The House of Lords held that no such balancing exercise was to be performed or that:

> "Putting it another way, if a balancing exercise was ever required in the case of legal professional privilege, it was performed once and for all in

---

[6] [1988] Ch. 317 at 331. This dictum was cited with approval by the House of Lords in *Three Rivers District Council v The Governor and Company of the Bank of England* [2005] 1 A.C. 610; [2004] UKHL 48.
[7] [1996] A.C. 487 at 507.
[8] [2002] UKHL 27; [2003] 1 A.C. 120.
[9] [2003] UKHL 21; [2003] 1 A.C. 563.
[10] [2003] UKPC 736; [2003] 2 A.C. 736.
[11] [2004] UKHL 48; [2005] 1 A.C. 610.
[12] [1996] A.C. 487.
[13] (1995) 183 C.L.R. 121. The effect of the decision was subsequently reduced by s.123 of the Evidence Act 1995 (Commonwealth and New South Wales).
[14] *R. v Ataou* [1988] Q.B. 798.

the 16th Century, and since then has applied across the board in every case, irrespective of the client's individual merits."[15]

R. v Derby Magistrates' Court was decided before the advent of the Human Rights Act 1998 and Lord Taylor expressly recorded[16] that their Lordships had heard no argument in relation to rights arising under the European Convention on Human Rights. In *Medcalf v Mardell*,[17] Lord Hobhouse suggested that:

> "It may be that, as in the context of articles 6 and 8 of the European Convention on Human Rights, the privilege may not always be absolute and a balancing exercise may sometimes be necessary... "

The re-examination of *R. v Derby Magistrates' Court* that Lord Hob- **18–008** house's suggestion would appear to entail has not yet been carried out in subsequent decisions of the House of Lords and Privy Council. In *R. (Morgan Grenfell) v Special Commissioner of Income Tax*, Lord Hobhouse recorded[18] that the parties accepted the absolute nature of privilege and repeated that this premise (along with others) would benefit from further examination, while Lord Hoffmann,[19] referring to *R. v Derby Magistrates' Court*, simply restated what can conveniently be labelled the "absolutist" view. *B v Auckland District Law Society* was a Privy Council case on appeal from the Court of Appeal of New Zealand and European Convention rights therefore did not arise directly for consideration.

In *Three Rivers District Council v Bank of England*, Lord Scott[20] **18–009** reaffirmed the absolutist view in emphatic terms:

> "The Supreme Court of Canada has held that legal professional privilege although of great importance is not absolute and can be set aside if a sufficiently compelling public interest for doing so, such as public safety, can be shown: see *Jones v Smith* [1999] 1 S.C.R. 455. But no other common law jurisdiction has, so far as I am aware, developed the law of privilege in this way. Certainly in this country legal professional privilege, if it is attracted by a particular communication between lawyer and client or attaches to a particular document, cannot be set aside on the ground that some other higher public interest requires that to be done."

In none of these cases was a direct attack made by any of the parties on **18–010** the decision in *R. v Derby Magistrates' Court*. Such an attack *was* made in *General Mediterranean Holdings S.A. v Patel*,[21] which concerned the extent

---

[15] [1996] A.C. 487, *per* Lord Taylor C.J. at 508.
[16] At 507.
[17] [2002] UKHL 27; [2003] 1 A.C. 120 at [60].
[18] At [43].
[19] At [16].
[20] At [25].
[21] [2000] 1 W.L.R. 272.

of the courts' powers to order disclosure of privileged material for the purposes of wasted costs applications. It was argued that the absolutist approach was inconsistent with Art.6. Toulson J. observed[22]:

> "The scope of the common law right to confidentiality has had its critics. In *Carter v Northmore Davy Hale and Leake* ... Toohey J. proposed a qualification in the following terms:
>
> > 'Where an accused facing trial satisfies the court that the production of documents subpoenaed by the accused is necessary for the proper conduct of his or her defence, then, subject to any proper objection that may be taken, other than on the ground of legal professional privilege, the court may order the production of those documents.'
>
> If ever there was a case for such a qualification, *Reg. v Derby Magistrates' Court, Ex parte B.* . . . might have been thought to be that case, but three connected factors caused the House of Lords to conclude that the principle of legal confidentiality should be maintained intact. One was that to admit any exception to the general principle would undermine the lawyer's ability to give an assurance of confidentiality to the client. The second was that there was a difference between setting bounds to the circumstances in which a duty of confidentiality would arise and giving a discretion to the court to override a duty of confidence which had arisen; and that to leave the matter to the court's discretion would be unsatisfactory both in terms of the nature of the task which the court would have to carry out and in terms of the client's inability to foretell in advance which way such a discretion might be exercised. The third was that there was no satisfactory way of limiting in advance what might be regarded as exceptional cases."

Toulson J. concluded[23]:

> "I do not accept the submission that the approach of the House of Lords in that case was in violation of article 6, or that the Convention requires a balancing exercise in individual cases of the kind which the House of Lords considered and rejected as a matter of English law."

18–011   In *Carter v Northmore Hale Davy & Leake*,[24] Deane J. suggested as a possibility that,

> " . . . if there were ever a case where it became apparent that refusal of access precluded a fair trial, it would be possible to invoke the inherent power of the courts to stay proceedings."

---

[22] At 294.
[23] At 296.
[24] (1995) 183 C.L.R. 121 at 138.

As the House of Lords has declared in a number of cases (most recently in R. v H[25]), it is:

" ... axiomatic that a person charged with having committed a criminal offence should receive a fair trial and that, if he cannot be tried fairly for that offence, he should not be tried for it at all."

However, discussion of that issue is outside the scope of this book.

Loss of privilege

Legal professional privilege is a right to resist the compulsory disclosure of information.[26] But it is now clear that the courts' ability to protect privileged communications is not confined to a narrow procedural rule but constitutes a much broader jurisdiction enabling them, for example, to restrain the further use or disclosure of privileged communications. Whatever the circumstances and manner of the court's intervention, it is founded ultimately on the public interest in upholding the confidential relationship which exists between a lawyer and his client. **18–012**

Particular problems have arisen in circumstances where a party has in fact obtained evidence of a privileged communication and proposes to adduce it, or to make some other use of it, without the consent of the person entitled to claim privilege. This has given rise to a number of questions: **18–013**

1. Can the doctrine of privilege prevent it?
2. Can the doctrine of confidentiality prevent it?
3. What, if any, discretion does the court have?
4. What amounts to waiver of privilege?

Underlying these questions there is an unresolved issue about what is meant by legal professional privilege. Is it simply a rule that a person entitled to the benefit of it cannot be required to disclose the privileged information or document (a shield against compulsory disclosure)? Or can it entitle a person to prevent someone else from using "privileged" information or materials in the course of litigation? If so, when does the fact that privileged information or materials have come to the knowledge or possession of another person involve a loss of privilege?

In addressing these issues the courts have been far from clear or consistent. Equitable principles of confidence have in some circumstances been prayed in aid in order to protect parties to litigation who have "lost" the benefit of the privilege to which they were entitled. In cases where the courts have had to deal with concepts both of confidence and privilege, there has sometimes been confusion, much of which has stemmed from the **18–014**

---

[25] [2004] UKHL 3; [2004] 2 A.C. 134 at [10]. See also R. v Ward [1993] 1 W.L.R. 619 at 681, and R. v Davis [1993] 1 W.L.R. 613 at 618, in the context of non-justiciable public interest immunity.
[26] B v Auckland District Law Society, at para.67.

unfortunate decision of the Court of Appeal in *Calcraft v Guest*[27] and subsequent attempts to obviate its consequences by reference to the doctrine of confidence.

Calcraft v Guest

18–015   In *Calcraft v Guest*, certain documents (including proofs of witnesses and rough notes of evidence) had been created to assist in the defence of an action for assault (*Fry v Stevens*) tried at the Dorchester Assizes in 1787. Privilege in the documents belonged to a Mr John Calcraft. After the action, the documents were retained by Mr John Calcraft's solicitor, a Mr Thomas Bartlett. In due course, the documents came into the possession of Mr Bartlett's great-great-grandson, a Mr C. L. O. Bartlett.

18–016   More than 100 years after *Fry v Stevens*, Mr John Calcraft's successor-in-title (also named Calcraft) commenced an action against a Mrs Drax to which the documents were relevant. Judgment was given in his favour. Shortly afterwards, the existence of the documents was discovered by Mr C. L. O. Bartlett. Before returning them to Mr Calcraft, he showed them to the solicitors acting for Mrs Drax, who had instructed Mr Bartlett's firm in other matters (though not on this occasion). Mrs Drax's solicitors took copies of the documents and sought to put them in evidence in an appeal. Mr Calcraft objected as Mr John Calcraft's successor-in-title, arguing that privilege in the documents had not been destroyed by Mr C. L. O. Bartlett's wrongful disclosure of the documents to Mrs Drax's solicitors.

18–017   Lindley M.R. (with whom Rigby and Vaughan Williams L.JJ. concurred) held that "the mere fact that documents used in a previous litigation are held and have not been destroyed does not amount to a waiver of the privilege."[28] He continued:

> "Then comes the next question. It appears that the appellant has obtained copies of some of these documents, and is in a position to give secondary evidence of them; and the question is whether he is entitled to do that."

Lindley M.R. cited a dictum of Parke B. in *Lloyd v Mostyn*[29]:

> " . . . Where an attorney intrusted confidentially with a document communicates the contents of it, or suffers another to take a copy, surely the secondary evidence so obtained may be produced. Suppose the instrument were even stolen, and a correct copy taken, would it not be reasonable to admit it?"

[27] [1898] 1 Q.B. 759.
[28] *Calcraft v Guest* [1898] 1 Q.B. 759 at 761–762.
[29] 10 M. & W. 478.

Lindley M.R. concluded that the case came within the scope of Parke B.'s dictum and that secondary evidence of the privileged documents was therefore admissible.

Is *Calcraft v Guest* right?

It is an odd proposition that one party could break into the offices of the opposing party's solicitors, take copies of privileged documents, and then introduce them at trial. Suppose that, instead of producing documents, one party chose to call a solicitor, who had previously acted for the other party, to give evidence of privileged matters. One would expect it to be said that his evidence would not be admissible without the consent of his former client.[30] **18–018**

It seems that in *Calcraft v Guest*, the court viewed privilege (1) as attaching to documents themselves, rather than to the information contained in them, and (2) as being a legitimate reason for refusing to produce material documents, but nothing more than that. **18–019**

There is a certain logic (though no merit) to the decision if, but only if, privilege is restricted to a rule exonerating a party from producing a document which is in his possession and satisfies the requirements of privilege.[31] **18–020**

The principle in *Calcraft v Guest* has been closely examined and rejected in New Zealand in the case of *R. v Uljee*.[32] It has also been the subject of a lengthy and learned judgment by Kellock Ag.J. in the Grand Court of Cayman in *J.P. Morgan Multi-Strategy Fund LP v Macro Fund Ltd*.[33] Analysing the subject-matter of *Calcraft* and the cases cited by the Court of Appeal in *Calcraft*, Kellock Ag.J. concluded[34]: **18–021**

> "It seems to me that *Calcraft* cannot be taken as deciding more than it actually decided and that the decision is limited to documents subject to deed privilege, or at most litigation privilege. Deed privilege has been abolished and there is still a debate as to the merit and scope of litigation privilege ... There is no statement in *Calcraft* to the effect that legal advice privilege in a document is lost if an attorney improperly discloses it, or the document is stolen. In addition, there is no statement that a document which remains subject to legal advice privilege (or a copy) may be admitted in evidence despite that privilege. It seems to me that *Calcraft* cannot be regarded as an authority for that

---

[30] *per* Sir John Strange in *Bishop of Winchester v Fournier* (1752) 2 Ves. Sen. 445 at 447. See *Wilson v Rastell* (1792) 4 T.R. 753, *per* Buller J. at 759, and *Bate v Kinsey* (1834) 1 C.M. & R. 38, *per* Lyndhurst C.B. at 43 and *R. v Derby Magistrates Court Ex p. B* [1996] A.C. 487, *per* Lord Taylor C.J. at 504–505.
[31] But see *Minter v Priest* [1930] A.C. 558, *per* Lord Atkin at 579.
[32] [1982] 1 N.Z.L.R. 561. *Calcraft* was cited without disapproval by the Supreme Court of South Australia in *Trevorrow v South Australia (No. 4)* [2006] SASC 42.
[33] [2003] C.I.L.R. 250.
[34] At para.94.

proposition and if it has been so regarded, it can no longer be seen as support for a proposition which to my mind is utterly inconsistent with the words used by Lord Taylor in *Derby Magistrates*... "Legal professional privilege is thus much more than an ordinary rule of evidence, limited in its application to the facts of a particular case. It is a fundamental condition on which the administration of justice as a whole rests."

18–022 There are difficulties in the way of an English court seeking to follow the bold course of simply disregarding *Calcraft v Guest* in relation to legal advice privilege. First, the relevant documents in *Calcraft v Guest* appear to have included documents in relation to which litigation privilege (at least) might be supposed to attach. If litigation privilege and legal advice privilege are but two sub-heads of a single integral legal professional privilege,[35] it is not clear why the effect of *Calcraft v Guest* should differ between them. Secondly, the Court of Appeal has consistently treated *Calcraft v Guest* as applicable to legal advice privilege. Thirdly, although it is true that the reasoning and decision in *Calcraft v Guest* does not sit comfortably with Lord Taylor's *dicta* in *R. v Derby Magistrates' Court*, it is not apparent that they are formally inconsistent.

18–023 In England, *Calcraft v Guest* has been criticised and distinguished (not always satisfactorily). In *English & American Insurance Co Ltd v Herbert Smith*.[36] Browne-Wilkinson V.C. said:

"I think that when this or some other case reaches the House of Lords it may well be that the absolute rule laid down in *Calcraft v Guest* is the suspect decision . . . ."

18–024 In *B v Auckland District Law Society*,[37] a law firm in New Zealand sought to recover documents that they had provided to the Auckland District Law Society's representative, a Mr Ennor, on terms that expressly preserved privilege in the documents. One argument raised by the Law Society was that, since the documents were now in its possession, the benefit of privilege had been lost. The Privy Council disagreed. Lord Millett said:

"The society's argument, put colloquially, is that privilege entitles one to refuse to let the cat out of the bag; once it is out of the bag, however, privilege cannot help to put it back."

He observed that this argument was not based on waiver (since the firm had expressly not waived privilege), but on the nature of privilege. He continued:

---

[35] As stated by Lord Carswell in *Three Rivers District Council v Bank of England* [2004] UKHL 48; [2005] 1 A.C. 610, at [105].
[36] [1988] F.S.R. 232 at 236–237.
[37] [2003] UKPC 38; [2003] 2 A.C. 736.

"The question is not whether privilege has been waived, but whether it has been lost. It would be unfortunate if it were. It must often be in the interests of the administration of justice that a partial or limited waiver of privilege should be made by a party who would not contemplate anything which would cause privilege to be lost, and it would be most undesirable if the law could not accommodate it . . .

The society argued that, once the documents were produced to Mr Ennor, they ceased to be privileged. Their Lordships consider that this is playing with words. It confuses the nature of the documents with the rights to which the arrangements with Mr Ennor gave rise. The documents are privileged because they were created for the purpose of giving or receiving legal advice. If they are not produced voluntarily, production cannot be compelled. If they are produced voluntarily, the right to withhold production no longer attaches to them. In that sense the privilege may be said to be lost. But they are the same documents, and it is not inappropriate to describe them as privileged. Their inherent characteristics are the same. The policy which protected them from unauthorised disclosure is the same. The cat is still a cat. It can be put back in the bag . . .

The fact that the claim to recover the documents is made on equitable grounds does not mean that it must yield to an overriding countervailing public interest. The documents are both confidential and privileged. Whether a claim to the return of such documents is based on a common law right or an equitable one, the policy considerations which give rise to the privilege preclude the court from conducting a balancing exercise. A lawyer must be able to give his client an unqualified assurance, not only that what passes between them shall never be revealed without his consent in any circumstances, but that should he consent in future to disclosure for a limited purpose those limits will be respected: see *Goddard v Nationwide Building Society* . . . per Nourse L.J."

Lord Millett must be right that there are circumstances in which it is "not inappropriate" to describe documents as privileged although they are in the hands of another person. At the most obvious level, a document can be privileged although it is in the hands of a client's lawyer, and in those circumstances the privilege belongs to the client. It would be very strange if the lawyer (or the client) could not disclose the document to another person (for example, an expert witness) without privilege being forfeited. Once that principle is recognised, there is no reason why it should not be appropriate to continue to regard a document as privileged in circumstances where it is obtained from the lawyer or client by improper means. That, however, is contrary to *Calcraft v Guest*, which concluded that privilege could not be claimed against a person in possession of a document, even if the possession was obtained by theft. The reasoning of the Privy Council is inconsistent with *Calcraft v Guest*, and is to be preferred, but *Calcraft v Guest* has yet to be overruled. **18–025**

18–026   As authority binding on the Court of Appeal and on lesser courts, *Calcraft v Guest* has thrown a long shadow over subsequent cases. Starting with *Ashburton v Pape*, the courts have resorted to the equitable doctrine of confidentiality to limit the effect of *Calcraft v Guest*, but in doing so have encountered complications.

Ashburton v Pape

18–027   Mrs Drax's leading counsel in *Calcraft v Guest* was Herbert Cozens-Hardy Q.C. He was also a member of the Court of Appeal which considered the consequences of that decision 15 years later, in the case of *Lord Ashburton v Pape*.[38] Pape was a bankrupt who sought discharge. Lord Ashburton, one of his creditors, opposed his discharge. In answer to a *subpoena*, a clerk from the firm of solicitors retained by Lord Ashburton attended court with a number of privileged letters from Lord Ashburton to his solicitors. Complaining of illness, he handed the letters over to Mr Pape's solicitors, who took copies and passed the originals to their client.

18–028   Lord Ashburton issued separate proceedings and obtained by interlocutory motion an order, both that Pape deliver up the original letters and that he, with various others, be restrained "until judgment or further order from publishing or making use of any of the copies of such letters or any information contained therein except for the purpose of the bankruptcy and subject to the direction of the Bankruptcy Court". Lord Ashburton appealed, seeking to vary the order so as to remove from it the specified exception. His appeal succeeded.

18–029   Interpretation of the Court of Appeal's decision is made more difficult by textual discrepancies between the various reports of it.[39] Nevertheless, it is most often read as doing much to mitigate the effects of the earlier decision in *Calcraft v Guest* by making it possible for a party claiming privilege in respect of a document to obtain an injunction restraining another party from deploying it (or a copy) in evidence, notwithstanding that it (or a copy) would otherwise be admissible.

18–030   Cozens-Hardy M.R. said[40]:

> "The rule of evidence as explained in *Calcraft v Guest* merely amounts to this, that if a litigant wants to prove a particular document which by reason of privilege or some circumstance he cannot furnish by the production of the original, he may produce a copy as secondary evidence although that copy has been obtained by improper means, and even, it may be, by criminal means. The court in such an action is not

[38] [1913] 2 Ch. 469; 109 L.T. 381; 82 L.J.Ch. 527; 29 T.L.R. 623; 57 S.J. 644.
[39] See, e.g. C. Tapper, "Privilege and Confidence" (1972) 35 M.L.R. 83, at 85ff., and N. H. Andrews, *The Influence of Equity upon the Doctrine of Legal Professional Privilege* (1989) 105 L.Q.R. 608 at 615ff.
[40] [1913] 2 Ch. 469, at 473.

really trying the circumstances under which the document was produced. That is not an issue in the case and the Court simply says 'Here
is a copy of a document which cannot be produced; it may have been
stolen, it may have been picked up in the street, it may have improperly
got into the possession of the person who proposes to produce it, but
that is not a matter which the Court in the trial of the action can go
into.' But that does not seem to me to have any bearing upon a case
where the whole subject-matter of the action is the right to retain the
originals or copies of certain documents which are privileged."

Swinfen Eady L.J. said,[41]

"The principle upon which the Court of Chancery has acted for many
years has been to restrain the publication of confidential information
improperly or surreptitiously obtained or of information imparted in
confidence which ought not to be divulged . . . There is here a
confusion between the right to restrain a person from divulging
confidential information and the right to give secondary evidence of
documents where the originals are privileged from production, if the
party has such secondary evidence in his possession. The cases are
entirely separate and distinct."

Comparison of *Calcraft* and *Ashburton*

Ashburton v Pape appears to set up a clear distinction between privilege,   **18–031**
which is lost or rendered useless by disclosure, and confidentiality, which
may continue to protect privileged communications which have come into
the possession of the other party as a result of a breach of confidence or by
accident.

However, the courts have not found it easy to set out clearly and   **18–032**
consistently the principles on which the equitable jurisdiction in *Ashburton
v Pape* will be exercised. In particular, different views have been expressed
as to whether the jurisdiction is subject to the usual incidents and
qualifications affecting the enforcement of obligations of confidence, or
whether it attracts to itself something of the absolute quality of legal
professional privilege.

Two issues which have arisen in a number of cases are: **18–033**

   (1) what, if any, discretion the court has when the *Ashburton v Pape*
      jurisdiction is invoked in relation to documents originally attract-
      ing privilege, which the person entitled to claim privilege did not
      intend to waive; and
   (2) what amounts to waiver of privilege.

---

[41] [1913] 2 Ch. 469 at 475–476.

Discretion

18-034   Differing views have been expressed whether a court has a discretion to refuse to give relief under the *Ashburton v Pape* jurisdiction in circumstances where a privileged document has come into the hands of another person as a result of improper conduct or inadvertence (not involving waiver).

18-035   In *Butler v Board of Trade*[42] the plaintiff sought a declaration that the Board of Trade, which had brought a prosecution against him, was not entitled to make any use of a letter written to him by his solicitor. A copy of the letter, together with other documents, had been handed over by his solicitor to the Official Receiver of a company in compulsory liquidation.

18-036   Goff J., having found that the original letter was privileged and the copy confidential, declined to grant relief on the principle in *Ashburton* because:

> "In my judgment it would not be a right or permissible exercise of the equitable jurisdiction in confidence to make a declaration at the suit of the accused in a public prosecution in effect restraining the Crown from adducing admissible evidence relevant to the crime with which he is charged. It is not necessary for me to decide whether the same result would obtain in the case of a private prosecution, and I expressly leave that point open."[43]

18-037   Goff J.'s distinction between private litigation and public prosecution was subsequently approved by the Criminal Division of the Court of Appeal in *R. v Tompkins*,[44] but has not been followed in New Zealand and was criticised by Nourse L.J. in *Goddard v Nationwide Building Society*.[45] In *R. v G*,[46] the Court of Appeal stated obiter:

> "There is no reason in principle why a Crown Court . . . should not similarly restrain the use of material inadvertently disclosed, although the particular circumstances of the case which dictate whether justice requires an order will, of course, be different."

18-038   In *Webster v James Chapman & Co*,[47] the plaintiff was injured at work and brought an action against his employer. A report by a firm of expert engineers was obtained by his solicitors, who requested the firm to reconsider some elements of its opinion. The plaintiff's solicitors inadvertently sent a copy of the unrevised report to the defendant's solicitors.

---

[42] [1971] 1 Ch. 680.
[43] [1971] Ch. 680 at 690.
[44] (1978) 67 Cr.App.R. 181.
[45] [1987] 1 Q.B. 670 at 686.
[46] [2004] EWCA Crim 1368; [2004] 1 W.L.R. 2932 at [16].
[47] [1989] 3 All E.R. 939.

The plaintiff sought an order that the defendant deliver up any copies of **18–039**
the unrevised report and be restrained from using its contents in any way.
Scott J. held[48]:

> "If a document has been disclosed, be it by trickery, accident or
> otherwise, the benefit and protection of legal privilege will have been
> lost . . . The question then will be what protection the court should
> provide given that the document which will have come into the
> possession of the other side will be confidential, and that use of it will
> be unauthorised."

Scott J. took the view that he was required to give broad consideration to all
the circumstances of the case, and concluded that the balance came down
against granting the relief sought.[49] His decision was subsequently disapproved by the Court of Appeal in *Pizzey v Ford Motor Company Ltd*,[50]
which held, citing the judgment of Dillon L.J. in *Derby & Co Ltd v Weldon
(No. 8)*,[51] that a balancing exercise was inappropriate (a matter in fact
conceded by the defendant in *Pizzey v Ford Motor Company Ltd*).

The weight of authority has tended, as in *Pizzey v Ford Motor Company* **18–040**
Ltd, towards a more "absolutist" view of the *Ashburton v Pape* jurisdiction
than was adopted in either *Butler v Board of Trade* or *Webster v James
Chapman & Co*. Both strands of opinion can be observed in the Court of
Appeal's decision in *Goddard v Nationwide Building Society*.[52] In that case,
a solicitor acted for both the plaintiff mortgagor and the defendant
mortgagee in relation to the purchase of a property by the plaintiff with the
assistance of a loan from the defendant. The plaintiff subsequently sued the
defendant in respect of alleged defects in the property. The solicitor had
made a file note while the transaction was proceeding of conversations he
had had with the plaintiff following receipt of information from the
defendant.

After the plaintiff had commenced proceedings, the solicitor sent the file **18–041**
note to the defendant, which pleaded the substance of its contents in its
defence. The plaintiff sought an injunction ordering that the defendant
should deliver up the file note and all copies thereof, and restraining the
defendant from using or relying upon it in any manner.

Having held that privilege in the document belonged to the plaintiff and **18–042**
that it should therefore not have been sent to the defendant, May L.J. and
Nourse L.J. went on to hold that the plaintiff was entitled to the relief
sought.

May L.J. appeared to subscribe to a view of *Ashburton v Pape* which **18–043**
placed the relief granted in that case within the scope of ordinary principles

---

[48] [1989] 3 All E.R. 939 at 946.
[49] *ibid.* at 947.
[50] Court of Appeal, 26 February 1993, partially reported in *The Times*, March 8, 1993.
[51] [1991] 1 W.L.R. 73.
[52] [1987] 1 Q.B. 670.

of confidentiality.[53] Nourse L.J., on the other hand, made a number of observations which suggested that the relief granted to Lord Ashburton was not simply to be equated with the injunctive relief available in an ordinary action for breach of confidence. He began by suggesting that it was no longer necessary for a party seeking *Ashburton v Pape* relief in ongoing litigation to initiate separate proceedings. He then stated that principles of confidentiality would assist a party seeking *Ashburton v Pape* relief only where the material was (or had been) privileged:

> "It cannot be the function of equity to accord a de facto privilege to communications in respect of which no privilege can be claimed. Equity follows the law."

He continued:

> " . . . the right of the party who desires the protection to invoke the equitable jurisdiction does not in any way depend on the conduct of the third party into whose possession the record of the confidential communication has come . . . equity gives relief against all the world, including the innocent, save only a bona fide purchaser for value without notice."

Moreover, he observed that:

> " . . . once it is established that a case is governed by *Lord Ashburton v Pape* [1913] 2 Ch. 469 there is no discretion in the court to refuse to exercise the equitable jurisdiction according to its view of the materiality of the communication, the justice of admitting or excluding it or the like. The injunction is granted in aid of the privilege which, unless and until it is waived, is absolute."

This is a significant passage. The obvious rationalisation of *Calcraft v Guest* and *Ashburton v Pape* was that, when a document has been mistakenly disclosed to the opposing party, the benefit of privilege is lost, but that the court has a discretion to grant equitable relief on the grounds of confidence so as to enable the mistaken party to recover his position. Here, on the other hand, Nourse L.J. suggested that the mere disclosure of a document does not involve the loss of privilege, and that a person has an absolute right to have the document treated as privileged unless and until there is some "waiver" of privilege in respect of it. This approach was followed in *Derby v Weldon (No. 8)*[54] by Vinelott J., who disagreed with Scott J.'s approach in *Webster v Chapman*.

---

[53] e.g. at 680A–B, though see the observations of Vinelott J. in *Derby & Co Ltd v Weldon (No. 8)* [1991] 1 W.L.R. 73 at 79.
[54] [1991] 1 W.L.R. 73 at 84; see also *per* Dillon L.J. at 99.

In *Istil Group Inc v Zahoor*,[55] the defendants obtained copies of e-mail **18–044**
communications between the claimants or their solicitors and an anonymous third party. They alleged that the e-mails revealed fraudulent conduct,
being strongly suggestive that a crucial document relied on by the claimants
was forged. They also claimed that the e-mails demonstrated that the
claimants had deliberately misled the court in affidavit evidence filed earlier
in relation to a freezing order. The claimants argued that the e-mails were
covered by litigation privilege. Lawrence Collins J. posed the following
question[56]:

> "What, then, is the extent of the discretion in the exercise of the *Lord
> Ashburton v Pape* line of authorities to restrain breach of confidence in
> relation to documents which have already been disclosed, but which
> would otherwise be privileged? In particular, can the court conduct a
> balancing exercise, and if so, on the basis of what factors?"

Having reviewed the authorities, he concluded[57] that relief could properly
be refused on grounds that it would be contrary to public interest to grant
it, but that the importance of the emergence of the truth was not a factor
which could be taken into account under the heading of public interest
"because the balance between privilege and truth has already been struck in
favour of the former by the establishment of the rules concerning legal
professional privilege". He refused to grant relief, holding that the combination of alleged forgery and misleading evidence made it a case where the
equitable jurisdiction to restrain breach of confidence gave way to the public
interest in the administration of justice.

In *J.P. Morgan Multi-Strategy Fund LP v The Macro Fund Ltd*,[58] Kellock **18–045**
Ag.J. observed[59] of the decision in *Istil* that:

> "Lawrence Collins J. was entitled if not obliged to refuse the injunction
> on general principles. That is to say, the grant of equitable relief is
> subject to the court's discretion and may be refused on the basis of the
> clean hands doctrine . . . I would respectfully disagree with Lawrence
> Collins J's assertion that it is necessary to invoke the general law
> relating to breach of confidence in these cases. The court should act in
> aid of the privilege."

The judgment of the Privy Council in *B v Auckland Law Society*[60] **18–046**
supports the view that there is no balancing exercise to be conducted. The
policy reasons for that view are the same as the policy reasons for

---

[55] [2003] EWHC 165 (Ch); [2003] 2 All E.R. 252.
[56] At para.88.
[57] At paras 89–94.
[58] [2003] C.I.L.R. 250 at para.113.
[59] At para.113.
[60] [2003] UKPC 38; [2003] 2 A.C. 736.

recognising legal professional privilege, and it is suggested that they are compelling.

18–047   There may, however, be other grounds for the court not to act in aid of the asserted privilege. In cases where the documents reveal strong evidence of misconduct by the party claiming relief under *Ashburton v Pape*, the claim might fail either on the grounds that the documents do not attract privilege because of the crime or fraud exception or on the grounds that relief should be refused under the clean hands doctrine, and in cases where a party entitled to assert privilege in respect of a document inadvertently discloses it to an opposing party questions of waiver may arise,

Waiver of privilege

18–048   In *English & American Insurance Co Ltd v Herbert Smith*[61] Browne-Wilkinson V.C. took a broad view of the jurisdiction recognised in *Ashburton v Pape* and *Goddard v Nationwide Building Society*, holding that the equitable right to restrain the use of confidential information could be enforced at any time before the information was tendered in evidence. He also rejected the argument that the jurisdiction was confined to cases in which the person seeking to use the information was improperly implicated in obtaining it.

18–049   In *Guinness Peat Properties Ltd v Fitzroy Robinson Partnership*,[62] a professional negligence action against architects, the defendants accidentally disclosed in a supplementary list of documents a letter sent by them to their insurers, containing their views as to the merits of the allegations made against them. The plaintiffs' solicitor inspected the letter, copied it and sent a copy to the plaintiffs' expert, who referred to it in his report. The defendants sought an injunction restraining the plaintiffs from using or relying upon the copy of the letter, and for the delivery up of all copies of the letter in the plaintiffs' possession or control. The defendants succeeded, both at first instance and in the Court of Appeal.

The plaintiffs argued, first, that:

> " . . . privilege is essentially privilege from compulsory disclosure . . . once a privileged document has not only been disclosed but also inspected in the course of discovery, it is too late to put the clock back; the privilege is lost."

Secondly, they distinguished the *Goddard* and *Herbert Smith* cases, on the grounds that neither of those two cases dealt with a loss of privilege occurring as a result of a step taken in the litigation by the party entitled to the privilege.

18–050   Slade L.J., delivering the leading judgment, accepted these submissions with one important reservation,

---

[61] [1989] 3 All E.R. 939.
[62] [1987] 1 W.L.R. 1027.

"My one reservation is this. I do not think that after inspection has taken place in the course of discovery, the court is inevitably and invariably powerless to intervene by way of injunction in exercise of the equitable jurisdiction exemplified by the *Ashburton, Goddard* and *Herbert Smith* cases if the particular circumstances warrant such intervention on equitable grounds."

The particular circumstances identified by Slade L.J. as warranting intervention were cases in which inspection had been procured by fraud or in which it was apparent to the inspecting party that an obvious mistake had been made.

In *Derby & Co Ltd v Weldon (No. 8)*,[63] the plaintiffs' solicitors **18–051** inadvertently allowed the defendants' solicitors to inspect a number of privileged documents. Despite the advice of counsel to the effect that they should first ascertain whether privilege had been intentionally waived, the defendants' solicitors requested and obtained copies of some of the privileged material. Subsequently the plaintiffs applied for an order requiring the defendants to deliver up all copies of some 14 documents and restraining the defendants from relying on any information contained in them.

At first instance, Vinelott J. acceded to the plaintiffs' application, except **18–052** in the case of three documents which, as he held, were not on their face clearly privileged. The Court of Appeal upheld his judgment, except that it allowed the plaintiffs' appeal in respect of the three documents which he had held to be beyond the scope of the relief sought.

Dillon L.J. gave the leading judgment in the Court of Appeal. Although **18–053** finding in the plaintiffs' favour, on the authority of *Guinness Peat* he rejected[64] the plaintiffs' broad submission that the court could always intervene in a case of mistaken disclosure. He distinguished *Goddard v Nationwide Building Society*[65] and *English & American Insurance Co Ltd v Herbert Smith*,[66] which were relied on by the plaintiffs in support of that proposition, on the grounds that they did not involve any question of waiver of privilege:

"The documents in question had got into the hands of the other party to the litigation, despite the wishes of the person entitled to privilege and in circumstances which could not amount to waiver of privilege."

He further held that the documents which the defendants were obliged to return should not be limited to those that were clearly privileged on their face, since the defendants were seeking to take advantage of an obvious general breakdown in the plaintiffs' system for excluding privileged documents from discovery. He saw this as a critical factor, drawing an analogy

[63] [1991] 1 W.L.R. 73.
[64] *ibid.* at 95.
[65] [1987] Q.B. 670.
[66] [1988] F.S.R. 232.

from rectification of a contract, where a species of equitable estoppel operates to prevent one party to a contract from relying on what he knows to be a mistake in his favour in the text of the contract.

18–054   He concluded[67]:

> "I see no reason why the first and second defendants should not be deprived of all the benefit from their having in those circumstances knowingly taken advantage of an obvious mistake."

It is not, however, clear whether he regarded the case as one in which the inspecting party was estopped by its conduct from asserting that there had been a loss of privilege, or simply as an application of *Ashburton v Pape* in a case where there had been loss of privilege.

18–055   The "obvious mistake" approach was taken a further stage by the Court of Appeal in *Pizzey v Ford Motor Co Ltd*,[68] which was followed by Aldous J. in *International Business Machines Corp v Phoenix International (Computers) Ltd*.[69] In these cases the question arose whether an injunction was obtainable if the person to whom the privileged material was disclosed in the course of inspection did not realise that it was privileged, but a reasonable solicitor would have so realised.

18–056   The Court of Appeal held that "the law ought not to give an advantage to obtusity and if the recipient ought to have realised that a mistake was evident then the exception applies." Aldous J. followed this test, but his decision illustrates the difficulties involved in applying it.

18–057   CPR 31.20 provides that, where a party inadvertently allows a privileged document to be inspected, the party who has inspected the document may use it or its contents only with the permission of the court. However, the introduction of the CPR has made no difference to the approach taken by the courts to issues relating to the waiver of privilege.[70] In *Fayed v The Commissioner of Police of the Metropolis*,[71] the Court of Appeal held that the following principles could be derived from the authorities:

> "i) A party giving inspection of documents must decide before doing so what privileged documents he wishes to allow the other party to see and what he does not.
>
> ii) Although the privilege is that of the client and not the solicitor, a party clothes his solicitor with ostensible authority (if not implied or express authority) to waive privilege in respect of relevant documents.

---

[67] *Derby & Co Ltd v Weldon (No. 8)* [1991] 1 W.L.R. 73 at 100.
[68] *The Times*, March 8 1993.
[69] [1995] 1 All E.R. 413.
[70] *Breeze v John Stacey & Sons Ltd, The Times*, July 8, 1999, CA; *Fayed v The Commissioner of Police of the Metropolis* [2002] EWCA Civ 780.
[71] [2002] EWCA Civ 780; *The Times*, June 17, 2002.

iii) A solicitor considering documents made available by the other party to litigation owes no duty of care to that party and is in general entitled to assume that any privilege which might otherwise have been claimed for such documents has been waived.

iv) In these circumstances, where a party has given inspection of documents, including privileged documents which he has allowed the other party to inspect by mistake, it will in general be too late for him to claim privilege in order to attempt to correct the mistake by obtaining injunctive relief.

v) However, the court has jurisdiction to intervene to prevent the use of documents made available for inspection by mistake where justice requires, as for example in the case of inspection procured by fraud.

vi) In the absence of fraud, all will depend upon the circumstances, but the court may grant an injunction if the documents have been made available for inspection as a result of an obvious mistake.

vii) A mistake is likely to be held to be obvious and an injunction granted where the documents are received by a solicitor and:

a) the solicitor appreciates that a mistake has been made before making some use of the documents; or

b) it would be obvious to a reasonable solicitor in his position that a mistake has been made;

and, in either case, there are no other circumstances which would make it unjust or inequitable to grant relief.

viii) Where a solicitor gives detailed consideration to the question whether the documents have been made available for inspection by mistake and honestly concludes that they have not, that fact will be a relevant (and in many cases an important) pointer to the conclusion that it would not be obvious to the reasonable solicitor that a mistake had been made, but is not conclusive; the decision remains a matter for the court.

ix) In both the cases identified in vii) a) and b) above there are many circumstances in which it may nevertheless be held to be inequitable or unjust to grant relief, but all will depend upon the particular circumstances.

x) Since the court is exercising an equitable jurisdiction, there are no rigid rules."

These guidelines provide a useful summary of the approach adopted by the courts but do not purport to elucidate the legal principles underlying it. The court considered that in principle there was much to be said for the view that an injunction ought not to be granted merely on the basis that the recipient ought to have appreciated that an obvious mistake had been made, because, if the test is unconscionability, subjective fault should be required, but it recognised that this view was not consistent with the decisions of the court in *Pizzey v Ford Motor Co* and *Breeze v John Stacey & Sons Ltd*.

18–058   In *R. v G*[72] the Court of Appeal considered the civil rules in the context of a criminal case. Five defendants were charged with conspiracy to defraud. Prior to the trial the judge ruled that on grounds of public interest immunity certain material should not be disclosed to the defence. The prosecution negligently and inadvertently disclosed some of the material, which was read by counsel for two of the defendants (one of whom informed his solicitors about it) before the mistake was realised. The judge made an order prohibiting those to whom the disclosure had been made from disseminating it to anyone else including their clients. The Court of Appeal accepted that he had jurisdiction to restrain the use of the material, by analogy with the jurisdiction of the civil court to prevent use of a privileged document inadvertently disclosed, but held that he was wrong to make the order. Rose L.J. observed[73] that a civil court will not prevent use of a privileged document inadvertently disclosed unless it would be unjust or inequitable to use it, and this question may well involve considering whether it is too late to restore the status quo: *Guinness Peat Properties Ltd v Fitzroy Robinson Partnership*.[74] The court considered the consequences of the judge's order and concluded that it would be impossible for those lawyers who had knowledge of the material to continue to act in the trial under the restraints imposed without causing serious unfairness.

18–059   If the recipient of a privileged document realises at once that it has been disclosed by mistake, the principle that he should not be permitted knowingly to take advantage of the mistake is plain. If he does not realise that there has been a mistake until later, to make the availability of relief under *Ashburton v Pape* depend on whether it would have been obvious to a reasonable solicitor in his position that a mistake had been made as the determinant is unsatisfactory and can give rise to unfairness in either direction.

18–060   The rule was first established by the Court of Appeal in *Pizzey v Ford Motor Co Ltd* on the basis that the law should not give an advantage to obtusity. It is a fundamental rule of the law of confidentiality that a person against whom a duty of confidentiality is alleged must have notice that the information is confidential.[75] What constitutes sufficient notice may vary according to the circumstances. Where information is imparted in the course of a relationship or venture which a reasonable person would regard as involving a duty of confidentiality, it is enough that a reasonable person in the recipient's position would regard the information as confidential. But parties on the different sides in litigation are not in such a relationship. The starting point is that a party who receives a document from another party, without reservation as to its use, is entitled to use it for the purposes of the litigation. If, through inexperience or for whatever reason, he does not appreciate that a mistake has been made, it is a strong thing to say that he nevertheless owes a duty of confidentiality in respect of the document

---

[72] [2004] EWCA Crim 1368; [2004] 1 W.L.R. 2932.
[73] *ibid.* at [15].
[74] [1987] 1 W.L.R. 1027 at 1046, *per* Slade L.J.
[75] *Att-Gen v Guardian Newspapers Ltd (No. 2)* [1990] 1 A.C. 109 at 281.

because it would have been obvious to a reasonable solicitor that a mistake had been made. The repercussions could be far reaching and unfair if it were not possible in practical terms to undo the situation. The client might have to instruct another professional team (depending on how far the knowledge had spread) and the client too might be in an impossible position if the solicitor had in good faith reported the information to him.

On the other hand, if the mistake was not immediately realised by the recipient and would not have been obvious to a reasonable solicitor, but the party which made the mistake realised it and notified the recipient before any lasting harm had been done (for example, before the recipient had fully studied the document), the party which made the mistake should be able to retrieve the position, on the principle that it would be unconscionable for the recipient to make use of a privileged document when he knew that it had been disclosed by mistake unless the receipt of the information had affected him in such a way that it would be impractical or unreasonable to expect him not to use it.   **18–061**

There are also practical difficulties arising from the test of what would have been obvious to a reasonable solicitor. It has proved to be troublesome to apply.[76] The reality is that in modern cases discovery is often on a voluminous scale, carried out by large teams. Not only are mistakes likely to be made, but there are many cases where the notion that each document is individually scrutinised at the time of inspection by a solicitor, evaluating in the context of his knowledge of the case whether the document is intended to be disclosed, is wholly unrealistic. It is unclear on the authorities what is the position where the recipient is a litigant in person and therefore does not have a solicitor acting for him.[77]   **18–062**

One further complication in the present case law must be mentioned. Although *Calcraft v Guest* has been outflanked to a large extent by the fashioning of relief under *Ashburton*, in *ITC Film Distributors Ltd v Video Exchange Ltd*[78] Warner J. was doubtful whether he could grant relief on that basis, but arrived at the same result by applying a version of the doctrine of public interest immunity.   **18–063**

One of the defendants had obtained possession of privileged documents, which had been left in the court. He exhibited copies of certain of the documents to a long affidavit, which was later read in part to the judge, and some of the documents were referred to and used for the purpose of cross-examining a witness. Warner J. found as a fact that the defendant concerned had obtained possession of the documents by a trick.   **18–064**

Warner J. considered that there were difficulties in granting *Ashburton* relief at that stage, but he accepted the plaintiff's alternative submission that he must: **18–065**

---

[76] See, for example, *International Business Machines Corp v Phoenix International (Computers) Ltd* [1995] 1 All E.R. 413 and *Fayed v Commissioner of Police of the Metropolis* [2002] EWCA Civ 780.
[77] The Court of Appeal discussed this in *Fayed v Commissioner of Police of the Metropolis* and left the point open.
[78] [1982] 1 Ch. 431.

"balance the public interest that the truth should be ascertained, which is the reason for the rule in *Calcraft v Guest* . . . against the public interest that litigants should be able to bring their documents into court without fear that they may be filched by their opponents, whether by stealth or by a trick, and then used by them in evidence."[79]

He held that documents obtained in such circumstances were exempt from forensic scrutiny as a matter of public interest and fell within the continuum of relevant evidence (in the words of Lord Simon[80]):

" . . . which may be excluded from the forensic scrutiny. This extends from that excluded in the interest of the forensic process itself as an instrument of justice . . . through that excluded for such and also for cognate interests . . . through again that excluded in order to facilitate the avoidance of forensic contestation . . . to evidence excluded because its adduction might imperil the security of that civil society which the administration of justice itself also subserves . . . "

However, Warner J. took the view that it was impossible for him to exclude those documents at which he had already looked, since they had been used in evidence, and it would be impossible for him to disregard the answers given by the witness when the documents had been put to him. Warner J.'s judgment was cited with approval by Nourse L.J. in *Goddard*.[81]

Conclusions

18–066   The present position needs to be simplified. It is clearly seen by the courts as desirable to afford a measure of protection to privileged material inadvertently disclosed to the opposing party, for reasons stated by Browne-Wilkinson V.C. in *English & American Insurance Ltd v Herbert Smith*[82]:

"Legal professional privilege is an important safeguard of a man's legal rights. It is the basis on which he and his advisers are free to speak as to matters in issue in litigation and otherwise without fear that it will subsequently be used against him. In my judgment, it is most undesirable if the security which is the basis of that freedom is to be prejudiced by mischances which are of every day occurrence leading to documents which have escaped being used by the other side."

[79] [1982] 1 Ch. 431 at 440.
[80] *D v National Society for the Prevention of Cruelty to Children* [1978] A.C. 171 at 233.
[81] [1987] 1 Q.B. 670 at 685. See also *Amwell View School Governors v Dogherty*, E.A.T., September 15, 2006.
[82] [1988] F.S.R. 232 at 239.

The first step towards a satisfactory solution would be to overrule **18–067** *Calcraft v Guest*. The right to privilege should be more than a right not to give compulsory disclosure (as it was interpreted in *Calcraft v Guest* and as was accepted in *Guinness Peat Properties Ltd v Fitzroy Robinson Partnership*). It should be a right not to have privileged information used in legal proceedings without the consent of the person entitled to privilege.

Where privileged information has been improperly or accidentally dis- **18–068** closed without the consent of the person entitled to the benefit of it, the court ought not to conduct a general balancing exercise in deciding whether to grant relief to protect the privilege. Such relief ought to be granted unless there are other grounds for not doing so (for example, that the information has already been deployed publicly or so widely that it can no longer sensibly be regarded as confidential). This is probably the present law, but it is not entirely settled.

There is also a need to clarify the concept of waiver of privilege. **18–069** Deliberate and unqualified waiver of privilege obviously terminates any privilege. There may be limited waiver for a specific purpose only, which would not amount to a general waiver of privilege.[83] A party who puts in evidence part of a privileged document, even accidentally, cannot prevent the whole document going in, unless there are points which relate to a different subject, in which case privilege may still be asserted in respect of the unrelated parts. The rationale is that the holder of the privilege should not be able to abuse it by using it to create an inaccurate or incomplete perception of the protected document.[84]

Where privileged information has been accidentally disclosed in the **18–070** course of litigation by a person entitled to the benefit of it (or by his agent) to another party, and the recipient is aware of the mistake before digesting the information, it is unconscionable conduct for the recipient knowingly to take advantage of the mistake. Where, however, the recipient is not aware of the mistake until later, the question whether he should be permitted to use it should depend on what is practical and just. It may be unrealistic for the person who has given disclosure to try to put the cat back in the bag (for example, where the material has become so widely circulated as to lose the quality of confidence, or where it has been not merely disclosed but used in evidence). Or it might put the recipient in position of unfairness or embarrassment to require him to put out of his mind information which will already have affected his understanding of the case. In such cases it will be too late for the person who has given disclosure to claim that he has not waived privilege.[85] Where there are no such obstacles, the party which has

---

[83] *British Coal Corporation v Dennis Rye (No. 2) Ltd* [1988] 1 W.L.R. 1113; *Goldman v Hesper* [1988] 1 W.L.R. 1238; *B v Auckland District Law Society* [2003] UKPC 38; [2003] 2 A.C. 736.
[84] *Att-Gen v Maurice* (1986) 161 C.L.R. 475 at 487–488.
[85] Scott J. might have arrived at the same decision on the facts of *Webster v James Chapman & Co* [1989] 3 All E.R. 939 as he reached applying a broad balancing test.

made accidental disclosure of privileged material should be allowed to retrieve its position. A similar test is applied in Australia.[86] As the Court of Appeal observed in *R. v G*,[87] "the essential question is what justice requires."

---

[86] *Att-Gen v Maurice* (1986) 161 C.L.R. 475 at 481 at 488. *Goldberg v Ng* (1995) 185 C.L.R. 83. (On the facts, the judgments of the minority may be considered more persuasive.)
[87] [2004] EWCA Crim 1368; [2004] 1 W.L.R. 2932 at [15].

CHAPTER 19

Public Interest Immunity

Origins and basis

Confidentiality is not by itself a ground of immunity from disclosure of information or documents in the course of litigation, whether by a party or by a non-party; but the desirability in the public interest that confidentiality in the relevant subject-matter should be preserved may give rise to public interest immunity.   **19–001**

The origin of this lies in the doctrine of Crown privilege, which is of considerable antiquity. However, the immunity is not a matter of privilege, nor is it confined to the Crown.[1] It is a protection given by the courts to documents and information whose disclosure in legal proceedings would be damaging to the public interest.   **19–002**

The corner-stone of the modern law is *Conway v Rimmer*,[2] in which the House of Lords departed from its own unanimous decision, 25 years earlier,   **19–003**

---

[1] See, e.g. *per* Lord Pearson in *R. v Lewes Justices Ex p. Home Secretary* [1973] A.C. 388 at 406, and *per* Lord Simon in *D. v N.S.P.C.C.* [1978] A.C. 171 at 235H.

[2] [1968] A.C. 910. See, e.g. *Air Canada v Secretary of State for Trade* [1983] 2 A.C. 394, *per* Lord Fraser of Tullybelton at 432.

in the case of *Duncan v Cammell, Laird & Co Ltd*.[3] It is necessary to regard with caution any case pre-dating *Conway v Rimmer*.[4]

Confidentiality and public interest immunity

19-004 Confidentiality is a necessary, but not a sufficient, basis for a claim for public interest immunity. In *Alfred Crompton Amusement Machines Ltd v Customs & Excise Commissioners*[5] Lord Cross said:

> " 'Confidentiality' is not a separate head of privilege, but it may be a very material consideration to bear in mind when privilege is claimed on the ground of public interest."

Lord Cross was speaking in the context of a claim for privilege in respect of documents of a confidential nature obtained from third parties, to whom a duty of confidence would be owed. That fact did not of itself make the documents privileged but was highly pertinent. Lord Cross's statement is not to be read as implying that public interest immunity could attach to documents which were not of a confidential character at all.

19-005 The object of a claim for public interest immunity is to prevent a document being placed before the court because its public disclosure would be damaging to the public interest. That cannot apply if the document itself does not warrant being treated as secret, for example because it has already lost all secrecy. So, in *Sankey v Whitlam*[6] Gibbs A.C.J. said:

> " . . . it may be necessary for the proper functioning of the public service to keep secret a document of a particular class, but once the document has been published to the world there no longer exists any reason to deny to the court access to that document, if it provides evidence that is relevant and otherwise admissible."

It would be different if, despite some prior publication, disclosure of the documents would still be capable of causing harm, for example, to national security.[7]

19-006 The additional ingredient which has to be established is that the public interest in preserving the secrecy of a particular document or class of documents overrides the public interest in the administration of justice,

---

[3] [1942] A.C. 624.

[4] Even of *Conway v Rimmer*, it was observed by Lord Keith of Kinkel in *Burmah Oil Co Ltd v Governor and Company of the Bank of England* [1980] 1 A.C. 1090 at 1131 that "no definitive body of binding rules universally applicable to future cases in the field is to be gathered from the speeches delivered".

[5] 1974 A.C. 405 at 433.

[6] [1978] 142 C.L.R. 1 at 45, High Court of Australia.

[7] *Thorburn v Hermon*, The Times, May 14, 1992.

which ordinarily requires that the parties should not be obstructed from placing relevant evidence before the court. As Lord Templeman said in *R. v Chief Constable of West Midlands Police Ex p. Wiley*[8]:

> "A claim to public interest immunity can only be justified if the public interest in preserving the confidentiality of the document outweighs the public interest in securing justice."

Class and contents claims

A common categorisation[9] of claims to immunity was to classify them as either contents claims or class claims. The former asserted that the disclosure of a document was objectionable because the public interest would be damaged by the disclosure of the contents of that particular document. The latter, in practice considerably more common, asserted that the disclosure of a document was objectionable because it belonged to a class of documents whose disclosure would damage the public interest.[10]   **19–007**

It had been said that there is no distinction in principle between a contents claim and a class claim,[11] but in practice class-based claims attracted a particularly high degree of judicial scrutiny. It was not possible, for example, for a class claim in respect of a number of documents to be based upon the administrative burden of checking individual documents to ascertain whether a contents claim could be made in respect of any of them.[12]   **19–008**

Although "the privilege is a narrow one, most sparingly to be exercised",[13] in *D v National Society for the Prevention of Cruelty to Children*[14] Lord Hailsham said: **19–009**

> "The categories of public interest are not closed, and must alter from time to time whether by restriction or extension as social conditions and social legislation develop."

---

[8] [1995] 1 A.C. 274 at 280.
[9] Described in *Burmah Oil Co Ltd v Governor and Company of the Bank of England* [1980] A.C. 1090, by Lord Wilberforce at 1111, as "rough but accepted", and by Lord Scarman at 1143, as "good working, but not logically perfect"; see also the exposition of the categories by Lord Edmund-Davies at 1124. Some dissatisfaction with the categories was expressed by, for example, Lord Hodson in *Conway v Rimmer* [1968] A.C. 910 at 979, and by Lord Keith in *Burmah Oil*, at 1132.
[10] The possibility that such a claim might be valid was denied by MacNaughton J. in *Spigelman v Hocken* (1934) 150 L.T. 256 at 262, but his view must yield to subsequent authority.
[11] In *Conway v Rimmer* [1968] A.C. 910, *per* Lord Morris at 971.
[12] *per* Lord Woolf in *R. v Chief Constable of West Midlands Ex p. Wiley* [1995] 1 A.C. 274 at 293.
[13] *Robinson v State of South Australia* [1931] A.C. 704, PC at 714.
[14] [1978] A.C. 171 at 230.

19–010   In *R. v Chief Constable of West Midlands Police Ex p. Wiley,*[15] however, Lord Woolf, though stating his agreement with Lord Hailsham's dictum, observed that,

> "The recognition of a new *class-based* public interest immunity requires clear and compelling evidence that it is necessary."[16] (Emphasis added.)

19–011   Following the recommendations made in Sir Richard Scott's report on the Matrix Churchill affair, the Attorney General, Sir Nicholas Lyell, entered into a process of consultation as to the approach that the Government should adopt to public interest immunity. In a statement to the House of Commons on December 18, 1996, he announced the adoption of a change in practice:

> "Under the new approach, Ministers will focus directly on the damage that disclosure would cause. The former division into class and contents claims will no longer be applied. Ministers will claim public interest immunity only when it is believed that disclosure of a document would cause real damage or harm to the national interest . . .
>
> It is impossible in advance to describe such damage exhaustively. The damage may relate to the safety of an individual, such as an informant, or to a regulatory process; or it may be damage to international relations caused by the disclosure of confidential diplomatic communications . . .
>
> This new, restrictive approach will require, so far as possible, the way in which disclosure could cause real damage to the public interest to be clearly identified. Public interest immunity certificates will in future set out in greater detail than before both what the document is and what damage its disclosure would be likely to do—unless to do so would itself cause the damage that the certificate aims to prevent. That will allow even closer scrutiny by the court, which is always the final arbiter."

It is suggested that the Government's approach is a sensible one, though there will remain cases in which the reason why it would be against the public interest to disclose a document is, at least in part, because release into the public domain of documents of that *kind* would be damaging (documents disclosing the identity of an informant being an obvious example).

---

[15] [1995] 1 A.C. 274 at 305.
[16] See also *R. v Lewes Justices Ex p. Home Secretary* [1973] A.C. 388 at 412, *per* Lord Salmon—"This immunity should not lightly be extended to any other class of document or information, but its boundaries are not to be regarded as immutably fixed".

Effect of the Human Rights Act 1998

Article 6 of the Convention provides that: **19–012**

> "In the determination of his civil rights and obligations or of any
> criminal charge against him, everyone is entitled to a fair and public
> hearing within a reasonable time by an independent and impartial
> tribunal established by law. Judgment shall be pronounced publicly but
> the press and public may be excluded from all or part of the trial in the
> interest of morals, public order or national security in a democratic
> society, where the interests of juveniles or the protection of the private
> life of the parties so require, or to the extent strictly necessary in the
> opinion of the court in special circumstances where publicity would
> prejudice the interests of justice."

Implicit in the unqualified right to a fair hearing provided by Art.6 are a
number of ancillary rights, including (particularly in the criminal sphere) a
right to disclosure of relevant evidence. These ancillary rights are not
themselves unqualified but are subject to implied limitations, where and to
the extent necessary, in respect of the fundamental rights of others or an
important public interest.[17] As the House of Lords said in *R. v H*[18]:

> "In such circumstances some derogation from the golden rule of full
> disclosure may be justified but such derogation must always be the
> minimum derogation necessary to protect the public interest in ques-
> tion and must never imperil the overall fairness of the trial."

In *R. v Brushett*,[19] the defendant, who had been convicted on 27 charges   **19–013**
of child abuse, contended that his Art.6 rights had been infringed by the
court's refusal to allow him access to documents in the social services files
relating to the complainants. The Court of Appeal dismissed his appeal,
observing that, in the context of the case, it saw no difference in principle
between the English common law and human rights jurisprudence.

Nevertheless, the introduction of the Human Rights Act 1998 has lent   **19–014**
impetus to an already existing process of development in English law, under
which the courts have tended to scrutinise claims to public interest
immunity more critically than before. The Court of Appeal referred in *Chief
Constable of the Greater Manchester Police v McNally*[20] to:

> " . . . a wider jurisprudential move away from near absolute protection
> of various categories of public interest in non-disclosure . . . Now, with

---

[17] *Fitt v United Kingdom* [2000] 30 E.H.R.R. 400; *Brown v Stott* [2003] 1 A.C. 681; *Edwards
and Lewis v UK* [2005] 40 E.H.R.R. 593.
[18] [2004] UKHL 3; [2004] 2 A.C. 134, at [18].
[19] (2001) Crim. L.R. 471.
[20] [2002] EWCA Civ 14, at [21].

the advent of Human Rights to our law, this move has the force of European jurisprudence behind it."

Reasons for immunity

19–015   It is impossible to compile a list of all reasons advanced for immunity, but they include the following:

(1) that disclosure would be prejudicial to national security or foreign relations[21];

(2) that disclosure would create or fan ill-informed or captious public or political criticism of the inner workings of Government,[22] and increase the difficulties of the decision-making process;

(3) that disclosure would impede the flow of information necessary in the public interest, in particular by discouraging candour in communications by or to persons with public responsibilities[23] or by discouraging informants from coming forward[24];

(4) that immunity is required to set a limit on the State's invasion of an individual's privacy.[25]

These reasons have provoked varying degrees of controversy, with the argument based on the encouragement of candour, in particular, being the subject of much judicial scepticism. While it is generally acknowledged that confidentiality may encourage frankness on the part of informants, doubts have often been expressed about the candour argument as applied to public officials or ministers.[26] In *Conway v Rimmer*[27] Lord Reid, in a much quoted passage, said:

"Virtually everyone agrees that Cabinet minutes and the like ought not to be disclosed until such time as they are only of historical interest. But I do not think that many people would give as the reason that

---

[21] e.g. *Burmah Oil Co Ltd v Governor and Company of the Bank of England* [1980] A.C. 1090, *per* Lord Salmon at 1121; *Balfour v Foreign and Commonwealth Office* [1994] 1 W.L.R. 681.

[22] *per* Lord Reid in *Conway v Rimmer* [1968] A.C. 910 at 952.

[23] *Burmah Oil Co Ltd v Governor and Company of the Bank of England* [1980] A.C. 1090, *per* Lord Wilberforce at 1112, and *per* Lord Scarman at 1145.

[24] *D. v N.S.P.C.C.* [1978] A.C. 171, *per* Lord Diplock at 218.

[25] *Re Joseph Hargreaves Ltd* [1900] 1 Ch. 347, as explained by Lord Reid in *Conway v Rimmer* [1968] A.C. 910 at 946F; *Lonrho plc v Fayed (No. 4)* [1994] Q.B. 775 at 787, *per* Bingham M.R.

[26] *Conway v Rimmer* [1968] A.C. 910, *per* Lord Reid at 952, *per* Lord Morris at 957, *per* Lord Pearce at 985 and *per* Lord Upjohn at 994; *Burmah Oil Co Ltd v Governor and Company of the Bank of England* [1980] A.C. 1090, *per* Lord Keith at 1132; *Sankey v Whitlam* (1978) 142 C.L.R. 1, *per* Stephen J. at 63 and *per* Mason J. at 97. But see also *Conway v Rimmer*, *per* Lord Hodson at 974; *Burmah Oil Co Ltd v Governor and Company of the Bank of England*, *per* Lord Wilberforce at 1112; *Air Canada v Secretary of State for Trade* [1983] 2 A.C. 394, *per* Lord Fraser at 433; *Sankey v Whitlam* (1978) 142 C.L.R. 1, *per* Gibbs A.C.J. 40.

[27] [1968] A.C. 910 at 952.

premature disclosure would prevent candour in the Cabinet. To my mind the most important reason is that such disclosure would create or fan ill-formed or captious public or political criticism. The business of government is difficult enough as it is, and no government could contemplate with equanimity the inner workings of the government machine being exposed to the gaze of those ready to criticise without adequate knowledge of the background and perhaps with some axe to grind."

Doubts have in turn been expressed whether the avoidance of "ill-informed or captious criticism" constitutes a satisfactory explanation for the protection of government documents.

In *Commonwealth of Australia v John Fairfax & Sons Ltd*,[28] Mason J. said: **19–016**

" . . . it can scarcely be a relevant detriment to the government that publication of material concerning its actions will merely expose it to public discussion and criticism. It is unacceptable in our democratic society that there should be a restraint on the publication of information relating to government when the only vice of that information is that it enables the public to discuss, review and criticize government action."

Moreover, it might reasonably be said that the problem of ill-informed public criticism of the government is more likely to be cured by a greater degree of openness in the inner workings of government than it is by the withholding of information on grounds of public interest immunity.

It is nevertheless generally agreed that the business of government must be attended by a degree of confidentiality, especially at high level. But if so, what is the basis and how does it explain the immunity that would attach to Cabinet minutes from, say, before the last election? **19–017**

Perhaps the best answer is that given by Mason J. in *Sankey v Whitlam*.[29] After setting out the relevant passage from Lord Reid's speech in *Conway v Rimmer*, he continued: **19–018**

"I agree with his Lordship that the possibility that premature disclosure will result in want of candour in cabinet discussions or in advice given by public servants is so slight that it may be ignored, despite the evidence to the contrary which was apparently given and accepted in *Attorney-General v Cape (Jonathan) Ltd*. I should have thought that the possibility of future publicity would act as a deterrent against advice which is specious or expedient. I also agree with his Lordship that the efficiency of government would be seriously compromised if

---

[28] (1980) 147 C.L.R. 39 at 52, approved in *Att-Gen v Guardian Newspapers Ltd (No. 2)* [1990] 1 A.C. 109, *per* Lord Keith at 258, Lord Griffiths at 270 and Lord Goff at 283. See para.5–005.
[29] (1978) 142 C.L.R. 1 at 97–98.

Cabinet decisions and papers were disclosed whilst they or the topics to which they relate are still current or controversial. But I base this view, not so much on the probability of ill-formed criticism with its inconvenient consequences, as upon the inherent difficulty of decision making if the decision-making processes of cabinet and the materials on which they are based are at risk of premature publication."

Since it is the power and duty of the court, as Lord Reid stated in *Conway v Rimmer*[30]:

"to hold a balance between the public interest, as expressed by a Minister, to withhold certain documents or other evidence, and the public interest in ensuring the proper administration of justice",

it is not bound by any ministerial certificate, although in the exercise of its judgment the court will normally attach considerable, and in some cases (those involving national security being the classic example) conclusive, weight to a ministerial certificate.

19–019   The court's ultimate responsibility was emphasised in *Air Canada v Secretary of State for Trade* by Lord Fraser, with whom Lord Edmund Davies and Lord Templeman agreed, when he said[31]:

"I do not think that even Cabinet minutes are completely immune from disclosure in a case where, for example, the issue in a litigation involves serious misconduct by a Cabinet Minister. Such cases have occurred in Australia (see *Sankey v Whitlam* (1978) 21 A.L.R. 505) and in the United States (see *United States v Nixon* (1974) 418 U.S. 683) but fortunately not in the United Kingdom: see also the New Zealand case of *Environmental Defence Society Inc. v South Pacific Aluminium Ltd (No. 2)* [1981] 1 N.Z.L.R. 153. But while Cabinet documents do not have complete immunity, they are entitled to a high degree of protection from disclosure."

19–020   It should be recognised that the application to the reported authorities of the reasons for immunity listed above[32] is in many cases an exercise in *ex post facto* rationalisation, since claims to Crown privilege in the past were rarely scrutinised as carefully as they are today. It was often successfully asserted on behalf of the Crown that production of specified documents would be contrary to the public interest, without any further explanation. Nevertheless, the categories remain a convenient basis for the examination of the classes of documents for which claims to immunity have been made.

---

[30] [1968] A.C. 910 at 952.
[31] [1982] A.C. 394 at 432.
[32] See para.19–015, above.

Documents whose disclosure would be prejudicial to national security or foreign relations

A question of national security or foreign relations is recognised as the most **19–021**
compelling basis for a claim to public interest immunity, whether the claim
is made on a class or a contents basis. In *Balfour v Foreign and Commonwealth Office*,[33] a former employee of the Foreign Office claimed that
he had been unfairly dismissed by his former employer. In proceedings
before an industrial tribunal, he sought discovery of certain documents from
the Foreign Office. The Foreign Secretary and Home Secretary each signed
certificates raising objection to:

> "the production of any evidence, documentary or otherwise, about the
> organisation of the security and intelligence services, their theatres of
> operation or their methods. Express reference was made to foreign
> powers and terrorist organisations and the threat to national security of
> disclosure."[34]

The certificates were held to be conclusive and Russell L.J. cited the dictum
of Lord Diplock in *Council of Civil Service Unions v Minister for the Civil
Service*[35]:

> "National security is the responsibility of the executive government;
> what action is needed to protect its interests is, as the cases cited by my
> learned friend, Lord Roskill, establish and common sense itself dictates,
> a matter upon which those upon whom the responsibility rests, and not
> the courts of justice, must have the last word. It is par excellence a non-
> justiciable question. The judicial process is totally inept to deal with the
> sort of problems which it involves."

National security, or the public safety, may also be one justification for the
immunity traditionally bestowed upon "documents pertaining to the general administration of the naval, military and air force services".[36] However,
most of the cases are more immediately explicable by reference to one of the
other categories dealt with below.

The protection of specific military secrets clearly falls within the national **19–022**
security category. Although the House of Lords departed in *Conway v
Rimmer* from their decision in *Duncan v Cammell, Laird & Co*,[37] their
Lordships were in no doubt that the decision in that case had been right on
its facts.

---

[33] [1994] 1 W.L.R. 681.
[34] *ibid.* at 684.
[35] [1985] A.C. 374 at 412.
[36] *Conway v Rimmer* [1968] A.C. 910, *per* Lord Upjohn at 993.
[37] [1942] A.C. 624.

19–023   The case arose from the loss of 99 lives at the sinking of the new submarine *Thetis* during trials in Liverpool bay in June 1939. Representatives and dependants of the deceased commenced an action against Cammell, Laird & Co., the makers of the submarine, claiming damages for negligence. The defendants declined to produce a number of documents included in their discovery, on the basis that the First Lord of the Admiralty objected to their production. These documents included the contract for the *Thetis*, correspondence relating to the vessel's trim, reports as to the submarine's condition when raised, various plans and specifications and the notebook of a foreman painter employed by the defendants. The First Lord duly swore an affidavit stating that in his opinion the disclosure of these documents to any person would be injurious to the public interest and his certificate was held to be conclusive.

19–024   Similar protection is given to diplomatic secrets and confidential communications between British authorities and other states. In *R. v Governor of Brixton Prison Ex p. Osman*,[38] Osman, who had been committed to custody to await return to Hong Kong to face criminal charges, applied for a writ of *habeas corpus* and sought discovery of various Government documents. In his certificate claiming immunity, the Minister of State for Foreign and Commonwealth Affairs divided them into three categories, including:

> "(A) Communications exchanged between ministers and/or officials of the Crown either in the United Kingdom or overseas concerning matters of policy, advice, judgment, action or prospective action within government. (B) Communications or reports of communications between British authorities (both in the United Kingdom and Hong Kong) and another sovereign state concerning matters of policy, advice, judgment, action or prospective action within government . . . ."[39]

The reasons given by the Minister for his belief that production of these documents would be detrimental to foreign relations were set out at length by Mann L.J., who observed[40] that:

> "It does not seem to be in dispute that the documents in categories (A) and (B) are documents eligible for a public interest claim. Were there such a dispute it could be given its quietus by examining the speeches of Lord Upjohn in *Conway v Rimmer* [1968] A.C. 910, 933, of Lord Salmon in *Burmah Oil Co. Ltd v Governor and Company of the Bank of England* [1980] A.C. 1090, 1121C and of Lord Keith of Kinkel and Lord Scarman in the same case at pp. 1132B and 1144G."

[38] [1991] 1 W.L.R. 281.
[39] *ibid.* at 286.
[40] *ibid.* at 287.

Documents whose disclosure would expose the inner workings of government to ill-informed and captious criticism and increase the difficulties of the decision-making process

It has been suggested above that mere avoidance of ill-informed criticism is **19–025** no satisfactory basis for a claim for immunity, and that the real question is whether disclosure would be sufficiently detrimental to the decision-making process to justify a claim for immunity. There is a great difference between documents relating to high affairs of state and more mundane communications between officials.

In *Re Grosvenor Hotel, London (No. 2)*,[41] Salmon L.J. said: **19–026**

"Again there may be classes of documents such as communications at a very high level, e.g., cabinet minutes, minutes of discussions between heads of departments, despatches from ambassadors abroad and the like which any right-minded person would say clearly ought not to be subject to protection in an action."

He continued:

"I can see no reason, unless compelled by authority to do so, for extending this privilege to routine communications between one civil servant and another."

This ground of public interest immunity can be used to protect only documents created for purposes of state, which in this context must mean national government rather than the broader apparatus referred to as the state by Lord Simon in *D. v National Society for the Prevention of Cruelty to Children*[42]:

"The state is the whole organisation of the body politic for supreme civil rule and government—the whole political organisation which is the basis of the civil government. As such it certainly extends to local—and, as I think, also statutory—bodies in so far as they are exercising autonomous rule."

Lord Reid observed in *Conway v Rimmer*[43]:   **19–027**

"There are now many large public bodies, such as British Railways and the National Coal Board, the proper and efficient functioning of which is very necessary for many reasons including the safety of the public. The Attorney-General made it clear that Crown privilege is not and

[41] [1965] 1 Ch. 1210 at 1258–1259; cited by Lord Morris in *Conway v Rimmer* [1968] A.C. 910 at 973.
[42] [1978] A.C. 171 at 236.
[43] [1968] A.C. 910 at 941.

cannot be invoked to prevent disclosure of similar documents made by them or their servants even if it were said that this is required for the proper and efficient functioning of that public service."

It is equally difficult to imagine a court upholding a class-based claim for immunity on the ground that it was necessary to protect the decision-making processes of local government or other statutory autonomous bodies.

19–028   In *R. v Chief Constable of West Midlands Police Ex p. Wiley*[44] Lord Woolf said of the decision in *D v National Society for the Prevention of Cruelty to Children*:

> "The significance of that case is that it made clear that the immunity does not only exist to protect the effective functioning of departments or organs of central government or the police, but also could protect the effective functioning of an organisation such as the NSPCC which was authorised under an Act of Parliament to bring legal proceedings for the welfare of children."

But the public interest recognised in that case was the public interest in protecting the free flow of information about child abuse *to* the NSPCC, rather than the public interest in protecting the internal decision-making processes *of* the NSPCC.

19–029   The scope of this category of immunity is particularly liable to change over time. Lord Keith noted in *Burmah Oil Co Ltd v Governor and Company of the Bank of England*,[45] that:

> "There can be discerned in modern times a trend towards more open governmental methods than were prevalent in the past. No doubt it is for Parliament and not for courts of law to say how far that trend should go."

It should not be assumed that the trend is irreversible. Lord Pearce commented in *Conway v Rimmer*[46]:

> "In theory any general legal definition of the balance between individual justice in one scale and the safety and well-being of the state in the other scale, should be unaffected by the dangerous times in which it is uttered. But in practice the flame of individual right and justice must burn more palely when it is ringed by the more dramatic light of bombed buildings. And the human mind cannot but be affected subconsciously, even in generality of definition, by such a contrast since

---

[44] [1995] 1 A.C. 274 at 291.
[45] [1980] A.C. 1090 at 1134. See also *per* Mason J. in *The Commonwealth of Australia v John Fairfax & Sons Ltd* (1980) 147 C.L.R. 39, at 52, cited above at para.5–005.
[46] [1968] A.C. 910 at 982.

it is certainly a matter which ought to influence the particular decision in the case."

Documents whose disclosure would discourage the free flow of information communicated for official purposes

Some kinds of official reports and records attract immunity. The scope of this category must now be regarded as uncertain in the light of the numerous judgments rejecting arguments that immunity is required to encourage candour in official reports; in recent years, its extent has certainly been greatly reduced.[47]

19–030

In *Ankin v London and North Eastern Railway Company*,[48] objection was successfully made to the production of a report furnished by the defendant to the Ministry of Transport pursuant to s.6 of the Railways Regulation Act 1871 following a railway accident. The case would unquestionably be decided differently today. Lord Reid said in *Conway v Rimmer*[49]:

19–031

> "*Ankin*'s case is a good example of what happens if the courts abandon all control of this matter. It was surely far fetched and indeed insulting to the managements of railway companies to suggest that in performing their statutory duty they might withhold information from the Minister because it might be disclosed later in legal proceedings."

The armed forces

The earlier cases often involved military matters and include claims to immunity successfully made for the minutes and proceedings of Army courts of enquiry,[50] admiralty collision reports[51] and naval and military medical records.[52] These cases should be regarded with particular caution in the light of *Conway v Rimmer* and more recent case-law. In *Barrett v Ministry of Defence*,[53] a naval airman died after a bout of heavy drinking. His widow commenced proceedings against the Ministry of Defence claiming damages for negligence and, prior to the service of a statement of claim, sought discovery of the report of a naval board of enquiry that had been convened to enquire into her husband's death.

19–032

---

[47] The private deliberations of an employer's disciplinary and appeal panel were held inadmissable in unfair dismissal proceedings in *Amwell View School Governors v Dogherty* E.A.T., September 15, 2006.
[48] [1930] 1 K.B. 527.
[49] [1968] A.C. 910 at 947.
[50] *Home v Bentinck* (1820) 2 Brod. & B. 130, at 162ff.; *Beatson v Skene* (1860) 5 H. & N. 838; *Dawkins v Lord Rokeby* (1873) L.R. 8 Q.B. 255 at 270. A claim for immunity was refused in *Dickson v The Earl of Wilton* (1859) 1 F. & F. 419.
[51] *The Bellerophon* (1875) 44 L.J.Adm. (N.S.) 5.
[52] *Gain v Gain* [1961] 1 W.L.R. 1469; *Anthony v Anthony* (1919) 35 T.L.R. 559.
[53] *The Times*, January 24, 1990.

19–033   On appeal, Popplewell J. refused her application but considered *obiter* a claim to immunity in respect of the report, which was made by the Ministry of Defence and backed by ministerial certificate. Dismissing this claim, he held that the absence of the alleged immunity would affect neither the candour of witnesses at future boards of enquiry nor the morale, discipline or safety of those in the service.

19–034   Although it appears from *Barrett* that there is no longer any blanket immunity in respect of all military boards of enquiry, it can easily be seen that different considerations might govern, on the one hand, an investigation into the death of an individual and, on the other hand, an investigation into matters of, say, potential technical significance. On the basis of *Barrett*, however, it appears that protection of the latter would result not so much from the need for candour as from considerations of national security.

Child care records

19–035   Child care records kept by local authorities have been held to be immune from production, even at the suit of their subject. The rationale of this is not the right of the child to confidentiality, but the necessity of such immunity if the child care services are to function properly. The leading authorities are the Court of Appeal's decisions in *Re D (Infants)*[54] and *Gaskin v Liverpool City Council*,[55] though the nature of the principle expressed in these cases has subsequently been the source of some doubts in the Court of Appeal.[56]

19–036   *Re D (Infants)* was cited in all the speeches given in the House of Lords in *D v NSPCC*,[57] without any expression of apparent disapproval or reservation, and in *Re G (A Minor) (Social Worker: Disclosure)*[58] Butler-Sloss L.J. observed:

> "There is a long line of authority that social service departments' case records and files are not produced on an application for discovery and are exempt from disclosure in court proceedings unless a judge rules to the contrary."

Official medical records

19–037   Official medical records have in the past been protected by the courts. For example, a doctor's report made to the Home Office after the exhumation

---

[54] [1970] 1 W.L.R. 599.
[55] [1980] 1 W.L.R. 1549.
[56] See, e.g., *per* Scarman LJ in *D v N.S.P.C.C.* [1978] A.C. 171 at 198, *per* Ackner L.J. in *Campbell v Tameside Metropolitan Borough Council* [1982] 1 Q.B. 1065 and *per* Ralph Gibson L.J. in *Brown v Matthew* [1990] 1 Ch. 662 at 675.
[57] [1978] A.C. 171.
[58] [1996] 1 W.L.R. 1407 at 1411.

and examination of a murder victim was held to be immune from production in *Williams v Star Newspaper Company Ltd.*[59]

Similarly, medical reports on the mental condition of a man confined in   **19–038**
the hospital wing of a prison were held to be immune from production in an action brought against the Home Office by another prisoner attacked and injured by that man.[60] However, the case caused both Devlin J. and the Court of Appeal great concern, and it is likely that it would be decided differently today.[61]

A better guide to the modern approach is provided by *R. v Secretary of*   **19–039**
State for the Home Department Ex p. Benson.[62] It was held that no immunity attached to a medical report produced in connection with the Home Secretary's consideration of the length of the term to be served by a person sentenced to life imprisonment, when production of the report was sought by its subject. The argument, advanced to protect the report of a prison doctor, that liability to production would result in a lack of candour was rejected.

The police

Police reports have been the subject of a number of decisions relating to   **19–040**
public interest immunity. As Lord Reid said in *Conway v Rimmer*[63]:

> "The position of the police is peculiar. They are not servants of the Crown and they do not take orders from the Government. But they are carrying out an essential function of government, and various Crown rights, privileges and exemptions have been held to apply to them."

Here too, the law has developed over the years. Reports on road traffic accidents produced by the police were held to be immune from disclosure in civil proceedings in the Scottish case of *McKie v The Western Scottish Motor Traction Co. Ltd.*[64] Earlier, in England, Macnaghten J. had rejected in *Spigelman v Hocken*[65] a class claim advanced in respect of a statement made to a police officer after a road accident by one of the defendants who was involved in the accident, but observed that there might be grave objections in the public interest to producing the police officer's actual report.

---

[59] (1908) 24 T.L.R. 297. Darling J. apparently made his decision on the strength of the existence of the minister's certificate alone, without consideration of the grounds for it. By way of contrast, see *Leigh v Gladstone* (1909) 26 T.L.R. 139: Lord Alvestone C.J. held that a prison doctor's report to the prison's Governor was not immune from production, though it does not appear that the objection to production in this case was backed by a ministerial certificate.
[60] *Ellis v Home Office* [1953] 2 Q.B. 135.
[61] See the comments of Lord Reid, in *Conway v Rimmer* [1968] A.C. 910 at 948; compare, also, the result in *Campbell v Tameside Metropolitan Borough Council* [1982] 1 Q.B. 1065.
[62] (Unreported, November 1, 1988); cited in *R. v Secretary of State for the Home Department Ex p. Duggan* [1994] 3 All E.R. 277 at 285.
[63] [1968] A.C. 910 at 953.
[64] (1952) S.C. 206.
[65] (1933) 150 L.T. 256.

19–041   In *Conway v Rimmer*,[66] however, Lord Pearce said:

> "One may perhaps take police reports of accidents as an extreme
> example of the malaise that can be produced by a total acceptance of
> the theory that all documents should be protected whenever the
> Minister says so on the basis that candour will be injured if there is
> production . . . When one considers the large public interest in a just
> decision of road accident cases, and the absence of any possible
> corresponding injury to the candour of police reports on accident cases,
> one realises to what a complete lack of common sense a general blanket
> protection of wide classes may lead. And it would be an equal
> departure from common sense to suppose that no great public injury
> could result from disclosure of police reports concerning their war on
> really serious crime."

In fact, police reports on accidents on the road or accidents on government
premises, or involving government employees, were among categories of
documents in respect of which the Lord Chancellor announced in a
statement in the House of Lords in 1956 that class-based immunity would
no longer be claimed.[67]

19–042   *Conway v Rimmer* itself concerned the status of police reports. A former
probationary police constable sued a police superintendent for damages for
malicious prosecution. The superintendent had been instrumental in bringing a charge of larceny against the plaintiff of which the plaintiff had been
acquitted. Shortly after his acquittal, the plaintiff had been dismissed. The
plaintiff sought discovery of five confidential police reports, of which four
were standard probationary or training reports and one was a report
submitted by the defendant to his chief constable for submission to the
Director of Public Prosecutions. The defendant was willing to release these
documents, but the Home Secretary swore an affidavit objecting to their
production.

19–043   The speeches in the House of Lords focused primarily on the duties and
powers of a judge when faced with a ministerial certificate claiming
immunity, and there was relatively little direct consideration of the question
whether the documents in question were in a class that prima facie attacted
immunity. The majority view appears to have been that the class claim in
respect of the probationary reports clearly failed, but that the class claim
in respect of the report to the chief constable might have more substance in
it.[68]

19–044   In *Evans v Chief Constable of Surrey*,[69] the plaintiff alleged wrongful
arrest and false imprisonment by the police following the murder of one of

---

[66] [1968] A.C. 910 at 985–986.
[67] See also the observations of Dillon L.J. in *Marcel v Commissioner of Police of the Metropolis*
[1992] Ch. 225 at 256E–F.
[68] See *per* Lord Reid at 954, Lord Morris at 972, Lord Hodson at 980, Lord Pearce at 988–989
and Lord Upjohn at 996.
[69] [1988] 1 Q.B. 588.

his friends. The plaintiff sought an order for the production of a report made by the police to the Director of Public Prosecutions, on the strength of which the Director of Public Prosecutions had advised that there was a prima facie case against the plaintiff and that he should be charged with the murder. The Attorney-General intervened and certified that it was in the public interest that the report should not be disclosed.

Wood J. held that the plaintiff had not shown that the discovery sought **19–045** was relevant to his case, but he added[70]:

> "It seems to me important, and very important in the functioning of the criminal process of prosecution, that there should be freedom of communication between police forces around the country and the Director of Public Prosecutions in seeking his legal advice without fear that those documents will become subject to inspection, analysis and detailed investigation at some later stage . . . I find the arguments in the Attorney-General's certificate to be convincing."

There is an obvious distinction between a police road accident report, which will be largely factual and will contain names and addresses of witnesses and what they said to the police, and communications between the police and the Director of Public Prosecutions containing legal analysis and advice.

A similar distinction has been drawn in the case of complaints made to **19–046** the Police Complaints Authority. Reports on the investigation of such complaints are immune from production in civil proceedings: *Taylor v Anderton*.[71] Witness statements taken in the course of the investigation and transcripts of disciplinary hearings are not immune,[72] though the confidential nature of witness statements taken by the Police Complaints Authority was re-emphasised by the House of Lords in *R. (Green) v Police Complaints Authority*.[73]

R. v Chief Constable of West Midlands Police Ex p. Wiley illustrates the **19–047** risk that public interest immunity can sometimes defeat its own purpose. In a line of cases beginning with *Neilson v Laugharne*[74] the Court of Appeal had previously held that statements taken under the statutory police complaints procedure were immune from production in civil proceedings. In *Wiley* two complainants sought undertakings from the police, before providing statements in support of their complaints, that the files created in the investigation of their complaints would not be used in civil proceedings which the complainants had either issued or intended to issue. On the police refusing to give such undertakings, the complainants challenged the lawfulness of the refusal by proceedings for judicial review. The heart of their

---

[70] [1988] 1 Q.B. 588 at 600.
[71] [1995] 1 W.L.R. 447; see also *O'Sullivan v Commissioner of Police of the Metropolis, The Times*, July 3, 1995.
[72] *R. v Chief Constable of West Midlands Police Ex p. Wiley* [1995] 1 A.C. 274.
[73] [2004] UKHL 6; [2004] 1 W.L.R. 725, *per* Lord Rodger of Earlsferry at [73].
[74] [1981] Q.B. 736.

complaint was that since, under *Neilson*, they would be unable to make use in the civil proceedings of information obtained by the police in the complaint investigations, the police should be put in a reciprocal position as regards information supplied by the complainants for the purpose of the complaint proceedings. The House of Lords held that *Neilson* and the cases that followed it had been wrongly decided. Lord Woolf observed[75] that the applicants' non co-operation in the complaints procedure was the direct result of the immunity recognised in *Neilson*, contrary to the very object which it was designed to achieve.

Financial regulator

19–048 *Wiley* was applied by Arden J. in *Kaufmann v Credit Lyonnais Bank*.[76] In this case, the plaintiff sought an order for the production of confidential reports, which had been made voluntarily on behalf of the defendant to the Security and Futures Authority ("the SFA"), its regulator for the purposes of the Financial Services Act 1986, together with assorted correspondence with the SFA. The defendant resisted the plaintiff's application, and an assertion of public interest immunity in respect of the documents was made both by the SFA and by the Bank of England, which had received copies of the documents in its capacity as the supervisory board of the defendant as a banking institution.

19–049 The claim to public interest immunity was class-based and the class was defined as documents containing:

> "information which was (i) disclosed to a regulator voluntarily and in confidence (ii) other than as a matter of routine (iii) brought into being for the purpose of enabling the regulator more effectively to discharge its functions or duties (iv) save where the disclosure of that information by the regulator was necessary for the proper performance of its functions and duties."

Arden J. declined to accept this class-based claim, observing:

> "Given the object of the 1986 Act is, so far as material, the protection of investors, the need for a class based immunity claim to public interest immunity which would result in the withholding of information from investors must in my judgment be clearly demonstrated."

Informants

19–050 In some circumstances, not only reports by officials, but also communications made to officials may attract immunity. The most prominent example of this is the immunity attaching to documents whose disclosure would

---

[75] [1995] 1 A.C. 274 at 305.
[76] *The Times*, February 1, 1995.

identify informants. This category is of very long standing. In *Home v Bentinck*,[77] Dallas C.J. said:

> "It is agreed, that there are a number of cases of a particular description, in which, for reasons of state and policy, information is not permitted to be disclosed. To begin with the ordinary cases, and those of a common description in the courts of justice. In these courts, for reasons of public policy, persons are not to be asked the names of those from whom they receive information as to the frauds on the revenue. In all the trials for high treason of late years, the same course has been adopted; and, if parties were willing to disclose the sources of their information, they would not be suffered to do it by the judges."[78]

In *Marks v Beyfus*[79] the plaintiff alleged that the defendants had maliciously conspired to have groundless criminal charges brought against him. The plaintiff called as a witness the Director of Public Prosecutions, who said in evidence that the prosecution had been instituted by himself and not the defendants. He had initiated it upon receipt of a written statement, but he declined to produce the statement or to reveal the identity of its author.　**19–051**

The Court of Appeal held that he had acted correctly. Lord Esher M.R. affirmed the rule that in a public prosecution a witness could not be asked (or permitted, even if willing, to answer) questions tending to disclose the informant, whether the informant was himself or a third person, but he added the important *caveat*:　**19–052**

> "I do not say it is a rule which can never be departed from; if upon the trial of a prisoner the judge should be of opinion that the disclosure of the name of the informant is necessary or right in order to shew the prisoner's innocence, then one public policy is in conflict with another public policy, and that which says that an innocent man is not to be condemned when his innocence can be proved is the policy that must prevail."[80]

In *R. v Keane*[81] the Court of Appeal observed that this passage was not a departure from, but an example of, the balancing exercise required where the application of public interest immunity would result in the withholding of relevant material in a criminal case. The court added:　**19–053**

> "If the disputed material may prove the defendant's innocence or avoid a miscarriage of justice, then the balance comes down resoundingly in favour of disclosing it."[82]

---

[77] (1820) 2 Brod. & B. 130.
[78] (1820) 2 Brod. & B. 130 at 162.
[79] (1890) 25 Q.B.D. 494.
[80] *ibid.* at 498.
[81] [1994] 1 W.L.R. 746.
[82] *ibid.* at 751–752.

The Court of Appeal has also warned of the need for careful scrutiny of the nature of the material and its potential significance to the defendant's case before concluding whether its non-disclosure might result in a miscarriage. In *R. v Turner*,[83] it was said:

> "We wish to alert judges to the need to scrutinise applications for disclosure of details about informants with very great care. They will need to be astute to see that assertions of a need to know such details, because they are essential to the running of the defence, are justified. If they are not so justified, then the judge will need to adopt a robust approach in declining to order disclosure. Clearly, there is a distinction between cases in which the circumstances raise no reasonable possibility that information about the informant will bear upon the issues and cases where it will. Again, there will be cases where the informant is an informant and no more; other cases where he may have participated in the events constituting, surrounding, or following the crime. Even when the informant has participated, the judge will need to consider whether his role so impinges on an issue of interest to the defence, present or potential, as to make disclosure necessary."

19–054   It would be an affront to the most basic principles of liberty that the interests of the general public could in any circumstances justify a person being wrongly convicted of a criminal offence, or that the doctrine of public interest immunity should ever be used in such a way as to have that effect. The House of Lords has repeatedly emphasised[84] that it is:

> " ... axiomatic that a person charged with having committed a criminal offence should receive a fair trial and that, if he cannot be tried fairly for that offence, he should not be tried for it at all."

However, it is not in the context of criminal cases alone that the public interest in maintaining the anonymity of an informant may yield to other considerations. In *Chief Constable of the Greater Manchester Police v McNally*,[85] a civil action against the police, the Court of Appeal rejected a submission that, as a matter of law, the public interest in the protection of informers should prevail over any countervailing interest, save where the party seeking disclosure was at risk of his liberty, or where the informer had consented to disclosure or there was some other exceptional circumstance, such as a threat to his safety. Holding that the judge at first instance had been entitled to balance the conflicting interests in the manner that she did, the court ordered that the Chief Constable should state whether or not an identified individual witness was a police informant. In doing so, it regarded as significant the fact that the scope for protecting the alleged informer was

---

[83] [1995] 1 W.L.R. 264 at 267.
[84] Most recently in *R. v H* [2004] UKHL 3; [2004] 2 A.C. 134 at [10].
[85] [2002] EWCA Civ 14.

limited by the fact that both sides knew who he was and the claimant believed, rightly or wrongly, that he was an informer.

Extension of the immunity of informants

The rule protecting informants in criminal cases has been extended by **19–055** analogy to other fields. In *R. v Lewes Justices Ex p. Secretary of State for Home Department*,[86] it was held by the House of Lords to apply to persons supplying information to the Gaming Board when it was considering whether to grant a gaming licence. Lord Salmon said[87]:

> "When one considers the grievous social ills which will undoubtedly be caused by gaming clubs if they get into the wrong hands, it is obviously of the greatest public importance that the law should give the board all its support to ensure that this does not occur. In my view, any document or information that comes to the board from whatever source and by whatever means should be immune from discovery. It is only thus that the board will obtain all the material it requires in order to carry out its task efficiently. Unless this immunity exists many persons, reputable or disreputable, would be discouraged from communicating all they know to the board."

This last sentence shows that the need to protect sources of information is not confined to cases where the moral fibre of potential informants is questionable. Nor indeed is it confined to cases where sources require protection from a possible threat posed by underworld elements.

In *D v National Society for the Prevention of Cruelty to Children*,[88] the **19–056** rule was applied in relation to an informant who reported to the defendants that the plaintiff was beating her child. Lord Diplock said:

> "I would extend to those who give information about neglect or ill-treatment of children to a local authority or the N.S.P.C.C. a similar immunity from disclosure of their identity in legal proceedings to that which the law accords to police informers. The public interests served by preserving the anonymity of both classes of informants are analogous; they are of no less weight in the case of the former than in that of the latter class, and in my judgment are of greater weight than in the case of informers of the Gaming Board to whom immunity from disclosure of their identity has recently been extended by this House."[89]

---

[86] [1973] A.C. 388.
[87] *ibid.* at 413.
[88] [1978] A.C. 171.
[89] *ibid.* at 219.

19–057   Documents created for the purpose of a private inquiry established by the Secretary of State for Foreign and Commonwealth Affairs, whose aim was to investigate the continuing supply of oil into Rhodesia notwithstanding the imposition of sanctions, were held to be immune by the House of Lords in *Lonrho Ltd v Shell Petroleum Co Ltd*.[90] Lord Diplock, giving the only speech, said[91]:

> "Even without the Minister's certificate I should not have needed evidence to satisfy me that the likelihood of success of an inquiry of this kind in discovering the truth as to what happened is greatly facilitated if those persons who know what happened come forward to volunteer information rather than waiting to be identified by the inquiry itself as likely to possess relevant information and having it extracted from them by question and answer. Nor would I need any evidence to satisfy me that without an assurance of complete confidentiality information is less likely to be volunteered; particularly where the inquiry is directed to matters that are the subject matter of a pending civil action to which the possessor of the information is a defendant."

The same rule has been applied in relation to persons providing information to the Audit Commission (which has statutory responsibilities with regard to the auditing of local government expenditure) about alleged wasted expenditure by a local authority.[92]

Documents whose disclosure would be oppressive

19–058   *Re Joseph Hargreaves Ltd*[93] concerned a summons for discovery under s.115 of the Companies Act 1862. The liquidators of an insolvent company sought to recover damages from the directors and auditors of the company. The summons was served on the local tax surveyor, requiring him to produce balance sheets submitted by the company. The Inland Revenue objected to production of the documents, and its objection was upheld by Wright J. and the Court of Appeal.

19–059   Lord Reid, commenting on the case in *Conway v Rimmer*,[94] observed:

> "If the state insists on a man disclosing his private affairs for a particular purpose it requires a very strong case to justify that disclosure being used for other purposes."

Substantial extensions in the state's powers to compel the production of information have caused the courts on a number of occasions to consider

---

[90] [1980] 1 W.L.R. 627.
[91] *ibid.* at 637.
[92] *Bookbinder v Tebbit (No. 2)* [1992] 1 W.L.R. 217.
[93] [1900] 1 Ch. 347.
[94] [1968] A.C. 910 at 946.

whether a document thereby obtained is immune from disclosure by the recipient to anyone else for any extraneous purpose ("the compulsion principle"). As Robert Walker J. observed in *Re Atlantic Computers plc*[95]:

> "The extension of statutory powers of investigation (both in their scope and the frequency of their exercise) in response to successive financial scandals has in the last decade produced a large number of important decisions of the High Court, the Court of Appeal and the House of Lords, and some of these important decisions are not easily understood or reconciled."

Some of those decisions relate to the privilege against self-incrimination, which is recognised both by the English common law and by European human rights jurisprudence; that privilege falls outside the scope of this book. But others relate to an immunity arising where self-incrimination is not in issue.

The compulsion principle as a head of public interest immunity

One issue not yet clearly resolved is the extent to which the compulsion principle is still properly to be regarded as giving rise to a head of public interest immunity at all. The proposition that tax documents provided to the Inland Revenue attract public interest immunity in the hands of the Inland Revenue was accepted by the majority of the Court of Appeal (Sir Thomas Bingham M.R. and Leggatt L.J.) in *Lonrho plc v Fayed (No. 4)*.[96] However, Leggatt L.J. made it clear that his acceptance of the proposition was based on authority, rather than principle, and Roch L.J. rejected the proposition (while acknowledging that the Inland Revenue would owe a duty of confidence in relation to the documents in its possession). The proposition was re-affirmed by the Privy Council (obiter) on appeal from the High Court of Justice of the Isle of Man in *Mount Murray Country Club Ltd v Macleod*.[97]

19–060

However, the Court of Appeal in *Lonrho plc v Fayed (No. 4)* rejected an argument that, because tax documents were protected in the hands of the Inland Revenue, it followed that they must also be protected in the hands of the taxpayer. (The plaintiff in an action for damages for conspiracy obtained an order for discovery of financial documents, including tax documents. The defendants appealed, arguing that public interest immunity would attach to the documents in the hands of the Inland Revenue and must also attach to them in the hands of the taxpayer.) Sir Thomas Bingham said[98]:

19–061

---

[95] [1998] B.C.C. 200, at 211.
[96] [1994] Q.B. 775.
[97] [2003] UKPC 53; (2003) STC 1525 at [33].
[98] *Lonrho plc v Fayed (No. 4)* [1994] Q.B. 775 at 788–789.

"There are some fields in which, if immunity covers a document in the hands of party A, it would be absurd to order production of a copy in the hands of B or to permit oral evidence of the contents of the document by C. In fields such as national security or the conduct of international relations, production of B's copy or the admission of C's evidence would injure the very public interest which the immunity exists to protect. But it does not follow that that need be so in all fields. It all depends on the facet of the public interest which is in question. Mr Sumption was, I think, right to pose the question: what is for present purposes the relevant public policy?

The answer to that question must be that which Lord Reid gave in commenting on *Re Joseph Hargreaves Ltd* [1900] 1 Ch. 347. The state must not, backed by compulsory powers, obtain information from the citizen for one purpose and use that information for another. It does not matter whether this is seen as a principle of good administration or statutory construction or ordinary morality or all three. That is the ratio which Lord Reid gave, as I understand him, and I do not think it bears on whether the taxpayer himself can be required to produce the documents or not."

He accordingly held that there was no public interest which entitled the defendants to claim immunity for the tax documents in their possession.

19–062   In *Wallace Smith Trust Co. Ltd v Deloitte Haskins & Sells*,[99] Simon Brown L.J. was prepared to assume ("as this court's decision in *Lonrho plc v Fayed (No. 4)* . . . strongly suggests") that the transcripts and tapes of interviews carried out by the Serious Fraud Office under its powers pursuant to s.2 of the Criminal Justice Act 1987 would be protected by public interest immunity in the hands of the SFO. He continued, however, that it was plain that the documents were not similarly protected in the hands of the defendants.

19–063   By contrast, in *Marcel v Commissioner of Police of the Metropolis*[1] the Court of Appeal allowing an appeal against a decision of Sir Nicolas Browne-Wilkinson V.C., held that the police owed a duty of confidentiality towards a citizen from whom documents were seized, but might be required to produce them on subpoena in circumstances where the owners of the seized documents might themselves be required to produce them on subpoena. In those circumstances, no public interest immunity prevented the disclosure from being given.

19–064   It is difficult to see any good reason why different rules should apply to confidential documents seized from a citizen by the police and confidential documents supplied by the citizen to the Inland Revenue under compulsion. In *Re Atlantic Computers plc*,[2] Robert Walker J., considered, obiter, the compulsion principle. Having observed that there had recently been a major shift in the government's approach to public interest immunity, restricting it

[99] [1997] 1 W.L.R. 257 at 274.
[1] [1992] Ch. 225; see para.3–014, above.
[2] [1998] B.C.C. 200.

"properly so called, to really cogent cases", he distinguished between the compulsion principle and "PII proper", stating[3]:

> "The narrower the scope of PII properly so called, the more frequent and the more difficult will be cases where the compulsion principle, rather than PII properly so called, may be relied on as a ground for resisting production of documents . . . "

He expressed the provisional view that authority was likely to preclude him from regarding the compulsion principle as an obstacle to disclosure.

In *British and Commonwealth Holdings plc v Barclays de Zoete Wedd Ltd*,[4] Neuberger J. ordered that disclosure should be given in civil litigation of transcripts of evidence that had been provided under compulsion to inspectors appointed by the DTI pursuant to s.432 of the Companies Act 1985. He started[5] from the proposition that the transcripts were not the subject of public interest immunity, without expressly setting out his reasoning. He continued: **19–065**

> " . . . one can see a powerful argument for saying that the court should not, save in exceptional circumstances, order disclosure of the transcripts in connection with civil proceedings . . . Support for such a view may be found in the observations of Sir Nicolas Browne-Wilkinson V.C. in *Marcel* . . . Like Robert Walker J. [in *Re Atlantic Computers plc*], however, while I might well have been inclined to give significant weight to what he helpfully called 'the compulsion principle' . . . I believe that that course is not open to me . . . "

Re Atlantic Computers plc and *British and Commonwealth Holdings plc v Barclays de Zoete Wedd Ltd* are both formally reconcilable with *Lonrho v Fayed (No. 4)*, on the basis that in those two cases the information in question was not in the hands of the organisation that had compelled its production. But they are also consistent with the rather different approach of the Court of Appeal in *Marcel*. The terms of Robert Walker J.'s discussion in *Re Atlantic Computers plc* do not encourage a broad view of any immunity arising from the compulsion principle. **19–066**

Whether the courts will develop the compulsion principle as a head of public interest immunity remains to be seen. Each case will require its own examination, but it may be that in this area *Marcel* will be seen in the future as providing more general guidance than *Lonrho plc v Fayed (No. 4)* and that documents obtained by compulsion will generally be regarded as subject to an obligation of confidentiality but not to public interest immunity. **19–067**

---

[3] At 213.
[4] [1999] 1 B.C.L.C. 86.
[5] At 95.

Disclosure for an authorised purpose

19–068 In any event, one significant limitation on any public interest immunity arising out of the compulsion principle is that it will not prevent an organisation from using compulsorily obtained information for a purpose that falls within the class of purposes for which the organisation was entitled to require the information.

19–069 In *Re Arrows*,[6] the House of Lords held that the Serious Fraud Office was entitled under s.2(3) of the Criminal Justice Act 1987 to require the liquidators of a company to provide transcripts and other documents relating to their compulsory examination of an individual under s.236 of the Insolvency Act 1986. Lord Browne-Wilkinson said[7]:

> "The statutory framework ... imposes a wide range of duties on liquidators to report, directly or indirectly, to the D.T.I. and prosecuting authorities cases of suspected criminal and dishonest conduct and to furnish them with all documents and information they may require. Such documents include transcripts of evidence given on a section 236 examination, which transcripts are admissible in evidence. The liquidator cannot be under any duty of confidence which will prevent the performance of these statutory duties."

Lord Browne-Wilkinson expressed the opinion, obiter, that the public interest in ensuring the free flow of information obtained informally under s.235 of the Insolvency Act 1986 was much greater than it was in relation to transcripts of s.236 examinations. However, the Court of Appeal in *R. v Brady*[8] held that the official receiver was entitled to disclose to the Inland Revenue statements obtained by him from the defendant under s.235:

> "Once it is accepted that one of the purposes for which section 235 material is obtained is the investigation of crime it would be entirely anomalous if that material could be used by the DTI for any criminal investigation it might undertake, but not by any other prosecuting authority interested in the same material, unless some elaborate balancing exercise was carried out or the sanction of the court was obtained on notice to the individual."

The nature of the protection afforded by immunity

19–070 In the nineteenth century, it was held that a document either attracted immunity in its entirety or not at all: it was not possible for arguably unobjectionable passages in immune documents to be received in evidence.[9]

---

[6] [1995] 2 A.C. 75.
[7] At 103.
[8] [2004] EWCA Crim 1763; [2004] 1 W.L.R. 3240, at [27].
[9] *per* Ellenborough C.J. in *Anderson v Hamilton* (1816), cited in *Home v Bentinck* (1820) 2 Brod. & B. 130, at 156n; *Stace v Griffith* (1869) L.R. 2 P.C. 420, *per* Lord Chelmsford in the course of argument at 425.

This may have been because the objection to disclosure generally affected every part of the document equally. In any event, it is now accepted that parts of a document may be disclosed while other parts are withheld.[10]

If immunity attaches to a document, its contents are protected from discovery and from production in court. The document's immunity does not necessarily prevent it from being used in other ways by the party in whose hands it is. **19–071**

In *R. v Commissioner of Police of the Metropolis Ex p. Hart-Leverton*,[11] the applicant sought judicial review of the Commissioner's decision to allow documents obtained in the course of a police complaints investigation and disciplinary hearing to be used by police legal advisers for purposes such as advising on evidence and taking statements from witnesses, so as to assist in the preparation of the defence to legal proceedings against the police commenced by the complainant. It was conceded by the Commissioner that the documents could not be used for the purpose of cross-examination. **19–072**

Nolan J. held that the guiding principle of immunity was to ensure that the protected material did not go before the court. There was nothing in the use of the documents by the police or their legal advisers which conflicted with the immunity. This view was departed from by the Court of Appeal in *Halford v Sharples*[12] and *R. v Chief Constable of West Midlands Police Ex p. Wiley*,[13] but its authority was restored by the House of Lords in the latter case.[14] **19–073**

One question is whether the concession made by the Commissioner in *Ex p. Hart-Leverton* was unnecessary: is it possible to use immune documents in cross-examination? In *Alfred Crompton Amusement Machines Ltd v Customs & Excise*,[15] Lord Cross of Chelsea remarked obiter[16] in relation to information for which immunity was claimed that: **19–074**

"No doubt it will form part of the brief delivered to counsel for the commissioners and may help him to probe the appellants' evidence in cross-examination; but counsel will not be able to use it as evidence to controvert anything which the appellants' witnesses may say."

The point was considered in some detail by the House of Lords in *R. v Chief Constable of West Midlands Police Ex p. Wiley*.[17] Lord Woolf, delivering the leading speech, quoted the statement of Lord Cross set out above and observed that his speech on that aspect of the case represented **19–075**

---

[10] See *Burmah Oil Co Ltd v Governor and Company of the Bank of England* [1980] A.C. 1090, *per* Lord Edmund-Davies at 1124; *R. v Chief Constable of West Midlands Police Ex p. Wiley* [1995] 1 A.C. 274, *per* Lord Templeman at 282 and *per* Lord Woolf at 307.
[11] *The Times*, February 6, 1990.
[12] [1992] 1 W.L.R. 736.
[13] [1994] 1 W.L.R. 114.
[14] [1995] 1 A.C. 274.
[15] [1974] A.C. 405.
[16] *ibid.* at 434, cited by Oliver L.J. in *Neilson v Laugharne* [1981] Q.B. 736 at 753.
[17] [1995] 1 A.C. 274 at 301.

the unanimous view of the House of Lords. He also stated as a matter of principle that,[18]

> "In general, the immunity is provided against disclosure of documents or their contents. It is not, at least in the absence of exceptional circumstances, an immunity against the use of knowledge obtained from the documents. It is impractical and artificial to erect barriers between a party and his legal advisers in an attempt to avoid that party having an advantage in the proceedings."

Lord Woolf went on to say that the legal advisers of a party in possession of material which is immune from disclosure should assist the court and the opposing party to mitigate any disadvantage as best they can by disclosing such information as is possible without production of the document; but that, in so far as this is not possible, the courts should not try to create a level playing field by orders of the kind made in that case (i.e. restricting internal use of the document by the party in possession of it).

19–076 It follows from this reasoning that the concession made by the Commissioner in *Ex p. Hart-Leverton* was too broad. He would have been entitled to use the material (even if it had been immune from production) for the purpose of cross-examination, provided that this was not done in such a way as to destroy the object of its immunity (for example, by putting the document to the witness).

19–077 The question has also arisen whether evidence about matters contained in a document, which is the subject of public interest immunity, may be adduced by other means, for example, by producing a copy of the document.

19–078 In many instances, a copy of an immune document will itself be immune, but this is not always the case, as is shown by *Lonrho plc v Fayed (No. 4)*,[19] where Sir Thomas Bingham M.R. observed that it depends in each case on identifying the aspect of the public interest which the immunity is intended to serve.

19–079 If, for example, the reason for the grant of immunity is not that the release of the information would be harmful in itself, but only that the provision of that information from a particular source would be against the public interest, because it would tend to dry up the free flow of information on matters of public importance, there would be no objection to the provision of the same information from another source.

Raising the objection

19–080 A claim to public interest immunity will often be made by ministerial certificate or certificate given by the Permanent Secretary of the relevant

---

[18] [1995] 1 A.C. 274 at 306.
[19] [1994] Q.B. 775 at 788. See para.19–060 above.

government department. However, in the absence of any governmental intervention,[20] an objection to production may be raised either by the holder or the owner of the document of which production is sought, or by any interested person, or by the court of its own motion.[21]

In *Re Barlow Clowes Gilt Managers Ltd*,[22] Millett J., holding that there **19–081** was a public interest in protecting from production the transcripts of interviews carried out by liquidators, observed[23]:

> "If the liquidation of insolvent companies were entrusted to the executive branch of government, the foregoing would be embodied in a certificate by the appropriate minister. As it is entrusted to the judicial branch, the place of the certificate must be taken by the doctrine of judicial notice."

The procedure to be adopted in criminal cases when the prosecution is in **19–082** possession of information which it believes to be immune on the grounds of public interest from disclosure to the defence has been the subject of scrutiny both in Europe and at the highest domestic level.[24] In *R. v H*[25] the House of Lords stated:

> "When any issue of derogation from the golden rule of full disclosure comes before it, the court must address a series of questions.
>
> (1) What is the material which the prosecution seek to withhold? This must be considered by the court in detail.
> (2) Is the material such as may weaken the prosecution case or strengthen that of the defence? If No, disclosure should not be ordered. If Yes, full disclosure should (subject to (3), (4) and (5) below) be ordered.
> (3) Is there a real risk of serious prejudice to an important public interest (and, if so, what) if full disclosure of the material is ordered? If No, full disclosure should be ordered.
> (4) If the answer to (2) and (3) is Yes, can the defendant's interest be protected without disclosure or disclosure be ordered to an extent or in a way which will give adequate protection to the public interest in question and also afford adequate protection to the interests of the defence? . . .
> (5) Do the measures proposed in answer to (4) represent the minimum derogation necessary to protect the public interest in

---

[20] Unless the relevant authority has already taken the decision not to pursue a claim to immunity (see below).
[21] See *Marcel v Commissioner of Police of the Metropolis* [1992] Ch. 225, *per* Dillon L.J. at 253; *R. v Lewes JJ. Ex p. Home Secretary* [1973] A.C. 388, *per* Lord Reid at 400; *Hennessy v Wright* (1888) 21 Q.B.D. 509 at 519 and 521.
[22] [1992] Ch. 208.
[23] *ibid.* at 223.
[24] *Edwards and Lewis v UK* [2003] E.C.H.R. 381; [2004] E.C.H.R. 560; [2005] 40 E.H.R.R. 593; *R. v H* [2004] UKHL 3; [2004] 2 A.C. 134.
[25] [2004] UKHL 3; [2004] 2 A.C. 134 at para.36.

question? If No, the court should order such greater disclosure as will represent the minimum derogation from the golden rule of full disclosure.

(6) If limited disclosure is ordered pursuant to (4) or (5), may the effect be to render the trial process, viewed as a whole, unfair to the defendant? If Yes, then fuller disclosure should be ordered even if this leads or may lead the prosecution to discontinue the proceedings to as to avoid having to make disclosure.

(7) If the answer to (6) when first given is No, does that remain the correct answer as the trial unfolds, evidence is adduced and the defence advanced?"

One of the difficulties facing the court may be that adversarial argument on these questions is impeded by the need to keep the relevant information from the defendant, with the result, for example, that applications are made by the prosecution in the absence of the defendant. In those circumstances, the court is required to take measures to ensure that its procedures counterbalance any difficulties caused to the defendant by the defendant's exclusion.[26] In some circumstances, these measures may extend to the appointment of independent special counsel to act on the defendant's behalf.

19–083   In *R. v H*,[27] the House of Lords warned against making a premature decision to seek the appointment of special counsel in cases where they were not necessary. They said:

" . . . the judge should involve the defence to the maximum extent possible without disclosing that which the general interest requires to be protected but taking full account of the specific defence which is relied on. There will be very few cases indeed in which some measure of disclosure to the defence will not be possible, even if this is confined to the fact that an ex parte application is to be made. If even that information is withheld and if the material to be withheld is of significant help to the defendant, there must be a very serious question whether the prosecution should proceed, since special counsel, even if appointed, cannot then receive any instructions from the defence at all".

19–084   In general, issues of public interest immunity should be dealt with in the proceedings in which they arise, and not by way of an application for injunctive or declaratory relief in ancillary proceedings. Where a summary trial is to be conducted by magistrates who have decided against the defendant on an issue of public interest immunity, the magistrates have a discretion to grant the defendant a hearing before a new bench.[28]

---

[26] *Rowe v UK* (2000) 30 E.H.R.R. 1; *Jasper v UK* (2000) 30 E.H.R.R. 441; *Fitt v UK* (2000) 30 E.H.R.R. 480.
[27] At para.37. See too the discussion of the role of special counsel at para.22.
[28] *R. v South Worcestershire Magistrates Ex p. Lilley*, *The Times*, February 22, 1995, DC.

Waiver

It has often been said that a claim to public interest immunity, in an **19–085** appropriate case, is not a right but a duty, and therefore cannot be waived in the same manner as, for example, legal professional privilege.[29] This statement requires substantial qualification.

First, in cases where the immunity is based upon a duty of confidence **19–086** owed to a person, a waiver of confidence by that person may operate as a negation of the immunity. As Lord Woolf said in *R. v Chief Constable of West Midlands Ex p. Wiley*[30]:

> "If the purpose of the immunity is to obtain the co-operation of an individual to the giving of a statement, I find it difficult to see how that purpose will be undermined if the maker of the statement consents to it being disclosed."

In *Savage v Chief Constable of Hampshire*[31] the plaintiff claimed to be a **19–087** police informer and sought to bring proceedings for payment for information that he had allegedly provided to the police. Judge L.J., who gave the leading judgment in the Court of Appeal, held that:

> " . . . if a police informer wishes personally to sacrifice his own anonymity, he is not precluded from doing so by the automatic application of the principle of public interest immunity at the behest of the relevant police authority."[32]

Judge L.J. commented that the police informer's own wishes were not necessarily conclusive because of the possibility that there was a significant public interest, extraneous to the informer and his safety, that would be damaged by disclosure. There was no evidence that any such consideration applied in that case.

Carnduff v Rock[33] involved a similar claim by a *soi-disant* police **19–088** informer. On this occasion, however, the majority of the Court of Appeal (Laws and Jonathan Parker L.JJ.) struck out the claim, holding that it was inevitable from the issues in the case that the proposed litigation would result in the disclosure of information harmful to the public interest. Waller L.J. dissented, suggesting that there should be a trial of the preliminary issue whether the contract alleged by the plaintiff had existed. If so,

---

[29] See, e.g., *D v N.S.P.C.C.* [1978] A.C. 171, *per* Lord Simon at 234; *R. v Lewes JJ.* [1973] A.C. 388, *per* Lord Salmon at 412; *Re S and W (Minors) (Confidential Reports)* (1983) 4 F.L.R. 290 *per* Eveleigh L.J. at 292; *Makanjuola v Commissioner of Police of the Metropolis* [1992] 3 All E.R. 617, *per* Bingham L.J. at 623.

[30] [1995] 1 A.C. 274, *per* Lord Woolf at 299. See also *Lonrho plc. v Fayed (No. 4)* [1994] Q.B. 775, *per* Sir Thomas Bingham M.R. at 786F, and *Campbell v Tameside Metropolitan Borough Council* [1982] 1 Q.B. 1065, *per* Lord Denning M.R. at 1073.

[31] [1997] 1 W.L.R. 1061.

[32] At 1067.

[33] [2001] EWCA Civ 680; [2001] 1 W.L.R. 1786.

"The court should then see whether there is machinery available to enable the questions that will arise thereafter to be tried fairly. I believe that machinery should and would if necessary be found, because it would not seem to me to be right in those circumstances that the police should simply be released from a binding contract that on this assumption they have made with their eyes open."[34]

The Court of Appeal's decision was arrived at without any express consideration of the claimant's Art.6 rights (perhaps because the decision under appeal was made shortly before the Human Rights Act 1998 came into force). It is possible that an analysis based on Art.6 would tend to favour the more cautious approach adopted by Waller L.J.

19–089   Secondly, in many instances, the courts will not query a decision by the executive or other relevant authority not to pursue a claim to immunity. This may occur for different reasons. On the one hand, it may be that the relevant authority decides that there is no public interest to be served by protection from disclosure because, for example, the proposed revelations pose no threat to national security.[35]

19–090   Alternatively, an argument for public interest in immunity may exist, but the executive or other authority may be able to decide the contest between (a) the aspect of the public interest supporting the immunity and (b) the aspect of the public interest supporting disclosure, in favour of the latter, without reference to the court.

19–091   Thus, in *R. v Chief Constable of West Midlands Ex p. Wiley*,[36] Lord Woolf said:

"If a Secretary of State on behalf of his department as opposed to any ordinary litigant concludes that any public interest in documents being withheld from production is outweighed by the public interest in the documents being available for purposes of litigation, it is difficult to conceive that unless the documents do not relate to an area for which the Secretary of State was responsible, the court would feel it appropriate to come to any different conclusion from that of the Secretary of State."

He later referred to[37]:

"a well known part of the speech of Lord Simon of Glaisdale in *R. v Lewes Justices Ex p. Secretary of State for the Home Department* [1973] A.C. 388 at 407, which is in these terms,

'It is true that the public interest which demands that the evidence be withheld has to be weighed against the public interest in the

---

[34] At [26].
[35] See, e.g., *A v Hayden* [1984] 156 C.L.R. 532.
[36] [1995] 1 A.C. 274 at 296; see also *Sankey v Whitlam* (1978) 142 C.L.R. 1 at 44–45 and 68.
[37] *ibid.* at 298.

administration of justice that courts should have the fullest possible access to all relevant material . . . but once the former public interest is held to outweigh the latter, the evidence cannot in any circumstances be admitted. It is not a privilege which may be waived by the Crown . . . or by anyone else.'

It will be observed from that passage that when Lord Simon said that the privilege was one which could not be waived, he was referring to the situation after it had been determined that the public interest against disclosure outweighed that of disclosure in the administration of justice."

Secretaries of State and the Attorney-General are capable of this form of disposal of the issue of immunity, but the situation may be different when parties other than government departments are involved.[38] It has been said that it would be appropriate for a chief constable to consult with other chief constables and possibly the Attorney-General and Home Secretary before deciding to disclose a document of a kind for which to the courts have previously recognised class immunity. When there is a doubt as to whether immunity can properly be waived, the prudent approach is to leave the matter to the court.[39] **19–092**

It is as yet unsettled whether an official's power to waive a claim to immunity where he decides that the public interest in immunity is outweighed by the public interest in the administration of justice brings with it a concomitant *duty* to make a claim *only* after taking this latter public interest into account. In *Bennett v Commissioner of Police of Metropolis*,[40] Rattee J., without deciding the matter, expressed the view that the existence of such a duty was arguable. The alternative view is that the responsible official is entitled to leave considerations of the administration of justice for the court to take into account to the extent that it chooses to do so. **19–093**

Where a party is not *bound* to assert public interest immunity and, during the course of litigation, accidentally discloses to the other side material in relation to which he is *entitled* to assert immunity, the Court of Appeal has said that the principles applicable to any application to restrain further use of the material are the same as in the case of the accidental disclosure of privileged material.[41] **19–094**

---

[38] See Lord Woolf's observations in *R. v Chief Constable of West Midlands Police Ex p. Wiley* [1995] 1 A.C. 274 at 297.

[39] *ibid.* at 297–298. In *Evans v Chief Constable of Surrey* [1988] 1 Q.B. 588, the Chief Constable was not entitled to waive the immunity attaching to a report relating to a murder suspect sent by him to the Director of Public Prosecutions in the face of objection made by the Attorney General

[40] [1995] 1 W.L.R. 488 at 495. See also Ganz, "Matrix Churchill and Public Interest Immunity: A Postcript" (1995) 58 M.L.R. 417.

[41] *Fayed v Metropolitan Police Commissioner* [2002] EWCA Civ 780 at [17]; *R. v G* [2004] EWCA Crim 1368; [2004] 1 W.L.R. 2932, at [15].

CHAPTER 20

Methods of Partial Protection

Restrictions on the manner in which confidential information is required to be disclosed

20–001 The courts may give partial protection to the confidentiality of information disclosed in litigation by ordering special restrictions on the circumstances and manner of its disclosure. These restrictions, which may be of a general nature or fashioned to meet the needs of particularly sensitive cases (for example, cases concerning trade secrets and children[1]) fall into two broad categories:

      (1) restrictions operating during pre-trial disclosure;
      (2) restrictions operating during and after trial.

Controls on the form of disclosure

20–002 The earlier authorities on this topic were reviewed by the Court of Appeal in *Warner-Lambert Co v Glaxo Laboratories Ltd*[2] Buckley L.J. concluded[3]:

> "None of these cases purports to lay down a form of order suitable for universal use. Nor, I think, does any of them indicate that the court

---

[1] In relation to children, see Ch.2.
[2] [1975] R.P.C. 354.
[3] *ibid*. at 358.

might not in appropriate circumstances at a later stage in the action have directed disclosure to a wider class of persons or on different terms. In my judgment, the court must in each case decide what measure of disclosure should be made, and to whom, and upon what terms, having regard to the particular circumstances of the case, bearing in mind that, if a case for disclosure is made out, the applicant should have as full a degree of appropriate disclosure as will be consistent with adequate protection of any trade secret of the respondent."

One possible control is to impose a restriction on the persons allowed to carry out inspection. In some circumstances, only a party's solicitors and a specified person or persons will be permitted to inspect documents, and then only on an undertaking not to disclose their content to any other persons. The specified person may sometimes be an independent expert,[4] but often inspection will need to be made by a person more familiar with the business of the parties.[5] Before agreeing to any restrictions that would prevent their legal representatives from communicating fully with them, parties should consider the difficulties that might arise as a result.[6]

Other possible controls include orders as to where the documents are to be inspected and stored, provision for the attendance at inspection of a representative of the party giving discovery, and restrictions on the making of copies or notes.   **20–003**

In deciding what condition to impose, the court may take into account its view of such factors as the susceptibility of the confidential information to memorisation.[7] The court may also take judicial notice of the standing of the party seeking discovery, if it is, for example, a reputable and well-known company.[8]   **20–004**

A failure to observe disclosure restrictions imposed by the court may result in proceedings for contempt.[9]   **20–005**

Restrictions operating during and after trial

The general rule is that court hearings are to be in public.[10] This rule covers not only final determinations on the merits but also procedural hearings of   **20–006**

---

[4] As in *Helitune Ltd v Stewart Hughes Ltd* [1994] F.S.R. 422, at 430 to 432.
[5] See, e.g. *Atari Incorporated v Philips Electronics and Associated Industries Ltd* [1988] F.S.R. 416; *Format Communications MFG Ltd v ITT (United Kingdom) Ltd* [1983] F.S.R. 473, CA; *Centri-Spray Corporation v Cera International Ltd* [1979] F.S.R. 175.
[6] The Court of Appeal discussed some of these, in another context, in *R. v G* [2004] EWCA Crim 1368; [2004] 1 W.L.R. 2932. See also the Court of Appeal's consideration of the effect of "confidentiality clubs" in *Lilly Icos Ltd v Pfizer Ltd (No. 2)* [2002] EWCA Civ 2; [2002] 1 W.L.R. 2253.
[7] *Centri-Spray Corporation v Cera International Ltd* [1979] F.S.R. 175 at 180–181.
[8] *Format Communications MFG Ltd v ITT (United Kingdom) Ltd* [1983] F.S.R. 473 at 486.
[9] See, for example, *Re a Solicitor (Disclosure of Confidential Records)* [1997] 1 F.L.R. 101.
[10] CPR 39.2(1).

the kind that were described, prior to the introduction of the CPR, as "hearings in chambers". The common law and statutory background to the rule was set out by Mance L.J. in *Department of Economics, Policy and Development of the City of Moscow v Bankers Trust* Co.[11] The rule accords with Art.6(1) of the European Convention on Human Rights, which entitles litigants to a fair and *public* hearing in the determination of their civil rights.[12]

20–007   Exceptionally, however, a party wishing to protect confidential material may seek an order restricting public attendance at, or public reporting of, proceedings that would normally be held in open court. CPR 39.2(3) provides that:

> "A hearing, or any part of it, may be in private if-
>
>   (a) publicity would defeat the object of the hearing;
>   (b) it involves matters relating to national security;
>   (c) it involves confidential information (including information relating to personal financial matters) and publicity would damage that confidentiality;
>   (d) a private hearing is necessary to protect the interests of any child or patient;
>   (e) it is a hearing of an application made without notice and it would be unjust to any respondent for there to be a public hearing;
>   (f) it involves uncontentious matters arising in the administration of trusts or in the administration of a deceased person's estate; or
>   (g) the court considers this to be necessary, in the interests of justice."

This part of the rule also accords with Art.6(1) of the European Convention on Human Rights,[13] which provides that:

> " . . . the press and public may be excluded from all or part of the trial in the interest of morals, public order or national security in a democratic society, where the interests of juveniles or the protection of the private life of the parties so require, or to the extent strictly necessary in the opinion of the court in special circumstances where publicity would prejudice the interests of justice."

20–008   The courts are generally reluctant to allow hearings to take place in private, for reasons that were set out by the House of Lords in *Scott v*

---

[11] [2004] EWCA Civ 314; [2005] Q.B. 207, at [11]–[25].
[12] Though, generally speaking, interim proceedings of an interlocutory nature do not engage Art.6: *APIS v Slovakia* (2000) 29 E.H.R.R. CD 105.
[13] As was held by the Divisional Court in *R. (Pelling) v Bow County Court* [2001] UKHRR 165.

Scott.[14] Lord Shaw of Dunfermline cited among various passages from the works of Bentham:

> "Publicity is the very soul of justice. It is the keenest spur to exertion and the surest of all guards against improbity. It keeps the judge himself, while trying, under trial."[15]

This passage was also cited by Lord Diplock in *Harman v Home Office.*[16]

Scott v Scott was considered by the Court of Appeal in *R. v Chief Registrar of Friendly Societies Ex p. New Cross Building Society.*[17] Sir John Donaldson M.R., with whom Griffiths and Slade L.JJ. on this point expressly indicated their agreement, said[18]:   **20–009**

> "The guidance which I get from their Lordships' speeches can be summarised as follows. The general rule that the courts shall conduct their proceedings in public is but an aid, albeit a very important aid, to the achievement of the paramount object of the courts which is to do justice in accordance with the law. It is only if, in wholly exceptional circumstances, the presence of the public or public knowledge of the proceedings is likely to defeat that paramount object that the courts are justified in proceeding in camera. These circumstances are incapable of definition. Each application for privacy must be considered on its merits, but the applicant must satisfy the court that nothing short of total privacy will enable justice to be done. It is not sufficient that a public hearing will create embarrassment for some or all of those concerned. It must be shown that a public hearing is likely to lead, directly or indirectly, to a denial of justice."

In the case before it, a judicial review of the Chief Registrar's adverse decision as to the suitability of a building society to continue to be a repository of trust funds and to accept moneys for investment, the Court of Appeal considered that publicity during the first instance hearing and subsequent appeal would have resulted in a loss of public confidence such that the society would have had to close even if it had proved successful (which, in the event, it did not). The hearings had therefore been rightly held *in camera.*

The court will reduce to a minimum the length of time spent in private.[19]   **20–010**
Arrangements may be made between the parties so that it is unnecessary for the public to be excluded at all.[20]

---

[14] [1913] A.C. 417.
[15] *Benthamia*, or *Select Extracts from the works of Jeremy Bentham* (1843) p.115.
[16] [1983] 1 A.C. 280 at 303.
[17] [1984] 1 Q.B. 227.
[18] *ibid.* at 235.
[19] For example, only while details of some secret chemical process are revealed: *Badische Anilin und Soda Fabrik v Levinstein* [1883] 24 Ch.D. 156.
[20] *Andrew v Raeburn* (1874) 9 Ch.App. 522: privacy not required since it was unnecessary to read out the contents of the confidential letters concerned.

Restrictions on the collateral use of information provided for the purposes of litigation

20–011 CPR 31 deals with disclosure and inspection of documents. CPR 31.22 provides that:

> "(1) A party to whom a document has been disclosed may use the document only for the purpose of the proceedings in which it is disclosed, except where—
>
> > (a) the document has been read to or by the court, or referred to, at a hearing which has been held in public;
> > (b) the court gives permission; or
> > (c) the party who disclosed the document and the person to whom the document belongs agree.
>
> (2) The court may make an order restricting or prohibiting the use of a document which has been disclosed, even where the document has been read to or by the court, or referred to, at a hearing which has been held in public.
> (3) An application for such an order may be made-
>
> > (a) by a party; or
> > (b) by any person to whom the document belongs."

20–012 CPR 32 deals with witness statements. CPR 32.12 provides that:

> "(1) Except as provided by this rule, a witness statement may be used only for the purpose of the proceedings in which it is served.
> (2) Paragraph (1) does not apply if and to the extent that—
>
> > (a) the witness gives consent in writing to some other use of it;
> > (b) the court gives permission for some other use; or
> > (c) the witness statement has been put in evidence at a hearing held in public."

20–013 CPR 18 deals with requests and orders for a party to provide further information to another. CPR 18.2 provides that:

> "The court may direct that information provided by a party to another party (whether given voluntarily or following an order made under rule 18.1) must not be used for any purpose except for that of the proceedings in which it is given."

Prior to the introduction of these rules, the recipients of information as the result of compulsory disclosure during the litigation process were bound at common law by an implied undertaking to the court not to use that information for any "ulterior or collateral purpose".[21] In *SmithKline*

---

[21] *Alterskye v Scott* [1948] 1 All E.R. 469.

Beecham plc v Generics (UK) Ltd,[22] the Court of Appeal accepted the submission that CPR 31.22 represented a complete code in relation to disclosed documents and, implicitly, that the previous implied undertaking to the court had been superseded.

A primary rationale for the existence of an implied undertaking[23] lay in the compulsory nature of disclosure under the litigation process, but the distinction between voluntary and involuntary disclosure proved problematic, especially where disclosure by one party was occasioned by a step taken by his opponent.[24] The Court of Appeal revisited the suggested distinction in *SmithKline Beecham v Generics (UK) Ltd*[25] and held that it did not affect the applicability of CPR 31.22 (although it might well be of relevance to the exercise of the court's discretion under CPR 31.22). The Court pointed out that "disclosure" was defined in CPR 31.2 in broad terms ("A party discloses a document by stating that the document exists or has existed") and concluded that this was determinative. Accordingly, a document referred to by a party in a witness statement had been "disclosed" for the purposes of CPR 31.22, even though it might be said that that party had chosen voluntarily to reveal the existence of the document. **20–014**

The Court of Appeal's broadening of the protection afforded by CPR 31.22 accords with the increased importance attached to the public interest in encouraging co-operation between the parties to litigation. A narrower approach might well constitute a disincentive to such co-operation (for example, by discouraging the voluntary disclosure of documents before it is formally required by the rules). **20–015**

It also appears that the applicability of CPR 31.22 does not depend upon the confidentiality of the documents in question (though their confidentiality will be relevant to the exercise of the court's discretion under CPR 31.22). As the Court of Appeal observed in *Lilly Icos Ltd v Pfizer Ltd*[26]: **20–016**

> "It may be mentioned that we have described the issue as one of confidentiality, and we will for convenience continue to describe it as such. However, it will be seen from CPR 31.22 that the basic prohibition in relation to disclosed documents is in terms of their *use*. A breach of that prohibition, such as in a patent case the use by the opponent of processes disclosed by the patentee, might not involve anything that would usually be characterised as a breach of *confidence*."

---

[22] [2003] EWCA Civ 1109; [2004] 1 W.L.R. 1479, *per* Aldous L.J. at [28] and [29].

[23] As described by Megaw L.J. in *Halcon International Inc v The Shell Transport and Trading Co* [1979] R.P.C. 97 at 121.

[24] See the contrasting approaches adopted by Sir Nicholas Browne-Wilkinson in *Derby & Co Ltd v Weldon (No. 2) The Times*, October 20, 1988; 132 S.J. 1755, and by Hugh Laddie Q.C. in *Lubrizol Corporation v Esso Petroleum Co Ltd (No. 2)* [1993] F.S.R. 53. See too the test proposed by Hobhouse J. in *Prudential Assurance Co Ltd v Fountain Page Ltd* [1991] 1 W.L.R. 756 at 765.

[25] Especially at [29].

[26] [2002] EWCA Civ 2; [2002] 1 W.L.R. 2253 at [4].

The rule thereby maintains the reasoning of the House of Lords in *Harman v Secretary of State for the Home Department*,[27] in which the House of Lords held that a solicitor who allowed a journalist to have access to documents obtained on discovery from the Home Office was in contempt of court, even though the documents had by then been read out in open court and had thereby entered the public domain.

20–017   In *EMI Records Ltd v Spillane*[28] Sir Nicolas Browne-Wilkinson V.C. held that the implied undertaking was not an absolute undertaking not to use the documents or permit their use for purposes other than the action in which discovery is given, but was an undertaking not without the consent of the party who gave discovery so to do. The effect of his decision has been preserved by the exception contained in CPR 31.22(1)(c). The addition, under that exception, of the *owner* of a disclosed document as a person entitled to object to its collateral use goes some way towards protecting the position of interested third parties but (as will be seen below) falls short of the protection that might be afforded under the general law of confidence.

20–018   The new rules do not remove the question whether a private law duty of confidentiality is owed by a person obtaining disclosure of confidential information in the course of litigation. In *Derby & Co Ltd v Weldon (No. 2)*,[29] Sir Nicholas Browne-Wilkinson V.C. said:

> "I have the greatest doubts whether such a separate duty of confidence can exist . . . . But even assuming (contrary to my inclination) that there is such a separate duty of confidence, such duty can only be implied from the circumstances of the case. Such private duty of confidence cannot, in my judgment, be wider than that imposed by the implied undertaking."

20–019   In *Prudential Assurance Co Ltd v Fountain Page Ltd*[30] Hobhouse J. observed that the implied undertaking was independent of any question of confidentiality. He cited *Derby & Co Ltd v Weldon (No. 2)* and stated[31]:

> "It is clear that where documents are produced in the course of legal proceedings, or information provided, the further use of that material must be governed by the legal principles or rules of court which relate to the use of such material and not by any private law rights. It is of course an *a fortiori* position where there were no antecedent private law rights in respect of that material; the use of material in litigation cannot itself give rise to that class of right."

---

[27] [1983] 1 A.C. 280. Following a compromise of Ms Harman's case before the European Court of Human Rights, RSC Ord.24, r.14A (the predecessor of CPR 31.22) was introduced.
[28] [1986] 1 W.L.R. 967.
[29] *The Times*, October 20, 1988; 132 S.J. 1755.
[30] [1991] 1 W.L.R. 756 at 765.
[31] *ibid.* at 767.

Rules of law governing the conduct of proceedings may undoubtedly provide wider protection than, or may qualify, the protection provided by principles of confidentiality; but it is difficult to see why such rules should necessarily oust the protection provided by the law of confidentiality. There are many examples of the law of confidentiality being applied by the courts in cases where documents have been improperly or mistakenly disclosed in the course of litigation.[32]

Ferris J. followed *Derby & Co Ltd v Weldon (No. 2)* and *Prudential* **20–020** *Assurance Co Ltd v Fountain Page Ltd* in *Apple Corps Ltd v Apple Computer Inc.*[33] In doing so, he was obliged to consider the problematic decision of the Court of Appeal in *Mainwaring v Goldtech Investments Ltd.*[34] In this case the defendants' solicitors had lodged various documents, including privileged papers, with the taxing master following an order for interlocutory costs made in the defendants' favour. The defendants' solicitors subsequently came off the record for the defendants and the taxation was abandoned. The taxing master did not return the papers to the defendants or their former solicitors, but handed them to the master who was in charge of the interlocutory proceedings between the parties.

The plaintiffs applied for and obtained an order against the defendants **20–021** for the production of various documents. When the defendants failed to comply with the order for production, the master looked through the documents in his possession and supplied those that fell within the terms of his order to one of the plaintiffs to enable her to take copies.

The defendants' counterclaim was dismissed when they failed to provide **20–022** security for the plaintiffs' costs, and judgment was also entered for the plaintiffs in default of defence. The plaintiffs issued a summons seeking an order that the defendants' former solicitors should personally bear the costs of the plaintiffs' actions. The master subsequently permitted the same plaintiff to inspect and to take copies of any of the documents in his possession, notwithstanding representations made on behalf of the defendants' former solicitors.

In due course, the plaintiffs' application for costs against the defendants' **20–023** former solicitors was dismissed and the defendants' former solicitors obtained an order from Hoffmann J. restraining the plaintiffs from making further use of the copy documents lodged by them for taxation purposes. One of the plaintiffs appealed from this order.

The Court of Appeal was of the view that any benefit of privilege in the **20–024** documents had been lost, bearing in mind the circumstances in which they came into the possession of Miss Mainwaring. However, it also held that the plaintiffs had obtained the taxation documents subject to an obligation of confidentiality owed, not only to the defendants, but also to the defendants'

---

[32] *Ashburton v Pape* [1913] 2 Ch. 469 and the line of authorities following it. The subject of documents obtained through impropriety or mistake is discussed more fully in Chs 3 and 18.
[33] [1992] 1 C.M.L.R. 969. See also *per* Millett J. in *Bank of Crete S.A. v Koskotas (No. 2)* [1992] 1 W.L.R. 919 at 925.
[34] *The Times*, February 19, 1991.

former solicitors, and that Hoffmann J. had exercised his discretion correctly in favour of the solicitors.

20–025   Ferris J. took the view in *Apple Corps Ltd v Apple Computer Inc.* that the continuing duty of confidentiality referred to by the Court of Appeal in *Mainwaring* was none other than that embodied in the plaintiffs' implied undertaking to the court. The fact that the Court of Appeal was told by counsel that the application to Hoffmann J. had been an application under Ord.24, r.14A supports Ferris J.'s interpretation, but there are two difficulties with it.

20–026   First, the Court of Appeal agreed with Hoffmann J. that the basis of the solicitors' right to keep the documents confidential was their status "as constituting confidential communications between themselves and counsel or themselves and their client, and that, as against the rest of the world, they were entitled to preserve their confidentiality." Secondly, the authorities referred to by the Court of Appeal—*Marcel v Commissioner of Police of the Metropolis*[35] and *Webster v James Chapman & Co*[36]—suggest that the proper test to be applied, in the court's view, was that applicable to the general law of confidence, rather than that applicable to undertakings impliedly given to the court on discovery.

20–027   In many cases the question whether the recipient of confidential information that has been provided for the purposes of litigation owes any private law duty of confidentiality in respect of that information will be of only academic concern. However, cases will from time to time arise (for example, in relation to documents improperly or mistakenly disclosed or in relation to the rights and obligations of third parties not directly involved in the litigation), in which it will matter.

20–028   Where information of a confidential nature is disclosed in the ordinary course, and for the purpose, of litigation (and, *a fortiori*, where it is disclosed at the recipient's request) the recipient ought to be under a general obligation, either by implied contract or under the equitable doctrine of confidence, or indeed under the recently developed jurisdiction based on privacy, not to use that information for other purposes.

20–029   In the case of arbitration, the voluntary nature of the proceedings has not precluded the courts from recognising such an obligation in relation to disclosed documents; on the contrary, it has caused them to do so.[37]

Third parties

20–030   Where confidential information is disclosed for the purposes of litigation by or to a person who is not a party to the litigation, but is either not referred to at a public hearing or is the subject of an order restricting its use (under

[35] [1992] Ch. 225.
[36] [1989] 3 All E.R. 939.
[37] *Dolling-Baker v Merrett* [1990] 1 W.L.R. 1205.

CPR 31.22), the question may arise whether the third party is entitled to assert, or is subject to, an obligation of confidentiality.

The issue whether a third party who received confidential documents **20–031** disclosed on discovery in an action which was settled before trial owed a duty of confidentiality to the party which had produced them arose in *Distillers Co (Biochemicals) Ltd v Times Newspapers Ltd.*[38] In the course of an action for personal injuries brought by users of the drug thalidomide against the pharmaceutical company which had marketed it, the company disclosed on discovery a large number of confidential documents. The claimants' solicitors passed them to a chemist retained by them as an expert witness. The action was settled, but shortly beforehand the expert witness agreed to sell the documents to *The Times*, which later decided to publish an article based on the documents and information provided to them by the expert witness. The pharmaceutical company brought an action against the newspaper claiming that publication of the article would be a misuse of confidential information, relying particularly on *Prince Albert v Strange*,[39] *Ashburton v Pape*,[40] *Saltman*[41] and *Fraser v Evans*.[42] Talbot J. accepted the company's submissions on the existence of a private duty of confidentiality, as well as a public need to protect the administration of justice.

Distillers Co. (Biochemicals) Ltd v Times Newspapers Ltd was approved **20–032** by the Court of Appeal in *Riddick v Thames Board Mills*.[43] In *Lilly Icos Ltd v Pfizer Ltd (No. 2)*,[44] the Court of Appeal considered in passing the extent to which a third party might be bound by an order under CPR 31.22(2) that a document was not to be used for any collateral purpose even after it had been referred to in open court:

> " . . . if the court does make an order under CPR r 31.22(2), but the document in question comes into the possession of a third party, for instance by accident or theft, then any use by the third party of the document with knowledge of the court's order will arguably be a contempt. We heard no sustained argument on that point, but as at present advised the conclusion just stated would appear to follow by analogy with the view taken by the House of Lords in *Attorney General v Times Newspapers Ltd* [1992] 1 A.C. 191."

Support for the Court of Appeal's position has since been provided by the **20–033** House of Lords' decision in *Attorney-General v Punch Ltd*,[45] which examined in detail the circumstances in which a third party could be guilty of contempt of court for impeding or prejudicing the purpose of a court

---

[38] [1975] 1 Q.B. 613.
[39] (1849) 1 Mac. & G. 25.
[40] [1913] 2 Ch. 469.
[41] (1948) 65 R.P.C. 203.
[42] [1969] 1 Q.B. 349.
[43] [1977] Q.B. 881 at 896, 901–902.
[44] [2002] EWCA Civ 2; [2002] 1 W.L.R. 2253 at [5].
[45] [2002] UKHL 50; [2003] 1 A.C. 1046.

order. Contempt of court was described as "the species of wrongful conduct which consists of interference with the administration of justice",[46] deliberate interference with the due administration of justice,[47] or a wilful interference with the administration of justice.[48] These definitions appear capable of extending, not only to the deliberate disregard of court orders, but also to the deliberate disregard of rules of court (such as CPR 31.22).

20–034   Aside from contempt, and whether or not an order has been made under CPR 31.22, it seems possible in principle for information disclosed in the course of litigation to possess the quality of confidentiality and be protectable as such, and moreover for that quality to subsist even where it has been referred to at a public hearing if on a practical view it has not become general public knowledge.

20–035   So far as the *protection* of third parties is concerned, a party may be required to disclose information in respect of which he owes a duty of confidence to someone else, if such information is relevant to the issues in the action. A person who is not a party may also be required, before a case comes to trial, to disclose documents, even if they contain information confidential to that person or in respect of which he owes a duty of confidentiality to someone else, if the court considers such disclosure necessary[49]; or to give evidence on deposition,[50] which may include information of a similar character. The law would be deficient if the receiving party did not in such circumstances owe an obligation to the relevant third party not to use such confidential information otherwise than for the purpose for which it was provided.

20–036   CPR 31.22 would prevent the recipient from using a disclosed document otherwise than for the purpose of the action without the consent of the party who provided the disclosure, but that party might not mind what the recipient did with it. The recipient's duty to the third party, it is suggested, would be a duty arising under the equitable doctrine of confidence.

20–037   In *Singh v Christie*,[51] a case under the former Rules of the Supreme Court, it was suggested by Drake J. that, even after disclosed documents had been referred to in open court, the implied undertaking was not relaxed to the extent necessary to permit the recipient of the documents to rely upon them for all purposes. In particular, the recipient was not entitled to found a libel action upon such documents. However, Drake J.'s suggestion was disapproved by the Court of Appeal in *Mahon v Rahn*[52] and has not been followed in subsequent first instance decisions.[53]

---

[46] *per* Lord Nicholls, at [2].
[47] *per* Lord Hoffmann, at [66].
[48] *per* Lord Hope, at [87].
[49] See Supreme Court Act 1981, s.34, County Courts Act 1984, s.53 and CPR 31.17.
[50] See CPR 34.
[51] *The Times*, November 11, 1993.
[52] [1998] Q.B. 424 (a decision itself subsequently disapproved by the House of Lords on other grounds in *Taylor v Director of the SFO* [1999] 2 A.C. 177) at 432–434, 449 and 455.
[53] See *Ruddy v Mercury Personal Communications Ltd*, QBD, Eady J., July 31, 2000, and *Colbeck v Ferguson*, QBD, Sir Ian Kennedy, January 24, 2002.

In *Dendron GmbH v Regents of the University of California*[54] Laddie J. **20–038**
considered the position in relation to depositions. The court had allowed
applications by the claimants for letters of request to be sent to courts in
Germany and the USA for the examination of expert witnesses in connection with patent litigation in England. The claimants wanted to be able to
use the evidence obtained in other proceedings in Europe and the USA. CPR
34 contains no restrictions on the use of a deposition taken from a non-
party. (Where an order is made requiring a party to be examined about his
assets for the purpose of a hearing other than the trial, CPR 34.12 contains
restrictions on the use which may be made of the deposition, but that is the
only restriction to be found in CPR 34 on the use of depositions.)

Laddie J. held that the claimants were subject to an implied obligation at **20–039**
common law not to use the depositions for any purpose other than the
English litigation except with the permission of the witness or of the court.
(Once the evidence was given in court, its status would be like any other
evidence.) He adopted the reasoning of Hobhouse J. in *Prudential Assurance plc v Fountain Page*[55] (applied also by Jacob J. in *Grapha Holding AG
v Quebecor Printing (UK) plc*[56]) that:

> " . . . where one party compels another, either by enforcement of a rule
> of court or a specific order of the court, to disclose documents or
> information whether the other party wishes to or not, the party
> obtaining this disclosure is given this power because the invasion of the
> other party's rights has to give way to the need to do justice between
> those parties in the pending litigation between them; it follows from
> this that the results of such compulsion should likewise be limited to
> the purpose for which the order was made . . . "

Laddie J. observed that there was no difference in principle between
documents provided under the disclosure rules and information provided
compulsorily during the course of litigation in some other form: the latter
required to be protected, no less than the former.

He was not referred to any authorities on confidentiality, and it does not **20–040**
appear that any consideration was given to the question of the confidentiality of the information sought from the witnesses. But his rationale is
consistent with the broader principle that a person who receives information in the exercise of a legal power owes an equitable obligation of
confidentiality not to use it for other purposes, at least in so far as the
information (or the fact that the supplier of the information has given it) is
information of a confidential nature.[57]

However, it is suggested that the form of rule as laid down by Laddie J., **20–041**
if it were considered as a rule of general application, would be too broad in
one respect and too narrow in another (neither of which he had cause to

---

[54] [2004] EWHC 589; [2005] 1 W.L.R. 200.
[55] [1991] 1 W.L.R. 756 at 765.
[56] [1996] F.S.R. 711.
[57] See Ch.2.

consider). If the evidence of a witness in his deposition contained some fact of a non-confidential kind, for example a fact about which there was widespread public knowledge, it is hard to see any principled reason why either party should not be free to use it. On the other hand, there may be circumstances in which the information supplied by a witness is obviously confidential to someone else (for example, medical information about someone else), and while it might suit both the witness and the party which deposed him to agree that the information should be disclosed for other purposes, their agreement to do so (for example, by selling it to the press, as the expert witness did in *Distillers Co (Biochemicals) Ltd v Times Newspapers Ltd*) should not automatically destroy any rights of confidentiality or rights under Art.8 belonging to the person concerned. (Since the dispute before Laddie J. was about a patent, he was not concerned with personal information or rights under Art.8.) Moreover, any duty of confidentiality in respect of information given by a witness in a deposition should not be restricted to the party which sought the order for the evidence to be given, but should apply equally to other persons to whom the deposition was supplied (such as other parties or other witnesses).

The scope of CPR 31.22

20–042   Whether or not a proposed use of information goes beyond use for the purpose of the proceedings in which it is disclosed is essentially a question of fact. In *Crest Homes plc v Marks*,[58] the Court of Appeal expressed the view, uncontradicted in the House of Lords (though regarded, on the facts of the case, as a technicality), that:

> "the use of documents disclosed in one action for the purposes of another action will usually, perhaps invariably, be a collateral or ulterior purpose."[59]

20–043   In *Sybron Corporation v Barclays Bank plc*,[60] the plaintiffs had commenced an action, in which they wished to involve further parties. For procedural reasons, they chose to commence a new action, rather than to add the new parties to the existing action. Although the causes of action in the two sets of proceedings were identical, Scott J. held that the implied undertaking still operated to prevent the plaintiffs without the leave of the court from using documents obtained in the first action for the purposes of the second action. The required leave was given.

20–044   Different considerations apply when a primary purpose of the proceedings in which discovery is obtained is to facilitate the conduct of other proceedings—for example, by means of a *Norwich Pharmacal* or search

---

[58] [1987] 1 A.C. 829 at 837.
[59] An action based on such documents will be struck out as an abuse of process: *Miller v Scorey* [1996] 1 W.L.R. 1122.
[60] [1985] 1 Ch. 299 at 318.

order (formerly an *Anton Piller* order). Prior to the introduction of the CPR, it was generally considered that the use of disclosed information for such purposes would not amount to an ulterior or collateral use of a kind that required the court's permission.[61] It is unclear that the introduction of CPR 31.22 was intended to alter this position and the phraseology employed in CPR 31.22 (which refers to use only for "the purpose" of the proceedings in which documentation is disclosed) would arguably not restrict use in the subsequent proceedings that the original proceedings were expressly intended to facilitate. Accordingly, although the safest course will be to seek permission from the court, it is doubtful whether the court's permission would in fact be required under CPR 31.22 for any use of disclosed documents which would not have constituted an "ulterior or collateral use" for the purposes of the implied undertaking.

In such cases the protection afforded by CPR 31.22 is still effective, even **20–045** if the court's permission is not required, inasmuch as the use to which the documents are put must still fall within the purpose allowed by CPR 31.22 (or must still not be ulterior or collateral to the purpose for which the discovery was obtained, as the case may be[62]). A party executing a search order is not necessarily obliged, however, to disregard all information incidentally acquired in the course of its execution.[63]

Similarly, the use of compulsorily obtained information for the purpose of **20–046** an interlocutory application for committal for contempt of court should also not represent a breach of CPR 31.22, provided that the application arises in the context of the proceedings in which the information has been obtained.[64] As Lord Oliver said in *Crest Homes Plc v Marks*[65]:

> "The proper policing and enforcement or [of?] observance of orders made and undertakings given to the court in an action are, in my judgment, as much an integral part of the action as any other step taken by the plaintiff in the proper prosecution of his claim."

CPR 31.22 and the effect of public hearings

In *Lilly Icos Ltd v Pfizer Ltd (No. 2)*,[66] the Court of Appeal considered both **20–047** the circumstances in which a public hearing would end the restriction otherwise imposed by CPR 31.22 on the use of a particular document and the circumstances in which the court would make an order under CPR 31.22(2), continuing the restriction after a document had been referred to at a public hearing.

---

[61] See *Sony Corporation v Anand* [1981] F.S.R. 398 (Browne-Wilkinson J.) and *Grapha Holding A.G. v Quebecor Printing (UK) plc* [1996] F.S.R. 711 at 715 (Jacob J.).
[62] *Bank of Crete S.A. v Koskotas (No. 2)* [1992] 1 W.L.R. 919; *Wilden Pump & Engineering Co. v Fusfield* [1985] F.S.R. 581.
[63] *Sony Corporation v Time Electronics* [1981] 1 W.L.R. 1293.
[64] *Aliter*, if the contempt proceedings are unrelated: see the decision of Laddie J. in *Cobra Golf Inc v Rata* [1996] F.S.R. 819.
[65] [1987] 1 A.C. 829 at 860.
[66] [2002] EWCA Civ 2; [2002] 1 W.L.R. 2253.

20–048   Enlarging on the Court of Appeal's earlier observations in *SmithKline Beecham Biologicals S.A. v Connaught Laboratories Inc*,[67] in which Lord Bingham C.J. expressed concern to avoid too wide a gap between theory and practice in the rules for determining what documents had passed into the public domain, the court confirmed that the effect of CPR 31.22(1)(a) could not be limited literally to what had happened in open court, given the extent to which practice had moved in the direction of the presentation of evidence and arguments in writing:

> " . . . it was necessary to take as falling under CPR 31.22(1)(a) any document preread by the judge, or referred to in for instance witness statements taken to stand as evidence, even if the document or the witness statement was not actually read out in court."[68]

In relation to pre-reading by the judge, the court added some practical guidance as to whether particular documents should be presumed to have formed part of a judge's pre-reading and as to the effect of that presumption. The court then commented:

> "The central theme of these rules is the importance of the principle that justice is to be done in public, and within that principle the importance of those attending a public court understanding the case."[69]

So far as applications under CPR 31.22(2) were concerned, the court warned against the direct importation of a test of "necessity" from the speeches in *Scott v Scott*,[70] before setting out its recommended approach[71]:

> "(i) The court should start from the principle that very good reasons are required for departing from the normal rule of publicity . . .
>
> (ii) When considering an application in respect of a particular document, the court should take into account the role that the document has played or will play in the trial, and thus its relevance to the process of [public scrutiny] . . .
>
> (iii) In dealing with issues of confidentiality between the parties, the court must have in mind any 'chilling' effect of an order upon the interests of third parties . . .

---

[67] [1999] 4 All E.R. 498 at 512. Lord Bingham referred to circumstances in which "there may be some degree of unreality in the proposition that the material documents in the case have (in practice as well as in theory) passed into the public domain. This is a matter which gives rise to concern".

[68] [2002] EWCA Civ 2; [2002] 1 W.L.R. 2253 at [7].

[69] At [8] and [9].

[70] [1913] A.C. 417.

[71] At para.25.

(iv) Simple assertions of confidentiality and of the damage that would be done by publication, even if supported by both parties, should not prevail. The court will require specific reasons why a party would be damaged by the publication of a document . . .

(v) It is highly desirable, both in the general public interest and for simple convenience, to avoid the holding of trials in private, or partially in private . . . The court should bear in mind that, if too demanding a standard is imposed under CPR r.31.22(2) in respect of documents that have been referred to inferentially or in short at the trial, it may be necessary, in order to protect genuine interests of the parties, for more trials or parts of trials to be held in private, or for instance for parts of witness statements or skeletons to be in closed form.

(vi) Patent cases are subject to the same general rules as any other cases, but they do present some particular problems and are subject to some particular considerations . . . "

Permission to use disclosed information for other purposes

In *Crest Homes plc v Marks*,[72] Lord Oliver stated that it was for a party   **20–049**
seeking release from the implied undertaking to demonstrate "cogent and persuasive reasons why it should be released". Referring to the authorities cited to the House of Lords in relation to this question, he said:

> "I do not, for my part, think that it would be helpful to review these authorities for they are no more than examples and they illustrate no general principle beyond this, that the court will not release or modify the implied undertaking given on discovery save in special circumstances and where the release or modification will not occasion injustice to the person giving discovery."[73]

That passage was cited by the Court of Appeal in *SmithKline Beecham plc v Generics (UK) Ltd*,[74] in the context of an application under CPR 31.22(2). The Court of Appeal also described as "useful" some guidance given as to relevant factors by Laddie J. in *Cobra Golf Inc v Rata*,[75] while reiterating that:

> "The most important consideration must be the interest of justice which involves considering the interest of the party seeking to use the documents and that of the party protected by the CPR 31.22 order. As Lord Oliver said each case will depend upon its own facts."[76]

[72] [1987] A.C. 829 at 859.
[73] *ibid.* at 860.
[74] [2003] EWCA Civ 1109; [2004] 1 W.L.R. 1479 at [36].
[75] [1996] F.S.R. 819.
[76] [2003] EWCA Civ 1109; [2004] 1 W.L.R. 1479 at [37].

However, the court added:

> "But a material consideration must be whether the documents could have been obtained under CPR 31.17. That rule enables the court to order disclosure from the third parties if the documents were likely to support SB's case and disclosure was necessary in order to dispose fairly of the claim."

20–050   The introduction of CPR 31.17, which greatly extended the scope of the courts' ability to make disclosure orders against non-parties, is clearly likely in the future to have a significant impact on applications for permission to use disclosed documents for other litigation: if the applicant would be entitled to apply in that other litigation for non-party disclosure of the relevant documents, there may be little sense in the court in the original proceedings declining to allow the applicant to use them in that other litigation.

20–051   In any event, the issue will only arise where the party seeking release is unable to obtain consent to his proposed use of the disclosed material from the person giving disclosure. The question whether such release will occasion injustice to that person will involve similar considerations to those which would arise if the question was whether the proposed disclosure should be restrained as a breach of an obligation of confidence.

CHAPTER 21

Children

Children's rights of confidence

21–001 A child may have a private law right of confidentiality no less than may an adult. Traditionally, the child's right to waive confidentiality has been a right to be exercised by the child's parents on its behalf,[1] but this general approach is subject to qualification.

21–002 In the first place, any such waiver is an exercise of parental responsibility, which the court is ultimately able to control—even in the face of parental opposition—by virtue of the provisions of the Children Act 1989.[2] Indeed, as Thorpe L.J. said in *Re G (Celebrities: Publicity)*[3]:

> " . . . there can be no doubt that the court has jurisdiction in personam to restrain any act by a parent that if unrestrained would or might adversely affect the welfare of the child the subject of the proceedings."

Secondly, the courts have in recent years increasingly recognised the autonomy of children mature enough to make informed decisions on their own behalf, a tendency accelerated by the incorporation into domestic law of both the European Convention and its rights-based jurisprudence.

---

[1] *Re Z (A Minor) (Identification: Restrictions on Publication)* [1997] Fam 1 at 25, *per* Ward L.J., who also observed that parents themselves owe their children a duty of confidentiality of uncertain ambit. In relation to medical treatment and advice, see para.11–040, above.
[2] *ibid.* at 25–27.
[3] [1999] 1 F.L.R. 409, at 414–415; see also *A v M (Family Proceedings: Publicity)* [2000] 1 F.L.R. 562 (Charles J.) at 565.

21-003   In *Torbay Borough Council v News Group Newspapers*,[4] Munby J. discussed this development in some detail. At the age of 12, Angela Roddy, became pregnant. The father ("X") was of about the same age. Following the birth of her daughter ("Y"), Angela fought an unsuccessful battle with her local authority, the outcome of which was an adoption order in respect of Y. She wanted to tell her story to the *Mail on Sunday* and later applied for the discharge of restrictive injunctions that prevented her from doing so. The hearing before Munby J. took place shortly before her 17th birthday. Citing the House of Lords' decision in *Gillick v West Norfolk and Wisbech Health Authority*,[5] Munby J. said[6]:

> "The courts must face reality. We must, as Lord Scarman said, be sensitive to human development and social change. Angela may not yet be quite 17 years old but she is a young woman with a mind of her own and, as her solicitor B has said, a mature and articulate young person. We no longer treat our 17-year old daughters as our Victorian ancestors did, and if we try to do so it is at our—and their—peril. Angela, in my judgment, is of an age, and has sufficient understanding and maturity, to decide for herself whether that which is private, personal and intimate should remain private or whether it should be shared with the whole world . . . "

He concluded[7]:

> "In fact Angela's decision is supported by her parents and not opposed by the local authority. But neither of those facts can be determinative. I wish to make it clear that, giving proper weight to Angela's evidence and the evidence of her solicitor, B, I should unhesitatingly have come to precisely the same conclusion even if Angela's wish to tell her story to the world had been opposed both by the local authority and by her parents."

The courts' jurisdiction

21-004   Since the decision of the House of Lords in *Re S (A Child) (Identification: Restrictions on Publication)*,[8] the courts' own jurisdiction to protect the

---

[4] [2003] EWHC 2927 (Fam); [2004] E.M.L.R. 8, at [45]–[60]. See also *Mabon v Mabon* [2005] EWCA Civ 634; [2005] Fam. 366, at [26] and [32], and the discussion in Jane Fortin's "Accommodating Children's Rights in a Post Human Rights Act Era" (2006) M.L.R. 299.
[5] [1986] A.C. 112.
[6] At para.56.
[7] At para.60. See also, in relation to an adult with learning disabilities, the decision of Munby J. in *E v Channel Four Television Corporation* [2005] EWHC 1144, Fam; [2005] E.M.L.R. 30.
[8] [2004] UKHL 47; [2005] 1 A.C. 593.

privacy of children, where it is not statutory,[9] has been based upon the application of Art.8 of the European Convention on Human Rights.

Prior to the introduction of the Human Rights Act 1998, the courts had **21–005** categorised their inherent jurisdiction to restrain publicity in relation to children into (a) a parental jurisdiction, directed at the welfare of the child and the child's upbringing, and (b) an ancillary jurisdiction, directed at the protection of the integrity and effectiveness of the courts' own proceedings.[10] However, in *Re S*[11] Lord Steyn, who gave the only speech, said:

> "The House unanimously takes the view that since the 1998 Act came into force in October 2000, the earlier case law about the existence and scope of inherent jurisdiction need not be considered in this case or in similar cases. The foundation of the jurisdiction to restrain publication in a case such as the present is now derived from Convention rights under the ECHR."

Lord Steyn said that previous case law might remain of some interest in regard to the ultimate balancing exercise to be carried out under the ECHR provisions and observed that the approach that had been adopted in the past was in fact "remarkably similar" to that to be adopted under the ECHR. However, just as would be the case if a child were seeking to enforce a private law right to privacy, the proper methodology for the courts is now that set out in *Campbell v MGN Ltd*.[12] Procedural guidance in relation to applications in the Family Division for reporting restriction orders was provided in the *President's Direction* of March 18, 2005[13] and the *CAFCASS Practice Note*[14] of the same date.

The nature of the necessary balancing exercise can be demonstrated by **21–006** comparing the outcome in *Re S* itself with the subsequent decision of Sir Mark Potter P. in *A Local Authority v W*,[15] in which the House of Lords' decision was distinguished.

In *Re S*, an order was made was made prohibiting publication of any **21–007** information that might identify S, a young boy whose brother had died and whose mother was facing trial for his brother's murder. The order was made subject to an exception providing that "Nothing in this order shall of itself prevent any person . . . publishing any particulars of or information relating to any part of the proceedings before any court other than a court sitting in private . . . ". S's representatives appealed against decisions by Hedley J. and the Court of Appeal that the exception should stand. The central question thereby raised for the House of Lords was whether it would be right to restrict the open reporting of the mother's forthcoming criminal trial. The

---

[9] e.g., s.39(1) of the Children and Young Persons Act 1933, cited at para.21–016 below.
[10] See, for example, *In re Z (A Minor) (Identification: Restrictions on Publication)* [1997] Fam. 1.
[11] At para.23.
[12] [2004] UKHL 22; [2004] 2 A.C. 457.
[13] [2005] 2 F.L.R. 120; [2005] Fam. Law 398.
[14] [2005] Fam. Law 398.
[15] [2005] EWHC 1564, Fam; [2006] 1 F.L.R. 1.

respondent newspapers accepted that they should not refer directly to S but wished, in particular, to publish the names and photographs of S's brother and his parents.

21–008   Lord Steyn accepted that both Arts 8 and 10 were engaged. However, the impact of publicity upon S would be "essentially indirect" and "not of the same order when compared with cases of juveniles, who are directly involved in criminal trials".[16] On the other hand, under the ECHR there was a general and strong rule in favour of unrestricted publicity for any proceedings in a criminal trial and the case was not covered by any of the numerous statutory exceptions to publicity that Parliament had seen fit to create. Lord Steyn also differed from the view expressed by Hale L.J. in the Court of Appeal that the public interest in the identification of defendants was greater after a conviction than it was before. He held that Hedley J. had analysed the case correctly and S's appeal was dismissed.

21–009   Lord Steyn went so far[17] as to suggest that, in view of the number of statutory exceptions to trial publicity:

> " . . . it needs to be said clearly and unambiguously that the court has no power to create by a process of analogy, except in the most compelling circumstances, further exceptions to the general principle of open justice."

21–010   The result in *A Local Authority v W*,[18] less than a year after the House of Lords' decision in *Re S*, demonstrates that the "most compelling circumstances" referred to by Lord Steyn may indeed arise. The facts were that the mother of two children pleaded guilty to a charge that she had knowingly infected the father of one of them with the HIV virus. One of the children had tested negative, but it was thought "more than a possibility" that the other child carried the virus. Both children were the subject of care proceedings and the local authority (opposed only by written submissions from the press) sought an injunction restraining publication of any information likely to lead to identification of the children.

21–011   Sir Mark Potter P. observed[19] that *Re S* raised difficulties of application, since it was not easy to reconcile the dictum of Lord Steyn quoted above with a balancing exercise that involved no presumption of priority as between the Art.10 rights of the press and the Art.8 rights of the child. Having concluded[20] that Lord Steyn had not intended to restore the presumptive priority of Art.10 that the House of Lords had rejected in *Campbell v MGN Ltd*, the President distinguished *Re S* on three grounds. First, unlike *Re S*, there had been no previous publicity and there was apparently a good prospect that, if the injunction were granted, the children would in large measure be protected from the fall out of future publicity.

---

[16] At [25]–[27].
[17] At [20]. See also the reference to "unusual or exceptional circumstances" at [18].
[18] [2005] EWHC 1564, Fam; [2006] 1 F.L.R. 1.
[19] At [24].
[20] At [53].

Secondly, there was evidence before the Court that refusal of the injunction might jeopardise the proper placement of the children, because of prejudice against those affected by the HIV virus. Thirdly, the danger for the children against which protection was sought was not the knowledge that their mother was a criminal but the personal attribution (mistaken or otherwise) of HIV infection. An injunction was accordingly granted.[21]

A potential complication arises from the terms of s.1 of the Children Act 1989, which provides that:

21–012

"(1) When a court determines any question with respect to—

(a) the upbringing of a child; or
(b) the administration of a child's property or the application of any income arising from it,

the child's welfare shall be the court's paramount consideration."

Re Z (A Minor) (Identification): Restrictions on Publication)[22] was such a case. Z was a child with particular educational needs. A television company wished to make a programme about the unusual and successful treatment she was receiving from a specialised foreign institution. To this end, Z's mother applied to the court for discharge or variation of earlier injunctions, which had restricted publicity relating to Z's education. The Court of Appeal dismissed her appeal from Cazalet J.'s refusal of her application. Ward L.J. distinguished other cases concerning minors and publicity, saying[23]:

"In my judgment a question of upbringing is determined whenever the central issue before the court is one which relates to how the child is being reared . . . This case is one where the mother wishes her child to perform for the making of the film. This mother wishes to bring up her child as one who will play an active part in a television film . . . The court is, therefore, required to determine a question with respect to the upbringing of the child."

However, even cases directly concerning the upbringing of a child may involve the Art.8 or Art.10 rights of other members of the child's family, or (in this context, probably less significantly) the Art.10 rights of media organisations. The absolute rule laid down by s.1 of the Children Act 1989

---

[21] Contrast *R. (Gazette Media Co Ltd) v Teeside Crown Court* [2005] EWCA Crim 1983; [2005] E.M.L.R. 34 and *A Local Authority v PD* [2005] EWHC 1832, Fam, another decision by Sir Mark Potter P. Further recent examples of the balancing exercise include *F v Newsquest Ltd* [2004] EWHC 762, Fam; (2004) E.M.L.R. 29 (Munby J.) and *British Broadcasting Corporation v Rochdale Metropolitan Borough Council* [2005] EWHC 2862 (Ryder J.).
[22] [1997] Fam 1. See also *Re X (A Minor) (Wardship: Jurisdiction)* [1975] Fam. 47, *per* Sir John Pennycuik at 62.
[23] *ibid.* at 110–111.

may at some point be the subject of challenge, mounted by reference to the balancing exercise required under the Convention.[24]

Family Court Proceedings

21–013   In family court proceedings, the privacy of children may be protected by:

(a) the exclusion of the public from hearings; and
(b) restrictions on the disclosure of information or documents relating to the proceedings.

Exclusion of the public

21–014   In recent years, the courts have expressed concern that the secrecy traditionally attendant upon their disposal of family matters has encouraged ill-informed and unjustified criticism of the family law system and should not be permitted to undermine the open administration of justice.[25] In *Clibbery v Allan*[26] the Court of Appeal held that the principle of open justice applied to all courts including the family courts, that the exclusion of the public had to be objectively justified and that such exclusion did not, of itself, have the consequence of a ban on subsequent publication. In evidence submitted to the Select Committee on Constitutional Affairs,[27] Dame Elizabeth Butler-Sloss P. expressed her personal view that the hearings of all children cases, except adoption hearings, should be opened to the press, though not the general public, unless there were good reasons to exclude them in a particularly sensitive child case—such as where sexual abuse allegations are raised. She also thought that the press, while maintaining anonymity, should have the right to report the judgment in the case and possibly the final submissions, but not the evidence given by the witnesses.

21–015   In its present state, the law reflects a long-standing recognition that children—and the court's exercise of its jurisdiction over them—represent a special case. Lord Shaw of Dumferline said in *Scott v Scott*[28]:

" . . . the jurisdiction over wards and lunatics is exercised by the judges as representing His Majesty as parens patriae. The affairs are truly private affairs; the transactions are transactions truly intra familiam; and it has long been recognised that an appeal for the protection of the Court in the case of such persons does not involve the consequence of placing in the light of publicity their truly domestic affairs."

[24] See the discussion in Jane Fortin's "Accommodating Children's Rights in a Post Human Rights Act Era" (2006) M.L.R. 299.
[25] See for example *Re B* [2004] EWHC 411, Fam; [2004] 2 F.L.R. 142, *per* Munby J., at [97]–[104]; *Re H (Children)* [2005] EWCA Civ 1325; [2006] 1 F.L.R. 815, *per* Wall L.J., at [26] and [29]–[32].
[26] [2002] EWCA Civ 45, [2002] Fam. 261.
[27] December 12, 2004.
[28] [1913] A.C. 417 at 483; see also *per* Viscount Haldane L.C. at 436–437.

The legislature has embodied this principle in a variety of statutory provisions. Proceedings under the Children Act 1989 are required by the Family Proceedings Rules 1991, r.4.16(7), to be held in chambers, unless the court otherwise directs.[29] The public is excluded from family proceedings in the magistrates' courts under the provisions of s.69 of the Magistrates' Courts Act 1980. Under s.101 of the Adoption and Children Act 2002, proceedings under the Act may be disposed of in private.[30]

Restrictions on the disclosure of information or documents relating to proceedings

Newspaper reporting of any case may be limited by an order under s.39(1) **21–016** of the Children and Young Persons Act 1933, which provides that:

> "In relation to any proceedings in any court the court may direct that—
>
> (a) no newspaper report of the proceedings shall reveal the name, address, or school, or include any particulars calculated to lead to the identification, of any child or young person concerned in the proceedings, either as being the person by or against or in respect of whom the proceedings are taken, or as being a witness therein;
>
> (b) no picture shall be published in any newspaper as being or including a picture of any child or young person so concerned in the proceedings as aforesaid;
>
> except in so far (if at all) as may be permitted by the direction of the court."[31]

Further restrictions on publication are common in proceedings where the court is acting in its parental role. Section 97(2) of the Children Act 1989 provides that:

> "No person shall publish to the public at large or any section of the public any material which is intended, or likely, to identify—
>
> (a) any child as being involved in any proceedings before the High Court, a county court or a magistrates' court in which any power under this Act or the Adoption and Children Act 2002 may be

---

[29] The European Court of Human Rights held in *B and P v United Kingdom* (2002) 34 E.H.R.R. 529 that this provision did not infringe the parties' Art.6 rights; see also *Pelling v Bruce-Williams* [2004] EWCA Civ 845; [2004] Fam. 155.
[30] The permissive nature of this provision may be contrasted with the rule imposed by its predecessor, s.64 of the Adoption Act 1976.
[31] See also s.49 of the Children and Young Persons Act 1933 (as amended), which restricts reporting of specified proceedings, including proceedings in juvenile courts. Section 39 is due to be replaced by s.45 of the Youth Justice and Criminal Evidence Act 1999 (not yet in force).

exercised by the court with respect to that or any other child; or

(b) an address or school as being that of a child involved in any such proceedings."

The Court of Appeal has rejected an argument that s.97 is incompatible with Art.6 of the European Convention on Human Rights.[32] However, the restriction imposed by s.97 applies only for the duration of the proceedings concerned.[33]

21–017   A consequence at common law of the privacy of proceedings where the court is acting in its parental role was that a person who published details of the proceedings exposed himself to liability for contempt of court.[34] Statutory notice of this was taken in s.12(1) (as amended) of the Administration of Justice Act 1960:

"The publication of information relating to proceedings before any court sitting in private shall not of itself be contempt of court except in the following cases, that is to say—

(a) where the proceedings—

(i)   relate to the exercise of the inherent jurisdiction of the High Court with respect to minors;

(ii) are brought under the Children Act 1989 or the Adoption and Children Act 2002; or

(iii) otherwise relate wholly or mainly to the maintenance or upbringing of a minor . . . "

21–018   In *Re B*,[35] Munby J. considered the scope of s.12 in detail and provided a summary of the relevant principles. He held that a communication constitutes a "publication" for the purposes of s.12 whenever the law of defamation would treat it as a publication:

"This means that most forms of dissemination, whether oral or written, will constitute a publication. The only exception is where there is a communication of information by someone to a professional, each acting in furtherance of the protection of children."[36]

However, he reiterated that the scope of s.12 is confined to the actual proceedings of the court and does not extend to other information relating

---

[32] *Pelling v Bruce-Williams* [2004] EWCA Civ 845; [2004] Fam. 155.
[33] *Clayton v Clayton* [2006] EWCA Civ 878.
[34] *Re Martindale* [1894] 3 Ch. 193. See also *per* Lloyd L.J. in *Att-Gen v Newspaper Publishing plc* [1988] 1 Ch. 333 at 380, citing *Arlidge and Eady, The Law of Contempt* (1982), p.244.
[35] [2004] EWHC 411 (Fam); [2004] 2 F.L.R. 142, at paras 62–82.
[36] At para.82.

to the child concerned. He referred to his previous statement in *Kelly v British Broadcasting Corporation*[37] that:

" . . . in essence, what section 12 protects is the privacy and confidentiality: (i) of the documents on the court file; and (ii) of what has gone on in front of the judge in his courtroom . . . "

Following Munby J.'s decision in *Re B*, r.4.23 of the Family Proceedings Rules 1991 (dealing with documents held by the court) has been repealed and replaced by r.10.20A(2) of the Family Proceedings Rules 1991,[38] which provides that: **21–019**

"For the purposes of the law relating to contempt of court, information relating to the proceedings[39] (whether or not contained in a document filed with the court) may be communicated—

(a) where the court gives permission;
(b) subject to any direction by the court, in accordance with paragraphs (3) and (4) of this rule; or
(c) where the communication is to—

    (i) a party,
    (ii) the legal representative of a party,
    (iii) a professional legal adviser,
    (iv) an officer of the service or a Welsh family proceedings officer,
    (v) the welfare officer,
    (vi) the Legal Services Commission,
    (vii) an expert whose instruction by a party has been authorised by the court, or
    (viii) a professional acting in the furtherance of the protection of children."

Subparagraphs (3) and (4) of the rule set out further categories of permitted communication by reference to a table.

The legislative history and the effect of Rule 10.20A were considered by Sumner J. in *Reading Borough Council v Angela D.*[40] He drew a distinction between disclosure of a document filed with the court (for which the court's permission was required) and disclosure of the information contained in **21–020**

---

[37] [2001] Fam. 59 at 72.
[38] Section 12(4) of the Administration of Justice Act 1960, as amended by the Children Act 2004, provides expressly that publication authorised by rules of court shall not be punishable as contempt of court.
[39] The rule applies to proceedings held in private where they relate to the exercise of the inherent jurisdiction of the High Court with respect to minors, are brought under the Children Act 1989, or otherwise relate wholly or mainly to the maintenance or upbringing of a minor: r.10.20A(1). It therefore extends to wardship proceedings, not previously covered by r.4.23. In relation to adoption proceedings, see also r.78 of the Family Procedure (Adoption) Rules 2005 and the supplementary Practice Direction.
[40] [2006] EWHC 1465, Fam.

such a document (which was now governed by Rule 10.20A), but it is questionable whether it was really the intention of Rule 10.20A to introduce such a formal distinction or what value it has. The object of Rule 10.20A is to control the supply of information relating to proceedings concerning children; it differs from the previous rule in that it is directed to the content of the information rather than the form in which it is held.

21–021   The matters to be considered by the court in considering an application for permission to disclose information relating to Children Act or similar proceedings were said by Swinton-Thomas L.J., giving the only judgment in *Re C (A Minor) (Care Proceedings: Disclosure)*,[41] to include the following ten factors:

> "(1) The welfare and interests of the child or children concerned in the care proceedings. If the child is likely to be adversely affected by the order in any serious way, this will be a very important factor.
>
> (2) The welfare and interests of other children generally.
>
> (3) The maintenance of confidentiality in children cases.
>
> (4) The importance of encouraging frankness in children's cases . . .
>
> (5) The public interest in the administration of justice. Barriers should not be erected between one branch of the judicature and another because this may be inimical to the overall interests of justice.
>
> (6) The public interest in the prosecution of serious crime and the punishment of offenders, including the public interest in convicting those who have been guilty of violent or sexual offences against children. There is a strong public interest in making available material to the police which is relevant to a criminal trial. In many cases, this is likely to be a very important factor.
>
> (7) The gravity of the alleged offence and the relevance of the evidence to it. If the evidence has little or no bearing on the investigation or the trial, this will militate against a disclosure order.
>
> (8) The desirability of co-operation between various agencies concerned with the welfare of children, including the social services departments, the police service, medical practitioners, health visitors, schools, etc. This is particularly important in cases concerning children.
>
> (9) In a case to which section 98(2)[42] applies, the terms of the section itself, namely that the witness was not excused from answering incriminating questions, and that any statement or admission would not be admissible against him in criminal proceedings. Fairness to the person who has incriminated himself and any others affected by the incriminating statement and any danger of oppression would also be relevant considerations.

---

[41] [1997] Fam. 76 at 85 and 86.
[42] Concerning a statement or admission made in an application for an order under Pt IV or Pt V of the Children Act 1989.

(10) Any other material disclosure which has already taken place."

Swinton-Thomas L.J. said that it was not possible to place these factors in any order of importance, because the importance of each of them would inevitably vary very much from case to case.

The Court of Appeal's guidance in *Re C (A Minor) (Care Proceedings:* **21–022** *Disclosure)* pre-dated the introduction of the Human Rights Act 1998, which now requires consideration also of the interests of anyone whose Art.6, Art.8 or Art.10 rights are engaged[43]; nevertheless, the validity of the guidance was confirmed by Wall J. in *A Chief Constable v A County Council.*[44]

Where material is relevant to criminal proceedings or a police investiga- **21–023** tion, the court's permission for disclosure is often given. In *Re W (Minors) (Social Workers: Disclosure)*,[45] Butler-Sloss L.J. said:

"In a case such as this where the police and the social workers are working together, a family judge should hesitate before refusing to provide relevant and significant information to the police. There will be cases where the evidence is peripheral and the harm of giving leave will outweigh the value of the information. But the police investigations require them to put together a jigsaw of information in order to carry out their important public duty. The family judges ought not to frustrate the investigation of potential crimes (which includes the dissipation of unfounded suspicions against the innocent) without good reason, even more so when the police are working alongside the social workers on the same case."

In *A Health Authority v X*[46] disclosure of case papers and GP records to **21–024** a health authority was permitted, but subject to conditions, including a condition that, save with the prior leave of the court, the authority should not disclose any of the documents, or communicate any information contained in them, to any person other than to a medical discipline committee or the National Health Service Tribunal or the General Medical Council. The Court of Appeal upheld both Munby J.'s jurisdiction to impose conditions and his decision to do so. Thorpe L.J. (who gave the only judgment) said[47]:

---

[43] The justification for disclosure may not always be a public law one: see the pre-Human Rights Act case of *Re X, Y and Z (Minors) (Wardship: Disclosure of Material)* [1992] Fam. 124, in which a newspaper unsuccessfully sought disclosure to assist its defence of justification to a libel action brought by two paediatricians.
[44] [2002] EWHC 2198, Fam; [2003] 1 F.L.R. 579; see also *Reading Borough Council v A* [2006] EWHC 1465 (Fam), *per* Sumner J. at [54]–[59].
[45] [1999] 1 W.L.R. 205, at para.19. *ND v JM* [2002] EWHC 2820, Fam; [2003] 1 F.L.R. 647, in which Hedley J. distinguished Wall J.'s decision in *A Chief Constable v A County Council* [2002] EWHC 2198, Fam; [2003] 1 F.L.R. 579, is an example of a case in which disclosure to the police was refused.
[46] [2001] EWCA Civ 2014; [2002] 2 All E.R. 780.
[47] At [19].

"There is obviously a high public interest, analogous to the public interest in the due administration of criminal justice, in the proper administration of professional disciplinary hearings, particularly in the field of medicine."

Munby J. had not been the judge who had tried the relevant Children Act proceedings and Thorpe L.J. also observed[48]:

" . . . despite the administrative difficulties that may result I am of the strong opinion that where the trial has been conducted by a judge of the [Family] Division, then a subsequent application by a third party for the release of the case papers must be to that judge rather than to another judge of the Division, absent exceptional circumstances."

Restricting disclosure to the parties themselves

21–025 In exceptional circumstances in adoption proceedings or family proceedings, confidential reports, or parts of them, may be withheld from the parties themselves (though available to the court). The principles on which the court should act were set out by the House of Lords in *Re D (Minors) (Adoption Reports: Confidentiality)*.[49] Lord Mustill, giving the only speech, said that there must be a strong presumption in favour of disclosure on grounds of natural justice:

" . . . the court should first consider whether disclosure of the material would involve a real possibility of significant harm to the child.

If it would, the court should next consider whether the overall interests of the child would benefit from non-disclosure, weighing on the one hand the interest of the child in having the material properly tested, and on the other both the magnitude of the risk that harm will occur and the gravity of the harm if it does occur.

If the court is satisfied that the interests of the child point towards non-disclosure, the next and final step is for the court to weigh that consideration, and its strength in the circumstances of the case, against the interest of the parent or other party in having an opportunity to see and respond to the material. In the latter regard the court should take into account the importance of the material to the issues in the case.

Non-disclosure should be the exception and not the rule. The court should be rigorous in its examination of the risk and gravity of the feared harm to the child and should order non-disclosure only when the case for doing so is compelling."[50]

21–026 In *Re B (Disclosure to Other Parties)*,[51] Munby J. considered the effect on those principles of the Human Rights Act 1998. He held that Lord Mustill's

---

[48] At [23].
[49] [1996] A.C. 593.
[50] At 615.
[51] [2001] 2 F.L.R. 1017 at paras 64–66.

guidance remained applicable, with the single qualification that it was no longer the case (if it ever had been) that the only interests capable of denying a litigant access to the documents in a proper case were the interests of the children involved in the litigation: the interests of any other person— whether child or adult—whose Art.8 rights were sufficiently engaged also had to be taken into account. Munby J.'s judgment was cited with approval by the Court of Appeal in *Re X (Children)*.[52] Guidance as to the procedure to be adopted in cases where the issue arises was given by Johnson J. in *Re C (Disclosure)*[53] and approved by the Court of Appeal in *Re M (A Minor) (Disclosure)*.[54]

[52] [2002] EWCA Civ 828; [2002] 2 F.L.R. 476.
[53] [1996] 1 F.L.R. 797.
[54] [1998] 2 F.L.R. 1028.

CHAPTER 22

Arbitrations

The duty of confidence

22–001   It has long been recognised by English law that arbitration is a private process, but the courts have experienced difficulty in formulating the nature and extent of the obligations of confidentiality that arise as a result.

22–002   In *Dolling-Baker v Merrett*[1] Parker L.J., giving the leading judgment in the Court of Appeal, stated:

> "As between parties to an arbitration, although the proceedings are consensual and may thus be regarded as wholly voluntary, their very nature is such that there must, in my judgment, be some implied obligation on both parties not to disclose or use for any other purpose any documents prepared for and used in the arbitration, or disclosed or produced in the course of the arbitration, or transcripts or notes of the evidence in the arbitration or the award, and indeed not to disclose in any other way what evidence had been given by any witness in the arbitration, save with the consent of the other party, or pursuant to an order or leave of the court. That qualification is necessary just as it is in the case of the implied obligation of secrecy between banker and customer."

The court was not concerned in that case to identify the nature or extent of any qualifications to the duty.

22–003   The subject of confidentiality in arbitrations was considered by the High Court of Australia in *Esso Australian Resources Ltd v Plowman*.[2] The appellants, Esso Australian Resources Ltd, made or were assignees of contracts with two public utilities for the sale of natural gas. The price was

---

[1] [1990] 1 W.L.R. 1205 at 1213.
[2] [1994–1995] 183 C.L.R. 10. For a copy of the judgments together with editorial comment, the salient parts of the experts' reports provided in the case by Stewart Boyd, Q.C. and others, and other learned articles, see *Arbitration International* [1995] 11(3) 231–340.

to be adjusted by taking into account the effect of any changes in taxes. The contracts required the sellers to provide the buyers with details of any price changes and the calculations on which they were based. Disputes between the sellers and the buyers were referred to arbitration. The Minister for Energy and Minerals had substantial powers to require the supply of information by the utilities. The Minister brought actions against the appellants and the utilities claiming declarations that information disclosed by the appellants to the utilities in the arbitrations was not subject to any obligation of confidence. The appellants cross claimed for declarations that the arbitrations were to be held in private and that any documents or information supplied by any party to any other party for the purpose of the arbitrations was to be treated in confidence between the parties and the arbitrators.

The trial judge decided in the Minister's favour. An appeal to the Supreme **22–004** Court of Victoria was allowed in part, but the court upheld declarations to the effect that the utilities were not restricted from disclosing information to the Minister and others by reason only that it was obtained from the appellants in the arbitration and had not otherwise been published. On further appeal by the sellers, the High Court remitted the declarations to the Supreme Court of Victoria for reformulation but otherwise dismissed the appeals.

The sellers argued that it was an implied term of the arbitration **22–005** agreements that the arbitrations should be conducted in private, and that the buyers were under an implied contractual, and equitable, obligation of confidence not to disclose, except for the purposes of the arbitration, information and documents provided to them for the purposes of the arbitration by the sellers, unless authorised by statute.

Mason C.J., with whom Dawson and McHugh JJ. agreed, recognised that **22–006** (subject to any manifestation of a contrary intention arising from the arbitration agreement) an arbitration was to be held in private. He preferred to describe the privacy attaching to an arbitration as an incident of the subject-matter of the agreement to arbitrate, rather than to attribute it to an implied term of the agreement, although he did not consider that it mattered greatly.

As to a general obligation of confidentiality, he said[3]: **22–007**

> "There is . . . a case for saying that, in the course of evolution, the private arbitration has advanced to the stage where confidentiality has become one of its essential attributes so that confidentiality is a characteristic or quality that inheres in arbitration. Despite the view taken in *Dolling-Baker* and subsequently by Colman J. in *Hassneh Insurance*, I do not consider that, in Australia, having regard to the various matters to which I have referred, we are justified in concluding that confidentiality is an essential attribute of a private arbitration imposing an obligation on each party not to disclose the proceedings or

---

[3] *Esso Australian Resources Ltd v Plowman* [1994–1995] 183 C.L.R. 10 at 30.

documents and information provided in and for the purposes of the arbitration."

22–008   Mason C.J. accepted, however, that there was an implied obligation to accord to documents disclosed by a party compulsorily, pursuant to an order of the arbitrator, the same confidentiality which would attach to them if the parties were litigating rather than arbitrating. He also said[4]:

> "In argument, reference was made to the principles governing the protection of confidential information generally. No doubt these principles may have some application to information in arbitration proceedings. But these principles do not support the broad claim for confidentiality made by the appellants."

In order for the principles of confidentiality to apply, the information must have the quality of confidence and must be received in circumstances importing an obligation of confidence. Mason C.J. would appear to accept that information disclosed in arbitration proceedings may satisfy both requirements, while rejecting the proposition that this applies to all such information.

22–009   Brennan J. and Toohey J. concurred in the result but by different reasoning. Brennan J. agreed with Mason C.J. that any duty of confidentiality would not arise merely from the privacy of the hearing. It must be derived from an implied term of the agreement to arbitrate. Some term could be implied from the fact that documents and information supplied for the purposes of arbitration were given solely for that purpose. But, to the extent that a party would not have agreed at the time of the arbitration agreement to keep documents or information confidential, the implied obligation of confidentiality must be qualified.

22–010   Brennan J. gave various examples. If a party was under a statutory or common law duty to communicate the document or information to a third party, no contractual obligation of confidentiality could prohibit performance of that duty. A party might be under a duty, not necessarily legal, to communicate documents or information to a party with a legitimate interest in the outcome of the proceedings (for example, a subsidiary company to its parent) or might wish to reveal them for the protection of its own interests. Nor should an obligation be implied that a party would keep confidential documents or information when he had an obligation, not necessarily legal, to satisfy a public interest—more than mere curiosity—in knowing what was contained in them.

22–011   Toohey J. considered that, subject to qualifications where disclosure was reasonably necessary to protect the interests of a party to the arbitration or in the public interest, an obligation of confidentiality did attach to the

---

[4] *Esso Australian Resources Ltd v Plowman* [1994–1995] 183 C.L.R. 10 at 30.

documents and information emanating from an arbitration by reason of an implied term of a commercial arbitration agreement. He said[5]:

> "The term is implied from the entry by the parties into a form of dispute resolution which they choose because of the privacy they expect to result. If this is said to confuse privacy and confidentiality, the answer is that they are not distinct characteristics. As Colman J. said in *Hassneh*:
>
> > 'The disclosure to a third party of [a note or transcript of the evidence] would be almost equivalent to opening the door of the arbitration room to that third party.'
>
> Any aspect of disclosure to third parties must infringe the privacy of the arbitration."

The majority of the Australian High Court therefore declined to infer from the undoubted privacy of arbitration proceedings the existence of a general duty of confidence between the parties requiring them to treat all aspects of the arbitration process as confidential.

In *Ali Shipping Corporation v Shipyard Trogir*,[6] the plaintiff sought to **22–012** restrain the defendant from using documents generated in the course of an arbitration between them for the purposes of separate arbitration proceedings between the defendant and other companies in common ownership with the plaintiff. The Court of Appeal granted an injunction to the plaintiff. Potter L.J. gave the only judgment. He referred to the decision of the High Court of Australia in *Esso v Plowman*, but concluded that an implied duty of confidentiality did arise in relation to arbitrations, stating[7]:

> "It seems to me that, in holding as a matter of principle that the obligation of confidentiality, whatever its precise limits, arises as an essential corollary of the privacy of arbitration proceedings, the court is propounding a term which arises 'as the nature of the contract itself implicitly requires' . . . As Lord Bridge of Harwich observed in *Scally v Southern Health and Social Services Board* [1992] 1 A.C. 294, 307, a clear distinction is to be drawn
>
> > 'between the search for an implied term necessary to give business efficacy to a particular contract and the search, based on wider considerations, for a term which the law will imply as a necessary incident of a definable category of contractual relationship.'
>
> In my view an arbitration clause is a good example of the latter type of implied term. The distinction referred to by Lord Bridge in *Scally's* case

---

[5] [1994–1995] 183 C.L.R. 10 at 47–48.
[6] [1999] 1 W.L.R. 314.
[7] At 326.

is of some practical importance in this case. This is because considerations of business efficacy... are likely to involve a detailed examination of the circumstances existing at the time of the relevant contract..., whereas the parties have indicated their presumed intention simply by entering into a contract to which the court attributes particular characteristics. While acknowledging that the boundaries of the obligation of confidence which thereby arise have yet to be delineated..., the manner in which that may best be achieved is by formulating exceptions of broad application to be applied in individual cases, rather than by seeking to reconsider, and if necessary adapt, the general rule on each occasion in the light of the particular circumstances and presumed intentions of the parties at the time of their original agreement."

Potter L.J. went on to identify the following recognised exceptions to the broad rule of confidentiality:

(i) consent of the party who produced the material;
(ii) order of the court (for example, an order for disclosure made in a later court action);
(iii) leave of the court;
(iv) disclosure when, and to the extent, reasonably necessary for the protection of the legitimate interests of an arbitrating party;
(v) disclosure where the public interest requires.

22–013   Potter L.J.'s views were subsequently questioned in *Associated Electric and Gas Insurance Services Ltd v European Reinsurance Co. of Zurich*,[8] a decision of the Privy Council on appeal from the Court of Appeal of Bermuda. The case concerned the proper construction of express confidentiality provisions in an arbitration agreement. It was held that they should not be construed in such a way as would prevent one party from relying on the award as giving him rights against the other. In a postscript Lord Hobhouse, delivering the judgment of the Privy Council, commented obiter on Potter L.J.'s approach as follows[9]:

"Their Lordships have reservations about the desirability or merit of adopting this approach. It runs the risk of failing to distinguish between different types of confidentiality which attach to different types of document or to documents which have been obtained in different ways and elides privacy and confidentiality. Commercial arbitrations are essentially private proceedings and unlike litigation in the public courts do not place anything in the public domain. This may mean that the implied restrictions on the use of material obtained in arbitration

[8] [2003] UKPC 11; [2003] 1 W.L.R. 1041.
[9] At para.20.

proceedings may have a greater impact than those applying in litigation. But when it comes to the award, the same logic cannot be applied. An award may have to be referred to for accounting purposes or for the purpose of legal proceedings . . . or for the purpose of enforcing the rights which the award confers. Generalisations and the formulation of detailed implied terms are not appropriate."

Subsequently, in *Department of Economics, Policy and Development of* **22–014**
the City of Moscow v Bankers Trust Co,[10] Mance L.J., giving the leading judgment in the Court of Appeal, reiterated that[11]:

"Among features long assumed to be implicit in parties' choice to arbitrate in England are privacy and confidentiality."

The authorities leave English law in a state of some uncertainty as to the nature and breadth of obligations of confidence arising in the context of arbitration proceedings.

Arbitration is a private process, but it is a process for determining legal **22–015**
rights. There may be strong reason for affording a high degree of confidentiality to the process, but less reason to afford the same degree of confidentiality to the existence of the rights and liabilities as determined by the arbitral tribunal. The establishment of those rights and liabilities may have relevance to a party's relations with others, to whom it may have good cause or a duty to disclose them.

An arbitral award may generate court proceedings between the same **22–016**
parties, either to enforce it or to challenge it. When this happens there is a meeting point between the essentially private process of arbitration and the essentially public process of the administration of justice by the courts.

Under the Arbitration Act 1996 a party may apply to the court to **22–017**
challenge an arbitral award for lack of substantive jurisdiction,[12] for serious irregularity[13] or by way of appeal on a point of law.[14] CPR 62.10 provides that the court may order that an arbitration claim be heard either in public or in private, but that, unless the court orders otherwise, an appeal on a question of law under s.69 will be heard in public but applications to challenge an award for want of jurisdiction or for serious irregularity or for leave to appeal under s.69 will be heard in private.

In *Department of Economics, Policy and Development of the City of* **22–018**
Moscow v Bankers Trust Co the issue was whether a judgment dismissing an application to challenge an award for serious irregularity under s.68 (or a summary) should be available for general publication or for limited publication to certain financial institutions. This involved a conflict between the value of open justice which (absent other considerations) would require

[10] [2004] EWCA Civ 314; [2005] Q.B. 207.
[11] At [2].
[12] s.67.
[13] s.68.
[14] s.69.

that a judgment of the court should be freely available and the value of protecting the private and confidential nature of the arbitral proceedings.

22–019   Mance L.J. said that the silence of the Arbitration Act about privacy and confidentiality did not detract from the long standing assumption that they are implicit in parties' choice to arbitrate in England. He referred to the report of the Departmental Advisory Committee on Arbitration Law, chaired by Lord Saville of Newdigate, which was heavily influential in the drafting of the Act. It was the difficulty of formulating the principles and the "myriad exceptions" and qualifications in the statutory terms that led the committee to conclude that the courts should be left to work them out "on a pragmatic, case-by-case basis".[15]

22–020   In relation to applications under s.68, Mance L.J. said that even though the hearing may have been in private the court should bear in mind in preparing and giving judgment that it should be given in public, where this could be done without disclosing significant confidential information.[16] He gave his reasons:

> "The public interest in ensuring appropriate standards of fairness in the conduct of arbitrations militates in favour of a public judgment in respect of judgments given on applications under section 68. The desirability of public scrutiny as a means by which confidence in the courts can be maintained and the administration of justice made transparent applies here as in other areas of court activity under the principles of *Scott v Scott* [1913] A.C. 417 and article 6. Arbitration is an important feature of international, commercial and financial life, and there is legitimate interest in its operation and practice. The desirability of a public judgment is particularly present in any case where a judgment involves points of law or practice which may offer future guidance to lawyers or practitioners."

As to confidentiality, and how this was to be set against the desirability of judgments being given in public, he said[17]:

> "The factors militating in favour of publicity have to be weighed together with the desirability of preserving the confidentiality of the original arbitration and its subject matter. There is a spectrum. At one end is the arbitration itself and at the other an order following a reasoned judgment under section 68 . . . A reasoned judgment under section 68 will in likelihood disclose very much less about the subject matter of the arbitration than will have been covered during the section 68 hearing itself. Moreover judges framing judgments are accustomed to concentrate on essentials, to avoid where possible unnecessary disclosure of sensitive material and in some cases to anonymise . . .

---

[15] At [2].
[16] [2004] EWCA Civ 314; [2005] Q.B. 207 at [39].
[17] *ibid.* at [40] and [41].

If . . . the court withholds publication where a party before it would suffer some real prejudice from publication or where the publication would disclose matters by the confidentiality of which one or both parties have set significant store, but publishes its judgments in other cases, businessmen can be confidant that their privacy and confidentiality in arbitration will, where appropriate, be preserved. The limited but necessary interface between arbitration and the public court system means that more cannot be expected. There can be no question of withholding publication of reasoned judgments on a blanket basis out of a generalised, and in my view unfounded, concern that their publication would upset the confidence of the business community in English arbitration."

Conclusions

Despite the reservations expressed by Lord Hobhouse in *Associated Electric and Gas Insurance Services v European Reinsurance Co of Zurich*,[18] broad questions of principle do arise in relation to the duty of confidentiality owed by parties to arbitrations and its qualifications. In developing the law of confidentiality, the courts should be capable, in this as in other fields, of formulating the qualifications with sufficient clarity and flexibility.   **22–021**

The starting point is that parties to an arbitration agreement are to be taken as impliedly agreeing to treat documents and information emanating from the arbitration as confidential. The implication arises from the nature of the arbitral process, ie that it is an essentially private process, and from what the courts have accepted to be the long held assumptions of those who use arbitration. However, as with other implied duties of confidentiality, it is subject to qualifications.   **22–022**

In *Department of Economics, Policy and Development of the City of Moscow v Bankers Trust Co*[19] Mance L.J. referred to a spectrum from the initial stages of an arbitration to the award and to a judgment in proceedings challenging the award. At different stages different circumstances may arise to warrant different degrees of disclosure.   **22–023**

At one end of the spectrum, for example, the confidentiality of documents produced by a party under compulsion pursuant to an arbitrator's order for disclosure should attract a high level of protection (and indeed the confidentiality of such documents was recognised by the High Court of Australia in *Esso v Plowman*).   **22–024**

On the other hand, there may be a wide range of reasons why a party to an arbitration legitimately requires to reveal the arbitrator's award to a third party. As the Privy Council observed in *Associated Electric and Gas Insurance Services*,[20] contrasting arbitration awards with material obtained in arbitration proceedings: **22–025**

---

[18] [2003] UKPC 11; [2003] 1 W.L.R. 1041 at [20].
[19] [2004] EWCA Civ 314; [2005] Q.B. 207, at [40].
[20] At [20].

> "But when it comes to the award, the same logic cannot be applied. An award may have to be referred to for accounting purposes or for the purposes of legal proceedings . . . or for the purposes of enforcing the rights which the award confers . . . "

Qualifications/exceptions

22–026   Of the qualifications identified by the Court of Appeal in *Ali Shipping Corporation v Shipyard Trogir*[21] (consent, court order, leave from the court, disclosure reasonably necessary for the protection of the legitimate interests of an arbitrating party and disclosure in the public interest), some merit further comment.

Leave of the court

22–027   It is axiomatic that a party to an arbitration should be entitled to disclose confidential information when a court has granted him permission to do so. However, as the Court of Appeal observed, this begs the question of the grounds on which such permission will be granted. It therefore appears that this "exception" is not in truth a separate category from the others; it may have been included out of caution, in order to meet unforeseen cases.

Disclosure in a party's own interests

22–028   In *Hassneh Insurance v Mew*[22] Colman J. held that the duty of confidence owed by an arbitrating party was subject to the qualification that it did not prevent disclosure of an arbitrator's award if it was reasonably necessary for the establishment or protection of that party's legal rights vis-à-vis a third party, and that in such a case the party wishing to make disclosure did not require to seek the approval of the court. In so holding, Colman J. based himself on the judgments in *Tournier v National Provincial and Union Bank of England*.[23]

22–029   The extent of this qualification was again considered by Colman J. in *Insurance Company v Lloyd's Syndicate*.[24] The case arose out of a reinsurance dispute between a Lloyd's syndicate and certain excess of loss reinsurers. The plaintiff reinsurers were the leading insurers on a slip subscribed also by five companies, who were not parties to the arbitration. In the arbitration between the syndicate and the leading insurers an interim award was issued in the syndicate's favour. The syndicate wished to disclose the award to the following market in order to persuade the following market to accept liability. Colman J. held that it was not entitled to do so, because as between the syndicate and the following market the award had no more status than if it had been an independent counsel's opinion. Disclosure might have been helpful to the syndicate in attempting to

---

[21] [1999] 1 W.L.R. 314 at 326 and 327.
[22] [1993] 2 Lloyd's Rep. 243 at 249.
[23] [1924] 1 K.B. 461.
[24] [1995] 1 Lloyd's Rep. 272.

persuade the following market to accept its claim, but was not necessary to enable the syndicate to establish or enforce its rights against the following market.

This may be thought a harsh decision. When the leading insurers **22–030** subscribed the slip, they had no knowledge on what terms other companies would subscribe, but as a matter of practicality it is common for the following market to follow the leader in matters such as settlements. If the following market had agreed to be bound by the leading underwriter's claims, settlements, decisions or arbitration awards, there is no doubt that the syndicate would have been entitled to disclose the arbitration award to the following market. If the leader had agreed to settle the syndicate's claim, the syndicate would have been entitled to tell the following market. If the arbitration had resulted in a decision that the leading underwriter was entitled to avoid the policy for non-disclosure, it would be surprising if the syndicate would have been entitled to prevent the following market from being told. It would in the circumstances seem not unreasonable to imply a qualification to the duty of confidentiality entitling the syndicate to inform the following market of the outcome of any claims made by it against the leaders of the slip as a step reasonably necessary to protect the syndicate's interest in obtaining prompt settlement and avoiding multiplicity of proceedings.

In *Ali Shipping Corporation v Shipyard Trogir*,[25] the Court of Appeal **22–031** endorsed the observations of Colman J. that it was not enough that an award or reasons might have a commercially persuasive impact on the third party to whom they were disclosed, nor that their disclosure would be "merely helpful, as distinct from necessary, for the protection of such rights", but at the same time suggested that the court should take a flexible approach to what was "reasonably necessary" for the protection of a party's legitimate interests.

It is suggested that it would be too narrow to limit the concept of **22–032** protection of a party's legitimate interests to cases where the object of disclosure is to enforce a party's legal rights. If, for example, the knowledge that a claim has been made against a party is affecting that party in its commercial relationships with business partners, its bank or others, it may have a good case for saying that it should be entitled to inform those parties of the outcome of an arbitration, without being entitled to disclose confidential documents or other details. It may also owe a duty to others, such as its bank, to inform them of the outcome.

Disclosure in the public interest

In *London & Leeds Estates Ltd v Paribas Ltd (No. 2)*[26], the question arose **22–033** whether an expert witness giving evidence in a rent review arbitration should be compelled to produce a proof of evidence provided by him in an earlier separate arbitration. Mance J. held:

---

[25] [1999] 1 W.L.R. 314 at 327.
[26] [1995] 2 E.G. 134.

"It does not seem to me that [the witness] has legitimate ground to object to cross-examination about his previous statements on the general subject of West End property market conditions in 1991. If a witness were proved to have expressed himself in a materially different sense when acting for different sides, that would be a factor which should be brought out in the interests of individual litigants involved and in the public interest."

22–034   In *Ali Shipping* Potter L.J. endorsed Mance J.'s view, while commenting[27]:

"As a matter of terminology, I would prefer to recognise such an exception under the heading 'interests of justice' rather than 'the public interest', in order to avoid the suggestion that use of that latter phrase is to be read as extending to the wider issues of public interest contested in *Esso Australia Resources Ltd v Plowman* . . . In that case, only the dissenting judgment of Toohey J. appears to me to treat the law of privacy and confidentiality in relation to arbitration proceedings on lines similar to English law. While it may well fall to the English court at a future time to consider some further exception to the general rule of confidentiality based on wider considerations of public interest, it is not necessary to do so in this case."

The precise scope of the "public interest defence" has long been a vexed question in the jurisprudence of confidentiality. However, it is suggested that there is no good reason why the general law on this topic[28] should not be applied also in the context of arbitration proceedings.

Others involved in arbitrations

22–035   An arbitrator by agreeing to act in that capacity must in principle owe an implied duty of confidentiality to the parties similar to that owed by the parties to each other. Those involved in arbitration proceedings as representatives of the parties or witnesses should by reason of their knowledge of the confidential nature of the proceedings, owe an equitable duty of confidentiality to the parties in respect of documents or information, but defining the boundaries of what is conscionable behaviour may involve difficulties. An expert witness giving evidence in a rent review dispute[29] may be aware of one or more highly relevant recent decisions by respected arbitrators, because he had been involved, and they may have had a strong bearing on the formation of his expert opinion. Or a solicitor applying on behalf of a client for permission to appeal against an arbitration award on a point of law under s.69 (under which there is a different threshold

---

[27] At 328.
[28] See Ch.16 above.
[29] See, for example, *London & Leeds Estates Ltd v Paribas Ltd (No. 2)* [1999] 1 W.L.R. 314.

according to whether the point of law is a one-off issue or a point of general importance) may wish to say that he is aware from his knowledge of other arbitrations that the point has regularly arisen with different arbitrators giving different answers. It is unlikely that the expert witness or the solicitor would be considered to be acting in breach of duty if he confined himself to saying that his evidence was based on experience in other anonymised cases, but, if challenged, to disclose the parties' identities, he would be unwise to do so without an order of the court.

INDEX